Special Edition

Using
HTML 3.2
Third Edition

Special Edition

USING
HTML 3.2
THIRD EDITION

Written by Jerry Honeycutt and Mark R. Brown
with

Jim O'Donnell • Eric Ladd • Robert Meegan • Bill Bruns
Robert Niles • David Wall • Mathew Brown • Rob Falla

Special Edition Using HTML 3.2, Third Edition

Library of Congress Catalog No.: 97-65026

ISBN: 0-7897-1097-8

99 98 97   6   5   4   3   2   1

Interpretation of the printing code: the rightmost double-digit number is the year of the book's printing; the rightmost single-digit number, the number of the book's printing. For example, a printing code of 97-1 shows that the first printing of the book occurred in 1997.

Screen reproductions in this book were created with Collage Plus from Inner Media, Inc., Hollis, NH.

Credits

PRESIDENT
Roland Elgey

PUBLISHER
Joseph B. Wikert

PUBLISHING MANAGER
Jim Minatel

EDITORIAL SERVICES DIRECTOR
Elizabeth Keaffaber

DIRECTOR OF MARKETING
Lynn E. Zingraf

ACQUISITIONS MANAGER
Cheryl D. Willoughby

ACQUISITIONS EDITOR
Philip Wescott

PRODUCT DIRECTORS
Mark Cierzniak
Steven M. Schafer

PRODUCTION EDITOR
Jim Bowie

EDITORS
Patricia R. Kinyon
Kelli M. Brooks
Kate O. Givens

PRODUCT MARKETING MANAGER
Kristine Ankney

ASSISTANT PRODUCT MARKETING MANAGERS
Karen Hagen
Christy M. Miller

STRATEGIC MARKETING MANAGER
Barry Pruett

TECHNICAL EDITORS
Andy Angrick
Matthew Brown
Jim Hofman
Eric Ladd
Jim O'Donnell
Tony Schafer
Jon Steever

TECHNICAL SUPPORT SPECIALIST
Nadeem Muhammed

ACQUISITIONS COORDINATOR
Jane K. Brownlow

SOFTWARE RELATIONS COORDINATOR
Susan D. Gallaher

EDITORIAL ASSISTANTS
Jennifer L. Condon
Andrea Duvall

BOOK DESIGNER
Ruth Harvey

COVER DESIGNER
Dan Armstrong

PRODUCTION TEAM
Marcia Brizendine
Bob LaRoche
Tim Neville
Paul Wilson

INDEXER
Kevin Fulcher

Composed in *Century Old Style* and *ITC Franklin Gothic* by Que Corporation.

In memory of William C. Niles   —Jerry Honeycutt

To my wife, Carol, and my daughter, Jenny, who are and have always been my inspiration, my foundation, and my best friends.   —Mark R. Brown

About the Authors

Jerry Honeycutt provides business-oriented technical leadership to the Internet community and software development industry. He has served companies such as The Travelers, IBM, Nielsen North America, IRM, Howard Systems International, and NCR. Jerry has participated in the industry since before the days of Microsoft Windows 1.0, and is completely hooked on Windows and the Internet.

Jerry is a leading author in the Internet field. He is the author of *Using Microsoft Plus!*; *Using the Internet with Windows 95*; *Windows 95 Registry & Customization Handbook*; *Special Edition Using the Windows 95 Registry*; *VBScript by Example*; *Special Edition Using the Internet, Third Edition*; *Using the Internet, Second Edition*; and *Windows NT and Windows 95 Registry Customization Handbook*, all of which are published by Que. Many of his books are sold internationally and have been translated into a variety of languages, including French, Italian, Korean, Japanese, Portugese, Russian, Spanish, and Turkish.

Jerry is also a contributing author on *Special Edition Using Windows 95*, *Special Edition Using Netscape 2*, *Platinum Edition Using Windows 95*, *Visual Basic for Applications Database Solutions*, *Special Edition Using Netscape 3*, *Windows 95 Exam Guide*, *Netscape Navigator 3 Starter Kit*, *Using Java Workshop*, *Using JScript*, *Internet Explorer ActiveX and Plug-Ins Companion*, and *Windows NT Server 4.0 Advanced Technical Reference*, all of which are published by Que. He has been printed in *Computer Language* magazine and is a regular speaker at Windows World, Comdex, and other industry trade shows on topics related to software development, Windows, and the Internet.

Jerry graduated from the University of Texas at Dallas in 1992 with a B.S. degree in Computer Science. He currently lives in the Dallas suburb of Frisco, Texas with two Westies: Corky and Turbo, and a bird called Opie. Jerry is an avid golfer, and has a passion for fine photography and international travel. Feel free to contact Jerry on the Internet at **jerry@honeycutt.com**.

Mark R. Brown has been writing computer books, magazine articles, and software manuals for over fourteen years. He was managing editor of *.info magazine*, when it was named one of the best computer magazines of the year by the Computer Press Association in 1991, and was nominated by the Software Publisher's Association for the Software Reviewer of the Year award in 1988. He's now a full-time freelance writer, who has contributed to over a half-dozen Que books, and is the author of Que's *Special Edition Using Netscape* series and the *WWW Plug-Ins Companion*. He is Webmaster of a Web site devoted to the topic of airships at **http://www2.giant.net/people/mbrown**, and can be reached via e-mail at **mbrown@avalon.net**.

Jim O'Donnell was born Oct. 17, 1963, in Pittsburgh, Pennsylvania (you may forward birthday greetings to **odonnj@rpi.edu**). After a number of unproductive years, he began his studies in electrical engineering at Rensselaer Polytechnic Institute. Jim liked that so much he spent 11 years at the school getting three degrees, graduating for the third (and final) time in the summer of 1992. When he isn't writing or researching for Que, he likes to run, row, play hockey, collect comic books and PEZ dispensers, and play the Best Board Game Ever, Cosmic Encounter. You can find Jim on the Web at **http://www.rpi.edu/~odonnj/**.

Eric Ladd (**erll@access.digex.net**) is a task leader for Advanced Technology Systems in McLean, Virginia, where he leads a group of Internet developers that support the FDIC.

By night, he toils endlessly for Macmillan Computer Publishing, coauthoring *Platinum Edition Using HTML 3.2, Java 1.1 and CGI* and *Special Edition Using Microsoft Internet Explorer 3* and contributing to several other titles. Eric lives in Washington, D.C., with his Boxer puppy, Zack.

Robert Meegan designs large software systems for manufacturing and research facilities. He has been working with computers for longer than he cares to recall. He can be reached at **rmeegan@ia.net**.

Bill Bruns is the Network Analyst at the Illini Student Union at the University of Illinois at Urbana-Champaign. He really wanted to work in television production, but got interested in computers while working on an undergraduate internship at Square One TV, a children's mathematics show produced by the Children's Television Workshop. Bill has been a technical editor for Que and has worked on such titles as *Platinum HTML 3.2, Java 1.1 and CGI*, *Running a Perfect Netscape Site*, and *10 Minute Guide to HTML Style Sheets*. Previously, he ran administrative computing at New York University's Tisch School of the Arts. Bill holds bachelors degrees in Telecommunications and English Literature from Indiana University, a Masters of Public Administration from New York University, and is a Certified Netware Engineer. You can reach him at **brunsl@prairienet.org**. He's also the Illini Union's Webmaster. Check out their pages at **www.union.uiuc.edu**.

Robert Niles is a systems administrator and Web programmer for InCommand Inc., a company located in Yakima, Washington that specializes in Internet and intranet applications.

Robert loves all things Internet, especially the Web and CGI. He has been online since 1983, exploring the very nature of the online world. In 1984, he entered the military service as a communications specialist, taking a one year intensive course at the Presidio of Monterey as a Czech linguist. After completing military service, he returned to his home in the Yakima Valley.

Currently, Robert can usually be found with his head almost stuck to a monitor—no matter where he is. He specializes in the UNIX environment, Perl, and SQL.

Robert lives in Selah, Washington (Apple Country) with his wife, Kimberly, his son, Michael, and his daughter, Shaela. You can find him on the Web at **http://www.selah.net/** or via e-mail at **rniles@selah.net**.

David Wall lives in Utah, where he distinguishes himself by belonging to neither an organized religious group nor a militia. Mainly, he skis, perfecting the fine points of the high-speed inverted face-plant.

Matthew Brown lives in the small town of Addison, TX with his fiancee Caroline, and their children Ramses, Cleo, and Bastian. Matthew currently works at National Knowledge Networks, Inc., as the Webmaster and local Windows NT expert. In his free time, Matthew enjoys listening to music, go-cart racing, and watching mindless television for hours.

Rob Falla (**rfalla@netroute.net**) is a professional HTML developer and part-time writer. He authored *HTML Style Sheets Quick Reference*. When not writing, Rob is usually on the Internet, learning about the next big trends before they become popular.

Acknowledgments

Wow. This book took a lot of work by many people. The authors, of course, contributed many hours of bone-racking work to this book. The editors made sure that this book's content was on the up-and-up. There are a couple of very special folks that I want you to be aware of, though:

- Philip Wescott put together a fine group of contributing authors in order to get this book done.
- Mark Cierzniak and Steve Schafer are the development editors for this book. They kept their heads cool and allowed the authors to put together the best book possible. Thanks.
- Jim Bowie, the production editor for this book, is a joy. He works with almost unbearable details and schedules, but manages to keep his head screwed on tight.
- The technical editors—Jim O'Donnell, Eric Ladd, Andy Angrick, Jim Hofman, Matthew Brown, Jon Steever, and Tony Schafer—did a fabulous job of making sure the technical details were correct. They scoured over every line of HTML in this book, as well as the text content. They didn't just verify the facts, either; they often came up with great ideas for new content.
- The copy editors—Patricia R. Kinyon, Kelli M. Brooks, and Kate O. Givens—made sure the gibberish the authors banged out on the keyboard was readable and conformed to some sense of English structure.
- The contributing authors—O'Donnell, Ladd, Matthew Brown, Bill Bruns, Robert Meegan, David Wall, Rob Falla, and Robert Niles—were shooting at fast-moving targets. They did good.
- The Internet community contributed ideas for content and often provided solutions to problems for which we were stumped.

Last, but not least, I'd like to thank my coauthor, Mark R. Brown. His contribution to this book was significant. It was more fun with him than it would have been without him.

—Jerry Honeycutt

Thanks, first of all, to the small group of knowledgeable writers who did the research and wrote down the words that comprise this book. Professionals all, I think that they have done a marvelous job of documenting a potentially formidable subject in an entertaining and enlightening manner.

I also extend my deepest thanks to the entire crew at Que. Please read their names on the masthead and try to imagine how hard these people had to work to make a huge and detailed book like this happen in such a short period of time. From this talented group, I'd like to single out Philip Wescott, Mark Cierzniak, and Jim Bowie for special thanks—Philip for his dogged discipline and diehard diligence in bringing together all the disparate elements of this tome; Mark for his sharp eye and controlled demeanor under incredible pressure, as always (it must be the cigars); and Jim for tying up all the loose ends. If you find yourself thinking that this book is pretty good, it's most likely due to something that these three did.

Closer to home, I'd like to thank Oran Sands for bringing me in the door at Que in the first place; Jim Oldfield for giving me my first chance (many, many years ago) to write professionally; and Benn Dunnington for an intense eight-year apprenticeship, which taught me to write improbably well under impossible deadlines. I'd also like to add to that list Mr. Frank Buston, my seventh grade English teacher, and Dr. Isacc Asimov, famed author of science books (both fact and fiction), for helping me to discover the seemingly disparate but surprisingly well-intertwined career paths of journalism and science.

Finally, I would like to thank my wife, Carol, for her continuing encouragement and support. We writers tend to make a big deal about how tough the writing life is, though it's often writers' spouses who suffer the most. She's suffered her share, and more.

—Mark R. Brown

We'd Like to Hear from You!

As part of our continuing effort to produce books of the highest possible quality, Que would like to hear your comments. To stay competitive, we *really* want you, as a computer book reader and user, to let us know what you like or dislike most about this book or other Que products.

You can mail comments, ideas, or suggestions for improving future editions to the address below, or send us a fax at (317) 581-4663. Our staff and authors are available for questions and comments through our Internet site, at **http://www.quecorp.com**, and Macmillan Computer Publishing also has a forum on CompuServe (type **GO QUEBOOKS** at any prompt).

In addition to exploring our forum, please feel free to contact me personally to discuss your opinions of this book: I'm **mcierzniak@que.mcp.com** on the Internet.

Thanks in advance—your comments will help us to continue publishing the best books available on new computer technologies in today's market.

Mark Cierzniak
Product Development Specialist
Que Corporation
201 W. 103rd Street
Indianapolis, Indiana 46290
USA

NOTE Although we cannot provide general technical support, we're happy to help you resolve problems you encounter related to our books, disks, or other products. If you need such assistance, please contact our Tech Support department at 800-545-5914 ext. 3833.

To order other Que or Macmillan Computer Publishing books or products, please call our Customer Service department at 800-835-3202 ext. 666. ▪

Contents at a Glance

VI | Web Site Management

VII | Web Site Tools

VIII | Examples

IX | Appendixes

Table of Contents

III | Advanced HTML

IV | Incorporating Objects

20 Video, Animation, and Multimedia 419

29 VBScript   663

VII | Web Site Tools

34 HTML Tag Editors   775

IX | Appendixes

Introduction

by Jerry Honeycutt and Mark Brown

You can't build a monument without bricks, and you can't make bricks without straw—everyone who has seen the film *The Ten Commandments* knows that. Likewise, if you plan to establish your own monumental presence on the World Wide Web, you have to start with the straw, and that's HTML.

The World Wide Web is built out of Web pages, and those pages are themselves created with the Hypertext Markup Language, or *HTML*. Though many folks talk about "HTML Programming" with a capital *P* (particularly recruiters), HTML is really not a programming language at all. HTML is exactly what it claims to be: a *markup language*. You use HTML to mark up a text document, just as you would if you were an editor using a red pencil. The marks you use indicate which format (or style) should be used when displaying the marked text. ■

What Is HTML?

If you have ever used an old word processing program (remember WordStar?), you already know how a markup language works. In those old programs, if you wanted text to appear in italics, you surrounded it with control characters. For example, you might surround a phrase with control characters that make it appear as bold text, like the following:

```
/Bthis text appears bold/b
```

When you printed the document, the first /B caused the word processor to start using bold characters. It printed all the characters in bold until it reached the second /b. The word processor didn't actually print the /B and /b. These just "marked up" the text sandwiched between them.

HTML works the same way. If you want text to appear on the Web page in bold characters, you mark it up like the following:

```
<B>this text appears bold</B>
```

The <B> turns on bold characters. The </B> turns off bold characters. These tags don't actually appear on the screen; they just cause the text sandwiched between them to appear in bold characters.

Why You Need This Book

Everything you create in HTML relies on tags like these. To be a whiz-bang HTML programmer, you need to learn which tags do what. Fortunately, that's what this entire book is about.

A few other topics are covered in this book: page-design techniques, the HTML extensions you find in Internet Explorer and Netscape Navigator, graphics creation, scripting, and much more. You'll look at HTML and graphics-editing tools, HTML code verification, and how to promote your site on the Web. You even take short side trips into Java programming, CGI programming, ActiveX controls, and the Virtual Reality Modeling Language (VRML).

But you explore these topics only as they relate to the main theme: creating your own Web pages using HTML. The major goal of this book is to help you learn as much as possible about HTML itself.

Ultimately, what you get out of this book will be different depending on how advanced you are:

- If you're a beginner, you'll find information on what other people are doing on the Web, what is appropriate to put on the Web, and how to use basic HTML tags to begin creating your own pages.
- If you're an intermediate user, you'll find tips, tricks, and techniques for creating Web pages that exploit the full potential of HTML.
- If you're an advanced user, you'll learn how to use powerful extensions to HTML and additional technologies such as JavaScript and Java applets to make your Web pages world class.

What's Changed in the Third Edition

The recent changes to HTML have lit a fire under our feet, We're motivated. Thus, we're turning around the third edition of *Special Edition Using HTML* in record time. Here's what we've changed in this edition:

- We've updated our coverage of HTML to include the latest and greatest HTML standards (HTML 3.2).

- We're including the latest information about all the related technologies, such as ActiveX controls, scripting, dynamic HTML, and style sheets.

- We've enhanced our coverage of HTML to take into account the fact that HTML is useful for much more than creating Web pages. It's now used to format e-mail messages, and Microsoft has even announced plans to produce help files using HTML.

- We've added countless new, real-world examples that you can learn from or even use on your own Web site.

Aside from the more dramatic changes we've made to this edition, each and every chapter has gone through more subtle changes. We've updated each chapter with new tips. Outdated information has been replaced with new information. And each chapter has been updated with the latest versions of each program.

How This Book Is Organized

Special Edition Using HTML 3.2, Third Edition provides comprehensive information about HTML and related technologies that you can use to build great Web pages. The new edition has nine parts, each dedicated to a particular concept, such as Web programming or objects. What follows is an overview of topics you'll find in each part of this book:

- Part I, "Overview of WWW Publishing," gives you a brief history of the Internet, World Wide Web, and HTML. In this part, you'll also learn about an approach to designing and implementing Web pages.

- Part II, "Basic HTML," introduces you to HTML. You learn how HTML documents are organized and formatted. You'll learn how to put text on a Web page. You'll also learn how to put graphics, lists, and tables on a Web page.

- Part III, "Advanced HTML," contains the meaty stuff. You learn how to use frames, forms, and imagemaps. You also learn about some of the recent innovations such as style sheets and dynamic HTML.

- Part IV, "Incorporating Objects," shows you how to use a variety of objects on your Web pages. You learn about using multimedia and graphics. You also learn how to use controls on the Web page.

- Part V, "Programming and Scripting," introduces you to some of the most exciting technology available for creating dynamic Web pages. Scripting (JavaScript, VBScript, and so forth) lets you glue together all the objects you put on the Web page. Using Java, you can create some pretty amazing applications and distribute them on the Web page.

- Part VI, "Web Site Management," shows you how to manage your entire Web site. You learn how to get your pages onto the Internet. You learn how to manage the files on your Web site, get your Web site noticed, and secure your Web site.

- Part VII, "Web Site Tools," describes the editors you can use to create great Web pages. It's a good idea that you learn about each individual HTML tag. Typically, however, you'll use an editor such as FrontPage to create your Web pages.

- Part VIII, "Examples," contains a variety of real-world examples that reinforce everything you've learned in this book. You'll find examples such as a database, a marketing site, a corporate intranet, and a personal Web site.

- Part IX, "Appendixes," provides a look at the future of HTML. You also get a look at WebTV and what's on the CD accompanying this book.

Conventions Used in This Book

This book uses various stylistic and typographic conventions to make it easier to use.

Shortcut key combinations are joined by + (plus) signs; for example, Ctrl+X means to hold down the Ctrl key, press the X key, and then release both.

Menu items and dialog-box selections often have a mnemonic key associated with them. This key is indicated by an underline on the item on-screen. To use these mnemonic keys, you press the Alt key and then the shortcut key. In this book, mnemonic keys are underlined like this: File.

This book uses the following typeface conventions:

Typeface	Meaning
Italic	Italics indicate new terms. They also indicate variables in commands and addresses.
Bold	Bold indicates text you type. It also indicates Internet addresses.
`Computer type`	Commands.

N O T E Notes provide additional information related to the topic at hand. ■

 Tips provide quick and helpful information to assist you along the way.

CAUTION

Cautions alert you to potential pitfalls or dangers in the operations discussed.

TROUBLESHOOTING

What are Troubleshooting notes? Troubleshooting notes answer questions that might arise while following the procedures in this book.

Special Edition Using HTML 3.2, Third Edition, uses references to point you to other places in the book with additional information relevant to the topic.

▶ **See** "Section Title," **p. xxx**

Overview of WWW Publishing

The Wide World of HTML Publishing

by Mark R. Brown

Though the experts aren't in total agreement, it is generally acknowledged that the jackknife was originally invented for whittling. But once someone had that first jackknife in hand, he found that it was also pretty good for cutting string, driving screws, and picking teeth. It wasn't long before some enterprising jackknife manufacturer added blades specifically designed for those (and other) tasks, and the humble jackknife quickly evolved into the some-what bulkier, but nonetheless more ubiquitously useful, Swiss Army Knife™.

The evolution of HTML has followed a similar path.

Originally developed for the creation of World Wide Web pages, HTML proved itself useful for many other, origi-nally unforeseen tasks, and has therefore evolved over time into a bulkier, but much more useful markup lan-guage. Though the Web is arguably still the place where it sees the most use, HTML is now also called into service for the creation of corporate intranets, for spicing up e-mail and news messages, and even for developing GUIs (Graphical User Interfaces) for stand-alone and net-centric applications. Along the way, new functions and features have been added to HTML, so that the current standard (3.2, as this is written) bears little resemblance to its much simpler and less ambitious precursors.

HTML's origin

HTML was originally used for the creation of pages on the World Wide Web.

HTML's growth

Corporate intranets are likely to become the main application for HTML in the near future.

HTML's destiny

Both Microsoft and Netscape are advocating HTML as the GUI-creation framework for application development.

HTML's expansion

Even news and e-mail are strongly integrating HTML content.

This chapter looks at how, in just a few short years, HTML has become such a widely used and useful development tool. ■

The Birth of the World Wide Web

Contrary to what the media would have you believe, the World Wide Web did not spring into being overnight. Though relatively new in human terms, the Web has a venerable genealogy for a computing technology. It can trace its roots back over 25 years, which is more than half the distance back to the primordial dawn of the electronic computing age.

The World Wide Web is actually just one of many applications that run on the Internet, a worldwide network of computer networks (or *internetwork*) which has been around in one form or another since 1961.

 If you're curious about the origins of the Internet, read Bruce Sterling's excellent article on the subject at **gopher://oak.zilker.net:70/00/bruces/F_SF_Science_Column/F_SF_Five_**.

By the mid-1970s, many government agencies, research facilities, and universities were on this internetwork (which was then called ARPAnet), but each was running on its own internal network developed by the lowest bidder for their specific project. For example, the Army's system was built by DEC, the Air Force's by IBM, and the Navy's by Unisys. All were capable networks, but all spoke different languages. What was clearly needed to make things work smoothly was a set of networking *protocols* that would tie together disparate networks and enable them to communicate with each other.

In 1974, Vint Cerf and Bob Kahn published a paper titled "A Protocol for Packet Network Internetworking" that detailed a design that would solve the problem. In 1982, this solution was implemented as *TCP/IP*. TCP stands for *Transmission Control Protocol;* IP is the abbreviation for *Internet Protocol*. With the advent of TCP/IP, the word *Internet*—which is a portmanteau word for *interconnected networks*—entered the language.

The Department of Defense quickly declared the TCP/IP suite as the standard protocol for internetworking military computers. TCP/IP has been ported to most computer systems, including personal computers, and has become the new standard in internetworking. It is the TCP/IP protocol set that provides the infrastructure for the Internet today.

TCP/IP comprises over 100 different protocols. It includes services for remote logon, file transfers, and data indexing and retrieval, among others.

 An excellent source of additional information on TCP/IP is the introduction to the TCP/IP Gopher site at the University of California at Davis. Check it out at **gopher://gopher-chem.ucdavis.edu/11/Index/Internet_aw/Intro_the_Internet/intro.to.ip/**.

 One of the best online guides to the Internet as a whole is the Electronic Freedom Foundation's Extended Guide to the Internet at **http://www.eff.org/papers/bdgtti/eegtti.html**.

The Web Explosion

There was a plethora of different data-indexing and retrieval experiments in the early days of the Net, but none was all-pervasive until, in 1991, Paul Lindner and Mark P. McCahill at the University of Minnesota created *Gopher*. Though it suffered from an overly cute (but highly descriptive) name, its technique for organizing files under an intuitive menuing system won it instant acceptance on the Net. The direct precursor, in both concept and function, to the World Wide Web, Gopher lacked hypertext links or graphic elements (see Figure 1.1). Although Gopher servers sprang up quickly all over the Internet, it was almost immediately apparent that something more was needed.

FIG. 1.1

Most Web browsers, like Netscape Navigator, can also display information on Gopher sites like this.

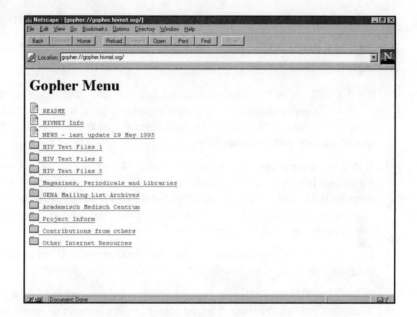

By the time "Gopherspace" began to establish itself on the Net, the European High-Energy Particle Physics Lab (CERN) had become the largest Internet site in Europe and was the driving force in getting the rest of Europe connected to the Net. To help promote and facilitate the concept of distributed computing via the Internet, Tim Berners-Lee created the World Wide Web in 1992.

The Web was an extension of the Gopher idea, but with many, many improvements. Inspired by Ted Nelson's work on Xanadu and the hypertext concept, the World Wide Web incorporated graphics, typographic text styles, and—most importantly—hypertext links.

N O T E The hypertext concept predates personal computers. It was first proposed by computer visionary Ted Nelson in his groundbreaking, self-published book *Computer Lib/Dream Machines* in 1974.

In a nutshell, electronic hypertext involves adding links to words or phrases. When selected, these links jump you to associated text in the same document or to another document altogether. For example, you could click an unfamiliar term and jump to a definition, or add your own notes that would be optionally displayed when you or someone else selected the note's hyperlink.

The hypertext concept has since been expanded to incorporate the idea of *hypermedia,* in which links can also be added to and from graphics, video, and audio clips. ■

The World Wide Web used three new technologies:

- ■ HTML (HyperText Markup Language) used to write Web pages.
- ■ HTTP (HyperText Transfer Protocol) to transmit those pages.
- ■ A Web browser client program to receive the data, interpret it, and display the results.

Using HTML, almost anyone with a text editor and access to an Internet site can build visually interesting pages that organize and present information in a way seldom seen in other online venues. In fact, Web sites are said to be composed of *pages* because the information on them looks more like magazine pages than traditional computer screens.

N O T E HTML is, itself, an outgrowth of the much more complex SGML, or Standard Generalized Markup Language. SGML is (rarely) also used for creating pages on the Web, though it takes a different browser to be able to view SGML pages. You can find out all about SGML at **http://www.w3.org/pub/WWW/MarkUp/SGML/**. ■

HTML is a markup language, which means that Web pages can only be viewed by using a specialized Internet terminal program called a *Web browser.* In the beginning, the potential was there for the typical computing "chicken and the egg problem": No one would create Web pages because no one owned a browser program to view them with, and no one would get a browser program because there were no Web pages to view.

Fortunately, this did not happen, because shortly after the Web was invented, a killer browser program was released to the Internet community—free of charge!

In 1993, the National Center for Supercomputing Applications (NCSA) at the University of Illinois at Champaign-Urbana released Mosaic, a Web browser designed by Marc Andreessen and developed by a team of students and staff at the University of Illinois (see Figure 1.2). It spread like wildfire through the Internet community; within a year, an estimated two million users were on the Web with Mosaic. Suddenly, everyone was browsing the Web, and everyone else was creating Web pages. Nothing in the history of computing had grown so fast.

 T I P For more information on NCSA Mosaic, check out the NCSA Web site at **http://www.ncsa.uiuc.edu/SDG/Software/Mosaic/**.

By mid-1993, there were 130 sites on the World Wide Web. Six months later, there were over 600. Today, there are over a quarter of a million Web sites in the world (more or less, depending on whose figures you believe).

FIG. 1.2

NCSA Mosaic, the browser that drove the phenomenal growth of the World Wide Web, is still available free of charge for Windows, Windows NT, Windows 95, UNIX, and Macintosh.

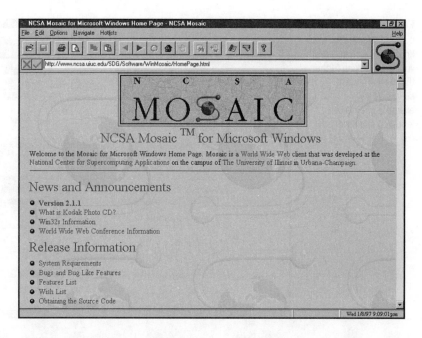

Mosaic's success—and the fact that its source code was distributed for free—spawned a wave of new browser introductions. Each topped the previous by adding new HTML commands and features. Marc Andreessen moved on from NCSA and joined with Jim Clark of Silicon Graphics to found Netscape Communications Corporation. They took along most of the NCSA Mosaic development team, which quickly turned out the first version of Netscape Navigator for Windows, Macintosh, and UNIX platforms. Because of its many new features and free trial preview offer, Netscape Navigator quickly became the most popular browser on the Web. The Web's incredible growth even attracted Microsoft's attention and, in 1995, it introduced its Internet Explorer Web browser to coincide with the launch of its new WWW service, The Microsoft Network (MSN).

Established online services like CompuServe, America Online, and Prodigy scrambled to meet their users' demands to add Web access to their systems. Most of them quickly developed their own versions of Mosaic, customized to work in conjunction with their proprietary online services. This enabled millions of established commercial service subscribers to spill over onto the Web virtually overnight; "old-timers" who had been on the Web since its beginning (only a year and a half or so before) suddenly found themselves overtaken by a tidal wave of Web-surfing *newbies*. Even television discovered the Web, and it seemed that every other news report featured a story about surfing the Net.

The World Wide Web didn't get its name by accident. It truly is a web that encompasses just about every topic in the world. A quick look at the premier index to the Web, Yahoo! (**http://www.yahoo.com**), lists topics as diverse as art, world news, sports, business, libraries, classified advertising, education, TV, science, fitness, and politics (see Figure 1.3). You can't get much more diverse than that! There are literally thousands of sites listed on Yahoo! and other online indexes.

FIG. 1.3
If you really want to know what's on the Web, you need look no further than Yahoo!, which serves as a good example of an excellent Web site itself.

T I P   For more information about the World Wide Web, consult the WWW FAQ at **http://www.boutell.com/boutell/**.

The Rise of the Corporate Intranet

The World Wide Web explosion shows no signs of slowing down. It proved so intuitive and so much fun to use that people almost immediately began to see other uses for the Web browsing "metaphor."

One of the first and most obvious was to build Webs that didn't communicate over the Internet at all, but were confined within the computer systems of individual companies and institutions. A term was quickly coined to distinguish these internal Webs: *intranets*.

The major difference between an intranet and a Web site—besides the obvious fact that the former is constrained to an individual site, while the latter is worldwide—is the audience. On a Web site, the content is aimed at the public, while an intranet addresses the needs of an organization's own employees (see Figure 1.4).

This means that intranets are more likely to contain company-specific—even confidential—data, such as sales reports, customer databases, training materials, and employee manuals.

FIG. 1.4
HTML-based corporate intranets like this one at National Semiconductor give employees quick-and-easy access to company databases and resources.

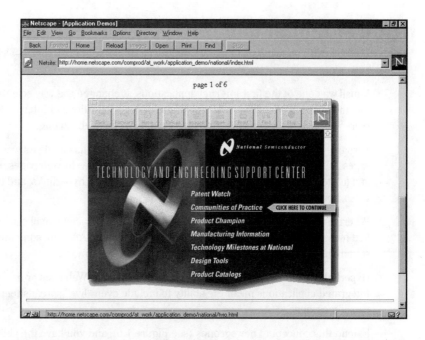

Though these kinds of data have been available on internal corporate networks for years, the difference with intranets is in the presentation. HTML and associated technologies are used to create user interfaces which are as fun and easy to use as those on most World Wide Web sites. Data which might have previously been locked up in difficult-to-use corporate databases can be made easily accessible to even computer novices.

Even with only a year or two of real-world usage, the utility of corporate intranets has already been proven beyond the shadow of a doubt. Netscape Communications Corporation, a publisher of Web-server and client software and one of the premier advocates of intranet development, says that a resounding majority of its intranet customers report substantial cost savings after installing corporate intranets. Some have claimed 1,000% returns on their investments, according to Netscape. In the world of business, this is a phenomenal rate of return, and a claim which has grabbed the attention of the majority of Fortune 500 companies—as well as many that are much, much smaller.

 To read Netscape Communication Corporation's study on intranet return-on-investment, go to **http://home.netscape.com/comprod/announce/roi.html**.

In fact, interest in intranets is so great that HTML server and client publishers like Netscape and Microsoft predict that the majority of their HTML-related income over the next few years will be generated by intranet development, not the World Wide Web.

HTML in E-Mail and News

HTML is also showing up in many other places you might not expect—electronic mail, for example.

E-mail was one of the first Internet applications. It changed the way scientists collaborated in the mid-60s, and continues to be one of the major applications of Internet technology. Millions more people use the Internet for e-mail than use it for Web surfing.

Perhaps, then, it should come as no surprise that HTML has made its way into e-mail messages. HTML affords the same benefits to e-mail as it does to Web pages or intranets: an easy and fun-to-use interface; integration of text and graphics; hyperlinks; and the ability to integrate video, sound, and applications inline, to name just a few.

Where e-mail is just a way to exchange text, HTML-enhanced e-mail can enhance and reinforce text messages with graphics or other "rich" information. After all, sometimes a picture—or sound bite, or video clip—is worth a thousand words, or more.

Hyperlinks mean the ability to link an e-mail message to Web sites or intranet information. Integrated applications mean the ability to include even "live" spreadsheets or other data into e-mail messages.

Extend this concept to newsgroups (see Figure 1.5), and you have the ability to turn static, all-text news postings into truly collaborative works. One worker can post an HTML message which contains an AutoCAD drawing, for example, and all the other members of the group can comment on it, adding notes or even making changes to the drawing itself.

FIG. 1.5

E-mail messages and newsgroup postings created with HTML can have all the look, feel, and functionality of Web pages.

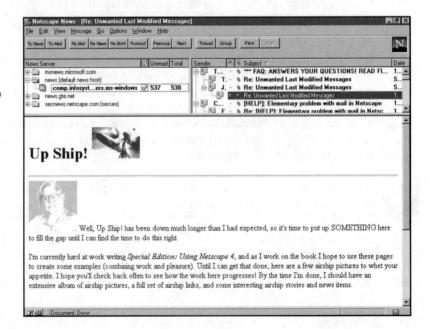

Clearly, HTML in messages—both e-mail and newsgroups—may have as much of an impact on the way people communicate and collaborate online as the Web or intranets have already had.

HTML for GUIs

But that's not the end of HTML's potential. Both Microsoft and Netscape are advocating that HTML be used as the basis for creating stand-alone applications, too.

That HTML's user interface is friendly and easy-to-use has certainly been well-established on the Web and corporate intranets. But, because HTML documents can also incorporate *active* objects like ActiveX controls and Java applets, HTML pages can act as containers for applications. HTML tags can be used to format text, graphics, interactive buttons, forms, and other objects on-screen which interact with the user just as any other GUI (Graphical User Interface). Incorporated into the HTML page are objects such as an ActiveX control or a Java applet (see Figure 1.6).

FIG. 1.6
This JavaScript-based online calculator is just a simple example of using HTML to create the user interface for an application program.

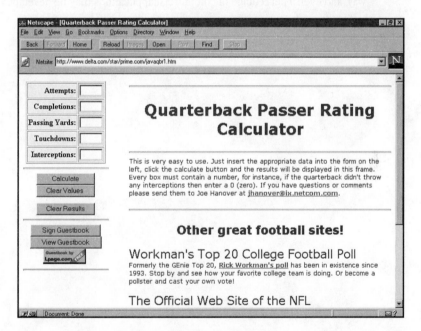

By using HTML as the GUI-development language, the developer gains a whole list of advantages:

- GUI development is sped up considerably. Rather than using a high-level language like C or C++, the GUI is created quickly with simple HTML.

- GUIs can be created by end users, or at least by relatively inexperienced personnel, which is cheaper and faster than tying up programmers.

- GUIs can be easily debugged and modified, further freeing up development resources.

- GUI development is not tied to application development. Applications can be of any type, from ActiveX controls to Java applets to JavaScript or VBScript applications.

- It's easy to develop applications that can access data locally, over a corporate intranet and over the Internet, without having to change the code.

- User interfaces are naturally easy to use and easy to learn, because they use the familiar Web metaphor.

Netscape is actively pushing Sun's Java as its development language of choice, while Microsoft would like to see developers using their ActiveX controls. But each supports the other and—most importantly—both advocate HTML as the GUI-development language.

As this concept catches on, you'll see more applications developed with HTML interfaces, and HTML will become important in its own right as a language for "gluing together" mini-application modules (or *applets*), no matter what language those applets have been written in. In time, it may be that the majority of special-purpose software and shareware is written in this way, and even a percentage of commercial applications may be developed in this manner. ●

## CHAPTER 2

HTML Page Design and Implementation

by Mark R. Brown

"**F**reedom of the press belongs to those who own one," wrote journalist and critic A.J. Liebling. But with the advent of the World Wide Web, almost anyone can own a "press," which can potentially reach a much larger audience (the world) at a much lower cost (practically free) than any other form of information distribution that has preceded it.

What do you print with this press? There are really two issues involved: content and presentation. Because HTML documents are such a visual medium (or *multi-medium*, to coin a term), the way in which information is presented can sometimes seem to almost bury the information itself.

Marshall McLuhan was the first to recognize this principle. In his landmark analysis of television's effect on society, he declared that "the medium is the message," and that's as true a statement when applied to HTML documents—especially the World Wide Web—as it was when he philosophized about TV. Because they represent a whole new way to present and interact with information, HTML documents can have a tremendous impact on the viewer's perception of the information contained in them.

Markup, not programming

HTML is not a programming language. It's a mark-up language, and there's a big difference between the two.

The Wright advice

Form follows function in architecture, and you find that's a good principle to follow when designing pages, too.

Keep in focus

HTML documents should be focused to draw the interest of your audience.

Reality intrudes

Real-world issues such as copyrights, plagiarism, legality, and morality assert themselves in HTML page design.

For example, a simple printed table of sales figures on paper can't convey the same levels and sublevels of information that those statistics communicate when placed in an HTML table, which includes links to the sales figures for the same periods in other years, a full set of charts and graphs which interpret those sales figures in multiple ways, and even photos and biographies of the company's top salespeople! It's clear that creating HTML documents demands a whole new way of thinking about information, and the ways in which that information is presented.

Before this chapter goes into the mechanics of creating pages with HTML, there are a few pages to get you thinking about what kinds of content you want in your HTML documents and how you might want to present that content. ■

What HTML Is

It isn't a programming language. HTML is exactly what it claims to be: a "mark-up language." You use HTML to mark up a text document, just as you would if you were an editor with a red pencil. The marks you use indicate which format (or presentation style) should be used when displaying the marked text.

If you have ever used an old word processor program, you already know how a mark-up language works. In older word processing programs, if you wanted text to appear in italics, you might surround it with control characters like this:

```
/Ithis is in italics/i
```

When the document was printed, the /I would kick your line printer into italics mode, and the following text would be printed in italics. The /i would then turn italics off. The printer didn't actually print the /I or /i. They were just codes to tell it what to do. The "marked up" text in between appeared in italics.

This is exactly how HTML works. If you want text to appear on a Web page in italics, you mark it like this:

```
<I>this is in italics</I>
```

The <I> turns italics on; the </I> turns them off. The <I> and </I> tags don't appear on-screen, but the text in between is displayed in italics.

Everything you create in HTML relies on marks, or *tags*, like these. To be a whiz-bang HTML "programmer," all you need to learn is which tags do what.

Of course, nothing in the real world is ever quite that simple. In truth, simple HTML gets a big boost in real-world page design from add-ons like Java and JavaScript, VBScript, CGI programming, style sheets, ActiveX controls, and other page-design extenders and expanders. Fortunately, this book covers those topics, as well. You can still get started in HTML page design by using nothing but a handful of basic HTML tags and a good text editor.

The Only Tool You Really Need

Because HTML is a tag-oriented text markup language that works with standard ASCII text, all you really need to begin creating HTML pages is a good text editor. If you're using a version of Windows, for example, good ol' NotePad will do just fine.

Listing 2.1 is a simple HTML document that you can re-create by using NotePad.

Part

I

Ch

2

Listing 2.1   A Sample HTML Document

```
<HTML>
<HEAD>
<TITLE>A Simple Sample HTML Document</TITLE>
</HEAD>
<BODY>
<H1>Welcome to the World of HTML</H1>
<HR>
HTML documents can be as simple as this Web page, which consists of just a
single page of <B>text</B> and <I>links</I>, or as complex as a 10,000
page corporate intranet site replete with Java applets and CGI database
access. <P>
In this book, we'll explore the possibilities of HTML, but we'll also
check out what can be done by adding other elements to your documents.<P>
Click <A HREF="sample.htm">HERE</A> to reload this page!<P>
</BODY>
</HTML>
```

Don't worry that you don't know what these markup tags mean for right now—they'll all be explained in the next few chapters. Just type this sample document into your text editor of choice, and save it using the file name "sample.htm." (Make sure your editor is set to save in simple ASCII text mode.) Then fire up your Web browser and load this file from disk. You should see a display similar to that in Figure 2.1.

 TIP   In Netscape Navigator, you can load a file from disk by selecting File, Open File from the menu. In Microsoft Internet Explorer, choose File, Open, then use the Browse button to locate the file you want. Other browser programs work similarly.

Of course, just as most carpentry projects are easier when you have a selection of power tools rather than just a couple of hand tools, the job of creating HTML documents is made easier if you have a selection of software tools to help you along. Chapters 34 ("HTML Tag Editors") and 35 ("WYSIWYG HTML Editors") discuss a variety of HTML editors that speed and simplify the task of editing HTML, and many of the other chapters in this book describe graphics editors and other software tools to ease the creation of the other elements you'll want to incorporate into your HTML documents.

FIG. 2.1

Netscape Navigator displays the simple sample HTML file from Listing 2.1.

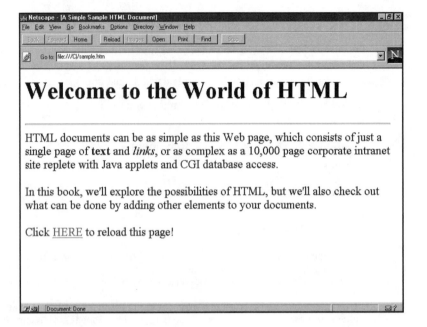

Image Is Not Everything

Billy Crystal's Fernando character on Saturday Night Live used to say, "As we all know, it is better to look good than to feel good...and you look mahvelous!" Unfortunately, it seems that many HTML developers have a similar attitude: They believe it is more important for their pages to look good than to actually be good. For example, you can find plenty of Web sites that are loaded with colorful graphics and have a multitude of links to click; they often lack good, solid content, however.

It might be better to follow the advice of the 20th Century's most famous architect, Frank Lloyd Wright, who coined the mantra of modern architecture: "Form follows function."

Because HTML documents can contain so many flashy elements—graphics, animations, video clips, and even interactive games—it's easy for the message to be overwhelmed. When designing HTML pages, you need to continually ask yourself: "Is this really necessary?"

Before adding a page-design element, it should be determined that the element will actually enhance and emphasize the message your document is trying to communicate. What are you trying to say? Does that graphic, sound bite, or table help you communicate your message? If the answer is "no," then you should rethink your page design.

The flip side of this is, of course, that if your HTML pages have excellent content but aren't visually appealing, people aren't likely to stay around long enough to find out just how good they are. People have a tendency to judge a book by its cover, and with so many well-done, visually attractive HTML documents out there, you're up against some stiff competition.

A case in point, chosen at random, is the Rutgers University Libraries Web site, listing resources on American and British history at **http://info.rutgers.edu/rulib/artshum/ amhist.html** (see Figure 2.2). Everything is here, from the autobiography of St. Patrick to the North American Free Trade Agreement (NAFTA). Unfortunately, this unadorned list of links is unlikely to be discovered by anyone except academics doing scholarly research. There's a lot of excellent information here, but it's hidden by unspectacular presentation. It's not even that the index is poorly done; in fact, the information is very well organized. It's just not presented in an appealing manner. (Note that this site has been awarded a "Top 5 Percent Web Site" recognition by Point Technologies, an award which was obviously based on its excellent content, not its presentation.)

FIG. 2.2

This list of American and British history resources at Rutgers contains good information and is well organized, but the site suffers from bland presentation.

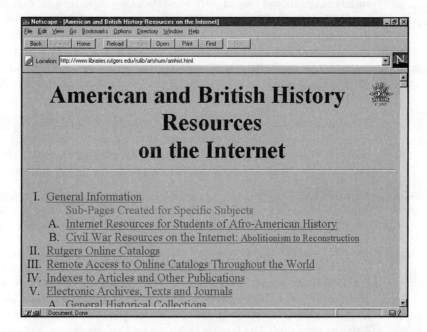

If you're going to draw people in, you have to present your pages the way a politician campaigns: you've only got the public's attention with a quick "sound bite," so you must make your impression up front.

NOTE Though you want to strive for good design, don't just shove a whole bunch of extra elements down your viewers' throats—give them a choice! If you want to add Java applications, animations, sound files, video clips, and even background graphics to your pages, make them optional. Don't make your visitors automatically load a home page that is overloaded with lots of noncritical elements. Viewers with slow modem connections will especially appreciate the opportunity to *not* view everything on your pages. ■

The Right Stuff

We've established that looks aren't everything, but that without looks you'll never get your message across. Now it's time to think about what that message will be.

Keep Focused

Here's your new motto: Keep in focus!

Your HTML documents should focus on a single topic or, at most, a cluster of closely associated topics. If you're developing a Web site, for example, there are millions of different Web surfers out there, and most of them won't even slow down for a generic, generalized site. They want to find information and entertainment that suits their personal needs, wants, and tastes. The odds are that you'll never find even a handful of individuals who share your dual interests in, say, windsurfing and Baroque music. It would be suicide to mix the two on a Web page— those who are interested in one topic will be turned off by the other, and move on. But if you put up a site devoted to one or the other, you'll pull in thousands of like-minded individuals. (And remember, there's nothing to keep you from putting two separate sites on the Web!)

Above all, your pages should be interesting. Whether you're developing a Web site or a corporate intranet, or even if you're just enhancing an e-mail or news message, your HTML documents should appeal to the audience you have identified for them, and should communicate your message clearly. The topic should be focused—the tighter, the better.

There are a million Web sites, for example, devoted to music or to farming. The odds of drawing much of a crowd with such generic topics are slim—you're sure to be overwhelmed by other bigger and better established Web sites with more resources to devote to the project.

However, if your Web site is focused on something specific, such as Lithuanian folk music or llama raising, you're sure to pull in a devoted following of true, die-hard advocates of the topic. Figure 2.3 is a perfect example of a Web site with a tightly defined subject matter. The St. Augustine page at the University of Pennsylvania (**http://ccat.sas.upenn.edu/jod/ augustine.html**) is a scholarly site devoted completely to the study of St. Augustine. There are complete texts (including some in Latin), images, commentaries, and essays, all presented in a well-organized and appealing way. And it's not stuffy—you'll even find the lyrics to Sting's rock-and-roll ballad, "St. Augustine in Hell"! This site won't attract many punk rockers or rocket scientists. However, its intended audience—philosophers and theologians, both amateur and professional—are sure to not only find it, but to keep coming back.

On the Links

Here's another motto for you: Think hyper!

Almost every HTML document features hypertext links; they're what make HTML unique. But I'm sure you've seen many Web sites which throw up a huge, unorganized list of links, some of which are more relevant to the topic at hand than others. A well-organized list of links— whether to associated Web pages or to a network database—can be a valuable asset to an HTML document.

FIG. 2.3

This page, devoted to the study of St. Augustine, is a perfect example of an HTML document that is focused, well-presented, and rich in content.

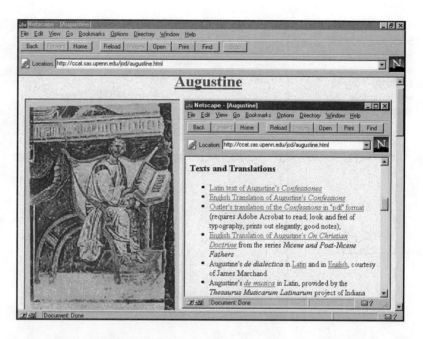

For example, Scott Yanoff began his list of must-see sites on the Internet back before the World Wide Web existed. People would download his list of informative Gopher, FTP, and Telnet sites every month or grab it off their UseNet news feed when it was updated. With the advent of the Web, Yanoff added Web sites to his list and set up a site of his own to host the list (**http://www.spectracom.com/islist/**). It is, and always has been, one of the best topically organized lists of resources on the Net (see Figure 2.4). Take a look at his site, and try to do as good a job of organizing your own hypertext link lists.

Timeliness

One of the reasons that people love the World Wide Web is because of its capability to deliver new information with an immediacy that can only be matched by other broadcast media, such as TV and radio. Whenever news breaks—whether it is a major world event, or just the release of the latest new software product—you can bet that the Web will have the information first. If you can keep the information on your site up-to-the-minute fresh, you're sure to attract loyal viewers.

Don't let your Web site lag behind. Keep it up-to-date. Always be on the lookout for new information and new links. Make sure to delete or update older information so that your site never, ever presents outdated or stale information. And, even if you're creating an internal intranet, you want to make sure the information contained therein is timely and accurate.

There are hundreds of daily news sites on the Web that do an amazing job of posting the latest news items every day. Even if your site isn't news-oriented, you can learn a few things by checking out how these sites keep up the pace. Figure 2.5 shows the Web site of the *Beloit Daily News*, one of the smaller newspapers keeping a daily presence on the Web—and doing an excellent job of it. Check out its site at **http://www.beloitdailynews.com/**.

FIG. 2.4

Scott Yanoff's topical list of Internet services is one of the most comprehensive and well-organized lists of resources on the Web.

FIG. 2.5

The *Beloit Daily News* is just one of hundreds of sites that present the latest news stories on the Web daily—or even hourly!

N O T E For general news updated on a daily basis, you can't beat CNN's Web pages at **http://www.cnn.com/**. For the best in computer-related daily news, check out c|net's site at **http://www.news.com/**.

Create a Vortex

So your HTML documents should be appealing, focused, organized, and up-to-date. That's not too much to ask, is it? The whole idea is to create an information vortex that draws in your audience like a spider draws in flies.

You've got to strike a careful balance between form and content, between innovation and familiarity. People long for the new, innovative, and unique—but, conversely, they are more comfortable with the recognizable and familiar. Everything must work together to make your pages appealing.

Everything in your documents should be directed toward delivering your message. All should point to the center: your focus topic. Graphics should illustrate, links should be relevant, and design should set a mood.

There are people accomplishing this every day on the World Wide Web. For example, take a look at Figure 2.6, the Web site for the Rock and Roll Hall of Fame at **http://www.rockhall. com**. The home page features a big, colorful, playful, clickable graphic menu that leads to fun and relevant areas of interest—from a tour of the museum itself to a list of the 500 top rock songs of all time. There's even a thoughtful link to the Cleveland home page. (This is a good tie in because the Rock Hall is a tourist attraction, and potential visitors want to know about travel, hotels, restaurants, and other tourist sites in the area).

Right up front are two very timely items: a link to Rock News and an item right below the menu showing what happened in rock-and-roll history on this date. The first thing you think when you check into this site is, "awesome!" But all of the information is relevant and up front, so the site accomplishes its real goal: to entice people to visit the Rock and Roll Hall of Fame.

FIG. 2.6
The Rock & Roll Hall of Fame Web site is the perfect example of what an HTML document should be: entertaining, appealing, and focused with a clear goal in mind.

The Wrong Stuff

So what shouldn't you put into your HTML documents? That's easy—just turn around everything we've said so far.

Remember to focus. Don't try to be everything to everybody. This is the number two problem of many personal sites on the World Wide Web. They haven't defined for whom or what they are there. They spew out whatever pops up in whatever areas interest them at the moment. You might see graphics of motorcycles, rock bands, comic book characters, and computer screens all mixed up like a nightmare collage.

"Wait a minute," you protest, "you said that's the number two problem of personal Web sites. What's number one?"

Even worse than a site that's burdened down with everything is one that contains nothing of interest at all. Many personal sites contain next to nothing: lists of CDs or comic books the person owns; pictures of his or her dog, gerbil, or fish; fuzzy photos of the site's owner goofing around with friends; and so on. Let's face it; except for a small circle of your very closest friends, nobody but nobody (not even your significant other) wants to know that much about you. So why put it up in public? It's a waste of bandwidth. It's boring!

What astounds me is many people are aware that it's mind-numbingly boring, and yet they put it up anyway! Some even seem to take pride in how boring they can make their sites, as shown by examples like the following page, appropriately titled "My *Boring* Life" (see Figure 2.7). Please don't ever put another site like this up on the Web. There are far too many of them already.

FIG. 2.7

There are already too many boring sites on the Web. Make sure yours isn't one of them.

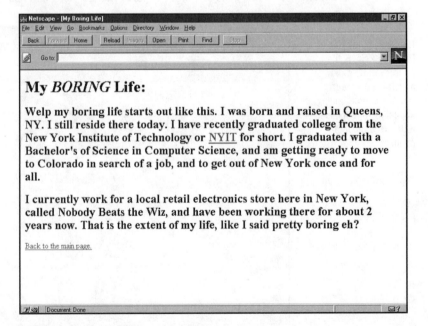

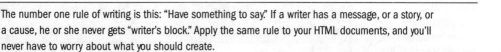

TIP The number one rule of writing is this: "Have something to say." If a writer has a message, or a story, or a cause, he or she never gets "writer's block." Apply the same rule to your HTML documents, and you'll never have to worry about what you should create.

Another thing you definitely don't want to do is to put up a page that consists of nothing but huge wads of unedited, unorganized links, such as the Web site shown in Figure 2.8. (And don't mistake alphabetical order for organization!) This site is like a library where the books are all stacked at random. It's almost worse than having none at all. People want useful links, but they also want to be able to find them easily.

FIG. 2.8

An unorganized list of random links is of no use to anyone. At least this site included short descriptions!

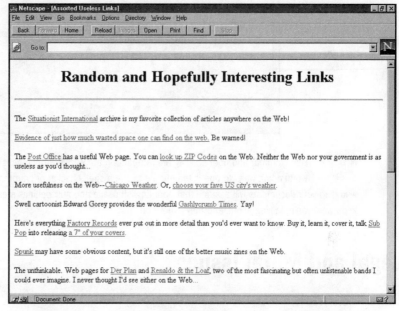

Everyone expects data in an HTML document—especially one on the Web—to be up-to-date and accurate. The worst thing you can do to your viewers is put up some purportedly useful data, only to have it go stale. It's better to take your site down completely than to let it sit there with outdated, useless information.

Figure 2.9 is an example of a site past its prime. It features graphs of card prices for the collectable trading card game, "Magic: the Gathering." Prices for these cards fluctuate wildly, and when the data was current, this was a valuable service for card collectors. Unfortunately, the site is still up, and as of this writing, the information is well over a year out of date. This is worse than useless, as someone is likely to consult these graphs and not notice that the information is outdated. He or she could make some bad decisions based on this old data. Don't ever do this to those who visit your site. If you can't keep it current, take it down.

FIG. 2.9
The data in these graphs is outdated and useless. Visitors to this site are going to be disappointed.

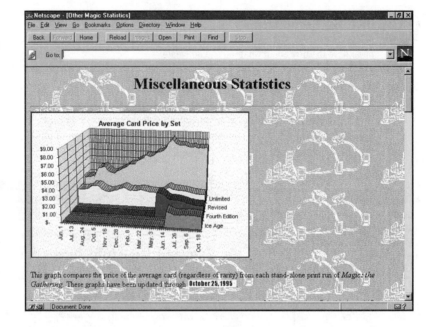

N O T E Bad grammar and poor spelling are rampant on the Web. If a document is worth doing, it's worth doing well. No one is too hurried to use a spell checker or grammar checker. People who read your documents will assume that poor English usage and misspellings mean that you don't know what you're talking about, and they'll move on. ■

Legal and Moral Issues

> **CAUTION**
>
> I am not a lawyer, and this section is not a legal guide. It is, rather, an overview of some of the legal issues to keep in mind when you are developing HTML documents. For advice on legal matters, consult an attorney.

When you're creating a private e-mail message, closed newsgroup post, or corporate intranet, you probably don't have to worry much about possible legal problems with your HTML documents. After all, your audience is all on the same team you are, and your communications are most likely governed by company policies and guidelines. However, when you create a site on the World Wide Web, you are subject to many of the same laws that govern printing, publishing, and broadcasting.

Be a Legal Eagle

The first amendment to the U.S. Constitution guarantees every American the right of free speech (and, of course, most other free nations have similar laws). This does not guarantee you the right to say anything you want with impunity. People who feel that you have treated them unfairly in public have legal recourse. You can be sued for libel and slander for anything you say on the Web, just as you could if you had printed it on paper. And in this litigious society, it is probably better to err on the side of caution than to strike out boldly and without forethought.

Part
I
Ch
2

Controversy and debate online are fine, but if you're diplomatic and noninflammatory, you'll not only avoid legal battles, you'll attract more sympathizers. After all, you're on the Web to share your ideas, not to entice someone to sue you. Before you post something questionable, consider the following: Even if you're sure you'd win, do you really want to spend your time sitting in court for months on end?

The right to privacy ties in closely with libel and slander issues. If you receive private information about any of your users—through a registration form, for example—you must be very, very careful about how it is used and who has access to it. Though there is no actual law guaranteeing U.S. citizens a right to privacy, there is a long-established legal precedent that says it is a basic right implied by the U.S. Constitution. It is best to keep all such information completely private, unless you have asked for and received specific permission to use it publicly.

Perhaps no laws are more openly flaunted on the Web than those concerning copyright and plagiarism. Everyone seems to steal text, graphics, programs, hypertext link lists, HTML code, and everything else from one another pretty freely and openly. However, the most recent U.S. copyright law says that all original, creative works in any medium (including electronic) are automatically assigned to their creator when created. No registration is necessary (though it is a good idea, so that ownership can be proven if challenged). Again, it's best to not "borrow" anything at all from anyone else's site, unless you have written permission to do so.

No Web-related topic has gotten more press than the issue of adult material on the Web and its accessibility by minors. It is such a hot topic that Congress included tough anti-pornography language directed at the Internet in the Telecommunications Act of 1996. Although this law was quickly challenged in the courts, it has made many ISPs very, very nervous about the content of pages posted through their sites. If you plan to post adult material on your site, you certainly should at least make people enter through a disclaimer page. And make sure you have the permission of your ISP beforehand, or you could be kicked unceremoniously offline at the first hint of controversy.

Got you scared now? You say you need advice? The Electronic Freedom Foundation is the champion of the rights of those online. If you have questions about copyrights, pornography, libel, or other legal issues online, the odds are good that you can find the answers on the EFF site at **http://www.eff.org** (see Figure 2.10).

FIG. 2.10

The Electronic Frontier Foundation home page features full coverage of the topic of legal issues online, including a lively discussion of the Telecommunications Act of 1996.

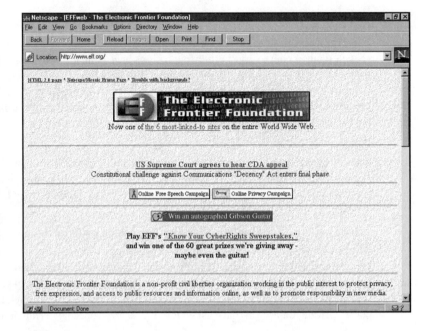

Electronic Morality

Once past the legal issues, you might want to stop a moment and ponder the fine line between rights and responsibilities. Are you the guardian of society's mores? Is it up to you to try to bolster a civilization that is sagging under its own decaying weight? I happen to think the answer to that question is a resounding "Yes!"

I've always considered it better to be positive than negative, to build up rather than to tear down. With a forum as wide-ranging as the World Wide Web, anyone putting up a Web site has a huge potential audience, and therefore a potential to do great good or great harm.

Nonetheless, there are legitimate issues, worthy of open discussion, that are the subjects of controversial Web sites. Take tax reform, for instance. Many sides of this issue are represented in force on the Web (see Figure 2.11), and all draw their share of criticism, harassment, and hate mail. I'm sure those who have chosen to establish these sites consider the controversy all part of the territory. There are religious denominations, environmentalists, pro-choice and pro-life organizations, neo-Nazis, and other controversial groups on the Web who are constantly drawing fire from others. Before you establish a site that's destined to become the center of controversy, you should answer just one question: Can you take the heat? If the answer is "yes," then by all means go online with your views.

FIG. 2.11
All sorts of controversial sites, such as this tax reform newsletter page, exist on the Web. Before you set one up, make sure you're willing to do battle for your cause.

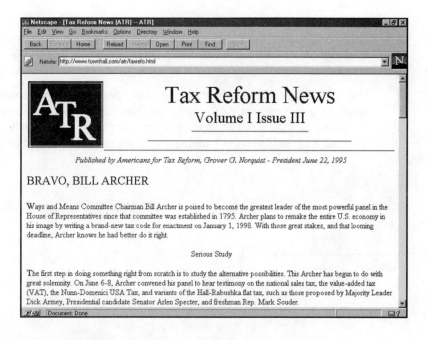

Sending Your Work Out into the World

As noted in Chapter 1, "The Wide World of HTML Publishing," HTML isn't just for Web pages, anymore. People are using HMTL to create corporate intranets, flashy e-mail and news postings, and even user interfaces for applications.

So what do you do with your HTML once you've written it? As you might expect, that depends on your application.

If your HTML pages are destined for the World Wide Web, you'll likely upload them to your ISP (Internet Service Provider). Finding an ISP to host your Web pages is a relatively simple task these days. If you're connected with an online service such as America Online, you probably already have space available to you, whether you know it or not. Most local ISPs also include a few megabytes of space for hosting your pages, all as a part of your dial-up service contract. Chapter 30, "Putting Your Pages Online," provides detailed information on how you can get your Web site up and running.

If you're developing for a corporate intranet, or if your Web pages will be hosted by your organization's own Web server, you'll need to set up the server computer to host your pages. The details will vary with different installations, and you need to work them out with your system administrator.

If your HTML is destined to dress up e-mail or newsgroup posts, you need to use an e-mail or newsgroup program that allows attaching HTML to messages. Netscape Communicator's Messenger (for e-mail) and Collabra (for news) applications include this capability, as do many others.

Finally, HTML for GUI (graphical user interface) development means your HTML code will be bundled together with controls, applets, and other bits and pieces of the application for distribution as a package. If you're not the sole developer of the application itself, the project coordinator will likely be in charge of making sure all the pieces come together as needed. ●

Basic HTML

HTML Document Architecture

by Robert Meegan

HTML documents are easy to create, after a few basic rules are understood. The rules provide the structure that allows many different browsers on almost every computer platform to display a document. As an HTML author, you have the responsibility to follow these rules. ■

The required elements for an HTML document

HTML documents are required to have certain features to direct the viewing software.

How to create relationships between documents

Documents do not generally exist in a vacuum. It is possible to specify the logical connections between documents.

About the attributes associated with the *BODY* element

The BODY element has a large number of attributes that determine how the text will appear when it is read.

How to add comments to your HTML source documents

Adding comments to an HTML document can help you remember why you did things a certain way.

How to create a template for your own use

The best way to develop HTML documents is to create a basic template that allows you to have a consistent format.

Starting with the Basics

The most fundamental of all the tags used to create an HTML document is, not surprisingly, the <HTML> tag. This tag should be the first item in your document and the corresponding end tag, </HTML>, should be the last. Together, these tags indicate that the material contained between them represents a single HTML document (see Listing 3.1). This is important because an HTML document is a plain text ASCII file. Without these tags, a browser or other program isn't able to identify the document format and interpret it correctly.

Listing 3.1   The Simplest HTML Document

```
<HTML>
<HEAD>
<TITLE>A Very Basic HTML Document</TITLE>
</HEAD>
<BODY>
This is where the text of the document would be.
</BODY>
</HTML>
```

N O T E   While most of the recent browsers properly interpret a document that is not contained within the <HTML> start and </HTML> end tags, it is still very important to use them. Many of the new uses for HTML documents, such as e-mail and UseNet postings, do not necessarily involve browsers, and the other programs are more likely to interpret an ASCII document as plain text without the hint that the <HTML> tag provides. ▓

The </HTML> end tag is just as important as the start tag. It is becoming possible to include HTML documents within e-mail messages and news postings. Without the </HTML>, the viewer does not know when to stop interpreting the text as HTML code.

The Document Heading

The document head container is not a required element, but a proper head can greatly increase the usefulness of a document. The purpose of the head is to provide information to the application that is interpreting the document. With the exception of the TITLE element, the elements within the HEAD element are not seen by the reader of the document, at least not directly.

Elements within the HEAD element do the following:

- ▓ Provide a title for the document.
- ▓ Lay out the relationships between multiple documents.
- ▓ Tell a browser to create a search form.
- ▓ Provide a method for sending special messages to a specific browser or other viewer.

Listing 3.2 shows an example of a document HEAD element.

Listing 3.2   A Fairly Detailed *HEAD* Element

```
<HTML>
<HEAD>
<TITLE>General Officers of the US Army in the Civil War</TITLE>
<LINK HREF="mailto:rmeegan@ia.net" REV="made">
<BASE HREF="http://www.ia.net/~rmeegan/civil">
<ISINDEX PROMPT="Enter the desired name">
<META HTTP-EQUIV="EXPIRES" CONTENT="31 Dec 1997">
<META NAME="Last Modified" CONTENT="16 Dec 1996">
<META NAME="Keywords" CONTENT="Yankee, Grand Army of the Republic,
 War Between the States">
<META NAME="Description" CONTENT="A listing of the general officers of the US
 Army in the Civil WAR">
</HEAD>
<BODY BGCOLOR="NAVY" TEXT="WHITE" LINK="RED" VLINK="BLUE" ALINK="GREEN">
<BASEFONT SIZE=3 FONT="Georgia, Century Schoolbook, Times New Roman">
<H1><FONT COLOR="YELLOW">Union Generals of the American Civil War</FONT></
H1><BR>
This listing contains the names of the general officers of the Regular Army
   and of the Volunteer Army, as well as the date of their appointment to the
   rank.<BR><BR>
 The names are taken from<BR>
<CITE>
Statistical Record by Frederick Phisterer<BR>
Published 1883, New York<BR><BR>
</CITE>
In all cases only the full rank is given. Many officers had a <EM>brevet</EM>
 (or temporary) rank that was often one or two ranks higher than the full rank.
 Remember also, that it was possible for an officer to have rank in a state
 militia, the Volunteer Army, and the Regular Army; all at the same time. With
 brevet ranks taken into account, it was possible for an individual to have as
 many as six ranks simultaneously, depending upon who he was dealing with.
</BODY>
</HTML>
```

The HEAD element is opened by the start tag, <HEAD>. This tag normally should immediately follow the <HTML> start tag. The end tag, </HEAD>, is used to close the element. The rest of the head element tags are located within this container.

Naming Your Document

The TITLE element is the only required element of the heading. It is used to give your document a name. This title is generally displayed in the title bar of the browser. The TITLE should not be confused with the file name of the document; instead, it is a text string that is completely independent of the name and location of the file, making it highly useful. The file name is generally constrained by the operating system of the computer that the file is located on.

The TITLE element is delimited by a <TITLE> start tag and a </TITLE> end tag. The actual title is located between these tags. Do not enclose the title in quotation marks unless you want it to appear with the quotes. It is most common for the TITLE element to be all on one line.

The title text is a string of unlimited length that can include any text except for the few special characters that are restricted in HTML. In practice, it is a good idea to keep the length of the title fairly short so that it fits on the title bar. Another thought to keep in mind when making up a title is that many browsers use the title as the caption for the icon when the browser is minimized. Try to make the first few characters particularly meaningful.

N O T E The TITLE is normally used as the default name when a user creates a bookmark to the document. To make this default as useful as possible, avoid having a title like Home Page or Index. Entries like this are nearly useless in a bookmark list. ■

Listing 3.3 is an example of a document TITLE. Figure 3.1 shows how Microsoft Internet Explorer uses the document TITLE as the title of the browser window.

Listing 3.3   An Example of the *TITLE* Element

```
<HTML>
<HEAD>
<TITLE>General Officers of the US Army in the Civil War</TITLE>
</HEAD>
<BODY>
</BODY>
</HTML>
```

FIG. 3.1
Titles provide your readers with a way to identify your documents.

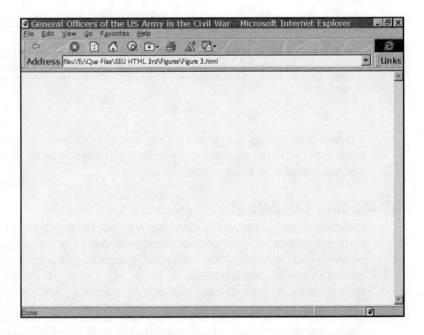

Indexing Your Document

One of the less commonly used <HEAD> elements is the <ISINDEX> tag. This tag originally predated the <FORM> element and the advanced search engines that are now available. The tag is used to inform the browser that a searchable index of the document is maintained on the server. The browser creates a prompt that allows the user to enter a word for which she would like to search the document.

▶ **See** "Working with HTML Forms Tags" for more information on the FORM element, **p. 198**

N O T E If you aren't certain that your server supports this function or if you don't know how to implement it, you probably should avoid using <ISINDEX>. Your readers are guaranteed to be frustrated by an index that doesn't work. ■

Although powerful search tools are available, if your server supports this feature, it is a very easy way to make large documents much more usable. Documents such as catalogs and phone lists are good examples of where a built-in index would be handy.

The attributes for the ISINDEX element are shown in Table 3.1.

Table 3.1 *ISINDEX* **Attributes and Their Functions**

Attribute	Function
ACTION	Points to the search program to which the response should be passed.
PROMPT	Defines a prompt to be used in place of the default prompt.

Listing 3.2 shows how the <ISINDEX> tag is used in an HTML document. This document contains the names of General Officers in the Grand Army of the Republic in the American Civil War, sorted by seniority. The list could have been automatically generated from a database. Because there are more than 2,600 names on the list, it would be difficult to find a particular person just by scanning the list. Figure 3.2 shows how the browser would open a search text field that can be used to enter a desired name. The reader would type the name and press Enter, and the search program on the server would locate the name in the document.

CAUTION

While testing the documents for this chapter, I discovered that Netscape Navigator 3.0 does not display text and background colors correctly if an <ISINDEX> tag is present.

Part II
Ch
3

FIG. 3.2

The browser displays an entry field that allows the reader to enter a search text string when a document has the `<ISINDEX>` tag in the HEAD section.

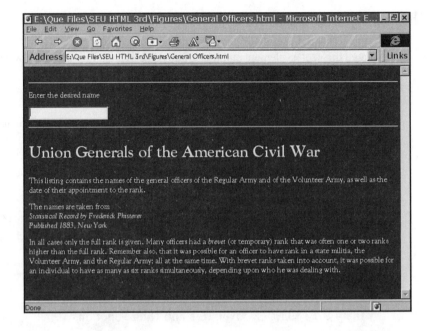

Creating a Document Hierarchy

HTML documents often have a relationship with other documents. This relationship is most frequently in terms of a link to another document. Links to other documents can be relative or absolute (see Listing 3.4). Each of these links poses its own problems. Absolute links can be long, cumbersome, and prone to breakage when the child document is moved. Relative links are easier to type and update, but they break when the parent document is moved. Both of these links are particularly vulnerable to a breaking when a document is moved from one machine to another.

Listing 3.4   Absolute and Relative Links

```
<HTML>
<HEAD>
<TITLE>News Links</TITLE>
</HEAD>
<BODY>
<IMG SRC=/gifs/news.gif ALT="News">          <--- Relative Link --->
<UL>
<BR><A HREF=http://www.cnn.com>CNN Interactive</A>
```

```
<BR><A HREF=http://www.usatoday.com>USA Today</A>
</UL>
<P>
<IMG SRC=//www.ia.net/~rmeegan/gifs/mags.gif ALT="mags">   <--- Absolute Link --->
<UL>
<BR><A HREF=http://www.infoworld.com>Infoworld Magazine</A>
<BR><A HREF=http://www.zdnet.com>Ziff-Davis Publications</A>
</UL>
<P>
</BODY>
</HTML>
```

This might sound unlikely, but consider that a long document might be downloaded to a user's machine so that he might read it when not online. Any links, such as a bibliography, would be unusable when the local copy was viewed. If the user wanted to link to other documents or images, he would first need to reopen the first document on the computer where it normally resides.

Fortunately, the designers of HTML anticipated this problem and have added two elements, BASE and LINK, that can be placed in a document head to help keep a document relationship straight.

> **N O T E** If you're just learning HTML, you might want to skim through this section. It isn't necessary to use the BASE and LINK elements until you start developing complicated documents that require many pages. ■

The *BASE* Element   The BASE element is used to specify the full, original URL of the document. This allows relative links to work, even if a document has been moved to another directory (or even to another machine!). In this way, a BASE element acts much like the DOS PATH statement; it allows the viewing software to find a document link, even when directed from a parent in a different location.

The BASE element has a single required attribute, HREF, which provides the full URL of the document. Listing 3.5 provides an example of how the <BASE> tag is used.

Listing 3.5   Using the *<BASE>* Tag

```
<HTML>
<HEAD>
<TITLE>News Links</TITLE>
<BASE HREF="//www.ia.net/~rmeegan">
</HEAD>
<BODY>
<IMG SRC=/gifs/news.gif ALT="News">
<UL>
<BR><A HREF=http://www.cnn.com>CNN Interactive</A>
<BR><A HREF=http://www.usatoday.com>USA Today</A>
</UL>
```

continues

Listing 3.5   Continued

```
<P>
<IMG SRC=/gifs/mags.gif ALT="mags">
<UL>
<BR><A HREF=http://www.infoworld.com>Infoworld Magazine</A>
<BR><A HREF=http://www.zdnet.com>Ziff-Davis Publications</A>
</UL>
<P>
</BODY>
</HTML>
```

Notice that the BASE element directs the viewer software where to look for the files. Even if a person has downloaded the file to his local machine, the little images for News and Mags can still be found, assuming that the reader's machine has access to the Internet.

The *LINK* Element   If the BASE element allows a browser to locate a document, there still exists the question of what the relationship between two documents might be. This becomes even more important as the complexity of your HTML document increases. To connect documents logically, HTML includes the LINK element.

The LINK element indicates the relationship between the document that contains the <LINK> tag and another document (or other object). It consists of an URL that points to the reference object and an attribute that serves as a description of the relationship. A document can contain as many LINK elements as needed to describe all of the relationships. Table 3.2 lists all of the attributes and their functions.

Table 3.2   *LINK* Attributes and Their Functions

Attribute	Function
HREF	Points to the URL of the other document.
REL	Defines the relationship between the current document and the other document.
REV	This is the opposite of the REL attribute and defines the relationship between the other document and the current document.
TYPE	Specifies the type and parameters for a linked style sheet.

There are many different relationships possible, and the list is not well defined in version 3.2 of the HTML specification. The most common REV relationship is "made", as in the following example:

```
<LINK HREF="mailto:nul@utexas.edu" REV="made">
```

This gives the URL for communicating with the document author. The URL in this instance is the instruction to open an e-mail message addressed to nul@utexas.edu. Sandia National

Laboratories, which is on the forefront of HTML document publishing, also recommends the following REV relationships: "author", "editor", "publisher", and "owner".

Some examples of relationships that can be used with the REL attribute are: "bookmark", " copyright", "glossary", "help", "home", "index", and "toc". There are also two relationships that are most commonly used in ordered documents: "next" and "previous". These are particularly useful relationships. Listing 3.6 shows the HEAD element for a document that is a chapter in an online manual.

Listing 3.6   Using the *<LINK>* Tag

```
<HTML>
<HEAD>
<TITLE>Using the Satellite Identification and Tracking System (SITS)</TITLE>
<LINK REV="made" HREF="mailto:rmeegan@ia.net">
<LINK REL="toc"   HREF="contents.htm">
<LINK REL="index"  HREF="index.htm">
<LINK REL="copyright"  HREF="copyright.htm">
<META NAME="Description" CONTENT="An on-line manual for the SITS">
</HEAD>
<BODY>
</BODY>
```

Part

II

Ch

3

Customized Heading Information

Although it might seem that the elements that can be placed in a document heading already cover every imaginable possibility, the truth is that they barely begin to scratch the surface. Because the procedure for the development and approval of a new HTML specification is rather slow, the companies that produce browser software often create several releases in the time between specification versions. To provide additional functionality, one final element is provided for the heading.

The META element allows a document author to define information that is outside of HTML. This *meta-information* can be used by the browser software to perform activities that are not yet supported by the official HTML specification. As a rule, META elements are not needed for a basic HTML document, but you should keep these elements in mind as you gain experience and as your pages become more sophisticated.

Figure 3.3 is an example of how the META element can be used to have the browser perform an action. Looking at the example, you can see the following line:

```
<META HTTP-EQUIV=refresh" CONTENT="60" URL="www.fdline.org/homepage.html">
```

This is interpreted by Netscape Navigator and Microsoft Internet Explorer as the instruction to wait 60 seconds and then load a new document. This kind of instruction is often used when a document is moved from one location to another. A small document can be left at the previous location to serve as an automatic pointer to the new location.

FIG. 3.3

A browser can interpret commands in the META element to perform actions such as loading a new page automatically.

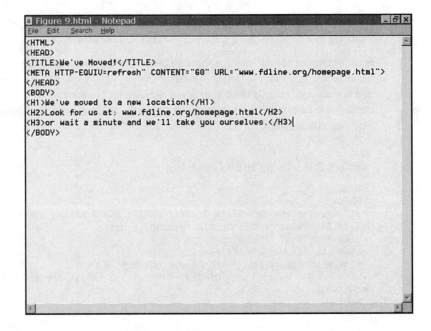

```
<HTML>
<HEAD>
<TITLE>We've Moved!</TITLE>
<META HTTP-EQUIV=refresh" CONTENT="60" URL="www.fdline.org/homepage.html">
</HEAD>
<BODY>
<H1>We've moved to a new location!</H1>
<H2>Look for us at: www.fdline.org/homepage.html</H2>
<H3>or wait a minute and we'll take you ourselves.</H3>
</BODY>
```

A similar command line

```
<META HTTP-EQUIV=refresh" CONTENT="60">
```

can be used to have the browser reload the page every 60 seconds. This is useful for a page that has frequently updated information, such as a stock price ticker.

N O T E Both of these techniques are known as *client-pull* because the client, your browser, requests the new document from the server. These are advanced techniques and you don't need to use except in circumstances when data is changing or the page needs to be reloaded. ▪

Finally, the most popular use of a META element at the present is to use the Keywords property. Many search engines preferentially use the words defined in this element to index the document. This can be used to provide additional keys to an index that might not actually appear in the document verbatim. Listing 3.7 shows how this works.

Listing 3.7 Using *META* Elements

```
<HTML>
<HEAD>
<TITLE>General Officers of the US Army in the Civil War</TITLE>
<META NAME="Keywords" CONTENT="Yankee, Grand Army of the Republic,
 War Between the States">
<META NAME="Description" CONTENT="A listing of the general officers of the US
 Army in the Civil WAR">
```

```
</HEAD>
<BODY BGCOLOR="NAVY" TEXT="WHITE" LINK="RED" VLINK="BLUE" ALINK="GREEN">
</BODY>
</HTML>
```

When designing a document that will be indexed by a search engine, it is also a good idea to use the Description property. Most indexes use this description for your page, if it is present. If no description is present, the index uses the first text available on the page, which can be confusing to some using the index.

N O T E The Keywords and Description properties are good first choices when you start to use META elements. Both of them are easy to understand, and they add a lot of value to your documents. ▪

The syntax for the META element includes the attributes shown in Table 3.3. Much like the relationships in the LINK element, the properties of the META element are not clearly defined in the current version of the HTML specification.

Table 3.3 *META* **Attributes and Their Functions**

Attribute	Function
HTTP-EQUIV	Defines the property for the element.
NAME	Provides an additional description of the element. If this attribute is missing, it is assumed to be the same as HTTP-EQUIV.
URL	Defines a target document for the property.
CONTENT	Provides the response value for the property.

Other Heading Elements

There are two additional elements that can be found in the document heading. Both of these are not fully defined in the HTML 3.2 specification but are supported by Netscape and Microsoft. The first is the SCRIPT element, which is described in Part V, "Programming and Scripting," and the second is the STYLE element.

▶ **See** "Exploring the Properties of a Style" for more information on style sheets, **p. 291**

The Document Body

Although the nature of the World Wide Web appears to be changing in the direction of increasing active content, most people who view your documents will still be interested in your text. This will be especially true for documents that are created for corporate intranets and for documents that serve as online manuals and texts. Because of this, whether you are converting existing documents or creating new ones, you will spend much of your time working in the body.

Starting with the Required Elements

Before you can fill in your document, you need to lay out a basic working framework. HTML documents must follow a defined pattern of elements if they are to be interpreted correctly. Rather than retype the elements that are used in every HTML document, it is a good idea for you to create a template to use for each of your pages so that you are less likely to leave out an important detail. At the end of this chapter, we build a template that you can use as a starter. Until then, we'll use the example presented in Listing 3.8.

Listing 3.8 A Basic HTML Document

```
<HTML>
<HEAD>
<TITLE>This is an example document</TITLE>
</HEAD>
<BODY>
Enter body text here.
</BODY>
</HTML>
```

This example begins with the `<HTML>` tag, which, as you have read, is necessary for every HTML document. Next is the `<HEAD>` tag, which opens up the heading part of the document. This contains the `TITLE` element. We've titled the document "This is an example document." The heading is closed with the `</HEAD>` tag. Finally, the `<BODY>` element follows. This is where you place the bulk of the material in your document. Remember to close the body element with the `</BODY>` tag and finish the page with the `</HTML>` tag.

Because HTML is a markup language, the body of your document is turned on with the start tag, `<BODY>`. Everything that follows this tag is interpreted according to a strict set of rules that tell the browser about the contents. The body element is closed with the end tag, `</BODY>`.

N O T E Strictly speaking, it isn't absolutely necessary to use the `<BODY>` start and end tags; HTML allows you to skip a tag if it is obvious from the context. However, it's still a good idea to use them. Some older browsers and other HTML programs can become confused without them and may not display the document correctly. ▪

In the preceding basic document, the body text is a single line. In your document, you replace this line with the main text of your document. Unless you are using a special HTML editor, you must enter your text using a strict ASCII format. This limits you to a common set of characters that can be interpreted by computers throughout the world. The text that you enter here—whether for the first time or from an existing document—must be completely free of any special formatting. Note that some ASCII characters can be added to the document using only a special coding scheme. This is discussed later in this chapter in "Special Characters."

N O T E Most browsers consider all nonblank white space (tabs, end-of-line characters, and so on) as a single blank. Multiple white spaces are normally condensed to a single blank. ▪

Attributes of the *BODY* Element

The BODY element supports a large number of attributes. These are all important for determining the general appearance of your document. Table 3.4 lists these attributes and their functions for your convenience, but we cover each of them in more detail.

Table 3.4 *BODY* Attributes and Their Functions

Attribute	Function
ALINK	Defines the color of an active link.
BACKGROUND	Points to the URL of an image to use for the document background.
BGCOLOR	Defines the color of the document background.
BGPROPERTIES	If this is set to FIXED, the background image does not scroll.
LEFTMARGIN	Sets the width of the left margin in pixels.
LINK	Defines the color of an unvisited link.
TEXT	Defines the color of the text.
TOPMARGIN	Sets the width of the top margin in pixels.
VLINK	Defines the color of an already visited link.

Coloring Your Documents

The first small step toward creating a document is to define the colors that will be used for the various text components. If you do not specify any colors, the default colors are used. These are normally set by the reader on her browser.

N O T E   Because you have no way of knowing which colors have been selected as defaults by the reader, it is considered good HTML practice to set all of the colors, if you set any. This way, the same color isn't used for more than one component. ▇

There is no simple rule that can be used to define a well-balanced palette, but remember that your readers must actually *read* your document. Try to maintain a high contrast between the text and the background and don't make the color differences too subtle.

Color Definitions   Colors are defined in HTML using a hexadecimal coding system. The system is based upon the three color components—red, green, and blue—which leads to the common name of RGB. Each of the components is assigned a hexadecimal value between 00 and FF (0 and 255 in decimal numbers). These three values are then concatenated into a single value that is preceded by a pound sign (#). An example of such a value is #800080, which is purple. Because few people can visualize colors based solely on a hexadecimal value, HTML 3.2 defines 16 standard color names, which are listed, along with their hexadecimal values, in Table 3.5.

Table 3.5 Standard Colors and Their Values

Color	Value
Black	#000000
Maroon	#800000
Green	#008000
Olive	#808000
Navy	#000080
Purple	#800080
Teal	#008080
Gray	#808080
Silver	#C0C0C0
Red	#FF0000
Lime	#00FF00
Yellow	#FFFF00
Blue	#0000FF
Fuchsia	#FF00FF
Aqua	#00FFFF
White	#FFFFFF

The Body Color Attributes   The BGCOLOR attribute is used for the document background color. If your document has a background image, the BGCOLOR should be as close to the primary color of the image as possible. This allows readers who may not be downloading images to see your text clearly. Many authors make this common mistake, which is particularly bad if the background image is primarily black and the text color that you selected was white. In this case, the reader of your document is greeted by the sight of what is apparently a blank page!

The TEXT attribute is the color used for the text in the document. Because most of your text appears in this color, it should be chosen to provide the reader with sufficient contrast. If you have elected to set the font, be aware that fonts with fine detail are often easier to read when they are dark against a bright background.

The LINK attribute is used by the browser for links that have not yet been followed. This color should be obviously different from the TEXT color so that readers can identify links.

The VLINK attribute is used to identify links that have already been visited. A common choice for VLINK is to use a darker version of the LINK color.

The ALINK attribute marks links that are currently active. This is a relatively recent develop-ment and is normally used for documents that have multiple frames. Quite frankly, choose your other colors first; the reader is least likely to see this color than any of the others.

▶ **See** "The *FRAME* Tag" for more information on using frames, **p. 178**

Having seen all of the things that can be colored in an HTML document, you might wonder if the results justify the effort. If you are creating a static document—such as a manual or a text-book—you might be best off to let the reader set the colors that she wishes to use. On the other hand, if your document is a high-energy page with a lot of graphics, then it is certainly worth the time to find the right blend of colors.

Filling In the Background

One popular way to dress up an HTML document is to add a background image. A background image is a graphics file that is visible under the document text. Using a background can help provide continuity to a document, or it can also serve to differentiate the various pages.

Most background images are small and are tiled across the viewer window like wallpaper. Images of textures are particularly popular for this purpose; bricks, marble, and cloth are often seen on HTML documents. Most of these serve only to fill in the blank space on the document, though. More interesting documents have a background that fits the theme of the page. Figure 3.4 shows an example of an astronomy page that uses a pattern of stars as the wallpaper.

Part

II

Ch

3

FIG. 3.4

Using a background image that "fits" your document is a nice, professional touch.

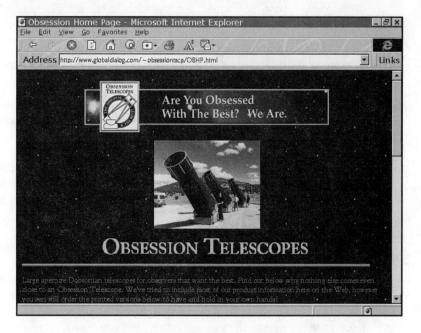

Other types of wallpaper that can make a document look good include a corporate logo or other image. These should be very subdued, almost monochrome, so as not to interfere with the foreground text. One way to accomplish this is to emboss an existing image using a graphics program. Chapter 17, "Graphics," discusses some of the tools available for creating these images. Figure 3.5 is an example of how this can be used.

FIG. 3.5

A company logo, embossed into a monochrome background, can give continuity to a collection of documents.

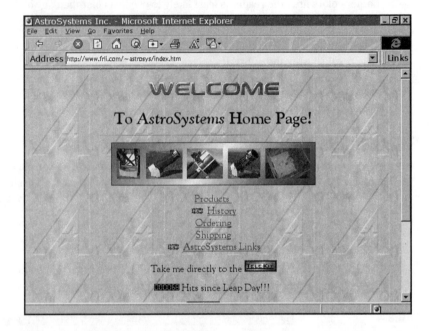

A background can also be created to watermark a document. This type of background can be used for an official seal or for a text message such as Draft or Confidential.

Background images look good, but they won't be seen by someone who's turned off the automatic loading of images. Remember the advice in the BGCOLOR section and set the background color to match the primary color of the image so that your page is readable even if the reader doesn't get to see the background.

N O T E The BGPROPERTIES attribute is unique to Microsoft Internet Explorer at this point. The only acceptable value for this attribute is FIXED. If BGPROPERTIES=FIXED, the background image does not scroll with the text. This is a nice effect with a wallpaper background and is useful if you've created a watermark background. ■

Setting the Margins

The LEFTMARGIN and TOPMARGIN attributes are used to set the margins between your text and the edges of the browser. There is no method provided to set either the right or bottom margin. This results from HTML documents being browser-independent. As an author, you don't know what size window the viewing software will have open.

The LEFTMARGIN sets the width of the space between the left edge of the browser window and the left edge of the text. The width of the margin is specified in pixels. This attribute is most often used when the background image has a pattern on the left edge that you would like to keep clear of text. Listing 3.9 is an example of this use for a left margin and Figure 3.6 shows how it looks in Internet Explorer.

Listing 3.9   A Basic HTML Document

```
<HTML>
<HEAD>
<TITLE>Demonstration of the LEFTMARGIN Attribute</TITLE>
</HEAD>
<BODY LEFTMARGIN="120" BACKGROUND="purplebg.jpg">
<H2>Note the handsome left border on this document.</H2>
<BR>
<H3>All of the text will line up so that it just barely clears the
border. This creates a visual edge that really sets your documents
apart from the rest.<H3>
</BODY>
</HTML>
```

Part
II

Ch
3

CAUTION

Unfortunately, Netscape Navigator does not support the LEFTMARGIN attribute at this time. If you don't know that your readers will be using Internet Explorer, you should use a background image with colors that allow the text to be read, even if the border is overwritten.

FIG. 3.6
The LEFTMARGIN attribute can be used with a background image to create an attractive border for your text.

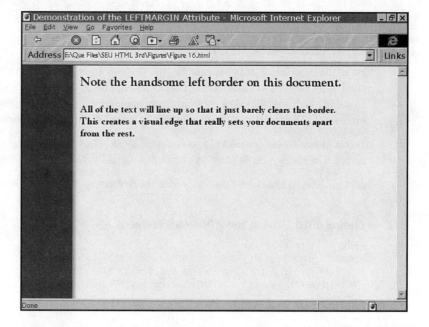

The TOPMARGIN attribute is used to set the height of the space between the top of the viewer window and the top of your text. This is normally used if the background image is particularly busy near the top. It can also be used simply to provide some space at the top of your document. Netscape Navigator 3.0 does not support this tag.

Commenting Your HTML Documents

It is possible to add comments to your HTML document that aren't seen by a reader. The syntax for this is to begin your comment with the <!-- tag and to end it with the --> tag. Anything located between the two tags is not displayed in the browser. This is a convenient way to leave notes for yourself or others. For example, you can enter a comment when new material is added to a document that shows the date of the new addition.

> **CAUTION**
>
> Don't assume your comments can't be seen by your readers. Most browsers allow the source of your document to be viewed directly, including any comments that you have added.

On the other hand, don't try to use comments to "comment out" any HTML elements in production documents. Some browsers interpret any > as the end of the comment. In any case, the chances of an older browser becoming confused are pretty good, resulting in the rest of your document being badly scrambled. If you are going to use comments to cut out HTML elements while you are testing the document, you should remove them in the final release.

A new use of comments is to hide scripts from browsers that cannot recognize them. This is discussed more thoroughly in Chapter 24, "Overview of Programming and Scripting."

The *ADDRESS* Element

One of the most important elements for your documents is the ADDRESS element. This is where you identify yourself as the author of the document and (optionally) let people know how they can get in touch with you. Any copyright information for the material in the page can be placed here as well. The ADDRESS element is normally placed at either the top or bottom of a document.

The ADDRESS element consists of text enclosed by an <ADDRESS> start tag and an </ADDRESS> end tag. The text within an ADDRESS element is normally displayed in italics.

Listing 3.10 is an example of one such address element and Figure 3.7 shows how it looks.

Listing 3.10   Using the *ADDRESS* Element

```
<HTML>
<HEAD>
<TITLE>Amateur Astronomy on the World Wide Web</TITLE>
<META NAME="Keywords" CONTENT="Astronomy, Telescope, Stargazing">
```

```
<META NAME="Description" CONTENT="Amateur Astronomy resources available on the
➥Web">
</HEAD>
<BODY BGCOLOR="WHITE" TEXT="BLACK" LINK="RED" VLINK="GREEN" ALINK="YELLOW" >
</HEAD>
<BODY>
<FONT SIZE=3 FACE="Verdana, Arial, Helvetica">
<BR>
<H1>Amateur Astronomy on the World Wide Web</H1>
<HR>
<H2>Magazines</H2>
<OL>
<LI><A HREF=http://www.astronomy-mall.com/Astronomy-Mall/?190,54>The Astronomy
➥Mall</A>
- A place to find many amateur astronomy companies.
<LI><A HREF=http://www.skypub.com>Sky On-line</A> - Publishers of <I>Sky and
Telescope</I> and <I>CCD</I> magazines.
</OL>
<HR>
<ADDRESS>
Created by Robert Meegan<BR>
Last Modified on 16 Dec 1996
</ADDRESS>
</BODY>
</HTML>
```

Part

II

Ch

3

N O T E A very important addition to the address is to indicate the date you created the document and the date of the last revision. This helps people determine if they have already seen the most up-to-date version of the document. ∎

FIG. 3.7
The ADDRESS element is used to identify the author or maintainer of the document.

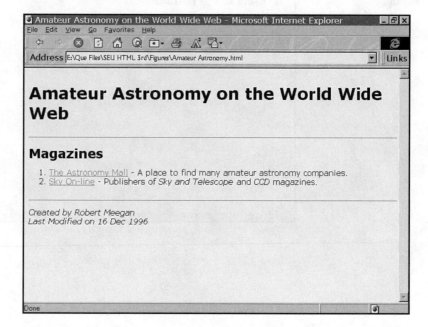

Special Characters

There are a number of special characters that are not found in the basic ASCII set. These include letters and characters used by other European languages, some mathematical symbols, and an assortment of other characters. These can be added to your document using the special character entity. The format of this entity is an ampersand (&) followed by the name of the character. The example in Listing 3.11 shows how you can use the special characters.

Listing 3.11 Using Special Characters

```
<H3>The Use of Character Format Elements</H3>
This is how to add &ltEM&gtemphasis&lt/EM&gt to a word.<BR>
Which gives the result:<BR>
This is how to add <EM>emphasis</EM> to a word.<BR>
```

The special characters < and > are inserted in the second line by using the &lt and &gt codes, respectively. If these codes weren't used, the browser would attempt to interpret whatever was between the characters as an HTML tag.

Figure 3.8 shows what this example looks like in Netscape.

FIG. 3.8

Special characters can be added to HTML documents using the special character entities.

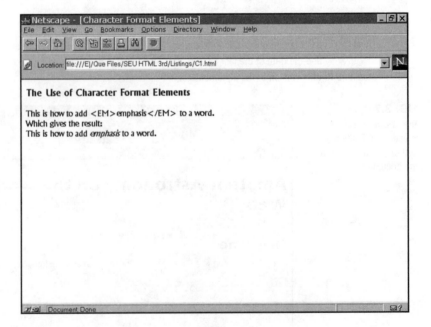

Creating a Document Template

Now, let's build a basic document template that you can use with your documents. This template allows you to start converting some of your existing documents to HTML. In the following chapters, you will see how to expand upon this template.

Let's begin with the required tags: `<HTML>`, `<HEAD>`, `</HEAD>`, `<BODY>`, `</BODY>`, and `</HTML>`. You also need to include the TITLE element, as this is a required element in HTML 3.2. Finally, put in a dummy line of text to remind yourself where to put the text. This gives you Listing 3.12.

Listing 3.12   A First Pass at a Basic Document Template

```
<HTML>
<HEAD>
<TITLE> A Basic Document Template </TITLE>
<HEAD>
<BODY>
Put the body text in here.
</BODY>
</HTML>
```

This would certainly suffice for a basic document, but you can do a lot better without much effort. First, let's add a simple, gray, textured background to the document, which changes the `<BODY>` tag to

```
<BODY BACKGROUND="greybg.jpg">
```

Earlier in the chapter you read that if you add a background image to a document, you should set the colors so that the reader can see your text. First, set the BGCOLOR attribute to GRAY. This is the closest match to the background. We'll also set the TEXT to BLACK, and LINK, ALINK, and VLINK to BLUE, GREEN, and RED, respectively. These additions change the `<BODY>` tag to

```
<BODY BACKGROUND="greybg.jpg" BGCOLOR="GRAY", TEXT="BLACK",
 LINK="BLUE", ALINK="GREEN", VLINK="RED">
```

You should have an ADDRESS element for the document, so add the following:

```
<ADDRESS>Created by Robert Meegan<BR>
Created on 16 December 1996</ADDRESS>
```

Of course, you'll want to put your own name in the ADDRESS element.

When all of these are added to the first pass of the template, you get Listing 3.13.

Listing 3.13   Your Final Basic Document Template

```
<HTML>
<HEAD>
<TITLE> A Basic Document Template </TITLE>
<HEAD>
```

Part

II

Ch

3

continues

Listing 3.13   Continued

```
<BODY BACKGROUND="greybg.jpg" BGCOLOR="GRAY", TEXT="BLACK",
 LINK="BLUE", ALINK="GREEN", VLINK="RED">
Put the body text in here.
<ADDRESS>Created by Robert Meegan<BR>
Created on 16 December 1996</ADDRESS>
</BODY>
</HTML>
```

The results of this template can be seen in Figure 3.9.

FIG. 3.9

The results of the basic
document template
opened Netscape
Navigator.

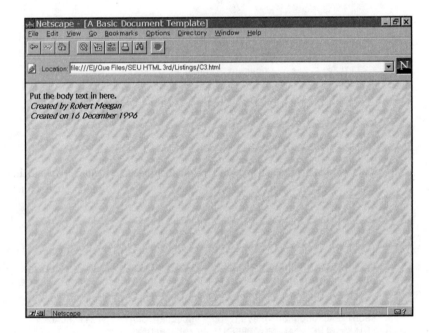

As you learn more about HTML, your template will grow and become more sophisticated.
Until then, this simple document should prove to be sufficient for most purposes. ●

## CHAPTER 4

Document Formatting

by Robert Meegan

Now that you've learned the basics of creating an HTML document, the next step is to expand upon that knowledge and make documents that are interesting to read. All published material has a structure; even something as visually flat as the stock quotations in the newspaper have been carefully designed to provide a maximum amount of information in an easy-to-use fashion. Imagine how many people would bother to look at these pages if they were formatted in a continuous stream of letters and numbers that filled the page from top to bottom and margin to margin.

The documents that you create have the same requirements. Whether you are writing Web pages, publishing manuals on a corporate intranet, or developing HTML-based hypertext books, you will need to format your work so that a reader can quickly skim the text to find the sections in which he or she is interested. ■

Break your text into paragraphs

You can organize your HTML text into paragraphs, just like you do with your favorite word processor.

Add structure to your document with headers

Headers provide a road map that your readers can use to get around your HTML document. This chapter shows you how to use them.

Divide your document by using horizontal lines

Horizontal lines, or rules, are useful for creating separate sections in your HTML document.

Create preformatted text

Typically, Web browsers automatically format your text. You can use preformatted text to lay out text yourself, however.

Create a specialized document template

With templates, you do the work on time, and then reuse it over and over. This chapter shows you how.

Breaking Text into Paragraphs

Your old English teacher taught you to break your writing up into paragraphs that expressed complete thoughts, and an HTML document shouldn't be an exception. Unfortunately, line and paragraph breaks are a little more complicated in HTML than you might expect.

As a mark-up language, HTML requires that you make no assumptions about your reader's machine. The readers of your document can set whatever margins and fonts they want to use. This means that text wrapping must be determined by the viewer software, as it is the only part of the system that knows about the reader's setup. Line feeds in the original document are ignored by the viewer, which then reformats the text to fit the context. This means that a document that may be perfectly legible in your editor (see Figure 4.1) is badly mashed together in the viewer, as shown in Figure 4.2.

FIG. 4.1

Line feeds separate the paragraphs in the editor.

The proper way to break text into paragraphs is by using paragraph elements. Place a paragraph start tag, <P>, at the beginning of each new paragraph, and the viewer will know to separate the paragraphs. Adding a paragraph end tag, </P>, is optional, as it is normally implied by the next start tag that comes along. Still, adding the </P> tag at the end of a paragraph can help to protect your documents against viewers that don't precisely follow the HTML 3.2 standard.

N O T E   Seriously consider using the beginning and ending paragraph tags. As style elements, which give you more control over the <P> tag, become more prevalent, this syntax becomes more important. ▪

FIG. 4.2

The viewer ignores the line feeds and runs the text together.

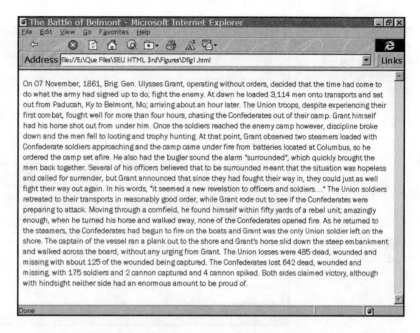

Figure 4.3 shows what the document looks like in the editor after the paragraph tags have been added. You can see the tags were added to the start of each paragraph and that the line feeds are still in the document. Because the viewer ignores the line feeds anyway, it is best to keep them in the source document to make it easier to edit later.

FIG. 4.3

If you want to separate paragraphs, you need to use the <P> tag.

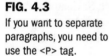

Paragraph tags

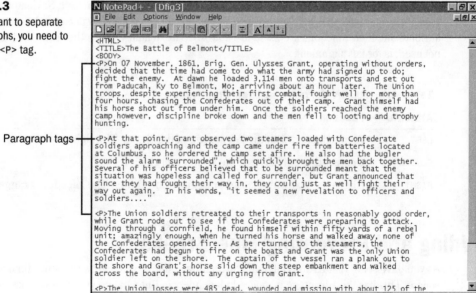

When you look at the document in Figure 4.4, you can see the viewer separated the paragraphs correctly by adding a double-spaced line between them.

FIG. 4.4
With paragraph elements, the text becomes much easier to read.

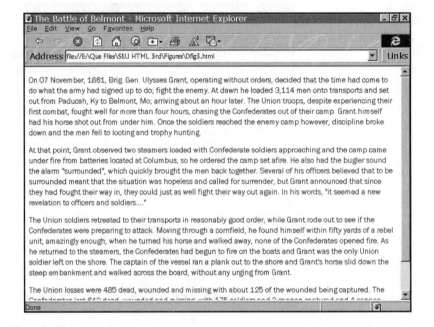

> **N O T E** In some HTML documents, you will see a paragraph start tag, `<P>`, used repeatedly in order to create additional white space. This is not supported in HTML, and most current viewers will ignore all of the `<P>` tags after the first one.

The paragraph element has one attribute that is supported by both Netscape Navigator and Microsoft Internet Explorer. This is the `ALIGN` attribute. The possible values for the `ALIGN` attribute and their functions are listed in Table 4.1. The default value, if the `ALIGN` attribute is not used, is for left alignment.

Table 4.1 *ALIGN* Values and Their Functions

Attribute	Function
`LEFT`	Aligns the text with the left margin of the viewer. The right edge is ragged.
`CENTER`	Centers the text between the viewer margins.
`RIGHT`	Aligns the text with the right margin of the viewer. The left edge is ragged.

Adding and Preventing Line Breaks

As you have seen, HTML does all of the formatting at the viewing software rather than at the source. This has the advantage of device independence. But what do you do if you have a reason to break up a line of text at a certain point?

The way to end a line where you want is to use the *line break tag*, <BR>. This forces the viewer to start a new line, regardless of the position in the current line. Unlike the paragraph element, the line break does not double-space the text. Because the line break element is not a container, it does not have an end tag.

One reason you might want to force line breaks is to show off your poetic muse, as shown in Listing 4.1.

**Listing 4.1 A Limerick Showing the Use of the *
* Tag**

```
<HTML>
<HEAD>
<TITLE>Creating an HTML Document</TITLE>
</HEAD>
<BODY>
<P>A very intelligent turtle<BR>
Found programming UNIX a hurdle<BR>
The system, you see,<BR>
Ran as slow as did he,<BR>
And that's not saying much for the turtle.<BR>
<CITE>Mercifully anonymous</CITE>
</BODY>
</HTML>
```

When this source is viewed in Figure 4.5, you can see how the line break element works.

FIG. 4.5

Use line breaks to force a new line in the viewer.

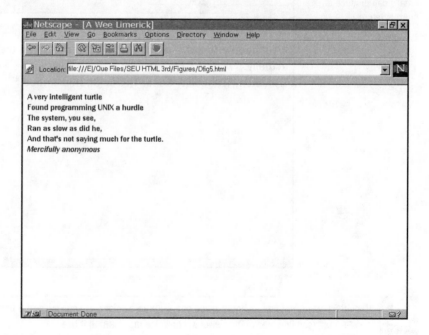

Part
II

Ch
4

> **CAUTION**
> You might think you can use multiple line breaks to provide extra white space in your document. Some browsers will condense multiple line breaks (multiple <BR> or <P> tags) to a single line break, however.

You need to be careful when using line breaks; if the line has already wrapped in the viewer, your break may appear after only a couple of words in the next line. This is particularly the case if the viewer that you test your documents on has wider margins than your reader's viewer. Figure 4.6 shows an example where the author saw that the break was occurring in the middle of the quotation, so she added a <BR>. Unfortunately, when displayed on a screen with different margins, the word "actually" ends up on a line by itself.

Just as there are instances in which it is convenient to break a line at a specified point, there are also times when you would like to avoid breaking a line at a certain point. Any text between a <NOBR> start tag and the associated end tag is guaranteed not to break across lines.

N O T E This can be very useful for items such as addresses, where an unfortunate line break can cause unexpected results. Don't overuse the <NOBR> element, however. Text can look very strange when the natural line breaks have been changed. ■

FIG. 4.6
Careless use of line breaks can produce an unexpected result.

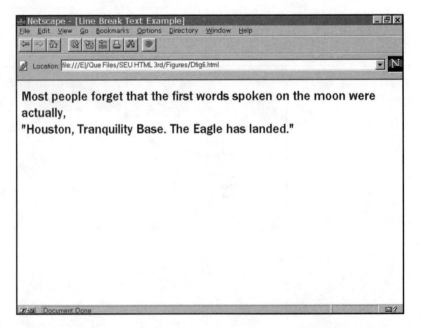

  TIP If you think you might need a break inside of a <NOBR> element, you can suggest a breaking point with a <WBR> tag (soft line break). The viewer will only use the <WBR> if it needs it.

Creating a Text Outline

So far, your HTML document probably looks a little dull. To make it more interesting, the first thing that you need to do is add a little more structure to it. Users of the Web want to be able to quickly scan a document to determine whether or not it has the information they are looking for. The way to make this scanning easier is to break the document up into logical sections, each covering a single topic.

After you have broken up the document, the next step is to add meaningful headers to each section, enabling your reader to quickly jump to the material of interest.

Adding Headings

Headings in HTML provide an outline of the text that forms the body of the document. As such, they direct the reader through the document and make your information more interesting and usable. They are probably the most commonly used formatting tag that you will find in HTML documents.

The heading element is a *container* and must have a start tag (<H1>) and an end tag (</H1>). HTML has six levels of headings: H1 (the most important), H2, H3, H4, H5, H6 (the least important). Each of these levels will have its own appearance in the reader's viewer, but you have no direct control over what that appearance will be. This is part of the HTML philosophy: You, as the document writer, have the responsibility for the content, while the viewer has the responsibility for the appearance. See the example in Listing 4.2.

Part
II
Ch
4

Listing 4.2   An HTML Document Showing the Use of Headings

```
<HTML>
<HEAD>
<TITLE>Creating an HTML Document</TITLE>
</HEAD>
<BODY>
<H1>Level 1 Heading</H1>
<H2>Level 2 Heading</H2>
<H3>Level 3 Heading</H3>
<H4>Level 4 Heading</H4>
<H5>Level 5 Heading</H5>
<H6>Level 6 Heading</H6>
</BODY>
</HTML>
```

▶ **See** "Text Properties," to learn more about using style sheets to change text properties for tags such as <H1>, **p. 301**

N O T E   Although it is not absolutely necessary to use each of the heading levels, as a matter of good practice you should not skip levels because it may cause problems with automatic document converters. In particular, as new Web indexes come online, they will be able to search Web documents and create retrievable outlines. These outlines may be confusing if heading levels are missing. ■

Figure 4.7 shows how these headings look when they are displayed in Microsoft Internet Explorer.

FIG. 4.7
Here are the six heading levels as they appear in Internet Explorer.

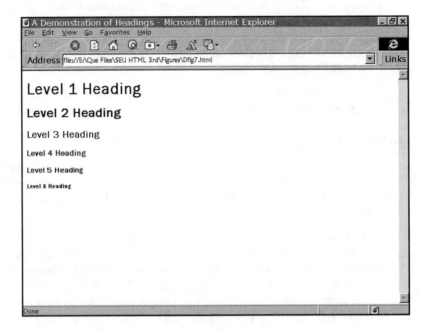

N O T E Remember that forgetting to add an end tag will definitely mess up the appearance of your document. Headings are containers and require both start and end tags. Another thing to remember is that headings also have an implied paragraph break before and after each one. You can't apply a heading to text in the middle of a paragraph to change the size or font. The result will be a paragraph broken into three separate pieces, with the middle paragraph in a heading format. ▪

The best way to use headings is to consider them the outline for your document. Figure 4.8 shows a document in which each level of heading represents a new level of detail. Generally, it is good practice to use a new level whenever you have two to four items of equal importance. If more than four items are of the same importance under a parent heading, however, try breaking them into two different parent headings.

Headings can use the ALIGN attribute, just as the <P> tag does. This is important to remember, because not all viewers will show all headings left-aligned. Figure 4.9 shows the use of the ALIGN attribute in a heading.

Adding Horizontal Lines

Another method for adding divisions to your documents is the use of horizontal lines. These provide a strong visual break between sections and are especially useful for separating the various parts of your document. Many viewers use an "etched" line that presents a crisp look and adds visual depth to the document.

FIG. 4.8
Headings provide an outline of the document.

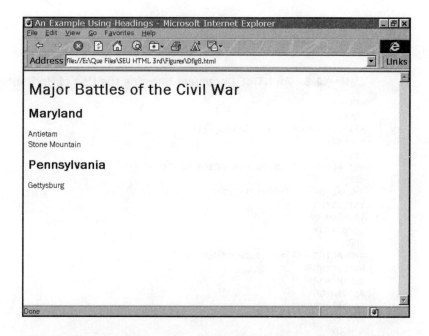

FIG. 4.9
Headings can be aligned on the left, right, or in the center.

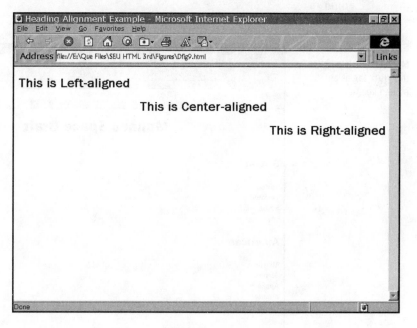

You can create a horizontal line by using the horizontal rule element, <HR>. This tag draws a shaded horizontal line across the viewer's display. The <HR> tag is not a container and does not require an end tag. There is an implied paragraph break before and after a horizontal rule.

Listing 4.3 shows how horizontal rule tags are used, and Figure 4.10 demonstrates their appearance in the Netscape Navigator viewer.

Listing 4.3   An HTML Document Showing the Use of Horizontal Rules

```
<HTML>
<HEAD>
<TITLE>Manned Space Craft</TITLE>
</HEAD>
<BODY>
<H1 ALIGN=CENTER>Manned Space Craft</H1>
<BR>
<H2 ALIGN=LEFT>Soviet</H2>
Vostok<BR>
Voskhod<BR>
Soyuz<BR>
<HR>
<H2 ALIGN=LEFT>American</H2>
Mercury<BR>
Gemini<BR>
Apollo<BR>
Shuttle<BR>
<HR >
</BODY>
</HTML>
```

FIG. 4.10

Most viewers interpret the <HR> tag as an etched line.

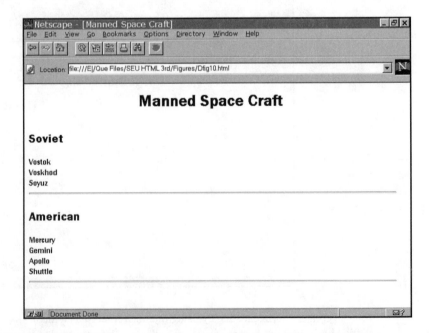

Table 4.2 lists the attributes of the <HR> tag. Listing 4.4 is similar to Listing 4.3, but shows how some of the attributes are used. Figure 4.11 shows the results as seen in Internet Explorer.

Table 4.2 *HR* Attributes and Their Functions

Attribute	Function
ALIGN	Can be set to LEFT, CENTER, or RIGHT.
WIDTH	Can be entered in pixels or as a percentage of the viewer window width. If a percentage is desired, add a percent sign to the number.
SIZE	The height of the ruled line in pixels.
NOSHADE	If this attribute is present, the viewer will not use a three-dimensional effect.
COLOR	Specifies the color of the ruled line. An RGB hexadecimal value or a standard color name can be used.

Listing 4.4 The Use of Attributes in Horizontal Rules

```
<HTML>
<HEAD>
<TITLE>Manned Space Craft</TITLE>
</HEAD>
<BODY>
<H1 ALIGN=CENTER>Manned Space Craft</H1>
<BR>
<H2 ALIGN=LEFT>Soviet</H2>
Vostok<BR>
Voskhod<BR>
Soyuz<BR>
<HR WIDTH=50% SIZE=6 ALIGN=LEFT COLOR=RED>
<H2 ALIGN=LEFT>American</H2>
Mercury<BR>
Gemini<BR>
Apollo<BR>
Shuttle<BR>
<HR WIDTH=50% SIZE=6 ALIGN=LEFT COLOR=NAVY>
</BODY>
</HTML>
```

Part

II

Ch

4

TIP The additional attributes that have been added in HTML 3.2 are very useful. Documents created using early versions of HTML often used a graphic image to provide a more colorful and obvious break. Of course, these would not appear in viewers that had image loading turned off. Even if the viewer was loading images, a color bar was another file that had to be copied and maintained. The new <HR> attributes allow you much more flexibility in the creation of your documents at virtually no loss of speed or ease of maintenance.

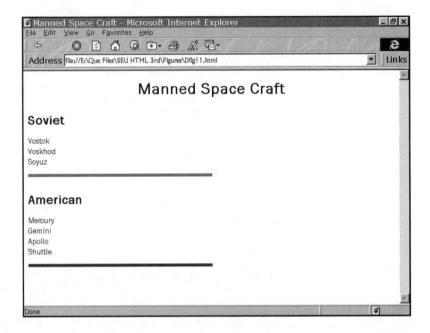

Horizontal rules should be reserved for instances when you want to represent a strong break in the flow of the text. Some basic guidelines for adding rules is that they should never come between a heading and the text that follows the heading. They should also not be used to create "white space" in your document.

Using Preformatted Text

Is it absolutely necessary to use paragraph and line break elements for formatting text? Well, not really; HTML provides a container that can hold preformatted text. This is text that gives you, the author, much more control over how the viewer displays your document. The trade-off for this control is a loss of flexibility.

The most common and useful of the preformatting tags is the <PRE> container. Text in a <PRE> container is basically freeform with line feeds causing the line to break at the beginning of the next clear line. Line break tags and paragraph tags are also supported. This versatility enables you to create such items as tables and precise columns of text. Another common use of the <PRE> element is to display large blocks of computer code (C, C++, and so on) that would otherwise be difficult to read if the browser reformatted it.

Text in a <PRE> container can use any of the physical or logical text formatting elements. You can use this feature to create tables that have bold headers or italicized values. The use of paragraph formatting elements, such as <Address> or any of the heading elements, is not permitted however. Anchor elements, which are described in Chapter 7, "Creating Document Links," can be included within a <PRE> container.

The biggest drawback to the <PRE> container is that any text within it is displayed in a monospaced font in the reader's viewer. This tends to make long stretches of preformatted text look clunky and out of place.

Figure 4.12 shows an example of some preformatted text in an editor. You can use the editor to line up the columns neatly before adding the character formatting tags. The result of this document is shown in Figure 4.13.

TIP HTML 3.2 introduces HTML tables. If you are not converting existing documents, the HTML tables are much more attractive than are the ones that you can create by using the <PRE> element. See Chapter 9, "Creating Tables," for more information on this topic.

CAUTION

Tab characters move the cursor to the next position, which is an integer multiple of eight. The official HTML specification recommends that tab characters not be used in preformatted text because they are not supported in the same way by all viewers. Spaces should be used for aligning columns.

FIG. 4.12
Preformatted text can be used to line up columns of numbers.

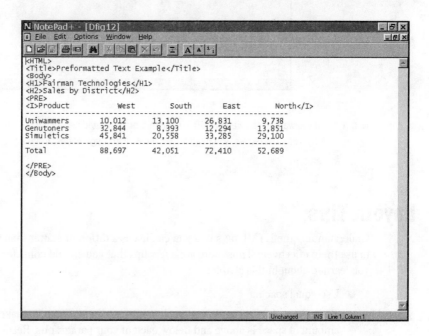

N O T E There are other preformatted container classes, but these have been declared as obsolete. The <XMP> and <LISTING> elements give you the capability to create text that is already laid out. There are some disadvantages to these in that other HTML elements are not permitted inside of them. Viewers are not allowed to recognize any mark-up tags except the end tag. Unfortunately, many viewers don't comply with this standard properly, and the results can be unpleasant.

The difference between the two elements are that <XMP> text must be rendered in a font size that permits at least 80 characters on a line and <LISTING> requires a font that permits 132 characters.

You should avoid using the <XMP> and <LISTING> elements unless it is absolutely necessary. Because they have been declared obsolete, viewers are not required to support them any longer. You will be more certain of what your readers are seeing if you use the <PRE> element instead. ■

FIG. 4.13
A preformatted table can be used in a document.

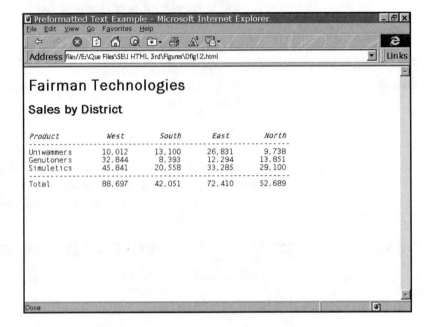

NOTE If you want to show actual HTML code in a preformatted section, or you just want to use the <or> characters, you need to use the &lt and &gt codes, like this:

&ltPRE&gt. ■

Layout Tips

Understanding the HTML tags that you can use is a different matter than understanding how to use them effectively. Thus, here are a few tips that you should consider when using the tags you learned about in this chapter:

■ Use equal spacing

Try to keep the spacing between elements consistent. That is, make sure the same amount of space is above and below each of your paragraphs. Readers will perceive uneven spacing as sloppiness on your part.

■ Avoid right- and center-justification

Don't right- or center-justify the main body of text. Right- and center-justified text is harder to read than left-justified text.

■ Don't go overboard with indents

Proper indentation depends on the size of the font you're using. A larger font requires a deeper indent and vice-versa.

■ Use `<NOBR>` with `<WBR>` to maintain control of line breaks

Sometimes you want to control exactly where the browser will break a line if it needs to. `<NOBR>` turns off line breaks while `<WBR>` provides hints to the browser that suggests a spot for a line break if necessary.

■ Consider dividing a page that uses `<HR>`

If you find yourself using rules to divide a Web page into individual topics, consider splitting that Web page into individual pages so each page remains focused on a single topic.

■ Give plenty of space to artwork

The images and tables in your HTML document should have enough white space around them so that they're set apart from the text. You don't want them to appear cramped.

■ Use headings to organize your text

Headings give readers a visual road map that helps them locate the information in which they're interested. Use them liberally.

Part

II

Ch

4

A Specialized Template

Using what we've learned in this chapter, we can create a more sophisticated template. Building upon the template that we laid out at the end of Chapter 3, let's use some of the features of this chapter to build a template that can be used for glossaries and related documents.

The first step is to bring the existing template into our editor. Once we've loaded it, we can make the appropriate changes to the elements that are already present. These can be seen in Listing 4.5.

Listing 4.5 The Glossary Template with the First Changes

```
<HTML>
<HEAD>
<TITLE>Glossary</TITLE>
<HEAD>
<BODY BACKGROUND="greybg.jpg" BGCOLOR="GRAY", TEXT="BLACK",
LINK="BLUE", ALINK="GREEN", VLINK="RED">
<ADDRESS>Created by Author<BR>
Created on Date</ADDRESS>
</BODY>
</HTML>
```

Now, we can add a title to the page and bracket the text with some horizontal rules. We make the decision that the terms to be defined will be level-two headings, left-aligned, and that the definitions themselves will be normal text. These decisions lead to Listing 4.6, which is a template that can now be saved and used anytime you need a glossary document. This same template would also work for a phone list or a catalog.

Listing 4.6   The Final Glossary Template

```
<HTML>
<HEAD>
<TITLE>Glossary</TITLE>
<HEAD>
<BODY BACKGROUND="greybg.jpg" BGCOLOR="GRAY", TEXT="BLACK",
LINK="BLUE", ALINK="GREEN", VLINK="RED">
<H1 ALIGN=CENTER>Glossary</H1>
<HR ALIGN=CENTER WIDTH=50% SIZE=5 COLOR=NAVY>
<H2 ALIGN=LEFT>Term 1</H2>
Type the definition for term 1 here.
<H2 ALIGN=LEFT>Term 2</H2>
Type the definition for term 2 here. And so on...
<HR ALIGN=CENTER WIDTH=50% SIZE=5 COLOR=NAVY>
<ADDRESS>Created by Author<BR>
Created on Date</ADDRESS>
</BODY>
</HTML>
```

An example of how this template could be used is shown in Figure 4.14.

FIG. 4.14

An example using the glossary template.

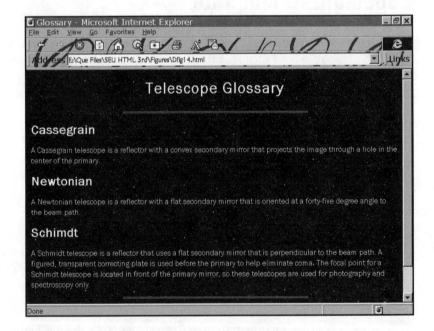

## CHAPTER 5

Text Formatting

by Robert Meegan

You've now seen how to create an HTML document and how to perform basic document formatting. The next step is exercising control over how the text looks. With the arrival of HTML 3.2, a document author now has a tremendous amount of discretion over the text formatting. You won't find quite as much detail as you might expect in the latest word processor, but you'll be amazed at how much there is. ■

Learn about logical and physical formatting

Logical formatting makes your documents portable across multiple platforms and browsers.

Format your text by using HTML text formatting tags

HTML provides a plethora of tags for formatting your text. This chapter describes each text formatting tag.

Take control of the fonts you use

HTML gives you a lot of control over the font in which the browser displays your text, including face, style, and size.

Create documents that are easy to read

This chapter describes some simple guidelines you can use to create an HTML document with text that's easy to read.

Text Formatting

Once you've created your document, much of the hard work is done. The text that you've written is neatly broken into paragraphs, headings are in place, and the miscellaneous items such as the title and the author information have been added. At this point, you could walk away satisfied, but something still seems to be missing.

One of the primary things that separates documents created on a word processor from those produced on a typewriter is the idea of text formatting. Word processors give the author control over how her text will look. She can choose the font that she likes in the appropriate size, and she can apply one or more of a myriad of options to the text. In HTML, you have this same capability. Your only real restrictions involve the importance of viewer independence.

▶ **See** "Attaching a Style Sheet to Your HTML Document," to learn how to attach a style sheet to your HTML document, **p. 286**

Logical Formatting

One of the ideas behind HTML is that documents should be laid out in a logical and structured manner. This gives the users of the documents as much flexibility as possible. With this in mind, the designers of HTML created a number of formatting elements that are labeled according to the purpose they serve rather than by their appearance. The advantage of this approach is that documents are not limited to a certain platform. Although they may look different on various platforms, the content and context will remain the same.

These logical formatting elements are as follows:

- ■ `<CITE>` The citation element is used to indicate the citation of a quotation. It can also be used to indicate the title of a book or article. An italic font is normally used to display citations.

    ```
    <CITE>Tom Sawyer</CITE> remains one of the classics of American literature.
    ```

- ■ `<CODE>` The code element is used to indicate a small amount of computer code. It is generally reserved for short sections, with longer sections noted by using the `<PRE>` tag described later. Code normally appears in a monospaced font.

    ```
    One of the first lines that every C programmer learns is:<BR>
    <CODE>puts("Hello World!");</CODE>
    ```

- ■ `<EM>` The emphasis element is used to indicate a section of text that the author wants to identify as significant. Emphasis is generally shown in an italic font.

    ```
    The actual line reads, "Alas, poor Yorick. I knew him, <EM>Horatio</EM>."
    ```

- ■ `<KBD>` The keyboard element is used to indicate a user entry response. A monospaced typewriter font is normally used to display keyboard text.

    ```
    To run the decoder, type <KBD>Restore</KBD> followed by your password.
    ```

- ■ `<SAMP>` The sample element is used to indicate literal characters. These normally are a few characters that are intended to be precisely identified. Sample element text normally is shown in a monospaced font.

```
The letters <SAMP>AEIOU</SAMP> are the vowels of the English language.
```

■ **<STRONG>** The strong element is used to emphasize a particularly important section of text. Text using strong emphasis is normally set in a bold font.

```
The most important rule to remember is <STRONG>Don't panic</STRONG>!
```

■ **<VAR>** The variable element is used to indicate a dummy variable name. Variables are normally viewed in an italic font.

```
The sort routine rotates on the <VAR>I</VAR>th element.
```

Note that all of these elements are containers and, as such, they require an end tag. Figure 5.1 shows how these logical elements look when seen in the Netscape viewer.

FIG. 5.1
Samples of the logical format elements are displayed in Netscape.

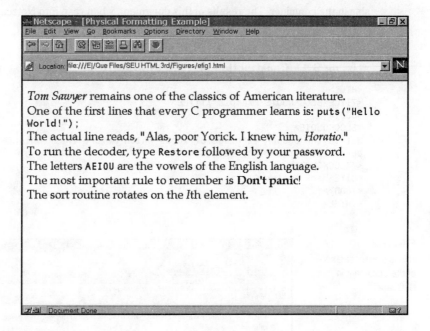

You have probably noticed that a lot of these format styles use the same rendering. The most obvious question to ask is why use them if they all look alike?

The answer is that these elements are logical styles. They indicate what the intention of the author was, not how the material should look. This is important because future uses of HTML may include programs that search the Web to find citations, for example, or the next generation of Web viewers may be able to read a document aloud. A program that can identify emphasis would be able to avoid the deadly monotone of current text-to-speech processors.

The <*BLOCKQUOTE*> Element

You may have the opportunity to quote a long piece of work from another source in your document. To indicate that this quotation is different from the rest of your text, HTML provides the

<BLOCKQUOTE> element. This container functions as a body element within the body element and can contain any of the formatting or break tags. As a container, the <BLOCKQUOTE> element is turned off by using the end tag.

The normal method used by most viewers to indicate a <BLOCKQUOTE> element is to indent the text away from the left margin. Some text-only viewers may indicate a <BLOCKQUOTE> by using a character, such as the "greater than" sign, in the leftmost column on the screen. Because most viewers are now graphical in nature, the <BLOCKQUOTE> element provides an additional service by enabling you to indent normal text from the left margin. This can add some visual interest to the document.

Listing 5.1 shows how a <BLOCKQUOTE> is constructed, including some of the formatting available in the container. The results of this document, when read into Netscape, can be seen in Figure 5.2.

Listing 5.1   Construction of a *<BLOCKQUOTE>*

```
<HTML>
<TITLE>BLOCKQUOTE Example</TITLE>
<BODY>
<BLOCKQUOTE>
Wit is the sudden marriage of ideas which before their union were not
perceived to have any relation.
</BLOCKQUOTE>
<CITE>Mark Twain</CITE>
</BODY>
</HTML>
```

FIG. 5.2

This is the appearance of the document in Netscape.

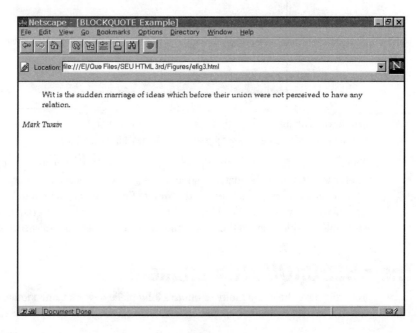

Physical Format Elements

Having said that HTML is intended to leave the appearance of the document up to the viewer, I will now show you how you can have limited control over what the reader sees. In addition to the logical formatting elements, it is possible to use physical formatting elements that will change the appearance of the text in the viewer. These physical elements are as follows:

- ▦ <B> The bold element uses a bold font to display the text.

  ```
  This is in <B>bold</B> text.
  ```

- ▦ <I> The italic element renders text using an italic font.

  ```
  This is in <I>italic</I> text.
  ```

- ▦ <TT> The teletype element displays the contents with a monospaced typewriter font.

  ```
  This is in <TT>teletype</TT> text.
  ```

- ▦ <U> The underline element causes text to be underlined in the viewer.

  ```
  This text is <U>underlined</U>.
  ```

- ▦ <STRIKE> The strikethrough element draws a horizontal line through the middle of the text.

  ```
  This is a <STRIKE>strikethough</STRIKE> example.
  ```

- ▦ <BIG> The big print element uses a larger font size to display the text.

  ```
  This is <BIG>big</BIG> text.
  ```

- ▦ <SMALL> The small print element displays the text in a smaller font size.

  ```
  This is <SMALL>small</SMALL> text.
  ```

- ▦ <SUB> The subscript element moves the text lower than the surrounding text and (if possible) displays the text in a smaller size font.

  ```
  This is a <SUB>subscript</SUB>.
  ```

- ▦ <SUP> The superscript element moves the text higher than the surrounding text and (if possible) displays the text in a smaller size font.

  ```
  This is a <SUP>superscript</SUP>.
  ```

If the proper font isn't available, the reader's viewer must render the text in the closest possible manner. Once again, each of these is a container element and requires the use of an end tag. Figure 5.3 shows how these elements look in the Internet Explorer.

Part
II

Ch
5

FIG. 5.3

Samples of the physical format elements are shown in the Internet Explorer.

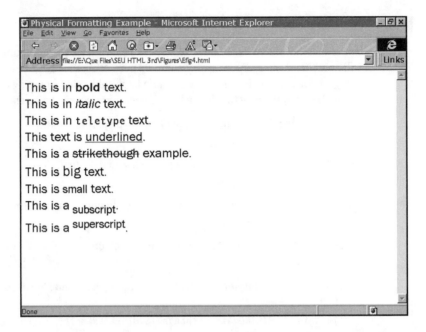

These elements can be nested, with one element contained entirely within another. On the other hand, overlapping elements are not permitted and can produce unpredictable results. Figure 5.4 gives some examples of nested elements and how they can be used to create special effects.

FIG. 5.4

Logical and physical format elements can be nested to create additional format styles.

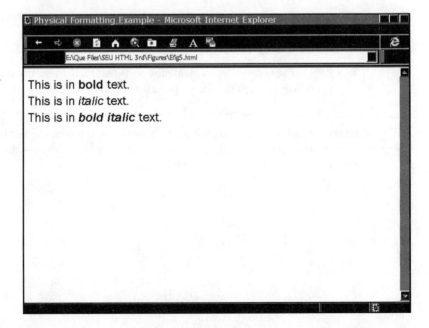

T I P There is a tag available only in Netscape Navigator that has acquired a particularly bad reputation: The `<BLINK>` tag is notorious in HTML circles. Unless you want people to speak ill of your documents, it's best to avoid this tag.

Fonts

One of the nicest features of HTML 3.2 is that you, as document author, now have the ability to control the appearance of the text in your documents. This capability was restricted entirely to the reader in previous versions of HTML. The problem with this ability is that you can only use fonts that exist on your readers' machines. So how do you know what your user might have available?

Unfortunately, you don't. If you are building documents to be used on an intranet, your organization should set standards as to which fonts should be found on every machine. As long as this is a reasonable set, it will be easy to maintain and you will be able to choose any of the standard fonts for your document. If you are developing for the Web, however, you have a more serious problem. In practice, you really don't know what fonts your readers might have. Even the most basic selection depends greatly upon the hardware that your readers are using. There are no really graceful ways around this problem at the present, although several companies are looking into ways of distributing font information with a document.

N O T E If you are developing for the Web and you would like to use some different fonts, you should be aware that Microsoft has several fonts available for free download on its Web site. These fonts are available in both Windows and Macintosh formats. If you decide to use any of these fonts in your documents, you might want to put a link to the Web page where your readers can download the fonts, if they don't already have them.

> http://www.microsoft.com/truetype/fontpack/default.htm ■

The *FONT* Element

The method that HTML uses for providing control over the appearance of the text is the FONT element. This element is new to HTML 3.2 and may not be supported by all viewers, but both Microsoft and Netscape make full use of it. The FONT element is a container that is opened with the `<FONT>` start tag and closed with the `</FONT>` end tag. Unless attributes are assigned in the start tag, there is no effect of using a FONT element.

The FONT element can be used inside of any other text container and it will modify the text based upon the appearance of the text within the parent container.

N O T E Netscape Navigator 3.0 does not support the FACE or COLOR attributes of BASEFONT. This support will likely appear in later versions, but to be strictly compatible, you probably would want to avoid them at this time. ■

N O T E The final version of Netscape Navigator 4.0 will provide Web developers the ability to temporarily download a font with a Web page, so that the user sees it as the developer intends. This eliminates the problem of using a font that the user doesn't have installed. ■

The *FACE* Attribute

The FACE attribute allows you to specify the font that you would like the viewing software to use when displaying your document. The parameter for this attribute is the name of the desired font. This name must be an exact match for a font name on the reader's machine, or the viewer will ignore the request and use the default font as set by the reader. Capitalization is ignored in the name, but spaces are required. Listing 5.2 shows an example of how a font face is specified and Figure 5.5 shows the page in Microsoft Internet Explorer.

Listing 5.2   An Example of *Font Face* Selection

```
<HTML>
<HEAD>
<TITLE>Font Selection Example</TITLE>
</HEAD>
<BODY>
<FONT FACE="Tolkien">
This is an example of font selection. </FONT>
</BODY>
</HTML>
```

FIG. 5.5

The FACE attribute of the FONT element lets you select the font in which the text will be displayed.

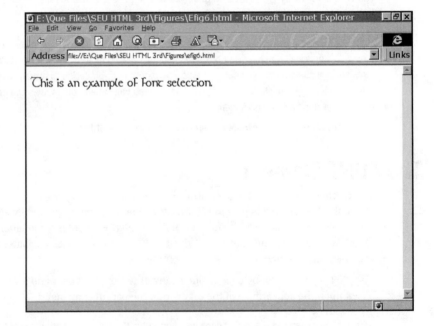

Since you don't know for certain what fonts the user might have on his system, the FACE attribute allows you to list more than one font, with the names separated by commas. This is especially useful because nearly identical fonts often have different names on Windows and Macintoshes. The font list will be parsed from left to right and the first matching font will be used. Listing 5.3 shows an example in which the author wanted to use a sans-serif font for his text.

Listing 5.3 Font Face Selection Can Use a List of Acceptable Choices

```
<HTML>
<HEAD>
<TITLE>Font Selection Example</TITLE>
</HEAD>
<BODY>
<FONT FACE="Verdana", "Arial", "Helvetica">
This is an example of font selection. </FONT>
</BODY>
</HTML>
```

In this example, the author wanted to use Verdana as his first choice, but listed Arial and Helvetica as alternatives.

The *SIZE* Attribute

The SIZE attribute of the FONT element allows the document author to specify character height for the text. Font size is a relative scale from 1 though 7 and is based upon the "normal" font size being 3. The SIZE attribute can be used in either of two different ways: The size can be stated absolutely, with a statement like SIZE=5, or it can be relative, as in SIZE=+2. The second method is more commonly used when a BASEFONT size has been specified.

Listing 5.4 shows how the font sizes are specified and Figure 5.6 shows how they would look.

Part

II

Ch

5

Listing 5.4 An Example of Font Size Selection

```
<HTML>
<HEAD>
<TITLE>Font Size Example</TITLE>
</HEAD>
<BODY>
<FONT SIZE=1>Size 1</FONT><BR>
<FONT SIZE=-1>Size 2</FONT><BR>
<FONT SIZE=3>Size 3</FONT><BR>
<FONT SIZE=4>Size 4</FONT><BR>
<FONT SIZE=+2>Size 5</FONT><BR>
<FONT SIZE=6>Size 6</FONT><BR>
<FONT SIZE=+4>Size 7</FONT><BR>
</BODY>
</HTML>
```

FIG. 5.6

Text size can be specified with the SIZE attribute of the FONT element.

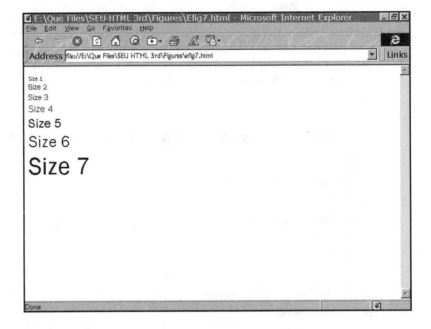

The *COLOR* Attribute

Text color can be specified in the same manner as the face or the size. The COLOR attribute accepts either a hexadecimal RGB value or one of the standard color names. Listing 5.5 is an example of how colors can be specified.

Listing 5.5   An Example of Font Color Selection

```
<HTML>
<HEAD>
<TITLE>Font Color Example</TITLE>
</HEAD>
<BODY>
<FONT COLOR="#FF0000">This text is red</FONT><BR>
<FONT COLOR="GREEN">This text is green</FONT><BR>
</BODY>
</HTML>
```

The *<BASEFONT>* Tag

The <BASEFONT> tag is used to establish the standard font size, face, and color for the text in the document. The choices made in the <BASEFONT> tag remain in place for the rest of the document, unless they are overridden by a FONT element. When the FONT element is closed, the BASEFONT characteristics are returned. BASEFONT attributes can be changed by another <BASEFONT> tag at any time in the document. Note that BASEFONT is a tag and not a container. There is no <BASEFONT> end tag.

BASEFONT uses the FACE, SIZE, and COLOR attributes just as the FONT element does.

Listing 5.6 is an example of the <BASEFONT> tag. Figure 5.7 shows how the example looks in Internet Explorer.

Listing 5.6   An Example of the <*BASEFONT*> Tag

```
<HTML>
<HEAD>
<TITLE>BASEFont Example</TITLE>
</HEAD>
<BODY>
This text is before the BASEFONT tag.<BR>
<BASEFONT SIZE=6 FACE="GEORGIA">
This text is after the BASEFONT tag.<BR>
Size changes are relative to the BASEFONT <FONT SIZE=-3>SIZE</FONT>.<BR>
</BODY>
</HTML>
```

FIG. 5.7

The <BASEFONT> tag can be used to control the text characteristics for the entire document.

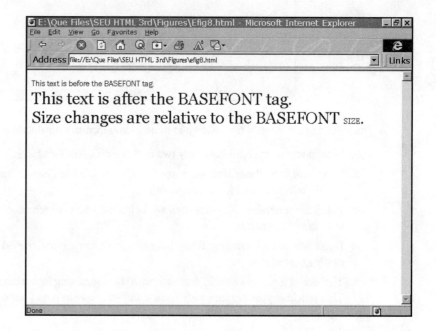

Part

II

Ch

5

Text Formatting Tips

Now that you have all of the tools to format your text, you need to decide how you are going to use them. It is possible to use so many different fonts, sizes, and formats that your document will be unpleasant to read. Figure 5.8 is a good example of how a document can use too many formats.

FIG. 5.8

The ability to select formats should not be overused.

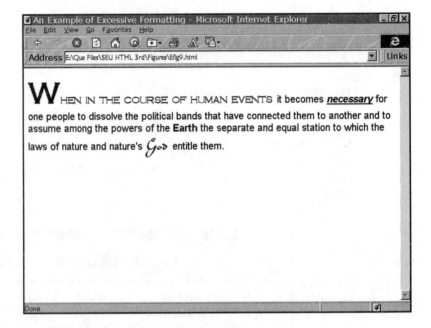

The following are general tips to keep in mind as you format your documents:

- Most documents should use only two or three different font faces.
- In general, if the body text is in a serif font, such as Times New Roman, the headings should be a sans-serif font, such as Arial.
- Italics are much less intrusive than are bold characters, which should be reserved for very important points.
- Don't overuse underlining. When long strings of text are underlined, the user's eyes easily get confused.
- The size of headings should decrease with the decreasing importance of the heading. This provides your readers with a quick and easy way to scan your documents.

## CHAPTER 6

Graphics Formatting

by Jerry Honeycutt and Robert Meegan

Images can make your HTML document more compelling than text alone. Imagine an HTML document that contains some fairly dry material; for example, the specification for the techno-widget that you invented. If you put only text in this document, the document would seem quite dull. On the other hand, a few well-placed graphics can break up the text, making it seem more readable, and making the document more visually appealing.

Images can often convey your message better than text alone. Can you picture this book without any figures? It wouldn't convey its message as well. Remember the old cliché: A picture is worth a thousand words? Beyond that, without figures you would probably have put this book right back on the shelf because it wouldn't look very appealing. I wouldn't blame you, either.

Up to this point, you've learned about the basic HTML required to add text to your document and how to format that text. This chapter stuffs your toolkit with another tool, inline images, that let you convey your message better and create a more visually attractive Web page. In this chapter, you learn how to add those images to your HTML documents. You also learn several tips and tricks that you need to know when using images in HTML. ▪

Use appropriate images in your HTML files

Before using an image, you need to concern yourself with its copyright. Also, you need to carefully consider how the image will affect your readers.

Choose the most appropriate graphics file format

There are several graphics file formats available for you to use, but this chapter recommends that you stick with GIF and JPEG, as they're pretty universal.

Easily add images to your HTML documents

Adding an image to your HTML document is a snap, with the `<IMG>` tag. This chapter shows you how to take full advantage of this tag and its attributes.

Learn the tricks of the trade

This chapter shows you some professional tips and tricks you can use to really enhance your HTML documents with images.

Understanding the Issues

You need to carefully consider each image that you add to your HTML documents. Yes, you should carefully consider the design and contents of each image, but, in this section, you learn about other issues. For example:

- Does the image add enough value to the Web page?
- Can I borrow an image? What about copyrights?
- What about offensive or pornographic images?

What Should I Know When Using Inline Images?

Before adding images to your HTML documents, you need to understand the issues. That doesn't mean you should avoid using images—you shouldn't. If you understand the issues, however, you're better able to choose appropriate images. Just keep these points in mind as you add each image to your document:

- **Graphics files are slow to download.** The average user with a 14.4K modem can wait several seconds or even several minutes while a graphics file downloads.

- **Search engines don't know what to do with images.** The search engines, such as AltaVista and Excite, can't index your images. Thus, if you depend heavily on images, your Web page isn't as likely to be hit upon by these search engines' users.

- **Many users don't have graphical browsers.** Thousands of folks are still using Lynx, for example, which is a UNIX-based, text-only browser. As well, Internet Explorer and Netscape users might disable inline images in order to open Web pages faster.

- **Images aren't always internationalized.** Such a big word, internationalized. Folks in cultures other than yours might not understand the significance or meaning of an image. Since HTML documents published on the Web have a worldwide audience, internationalized images might be important.

- **Color images aren't always portable.** A color image that looks good on your computer might not look quite as good on another user's computer. Thus, you need to pay particular attention to how you use colors in an image.

  ▶ **See** "Bandwidth Issues," **p. 358**

Do I Have to Worry About an Image's Copyright?

The growth in electronic publishing has given rise to a startling new crime wave. Many people who are perfectly honest in all of their day-to-day dealings think nothing of using a clever graphic that they found on the Web. After all, once they download it, the image has lost all of its ties to the original author. Regardless, the copyright laws apply to electronic images just as much as they do to works like this book. If you use an image that has been copyrighted, the author can sue for damages.

How can you tell if a graphic has been copyrighted? It's not as easy as looking for a little copyright symbol in the image. Here are some tips to help you tell if an image is copyrighted:

- Look at the original document that contained the image for a copyright notice.
- If you borrowed the image from clip art or an image library, look in the library's document for a copyright notice.
- If you scanned the image from a magazine or book, you can bet the image is copyrighted.
- If you downloaded an image from a commercial site, such as an online magazine, the image is probably copyrighted.

N O T E Images that are obviously commercially oriented are usually copyrighted. These include images of people, logos, cartoon characters, and other unique images. As well, interesting decorations, such as bullets or horizontal rules, probably come from a clip art library, which grants rights to use those images only to the purchaser of the library. ■

Can you plead ignorance if you're busted using a copyrighted image? Nope. You have the total responsibility for determining whether or not an image is copyrighted. Since this is not always practical, the best advice is to use only images that you're completely certain are not copyrighted, those to which you have been granted the right to use, or those for which you hold the copyright.

CAUTION

Changing a copyrighted work does not revoke the copyright. The copyright holder has rights to all derived works. This means that you cannot download an image, change it in some fashion, and then freely use the new version.

As you can see, copyright law is a tricky thing. Your best bet is to assume that all images are copyrighted unless proven otherwise. If you have any questions or if you're developing a high-profile Web site, you should probably contact an attorney who specializes in copyright law.

Can I Get into Trouble for Pornographic Images?

Maybe. A simple rule of thumb is that you should avoid pornographic images. From a practical point of view, a Web site that has pornographic images on it is likely to be overwhelmed with traffic. As a result you may run afoul of your Internet service provider, who is almost certainly not going to be pleased with hundreds of megabytes of downloads from a single Web page.

There are a couple of legal aspects to this issue, as well:

- Most pornography has been scanned from published sources and is in violation of the copyright laws. These publishers are among the most aggressive plaintiffs in pursuit of legal damages.

■ A variety of states and countries have laws regarding what is obscene. Since the Web is a worldwide medium, you might violate laws that you don't even know exist.

> **CAUTION**
>
> The information you read in this section is common sense. This information doesn't replace your legal counsel, however, in cases where you have real questions about pornographic images.

Picking the Right Graphics File Format

You'll find dozens of graphics file formats that you can use to store images. GIF, JPEG, PCX, WMF, and so on. When creating images for use in an HTML document, however, you're better off sticking with those file formats that most browsers understand: GIF or JPEG.

Each file format has certain tradeoffs. While one file format downloads faster, for example, the other format maintains more image detail. This section helps you pick the right file format by describing these tradeoffs. First, it briefly describes each file format. Then, it compares the speed, color depth, "loss-y-ness," and browser support of each file format.

> **N O T E**   If want to get right to the bottom line, I recommend that you use GIF. It's widely supported by most Web browsers (whereas PNG is not). It's interlaced, which lets users view an image before it's finished downloading. It does transparency, too, so you can create great looking imagemaps with transparent backgrounds. ▩

Formats

Chapter 17, "Graphics," describes each file format you read about here in great detail. For your convenience, however, the following sections contain an overview of each file format.

▶ **See** "Web Graphic Formats, **p. 349**

GIF   The most common file format on the Web is GIF (CompuServe Graphical Interchange Format). More specifically, GIF89A. This format was developed for CompuServe. It's been through a number of revisions and now includes many important features that you learn about in Chapter 17, including:

■ It uses a lossless compression scheme, so images don't lose detail when they're compressed.

■ It supports transparent backgrounds, so you can create images with transparent regions.

■ It's an interlaced file format (see Figure 6.1), so the user can view the image before the browser has finished downloading it.

■ It's widely supported by most browsers, so most users can view this file format inline.

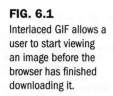

FIG. 6.1
Interlaced GIF allows a
user to start viewing
an image before the
browser has finished
downloading it.

Interlaced image, —
which is partially
loaded

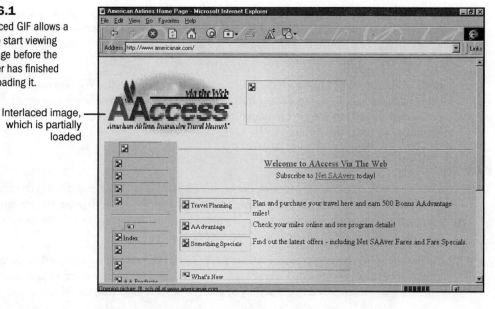

N O T E GIF has recently made the headlines. GIF, like several other compressed file formats, uses
an algorithm known as *LZW*, which is patented by Unisys. In late 1994, Unisys announced
that, in order to protect its rights, anyone producing software that used GIF would need a license from
Unisys. This requirement is for the developers of that software and does not affect end users. In fact,
the Unisys press release specifically states that using GIF on a Web page is acceptable and doesn't
require a license. ■

JPEG   Another popular format for graphics is JPEG. This was developed by the Joint Photographic Experts Group to provide a standard "lossy" compression scheme for photographic
images. Here's an overview of JPEG:

- It uses a lossy compression scheme, so images lose detail when they're compressed.
- It produces smaller images than GIF, so they download faster.
- It supports 16.7 million colors, so it reproduces photographic images very well.
- It loses detail around sharp edges, so it's not suitable for images that contain sharp
  images or text.

PNG   The Portable Network Graphics (PNG) format was developed as a result of the confusion and concern that followed the Unisys/CompuServe GIF announcement. Early in 1995, a
group of graphics programmers started to develop a new lossless format that would avoid the
licensing issues of GIF, while resolving some of the technical problems that GIF has. The new
format, PNG (pronounced "ping"), was released in March of 1995.

Part
II

Ch
6

Since that time, PNG has become ever more common and will probably replace GIF completely within the next few years. It provides better compression and supports a larger number of colors than does GIF. At this time, add-ins are available to give PNG display capabilities to both Netscape Navigator and Microsoft Internet Explorer.

BMP   A bitmap (BMP) file is a format commonly encountered in the Windows and OS/2 operating systems. These files are completely uncompressed and take inordinate amounts of time to download. Only Internet Explorer supports BMP files, and I recommend *very* strongly that you avoid using this format.

File Speed

When choosing a graphics file format, the most important issue to keep in mind is download speed versus image quality. If you're going to use an image in your Web page, you obviously want to store that image in a format that downloads as quickly as possible. On the other hand, you trade image quality for faster download speeds.

The best possible choices are GIF, PNG, and JPEG. BMP files aren't compressed at all, thus it is the slowest of all file formats to download. GIF, PNG, and JPEG all provide an acceptable experience when compared to the variety of other formats available on the Web:

- GIF and PNG files are larger than JPEG files, but GIF and PNG files decode faster and maintain more image detail.
- JPEG files download faster than GIF and PNG, but they decode slower and maintain less image detail.

TIP   GIF does an extremely good job compressing images that contain only a handful of colors.

Colors

GIF supports 256 colors. JPEG supports 16.7 million colors. Thus, if color depth is not important, or you're using a limited number of colors in an image, you can be comfortable using GIF. On the other hand, if you want to maintain a photographic quality color depth, then you might consider using JPEG.

Loss

Lossy compression schemes cause an image to lose detail when the graphics program saves it. This is how these schemes compress the file so much. Lossless compression schemes, on the other hand, don't cause an image to lose any detail at all. Table 6.1 describes each file format's compression scheme.

Table 6.1 Compression Schemes

Format	Scheme	Description
GIF	Lossless	GIF compresses without losing any detail. Thus, if you're concerned more with maintaining detail than download speed, use GIF.
PNG	Lossless	PNG also compresses without losing any detail. PNG is a good alternative to GIF, except that it's not directly supported by most Web browsers.
JPEG	Lossy	JPEG causes an image to lose detail when you save it. If you're concerned more with file size than with detail, however, use JPEG.
BMP	N/A	BMP provides no compression. You should avoid this file format for that reason.

Browser Support

You really don't want readers to have to install a helper application to view the images in your HTML documents. Thus, you should stick with those file formats that are directly supported by the most popular browsers. These formats include GIF and JPEG. PNG is not yet supported by a majority of the Web browsers, so you should shy away from this format for now.

Adding Inline Images to Your HTML Document

Putting an image in an HTML document is incredibly easy. You use the <IMG> tag with its SRC attribute. Add the following tag to your HTML document at the location in which you want to display the image. Then, replace *filename* with the URL of the image you want to display.

```
<IMG SRC="filename">
```

By default, the browser displays the image inline. Thus, the browser displays it immediately to the right of any text or any other object that immediately precedes the image. Take a look at Listing 6.1, for example. It shows the same image three different times. Each time, the image is shown inline. That is, the browser displays the image immediately to the right of any text preceding it as shown in Figure 6.2.

Listing 6.1 Using the <IMG> Tag

```
<HTML>
<HEAD>
  <TITLE>Using the IMG tag</TITLE>
</HEAD>
<BODY>
```

continues

Part

II

Ch

6

Listing 6.1 Continued

```
<P>
  <IMG SRC="book.gif">
  This text immediately follows the image.
</P>
<P>
  This text is interrupted
  <IMG SRC="book.gif">
  by the image.
</P>
<P>
  In this case, the image appears inline after this text.
  <IMG SRC="book.gif">
</P>
</BODY>
</HTML>
```

FIG. 6.2

You can insert an image anywhere in an HTML document that you like.

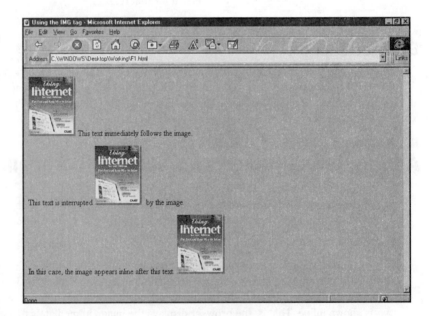

 T I P Consider storing all of your images in a single directory off of your Web site's root folder. Then, you can use relative paths in combination with the <BASE> tag (see Chapter 7, "Creating Document Links") to access your images without specifying a full URL.

Aligning Text with an Inline Image

By default, when you insert an image inline with text, the text is aligned with the bottom of the image. Chances are good that you won't like this default alignment. You can change it, using the <IMG> tag's ALIGN attribute. Table 6.2 describes each value you can assign to this attribute.

Table 6.2   Values for the *ALIGN* attribute

Value	Description
TOP	Aligns the text with the top of the image.
MIDDLE	Aligns the text with the middle of the image.
BOTTOM	Aligns the text with the bottom of the image.

Listing 6.2 shows you an HTML document that inserts three images, each of which uses one of the alignment values shown in Table 6.2. Figure 6.3 shows the resulting Web page.

Listing 6.2   Using the *<IMG>* Tag's *ALIGN* Attribute

```
<HTML>
<HEAD>
  <TITLE>Using the IMG tag's ALIGN attribute</TITLE>
</HEAD>
<BODY>
  <P>
    <IMG SRC="book.gif" ALIGN=TOP>
    This text is aligned with the top of the image.
  </P>
  <P>
    <IMG SRC="book.gif" ALIGN=MIDDLE>
    This text is aligned with the middle of the image.
  </P>
  <P>
    <IMG SRC="book.gif" ALIGN=BOTTOM>
    This text is aligned with the bottom of the image.
  </P>
</BODY>
</HTML>
```

Positioning an Image on the Web Page

By default, the browser displays images inline. That is, it displays an image immediately to the right of the previous content. Text does not wrap around it, either. You can display an image on the left or right side of the Web page, however, allowing the surrounding content to flow around the image. This type of image is called a *floating* image.

You create a floating image using the <IMG> tag's ALIGN attribute. This is the same attribute you use to align the surrounding text with an image. Table 6.3 describes each value you can assign to this attribute.

Part
II

Ch
6

FIG. 6.3
By default, the baseline of the text is aligned with the bottom of an inline image.

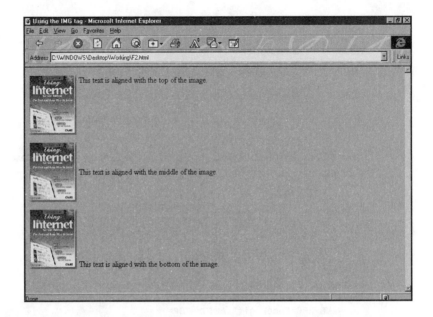

Table 6.3   Values for the *ALIGN* Attribute

Value	Description
LEFT	Displays image on left side and surrounding content flows around the image.
RIGHT	Displays image on the right side of the window and surrounding content flows around the image.

Listing 6.3 shows an HTML document that inserts two images, each of which uses one of the alignment values shown in Table 6.3. Figure 6.4 shows the resulting Web page.

Listing 6.3   Using the *<IMG>* Tag's *ALIGN* Attribute

```
<HTML>
<HEAD>
  <TITLE>Using the IMG tag's ALIGN attribute</TITLE>
</HEAD>
<BODY>
  <P>
    <IMG SRC="book.gif" ALIGN=LEFT>
    This text will wrap around the right-hand and bottom of the image.
    This text will wrap around the right-hand and bottom of the image.
    This text will wrap around the right-hand and bottom of the image.
    This text will wrap around the right-hand and bottom of the image.
    This text will wrap around the right-hand and bottom of the image.
    This text will wrap around the right-hand and bottom of the image.
    This text will wrap around the right-hand and bottom of the image.
    This text will wrap around the right-hand and bottom of the image.
```

```
      This text will wrap around the right-hand and bottom of the image.
      This text will wrap around the right-hand and bottom of the image.
      This text will wrap around the right-hand and bottom of the image.
      This text will wrap around the right-hand and bottom of the image.
   </P>
   <P>
   <IMG SRC="book.gif" ALIGN=RIGHT>
      This text will wrap around the left-hand and bottom of the image.
      This text will wrap around the left-hand and bottom of the image.
      This text will wrap around the left-hand and bottom of the image.
      This text will wrap around the left-hand and bottom of the image.
      This text will wrap around the left-hand and bottom of the image.
      This text will wrap around the left-hand and bottom of the image.
      This text will wrap around the left-hand and bottom of the image.
      This text will wrap around the left-hand and bottom of the image.
      This text will wrap around the left-hand and bottom of the image.
      This text will wrap around the left-hand and bottom of the image.
      This text will wrap around the left-hand and bottom of the image.
      This text will wrap around the left-hand and bottom of the image.
      This text will wrap around the left-hand and bottom of the image.
   </P>
   </BODY>
   </HTML>
```

FIG. 6.4

With the ALIGN attribute, text can wrap around figures to the left or the right side of the window.

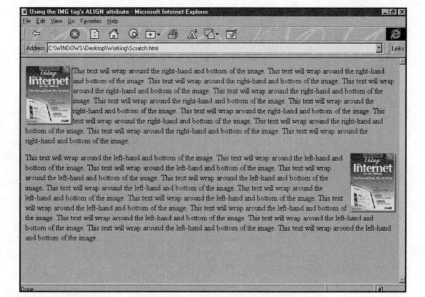

Part

II

Ch

6

Giving the Browser Size Hints

Providing the browser a size hint means that you explicitly state the height and width of the image within the `<IMG>` tag. This has two benefits that make it a must:

■ **Size hints help users who've disabled inline images.** If a user has disabled inline images, and you're not using size hints, she will see a small icon in place of the image. Thus, the Web page will not be formatted quite like you expect. Size hints cause the browser to display an empty box that is the same size as the image.

■ **Size hints make the Web page render faster.** A browser displays the HTML document first. Then, it displays the image. If you provide size hints for your inline images, the browser can display the formatted HTML document while it finishes downloading the images. Thus, the user sees the Web page faster.

You use the `<IMG>` tag's `HEIGHT` and `WIDTH` attributes to provide size hints to the browser. You set the `HEIGHT` attribute to the exact height and the `WIDTH` attribute to the exact width in pixels that you want to reserve for the image. Listing 6.4 shows what an HTML document looks like that sets the height and width of an image. Figure 6.5 shows what this HTML document looks like when inline images are disabled.

Listing 6.4 Using *HEIGHT* and *WIDTH* to Give Size Hints

```
<HTML>
<HEAD>
  <TITLE>Using HEIGHT and WIDTH to give size hints</TITLE>
</HEAD>
<BODY>
<IMG SRC="book.gif" WIDTH=320 HEIGHT=240>
</BODY>
</HTML>
```

If the size you specify by using the `HEIGHT` and `WIDTH` attributes isn't the same as the actual size of the image as determined in your favorite graphics editor, the browser scales the image. The following sections describe the result of scaling the image down and scaling the image up.

Scaling an Image Down   Scaling the image down means the actual image is larger than the space you reserved for it using the `HEIGHT` and `WIDTH` attributes. In this case, the browser shrinks the image so that it fits the reserved space.

You can easily distort an image if you're not careful how you specify its size. For example, if you decrease the image's height by 50 percent and the width by 25 percent, the image will look funny in the browser (see Figure 6.6).

CAUTION

Specifying a height and width that are smaller than the actual image's height and width doesn't save any download time. The browser still downloads the entire image before it scales it to fit the reserved area.

FIG. 6.5
Without size hints, all you'd see in this image is a small box with an icon in it.

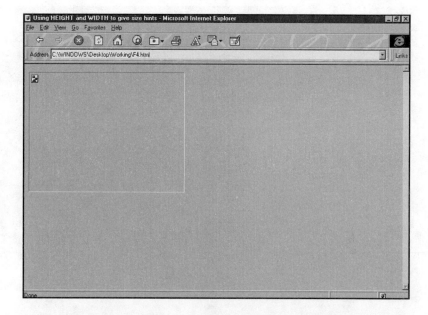

FIG. 6.6
Equally scaling an image's height and width is also known as maintaining the image's aspect ratio.

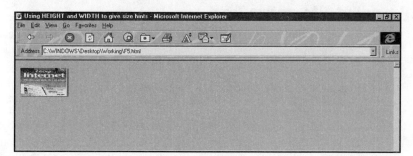

Scaling an Image Up   Scaling the image up means the actual image is smaller than the space you reserved for it by using the HEIGHT and WIDTH attributes. In this case, the browser enlarges the image so it fits the reserved space.

Just as with scaling an image down, you have to be concerned with maintaining an image's aspect ratio when you scale it up.

Unlike scaling an image down, however, you also have to worry with pixelation. That is, when you enlarge an image, the image's contents are expanded to fill the area. Where are the additional details coming from, though? The browser makes each pixel bigger so that it fills more space. This effect is sometimes very unattractive, as shown in Figure 6.7.

Part
II

Ch
6

FIG. 6.7
You can sometimes use pixelation to create special effects.

Providing Alternative Text

So, you've dumped a bunch of images into your HTML document. What about those folks who aren't viewing images? You can provide alternative text to them that, at least, tells them about the image. You do that with the `<IMG>` tag's `ALT` attribute, like this:

```
<IMG SRC="filename" ALT="Description">
```

If the user's browser isn't displaying images, he or she will see the alternative text in the image's place. For those users whose browser is displaying images, they'll see the alternative text until the browser is ready to display the image. Better yet, if you combine alternative text with size hints, they'll see a box that's correctly sized with the alternative text within its borders.

Listing 6.5 is an HTML document that uses alternative text to provide a description of the image. Figure 6.8 shows you what this document looks like in a browser that's not displaying inline images.

Listing 6.5   Using the *ALT* Attribute

```
<HTML>
<HEAD>
  <TITLE>Using the ALT attribute</TITLE>
</HEAD>
<BODY>
<IMG SRC="book.gif" WIDTH=320 HEIGHT=240 ALT="A picture of my latest book's
cover">
</BODY>
</HTML>
```

FIG. 6.8
Internet Explorer
displays the image's
alternative text in a
pop-up window when
the mouse pointer
lingers over the image
for more than a few
seconds.

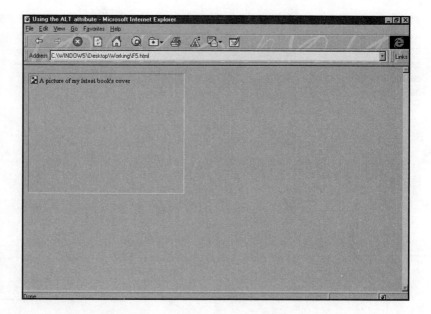

Framing an Image with a Border

By default, the user's browser will display a border around each inline image that you're using
as an anchor. You have a lot of control over that border and the white space around the image.

You set the `<IMG>` tag's BORDER attribute to the width of the border in pixels. If you want the
border to be 10 pixels in width, set this attribute to 10. Listing 6.6 shows an HTML document
with three images, each of which has a different border width. Figure 6.9 shows the result in
the browser.

Listing 6.6   Using the *BORDER* Attribute

```
<HTML>
<HEAD>
  <TITLE>Using the BORDER attribute</TITLE>
</HEAD>
<BODY>
<A HREF=""><IMG SRC="book.gif" BORDER=0></A>
<BR>
<A HREF=""><IMG SRC="book.gif" BORDER=5></A>
<BR>
<A HREF=""><IMG SRC="book.gif" BORDER=10></A>
</BODY>
</HTML>
```

▶ **See** "Anchors," **p. 107**

Part
II

Ch
6

FIG. 6.9
If you don't want the browser to draw a border around an image, set the BORDER attribute to 0.

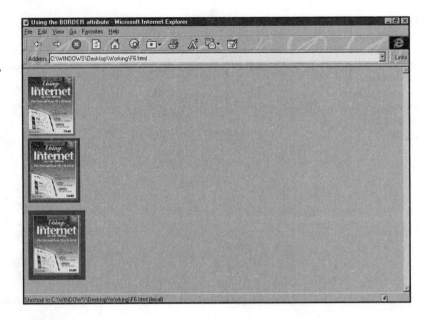

Giving an Image Space

You might not like how the text surrounding an image is crowding it. If so, you can use the VSPACE and HSPACE attributes to add vertical and horizontal space around the image, respectively. You set each of these attributes to the amount of space, in pixels, you want to allow between the surrounding content and the image. Listing 6.7 shows you an example of an image that adds additional space around the image to separate it from the text. Figure 6.10 shows you the result.

Listing 6.7   Using the *VSPACE* and *HSPACE* Attributes

```
<HTML>
<HEAD>
  <TITLE>Using the BORDER attribute</TITLE>
</HEAD>
<BODY>
<IMG SRC="book.gif" VSPACE=20 HSPACE=20 ALIGN=LEFT>
This text will wrap around the image.
This text will wrap around the image.
This text will wrap around the image.
This text will wrap around the image.
This text will wrap around the image.
This text will wrap around the image.
This text will wrap around the image.
This text will wrap around the image.
This text will wrap around the image.
This text will wrap around the image.
This text will wrap around the image.
```

```
This text will wrap around the image.
This text will wrap around the image.
This text will wrap around the image.
This text will wrap around the image.
This text will wrap around the image.
This text will wrap around the image.
This text will wrap around the image.
This text will wrap around the image.
This text will wrap around the image.
This text will wrap around the image.
This text will wrap around the image.
This text will wrap around the image.
This text will wrap around the image.
This text will wrap around the image.
This text will wrap around the image.
This text will wrap around the image.
This text will wrap around the image.
This text will wrap around the image.
This text will wrap around the image.
This text will wrap around the image.
This text will wrap around the image.
</BODY>
</HTML>
```

FIG. 6.10
Adding additional white space around an image keeps it from looking too cramped.

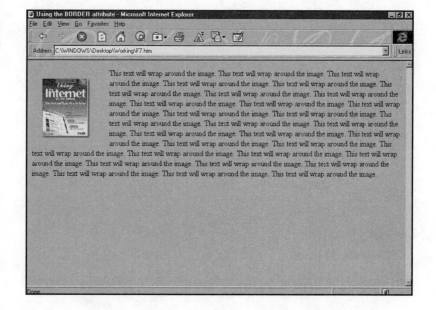

Part

II

Ch

6

Using an Image as an Anchor

Chapter 7, "Creating Document Links," describes how to use an image as a link to another resource. It's easy, however. You enclose an image within the <A> tag as shown here:

```
<A HREF="http://www.mysite.com"><IMG SRC="image.gif"></A>
```

▶ **See** "Anchors," **p. 107**

Creating Document Links

by Jerry Honeycutt and John Jung

By now, you've noticed the references to other chapters that are scattered all through this book. They serve a similar purpose as links on a Web page—albeit a little low-tech. They refer you to other places in this book that might be useful or interesting to read. Without these references, you would have to resort to flipping through the pages looking for what you need.

Links on a Web page are even more vital. You have all the pages of this book right in front of you. At least you would know where to start looking. On the other hand, you have no idea where to find all the Web pages on the Internet. And there are too many to keep track of anyway. Therefore, links are the only reasonable way to go from one Web page to another related Web page. ■

What is hypertext? Hypermedia?

Hypertext and hypermedia are the basic concepts behind the Web. This chapter refreshes your memory.

Learn about each part of a link

This chapter breaks down a link into its individual parts so that you can better understand it.

Add links to your HTML documents

You can link the text and graphics on your Web page to another document or file on the Internet.

Link your Web page to other Internet resources

Link your Web page to other Internet resources, such as Gopher, FTP, e-mail, and UseNet news.

Use the <*BASE*> tag in your HTML file

Simply your relative URLs using the <BASE> tag.

Understanding Hypertext and Hypermedia

Hypertext is a term you'll frequently hear associated with the Web. A hypertext document is a document that contains links to other documents—allowing you to jump between them by clicking the links. It's also a term associated with help files and other types of documents that are linked together. For example, if you've published a report that cites several sources, you can link the references of those sources to related works. Likewise, if you're discussing the migratory habits of the nerd-bird, you can provide links to Web pages where nerd-birds are known to frequent.

Hypermedia is based upon hypertext but it contains more than text. It contains multimedia such as pictures, videos, and audio, too. In hypermedia documents, pictures are frequently used as links to other documents. You can link a picture of Edinburgh to a Web site in Edinburgh, for example. There are countless types of multimedia you can include on a Web page, and some of those can serve as links to other Internet documents and resources. Figure 7.1 shows you an example of a hypermedia document.

FIG. 7.1
Hypermedia documents contain much more than just text; they contain graphics, sounds, and video, too.

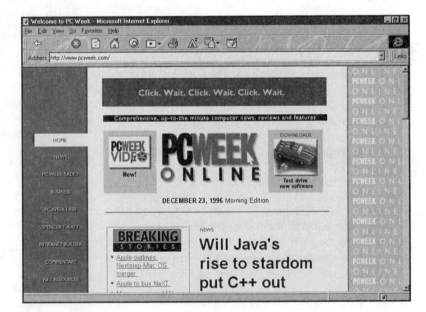

Understanding Links

A link really has two different parts. First, there's the part you see on the Web page—called an *anchor.* There's also the part that tells the browser what to do if you click that link—called the *URL reference.* When you click a link's anchor, the browser loads the file or document given by the link's corresponding URL reference. You'll learn about both parts of a link in the following sections.

Anchors

A link's anchor can be a word, group of words, or a picture. Exactly how an anchor looks in the browser depends largely on what type of anchor it is, how the user has configured the browser to display links, and how you created it. There are only two types of anchors though: text and graphical. You'll learn about both types in this section.

Text Anchors   Most text anchors look somewhat the same. A text anchor is one or more words the browser underlines to indicate it represents a link. The browser also displays a text anchor using a different color than the rest of the text around it (the color and appearance of links are under the author and user's control).

Figure 7.2 shows a Web page that contains three text anchors. In particular, notice how the text anchors on this Web page are embedded in the text. That is, they aren't set apart from the text, like the references in this book, but are actually an integral part of it. Clicking one of these links will load a Web page that is related to the link. You'll find many text anchors used this way. The HTML for the first text link looks a bit like this (you'll learn more about the <A> tag later in this chapter):

```
<A HREF="vero.html">Vogon Earth Reconnaissance Office</A>
```

FIG. 7.2
You'll find Vogon's Hitch-Hiker's Guide to the Galaxy Page at **http://www. metronet.com/ ~vogon/hhgttg.html**.

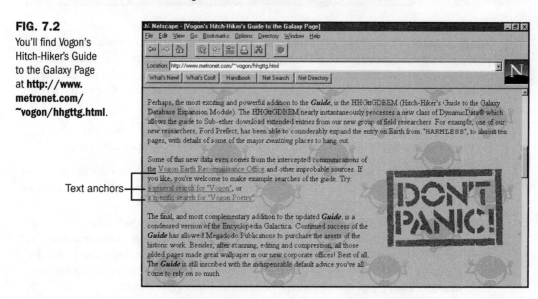

Figure 7.3 shows another Web page with a lot of text anchors. These anchors aren't embedded in the text, however. They are presented as a list or index of links from which you can choose. Web page authors frequently use this method to present collections of related links.

Part

II

Ch

7

FIG. 7.3
To learn how to list your
Web site in Yahoo!,
see Chapter 32,
"Search Engines
and Advertising."

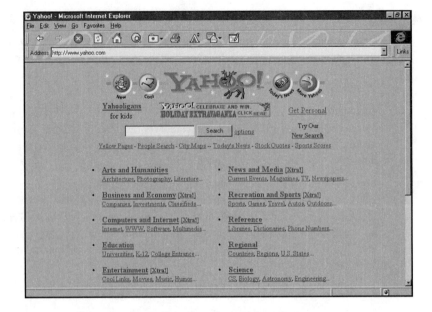

Graphical Anchors   A *graphical anchor* is similar to a text anchor. When you click a link's graphical anchor, the browser loads the Web page that the link references. Graphical anchors aren't underlined or displayed in a different color, but you can display a border around them. And no two graphical anchors need to look the same, either. It depends entirely on the picture that you choose to use.

Versatility is the strong suit of graphical anchors. You can use them for a variety of reasons. Here are some examples of the ways you'll find graphical anchors used on a Web page:

- *Bullets.* Graphical anchors are frequently used as list bullets. You can click the picture to go to the Web page described by that list item. Frequently, the text in the list item is also a link. You can click either the picture or the text.

- *Icons.* Many Web sites use graphical anchors in a similar manner to Windows 95. They are common on home pages, and represent a variety of Web pages available at that site. Figure 7.4 shows a Web site that uses graphical anchors in this manner. The HTML for the icon on the left side of this Web page that says "Whats New!" might look a bit like this (you'll learn how to create graphical anchors later in this chapter):

```
<A HREF="whatsnew.htm"><IMG SRC="whatsnew.gif" BORDER=0></A>
```

Advertisements   Many Web sites have sponsors that pay to advertise on the site. This makes the Web site free to you and me, while the site continues to make money. You'll usually find advertisements, such as the one shown in Figure 7.5, at the top of a Web page. Click the advertisement, and the browser will load the sponsor's Web page.

FIG. 7.4
GolfWeb's home page uses graphical anchors to represent a variety of its pages you can load.

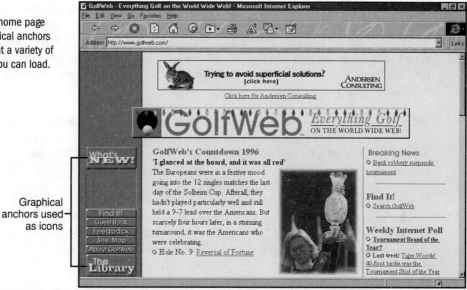

Graphical anchors used as icons

FIG. 7.5
HomeArts is an online magazine that uses sponsors to pay the bills so that the service remains free.

Graphical anchor used as an advertisement

URL References

The other part of a link is the URL reference. This is the address of the Web page the browser will load if you click the link. Every type of link, whether it uses a text or graphical anchor, uses either a relative or absolute reference. You'll learn about each type in this section.

Relative References   A URL reference to a file on the same computer is also known as a *relative reference*. It means that the URL is relative to the computer and directory from which the browser originally loaded the Web page. If the browser loadsa page at **http://www.mysite.com/page**, for example, then a relative reference to**/picture** would actually refer to the URL **http://www.mysite.com/page/picture**. Relative references are commonly used to refer to Web pages on the same computer.

> **N O T E**   Relative references work differently if you use the <BASE> tag in your HTML file. If you do use the <BASE> tag, as described later in this chapter, relative references are always relative to the URL given in the tag. They're not relative to the URL page on which the reference appears. ■

The primary reason you use a relative reference is convenience. It's much simpler to just type the file name, instead of the entire URL. It also makes it easier for you to move Web pages around on the server. Since the URL references are relative to the Web page's computer and directory, you don't have to change all the links in the Web page every time the files move to a different location.

Absolute References   An URL reference that specifies the exact computer, directory, and file for a Web page is an *absolute reference*. Whereas relative references are common for links to Web pages on the same computer, absolute references are necessary for links to Web pages on other computers.

Linking to Documents and Files

Now that you have the terminology down (anchors, links, relative references, and so on), you're ready to start adding links to your own Web pages. It's truly very simple. You have to tell the browser what element in the HTML file is the anchor and the address of Internet document or resource to which you're linking. You do both things with one tag: <A>.

The following example shows you what the <A> tag looks like. This is its simplest form used for linking to another Web page on the Internet. It's only attribute is HREF, which specifies the URL to which you're linking. The URL can be any valid abosolute or relative reference, such as **http://www.server.com/home/index.htm**. Since the <A> tag is a container, you must put the closing </A> tag on the other side of the anchor. That is, the opening <A> tag tells the browser where the anchor (text or graphical) starts and the closing </A> tag tells the browser where the anchor ends.

```
<A HREF=URL>Anchor</A>
```

The following bit of HTML shows you how to add a text anchor to your HTML file. In this example, HREF references my home page on the Internet. The anchor, which is underlined in the Web browser, is "Jerry Honeycutt's." The text before and after the <A> container isn't part of the anchor and is therefore not underlined. For that matter, nothing will happen when the user clicks the text outside of the container. On the other hand, when the user clicks

"Jerry Honeycutt's," the browser will load my home page in the browser. Figure 7.6 shows what this anchor looks like in Internet Explorer.

```
While you're here, why don't you visit
<A HREF="http://rampages.onramp.net/~jerry">Jerry Honeycutt's</A> homepage
```

FIG. 7.6

You can control the appearance of links by using the <BODY> tag, as described in Chapter 3, "HTML Document Architecture."

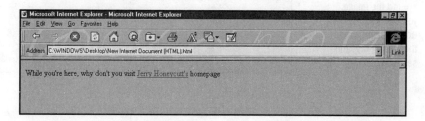

N O T E The examples you've seen thus far all use absolute references. You can also use relative references. Relative references can get a bit out of hand, however, if you store different Web pages in different directories. You'll have a difficult time remembering exactly in which directory an HTML file is stored and thus how to formulate the relative reference.

To remedy this problem, you can add the <BASE> tag to the top of your HTML file. In the absence of the <BASE> tag, all relative references are based upon the URL of the current HTML file. Adding the <BASE> tag provides an URL on which all relative references in the HTML file are based. It affects relative references in every HTML tag, including the <A> tag, <IMG> tag, and so on.

Thus, if you add

```
<BASE HREF="http://www.server.com">
```

to your HTML file, all relative references are based upon that address, instead of the address of the current HTML file. In this case, the relative reference "images/face.gif" would resolve to **http://www.server.com/images/face.gif**.

Note that the <BASE> tags original intention was to provide the URL of the document in which it's found. This allows folks who are viewing the document out of context to locate the document on the Internet. It works perfectly well for the purpose of dereferencing relative URLs, however, and is documented by W3C in this manner. ■

  Some browsers support tooltip style help for links. That is, when the user holds the mouse over a link for a certain period of time, the browser will display the contents of the <A> tags TITLE attribute in a small popup window. Thus, if you want to provide additional information about the link to the user, assign it to the TITLE attribute, like this: <A HREF="page.html" TITLE="Go to page.html">.

The previous example showed you how to create a text anchor. Creating a graphical anchor isn't much different. Instead of enclosing text in the <A> container, you put an image. Consider the following HTML, which is very similar to the previous example. Figure 7.7 shows what it looks like. The HREF references my home page, but, instead of using a text anchor, it uses the <IMG> tag to create a graphical anchor. When the user clicks anywhere on the picture, the browser opens the Web page referred to by the <A> tag.

Part

II

Ch

7

```
<A HREF="http://rampages.onramp.net/~jerry"><IMG SRC="photo.gif"></A>
```

FIG. 7.7

If you don't want to display a border around the image, you can add the BORDER attribute to the <IMG> tag, and set its value to 0.

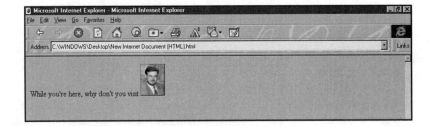

N O T E Imagemaps are becoming much more common. They let you map certain portions of an image to different URLs. For more information about creating imagemaps, see Chapter 12, "Imagemaps." ∎

Internal Links

As well as providing links to other HTML files, you can link to an anchor within the current document. For example, you can provide a table of contents for the current Web page at the top of the page. You can then link each entry to a different section within the current Web page.

There are two steps to do this. First, you must create an anchor in the HTML file that indicates the location to which you're linking. For example, if you want to provide a link to the middle portion of your Web page, you'd create an anchor in the middle and give it a name using the NAME attribute. You name the anchor so that you can refer to that name in your link. Note that since you're only naming an anchor, instead of creating a link, you don't set the HREF attribute. You still have to use the opening and closing <A> tags, but the browser doesn't highlight the contents of the <A> tag because you're not using it as a link. Here's what the named anchor looks like:

```
<A NAME=MIDDLE>Middle Section in Web Page</A>
```

After you've created the named anchor, you create a link to it. You use a special notation to link to that anchor. Instead of setting the HREF attribute to the URL of another Web page, you set it to the name of the anchor. You prefix the anchor's name with a pound sign (#), though. Consider the following example. The HREF attribute refers to the named anchor shown in the previous example. The name is prefixed with the pound sign to indicate to the browser that you're making an internal link. When the user clicks Jump to the middle, the browser will align the anchor in the previous example to the top of the browser window.

```
<A HREF="#MIDDLE">Jump to the middle</A>
```

N O T E Some browsers will not move the named anchor to the top of the browser window if the anchor is already displayed in the window. That is, if your internal link is at the top of the Web page, and the named anchor is displayed somewhere in the middle of the Web page, when the user clicks the internal link, the browser will do nothing. ∎

Files, Plug-In Content, and So On

When the user clicks a link to another Web page, the browser opens that Web page in the browser window. On the other hand, if the user clicks a link to a different type of document, it downloads the document to the user's computer and then decides what to do with it. One of two things will happen as a result:

- The browser will know how to handle the file, which is the case with many graphics formats, and will display the file in the browser window. For example, if you create a link to a GIF file and the user clicks that link, the browser will download the GIF file, clear the current Web page from the browser window, and display the GIF file in the window as shown in Figure 7.8. In some cases, however, the browser can use a plug-in to display the file in the browser window without actually opening a separate window, even though the browser itself doesn't know what to do with the file.

FIG. 7.8

Linking to a file, such as a GIF file, is not the same thing as inserting or embedding that file in your Web page.

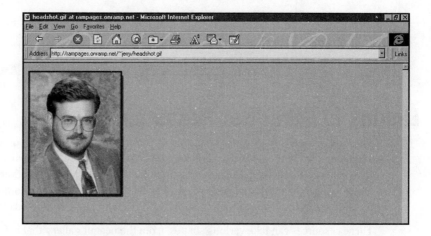

- The browser will not know how to handle the file, which is the case for a variety of documents and many types of plug-in content. In this case, the browser will download the file and look for a helper application that knows what to do with it. If it finds one, it'll launch the helper application and pass it the downloaded file. For example, if the user clicks a link to an AVI video, the browser will download the file, find a helper application to play AVI files, and launch that file in the application. In most cases, the application will display the file in a separate window, as shown in Figure 7.9.

T I P Digital InfoWorks sells a product called Cyberlinks that you can use to create links in any OLE-enabled product, such as Wordpad. This means you can create hypertext links in your documents just like you can in your Web pages. For more information, see **http://www.pioneersys.com**.

Part

II

Ch

7

FIG. 7.9

You can cause the browser to play AVI files inline by embedding them, instead of linking to them (see Chapter 20, "Video, Animation, and Multimedia," for more information).

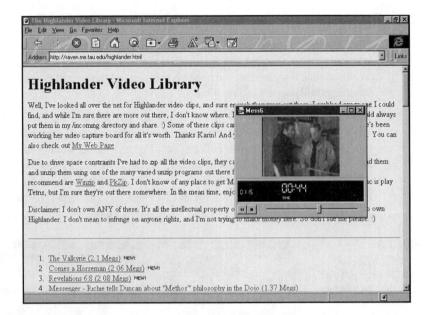

Linking to Other Net Resources

The World Wide Web is a popular part of the entire Internet, but many other resources are available. Most of them were around long before the Web was even born and, as a result, they have a lot of stuff on them. Also as a result of the Web's newness, the other resources sometimes have a much wider audience base. Whether you're designing a home page for yourself or for your company, you may want to know how to link to those resources.

These resources can take various shapes, from the peanut gallery that is UseNet news, to personal e-mail, to the capability to access other computers through Telnet. Although you can create your own versions of these resources by using forms (see Chapter 11, "Forms"), most of the time you wouldn't want to do so. For example, you could easily create a page with many HTML form tags, text elements, and a submit button for e-mail, but simply creating a link to e-mail with a particular address would be easier. This way, you can more easily update the page because you don't have to worry about which forms to read. Also, sometimes browsers have built-in support for some of the other resources, giving the user faster response time.

You especially want to create links to other resources on the Net if you're already using a resource. If you already have a Gopher site with information that's updated automatically, why rebuild it to fit the Web? Just adding a hyperlink to your Gopher site makes more sense. Similarly, if you're running a BBS that's on the Internet, putting in a Telnet link to it makes more sense. There's no reason for re-creating, or even mirroring, your BBS through forms for the Web.

Creating a Link to E-Mail

The single most popular activity on the Internet is sending e-mail. More people use e-mail than any other resource on the Net. The reason is quite simple: If you're on the Internet, you have an e-mail address. The provider that gives you access to the Net often has at least one e-mail program available for your use. Most modern e-mail programs offer a friendly interface, with no complex commands to learn.

You'll most likely want to put in an e-mail link when you want people to give you feedback on a particular topic. Whatever it is you want comments on—be it your home page or your company's product—if you want to know what people think use an e-mail link. E-mail links are also useful for reporting problems, such as a problematic or missing link. Typically, the Webmaster of a particular site should put these types of links to himself or herself. You really have no reason not to put in a link to your e-mail address.

Creating a link to an e-mail address is similar to creating a link to another home page. The only difference is the reference for your anchor element. Normally, you put a link to a home page around some text as in the following:

```
<A HREF="http://www.mycom.com/myhome.html">Go to my home page</A>.
```

Linking to e-mail is just as simple. Instead of entering **http**, which specifies a Web address, use **mailto:** to specify an e-mail address. And instead of specifying an URL, put in your full e-mail address. The preceding example now looks like this:

```
<A HREF="mailto:me@mycom.com">Send me E-mail</A>.
```

The link created with the preceding HTML will look like any other hypertext link. You can easily mix and match hyperlinks to different resources, and they'll all look the same (see Figure 7.10). When this link is selected, the browser opens its own e-mail interface for the user. Each interface is different, but most of them automatically get your e-mail address and real name, and prompt you for a subject.

FIG. 7.10
E-mail links look just like regular hypertext links.

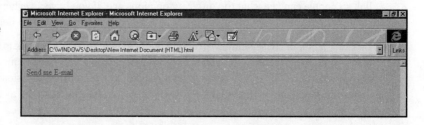

Because the e-mail link is a standard URL and easily implemented, many browsers have built-in support for it. As a result, when people click an e-mail link, the Web browser will put up a primitive mail program. A few companies offer a full set of Internet applications, from an e-mail program, to a newsreader, to a Web browser. Often times, these work in conjunction with each other. Consequently, when you click an e-mail link, these Internet packages will start up their own e-mail program (see Figure 7.11).

Part
II

Ch
7

FIG. 7.11
Internet Explorer will
launch its own full-
featured e-mail program
when you click an
e-mail link.

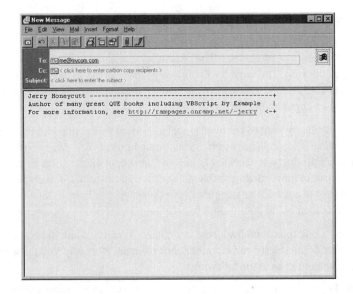

Creating a Link to UseNet News

UseNet is one of the best, or worst, resources on the Net, depending on whom you ask. Any-body with an opinion can tell you what he or she thinks. They may not know what they're talking about, but they'll let you know their opinion. UseNet is the ultimate embodiment of the freedom of speech, letting everybody say anything they want.

This ability of anybody anywhere on the Net having a voice could be an asset to your home page. Often, you may want to put in a link to UseNet when you want people to read for more information. If your home page has some information about HTML authoring, for example, you might want readers to go to a particular newsgroup for more help. You can also include such a link so people can see what the differing opinions are. If you have a certain political view and want others to see what the opposition is, a UseNet news link would be helpful.

Creating a link to a UseNet newsgroup is pretty simple; this kind of link is also just a derivative of the basic hypertext link. As you did with the e-mail link, you need to modify two parts in the anchor reference. When you're creating a UseNet link, enter **news:** instead of **http:**. Likewise, instead of specifying a particular URL, you put in a specific newsgroup, as follows:

```
For more information, see
<A HREF="news:news.newusers.questions">news.newusers.questions</A>.
```

As you can see in Figure 7.12, the UseNet news hyperlink looks identical to other links. When a user selects such a link, the browser tries to access the user's UseNet news server. If the news server is available to that person, the browser goes to the specified newsgroup. The user can then read as much as he or she likes in that particular group.

FIG. 7.12
UseNet news links allow you to make a point to people interested in your topic.

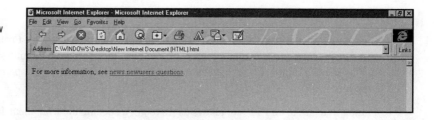

CAUTION

When a user clicks a UseNet news link, his or her browser tries to access the newsgroup in question. Because it's this user's browser and environment, he or she might not have access to the group you specified. Not all Internet providers have access to the same newsgroups. When you're creating such links, be mindful that not everybody will necessarily be able to access them.

How a UseNet hyperlink is handled is left entirely up to the Web browser the person is using. Many of them treat each article in a newsgroup as an individual hyperlink. Often, there's little in the way of sophisticated newsreading features. Some companies, such as Netscape and Microsoft, offer an entire suite of programs, including a UseNet newsreader (see Figure 7.13). In these cases, the newsreader of that suite is started.

FIG. 7.13
When a UseNet link is accessed, some sophisticated Web browsers will start up their own newsreader.

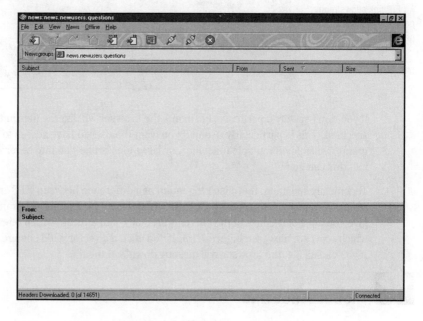

Part
II

Ch

Making FTP Available on Your Site

Another popular activity is accessing an FTP site. FTP, or File Transfer Protocol, allows users to copy files from other computers (the FTP site) onto their own computers. This popular method allows companies to distribute their demonstration software or patches to their products.

Putting in a link to an FTP site allows users to get a specific file from a particular location. This capability is useful for companies and shareware authors in making their products available. This type of link is also great for people who review software, allowing them to let users get the files being reviewed. People who have files, such as FAQs and interesting pictures that they want others to get to easily, might want to put in a link to an FTP site.

You create a link to an FTP site the same way you create other links, and they look the same, too (see Figure 7.14). You enter **ftp:** instead of the usual **http:**, and you change the URL address to **//*sitename/path***. Simply put, the site name looks the same as the URL address. You need to make sure the site name you specify points to a machine that accepts anonymous FTP connections. FTP links are almost always supported by the browser natively. You can create a typical FTP link as follows:

```
You can get the FAQ <A HREF="ftp://ftp.mysite.com/pub/FAQ">here</A>.
```

FIG. 7.14

An FTP link allows many people to access a particular file.

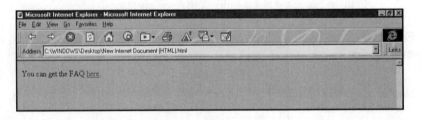

If you don't specify a particular file name, the browser will list the files in the directory you specified. This is particularly useful if you want the user to have access to multiple files. Programs available on multiple machines, or large files broken up into several chunks, typically fall into this category.

Technically speaking, there isn't too much of a difference between FTP and the Web. As a result, Web browsers support FTP links without needing another program. The browsers will give you a list of the files in the current directory, and indicate which ones are directories and which ones are files (see Figure 7.15). If you click a directory, it'll change into that directory. If you click a file, the browser will directly download the file.

TROUBLESHOOTING

Some people can't access some of my FTP links. If a lot of people are reporting they can't access some of your FTP links, try finding others. This error usually comes up when you have an FTP link to a particularly busy FTP site. You should try and locate other (less busy) FTP sites that have the same file you're pointing to.

FIG. 7.15
Web browsers will have no problems handling FTP links by themselves.

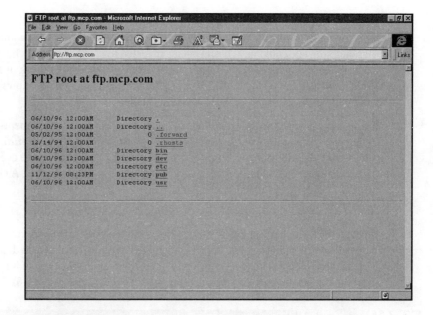

FTP root at ftp.mcp.com

```
06/10/96 12:00AM    Directory .
06/10/96 12:00AM    Directory ..
05/02/95 12:00AM           0 .forward
12/14/94 12:00AM           0 .rhosts
06/10/96 12:00AM    Directory bin
06/10/96 12:00AM    Directory dev
06/10/96 12:00AM    Directory etc
11/12/96 08:23PM    Directory pub
06/10/96 12:00AM    Directory usr
```

N O T E   By default, when FTP links are activated, the FTP connection that's made is known as anonymous FTP. This means that the FTP site the user is trying to access doesn't care who the user is. All the anonymous FTP site cares about is sending and receiving files to anybody who logs in with the username "anonymous." The password is often the e-mail address of the user, but this isn't necessary. Anonymous FTP allows software companies and the like to distribute their products to a very wide audience.

A nonanonymous FTP is where the FTP site is very particular about who can access it. To get access to a nonanonymous FTP site, you must have an account on the FTP site itself. Basically, you can't get into a nonanonymous FTP site unless you're already in. This is probably the most widely used FTP site around, as many companies allow employees to FTP into their own accounts. ▪

N O T E   You can easily change an anonymous FTP link into a nonanonymous one. Simply put, a user name and the "@" sign before the site name. This will cause most Web browsers to automatically attempt to log in as user name. The browser will then prompt the user for the password for the login id. ▪

Linking Your Home Page to a Gopher Site

Before there was the World Wide Web, there was something known as Gopher. It was originally designed by the University of Minnesota (the Golden Gophers) as a way of making information that was spread out easily available. Gopher has probably been the Internet resource most affected by the Web, often being superseded by it. The biggest difference between Gopher and the Web is that it is very difficult for individual people to create their own Gopher sites or holes.

Part
II

Ch
7

Although Gopher sites are not as prevalent as they once were, they still have a strong following. You can typically find Gopher sites at places that dispense a lot of automated information. Although the site could have easily been converted to HTML, it simply hasn't bothered to. This conversion of Gopher data into usable HTML code is typically the work of a programmer, and often not worth the effort. Putting in an HTML link to a Gopher site allows people browsing your page easy access to a great deal of information.

You can create a link to a Gopher hole by modifying the same two elements of the anchor reference. Change the **http:** to **gopher:**, and change the URL to **//*sitename***. The site name must be a valid Internet host name address. The link created looks like every other type of hypertext link, and built-in support is provided by most Web browsers. A Gopher hole link usually looks something like the following:

```
For more information, go <A HREF="gopher://gopher.mysite.com">here</A>.
```

Just like FTP, Gopher is a Net resource that is built into HTML. Consequently, most Web browsers will support any links to a Gopher site internally. That is, you don't need a Gopher-specific application to go to a Gopher site, the browser will take care of it for you. But just like FTP, the built-in support for Gopher is often very bland (see Figure 7.16).

FIG. 7.16

There's only so much a Web browser can do to liven up the text-based Gopher resource.

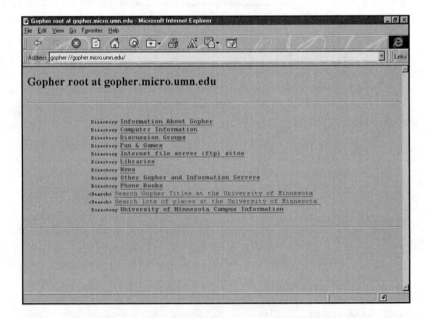

Providing Access to a Large Database with a WAIS Link

WAIS stands for Wide Area Information System, which basically means "lots of large databases you can search through." WAIS was specially designed by WAIS Corp. as a way of accessing large amounts of information. This capability is very different from what Gopher and the Web do in that WAIS was intended to cover very large chunks of information. Typically, databases that contained several million entries were considered appropriate for WAIS.

WAIS is typically accessed through a search engine because most people don't want to plod through such large stores of information. When WAIS was first introduced, custom front ends allowed easy access to a WAIS database. With the advent of the Web, however, most WAIS databases now have HTML front ends to their databases. Now, you can simply fill out a Web form and click a button, and the WAIS search is underway.

You can create a link in your home page to a WAIS database as easily as you do with all the other links. You have to modify the same two anchor reference elements to hold the correct information. Instead of using **http:**, enter the prefix **wais:**, and change the URL location to be the address of a WAIS database:

```
To search for a number in your area, click
<A HREF="wais://wais.mysite.com">here</A>.
```

N O T E Most browsers don't have built-in support of WAIS database searches. If you put in a link to one of these databases, be sure to include some sort of reference to where users can get a WAIS client. Of course, if the WAIS database you're pointing to has HTML forms support, you don't need to worry about including such information. ■

Accessing Remote Computers with Telnet Links

The capability to access other computers is not something new to the Web; it's been around for a long time. This access has always been achieved with a UNIX program called Telnet, which doesn't stand for anything in particular. Telnet allowed people to try to log into a remote machine, much the same way as some people access their Internet providers. The Web allows for support of accessing remote machines through a Telnet link to a remote computer.

Usually, people trying to get on a secure system are the people for whom you want to provide a Telnet link. People who provide access to a private, Internet-accessible BBS will most likely want to put in a Telnet link. Also, companies that offer a BBS for customer support may want to make use of a link to a Telnet site. Generally speaking, for most home pages, you have little or no reason to include a link to a remote site.

As you might have guessed, creating a Telnet link to a remote site requires modifying the anchor reference element. You change the **http:** to **telnet:**. You also need to change the URL part of the anchor reference to hostname. Hypertext links that refer to Telnet sites look the same as other links. A typical Telnet link takes the following form:

```
Click <A HREF="wais://wais.mysite.com">here</A> to access our BBS.
```

N O T E Most Web browsers do not support Telnet activity natively. They typically depend on an external application to talk correctly to the remote machine. If you put in a link to Telnet to another site, be sure to also include some reference to a Telnet client. ■

N O T E There are a few operating systems that have built-in Telnet capability. Among the OSes that have this are Windows 95, Windows NT, and UNIX. ■

Part
II

Ch
7

Even though Telnet is a rather simple Net resource, it also has some problems. Among the many problems are issues of how to display the remote session and how to interpret keypresses. As simple as these problems may appear, they're hard to implement in a Web browser. For these reasons, most Web browsers don't have support for Telnet. Rather, they leave it up to the individual person to find a Telnet program and set it up (see Figure 7.17).

FIG. 7.17

Most Web browsers don't support the Telnet links internally, so you need another program to access these links.

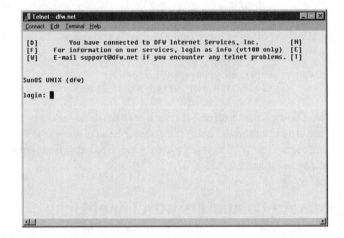

Some Web browsers allow something extra in the anchor reference. Simply add the user name you want the person to log in as, followed by the "@" sign before the site name. So that instead of:

```
Access my <A HREF="telnet://mysite.com/">system!</A>
```

You can have:

```
Access my <A HREF="telnet://john@mysite.com/">system!</A>
```

On those browsers that support this, the Web browser will pop up a little notice. This notice tells the user what login name should be used to access the system.

How Links Work Together

You may be wondering how well these hypertext links work with each other. The answer is: very well. Even though the links are different, they all look and behave the same. This common behavior exists because of the anchor reference that all hyperlinks use. Some may need client programs not built into a Web browser, but that's not a big deal. This identical look and feel of various hypertext links allows home pages to have a consistent feel. Consistency in a home page is important because it allows people to simply "know" they're in your home page without looking at the current URL.

The best thing you can do is to treat all hypertext links in the same manner, with slightly different formats. Just take the same basic anchors, add a reference, and put in the correct pointer to that reference (see Table 7.1). As a Web author, you must always remember that each person looking at your home page could be using any browser available. No hard and fast rules about what resources all browsers will support even exists. Whatever resource you want to link to, though, try to include a link to a location where the user can get a client.

Table 7.1   Sample Formats for Creating Links

Link to	What to Use	Sample Link
Web page	http://*sitename*/	http://www.mysite.com/
E-mail	mailto:*address*	mailto:me@mysite.com
Newsgroup	news:*newsgroupname*	news:news.newusers.questions
FTP	ftp://*sitename*/	ftp://ftp.mysite.com/
Gopher	gopher://*sitename*/	gopher://gopher.mysite.com/
WAIS	wais://*sitename*/	wais://wais.mysite.com/
Telnet	telnet://*sitename*/	telnet://bbs.mysite.com/

Part

II

Ch

7

Creating Lists

by Jerry Honeycutt and Jim O'Donnell

You can organize information for presentation in many different ways. One of the most effective formats is the list. Lists are both functional and easy to read; they can define sequential procedures, relative importance, available decision options, collections of related data, and data ordering. We see lists everywhere and every day. From restaurant menus to encyclopedias to phone books, lists are a fundamental way that we organize and disseminate information.

HTML provides container elements for creating lists in HTML documents. The basic list types available are numbered, bulleted, menu, directory, and definition. You can mix these types to create a variety of display and organizational effects, too. ■

Learn about the types of lists available

In HTML, you can create numbered, bulleted, menu, directory, and definition lists.

Create each different type of list

This chapter shows you the HTML tags you use to create each type of list.

Create a custom-list format

You can create your own list format. This chapter shows you how.

Creating an Ordered List

A basic list in HTML consists of a list-identifier container plus the standard list items tag. (In HTML, all list items use one tag, <LI>, while the lists themselves are differentiated by their container tags.) An ordered list, also called a numbered list, is used to create a sequential list of items or steps. When a Web browser sees the tag for an ordered list, it sequentially numbers each list item by using standard numbers, such as 1, 2, 3, and so on.

Using the *<OL>* Tag

Ordered (or numbered) lists begin with the <OL> tag, and each item uses the standard <LI> tag. If needed, you can create a list heading by using the <LH> tag. Close the list with the </OL> tag to signal the end of the list to the browser. List containers provide both a beginning and ending line break to isolate the list from the surrounding text; it's not necessary (except for effect) to precede or follow the list with the paragraph <P> tag.

N O T E   Lists support internal HTML elements. One of the most useful elements is the paragraph tag (<P>), which enables you to separate text in a list item. Other useful tags include both logical and physical style tags (such as <EM> and <I>) and HTML entities. Headings are not appropriate for use in lists; although they're interpreted correctly, their forced line breaks make for an ugly display. SGML purists also object to them because heading tags are meant to define relationships in paragraphs, not lists.

Listing 8.1 shows how you can use the OL list container. Pay particular attention to include closing tags, especially in nested lists. You can use leading blanks and extra lines to make your list code easier to read, but Web browsers ignore them. Figure 8.1 shows how Netscape Navigator interprets this HTML code.

Listing 8.1   Ordered List Example

```
<HTML>
<HEAD>
<TITLE>ordered List Example</TITLE>
</HEAD>
<BODY>
<OL>
     <LH><EM>Colors of the Spectrum:</EM><BR>
     <LI>Red
     <LI>Orange
     <LI>Yellow
     <LI>Green
     <LI>Blue
     <LI>Indigo
     <LI>Violet
</OL>
</BODY>
</HTML>
```

FIG. 8.1
Web browsers display internal HTML elements according to their defined usage.

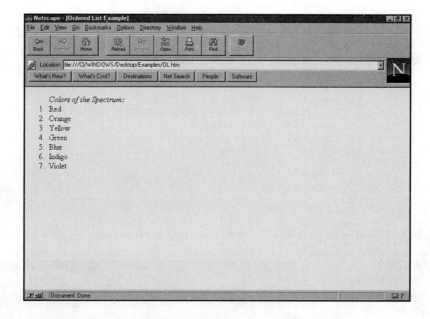

TIP The line break tag, <BR>, after the list header is not necessary for Netscape Navigator, but it is necessary for Microsoft's Internet Explorer, which will otherwise put the first list item on the same line as the header.

It is also possible to nest ordered lists, creating a document that looks more like an outline. Listing 8.2 shows the HTML code for such a list, which is rendered in Figure 8.2.

Listing 8.2   Nested Ordered List Example

```
<HTML>
<HEAD>
<TITLE>Nested Ordered List Example</TITLE>
</HEAD>
<BODY>
<OL>
     <LH><EM>Planets of the Solar System:</EM><BR>
     <LI>Mercury
     <OL>
          <LI>57.9 million kilometers from the sun
          <LI>no satellites
     </OL>
     <LI>Venus
     <OL >
          <LI>108 million kilometers from the sun
          <LI>No satellites
     </OL>
     <LI>Earth
     <OL>
```

continues

Listing 8.2 Continued

```
            <LI>149.6 million kilometers from the sun
            <LI>one satellite: The Moon
        </OL>
        <LI>Mars
        <OL>
            <LI>227.9 million kilometers from the sun
            <LI>two satellites
            <OL>
                <LI>Phobos
                <LI>Deimos
            </OL
        </OL>
    </OL>
    </BODY>
    </HTML>
```

FIG. 8.2

Sublists are automatically indented to create an outline effect.

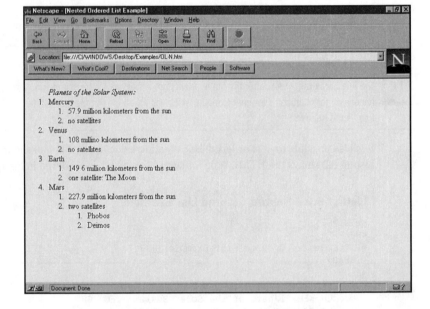

 T I P Use indentations and blank lines to organize your data when creating HTML documents. Web browsers don't care how the text is aligned or run together, but you will appreciate the extra effort when rereading and editing the HTML code.

New HTML 3.2 *<OL>* Attributes

HTML 3.2 defines a handful of new attributes for the <OL> tag. These attributes' previous incarnation was as Netscape extensions. Now that these attributes have gained more acceptance, they're part of the HTML 3.2 specification.

These attributes give you control over the appearance of the item markers and the beginning marker number. Table 8.1 lists these new attributes and their functions.

Table 8.1   New HTML 3.2 Attributes for *<OL>*

Attribute	Description
COMPACT	Renders the list in a more compact form.
TYPE=A	Sets markers to uppercase letters.
TYPE=a	Sets markers to lowercase letters.
TYPE=I	Sets markers to uppercase Roman numerals.
TYPE=i	Sets markers to lowercase Roman numerals.
TYPE=1	Sets markers to numbers.
START=n	Sets beginning value of item markers in the current list.

Varying the marker style enables you to create distinctions between numbered lists in the same document. Listing 8.3 shows how an HTML document incorporates these new attributes, and Figure 8.3 shows how these attributes can enhance a document.

Listing 8.3   Nested Ordered List Example Using Type

```
<HTML>
<HEAD>
<TITLE>Nested Ordered List Example Using Type</TITLE>
</HEAD>
<BODY>
<OL>
     <LH><EM>Planets of the Solar System:</EM><BR>
     <LI>Mercury
     <OL TYPE=A>
         <LI>57.9 million kilometers from the sun
         <LI>no satellites
     </OL>
     <LI>Venus
     <OL TYPE=A>
         <LI>108 million kilometers from the sun
         <LI>No satellites
     </OL>
     <LI>Earth
     <OL TYPE=A>
         <LI>149.6 million kilometers from the sun
         <LI>one satellite: The Moon
     </OL>
     <LI>Mars
     <OL TYPE=A>
         <LI>227.9 million kilometers from the sun
         <LI>two satellites
```

continues

Listing 8.3   Continued

```
            <OL>
                <LI>Phobos
                <LI>Deimos
            </OL
        </OL>
    </OL>
    </BODY>
    </HTML>
```

FIG. 8.3
Controlling the
appearance of lists
is useful for both
functional and aesthetic
purposes.

Ordered list uses
uppercase Roman
numerals

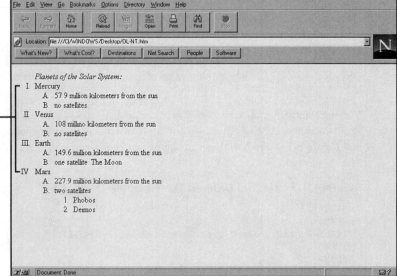

TROUBLESHOOTING

**I'm creating a list of items, and I need to interrupt the list for a regular paragraph of text. How
can I make the list pick up where it left off and continue numbering the items sequentially?**
The HTML 3.2 specification includes an attribute to the <OL> tag called START. Ideally then, you could
pick up, say, at item seven by specifying <OL START=7>.

The number 7 is just an example. Put whatever value you want the numbering to start with.

Creating an Unordered List

HTML also supports the unordered or bulleted list: a list of items that does not define a specific
structure or relationship among the data.

Using the *<UL>* Tag

Unordered lists (bulleted lists) use the <UL> container tag. Just like ordered lists, bulleted lists provide beginning and ending line breaks and support internal HTML elements and sublists. Also, like ordered lists, they require closing tags; include the </UL> tag to signal the end of the list to the browser. Web browsers support and automatically indent sublists, and some will also vary the bullet icon based on the relative level of the list. These icons vary depending on the client software viewing the HTML document.

Listing 8.4 shows how to use the <UL> list container. Again, to make the HTML document easier to read, you can include leading blanks and extra lines, but Web browsers will ignore them. Figure 8.4 shows how Netscape Navigator will render this HTML code.

Listing 8.4   Nested Unordered List Example

```
<HTML>
<HEAD>
<TITLE>Nested Unordered List Example</TITLE>
</HEAD>
<BODY>
<UL>
     <LH><EM>Planets of the Solar System:</EM><BR>
     <LI>Mercury
     <UL >
          <LI>108 million kilometers from the sun
          <LI>no satellites
     </UL>
     <LI>Venus
     <UL >
          <LI>108 million kilometers from the sun
          <LI>No satellites
     </UL>
     <LI>Earth
     <UL>
          <LI>149.6 million kilometers from the sun
          <LI>one satellite: The Moon
     </UL>
     <LI>Mars
     <UL>
          <LI>227.9 million kilometers from the sun
          <LI>two satellites
          <UL>
               <LI>Phobos
               <LI>Deimos
          </UL
     </UL>
</UL>
</BODY>
</HTML>
```

FIG. 8.4
Web browsers automatically indent sublists and apply the corresponding markers.

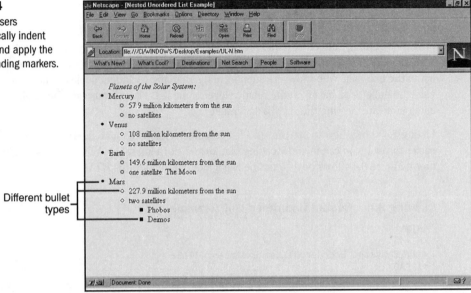

Different bullet types

New HTML 3.2 *<UL>* Attributes

Like the <OL> tag, HTML 3.2 has adopted some of Netscape's extensions for the <UL> tag. You can manually control the appearance of item markers as either circles, squares, or discs. This feature is meant to give you more control over the look of bulleted lists.

You use the TYPE attribute to change the bullet used in the list. Its value can be one of disc, square, or circle. Listing 8.5 demonstrates its use in an HTML document, which is rendered by Netscape Navigator in Figure 8.5.

Listing 8.5   Nested Unordered List Example Using Type

```
<HTML>
<HEAD>
<TITLE>Nested Unordered List Example Using Type</TITLE>
</HEAD>
<BODY>
<UL TYPE=SQUARE>
    <LH><EM>Planets of the Solar System:</EM><BR>
    <LI>Mercury
    <UL TYPE=CIRCLE>
        <LI>108 million kilometers from the sun
        <LI>no satellites
    </UL>
    <LI>Venus
    <UL TYPE=CIRCLE>
        <LI>108 million kilometers from the sun
        <LI>No satellites
```

```
    </UL>
    <LI>Earth
    <UL TYPE=CIRCLE>
        <LI>149.6 million kilometers from the sun
        <LI>one satellite: The Moon
    </UL>
    <LI>Mars
    <UL TYPE=CIRCLE>
        <LI>227.9 million kilometers from the sun
        <LI>two satellites
        <UL TYPE=DISC>
            <LI>Phobos
            <LI>Deimos
        </UL
    </UL>
</UL>
</BODY>
</HTML>
```

FIG. 8.5
It's easy to control the display of bullet markers for your Netscape Navigator audience.

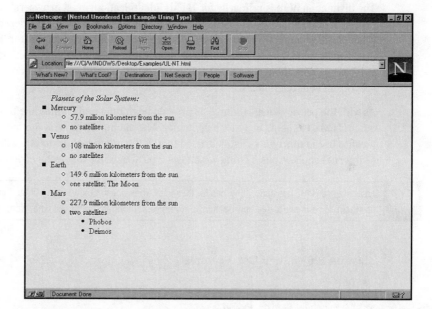

CAUTION

There is a reason why HTML and its client software support multiple item markers: to provide a visual differentiation for sublists. By manually controlling the markers, however, you're working against the user's expectations and potentially weakening the communication of your document's information. After all, the less work the user has to do to recognize subsets of lists, the easier any browser can read the document. Use this manual control with care.

N O T E Besides the new attributes for the <OL> and <UL> elements, HTML 3.2 also provides extensions for individual list items. The extensions are based on those available to the list container that the item is in (ordered or unordered). Ordered lists pass on the capability to change the current TYPE of list items and also the VALUE they begin with—by using the VALUE tag, you can begin a list with a value other than one, or change the numbering within a list. This would be another good way to continue a list that has been interrupted by some other type of HTML object. (All subsequent items adopt the extension changes until the list closes.) You can modify unordered list items with the TYPE extension; all subsequent items in the container use the new item marker. ■

Like the <OL> tag, <UL> also supports the COMPACT attribute, which causes the browser to render the list in a more compact form.

Creating Menu Lists

You can create menu lists with another list type supported by HTML and Web browsers. The distinction here is primarily for HTML identification; most browsers' default display for the <MENU> container is very similar to the font and style used for the unordered list container. The value of this element is enhanced if you select a distinct screen format for the menu paragraph in a Web browser's preferences. The container might also be more functional in future versions of HTML and its client software, enabling browsers and other applications to identify the menu sections in your documents.

As with the previous lists, menu lists provide beginning and ending line breaks and can include other HTML elements in a menu container. The anchor element is the most likely HTML element to use in this type of list; it is used to link the menu listings to other document resources or Internet applications. Listing 8.6 shows typical uses for the <MENU> container.

T I P Just because HTML has specific names for these list types doesn't mean you're limited in how you can use them. Experiment to see how each list delivers your information and use what works best.

Listing 8.6   Menu List Example

```
<HTML>
<HEAD>
<TITLE>Menu Listing Example</TITLE>
</HEAD>
<BODY>
<MENU>
     <LH><EM>Planets of the Solar System:</EM><BR>
     <LI><A HREF="mercury.htm">Mercury</A>
     <LI><A HREF="venus.htm"> Venus </A>
     <LI><A HREF="earth.htm"> Earth </A>
     <LI><A HREF="mars.htm"> Mars </A>
     <LI><A HREF="jupiter.htm"> Jupiter </A>
     <LI><A HREF="saturn.htm"> Saturn </A>
     <LI><A HREF="uranus.htm"> Uranus </A>
```

```
        <LI><A HREF="neptune.htm"> Neptune </A>
        <LI><A HREF="pluto.htm"> Pluto </A>
    </MENU>
    </BODY>
    </HTML>
```

Again, the current implementation of <MENU> by most Web browsers doesn't provide a visual distinction between menu and unordered lists. Netscape Navigator displays menu lists and unordered lists identically (see Figure 8.6), while Microsoft Internet Explorer displays them identically except it omits the bullets in the latter.

N O T E   Menu items (and other list types) can contain hypertext links to other documents or Internet resources. Use the <A> container to create the links, as follows:

```
<A HREF="home.htm">Jump to My Home Page</A>
```

Click the text, `Jump to My Home Page`, and the browser retrieves the document HOME.HTM. ▓

FIG. 8.6
The <MENU> tag hasn't changed much since it was incorporated into HTML 2.0.

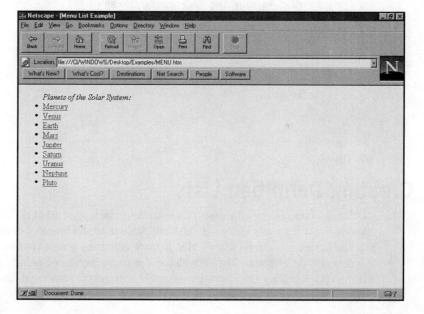

Creating Directory Lists

The <DIR> element functions much like the <MENU> element; it provides HTML identification to the section of text that has more potential usefulness than real functional value right now. Similar to <MENU>, <DIR> containers display with the same default settings as unordered lists. As browsers and other applications begin to support <DIR> as it's intended, it'll become more common.

The intended use for the <DIR> container limits items to 24 characters and displays the items in rows (like file directories in UNIX, or in DOS using the /W parameter). Current browsers don't support this interpretation. The `<DIR>` element also isn't intended to include other HTML elements, browsers interpret them correctly. When using `<DIR>`, remember to close the container with the ending `</DIR>` tag. Listing 8.7 shows typical uses of the `<DIR>` container.

Currently, browsers don't provide, by default, any unique display attributes for the `<DIR>` element. As with menu lists, Netscape Navigator and Microsoft Internet Explorer render directory lists just like unordered lists (Microsoft Internet Explorer without the bullets). My version of NCSA Mosaic also renders them as unordered lists, though in a different font and style.

Listing 8.7   Dir List Example

```
<HTML>
<HEAD>
<TITLE>Dir List Example</TITLE>
</HEAD>
<BODY>
<DIR>
      <LH><EM>Colors of the Spectrum:</EM><BR>
      <LI>Red
      <LI>Orange
      <LI>Yellow
      <LI>Green
      <LI>Blue
      <LI>Indigo
      <LI>Violet
</DIR>
</BODY>
</HTML>
```

Creating Definition Lists

Definition lists, also called glossary lists, are a special type of list in HTML. They provide a format like a dictionary entry, with an identifiable term and indented definition paragraph. This format is especially useful when listing items with extensive descriptions, such as catalog items or company departments. The `<DL>` element provides both a beginning and ending line break. In the `<DL>` container, the `<DT>` tag marks the term and the `<DD>` tag defines the paragraph. These are both open tags, meaning they don't require a closing tag to contain text.

The standard format of a definition list is as follows:

```
<DL>
<DT>Term
<DD>Definition of term
</DL>
```

The `<DT>` tag's text should fit on a single line, but it will wrap to the next line without indenting if it runs beyond the boundary of the browser window. The `<DD>` tag displays a single paragraph, continuously indented one or two spaces beneath the term element's text (depending on how the browser interprets a definition list).

The HTML 3.2 specification provides an important optional attribute for <DL>: COMPACT. This attribute is supposed to be interpreted as a list with a different style, presumably with a smaller font size for more compactness. This could be useful for embedded definition lists (those inside other definition, numbered, or bulleted lists), or for graphic effect. Most browsers, however, ignore the attribute, displaying the definition list to the standard format.

Definition lists can include other HTML elements. The most common are physical and logical styles and other list containers. Although Web browsers can correctly interpret elements, such as headings, this is bad HTML; their forced line breaks are not pretty to look at, and heading tags are usually meant to define relationships in paragraphs—not within lists. Listing 8.8 shows examples of how you can create definition lists.

Figure 8.7 shows how this document displays in Netscape Navigator. Other browsers may format this text differently.

TIP In Netscape Navigator, use a horizontal rule, <HR>, on a <DD> tagged line in a definition list. The rule indents with the rest of the <DD> lines, providing an easy-to-read separator for your definition text.

Listing 8.8   Definition List Example

```
<HTML>
<HEAD>
<TITLE>Definition List Example</TITLE>
</HEAD>
<BODY>
<DL>
     <DT>Mercury
     <DD>The smallest of the planets and the one nearest the sun,
     having a sidereal period of revolution about the sun of 88.0
     days at a mean distance of 58.3 million kilometers (36.2
     million miles) and a mean radius of appropriately 2,414
     kilometers (1,500 miles).

     <DT>Venus
     <DD>The second planet from the sun, having an average radius
     of 6,052 kilometers (3,760 miles), a mass 0.815 times that of
     Earth, anda sidereal period of revolution about the sun of
     224.7 days at a mean distance of approximately 100.1 million
     kilometers (67.2 million miles).

     <DT>Earth
     <DD>The third planet from the sun, having a sidereal period
     of revolution about the sun of 365.26 days at a mean distance
     of approximately 149 million kilometers (92.96 million miles),
     an axial rotation period of 23 hours 56.07 minutes, an average
     radios of 6,374 kilometers (3,959 miles), and a mass of
     approximately 29.11 x 10^24 kilograms (13.17 x 10^24 pounds).
</DL>
</BODY>
</HTML>
```

Part

II

Ch

8

FIG. 8.7
Definition lists appear
much the same as
dictionary entries and
enable easy reading of
each term.

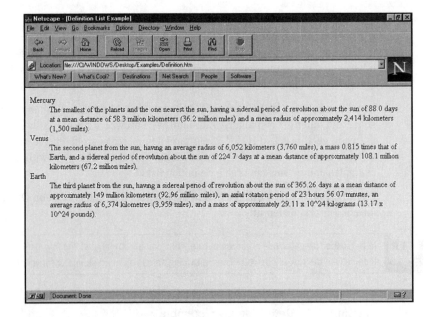

Combining List Types

There are times when it's necessary to use sublists of more than one type within a single list.
For instance, you may have a numbered list that includes a list as one of the numbered elements. Instead of just creating an ordered sublist, which numbers each of its items, you might
prefer to display an unordered list to differentiate the sublist (while avoiding ordering the
information as well). HTML supports embedded combinations of all of the list types. Listing 8.9
shows a sample of combined lists.

Listing 8.9   Combined List Example

```
<HTML>
<HEAD>
<TITLE>Combined List Example</TITLE>
</HEAD>
<BODY>
<OL>
     <LH><EM>Planets of the Solar System:</EM><BR>
     <LI>Mercury
     <UL>
        <UL>
             <LI>Roman god of commerce, travel, and thievery
             <LI>Dictionary Definition
             <DL>
```

```
            <DT>Mercury
            <DD>The smallest of the planets and the one
            nearest the sun, having a sidereal period of
            revolution about the sun of 88.0 days at a
            mean distance of 58.3 million kilometers (36.2
            million miles) and a mean radius of appropriately
            2,414 kilometers (1,500 miles).
        </DL>
    </UL>
</UL>
<LI>Venus
<UL>
    <UL>
        <LI>Roman goddess of sexual love and physical beauty
        <LI>Dictionary Definition
        <DL>
            <DT>Venus
            <DD>The second planet from the sun, having an
            average radius     of 6,052 kilometers (3,760 miles),
            a mass 0.815 times that of Earth, anda sidereal
            period of revolution about the sun of 224.7 days
            at a mean distance of approximately 100.1 million
            kilometers (67.2 million miles).
        </DL>
    </UL>
</UL>
</OL>
</BODY>
</HTML>
```

In Listing 8.9, I used three list types: numbered, bulleted, and definition. The primary list is a numbered list of planets. Each planet has a bulleted sublist indicating the Roman god after whom it was named, followed by its dictionary definition. I'm relying on the user's browsers to indent embedded lists; if I want to force more indentation, I can embed the lists inside additional, empty lists. For instance, instead of the following:

```
<OL>
    <LI>Small example list
    <LI>That I want to indent more
</OL>
```

I can force more indentation by using:

```
<OL><OL>
    <LI>Small example list
    <LI>That I want to indent more
</OL></OL>
```

Because the primary difference between list types involves either the list item markers or the format of the elements—and not the actual text representation itself—combined lists tend to display very well. Figure 8.8 shows how the samples in Listing 8.9 display in a typical Web browser.

FIG. 8.8

Embedded list types inherit certain formatting characteristics from the original list styles.

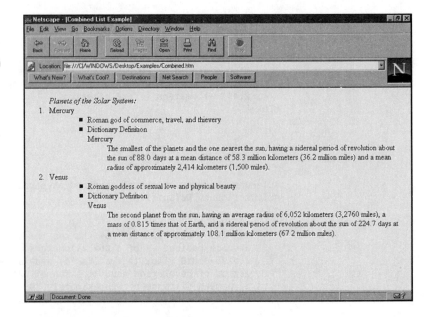

Manually Formatting Lists

It is possible to create your own custom bullets with a little manual effort in your HTML code. Consider the HTML code shown in Listing 8.10.

The <UL> and </UL> tags are used to instruct the Web browser to set up the formatting and indentation to support an unordered list. However, no <LI> tags are used: because you don't want the standard bullets, you can't use the standard list-item tag. Instead, each item in the list is specified similar to the following example:

```
<IMG SRC="cube.gif" ALIGN=TOP>Red<BR>
```

The <IMG> tag is used to specify and align the graphic you want to use as your bullet, followed by the list item. Because you're not using the standard <LI> tag to set off each item, you need to use the <BR> tag to insert a line break after each one. This HTML code is rendered as shown in Figure 8.9.

Listing 8.10   Manual List Example

```
<HTML>
<HEAD>
<TITLE>Manual List Example</TITLE>
</HEAD>
<BODY>
<IMG SRC="BulletSquiggle.gif" ALIGN=TOP><em>Colors of the Spectrum:</EM><BR>
<UL>
     <IMG SRC="BulletCheck.gif" ALIGN=TOP>Red<BR>
     <IMG SRC="BulletCheck.gif" ALIGN=TOP>Orange<BR>
```

```
            <IMG SRC="BulletCheck.gif" ALIGN=TOP>Yellow<BR>
            <IMG SRC="BulletCheck.gif" ALIGN=TOP>Green<BR>
            <IMG SRC="BulletCheck.gif" ALIGN=TOP>Blue<BR>
            <IMG SRC="BulletCheck.gif" ALIGN=TOP>Indigo<BR>
            <IMG SRC="BulletCheck.gif" ALIGN=TOP>Violet<BR>
        </UL>
        </BODY>
        </HTML>
```

FIG. 8.9

With a little added work, nonstandard formatting and bullets can be used on your Web pages.

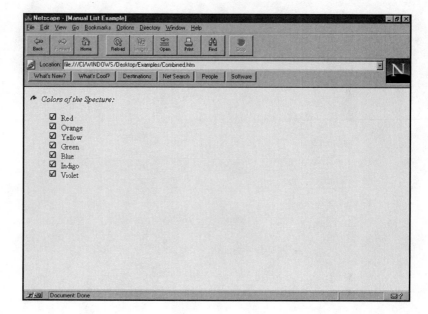

## CHAPTER 9

Creating Tables

by Jerry Honeycutt and Jim O'Donnell

As a tool for governmental, commercial, educational, and personal Web applications, HTML has many needs and expectations to meet. It's the language behind the most popular resource on the Internet and, as such, is required to support a greater range of uses today than perhaps its original creators had first imagined. For example, you might design a corporate Web site similar to a marketing brochure, while you'd design a government publication to present static data in tabular form. In most cases, you can use tables to better present these types of Web pages.

In print publications, tables are a basic design element. They're used to present data in rows and columns. They make comparative analysis more understandable. They're also used (albeit invisibly) to divide the printed page into sections for layout purposes. Tables should be a basic design element in your Web pages, too.

On the Web, tables have been used for a while now, thanks to Netscape and subsequently Microsoft, but they've never been an official part of the HTML standard. With HTML 3.2, however, all that changes. Tables are now a formally defined part of HTML. This chapter shows you how to use HTML 3.2 tables to organize content on your Web page or even to help lay out your Web page. ■

What table tags does HTML 3.2 support?

Finally. Tables are a formally defined HTML standard. Learn about which tags are in HTML.

Create tables in your HTML documents

This chapter shows you how to design and add tables to your own Web pages. It's easy.

Learn about alternatives to using tables

In many cases, you can achieve the same results of tables by using other methods such as lists.

Apply the design techniques you learn here

You can use tables for more than just presenting data; you can use them as a layout tool.

Introducing Tables

HTML 3.2 defines tables in much the same way it defines list containers. The <TABLE> element is the container for the table's data and layout.

HTML tables are composed row by row: you indicate a new row with the <TR> (table row) tag and you separate the data with either the <TH> (table header) or <TD> (table data) tags. Think of the <TR> tag as a line break, signaling that the following data starts a new table row. Table headers are generally shown in bold and centered by WWW browsers, and table data is shown in the standard body-text format. Whereas you can think of a row as a line in a table, a cell represents each box within the table.

Understanding the Basic Tags

The HTML for a basic table is shown in Listing 9.1. All of the HTML 3.2 table elements used are supported by the latest versions of the most popular Web browsers: Netscape Navigator, Microsoft Internet Explorer, and NCSA Mosaic. This table, as rendered by Internet Explorer, is shown in Figure 9.1.

Listing 9.1   A Basic Table

```
<HTML>
<HEAD>
<TITLE>Basic Table Examples</TITLE>
</HEAD>
<BODY>
<TABLE BORDER>
   <TR>
     <TH>Colors</TH><TH>Of</TH><TH>The Rainbow</TH>
     <TR>
       <TD>Red</TD><TD>Orange</TD><TD>Yellow</TD>
     </TR>
     <TR>
       <TD>Green</TD><TD>Blue</TD><TD>Violet</TD>
     </TR>
</TABLE>
<HR>
<TABLE BORDER>
  <CAPTION>My Favorite Groups</CAPTION>
  <TR><TH>Rock</TH><TD>Pink Floyd</TD>
                  <TD>Led Zepplin</TD>
                  <TD>The Dobbie Brothers</TD></TR>
  <TR><TH>Soft</TH><TD>Simon and Garfunkel</TD>
                  <TD>Peter, paul, & Mary</TD>
                  <TD>Neil Young</TD></TR>
  <TR><TH>New Age</TH><TD>Enya</TD>
                  <TD>Clannad</TD>
                  <TD>Steamroller</TD></TR>
</TABLE>
</BODY>
</HTML>
```

FIG. 9.1

Most of the HTML 3.2 table tags are supported by the most popular Web browsers.

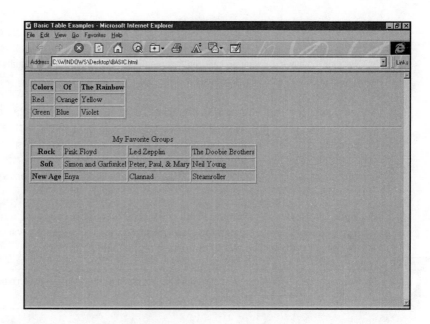

The basic HTML table tags shown in Figures 9.1 and 9.2 are as follows:

- **<TABLE></TABLE>**—These HTML tags are the containers for the rest of the table data.
- **<TR></TR>**—Each row in the table is contained by these tags. You can optionally leave off the closing </TR> tag.
- **<TD></TD>**—Defines a cell. Table data is contained within these tags. You can also nest additional tables within a single cell. You can optionally leave off the closing </TD> tag.
- **<TH></TH>**—These table header tags are used to define headers, usually in the first row or column of the table. You can optionally leave off the closing </TH> tag.

In addition to the basic tags shown here, some other characteristics should be noted from the example shown in Figures 9.1 and 9.2:

- **BORDER attribute**—By using the BORDER attribute of the <TABLE> tag, borders are put around the table. You set the value of this attribute to the number of pixels wide you want the border, like this: BORDER=1. If you set this attribute to 0, the browser will not display a border.
- **ALIGN attribute**—The ALIGN attribute can be specified in the <TABLE> tag with possible values of LEFT, RIGHT, and CENTER (the default is LEFT).
- **Table heads**—In most browsers, table heads enclosed by the <TH></TH> tags are emphasized and centered.
- **Table data**—In most browsers, table data enclosed by the <TD></TD> tags are shown in the normal font and are left-justified.

N O T E   If you're concerned about browsers displaying your header text correctly (as emphasized
text, preferably in a bold font), you can use style tags to force the issue. Be careful what
you wish for, though: if you want an italicized font but the browser automatically formats the text bold,
you can wind up with bold italicized headers.

Cells do not necessarily have to contain data. To create a blank cell, either create an empty cell
(for instance, `<TD></TD>`), or create a cell containing nothing visible (`<TD> </TD>`). Note
that   is an HTML entity, or special character, for a nonbreaking space. Though you
would think these two methods would produce the same result, as you will see later in this
chapter in the section "Empty Cells and Table Appearance," different browsers treat them
differently.

It's not really necessary to create blank cells if the rest of the cells on the row are going to be
blank; the `<TR>` element signals the start of a new row, so the Web browsers automatically fill in
blank cells to even out the row with the rest of the table.

TIP   Tables are necessarily uniform with equal numbers of cells in each row and in each column.
No "L-shaped" tables (or worse!) allowed.

Aligning Table Elements

It is possible, through the use of the `ALIGN` and `VALIGN` attributes, to align table elements within
their cells in many different ways. These attributes can be applied in various combinations to
the `<CAPTION>`, `<TR>`, `<TH>`, and `<TD>` table elements. The possible attribute values for each of
these elements are as follows:

- ▪ **`<CAPTION>`**—The `ALIGN` attribute can be specified for this element with possible values of
  `TOP` and `BOTTOM` (the default is `TOP`); this places the table caption above or below the table.

- ▪ **`<TR>`**—The `ALIGN` attribute can be specified for this element with possible values of `LEFT`,
  `RIGHT`, and `CENTER` (the default is `LEFT` for table-data elements and `CENTER` for table-
  header elements); the `VALIGN` attribute can be specified with possible values of `TOP`,
  `BOTTOM`, `MIDDLE`, and `BASELINE` (the default is `MIDDLE`). If specified, this will give the
  default alignment for all the table elements in the given row, which can be overridden in
  each individual element. The `BASELINE` element applies to all elements in the row and
  aligns them to a common baseline.

- ▪ **`<TH>`**—The `ALIGN` attribute can be specified for this element with possible values of `LEFT`,
  `RIGHT`, and `CENTER` (the default is `CENTER`); the `VALIGN` attribute can be specified with
  possible values of `TOP`, `BOTTOM`, and `MIDDLE` (the default is `MIDDLE`).

- ▪ **`<TD>`**—The `ALIGN` attribute can be specified for this element with possible values of `LEFT`,
  `RIGHT`, and `CENTER` (the default is `LEFT`); the `VALIGN` attribute can be specified with
  possible values of `TOP`, `BOTTOM`, and `MIDDLE` (the default is `MIDDLE`).

These alignments are illustrated by the HTML document shown in Listing 9.2 and are rendered by Netscape Navigator in Figure 9.2.

Listing 9.2   Table Alignments

```
<HTML>
<HEAD>
<TITLE>Table Alignments</TITLE>
</HEAD>
<BODY>
<TABLE BORDER>
  <CAPTION ALIGN=BOTTOM>A Really Ugly Table</CAPTION>
  <TR>
    <TH></TH><TH>##########</TH><TH>##########</TH>
    <TH>##########</TH>
  </TR>
  <TR ALIGN=RIGHT>
    <TH>Row 1</TH><TD>XX<BR>XX</TD><TD ALIGN=CENTER>X
    </TD><TD>XXX</TD>
  </TR>
  <TR VALIGN=BASELINE>
    <TH ALIGN=LEFT>Second Row</TH><TD>XXX<BR>XXX</TD><TD>XXX</TD>
    <TD>XXX<BR>XXXXX<BR>XXX</TD>
  </TR>
  <TR ALIGN=LEFT>
    <TH>This Is<BR>The Bottom Row of <BR>The Table</TH>
    <TD VALIGN=BOTTOM>XXXXX</TD>
    <TD VALIGN=TOP>XXX<BR>XXXXX</TD>
    <TD VALIGN=MIDDLE>XXXXX</TD>
  </TR>
</TABLE>
</BODY>
</HTML>
```

FIG. 9.2
Table element
alignment can be
specified row by row or
for each individual
element in the table.

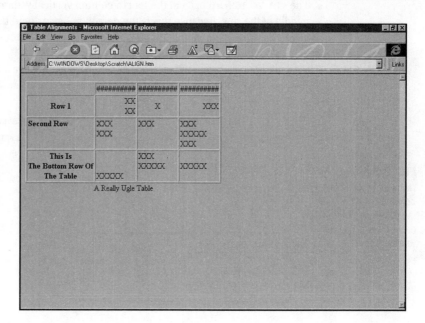

Although this table is pretty ugly, it illustrates the capabilities of the different ALIGN and VALIGN attributes, as follows:

- **Table Caption:** <CAPTION ALIGN=BOTTOM> places the caption underneath the table—overriding the default value, which would put the caption on top.

- **"Row 1":**
  - The <TR ALIGN=RIGHT> sets a default horizontal alignment to the right margin for each element in the row.
  - The <TD ALIGN=CENTER> in the third column overrides the default set in the <TR> element for just this table element.

- **"Second Row":**
  - The <TR VALIGN=BASELINE> aligns all of the cells in the row vertically so that their baselines match.
  - The <TH ALIGN=LEFT> in the first column overrides the default table header alignment and aligns the table header along the left side.

- **"This Is The Bottom Row Of The Table":**
  - The <TR ALIGN=LEFT> sets a default horizontal alignment to the left margin for each element in the row.
  - The <TD VALIGN=BOTTOM> in the second column vertically aligns the element on the bottom of the row.
  - The <TD VALIGN=TOP> in the third column vertically aligns the element on the top of the row.
  - The <TD VALIGN=MIDDLE> in the fourth column vertically aligns the element in the middle of the row. Because this is the default behavior (and hasn't been overridden in the <TR> element for this row), this attribute isn't necessary.

N O T E Sitting down with your favorite text editor and hacking out the HTML for a table isn't always the best way to do it. There comes a time when a piece of paper and a no. 2 pencil are the best design tools you can use.

Take a look at Figure 9.3. It shows a sketch for a table that has two rows and four columns. The first two columns of the first row are joined, and the last two columns of the last row are joined.

FIG. 9.3
Laying out your table before you start writing the HTML code is the easiest way to design your tables.

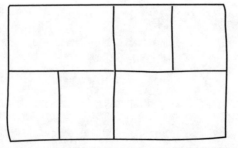

To make your HTML coding job easier, you can hand write a <TABLE> tag above the table and a </TABLE> tag below the figure. Then, hand write a <TR> at the beginning of each row, and a </TR> tag at the end of each row. Last, hand write a <TD> and </TD> within each cell. If a cell is spanned, then write the number of cells it spans next to the <TD> tag and indicate if it spans rows or columns. Figure 9.4 shows you an example of such a sketch.

FIG. 9.4
After you mark up your sketch with tags, start at the top and work your way to the bottom, left to right.

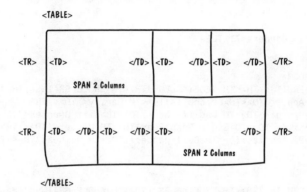

Part
II

Ch
9

With your marked-up sketch in hand, you're ready to write the HTML. Start at the top and work towards the bottom of the sketch in a left to right fashion. Type each tag as you encounter it. If you noted that a cell is spanned, be sure to add the ROWSPAN or COLSPAN attribute to the <TD> tag. The following listing shows you the HTML that results from the previous sketch. (Note that indenting the code can help clarify the row and column breaks.)

```
<TABLE>
<TR>
<TD COLSPAN=2> </TD>
<TD> </TD>
<TD> </TD>
</TR>
<TR>
<TD> </TD>
<TD> </TD>
<TD COLSPAN=2> </TD>
</TR>
</TABLE>
```

Working with Advanced Tables

There are more sophisticated things that can be done with tables, both by using additional table attributes and by different uses of some of the ones you already know about.

Creating Borderless Tables

As mentioned previously, the BORDER attribute to the <TABLE> element is what creates the borders around the table elements. Even though this attribute is off by default, for most conventional tables—those used to organize information in a tabular format—borders are usually used to accentuate the organization of the information. Consider the HTML document shown in Listing 9.3 and rendered in Figure 9.5. In this case, the organization of the information is much easier to see in the version that includes borders.

Listing 9.3 Table Borders

```
<HTML>
<HEAD>
<TITLE>Table Borders</TITLE>
</HEAD>
<BODY>
<TABLE BORDER>
  <TR><TH>FRUITS</TH><TH>VEGETABLES</TH><TH>WHOLE GRAINS</TH></TR>
  <TR><TD>Apple</TD><TD>Broccoli</TD><TD>Barley</TD></TR>
  <TR><TD>Orange</TD><TD>Cauliflower</TD><TD>Weat Berries</TD></TR>
  <TR><TD>Kiwi</TD><TD>Sugar Snap Pea</TD><TD>Millet</TD></TR>
  <TR><TD>Pineapple</TD><TD>Bell pepper</TD><TD>Quinoa</TD></TR>
</TABLE>
<HR>
<TABLE>
  <TR><TH>FRUITS</TH><TH>VEGETABLES</TH><TH>WHOLE GRAINS</TH></TR>
  <TR><TD>Apple</TD><TD>Broccoli</TD><TD>Barley</TD></TR>
  <TR><TD>Orange</TD><TD>Cauliflower</TD><TD>Weat Berries</TD></TR>
  <TR><TD>Kiwi</TD><TD>Sugar Snap Pea</TD><TD>Millet</TD></TR>
  <TR><TD>Pineapple</TD><TD>Bell pepper</TD><TD>Quinoa</TD></TR>
</TABLE>
</BODY>
</HTML>
```

FIG. 9.5

In many cases, borders accentuate the organization of the information.

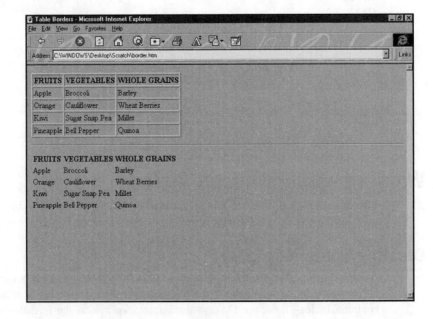

However, HTML tables can be used in other ways, besides the simple tabular display of data. They give an HTML author great flexibility in presenting information, grouping it, and formatting it along with other information. Consider the HTML document shown in Listing 9.4 and rendered in Figure 9.6. In this case, the use of a borderless table allows the descriptive text of the image to be displayed alongside the image.

Part
II

Ch
9

Listing 9.4 Table Borders

```
<HTML>
<HEAD>
<TITLE>Table Borders</TITLE>
</HEAD>
<BODY>
<TABLE>
  <TR>
    <TD><IMG SRC="lion.gif"></TD>
    <TD>
The rampant lion is a symbol from Scottish heraldry. It symbolizes
a duty and willingness to defend one's ideals and values, such as
aret&ecirc. The color of the lion, White, is for the purity of the
brotherhood of PEZ, void of the negativity associated with some
fraternities. This White symbolizes how PEZ is a practice of the
pure theory of brotherhood. This brotherhood has its roots in common
ties and support rather than hazing and the like.
    </TD>
  </TR>
</TABLE>
</BODY>
</HTML>
```

FIG. 9.6

Side-by-side presentation of information elements can be achieved by using HTML tables.

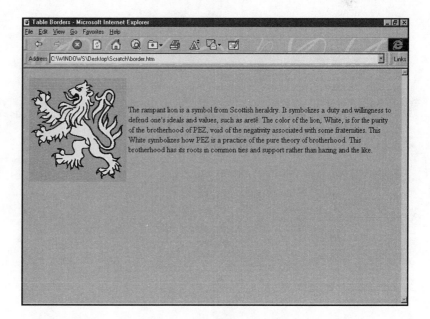

Spanning Rows and Columns

Rows and columns can be spanned—combined with adjacent cells to create larger cells for the data. For instance, in a table with five rows and five columns, the first row could be spanned across all five columns to create a banner header for the whole table. In the same table, each of the columns could have elements that spanned multiple rows. It would be possible, through spanning, to create rectangular table elements that span both multiple rows and columns, up to the full size of the table.

To span two adjacent cells on a row, use the ROWSPAN attribute with <TH> or <TD>, as follows:

```
<TD ROWSPAN=2>
```

To span two adjacent cells in a column, use the COLSPAN attribute with <TH> or <TD>, as follows:

```
<TD COLSPAN=2>
```

 T I P Don't forget to close your table data with the </TABLE> closing tag.

Listings 9.5 and 9.6 show an HTML document that makes use of row and column spanning. This example is shown in Figure 9.7, which shows some of the trouble you can get yourself into with row and column spanning. The table shown on the left is formatted correctly. However, HTML will allow you to overlap rows and columns if you aren't careful with your spanning, and the results of this can (and usually will) be unpredictable.

Listing 9.5   Row and Column Spanning

```
<HTML>
<HEAD>
<TITLE>Row and Column Spanning</TITLE>
</HEAD>
<BODY>
<TABLE BORDER>
  <TR><TH COLSPAN=3>DC nationals</TH><TR>
  <TR><TH>Offense</TH><TH>Defense</TH><TH>Goalie</TH></TR>
  <TR>
    <TD>Husmann</TD><TD>O'Donnell</TD><TD ROWSPAN=5>Weinberg</TD>
  </TR>
  <TR>
    <TD COLSPAN=2>Popplewell</TD>
  </TR>
  <TR>
    <TD>McGilly</TD><TD>Longo</TD>
  </TR>
  <TR>
    <TD>Donahue</TD><TD>Seymour</TD>
  </TR>
  <TR>
```

```
        <TD>Camillo</TD><TD>Walsh</TD>
    </TR>
</TABLE>
</BODY>
<HTML>
```

Listing 9.6 Row and Column Spanning

```
<HTML>
<HEAD>
<TITLE>Row and Column Spanning</TITLE>
</HEAD>
<BODY>
<TABLE BORDER>
  <TR><TH COLSPAN=3>DC nationals</TH><TR>
  <TR><TH>Offense</TH><TH>Defense</TH><TH>Goalie</TH></TR>
  <TR>
    <TD>Husmann</TD><TD>O'Donnell</TD>
    <TD ROWSPAN=5>
      Weinberg<BR>Weinberg<BR>Weinberg<BR>
      Weinberg<BR>Weinberg<BR>Weinberg<BR>
    </TD>
  </TR>
  <TR>
    <TD COLSPAN=2>Popplewell</TD>
  </TR>
  <TR>
    <TD>McGilly</TD><TD>Longo</TD>
  </TR>
  <TR>
    <TD>Donahue</TD><TD>Seymour</TD>
  </TR>
  <TR>
    <TD>Camillo</TD><TD COLSPAN=2>Walsh Walsh Walsh</TD>
  </TR>
</TABLE>
</BODY>
<HTML>
```

N O T E When you create larger cells in an HTML table, you might find your cell data acts a bit unruly: not breaking properly, wrapping text when it shouldn't, and crowding too close to the cell divisions. Like other HTML documents, tables support internal HTML elements, such as
 (to create a line break in the data), hypertext link anchors, inline images, and even forms.

Use an HTML table in the same manner you would a spreadsheet: for data display, for creating data layouts (such as inventory lists or business invoices), and for calculation tables (when combined with a CGI script that can take your form input and generate output data that's displayed in your HTML table). The uses for tables are limited only by your data and your creativity. ■

Part
II

Ch
9

FIG. 9.7

If you aren't careful, you can overlap rows and columns when using spanning, which tends to give ugly results.

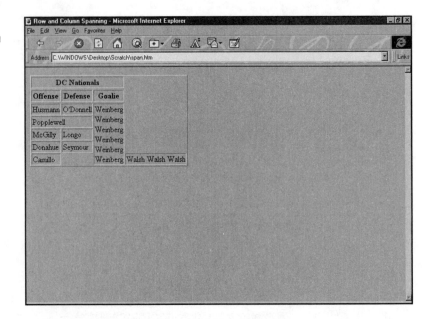

Understanding Empty Cells

As mentioned earlier, there is sometimes a difference between an empty cell in a table and one with nothing visible in it. This is particularly true with Netscape Navigator and Internet Explorer, which will display the two differently. Consider the HTML document shown in Listing 9.7, which shows two tables. In the top table, there are several empty table cells—cells with only white space in them, which Netscape Navigator will not treat as data. In the lower table, these same cells have something in them: the HTML entity , which is a nonbreaking space (an invisible character).

As shown in Figure 9.8, Internet Explorer will display these two tables differently. As you can see, it is now mainly an aesthetic difference.

Listing 9.7   Table Example: Empty Cells

```
<HTML>
<HEAD>
<TITLE>Table Example: Empty Cells</TITLE>
</HEAD>
<BODY>
<TABLE BORDER>
  <TR><TD>Amaranth</TD><TD>        </TD><TD>Buckwheat</TD></TR>
  <TR><TD>Barley   </TD><TD>Rye   </TD><TD>           </TD></TR>
  <TR><TD>Quinoa   </TD><TD>Wheat</TD><TD>           </TD></TR>
</TABLE>
<HR>
```

```
<TABLE BORDER>
  <TR><TD>Amaranth</TD><TD> </TD><TD>Buckwheat</TD></TR>
  <TR><TD>Barley  </TD><TD>Rye  </TD><TD>     </TD></TR>
  <TR><TD>Quinoa  </TD><TD>Wheat</TD><TD>     </TD></TR>
</TABLE>
<BODY>
<HTML>
```

FIG. 9.8

Netscape Navigator will display tables with empty cells differently from those that contain invisible characters.

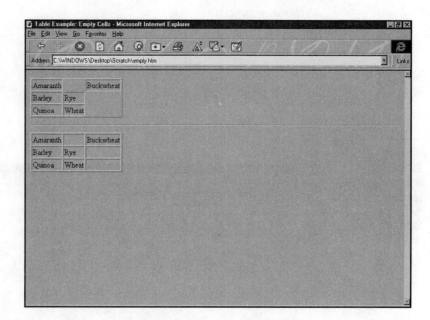

Controlling Table Layout

HTML 3.2 introduces several attributes that you can use to increase the degree of control you have over how tables are displayed. These attributes were once Netscape enhancements, supported by Internet Explorer, but are now a part of the HTML 3.2 standard. Listing 9.8 shows the HTML document for these attributes, which are rendered by Internet Explorer in Figure 9.9.

Listing 9.8 Formatting Example

```
<HTML>
<HEAD>
<TITLE>Formatting Example></TITLE>
</HEAD>
<BODY>
<TABLE BORDER=10 CELLPADDING=10 CELLSPACING=10 WIDTH=100%>
  <TR>
    <TD>Width 100%</TD>
```

continues

Listing 9.8   Continued

```
    <TD>Border<BR>CellPadding = 10<BR>CellSpacing</TD>
  </TR>
  <TR>
    <TD>
      <TABLE BORDER=5 CELLPADDING=5 CELLSPACING=5 WIDTH=75%>
        <TR>
          <TD>Width 75%</TD>
          <TD>Border<BR>CellPadding = 5<BR>CellSpacing</TD>
        </TR>
      </TABLE>
    </TD>
    <TD>Have a nice day!</TD>
  </TR>
</TABLE>
<BODY>
</HTML>
```

FIG. 9.9
HTML 3.2 gives you
complete control over
the appearance of HTML
tables.

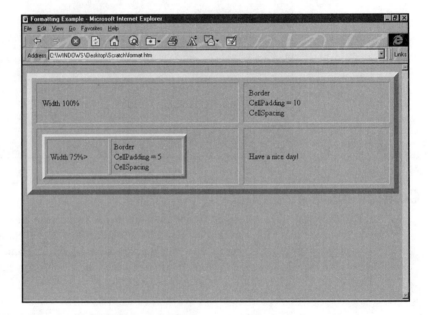

The attributes shown in Figure 9.9 are as follows:

- **WIDTH attribute**—This enables you to specify the width of the table, either in pixels or as a percentage of the width of the browser window. You can also use this attribute with individual cells.

- **HEIGHT attribute**—This enables you to specify the height of the table, either in pixels or as a percentage of the height of the browser window. You can also use this attribute with individual cells.

- **BORDER attribute**—This attribute puts a border around the table. You specify the width of the border in pixels, like this: BORDER=2.

- **CELLPADDING and CELLSPACING**—These numerical attributes include extra space within each cell in the table and/or within the borders of the table. If the border is not being displayed, they are equivalent.

Using Color in Tables

HTML 3.2 makes no provision for setting a table's or cell's color. However, both Netscape and Internet Explorer 3.0 provide extensions that let you change the color of cells and borders. You use the BGCOLOR attribute to change the color of a cell's background, before any text or images are placed into the cell. You use the BORDERCOLOR attribute to change the color of the border around the cell. Both Netscape and Internet Explorer support these attributes.

The <TABLE>, <TD>, <TH>, and <TR> tags all support BGCOLOR and BORDERCOLOR attributes. Thus, you can apply colors to the entire table, an individual cell, or an individual row of the table. The example in Listing 9.9 shows you the HTML for three tables, which show you an example of each case. Figure 9.10 shows you how these tables are rendered in Internet Explorer.

Listing 9.9   Formatting Example

```
<HTML>
<HEAD>
<TITLE>Formatting Example</TITLE>
<HEAD>
<BODY>
<TABLE BORDER BORDERCOLOR=BLACK BGCOLOR=WHITE>
  <TR><TD>1-one</TD><TD>2-two</TD><TD>3-three</TD></TR>
  <TR><TD>4-four</TD><TD>5-five</TD><TD>6-six</TD></TR>
  <TR><TD>7-seven</TD><TD>8-eight</TD><TD>9-nine</TD></TR>
</TABLE>
Changing the entire table's color
<HR>
<TABLE BORDER>
  <TR BORDERCOLOR=BLACK BGCOLOR=WHITE><TD>1-one</TD>
          <TD>2-two</TD><TD>3-three</TD></TR>
  <TR><TD>4-four</TD><TD>5-five</TD><TD>6-six</TD></TR>
  <TR><TD>7-seven</TD><TD>8-eight</TD><TD>9-nine</TD></TR>
</TABLE>
Changing a single row's color
<HR>
<TABLE BORDER>
  <TR><TD BORDERCOLOR=BLACK BGCOLOR=WHITE>1-one</TD><TD>2-two</TD>
          <TD>3-three</TD></TR>
  <TR><TD>4-four</TD><TD>5-five</TD><TD>6-six</TD></TR>
  <TR><TD>7-seven</TD><TD>8-eight</TD><TD>9-nine</TD></TR>
</TABLE>
Changing a single cell's color
</BODY>
</HTML>
```

FIG. 9.10

Changing the color of a cell without changing the color of the surrounding border looks very odd.

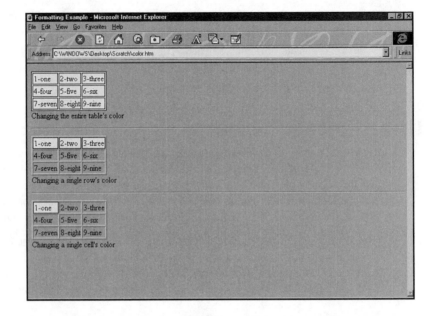

N O T E HTML 3.2 defines the following color names. For your convenience, you'll also find the equivalent hexadecimal RGB values next to each color.

BLACK	#000000
SILVER	#C0C0C0
GRAY	#808080
WHITE	#FFFFFF
MAROON	#800000
RED	#FF0000
PURPLE	#800080
FUCHSIA	#FF00FF
GREEN	#008000
LIME	#00FF00
OLIVE	#808000
YELLOW	#FFFF00
NAVY	#000080
BLUE	#0000FF
TEAL	#008080
AQUA	#00FFFF

Using a Table Alternative

Table support has become very widespread with most of the popular Web browsers, so there is less reason to avoid using tables. Still, there are folks out on the Web, either because of their Internet service provider or because of the type of connection to the Internet they have, who are forced to use Web browsers that do not have table support. If you are worried about missing such people, there are some alternatives that you can use, either instead of, or in addition to, using tables themselves.

Listing 9.10 shows an HTML document for a fairly simple table, which is shown in Figure 9.11. Some other ways of displaying this information, not using tables, are as follows:

Part
II
Ch
9

Listing 9.10   Row and Column Spanning

```
<HTML>
<HEAD>
<TITLE>Row and Column Spanning</TITLE>
</HEAD>
<BODY>
<TABLE BORDER>
  <TR><TH COLSPAN=3>DC nationals</TH><TR>
  <TR><TH>Offense</TH><TH>Defense</TH><TH>Goalie</TH></TR>
  <TR>
    <TD>Husmann</TD><TD>O'Donnell</TD>
    <TD VALIGN=TOP ROWSPAN=5>Weinberg</TD>
  </TR>
  <TR>
    <TD COLSPAN=2>Popplewell</TD>
  </TR>
  <TR>
    <TD>McGilly</TD><TD>Longo</TD>
  </TR>
  <TR>
    <TD>Donahue</TD><TD>Seymour</TD>
  </TR>
  <TR>
    <TD>Camillo</TD><TD>Walsh</TD>
  </TR>
</TABLE>
</BODY>
<HTML>
```

■ Use a list. Information that is relatively straightforward can be displayed instead as a list. This information can be displayed just as well as a list, as coded in Listing 9.11 and rendered by Internet Explorer in Figure 9.12.

FIG. 9.11

A sample table showing a fairly straightforward organization of information.

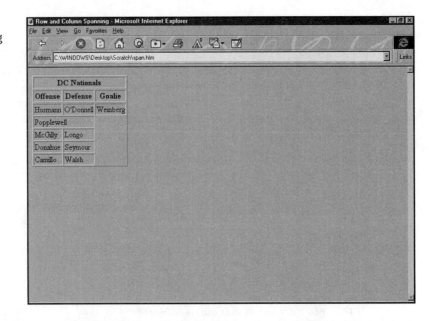

Listing 9.11   Row and Column Spanning

```
<HTML>
<HEAD>
<TITLE>Row and Column Spanning</TITLE>
</HEAD>
<BODY>
  <STRONG>DC Nationals</STRONG>
  <UL>
    <LI><EM>Offense</EM>
      <UL>
        <LI>Husmann
        <LI>Popplewell
        <LI>McGilly
        <LI>Donahue
        <LI>Camillo
      </UL>
    <LI><EM>Defense</EM>
      <UL>
        <LI>O'Donnell
        <LI>Popplewell
        <LI>Longo
        <LI>Seymour
        <LI>Walsh
      </UL>
    <LI><EM>Goalie</EM>
      <UL>
        <LI>Weinberg
      </UL>
  <UL>
<BODY>
</HTML>
```

FIG. 9.12
Because support for lists is more wide-spread than that for tables, they can sometimes be a good alternative.

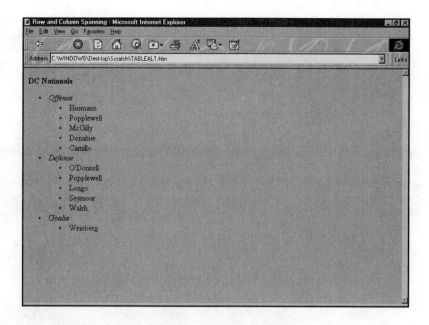

■ Use an image instead. By creating the table in a word processor, or even in your own copy of a Web browser such as Netscape Navigator, and then taking a screen shot and cropping it down to the size of the displayed table, you can include the table in your HTML document as an image. This may not be the best alternative, however, as Web browsers that do not support tables may not support images, either.

■ Use preformatted text. This will give you a table that is aesthetically unappealing, but it has the advantage of being displayed correctly in just about every Web browser, including text-only browsers such as Lynx. An example of this is shown in Listing 9.12 and Figure 9.13.

Listing 9.12　Row and Column Spanning

```
<HTML>
<HEAD>
<TITLE>row and Column Spanning</TITLE>
</HEAD>
<BODY>
<PRE>
+-------------------+---------------------+--------------------+
¦ Offense           ¦ Defense             ¦ Goalie             ¦
+-------------------+---------------------+--------------------+
¦ Husmann           ¦ O'Donnell           ¦                    ¦
¦ Popplewell        ¦                     ¦                    ¦
¦ McGilly           ¦ Longo               ¦ Weinberg           ¦
```

continues

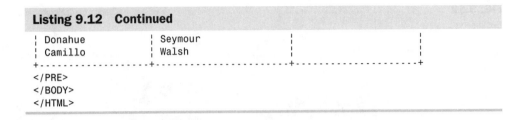

Listing 9.12   Continued

```
¦  Donahue           ¦  Seymour           ¦                    ¦                    ¦
¦  Camillo           ¦  Walsh             ¦                    ¦                    ¦
+-------------------+--------------------+--------------------+--------------------+
</PRE>
</BODY>
</HTML>
```

FIG. 9.13
A preformatted table isn't very pretty, but it will be displayed correctly in just about any Web browser.

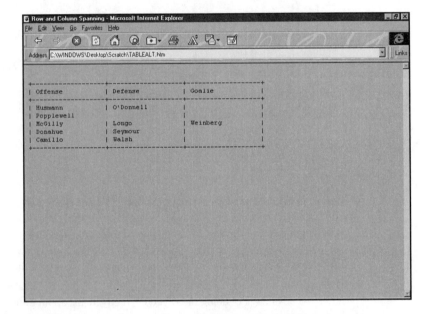

Table Examples

The use of tables to display tabular information is, by definition, pretty obvious. Tables can also come in handy when using HTML forms, as they give you the capability to create a very well-organized form for entering information. Tables can be used in other ways as well, as mentioned briefly earlier. Because they give you the ability to group text and graphics with one another in many different ways, tables can be used to enhance the way a page is displayed.

▶ **See** "Using HTML Tables to Line Up Forms," **p. 218**

Using Tables as a Layout Tool

Consider the HTML document shown in Listing 9.13. This document includes graphics and text information, and is meant to display it as a sort-of business card. This document is shown, as rendered by Internet Explorer, in Figure 9.14.

Listing 9.13   Using Tables to Display Information

```html
<HTML>
<HEAD>
<TITLE>Using Tables to Display Information</TITLE>
</HEAD>
<BODY>
<TABLE>
  <TR>
    <TD ROWSPAN=4 VALIGN=BOTTOM><IMG SRC="init.gif"><TD>
    <TH VALIGN=TOP>Jerry Honeycutt</TH>
  </TR>
  <TR>
    <TD VALIGN=TOP><EM>Books:</EM><BR>
      Using the Internet with Windows 95<BR>
      Windows 95 Registry and Customization Handbook<BR>
      Special Edition Using the Windows 95 Registry<BR>
      VBScript by Example<BR>
      Using the Internet 2E<BR>
      Special Edition Using the Internet 3E<BR>
    </TD>
  </TR>
  <TR><HR></TR>
  <TR>
    <TD ALIGN=CENTER VALIGN=BOTTOM>Send e-mail to <EM>
            jerry@honeycutt.com</EM></TD>
  </TR>
</TABLE>
<BODY>
</HTML>
```

Part

II

Ch

9

FIG. 9.14

Though at first glance this does not look like a "table," the use of an HTML table to organize the information has made the display more effective.

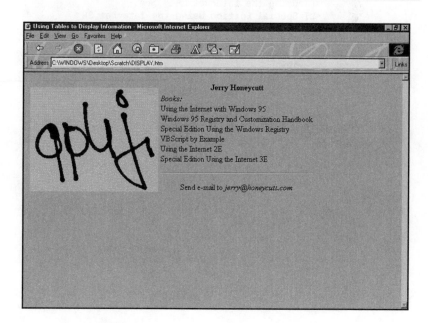

Combining Text and Lists

To refine this Web page further, some of the information presented within it can be displayed differently—in this case, by using an HTML list (an unordered list, but any other kind of list could be used just as easily). The HTML code for this page is shown in Listing 9.14—it makes sense to group lists of data by using HTML list elements, and the ability to include these within a table allows the information to be conveyed more clearly. The revised Web page is shown in Figure 9.15.

Listing 9.14   Using Tables to Display Information

```
<HTML>
<HEAD>
<TITLE>Using Tables to Display Information</TITLE>
</HEAD>
<BODY>
<TABLE>
  <TR>
    <TD ROWSPAN=4 VALIGN=BOTTOM><IMG SRC="init.gif"><TD>
    <TH VALIGN=TOP>Jerry Honeycutt</TH>
  </TR>
  <TR>
    <TD VALIGN=TOP><EM><Books:</EM><BR>
      <UL>
        <LI>Using the Internet with Windows 95
        <LI>Windows 95 Registry and Customization Handbook
        <LI>Special Edition Using the Windows 95 Registry
        <LI>VBScript by Example
        <LI>Using the Internet 2E
        <LI>Special Edition Using the Internet 3E
      </UL>
    </TD>
  </TR>
  <TR><HR></TR>
  <TR>
    <TD ALIGN=CENTER VALIGN=BOTTOM>Send e-mail to <EM>
           jerry@honeycutt.com</EM></TD>
  </TR>
</TABLE>
</BODY>
</HTML>
```

FIG. 9.15
Combining lists and tables gives you powerful means for organizing and displaying information within your Web pages.

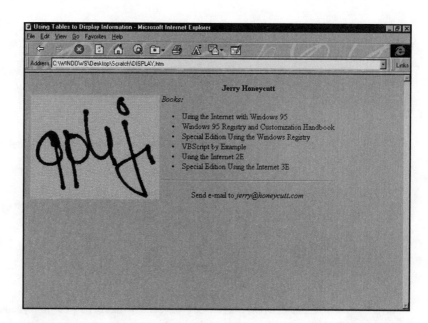

Nesting HTML Tables

Another way to display this information is to use tables within a larger table. The list items are composed of both a team name and a year (or range of years). Couldn't this information also be displayed in a table? In HTML 3.2, you can nest tables within other tables.

Listing 9.15 shows the HTML code for the business-card Web page using nested tables. It is displayed in Figure 9.16. Notice the nested tables are displayed with borders (and with cell spacing and padding reduced to make them more compact), while the outer table used to structure the whole page is not.

Listing 9.15   Using Tables to Display Information

```
<HTML>
<HEAD>
<TITLE>Using Tables to Display Information</TITLE>
</HEAD>
<BODY>
<TABLE>
  <TR>
    <TD ROWSPAN=4 VALIGN=BOTTOM><IMG SRC="init.gif"><TD>
    <TH VALIGN=TOP>Jerry Honeycutt</TH>
  </TR>
```

continues

Listing 9.15   Continued

```
<TR>
  <TD VALIGN=TOP><EM><Books:</EM><BR>
    <TABLE BORDER CELLSPACING=1 CELLPADDING=1>
      <TR><TH>Book</TH><TH>Year</TH><TR>
      <TR><TD>Using the Internet with Windows 95</TD>
            <TD>1995</TD></TR>
      <TR><TD>Windows 95 Registry and Customization Handbook
            </TD><TD>1996</TD></TR>
      <TR><TD>Special Edition Using the Windows 95 Registry
            </TD><TD>1996</TD></TR>
      <TR><TD>VBScript by Example</TD><TD>1996</TD></TR>
      <TR><TD>Using the Internet 2E</TD><TD>1996</TD></TR>
      <TR><TD>Special Edition Using the Internet 3E</TD>
            <TD>1996</TD></TR>
    </TABLE>
  </TD>
</TR>
<TR><HR></TR>
<TR>
  <TD ALIGN=CENTER VALIGN=BOTTOM>Send e-mail to <EM>jerry@honeycutt.com</EM>
  ➥</TD>
</TR>
</TABLE>
<BODY>
</HTML>
```

FIG. 9.16

Nested tables are another way to organize information effectively within a Web page.

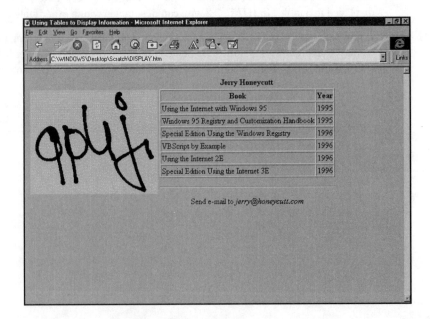

Using an Image as a Table Header

You can easily spruce up a table by using an image as the table's header. That is, instead of displaying a plain-text heading for the table, create a snazzy image and use that instead. Listing 9.16 shows you the HTML for such a table, and Figure 9.17 shows you this table rendered in Internet Explorer. There are a couple of things you should note about this example:

- The width of the table is specified to be exactly the width of the image by using the WIDTH attribute, like this: <TABLE WIDTH=500>.

- In the <TABLE> tag, CELLSPACING is set to 0 in order to make sure the image lines up with the table correctly.

- The table heading is spanned across all columns in order to accommodate the image. In this case, the tag <TH COLSPAN=2> spans across the top two columns of the table.

- The <IMG> tag is used to insert the image into the spanned columns. Note that the border is disabled by using BORDER=0, and the height and width are set to the exact dimensions of the image by using the HEIGHT and WIDTH attributes.

Part

II

Ch

9

Listing 9.16   Pictures in Headings

```
<HTML>
<HEAD>
<TITLE>Pictures in Headings</TITLE>
</HEAD>
<BODY BGCOLOR=WHITE>
<TABLE WIDTH=500 CELLSPACING=0 CELLPADDING=2 BORDER=0>
  <TR>
    <TH COLSPAN=2>
      <IMG SRC="head.gif" BORDER=0 HEIGHT=25 WIDTH=500>
    </TH>
  </TR>
  <TR>
    <TD VALIGN=TOP>
      <IMG SRC="internet.gif">
    </TD>
    <TD VALIGN=TOP>
      This book will show you how to get the most out of the
      Internet. You won't find intimidating, technical language
      here. You'll find no-nonsense instructions for using e-mail,
      UseNet, FTP, and the World Wide Web. You'll also learn how
      to find your way around the World Wide Web, read the UseNet
      newsgroups, and more.
    </TD>
  </TR>
</TABLE>
</BODY>
</HTML>
```

FIG. 9.17

When using an image for a table heading, use your favorite paint program to fade the image before adding headings.

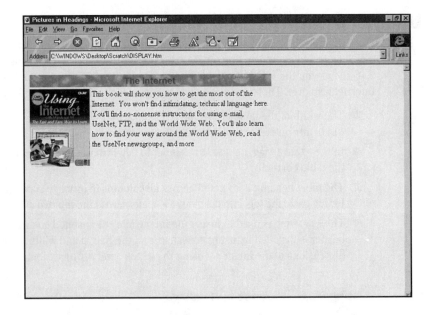

Using a Table to Lay Out a Home Page

Figure 9.18 shows you an example of a home page that uses tables extensively for layout purposes. This happens to be Microsoft's home page. Note that the toolbar at the top of the page is actually defined as a table. As well, each layout region on this page is actually a cell within the table.

FIG. 9.18

Use tables to split an HTML document into individual regions in which you put your elements.

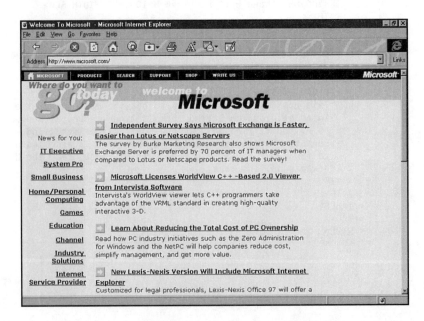

## PART III

Advanced HTML

## CHAPTER 10

Frames

by Mark R. Brown

Sometimes, just the right frame can make a painting
look perfect—and the wrong frame can ruin it. Likewise, prudent use of frames can help make your HTML
documents better organized, more easily navigable,
and more impressive looking. But used incorrectly or to
excess, frames can ruin your site by making information
inaccessible, fragmented, and just plain ugly.

You might wonder if you should even use frames on your
pages at all, since they aren't supported by all browsers
and are not a part of the current HTML standard. While
it's true that not all browsers support frames, the top
two—Netscape Navigator and Microsoft Internet Explorer—certainly do. That's well over 90 percent of your
audience on the Web. If you can live with potentially alienating the other 10 percent who use nonframes-capable
browsers (like the all-text UNIX browser, Lynx), frames
can add a touch of class to your Web site. You'll find later
in this chapter that this isn't necessarily an "either/or"
decision, anyway—the HTML syntax for creating frames
lets you provide alternate content for those who cannot
display them. And if you're working on a corporate
intranet that has standardized on Navigator or Explorer as
the browser for all your users, of course compatibility isn't
an issue at all. ■

**Create navigational menus
with frames**

If having a stay-put navigational
menu would be of benefit to your
site, then frames are the answer.

**How do you associate a link
with a frame?**

Frames accomplish much of their
magic through targeted hyperlinks,
which identify in which frame an
URL is loaded.

**Learn how to create complex
frames**

Though simple frames are easy to
create, more complex arrangements
of frames can be difficult to understand and to implement.

The Frames Concept

First introduced in Netscape Navigator 2.0, HTML frames create independently changeable and (sometimes) scrollable windows that tile together to break up and organize a display so that it's not only more visually appealing, but easier to work with. Frames are similar in many ways to HTML tables. If you understand how tables work, you'll have a jump start on how to work with frames.

▶ If you want to check out how tables work before starting with frames, **see** Chapter 9, "Creating Tables," **p. 143**

However, unlike tables, frames not only organize data, they organize your browser's display window, too. In fact, they break up the window into individual, independent panes or frames. Each frame holds its own HTML file as content, and the content of each frame can be scrolled or changed independently of the others. In a way, it's almost as though each frame becomes its own "mini-browser."

Perhaps the best way to get a feel for what you can do with frames is to look at a few real-world examples.

Netscape's DevEdge Site

As you might expect, Netscape—the inventor of frames—has some excellent examples of frames on its Web sites. Figure 10.1 is taken from its DevEdge developer's site and shows a window that is broken into four separate frames.

FIG. 10.1
Netscape's DevEdge site at **http://developer. netscape.com** showcases some excellent examples of using frames to separate information from navigation.

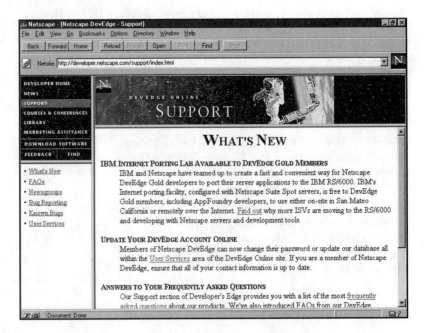

The frames on this page show how Netscape has split information display into the two frames on the right, while reserving navigation functions for the two frames on the left.

The top-right frame—which occupies about 80 percent of the width of the screen, but only about 20 percent of its height—holds a title graphic, which serves as a "landmark" to help you remember where you are. This is an important function, as HTML documents created using frames can get very complex very quickly. "Road signs" like this header graphic can help you get your bearings.

The top-left frame—which takes up about 20 percent of the horizontal real estate, and approximately 30 percent of the screen height—contains a top-level navigation menu, which stays in place wherever you go on the DevEdge site. Making a selection from this menu moves you to a new information category such as the support area or the library. This graphic menu also serves as a placeholder, since it shows the currently selected area as highlighted.

The bottom-left frame—about 20 percent of the screen width and 70 percent of its height—is a list of text-based hyperlinks, which makes up the information menu for the currently selected category. A new text menu is displayed in this frame whenever the user selects a new category from the graphic category menu in the frame above it.

 Note how Netscape has saved itself a great deal of time and development work by making only the category-level menus graphic, while using much easier-to-create, text-only lists of links for the more numerous subcategory menus.

Finally, the bottom-right frame—which occupies the majority of the screen area, about 80 percent of its width and 70 percent of its height—contains all of the actual information displayed on this site. The information in this window is selected from the category-specific text link menu in the frame to its left.

This site can definitely serve as a template for good frames-based HTML document design for any information that is hierarchically organized by category.

The CyberDungeon

But frames aren't just for business documents. Take a look at Figure 10.2, which depicts the online CyberDungeon adventure game. I doubt that you will ever find 10 frames used as gracefully as they are on this site. (Usually it's bad practice to use more than 4–6 frames at a time.) This artfully done Web site anticipates the recent mantra of both Microsoft and Netscape, who are now encouraging developers to use HTML to create graphical user interfaces (or GUIs) for application programming.

The CyberDungeon site uses a set of frames down the left side of the screen to hold graphical icons of objects you (the resident adventurer) pick up in your explorations. The top frame of the center set of three displays the text description of your current location, while the larger frame below it shows a picture of the same scene. The bottom frame gives you choices to make along the way.

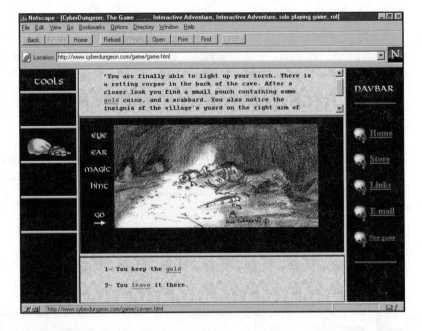

Finally, the tall right frame keeps the navigational menu for the CyberDungeon site handy as you play.

This site provides a wonderful example of how a well-designed HTML document using frames can replicate applications that previously had to be written in high-level languages like C or C++.

The Mondrian Machine

A final example is a wonderful lampoon of the too-ambitious use of frames. The Mondrian Machine site takes the overuse of frames—normally an ugly and heinous practice—and turns it into an art form (see Figure 10.3).

Clicking a selection in the table shown in Figure 10.3 brings up one of several different Mondrian Machines. Each, in its own unique way, creates an HTML document composed of a wild collection of frames which rapidly take over the entire screen. Each frame has no content except a background color, so the end effect is that of a painting by Mondrian, who became famous for dividing his canvases into so many colored rectangles. The effect, though humorous and somehow compelling, shows just how much trouble you can get into if you overdo the use of frames on your own pages.

That warning having been sounded, you'll now see how frames are created.

FIG. 10.3
The Mondrian Machine (**http://www.desires. com/2.1/Toys/ Mondrian**) serves as both a fun Web toy and a graphic illustration of what can happen if you go too crazy with frames!

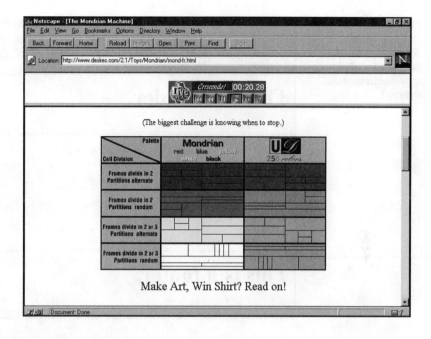

Frame Creation Basics

Diving in head first, take a look at an entire block of HTML that creates a frame document of medium complexity:

```
<HTML>
<HEAD>
</HEAD>
<FRAMESET ROWS="25%,50%,25%">
    <FRAME SRC="header.htm">
    <FRAMESET COLS="25%,75%">
        <FRAME SRC="label.htm">
        <FRAME SRC="info.htm">
    </FRAMESET>
    <FRAME SRC="footer.htm">
</FRAMESET>
<NOFRAMES>
Your browser cannot display frames.
</NOFRAMES>
</HTML>
```

This example, Frames1.htm, produces the frames page shown in Figure 10.4. As you can see, this HTML code produces four frames. The top frame spans the page and includes a header. There are two central frames, one for a label on the left, which takes up 25 percent of the screen width, and one for information on the right, which takes up the remaining space. Another frame fills the entire width of the bottom of the screen and contains a footer.

FIG. 10.4
This is the frame document produced by the preceding HTML code, as displayed by Netscape.

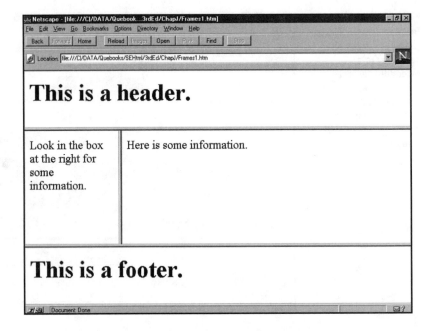

Though you won't get into the details for a couple more pages, it's important to note that this document calls four other HTML documents—header.htm, label.htm, info.htm, and footer.htm—containing the actual information that is displayed in each of the individual frames.

The *FRAMESET* Container

Frames are contained in a structure called a FRAMESET, which takes the place of the BODY container on a frames-formatted page. An HTML document which contains a FRAMESET definition has no BODY section in its HTML code, and a page with a BODY section cannot use the FRAMESET tag.

> **CAUTION**
>
> If you define a BODY section for a page that you compose with FRAMESET and FRAME commands, the frame structure will be completely ignored by browser programs, and none of the content contained in the frames will be displayed. Instead, you will only see the content contained in the BODY section.
>
> Because there is no BODY container, FRAMESET pages can't have background images and background colors associated with them. (Remember, these are defined by the BACKGROUND and BGCOLOR attributes of the BODY tag, respectively.) However, the HTML files which contain the content for the individual frames can use background colors and images, since they do use the BODY tag.
>
> Make sure you don't accidentally use BODY and FRAMESET within the same HTML document.

The `<FRAMESET></FRAMESET>` tag pair surrounds each block of frame definitions. Within the FRAMESET container you can only have FRAME tags or nested FRAMESET containers.

Defining Rows and Columns

The FRAMESET tag has two major attributes: ROWS and COLS (columns). Here's a fully decked-out (but empty) generic FRAMESET container:

```
<FRAMESET ROWS="value_list" COLS="value_list">
</FRAMESET>
```

You can define any reasonable number of ROWS or COLS, or both, but you have to define something for at least one of them.

> **CAUTION**
>
> If you don't define more than one row or column, browser programs will ignore your frames completely. Your screen will be left totally blank. In other words, you can't have a FRAMESET of just one row and one column, which would just be a single window, anyway. If you've defined at least two of either ROWS or COLS, however, you can safely omit the other attribute, and a value of 100 percent will be assumed for it.

The `"value_list"` in your generic FRAMESET line is a comma-separated list of values which can be expressed as pixels, percentages, or relative scale values. The number of rows or columns is set by the number of values in their respective value lists. For example, the following:

```
<FRAMESET ROWS="100,240,140">
```

defines a frame set with three rows. These values are in absolute number of pixels. In other words, the first row is 100 pixels high, the second 240 pixels high, and the last 140 pixels high.

Setting row and column height by absolute number of pixels is bad practice, however. It doesn't allow for the fact that browsers run on all kinds of systems on all sizes of screens. While you might want to define absolute pixel values for a few limited uses—such as displaying a small image of known dimensions—it is usually better practice to define your rows and columns using percentages or relative values like the following:

```
<FRAMESET ROWS="25%,50%,25%">
```

This example would create three frames arranged as rows, the top row taking up 25 percent of the available screen height, the middle row 50 percent, and the bottom row 25 percent.

 Don't worry about having to do the math just right—if the percentages you give for the ROWS or COLS attributes don't add up to 100 percent, they will be scaled up or down proportionally to equal 100 percent.

Proportional values look like the following:

```
<FRAMESET COLS="*, 2*, 3*">
```

The asterisk is used to define a proportional division of space. Each asterisk represents one piece of the overall pie. You get the denominator of the fraction by adding up all the asterisk values (if there is no number specified, 1 is assumed). In this example, with an overall pie that has six slices, the first column would get 1/6 of the total width of the window, the second column would get 2/6 (or 1/3), and the final column would get 3/6 (or 1/2).

Remember that bare numeric values assign an absolute number of pixels to a row or column, values with a percent sign assign a percentage of the total width (for COLS) or height (for ROWS) of the display window, and values with an asterisk assign a proportional amount of the remaining space.

Here's an example using all three in a single definition:

```
<FRAMESET COLS="100, 25%, *, 2*">
```

This example assigns the first column an absolute width of 100 pixels. The second column gets 25 percent of the width of the entire display window, whatever that is. The third column gets 1/3 of what's left, and the final column gets the other 2/3.

So what are the space-allocation priorities? Absolute pixel values are always assigned space first, in order from left to right. These are followed by percentage values of the total space. Finally, proportional values are divided up based on what space is left.

> **CAUTION**
>
> Remember, if you do use absolute pixel values in a COLS or ROWS definition, keep them small so you are sure they'll fit in any browser window, and balance them with at least one percentage or relative definition to fill the remainder of the space gracefully.

If you use a FRAMESET with both COLS and ROWS attributes, it will create a grid of frames. Here's an example:

```
<FRAMESET ROWS="*, 2*, *" COLS="2*, *">
```

This line of HTML creates a frame grid with three rows and two columns. The first and last rows each take up 1/4 of the screen height, and the middle row takes up half. The first column is 2/3 as wide as the screen, and the second is 1/3 the width.

`<FRAMESET></FRAMESET>` sections can be nested inside one another, as shown in your initial example. But don't get ahead of yourself. You need to look at the FRAME tag first.

The *FRAME* Tag

The FRAME tag defines a single frame. It must sit inside a FRAMESET container. For example,

```
<FRAMESET ROWS="*, 2*">
<FRAME>
```

```
<FRAME>
</FRAMESET>
```

Note that the FRAME tag is not a container so, unlike FRAMESET, it has no matching end tag. An entire FRAME definition takes place within a single line of HTML code.

You should have as many FRAME tags as there are spaces defined for them in the FRAMESET definition. In this example, the FRAMESET established two rows, so you needed two FRAME tags. However, this example is very, very boring, since neither of your frames has anything in it! (Frames like these are displayed as blank space.)

The FRAME tag has six associated attributes: SRC, NAME, MARGINWIDTH, MARGINHEIGHT, SCROLLING, and NORESIZE. Here's a complete generic FRAME:

```
<FRAME SRC="url" NAME="window_name" SCROLLING=YES¦NO¦AUTO MARGINWIDTH="value"
MARGINHEIGHT="value" NORESIZE>
```

Fortunately, frames hardly ever actually use all of these options.

Going to the Source

The most important FRAME attribute is SRC (source). You can (and quite often do) have a complete FRAME definition using nothing but the SRC attribute. For example,

```
<FRAME SRC="url">
```

SRC defines the URL of the content of your frame. This is usually an HTML file on the same system (paths are relative to the page containing the FRAMESET), so it usually looks something like the following:

```
<FRAME SRC="sample.htm">
```

Note that any HTML file called by the SRC attribute in a FRAME definition must be a complete HTML document, not a fragment. This means it must have HTML, HEAD, and BODY containers, and so on. For example, the file called by the SRC attribute in this example, sample.htm, might look like the following:

```
<HTML>
<HEAD>
<TITLE>
</TITLE>
</HEAD>
<BODY>
This is some Sample Text.
</BODY>
</HTML>
```

Of course, SRC can point to any valid URL. If, for example, you wanted your frame to display a GIF image that was located somewhere in Timbuktu, your FRAME might look like the following:

```
<FRAME SRC="http://www.timbuktu.com/budda.gif">
```

If you specify an URL the browser can't find, space will be allocated for the frame, but it won't be displayed, and you will get a nasty error message from your browser. Note that the effect is

Part
III

Ch
10

quite different than simply specifying a FRAME with no SRC at all. <FRAME> will always be created, but left blank; <FRAME SRC="unknown URL"> will not be created at all—the space will be allocated and left completely empty. The former will fill with background color, while the latter will remain the browser's border color.

CAUTION

Plain text, headers, graphics, and other elements cannot be used directly in a FRAME document. All of the content must come from the URL defined by the SRC attribute of the FRAME tags. If any other content appears on a FRAMESET page, it will be displayed and the entire set of frames will be ignored.

Providing Alternate Content

"All of this is well and good," you say, "and I really, really want to use frames in my HTML documents. But I can't help feeling guilty about all those users who don't have frames-capable browsers. They won't be able to see my beautiful pages!" Don't worry. Here's where you can provide for them, too.

The <NOFRAMES></NOFRAMES> container is what saves you. By defining a NOFRAMES section and marking it up with normal HTML tags, you can provide alternate information for those without forms-capable browsers. This is how it works:

```
<NOFRAMES>
All your alternate HTML goes here.
</NOFRAMES>
```

You can safely think of this as an alternative to the BODY structure of a normal HTML page. Whatever you place between the <NOFRAMES> and </NOFRAMES> tags will appear on browsers without frames capability. Browsers with frames will throw away everything between these two tags.

NOTE If you want to include background graphics or images, you can add the BODY tag to your alternate content. For example,

```
<NOFRAMES>
<BODY BGCOLOR="red" BACKGROUND="bgimage.gif">
content...
</BODY>
</NOFRAMES>
```

As long as the BODY container is kept within the bounds of the NOFRAMES container, your document will work just fine. But there's no need to use the BODY tag within the NOFRAMES container unless you want to take advantage of its special attributes. ■

A Few Simple Frame Examples

Frames are very flexible, which means they can get complicated quickly. Now that you understand the basics, take a look at a few frame examples so you can get your bearings.

A Simple Page with Two Frames

The simplest possible frame setup is one with two frames, like the following:

```
<HTML>
<HEAD>
</HEAD>
<FRAMESET COLS="*, 2*">
    <FRAME SRC="label.htm">
    <FRAME SRC="info.htm">
</FRAMESET>
</HTML>
```

This HTML code (2Frames.htm) defines a page with two frames, organized as two columns. The first column takes up 1/3 the width of the screen and contains the HTML document label.htm, and the second takes up the other 2/3 and contains the document info.htm. Figure 10.5 shows how Netscape Navigator displays this page.

Part

III

Ch

10

FIG. 10.5

Netscape displays the simple two-column FRAMESET defined by the HTML code above.

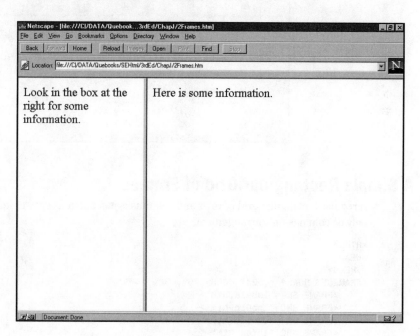

You could just as easily create 10 or more columns or use the same syntax, substituting the ROWS attribute to create two (or 10) rows. However, 10 columns or rows is way too many for any browser to handle gracefully. Your pages should probably never have more than three or four rows or columns.

N O T E If you want to display more information than three or four rows or columns, you should probably be using tables rather than frames. Remember, frames are most useful when you want to add an element of control in addition to formatting the display or if you need to update displayed data dynamically. Tables are best if all you want to do is format static data into rows and columns.

Too many frames can actually crash your browser. For a real-world example (if you don't mind your browser program crashing) check out **http://www.newdream.net/crash/** (see Figure 10.6). ■

FIG. 10.6
This Web site sets out to deliberately crash your browser by creating too many frames—and succeeds! Don't cause the same problem for your viewers.

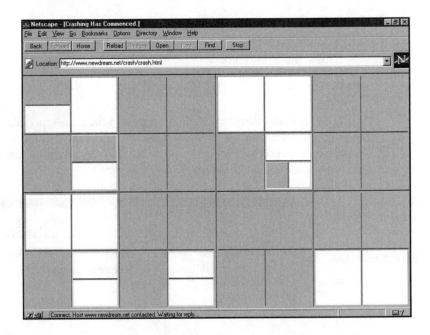

A Simple Rectangular Grid of Frames

A regular rectangular grid of rows and columns is just about as easy to implement as a rows-only or columns-only arrangement:

```
<HTML>
<HEAD>
</HEAD>
<FRAMESET ROWS="*, 2*" COLS="20%, 30%, 40%">
     <FRAME SRC="labela.htm">
     <FRAME SRC="labelb.htm">
     <FRAME SRC="labelc.htm">
     <FRAME SRC="infoa.htm">
     <FRAME SRC="infob.htm">
     <FRAME SRC="infoc.htm">
</FRAMESET>
</HTML>
```

This example (2by3Grid.htm) creates a grid with two rows and three columns (see Figure 10.7). Since you defined a set of six frames, you've provided six FRAME definitions. Note that they fill in by rows. That is, the first FRAME goes in the first defined column in the first row, the second frame follows across in the second column, and the third finishes out the last column in the first row. The last three frames then fill in the columns of the second row going across.

Also, note that the math didn't work out very well, since the percentage values in the COLS definition only add up to 90 percent. No problem, because the browser has adjusted all the columns proportionally to make up the difference.

FIG. 10.7
This two-by-three grid of frames was created by the preceding HTML example.

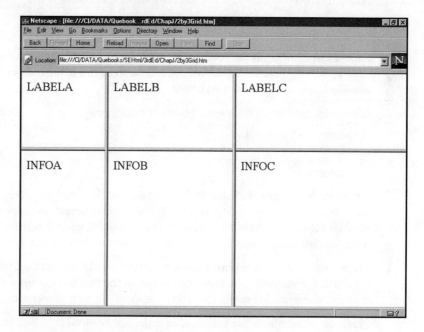

Part
III

Ch
10

Creating a Complex Grid of Frames

A bit tougher is the problem of creating a more complex grid of frames. For that, return to the example that opened this discussion (refer to Figure 10.4):

```
<HTML>
<HEAD>
</HEAD>
<FRAMESET ROWS="25%,50%,25%">
    <FRAME SRC="header.htm">
    <FRAMESET COLS="25%,75%">
        <FRAME SRC="label.htm">
        <FRAME SRC="info.htm">
    </FRAMESET>
    <FRAME SRC="footer.htm">
```

```
</FRAMESET>
<NOFRAMES>
Your browser cannot display frames.
</NOFRAMES>
</HTML>
```

This example (Frames1.htm) makes use of nested FRAMESET containers. The outside set creates three ROWS, with 25 percent, 50 percent, and 25 percent of the window height, respectively:

```
<FRAMESET ROWS="25%,50%,25%">
```

Within this definition, the first and last rows are simple frames:

```
<FRAME SRC="header.htm">
<FRAME SRC="footer.htm">
```

Each of these rows runs the entire width of the screen. The first row at the top of the screen takes up 25 percent of the screen height, and the third row at the bottom of the screen also takes up 25 percent of the screen height.

In between, however, is this nested FRAMESET container:

```
<FRAMESET COLS="25%,75%">
    <FRAME SRC="label.htm">
    <FRAME SRC="info.htm">
</FRAMESET>
```

This FRAMESET defines two columns that split the middle row of the screen. The row these two columns reside in takes up 50 percent of the total screen height, as defined in the middle row value for the outside FRAMESET container. The left column uses 25 percent of the screen width, while the right column occupies the other 75 percent of the screen width.

The frames for the columns are defined within the set of FRAMESET tags, which include the column definitions, while the FRAME definitions for the first and last rows are outside the nested FRAMESET command but within the exterior FRAMESET in their proper order.

This is not as confusing if you think of an entire nested FRAMESET block as a single FRAME tag. In this example, the outside FRAMESET block sets up a situation in which you have three rows. Each must be filled. In this case, they are filled by a FRAME, then a nested FRAMESET two columns wide, and then another FRAME.

By now you may be asking yourself, "I wonder if it is possible for a FRAME to use as its SRC a document that is, itself, a FRAMESET?" The answer is "Yes." In this case, you simply use the FRAME tag to point to an HTML document which is the FRAMESET you would have otherwise used in place of the FRAME.

Redefine the previous example (which used nested FRAMESETs) in terms of referenced FRAME documents instead. All you're doing is moving the nested FRAMESET to its own document. Here's the first (outside) file (Frames2.htm):

```
<HTML>
<HEAD>
</HEAD>
<FRAMESET ROWS="25%,50%,25%">
     <FRAME SRC="header.htm">
     <FRAME SRC="nested.htm">
     <FRAME SRC="footer.htm">
</FRAMESET>
<NOFRAMES>
Your browser cannot display frames.
</NOFRAMES>
</HTML>
```

And here's the second (inside) file ("Nested.htm").

```
<HTML>
<HEAD>
</HEAD>
<FRAMESET COLS="25%,75%">
     <FRAME SRC="label.htm">
     <FRAME SRC="info.htm">
</FRAMESET>
</HTML>
```

Part
III

Ch
10

In this case, the top and bottom rows behave as before. But the second row in the "outside" file is now just a simple FRAME definition like the others. However, the "inside" file that its SRC points to is frameset.htm, which you created with a FRAMESET all its own. When inserted into the original FRAMESET, it will behave just as if it appeared there verbatim. The resulting screen is identical to the original example (compare Figure 10.8 to Figure 10.4).

FIG. 10.8
FRAMESET containers can be nested or can call other documents containing their own FRAMESETs. The end result is the same.

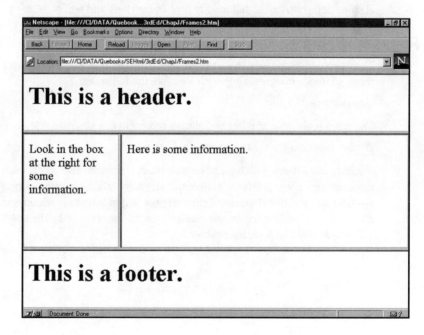

CAUTION

Though it's possible to create nested FRAMESETs by using FRAME tags which call the same URL, it certainly isn't a good idea. This is called *infinite recursion*, which creates an infinite loop in a computer that consumes all memory and crashes the machine. Fortunately, frames-aware browsers check for this—if an SRC URL is the same as any of its ancestors it's ignored, just as if there were no SRC attribute at all.

By using nested FRAMESET containers in clever combinations, it is possible to create just about any grid of frames you can dream up. But remember that you're trying to create a friendly, useful interface, not show off how clever you can be with frames.

N O T E In Netscape Navigator 2.0, the toolbar's Back button didn't back you out of a frame, it backed you out of the whole FRAMESET to the previous page.

With versions 3.0 and above, choosing the Back button returns you to the previous state of the currently selected frame.

To navigate forward or backward within a frame, make sure you make the frame active first by clicking in it somewhere; then use the Forward or Back buttons or menu selections to navigate within that frame. ▨

Modifying a Frame's Look and Feel

Now that you understand how framesets are used to create various grids of frames, take a look at some of the attributes that modify how frames look and feel.

Frame Margins

The FRAME attributes MARGINWIDTH and MARGINHEIGHT give you control over the width of the frame's interior margins. They both look like the following:

```
MARGINWIDTH="value"
```

The value is always a number and always represents an absolute value in pixels. For example,

```
<FRAME MARGINHEIGHT="5" MARGINWIDTH="7">
```

would create a frame with top and bottom interior margins five pixels wide, and left and right margins seven pixels wide. Remember, you're talking interior margins here, not borders. MARGINWIDTH and MARGINHEIGHT define a space within the frame within which content will not appear. Border widths are set automatically by the browser or by the BORDER attribute, which will be discussed later in this chapter.

Frame Scrollbars

Your frames will automatically have scrollbars if the content you've specified for them is too big to fit the frame. Sometimes this ruins the aesthetics of your page, so you need a way to control them. That's what the SCROLLING attribute of the FRAME tag is for. Here's the format:

```
<FRAME SCROLLING="yes¦no¦auto">
```

There are three valid values for SCROLLING: YES, NO, and AUTO. AUTO is assumed if there is no SCROLLING attribute in your FRAME definition. YES forces the appearance of a scrollbar. NO keeps them away at all costs. For example, this FRAME definition turns on scrollbars:

```
<FRAME SCROLLING=YES>
```

Frame Resizing

Frames are normally resizable by the user. But if you let the user drag your frames around, it can quickly muck up the look and feel of your beautifully designed frames. You will therefore almost always want to use the NORESIZE attribute of the FRAME tag to keep users from resizing your frames. Here's how:

```
<FRAME NORESIZE>
```

That's it. No values. Of course, when you set NORESIZE for one frame, none of the adjacent frames can be resized, either. Depending on your layout, using NORESIZE in a single frame will often be enough to keep users from resizing all the frames on the screen.

When you move over a resizable frame border with the mouse cursor, it will change to a double-arrow (see Figure 10.9), indicating that the frame can be resized. If you don't get the double-arrow, it means that resizing has been turned off with the NORESIZE attribute. To resize a resizable frame, grab the frame border by clicking and dragging it with your mouse to a new position.

TROUBLESHOOTING

I've created a frame using the NORESIZE attribute. What do I do about users who are using small screens on which the entire contents of the frame may not fit? Your best bet is to make sure the frame will hold all of its content at lower screen resolutions. That is, redesign the frame. Otherwise, consider reenabling, resizing, or adding scrollbars to the frame.

Figure 10.9 shows an example of a frames page where the lower-left frame has had its MARGINHEIGHT set to 50, MARGINWIDTH set to 100, and SCROLLING set to YES. The NORESIZE attribute has not been used, so you can see what the resizing cursor looks like.

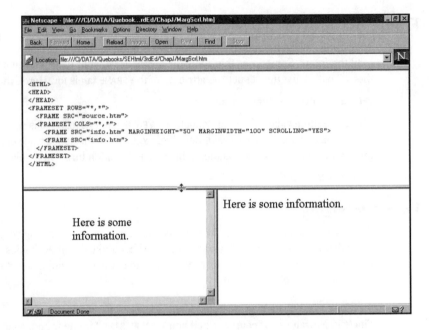

```
<HTML>
<HEAD>
</HEAD>
<FRAMESET ROWS="*,*">
   <FRAME SRC="source.htm">
   <FRAMESET COLS="*,*">
      <FRAME SRC="info.htm" MARGINHEIGHT="50" MARGINWIDTH="100" SCROLLING="YES">
      <FRAME SRC="info.htm">
   </FRAMESET>
</FRAMESET>
</HTML>
```

Here is some information.

Here is some
information.

Frame Borders

You use the BORDER, FRAMEBORDER, and BORDERCOLOR attributes to set the look and feel of the
borders for your frameset. The BORDER attribute is used only with the FRAMESET tag, and sets
the width of all the borders in the frameset. It is assigned a value in pixels, like the following:

```
<FRAMESET BORDER="5">
```

This example would set the width of the frame borders to five pixels. BORDER can be assigned a
value of "0", in which case all the frames in your frameset will be borderless.

The default value of BORDER is 5.

The FRAMEBORDER attribute can be used with either the FRAMESET or FRAME tag. It has two legitimate values, YES and NO. If FRAMEBORDER=YES, then frame borders are drawn with a 3-D look.
If FRAMEBORDER=NO, frame borders are invisible, which really means that they are drawn in the
default background color of the browser.

The default value of FRAMEBORDER is YES, which means that browser programs generally display
3-D frame borders.

The border for a frame will be invisible (not 3-D) only if FRAMEBORDER="NO" is set for all surrounding frames.

 T I P To create a page with entirely borderless frames, set FRAMEBORDER="NO" and BORDER="0" in the top FRAMESET definition.

The BORDERCOLOR attribute can be used with the FRAMESET tag or with the FRAME tag. BORDERCOLOR can be assigned a named color value or a hexadecimal RGB color value. Here's an example:

```
<FRAMESET BORDERCOLOR="red" ROWS="*,*">
    <FRAME SRC="info.htm" BORDERCOLOR="#FF00FF">
    <FRAME SRC="info.htm">
</FRAMESET>
```

In this example, the outer FRAMESET tag sets the BORDERCOLOR to "red", one of the named colors for most browsers. But the following FRAME tag sets BORDERCOLOR to the hexadecimal value #FF00FF (which happens to be purple). The lowest level definition takes precedence. Though the FRAMESET BORDERCOLOR is defined as "red", the border color of the first frame will instead be set to the hexadecimal RGB value #FF00FF. The adjacent frame, which has no BORDERCOLOR definition, will have a border of #FF00FF on the edge it shares with the other frame, but a color of "red" on borders it does not share with that frame.

N O T E RGB hexadecimal color values are precise but obscure. (Exactly what color *is* #FA10D7?) Named colors are easier to comprehend, but not all browsers support the same color names. In general, if you stick with the 16 common color names listed here, you'll be safe: aqua, black, blue, fuchsia, gray, green, lime, maroon, navy, olive, purple, red, silver, teal, white, and yellow. ■

 T I P If two adjacent frames of the same priority attempt to define their own BORDERCOLOR, neither will take effect. They will revert to the BORDERCOLOR defined at the next higher FRAMESET level.

Figure 10.10 shows an example of using the BORDER, FRAMEBORDER, and BORDERCOLOR attributes to control the look and feel of your frame borders. Note that the only frame to maintain the BORDERCOLOR defined in the outside FRAMESET definition is the one in the upper right, the only frame which doesn't share a border with the left-most center frame, which redefines the BORDERCOLOR. Actually, the right-most center frame would have also had a red border on the left, but it has had its left border turned off by the FRAMEBORDER="NO" attribute it shares with the central frame. Note this complex interplay of attributes carefully. If you use them often, their interrelationships are sure to throw you for a loop more often than they make sense.

Part

III

Ch

10

FIG. 10.10
The HTML source for this border-manipulating example is shown in the top frame.

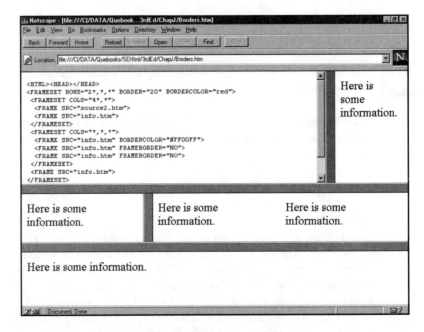

Targeted Hyperlinks

Though you've examined in depth how to create and nest framesets and how to control the look and feel of frames, you have yet to understand how to use frames to control navigation, which is their major application. To use frames to their full advantage, you need to know how to name and target frames.

Naming and Targeting Frames

The NAME attribute assigns a name to a frame that can be used to link to the frame, usually from other frames in the same display. This example,

```
<FRAME SRC="info.htm" NAME="Joe">
```

creates a frame named "Joe", which can be referenced via a hyperlink like the following:

```
<A HREF="moreinfo.htm" TARGET="Joe">Click Here to Jump to Joe</A>
```

Note the TARGET attribute in the hypertext link that references the name of your frame. When selected, this hyperlink will replace the content of the named frame "Joe"—which was given the content file info.htm when it was created—with the content in the file moreinfo.htm. Note that, while a hyperlink without a named TARGET replaces the content in its own window or frame with the content named in the HREF attribute, a hyperlink with a named TARGET instead replaces the content in the targeted frame or window with the content named in the HREF attribute. This is the only trick you need to know for creating killer frames-based navigational systems. Of course, there are some fine points.

Legitimate Names

If you don't create an explicit name for a frame, it will simply have no name, and you won't be able to use links in one frame to open documents or images in another. You'll want to name all frames whose content will be changed by clicking a link in a different frame.

All frame names must begin with an alphanumeric character. Don't use an underscore as the first character in a frame name. Other than that, you're pretty much on your own.

However, there are four reserved *implicit* names built into HTML, and all of them *do* start with an underscore. These are listed in Table 10.1 below. All other names starting with an underscore will be ignored.

Table 10.1   Reserved Implicit Frame Names

Name	Purpose
_blank	Load content directed to this name into a new, unnamed window. This name is used to completely wipe out the current frameset and start with a new, blank window.
_self	Load content directed to this name into the calling frame.
_parent	Load content directed to this link to the calling frame's parent frameset window. If it has no parent frameset, this is the same as using the name _self.
_top	Load content directed to this link to the top level frameset related to the calling frame. If the calling frame is already the top level, this is the same as using the name _self.

Here are a few examples to help clarify how these reserved names work.

If a frame contains the following link:

```
<A HREF="stuff.htm" TARGET="_blank">
```

then clicking the link will launch a new, unnamed browser display window which will contain the content defined in stuff.htm. This can be a simple HTML document or an entirely new FRAMESET definition. Whichever, this call wipes the slate clean and starts completely over.

Part

III

Ch

10

If a frame contains the following link:

```
<A HREF="stuff.htm" TARGET="_self">
```

then clicking the link will simply cause the frame which contains the link to clear, and its content will be replaced with whatever is in stuff.htm.

If a frame contains the following link:

```
<A HREF="stuff.htm" TARGET="_parent">
```

then the frameset which contains the frame that contains this link will be replaced by stuff.htm.

Finally, if a frame contains the following link:

```
<A HREF="stuff.htm" TARGET="_top">
```

then clicking the link replaces the entire browser window with the contents of stuff.htm.

> **N O T E**   Hyperlinks using the <A> tag aren't the only tags that can make use of the TARGET attribute. The AREA, FORM, and BASE tags also use the TARGET attribute and can be used effectively to extend and expand the utility of named frames.
>
> Remember, too, that windows can also be named by using the TARGET attribute within the <A> tag; using named windows in conjunction with named frames adds a whole new dimension to HTML document navigation. ■

Updating More Than One Frame at a Time

You've seen that you can click a link in one frame to change the content in another by naming the target frame by using the NAME attribute of the FRAME tag when creating the target frame, and then using the TARGET attribute of the <A> hyperlink tag when defining the link, as in this example:

```
<FRAME SRC="info.htm" NAME="Joe">
<A HREF="moreinfo.htm" TARGET="Joe">Click Here to Jump to Joe</A>
```

The first line of the preceding HTML is used in the frame definition document, and the second line is used in the document which links to the first.

You've also seen that you can use special implicit names to target some frames and framesets, depending on their relationship to the frame which contains the calling link. But what if you want to update more than one frame by clicking a single link? This is possible if you set up your document correctly. The key is to update a frameset, not a single frame. To do this, you need to create a subframeset that is contained in its own file, as was done earlier in the example shown back in Figure 10.8. If you recall, you began with an HTML document that included one frameset nested inside another:

```
<HTML>
<HEAD>
</HEAD>
<FRAMESET ROWS="25%,50%,25%">
    <FRAME SRC="header.htm">
    <FRAMESET COLS="25%,75%">
        <FRAME SRC="label.htm">
        <FRAME SRC="info.htm">
    </FRAMESET>
    <FRAME SRC="footer.htm">
</FRAMESET>
</HTML>
```

Then you took the nested frameset out and put it into its own file.

Here's the original file, with the nested frameset replaced by the FRAME definition pointing to the second file, nested.htm. Note that you'll name this frame this time using the NAME attribute, calling it "Inner":

```
<HTML>
<HEAD>
</HEAD>
<FRAMESET ROWS="25%,50%,25%">
    <FRAME SRC="header.htm">
    <FRAME SRC="nested.htm" NAME="Inner">
    <FRAME SRC="TestLink.htm">
</FRAMESET>
</HTML>
```

Also note the last FRAME SRC file has been renamed TestLink.htm—this file will contain the targeted link you want to test. Call this modified file NameTest.htm. Now here's the file (nested.htm) that the frame named "Inner" calls:

```
<HTML>
<HEAD>
</HEAD>
<FRAMESET COLS="25%,75%">
    <FRAME SRC="label.htm">
    <FRAME SRC="info.htm">
</FRAMESET>
</HTML>
```

The file which occupies the bottom frame contains the file TestLink.htm, which is listed here:

```
<HTML>
<HEAD>
<TITLE>
</TITLE>
</HEAD>
<BODY>
<A HREF="NewStuff.htm" TARGET="Inner">Click me</A>
to put new stuff into the upper center frameset.
</BODY>
</HTML>
```

The frameset created by these two files (and their associated content files) is shown in Figure 10.11.

FIG. 10.11

Here's your test page, all set to change two frames with one mouse click.

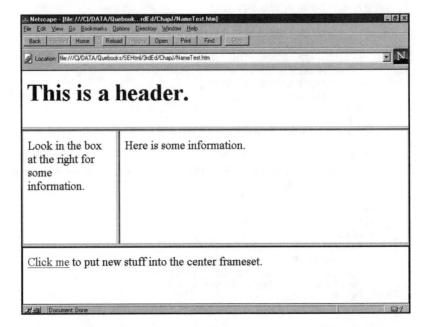

When the link Click me in the bottom window is clicked, it will replace the two frames in the center frameset (which was defined in the file nested.htm) with new information from the document NewStuff.htm. Say that the following is the content of NewStuff.htm:

```
<HTML>
<HEAD>
<TITLE>
</TITLE>
</HEAD>
<BODY>
Here is some NEW STUFF!
</BODY>
</HTML>
```

When you click the link in the bottom window, you now get the result shown in Figure 10.12.

With one click, you've replaced the two frames of the central frameset with a single frame containing new content. You could just as easily have replaced the two frames with two new frames—the same size or different sizes—or with three frames or with a whole new frameset. All you would have to do is define the new frameset in your new content file, NewStuff.htm.

If you're careful and think ahead when defining your framesets, you can easily create hyperlinks that can update almost any combination of frames with a single mouse click.

FIG. 10.12
Clicking the hyperlink in the bottom window has replaced the two-frame central frameset with the single frame of content from a different file.

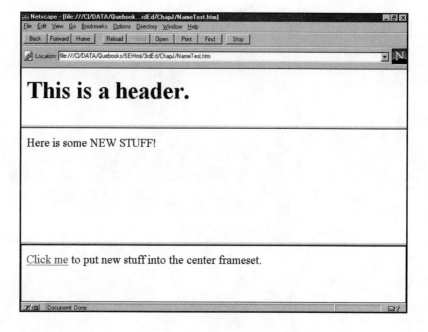

TROUBLESHOOTING

I have two frames that don't have the same parent frameset. Can I update both of them with one hyperlink? Yes. You will have to write a JavaScript or VBScript application to handle them. In fact, this is how Netscape Communications has done multiframe updates from single hyperlinks on its own Web site.

See Chapter 27, "JavaScript/JScript," for information on how to get started writing your own JavaScript applications. Also, see Chapter 29, "VBScript," to learn more about writing VBScripts.

## CHAPTER 11

Forms

by Jerry Honeycutt and Jim O'Donnell

Forms are one of the most popular, interactive features on the World Wide Web. They enable users to interact with the text and graphics that are displayed on your machine. You can make forms with simple yes or no questions; you can make highly complex order forms; or you can make forms for people to send you comments.

You create forms by providing a number of fields in which a user can enter information or choose an option. Then, when the user submits the form, the information is returned to a server-side script. A script is a short program that is written specifically for each form. You can create scripts to do any number of things. You can also handle the contents of a form by using a client-side script, which you learn about in Part V, "Programming and Scripting." ■

What are HTML forms? What are they useful for?

This chapter introduces you to HTML forms, and shows you some of the things you can do with them.

Add forms to your own Web pages

Adding a form to your HTML file is easy; and it's exciting to see a user interface pop up, too.

Design and lay out your HTML forms

You can use a number of the tips and tricks from this chapter to create great-looking forms.

Introducing HTML Forms

HTML forms give you the opportunity to gather input from people reading your Web page. Just as HTML provides many mechanisms for outputting information, the use of HTML forms enables input. These forms can be used to solicit free-form text information, get answers to yes or no questions, and get answers from a set of options.

You can add forms to your Web page with many different results in mind. You can do something simple, like asking visitors to sign a guest book (see Figure 11.1) or comment about your Web site. You can also use forms to gather input for a discussion group or, when combined with a secure method of transmission, take online orders for your $10 widgets. These and many other uses can be achieved with HTML forms.

FIG. 11.1

Guestbooks are easy to create, using forms.

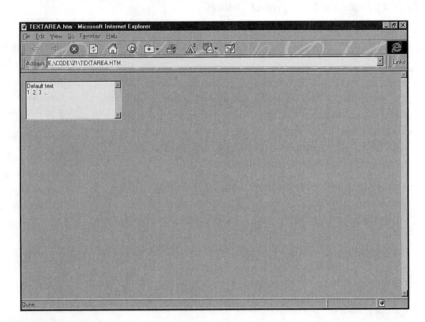

Working with HTML Forms Tags

The HTML tags you use to display forms are straightforward. There are three types of tags for creating fields: `<TEXTAREA>`, `<SELECT>`, and `<INPUT>`. You can put any number of these tags between the `<FORM>` and `</FORM>` container tags. The following is a brief description of each tag (you'll learn more about each a bit later in this chapter):

`<TEXTAREA>`	This tag defines a field in which the end user can type multiple lines of text.
`<SELECT>`	This tag enables the end user to choose among a number of options in either a scroll box or pop-up menu.

`<INPUT>`   This tag provides all of the other types of input: single lines of text, radio buttons, check boxes, and the buttons to submit or clear the form.

<FORM>

The `<FORM>` tag comes at the beginning of any form. When you create a `<FORM>` tag, you also define the script it uses and how it sends data using the `ACTION` and `METHOD` attributes:

`ACTION`   This attribute points the form to an URL that will accept the form's information and do something with it. If you don't specify an `ACTION`, it sends the information back to the same URL the page came from.

`METHOD`   This attribute tells the form how to send its information back to the script. The most common method is `POST`, which sends all the information from the form separately from the URL. The other option for `METHOD` is `GET`, which attaches the information from the form to the end of the URL.

The following is an example of a `<FORM>` tag:

```
<FORM METHOD="POST" ACTION="/cgi-bin/comment_script">
...
</FORM>
```

This example says that you want the browser to send the completed form to the script `comment_script` in the `cgi-bin` directory on your server and to use the `POST` method to send it.

> **CAUTION**
>
> You can put any number of forms on the same HTML page, but be careful not to nest one form inside another. If you put in a `<FORM>` tag before finishing the last one, that line is ignored, and all the inputs for your second form are assumed to go with the first one.

<TEXTAREA>

With `<TEXTAREA>`, you can provide a field for someone to enter multiple lines of information. By default, a `<TEXTAREA>` form shows a blank field 4 rows long and 40 characters wide. You can make it any size you want by using the ROWS and COLS attributes in the tag. You can also specify some default text by simply entering it between the `<TEXTAREA>` and `</TEXTAREA>` tags.

 TIP   `<TEXTAREA>` fields are ideal for having users enter comments or lengthy information because they can type as much as they want in the field.

The options for the `<TEXTAREA>` tag are as follows:

NAME   This is required. It defines the name for the data.

ROWS   This sets the number of rows in the field.

COLS   This sets the width of the field in characters.

Default text   Any text between the <TEXTAREA> and </TEXTAREA> tags is used as
                        default text and shows up inside the field.

While the ROWS and COLS attributes are not required, there is no default value for these that you
are guaranteed to get on every Web browser, so it's always a good idea to set them. Listing 11.1
shows you an example using the <TEXTAREA> tag. Figure 11.2 shows you what this example
looks like.

 All input fields in a form—<TEXTAREA>, <SELECT>, and <INPUT>—must each have a NAME defined
for its information.

Listing 11.1   TEXTAREA.HTM—*<TEXTAREA>* Default Text

```
<HTML>
<HEAD>
<TITLE>TEXTAREA.HTM</TITLE>
</HEAD>
<BODY>
<FORM>
<TEXTAREA NAME="comments" ROWS=4 COLS=40>Default text
1 2 3 ...
</TEXTAREA>
</FORM>
</BODY>
</HTML>
```

FIG. 11.2

The default text is shown
as preformatted text in
the <TEXTAREA>
element.

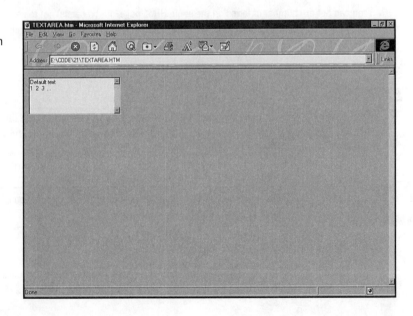

\<SELECT>

The \<SELECT> element shows a list of choices in either a pop-up menu or a scrolling list. It's set up as an opening and closing tag with a number of choices listed in between. Just like the \<TEXTAREA> element, the \<SELECT> tag requires you to define a name. You can specify how many choices to show at once by using the SIZE attribute.

The options for the \<SELECT> element are as follows:

NAME	This is required. It defines the name for the data.
SIZE	This attribute determines how many choices to show. If you omit SIZE or set it to 1, the choices are shown as a drop-down list. If you set it to 2 or higher, it shows the choices in a scroll box. If you set SIZE larger than the number of choices you have within \<SELECT>, a nothing choice is added. When the end user chooses this, it's returned as an empty field.
MULTIPLE	This allows multiple selections. If you specify multiple, a scrolling window displays—regardless of the number of choices or the setting of SIZE.

TIP Some WWW browsers don't properly display a scrolling window if the SIZE is 2 or 3. In that case, leave it as a drop-down list or think about using the \<INPUT> field's radio buttons.

You present the choices the end user can make within the \<SELECT> and \</SELECT> tags. The choices are listed inside the \<OPTION> tag and don't allow any other HTML markup.

The options for the \<OPTION> tag are the following:

VALUE	This is the value to be assigned for the choice, which is what is sent back to the script, and doesn't have to be the same as what is presented to the end user.
SELECTED	If you want one of the choices to be a default, use the SELECTED option in the \<OPTION> tag.

Consider Listing 11.2, the results of which are shown in Figures 11.3 and 11.4. This HTML adds a list called network to the document that contains four options: ethernet, token16, token5, and localtalk.

Listing 11.2   SELECT1.HTM—Selection via Drop-Down List

```
<HTML>
<HEAD>
<TITLE>SELECT1.HTM</TITLE>
</HEAD>
<BODY>
```

continues

Part
III

Ch
11

Listing 11.2   Continued

```
What type of connection:
<FORM>
<SELECT NAME="network">
        <OPTION SELECTED VALUE="ethernet"> Ethernet
        <OPTION VALUE="token16"> Token Ring - 16MB
        <OPTION VALUE="token4"> Token Ring - 4MB
        <OPTION VALUE="localtalk"> LocalTalk
</SELECT>
</FORM>
</BODY>
</HTML>
```

FIG. 11.3

The <SELECT> tag uses the default of a drop-down list (size=1).

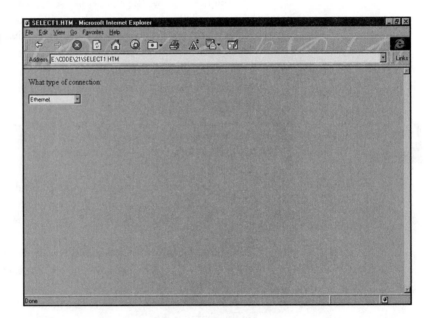

Suppose you set the tag as shown in Listing 11.3, the result of which is shown in Figure 11.5.

Listing 11.3   SELECT2.HTM—Selection via Scrollable List

```
<HTML>
<HEAD>
<TITLE>SELECT2.HTM</TITLE>
</HEAD>
<BODY>
<FORM>
What type of Connection:
<SELECT MULTIPLE NAME="network">
        <OPTION SELECTED VALUE="ethernet"> Ethernet
        <OPTION VALUE="token16"> Token Ring - 16MB
```

```
            <OPTION VALUE="token4"> Token Ring - 4MB
            <OPTION VALUE="localtalk"> LocalTalk
    </SELECT>
    </FORM>
    </BODY>
    </HTML>
```

FIG. 11.4

The width of the drop-down list is determined by the size of the entries listed with the <OPTION> tags.

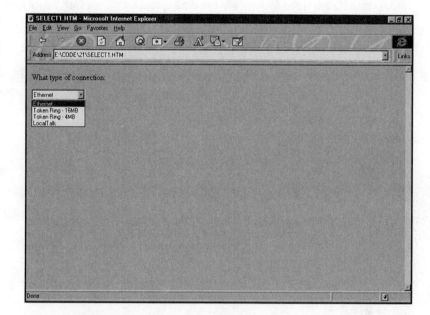

FIG. 11.5

If you use MULTIPLE within the <SELECT> tag, then the field becomes a list of choices.

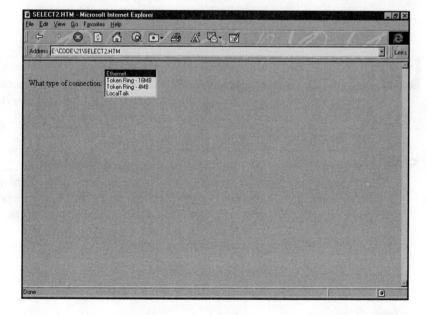

Part
III

Ch
11

TROUBLESHOOTING

I know the most common choices I want to present, but I want to allow people to enter their own value if they want to. How can I do that? Your best bet is to display the common choices in a <SELECT> box or pop-up menu, with one of the options set to Other. Then include an <INPUT> text field or a <TEXTAREA> field right after the list of choices (see Listing 11.4).

Listing 11.4   SELECT3.HTM—Selection with Other Option

```
<HTML>
<HEAD>
<TITLE>SELECT3.HTM</TITLE>
</HEAD>
<BODY>
<FORM>
What type of Connection:
<SELECT MULTIPLE NAME="network">
        <OPTION SELECTED VALUE="ethernet"> Ethernet
        <OPTION VALUE="token16"> Token Ring - 16MB
        <OPTION VALUE="token4"> Token Ring - 4MB
        <OPTION VALUE="localtalk"> LocalTalk
        <OPTION VALUE="other"> Other...
</SELECT>
<BR>
If other, please specify:<INPUT TYPE="text" NAME="network_other">
</FORM>
</BODY>
</HTML>
```

The result of Listing 11.4 is shown in Figure 11.6.

TIP You can use the <SELECT> tag as a navigational aid in your Web pages. You can provide a number of URLs in a list. The user then can choose one, click a SUBMIT button, and have the server-side or client-side script jump to the URL indicated by that choice. Microsoft uses this method to direct users to different international Web sites (see **http://www.microsoft.com**).

<INPUT>

<INPUT>, unlike <TEXTAREA> and <SELECT>, is a single tag option for gathering information. <INPUT> contains all of the other options for acquiring information, including simple text fields, password fields, radio buttons, check boxes, and the buttons to submit and reset the form.

FIG. 11.6

This type of form layout provides both a common list and a place for exceptions.

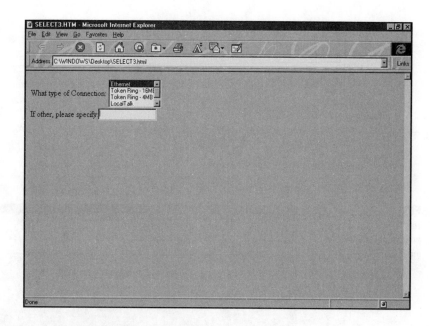

The attributes for the <INPUT> tag are the following:

NAME	This defines the name for the data. This field is required for all the types of input except SUBMIT and CLEAR.
SIZE	This is the size of the input field in number of characters for text or password.
MAXLENGTH	This specifies the maximum number of characters to be allowed for a text or password field.
VALUE	For a text or password field, it defines the default text displayed. For a check box or radio button, it specifies the value that is returned to the server if the box or button is selected. For the SUBMIT and RESET buttons, it defines the text inside the button.
CHECKED	This sets a check box or radio button to on. It has no meaning for any other type of <INPUT> tag.
TYPE	This sets the type of input field you want to display. (See the types in the following section.)

Setting the *<INPUT>* Tag's *TYPE*

This section describes the possible values for the INPUT tag's TYPE attribute.

TEXT   TEXT, the default input type, gathers a simple line of text. You can use the attributes NAME (this is required), SIZE, MAXLENGTH, and VALUE with TEXT. For example, consider Listing 11.5, the result of which is shown in Figure 11.7.

Part

III

Ch

11

Listing 11.5 INPUT1.HTM—Text Input Box

```
<HTML>
<HEAD>
<TITLE>INPUT1.HTM</TITLE>
</HEAD>
<BODY>
<FORM>
A Phone Number: <INPUT TYPE="text" NAME="Phone" SIZE="15" MAXLENGTH="12">
</FORM>
</BODY>
</HTML>
```

FIG. 11.7

The TEXT input type provides a very flexible input field.

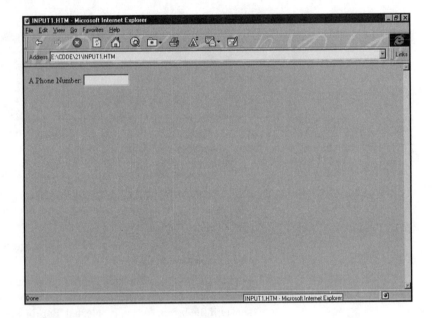

TROUBLESHOOTING

I want to let someone put in a very long URL, but the screen is not wide enough. How do I do that? A good way to enable someone to put in an extremely long text line is to simply set the size to 60 or 80 characters and not set a maximum length. This allows a user to put in a very long string, even if you can't see it all at once.

PASSWORD PASSWORD, a modified TEXT field, displays typed characters as bullets instead of the characters actually typed. Possible attributes to include with the type PASSWORD include NAME (required), SIZE, MAXLENGTH, and VALUE. Consider Listing 11.6, the result of which is shown in Figure 11.8.

Listing 11.6 INPUT2.HTM—Text Input Box with No Echo

```
<HTML>
<HEAD>
<TITLE>INPUT2.HTM</TITLE>
</HEAD>
<BODY>
<FORM>
Enter the secret word: <INPUT TYPE="password" NAME="secret_word" Size="30"
MAXLENGTH="30">
</FORM>
</BODY>
</HTML>
```

FIG. 11.8

Although it will look different in different browsers, the PASSWORD element hides the text that is typed.

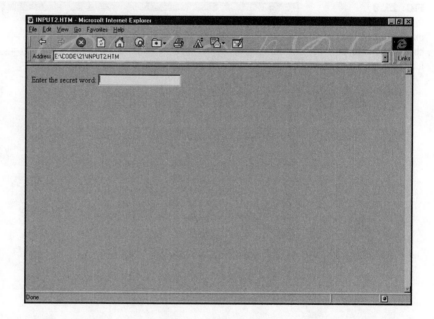

Part III

Ch 11

CHECK BOX CHECKBOX displays a simple check box that can be checked or left empty; use a check box when the choice is yes or no and doesn't depend on anything else. Possible attributes to include with the TYPE text include NAME (required), VALUE, and CHECKED (which defaults the check box as checked). Consider Listing 11.7, the result of which is shown in Figure 11.9. Check boxes are useful when you have a list of options, more than one of which can be selected at a time.

Listing 11.7 CHECK BOX.HTM—Check Box Form Input

```
<HTML>
<HEAD>
<TITLE>CHECKBOX.HTM</TITLE>
```

continues

Listing 11.7   Continued

```
</HEAD>
<BODY>
<FORM>
<INPUT TYPE="checkbox" NAME="checkbox1" VALUE="checkbox_value1">
A checkbox
<INPUT TYPE="checkbox" NAME="checkbox2" VALUE="checkbox_value2"
CHECKED>A pre-selected checkbox
</FORM>
</BODY>
</HTML>
```

FIG. 11.9

Select the check boxes that are commonly checked to make the form easier to use.

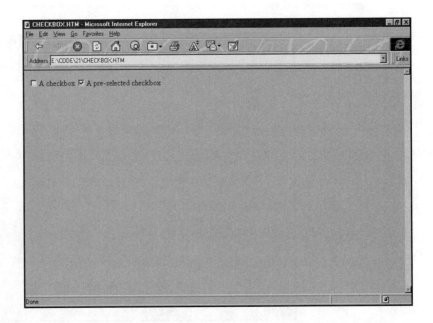

CAUTION

You want to be especially careful when using check boxes and radio buttons in HTML documents with custom backgrounds or background colors. Depending on the Web browser used, check boxes and radio buttons sometimes do not show up with dark backgrounds.

RADIO   RADIO is a more complex version of a check box, allowing only one of a related set to be chosen. You can group radio buttons together by using the NAME attribute; this keeps all buttons in the same group under one NAME. Possible attributes to include with the TYPE text include NAME (required), VALUE, and CHECKED. Consider Listing 11.8, the result of which is shown in Figure 11.10.

Listing 11.8 RADIO1.HTM—Radio Button Form Input

```
<HTML>
<HEAD>
<TITLE>RADIO1.HTM</TITLE>
</HEAD>
<BODY>
Form #1:
<FORM>
        <INPUT TYPE="radio" NAME="choice" VALUE="choice1"> Yes.
        <INPUT TYPE="radio" NAME="choice" VALUE="choice2"> No.
</FORM>
<HR>
Form #2:
<FORM>
        <INPUT TYPE="radio" NAME="choice" VALUE="choice1" CHECKED> Yes.
        <INPUT TYPE="radio" NAME="choice" VALUE="choice2"> No.
</FORM>
</BODY>
</HTML>
```

FIG. 11.10

In the top form, without selecting yes or no, the end user can send back a "blank" value for this selection because none of the boxes were preselected with the CHECKED field.

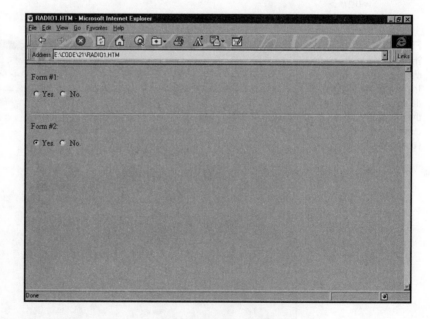

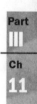

Part

III

Ch

11

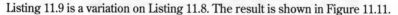

Listing 11.9 is a variation on Listing 11.8. The result is shown in Figure 11.11.

Listing 11.9   RADIO2.HTM—Radio Button Form Input with More Choices

```
<HTML>
<HEAD>
<TITLE>RADIO2.HTM</TITLE>
</HEAD>
<BODY>
<FORM>
One Choice:<BR>
        <INPUT TYPE="radio" NAME="choice1" VALUE="choice1" CHECKED>(1)
        <INPUT TYPE="radio" NAME="choice1" VALUE="choice2">(2)
        <INPUT TYPE="radio" NAME="choice1" VALUE="choice3">(3)
<BR>
One Choice:<BR>
        <INPUT TYPE="radio" NAME="choice2" VALUE="choice1" CHECKED>(1)
        <INPUT TYPE="radio" NAME="choice2" VALUE="choice2">(2)
        <INPUT TYPE="radio" NAME="choice2" VALUE="choice3">(3)
        <INPUT TYPE="radio" NAME="choice2" VALUE="choice4">(4)
        <INPUT TYPE="radio" NAME="choice2" VALUE="choice5">(5)
</FORM>
</BODY>
</HTML>
```

FIG. 11.11

The end user has more choices in this variation. The first choice was the default in each list; this choice has been overridden in the second list.

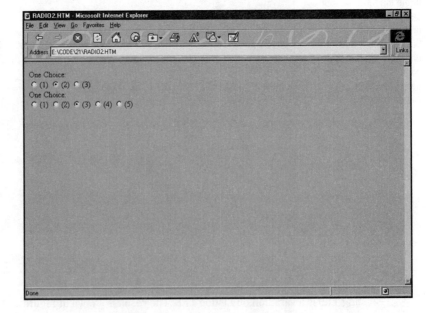

 T I P   If you want to provide a long list of choices, use the <SELECT> tag so the choice doesn't take up as much space on the page.

CAUTION

If you don't specify a set of radio buttons or check boxes with one of the values as CHECKED, then you could receive an empty field for that <INPUT> name.

RESET   RESET displays a push button with the preset function of clearing all the data in the form to its original value. You can use the VALUE attribute with the RESET tag to provide text other than Reset (the default) for the button. For example, consider Listing 11.10. The result is shown in Figure 11.12.

Listing 11.10   RESET.HTM—Form Reset Button

```
<HTML>
<HEAD>
<TITLE>RESET.HTM</TITLE>
</HEAD>
<BODY>
<FORM>
        <INPUT TYPE="reset">
        <BR>
        <INPUT TYPE="reset" VALUE="Clear that form!">
</FORM>
</BODY>
</HTML>
```

Part
III

Ch
11

FIG. 11.12

The top button shows the default text for the RESET element.

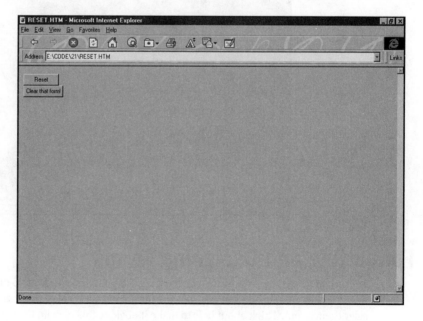

SUBMIT SUBMIT displays a push button with the preset function of sending the data in the form to the server to be processed by a server-side script. You can use the VALUE attribute with SUBMIT to provide text other than Submit Query (the default) for the button. Consider, for example, Listing 11.11. The result is shown in Figure 11.13.

Listing 11.11 SUBMIT.HTM—Form Submit Button

```
<HTML>
<HEAD>
<TITLE>SUBMIT.HTM</TITLE>
</HEAD>
<BODY>
<FORM>
        <INPUT TYPE="submit">
        <BR>
        <INPUT TYPE="submit" VALUE="Send in the data!">
</FORM>
</BODY>
</HTML>
```

FIG. 11.13
The top button shows the default text for the SUBMIT element.

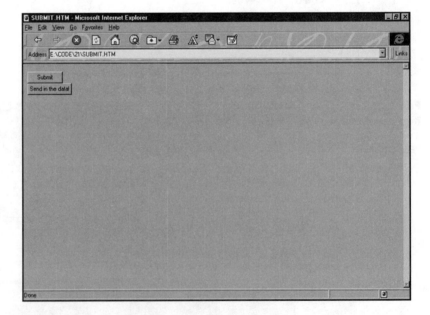

Formatting and Designing Forms

Forms can be easy to read, simple one- or two-entry affairs with little to display; they can also be terrifically complex devices. As your forms get more complex, you need to carefully consider their layout. Think about how to make it obvious that certain titles are connected to certain fields, and think about how to make your forms easy for anyone to use. People are often put off by complex forms that are hard to understand, so it's in your best interest to make them easy and fun to use—regardless of their complexity.

Using Line Break Tags

When you mark up HTML documents, you usually just let the words wrap across the screen. Although this flexibility is wonderful to have for segments of text, it can make reading a form incredibly difficult. A quick and simple solution is to include the line break tag, <BR>, to move something to the next line.

Forcing Fields onto Separate Lines If you want to have two fields, Name and E-Mail Address, for example, you can simply mark them up as shown in Listing 11.12.

Listing 11.12 LB1.HTM—Forms Without Line Breaks

```
<HTML>
<HEAD>
<TITLE>Form Layout and Design</TITLE>
</HEAD>
<BODY>
<H1>Line Break Tags</H1>
<FORM>
        Name: <INPUT NAME="name" SIZE="30">
        E-Mail Address: <INPUT NAME="email" SIZE="40">
</FORM>
</BODY>
</HTML>
```

Although this might look great now, it can wrap strangely on some WWW browsers and look shabby when displayed (see Figure 11.14).

To split these lines and make them more readable, you need to include the line break tag <BR> between them, as shown in Listing 11.13.

Listing 11.13 LB2.HTM—Line Breaks Within Forms

```
<HTML>
<HEAD>
<TITLE>Form Layout and Design</TITLE>
</HEAD>
<BODY>
<H1>Line Break Tags</H1>
<FORM>
        Name: <INPUT NAME="name" SIZE="30">
        <BR>
        E-Mail Address: <INPUT NAME="email" SIZE="40">
</FORM>
</BODY>
</HTML>
```

Part
III

Ch
11

FIG. 11.14

Without some type of organization, your forms can be very hard to read.

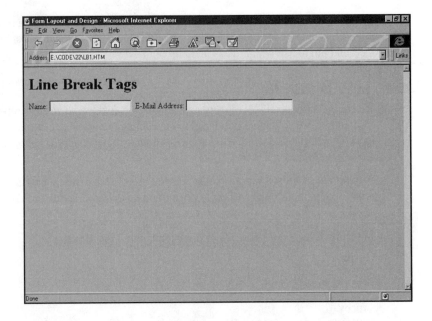

Adding the <BR> tag between the two fields forces the browser to wrap the field to the next line, regardless of the width of the screen. The result of Listing 11.13 is shown in Figure 11.15.

FIG. 11.15

The <BR> tag enables you to control the placement of form text.

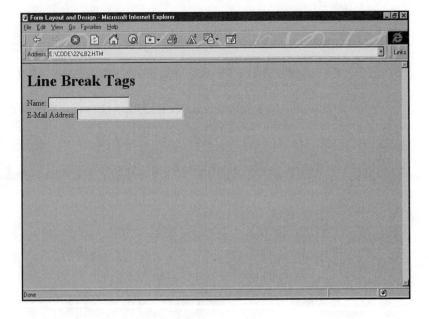

N O T E   The wrapping feature of HTML can work for you to help keep a form small in size. If you have several multiple-choice items that could take up huge amounts of space on your form, you can try to keep them small and let them wrap closely together on the page.

If you're using the <SELECT> tag, the width of the pop-up menu on the screen is directly related to the words in the options to be selected. If you keep all the words small, you can provide a relatively large number of choices in a small area. ■

Working with Large Entry Fields   If you're working with long text entry fields or perhaps with a <TEXTAREA> field, it's often easier to put the text just above the field and then separate the different areas with paragraph breaks.

For example, if you have a text input line that is very long or a long field description, it doesn't work well to put them side by side. Also, if you want to leave a space for comments, it's easier—and looks nicer—to have the field description just above the comment area. This makes it appear that there's more space to write in. Listing 11.14 is an example of this sort of design. The result of this code is shown in Figure 11.16.

Listing 11.14   LARGE.HTM—Large Fields for Text Input

```
<HTML>
<HEAD>
<TITLE>Form Layout and Design</TITLE>
</HEAD>
<BODY>
<H1>Line Break Tags</H1>
<FORM>
        Please enter the new title for the message:<BR>
        <INPUT NAME="name" SIZE="40">
        <HR>
        Your comments:<BR>
        <TEXTAREA ROWS="6" COLS="70"></TEXTAREA>
</FORM>
</BODY>
</HTML>
```

Part

III

Ch

11

N O T E   Most browsers automatically wrap a large field to the next line, treating it like an image. Because you don't know how wide (or narrow!) the client screen is, take steps to ensure the form will look as you want. If, for example, you want the field to be on the next line, put in a <BR> tag to make sure it will be! ■

Using the Preformatted Text Tag to Line Up Forms   A very common sight on many forms are simple text entry fields aligned haphazardly. A great trick for aligning text fields is to use the <PRE> tag. This ensures that some spaces appear before the field.

FIG. 11.16

Using the line break tags enables you to put a label just above the field.

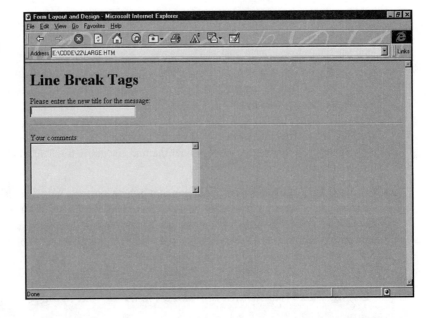

CAUTION

If you're using the <PRE> tags to line up fields, don't use any other HTML tags inside that area. Although the tags won't show up, they'll ruin the effect of lining everything up perfectly.

Listing 11.15 is an example of an entry form that only uses line breaks. The result of this code is displayed in Figure 11.17.

Listing 11.15 PRE1.HTM—Form Fields Not Aligned by Default

```
<HTML>
<HEAD>
<TITLE>Form Layout and Design</TITLE>
</HEAD>
<BODY>
<H1>Using PRE tags</H1>
<FORM>
      Name: <INPUT TYPE="text" NAME="name" SIZE="50"><BR>
      E-Mail: <INPUT TYPE="text" NAME="email" SIZE="50"><BR>
      Street Address: <INPUT TYPE="text" NAME="street1" SIZE="30"><BR>
      <INPUT TYPE="text" NAME="street2" SIZE="30"><BR>
      City: <INPUT TYPE="text" NAME="city" SIZE="50"><BR>
      State: <INPUT TYPE="text" NAME="state" SIZE="2"><BR>
      Zip: <INPUT TYPE="text" NAME="zip" SIZE="10">
</FORM>
</BODY>
</HTML>
```

FIG. 11.17
These fields were organized only with line breaks, so they align haphazardly.

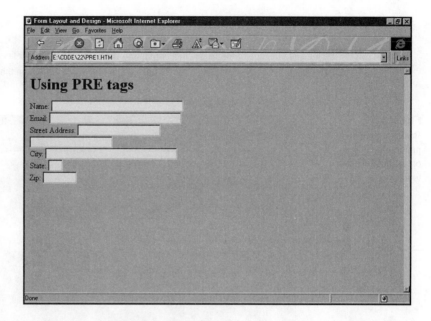

If you space things out and use the tags for preformatted text, you can create a very nice looking form. Listing 11.16 is an example of aligning fields by using the <PRE> tag, which produces the layout shown in Figure 11.18.

Listing 11.16   PRE2.HTM—Aligning Forms Fields with Preformatted Text

```
<HTML>
<HEAD>
<TITLE>Form Layout and Design</TITLE>
</HEAD>
<BODY>
<H1>Using PRE tags</H1>
<FORM>
    <PRE>
    Name:           <INPUT TYPE="text" NAME="name" SIZE="50">
    E-Mail:         <INPUT TYPE="text" NAME="email" SIZE="50">
    Street Address: <INPUT TYPE="text" NAME="street1" SIZE="30">
                    <INPUT TYPE="text" NAME="street2" SIZE="30">
    City:           <INPUT TYPE="text" NAME="city" SIZE="50">
    State:          <INPUT TYPE="text" NAME="state" SIZE="2">
    Zip:            <INPUT TYPE="text" NAME="zip" SIZE="10">
    </PRE>
</FORM>
</BODY>
</HTML>
```

CAUTION

Make sure you keep the size of the fields smaller than the general browser, or your lines will wrap off the screen. If the input fields have to be large, you can use a line break to put them on their own line.

FIG. 11.18

The layout of the preformatted text is organized and easy to follow.

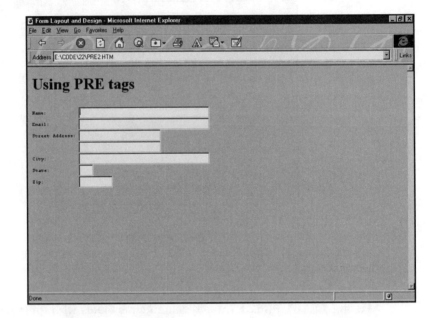

 TROUBLESHOOTING

When I set up the preformatted text, it doesn't come out aligned in my HTML document! Why doesn't it match up? In some text editors, the width of each letter on the screen isn't the same. If you're creating HTML documents with a text editor or word processor, make sure you use a monospaced font such as Courier New (each character, including spaces, takes up exactly the same amount of space). That should solve the problem.

Using HTML Tables to Line Up Forms   Another way to line up form fields is to place them in an HTML table. This can produce an effect similar to using preformatted text but, because you are using regular HTML rather than preformatted text, you can also include other HTML constructs within the form. So, by using a table rather than preformatted text to align your form, you're also able to include images, hypertext links, or other HTML elements as part of the form.

Listing 11.17 is an example of the entry form shown in Figures 11.17 and 11.18, formatted using an HTML table. The result of this code is displayed in Figure 11.19.

Listing 11.17   TABLE.HTM—Aligning Forms Fields with Tables

```
<HTML>
<HEAD>
<TITLE>Form Layout and Design</TITLE>
</HEAD>
<BODY>
<H1>Using HTML Tables</H1>
<FORM>
        <TABLE>
                <TR><TD>Name:</TD><TD><INPUT TYPE="text"
                NAME="name" SIZE="50"></TD></TR>
                <TR><TD>E-Mail:</TD><TD><INPUT TYPE="text"
                NAME="email" SIZE="50"></TD></TR>
                <TR><TD>Street Address:</TD><TD><INPUT TYPE="text"
                NAME="street1" SIZE="30"></TD></TR>
                <TR><TD></TD><TD><INPUT TYPE="text" NAME="street2"
                SIZE="30"></TD></TR>
                <TR><TD>City:</TD><TD><INPUT TYPE="text" NAME="city"
                SIZE="50"></TD></TR>
                <TR><TD>State:</TD><TD><INPUT TYPE="text" NAME="state"
                SIZE="2"></TD></TR>
                <TR><TD>Zip:</TD><TD><INPUT TYPE="text" NAME="zip"
                SIZE="10"></TD></TR>
        </TABLE>
</FORM>
</BODY>
</HTML>
```

Part
III

Ch
11

FIG. 11.19

HTML tables text can be
combined with forms to
enable the aligning of
different form fields.

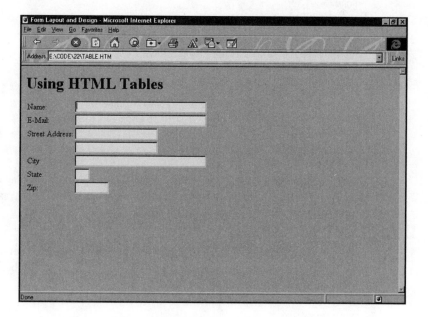

Some people use browsers, particularly text-only ones, that don't support tables. If you use tables with your forms, consider including an alternate page without tables for these folks. See Chapter 9, "Creating Tables," for alternatives for browsers that don't support tables.

Using Paragraph Marks to Separate Form Sections   If you have a large form with different sections, it's handy to separate those sections. The paragraph container tag, `<P>...</P>`, provides a way of adding some space without making the delineation so hard that it appears to be another form. Note that Web browsers also allow you to use the `<P>` opening tag without the `</P>` closing tag to give identical results.

For example, a simple comment form might have places for a name and an e-mail address, but these might not be a required part of the form. In this case, separate the comment part of the form from the area that's optional. It's also possible to make it more obvious by simply making some comments in the form, such as a small heading titled Optional. A simple comment form with optional Name and E-Mail fields can have the code shown in Listing 11.18.

Listing 11.18   P.HTM—Using Paragraphs to Improve Spacing

```
<HTML>
<HEAD>
<TITLE>Form Layout and Design</TITLE>
</HEAD>
<BODY>
<H1>Using &lt;P&gt; tags</H1>
<FORM>
        <PRE>
        <I><B>Optional:</B></I>
        Name:   <INPUT TYPE="text" NAME="name" SIZE="50">
        E-Mail: <INPUT TYPE="text" NAME="email" SIZE="50">
        </PRE>
        <P>
        Your comments:<BR>
        <TEXTAREA ROWS="6" COLS="70"></TEXTAREA>
</FORM>
</BODY>
</HTML>
```

Listing 11.18, using both `<PRE>` tags and line break tags, produces the layout shown in Figure 11.20. A similar effect can be achieved by using a table instead of preformatted text.

Using List Tags

There are a few occasions when line breaks and paragraph tags can't set up the form exactly as you'd like. At these times, list tags can provide just the right look! The best use of list tags is for the indenting and numbering of text.

FIG. 11.20
Combining
preformatted and
wrapped areas can
make your form very
easy to use.

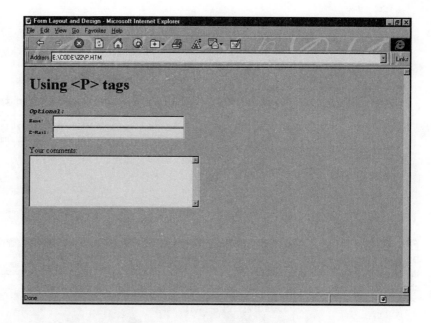

Indenting Form Entries with Descriptive Lists On the WWW, it's common to see order forms for merchandise. Finding out the method of payment is a perfect use for descriptive list tags to lay out the choices. Indenting some items more than others makes the options obvious and easy to read.

N O T E When you lay out lists, consider indenting the areas in your HTML documents that will be indented on-screen. This makes it easier to remember to finish with the descriptive list tag, </DL>. ■

For example, Listing 11.19 shows how to separate a section of credit cards from the rest of the payment methods. The result of this code is shown in Figure 11.21.

Listing 11.19   LIST1.HTM—Organizing Forms Using a Descriptive List

```
<HTML>
<HEAD>
<TITLE>Form Layout and Design</TITLE>
</HEAD>
<BODY>
<H1>Descriptive List Tags</H1>
<FORM>
        <DL>
        <DT>How would you like to pay for this?
        <DD><INPUT NAME="pay" TYPE="radio" VALUE="cash" CHECKED>Cash
```

continues

Part
III

Ch
11

Listing 11.19 Continued

```
        <DD><INPUT NAME="pay" TYPE="radio" VALUE="check">Check
        <DD><INPUT NAME="pay" TYPE="radio" VALUE="debit">Debit Card
            <DL>
            <DT>Credit Card
            <DD><INPUT NAME="pay" TYPE="radio" VALUE="mc">Mastercard
            <DD><INPUT NAME="pay" TYPE="radio" VALUE="visa">Visa
            <DD><INPUT NAME="pay" TYPE="radio" VALUE="disc">Discover
            <DD><INPUT NAME="pay" TYPE="radio" VALUE="ae">American Express
            </DL>
        </DL>
    </FORM>
    </BODY>
    </HTML>
```

FIG. 11.21
Descriptive lists make
the breakdown of
choices obvious.

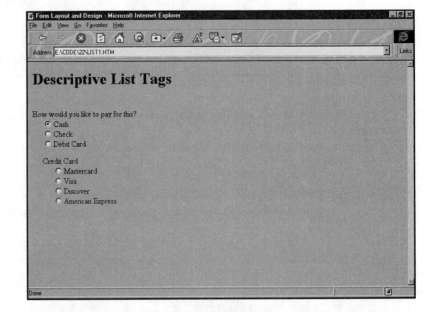

Using Ordered Lists to Number Fields   It's easy to display a numbered list if you use the ordered list tag, <OL>. Listing 11.20 uses the <OL> tag to automatically number the fields. The result of this code is shown in Figure 11.22.

Listing 11.20   LIST2.HTM—Organizing Forms by Using an Ordered List

```
<HTML>
<HEAD>
<TITLE>Form Layout and Design</TITLE>
</HEAD>
```

```
<BODY>
<H1>Ordered List Tags</H1>
<FORM>
        What are your three favorite books?
        <OL>
        <LI><INPUT NAME="1st" SIZE="20">
        <LI><INPUT NAME="2nd" SIZE="20">
        <LI><INPUT NAME="3nd" SIZE="20">
        </OL>
</FORM>
</BODY>
</HTML>
```

FIG. 11.22

Using ordered lists, you can reorder fields without retyping all those numbers!

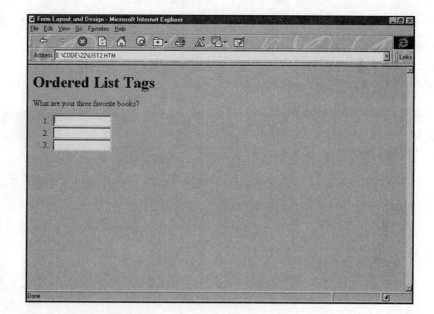

Part
III

Ch
11

Check Box and Radio Button Layouts

Check boxes and radio buttons can provide a great deal of simple yes or no input. They can also be some of the hardest parts of a form to understand if they're not laid out correctly. There are three straightforward methods of layout: setting up the check boxes and radio buttons in a line horizontally, using a list to order them vertically, or setting them up in a grid pattern.

Setting Up Check Boxes or Radio Buttons in a Line   Probably the easiest method of layout is listing the check boxes in a line horizontally (see Listing 11.21). It has the benefits of being very simple to set up, relatively compact on the browser, and easy to understand. The only caution is to make sure there aren't too many items for one line. The intent of the form might not be obvious if you let check boxes wrap unintentionally. The result of Listing 11.21, which specifies a horizontal line of radio buttons, is shown in Figure 11.23.

Listing 11.21   BUTTON1.HTM—Organizing Forms Check Boxes and Radio Buttons

```
<HTML>
<HEAD>
<TITLE>Form Layout and Design</TITLE>
</HEAD>
<BODY>
<H1>Checkboxes and Radio Buttons</H1>
<FORM>
        What size would you like?<BR>
        <INPUT NAME="size" TYPE="radio" VALUE="sm">Small
        <INPUT NAME="size" TYPE="radio" VALUE="md">Medium
        <INPUT NAME="size" TYPE="radio" VALUE="lg">Large
        <INPUT NAME="size" TYPE="radio" VALUE="x">X-Large
        <INPUT NAME="size" TYPE="radio" VALUE="xx">XX-Large
</FORM>
</BODY>
</HTML>
```

FIG. 11.23

This method works well
for check boxes too!

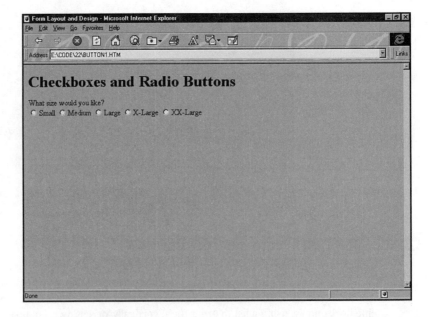

 TIP When creating a Web page with a line of buttons, check it with your Web browser set to the width of a
640×480 screen to make sure your line doesn't wrap.

Lists of Check Boxes   When the choices get more complex than a simple line selection, it's
best to forgo compactness and spread out the choices in a list, as specified in Listing 11.22.
The result of using a descriptive list in this code is shown in Figure 11.24.

Listing 11.22 BUTTON2.HTM—Organizing Forms Buttons by Using Lists

```
<HTML>
<HEAD>
<TITLE>Form Layout and Design</TITLE>
</HEAD>
<BODY>
<H1>Checkboxes and Radio Buttons</H1>
<FORM>
        <DL>
        <DT>What machines do you work on?
        <DD><INPUT NAME="mac" TYPE="checkbox">Macintosh
        <DD><INPUT NAME="pc" TYPE="checkbox">IBM Compatible PC
            <DL>
            <DT>UNIX Workstation
            <DD><INPUT NAME="sun" TYPE="checkbox">Sun
            <DD><INPUT NAME="sgi" TYPE="checkbox">SGI
            <DD><INPUT NAME="next" TYPE="checkbox">NeXT
            <DD><INPUT NAME="aix" TYPE="checkbox">AIX
            <DD><INPUT NAME="lin" TYPE="checkbox">Linux
            <DD><INPUT NAME="other" TYPE="checkbox">Other...
            </DL>
        </DL>
</FORM>
</BODY>
</HTML>
```

Part
III

Ch
11

FIG. 11.24
Complex choices
are often easier to
understand in a list
format.

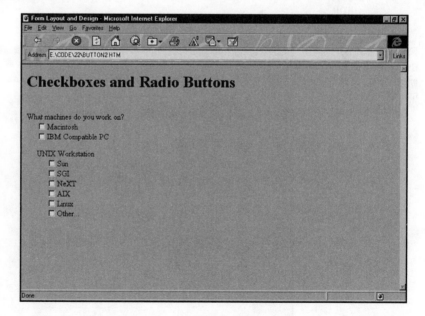

Making a Grid   The most complex method for displaying check boxes is in a grid. Using tables, you can space out the display to create a grid effect (see Listing 11.23). You can also create a grid of radio buttons by substituting radio for checkbox in the <INPUT> tags. The result of setting up the grid in Listing 11.23 is shown in Figure 11.25.

Listing 11.23   GRID.HTM—Creating a Grid of Buttons by Using Tables

```
<HTML>
<HEAD>
<TITLE>Form Layout and Design</TITLE>
</HEAD>
<BODY>
<H1>Checkboxes and Radio Buttons</H1>
<FORM>
        What combinations?
        <TABLE>
                <TR><TD></TD><TD>Red</TD><TD>Blue</TD></TR>
                <TR><TD>Small</TD><TD><INPUT NAME="sr" TYPE="checkbox"></TD>
                        <TD><INPUT NAME="sb" TYPE="checkbox"></TD></TR>
                <TR><TD>Medium</TD><TD><INPUT NAME="mr" TYPE="checkbox"></TD>
                        <TD><INPUT NAME="mb" TYPE="checkbox"></TD></TR>
                <TR><TD>Large</TD><TD><INPUT NAME="lr" TYPE="checkbox"></TD>
                        <TD><INPUT NAME="lb" TYPE="checkbox"></TD></TR>
        </TABLE>
</FORM>
</BODY>
</HTML>
```

FIG. 11.25

Grids provide a very intuitive method of making a choice.

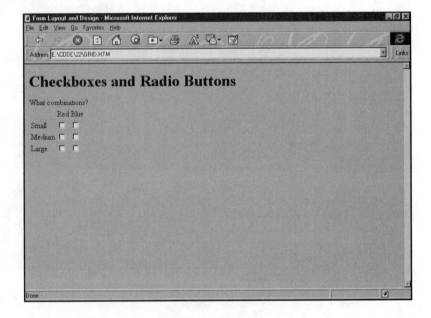

Multiple Forms in a Document

It's quite possible to put multiple forms in a single document; it often makes the document more concise and easier to understand. An example of using multiple forms is a document with a number of different methods for searching. From one form, you can choose to do a search from any of a number of locations by having each <FORM> point to a different search method.

TIP Also consider using multiple forms when your form is too large to fit on one or two screens; this makes it easier for your readers to use the form.

When including multiple forms in a document, visibly separate them to make them easier to understand. A common way to break up a form is to use the horizontal rule tag, <HR>, or a wide image that looks like a horizontal rule in an <IMG> tag. Put line breaks before and after the tags. For example, Listing 11.24 shows how to separate three forms by using <HR> tags to break them up. The result of this code is shown in Figure 11.26.

Listing 11.24 MULTIPLE.HTM—Using Multiple Forms in a Single HTML Document

```
<HTML>
<HEAD>
<TITLE>Form Layout and Design</TITLE>
</HEAD>
<BODY>
<H1>Multiple Forms in a Document</H1>
<FORM>
        What size would you like?<BR>
        <INPUT NAME="size" TYPE="radio" VALUE="sm">:Small
        <INPUT NAME="size" TYPE="radio" VALUE="md">:Medium
        <INPUT NAME="size" TYPE="radio" VALUE="lg">:Large
        <INPUT NAME="size" TYPE="radio" VALUE="x">:X-Large
        <INPUT NAME="size" TYPE="radio" VALUE="xx">:XX-Large
        <P>
        <INPUT TYPE="submit">
</FORM>
<HR>
<FORM>
        <TABLE>
                <TR><TD>Name:</TD><TD><INPUT TYPE="text" NAME="name"
                SIZE="50"></TD></TR>
                <TR><TD>E-Mail:</TD><TD><INPUT TYPE="text" NAME="email"
                SIZE="50"></TD></TR>
                <TR><TD>Street Address:</TD><TD><INPUT TYPE="text"
                NAME="street1" SIZE="30"></TD></TR>
                <TR><TD></TD><TD><INPUT TYPE="text" NAME="street2"
                SIZE="30"></TD></TR>
                <TR><TD>City:</TD><TD><INPUT TYPE="text" NAME="city"
                SIZE="50"></TD></TR>
                <TR><TD>State:</TD><TD><INPUT TYPE="text" NAME="state"
```

continues

Listing 11.24 Continued

```
                SIZE="2"></TD></TR>
                <TR><TD>Zip:</TD><TD><INPUT TYPE="text" NAME="zip"
                SIZE="10"></TD></TR>
        </TABLE>
<P>
<INPUT TYPE="submit">
</FORM>
<HR>
<FORM>
        <DL>
        <DT>How would you like to pay for this?
        <DD><INPUT NAME="pay" TYPE="radio" VALUE="cash" CHECKED>Cash
        <DD><INPUT NAME="pay" TYPE="radio" VALUE="check">Check
        <DD><INPUT NAME="pay" TYPE="radio" VALUE="debit">Debit Card
            <DL>
            <DT>Credit Card
            <DD><INPUT NAME="pay" TYPE="radio" VALUE="mc">Mastercard
            <DD><INPUT NAME="pay" TYPE="radio" VALUE="visa">Visa
            <DD><INPUT NAME="pay" TYPE="radio" VALUE="disc">Discover
            <DD><INPUT NAME="pay" TYPE="radio" VALUE="ae">American Express
            </DL>
        </DL>
        <P>
        <INPUT TYPE="submit">
</FORM>
</BODY>
</HTML>
```

FIG. 11.26

By using horizontal rules to break up the multiple forms in this document, the intent of the form is easily apparent.

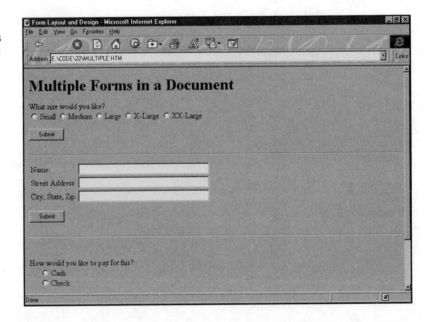

TROUBLESHOOTING

I put multiple forms in one document, but I only see one. Why aren't both showing up? Check to make sure you finished one form before beginning another. If you didn't include the </FORM> tag to stop the first form, the second <FORM> tag is just ignored.

Combining Forms with Tables

As discussed earlier in this section, forms can be used very effectively with HTML tables, allowing more control of the positioning of different fields. Listing 11.25 shows an address entry form that uses a table to align the different fields. The resulting Web page is shown in Figure 11.27.

Listing 11.25   TABLE2.HTM—Combining Forms and Tables

```
<HTML>
<HEAD>
<TITLE>Form Layout and Design</TITLE>
</HEAD>
<BODY>
<H1>More HTML Tables and Forms</H1>
<FORM>
        <TABLE>
                <TR><TD ALIGN=RIGHT>Name:</TD>
                    <TD COLSPAN=4><INPUT TYPE="text" NAME="name" SIZE="40">
                </TD></TR>
                <TR><TD ALIGN=RIGHT>Street Address:</TD>
                    <TD COLSPAN=4><INPUT TYPE="text" NAME="street1" SIZE="40">
                </TD></TR>
                <TR><TD ALIGN=RIGHT>City, State, Zip:</TD>
                    <TD><INPUT TYPE="text" NAME="city" SIZE="30"></TD><TD>,</TD>
                    <TD><INPUT TYPE="text" NAME="state" SIZE="2"></TD>
                    <TD><INPUT TYPE="text" NAME="zip" SIZE="15"></TD></TR>
        </TABLE>
</FORM>
</BODY>
</HTML>
```

Part

III

Ch

11

This idea can be taken even further, including other form elements such as check boxes or radio buttons, to allow the user more input options. A further refinement of the address entry form, allowing the user to input both a home and business address and specify which is preferred, is shown in Listing 11.26—the corresponding Web page is shown in Figure 11.27.

FIG. 11.27

The capability of tables to position items side by side and align them in many different ways makes them a natural for use with forms.

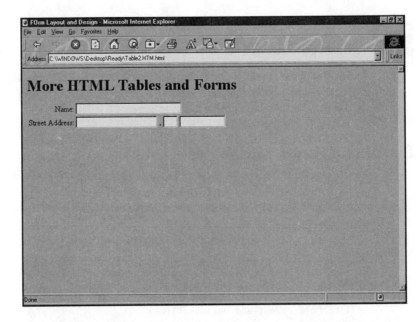

Listing 11.26   TABLE3.HTM—More on Combining Forms and Tables

```
<HTML>
<HEAD>
<TITLE>Form Layout and Design</TITLE>
</HEAD>
<BODY>
<H1>More HTML Tables and Forms</H1>
<FORM>
        <TABLE>
                <TR><TH ALIGN=LEFT COLSPAN=5>HOME ADDRESS</TH><TD><EM>Preferred?
                ➥</EM></TR>
                <TR><TD ALIGN=RIGHT>Name:</TD>
                    <TD COLSPAN=4><INPUT TYPE="text" NAME="name" SIZE="40"></TD>
                    <TD ALIGN=CENTER><INPUT TYPE="radio" NAME="pref"
                    ➥VALUE="home"></TD></TR>
                <TR><TD ALIGN=RIGHT>Street Address:</TD>
                    <TD COLSPAN=4><INPUT TYPE="text" NAME="street1" SIZE="40">
                    ➥</TD></TR>
                <TR><TD ALIGN=RIGHT>City, State, Zip:</TD>
                    <TD><INPUT TYPE="text" NAME="city" SIZE="25"></TD><TD>,</TD>
                    <TD><INPUT TYPE="text" NAME="state" SIZE="2"></TD>
                    <TD><INPUT TYPE="text" NAME="zip" SIZE="15"></TD></TR>
                <TR><TD COLSPAN=6><HR></TD></TR>
```

```
                        <TR><TH ALIGN=LEFT COLSPAN=5>BUSINESS ADDRESS</
TH><TD><EM>Preferred?</EM></TR>
                <TR><TD ALIGN=RIGHT>Name:</TD>
                    <TD COLSPAN=4><INPUT TYPE="text" NAME="name" SIZE="40"></TD>
                    <TD ALIGN=CENTER><INPUT TYPE="radio" NAME="pref" VALUE="bus"></
                    ➥TD></TR>
                <TR><TD ALIGN=RIGHT>Street Address:</TD>
                    <TD COLSPAN=4><INPUT TYPE="text" NAME="street1" SIZE="40"></
                    ➥TD></TR>
                <TR><TD ALIGN=RIGHT>City, State, Zip:</TD>
                    <TD><INPUT TYPE="text" NAME="city" SIZE="25"></TD><TD>,</TD>
                    <TD><INPUT TYPE="text" NAME="state" SIZE="2"></TD>
                    <TD><INPUT TYPE="text" NAME="zip" SIZE="15"></TD></TR>
            </TABLE>
        </FORM>
        </BODY>
        </HTML>
```

FIG. 11.28
HTML tables allow you to combine many different form fields and position them logically.

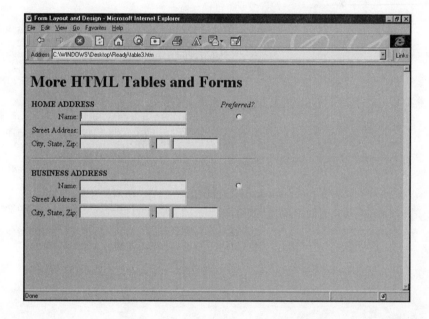

Part
III

Ch
11

One final refinement of the address entry form (see Figure 11.29) substitutes different submit buttons for the radio buttons, shown in Figures 11.27 and 11.28. This allows the user to enter the information on the form and then specify which is the preferred address by his choice of submit button. Specifying a NAME attribute for the submit button enables the choice of button to be determined.

Listing 11.27   TABLE4.HTM—Another Example of Forms and Tables

```
<HTML>
<HEAD>
<TITLE>Form Layout and Design</TITLE>
</HEAD>
<BODY>
<H1>More HTML Tables and Forms</H1>
<FORM>
        <TABLE>
                <TR><TH ALIGN=LEFT COLSPAN=5>HOME ADDRESS</TH>
                    <TD ALIGN=CENTER><EM>Preferred?</EM></TD></TR>
                <TR><TD ALIGN=RIGHT>Name:</TD>
                    <TD COLSPAN=4><INPUT TYPE="text" NAME="name" SIZE="40"></TD>
                    <TD ALIGN=CENTER><INPUT TYPE="submit" NAME="home" VALUE="Home">
                </TD></TR>
                <TR><TD ALIGN=RIGHT>Street Address:</TD>
                    <TD COLSPAN=4><INPUT TYPE="text" NAME="street1" SIZE="40">
                </TD></TR>
                <TR><TD ALIGN=RIGHT>City, State, Zip:</TD>
                    <TD><INPUT TYPE="text" NAME="city" SIZE="25"></TD><TD>,</TD>
                    <TD><INPUT TYPE="text" NAME="state" SIZE="2"></TD>
                    <TD><INPUT TYPE="text" NAME="zip" SIZE="15"></TD></TR>
                <TR><TD COLSPAN=6><HR></TD></TR>
                <TR><TH ALIGN=LEFT COLSPAN=5>BUSINESS ADDRESS</TH>
                    <TD ALIGN=CENTER><EM>Preferred?</EM></TD></TR>
                <TR><TD ALIGN=RIGHT>Name:</TD>
                    <TD COLSPAN=4><INPUT TYPE="text" NAME="name" SIZE="40"></TD>
                    <TD ALIGN=CENTER><INPUT TYPE="submit" NAME="bus"
                VALUE="Business"></TD></TR>
                <TR><TD ALIGN=RIGHT>Street Address:</TD>
                    <TD COLSPAN=4><INPUT TYPE="text" NAME="street1" SIZE="40">
                </TD></TR>
                <TR><TD ALIGN=RIGHT>City, State, Zip:</TD>
                    <TD><INPUT TYPE="text" NAME="city" SIZE="25"></TD><TD>,
                </TD>
                    <TD><INPUT TYPE="text" NAME="state" SIZE="2"></TD>
                    <TD><INPUT TYPE="text" NAME="zip" SIZE="15"></TD></TR>
        </TABLE>
</FORM>
</BODY>
</HTML>
```

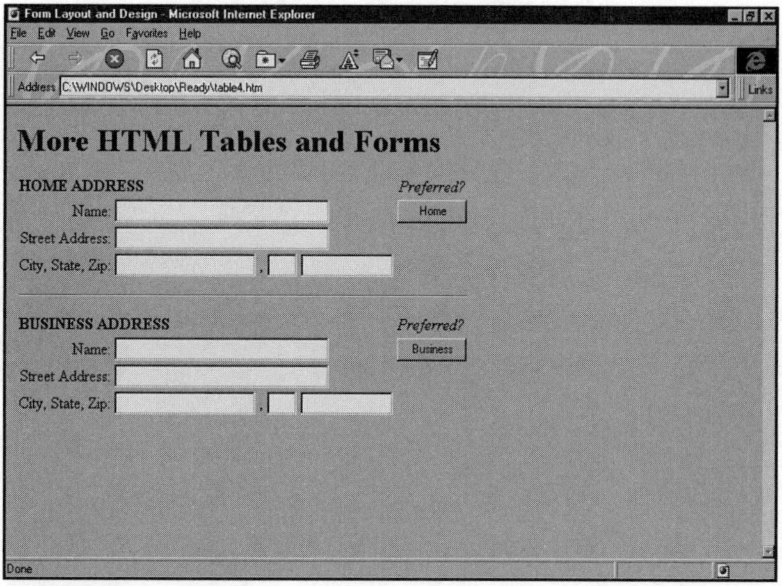

FIG. 11.29

The options available for using forms with HTML tables are limited only by your imagination.

Final Notes on Form Layouts

When you're creating forms, it's always a good idea to keep the form on a single page. Further, because you can't control what browser someone uses to look at your pages, you need to observe some general guidelines, as follows:

- If your form is very short, keep it under 14 lines. This ensures that it will fit on one page in most browsers. It doesn't always work, but it does create a compact page that's easy for most people to see. A good trick for keeping the pages compact is using <SELECT> tags with the size set to 1 (to show a pop-up menu) or 3 or 4 (for a small scrolling window for multiple choices), instead of having large numbers of check boxes and radio buttons.

- If your form is large (more than two pages on any browser), don't put the <SUBMIT> or <RESET> buttons in the middle of the form. If you do, someone reading the form might not continue beyond those buttons and might miss an important part of the form.

- Put the fields on your form in a logical order. This sounds obvious, but it's easy to forget.

- Think about your forms well before you start creating them. If you know what choices you want to provide, it makes your final layout much easier.

## CHAPTER 12

Imagemaps

by Jerry Honeycutt and John Jung

A large number of advanced Web pages use *imagemaps* as a sort of graphical menu from which the user chooses a Web page to open. Imagemaps are just pictures on which well-defined areas of the image are linked to other Web pages (or any other Internet resource). Virtually every corporate home page uses an imagemap. Some use an imagemap on the home page as the home page's primary content; others use an imagemap as a toolbar, or navigational aid. For example, take a look at Hewlett Packard's Web site: **http://www.hp.com**.

You may think that adding an imagemap to your Web site is a lot of work. Once upon a time, it was a lot of work. Not anymore. Considering the difficulty of everything else you do as a Webmaster, imagemaps are child's play. They also add a good bit of class to your Web site and so are worth careful consideration. On the other hand, there are a few drawbacks to using imagemaps, so you should carefully consider the issues described in this chapter before doing so. ■

Learn how server- and client-side imagemaps work

Imagemaps aren't nearly as difficult as you might think. This chapter shows you how to create them.

What makes a good graphic for an imagemap?

Not all graphics are created equal. You must carefully design them, just like menus in a program.

Create both server- and client-side imagemaps

Creating an imagemap is easy. You create an image and map definition; and insert the HTML.

Stick to the guidelines

You can create great imagemaps if you stick to the guidelines contained in this chapter.

Are there any programs that create imagemaps

You don't have to create imagemaps by hand; learn about programs you can use to create imagemaps.

Use an alternative to imagemaps

If you're not in the mood for an imagemap, you can use this slick alternative to get the same effect.

Introducing Imagemaps

Because imagemaps make use of pictures, they let users navigate content-related links in a friendly fashion. The Web uses the first Internet standard (HTML) that allows for the easy display of graphics. This is in sharp contrast to past standards, which were all text-based, such as Gopher, WAIS, and FTP. Although these older standards could transport images; this capability was never designed into them (see Figure 12.1).

FIG. 12.1

Using imagemaps is easier than text links because most folks relate to pictures better than the written word.

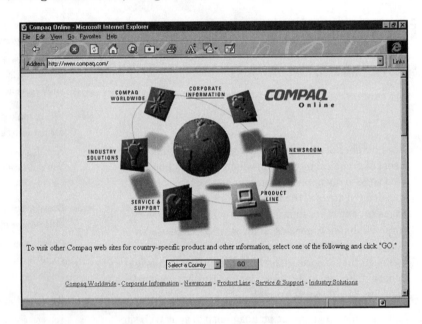

TIP In the wide world of HTML, you'll also see imagemaps referred to as *area maps* or *clickable maps*.

Different parts of an imagemap's graphic point to different URLs. Because the user has to know where these clickable regions are in the imagemap, you'll often find borders around each region, as shown in Figure 12.2. Note these borders are part of the graphic itself, and are not created by the Web server.

You can use two different types of imagemaps: server side and client side. Here's how each type of imagemap works:

Server side The browser sends the coordinates of the mouse pointer to the Web server when the user clicks somewhere on the imagemap. Then, the server looks up the coordinates and determines the region on which the user clicked. Armed with this information, the server looks up the corresponding URL and returns it to the browser. As a result, the browser opens the URL.

Client side   You define an imagemap's region within the Web page. When the user clicks somewhere on the imagemap, the browser looks up the region in the HTML file, determines the associated URL, and opens that URL. The browser doesn't communicate with the Web server at all.

FIG. 12.2

For imagemaps to be useful, the user must be able to easily distinguish each region in the imagemap.

Regions—

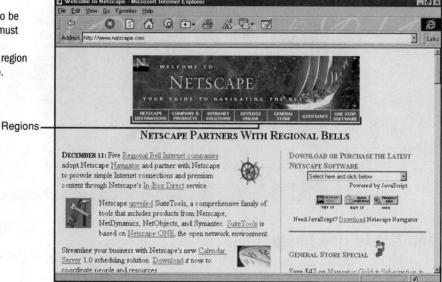

When to Use Imagemaps

In many situations, you should consider using imagemaps instead of hypertext links. Here's a short list of some times when using imagemaps is appropriate:

- **When you want to represent links that have a physical relation to each other.** For example, clicking a map of the world is easier than picking from a list of countries.

- **When you want to enable users to go to important points on your site at any time.** You can even make imagemaps a constant staple in every page on your Web site—like a toolbar.

- **When you want to give your Web site a sense of consistency.** Whenever you add new pages to your Web site, you'll probably want to add the navigation imagemap graphic to them (see Figure 12.3).

Part
III

Ch
12

FIG. 12.3
By using imagemaps as a navigational tool for the user, you make getting around your home page easier.

Imagemap used as a Toolbar

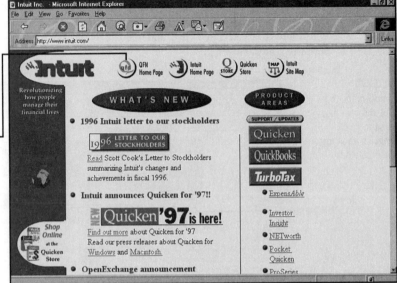

When Not to Use Imagemaps

Although imagemaps might be useful in most situations, sometimes you shouldn't use them. For example:

- **Server-side imagemaps require a Web server capable of handling them properly.** You can get a free copy of Microsoft's Personal Web Server at Microsoft's Web site: **http://www.microsoft.com**.

- **Server-side imagemaps can't be tested without a Web server.** This means that while you're designing your imagemaps, you can't test them easily. You either have to get Web server software loaded on your own computer, or put the imagemap files on your server.

- **You should consider nongraphical browsers when designing your Web pages.** Many people still use text-based browsers when surfing the Web. Still more folks disable images in their browser so they can open Web pages faster. You should provide a textual alternative to your imagemaps as shown in Figure 12.4.

- **If you're concerned about your Web site's performance, you should avoid using imagemaps (or consider using text alternatives).** Because imagemaps can be rather large, they can take a while to download (particularly if the user has a 14.4Kbps modem). Also, network traffic can sometimes make large graphics take longer than normal to download.

FIG. 12.4
Making textual alternatives for your imagemaps is essential for users with text-based browsers or users who have disabled graphics in their graphical browser.

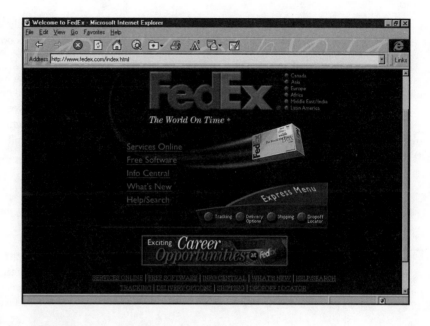

Using Server-Side Imagemaps

In order to add a server-side imagemap to your Web page, you need four things:

- imagemap graphic
- imagemap definition file
- imagemap program or script
- HTML tags

Creating the Imagemap Graphic

The first thing you want to look at when building an imagemap is the imagemap graphics. If you're building a company Web site, for example, you might want to duplicate the look and feel of your corporate stationery. Chapter 17, "Graphics," has some good information if you're planning to create fresh, new graphics or modify existing ones. Chapter 17 describes the image file formats you can use as an imagemap as well as the programs you can use to create imagemaps.

In choosing your imagemap graphic, you have many considerations:

- **Store the imagemap graphic in the GIF graphics format.** Because you want as many people as possible to see your imagemap, you should make it as basic as possible. All Web browsers support GIF and most support JPEG. But, a few browsers still don't handle JPEG images.

- **Save the imagemap graphic as an Interlaced GIF.** This format allows an image to be displayed progressively. As the image file is downloaded, more detail is added on the

Part
III

Ch
12

screen. By using this format, you let users see where the larger clickable regions are. By using interlaced GIFs as your imagemap graphic, you also help people who have slower modems.

- **Keep the resolution of your imagemap graphic small.** Try to keep your image from being more than 600 pixels wide by 400 pixels tall. Many different computers will be accessing your page, each with a different configuration. The lowest resolution for most modern computers is 640×480. With the 600×400 resolution recommendation, you make sure almost everybody can see your image without having to scroll.

- **Try to reduce the number of colors each of your imagemap graphics uses.** Using fewer colors makes the size of the file smaller. The smaller file size translates into a faster download for each user.

  ▶ **See** "Useful Graphics Tools," for more information about creating images by using the most popular graphics programs, **p. 360**

N O T E If you use Transparent GIFs as imagemap graphics, define a default region type as described later in this chapter. When you use Transparent GIFs (see Chapter 16, "Graphics") as imagemap graphics, users might be confused, because the imagemap doesn't have any borders (see Figure 12.5). ■

FIG. 12.5
Yahoo's main masthead is a transparent GIF and the main user navigational interface. It's not always obvious when you're in the imagemap and when you're not.

Transparent GIF used as an imagemap

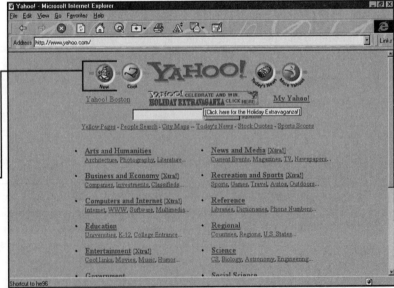

Understanding Imagemap Definition Files

To create a server-side imagemap, you're going to need more than just a pretty picture. You're going to need an imagemap definition file, which identifies where each specific region is within the imagemap.

An imagemap definition file can come in two forms: CERN and NCSA. Both contain the same basic information for the clickable regions within an imagemap. Both of them also use the same region types. The coordinates used to define the regions are also the same. The only difference between the two is the manner in which the information is presented. Because of this incompatibility, you must find out from your system administrator which format your Web server supports.

All entries in an imagemap definition file must include the URL to be accessed (see Listing 12.1). The URL can either be an absolute path or a relative path. If you're using relative paths to specify a URL, be sure to make them relative to the directory where the imagemap definition file resides, not where the imagemap resides.

▶ **See** "Understanding Links," to learn about the differences between absolute and relative links, **p. 106**

Listing 12.1   Imagemap Definition File

```
#
# Sample Imagemap Definition File
# File Format: NCSA
#

# Define the default region
default http://www.myserver.com/mypage/index.htm

# Define a rectangle region
rect http://www.myserver.com/mypage/rectangle.htm 50,40 100,120

# Define a circle region
circle http://www.myserver.com/mypage/rectangle.htm 50,40 100,60

# Define a polygon region
poly http://www.myserver.com/mypage/rectangle.htm 10,20 24,70 84,45 07,11 10,20
```

Part
III

Ch
12

The CERN Format   Originally, CERN (Conseil Europeen pour la Recherche Nucleaire) was founded as a research group of European physicists. The group slowly expanded their research into the field of computers. Because they were the ones who first thought of the idea, they rightfully claim the honor of being "the birthplace of the Web." When imagemaps were deemed necessary, CERN developed their format for the imagemap definition file. On Web servers that follow the CERN format, you can find files that look like this:

```
region_type (x1,y1) (x2,y2) ... URL
```

The horizontal (*x1* and *x2*) and vertical (*y1* and *y2*) coordinates must be in parentheses and separated by a comma. Each pair of coordinates means something different for each region type. The ... specifies additional coordinates, such as for the *poly* region type (see "Working with Imagemap Region Types" later in the chapter). Here's an example of a CERN imagemap definition:

```
rect (60,40) (340,280) http://www.rectangle.com/
```

The NCSA Format   The first wildly popular browser, Mosaic, came from the University of Illinois' National Center for Supercomputing Applications (NCSA). When this group heard about the demand for imagemaps, they came up with their own imagemap definition file format. A typical entry in one of their files would look like this:

```
region_type URL x1,y1 x2,y2 ...
```

Subtle (but significant) differences distinguish the CERN and NCSA formats. The URL for the region type comes before the coordinates with NCSA, not after, like CERN. The coordinates defining the region need to be separated by commas, but they don't need the parentheses around them. Here's an example of an NCSA imagemap definition:

```
rect http://www.rectangle.com/ 60,40 340,280
```

N O T E   You can put comments to yourself in an imagemap definition file. Simply put a pound character (#) at the beginning of any line. Everything else on the same line after the pound sign will be ignored by the Web server. Comments are useful for putting in bits of information to yourself about the referenced URL, the imagemap graphic, or anything else. For corporate Web pages, comments are particularly useful for telling others when the file was last modified, who did it, and why it was changed.

The pound sign at the beginning of the line is different than the pound sign in the middle of a URL. When a pound sign is in the middle of a URL, it specifies an internal destination point. ■

Working with Imagemap Region Types   Each entry in the definition file specifies a region type. It also tells the exact points that define the region for that type. The coordinates used by each region type are an offset, in pixels, from the upper-left corner of the imagemap graphic. The available region types are mostly geometric (see Figure 12.6).

FIG. 12.6

You can use any combination of these region types, except for the default type.

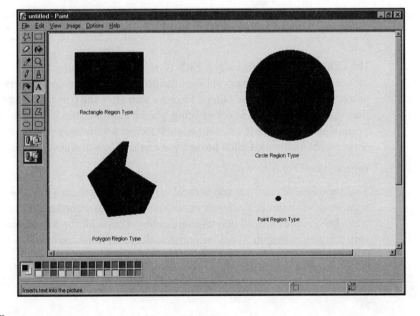

N O T E   Each imagemap depends on its own imagemap definition file to hold the information about clickable regions. This means that if your Web site has many different imagemaps, you need an imagemap definition file for each of them. ∎

The Rectangle Region   To get a clickable rectangle in your imagemap, use the *rect region type*. This element takes in two coordinates, the upper-left and lower-right corners of the rectangle. Any mouse clicks inside the rectangle that are within these corners activate the region. Here's an example using the NCSA format:

```
rect http://www.rectangle.com/ 100,100 120,120
```

If your Web server is a CERN imagemap server, the previous example will look like this:

```
rect (100,100) (120,120) http://www.rectangle.com/
```

T I P   Whenever multiple-region types overlap, the first one with an entry in the imagemap definition file is used.

The Polygon Region   To specify a geometric shape of an arbitrary number of sides, use the *poly region type*. This element looks for up to 100 coordinates, each referring to a vertex of the polygon. The active region is the area within the polygon. Note that you should close the polygon. That is, the first and last set of coordinates should be the same. Here's an example using the NCSA format:

```
poly http://www.polygon.com/ 0,0 100,100 120,120 80,60 40,50 10,10 0,0
```

If your Web server is a CERN imagemap server, the previous example will look like this:

```
poly (0,0) (100,100) (120,120) (80,60) (40,50) (10,10) (0,0) http://
➥www.polygon.com/
```

The Circle Region   To get a hot spot in the shape of a circle, you should use the *circle region type*. This element takes in two coordinates, but they are different values for different Web servers. If your Web server is an NCSA imagemap server, the two coordinates specify the coordinates for the center of the circle and a point on that circle, like this:

```
circle http://www.circle.com/ 100,100 150,150
```

If your Web server is a CERN imagemap server, you really need only one coordinate and one value. The coordinates specify the center of the circle, whereas the value defines its radius. The clickable region of this type is everything enclosed within the circle. Here's an example:

```
circle (100,100) 50 http://www.circle.com/
```

The Point Region   You can easily create hot spots the size of small circles with the *point region type*. This element requires just one set of coordinates to specify the center of the circle. The area enclosed within that point is considered the active region. For example:

```
point http://www.point.com/ 88,65
```

The Default Region   If the user clicks in an imagemap and doesn't activate any region, the *default region type* is used. This element requires no coordinates. For example, assume you have the following two lines in your imagemap definition file:

```
rect http://www.rectangle.com/ 0,0 100,100
default http://www.rectangle.com/helpme
```

If the user clicks anywhere within the first rectangle, the browser opens **http://www.rectangle.com**. On the other hand, if the user clicks anywhere outside of the first rectangle, the browser opens **http://www.rectangle.com/helpme** because this URL is associated with the default region.

CAUTION

Whenever possible, try to avoid putting in a point alone with a default-region type. Because the point region is so small, a user can easily miss it. As a result, the default region will be accessed instead. The user will be frustrated by not getting to the URL he or she wants. Try using small circles, instead.

 An imagemap definition file should, whenever possible, be configured with a default region. The default region opens a specified URL when the user clicks outside of any region. This URL can provide the user with feedback or helpful information about using that particular imagemap.

▶ **See** Chapter 7, "Creating Document Links," **p. 105**

Creating Imagemap Definition Files   Creating the imagemap definition file can be a tiring part of creating the imagemap for your Web site. You can create this file in two ways: the easy way and the hard way. The easy way is to use an imagemap creation program. This type of program lets you draw imagemap region types on top of an imagemap graphic of your choice and specify the appropriate URL. You learn more about these programs in "Working with Imagemap Editing Programs," later in this chapter.

The hard way of creating the file is to do it by hand. Creating the file this way really isn't as difficult as you might think, but it is dull and repetitious. You need two programs to create an imagemap definition file by hand: a graphics program and a text editor. Here's how:

1. Print a hard copy of the image you're using as an imagemap and mark where you want each clickable region to be.
2. Load the image in a graphics program (the program should display the coordinates of the mouse).
3. Create a new text file for your imagemap and open it in your favorite text editor (Notepad). Consider using the .MAP file extension as this is standard across the Internet.
4. For each region in your sketch, add an entry to the imagemap definition file. Use the graphics program to locate the coordinates required for each region. For example, if you are creating a region for the rectangle in Figure 12.6, place your mouse pointer at the top-left corner of the rectangle and note the coordinates (30,20); place the mouse pointer at the bottom-right corner of the rectangle and note the coordinates (130, 80); and add the following entry to your imagemap definition file:

   ```
   rect http://www.myserver.com/mypage/rectangle.htm 30,20 130,80
   ```
5. Save your imagemap definition file.

CAUTION

When using a graphics program to get coordinates for use in an imagemap, be careful not to actually change the image.

 If you choose to have multiple imagemaps using different imagemap graphics, you should organize everything. A good way to do this is to create a separate directory for each group of files for each imagemap. Another way of keeping multiple imagemap files distinct from each other is to keep the same file name for each imagemap component, where each will have the appropriate extension.

Using a CGI Program to Look Up Mouse Clicks

As noted earlier in this chapter, you must use a CGI program to translate a user's mouse click into a URL. The user's browser invokes your CGI program, passing to it the coordinates of the mouse click. Then, within your imagemap definition file, your program finds the region in which the user clicks. If the program finds a matching region, it returns the corresponding URL; otherwise, it returns an error.

Chapter 25, "All About CGI Scripts," shows you how to create CGI programs. In most cases, however, your ISP already provides a CGI program that you can use to look up URLs in an imagemap definition file.

Invoking the CGI Program   I hope that by now you've asked yourself how you invoke the CGI script from within the Web page. You'll learn more about the HTML you use to create imagemaps in the next section. For now, however, imagemaps within your HTML look a bit like the following example:

```
<A HREF="http://www.myserver.com/cgi-bin/mapfile.map"><IMG SRC=imagemap.gif
➥ISMAP></A>
```

The HREF in the example anchor specifies a link, not to another Web page or Internet resource, but to an imagemap. Depending on how you create your imagemap and how your ISP works with imagemaps, you may also link to the actual CGI program. When the user clicks the imagemap, the browser attempts to open this URL, passing to it the coordinates of the mouse pointer as a parameter. The server then replies by returning the URL that the CGI program determined is associated with those coordinates.

Working with an ISP   Most ISPs do work alike, down to the tilde (~) many prefix to your user name when creating the directory for your home page. Thus, if you're creating a personal home page on an ISP's Web server, you can bet that you'll use a format similar to the following when invoking an imagemap:

```
<a href="/cgi-bin/imagemap/~username/image.map">
<img src="myimage.gif"></a>
```

The HREF points to /cgi-bin/imagemap/~*username*/*image.map*. You simply substitute your user name for *username* and the name of your imagemap file for *image.map*. Also note that most

Part III

Ch 12

ISPs have requirements for how you store your map files. For example, my ISP requires that I store all imagemap files in the root directory of my home page, called /PUBLIC_HTML, regardless of the directory structure that my Web site uses. Your ISP may have different requirements.

Putting the HTML on the Web Page

Now that you have all the elements in place for an imagemap, you're ready to actually put it in your Web page. You do so by building from what you learn in Chapter 17, "Graphics." There, you saw how to make an image clickable and go to a certain URL. All you have to do is enclose the <IMG SRC> tag within an anchor element and have the anchor reference point to the appropriate Web page.

Two steps are needed to make an imagemap an integral part of a Web page on your site. First, you need to change the anchor element reference from an HTML document to point to your imagemap definition file. Second, you must add the attribute ISMAP to the <IMG SRC> tag. For example, say that you've created an imagemap definition file called MAPFILE.MAP, and its graphic is called IMAGEMAP.GIF. To put an imagemap in an HTML document, you use the following HTML code:

```
<A HREF="http://www.myserver.com/cgi-bin/mapfile.map">
<IMG SRC=imagemap.gif ISMAP></A>
```

When the imagemap is selected, the Web server runs the imagemap CGI program. The program then takes over and translates the mouse-click coordinates into a corresponding URL.

N O T E Be sure to ask your Webmaster where the imagemap definition file will be stored. These file locations are determined by the configuration of your Web server. ▪

N O T E You can use the ISMAP attribute with any other image attributes. Just because you're specifying an imagemap doesn't restrict your ability to control the graphic. You can still use any other image-controlling attributes you want. ▪

Putting Your Imagemap Through a Dry Run

After you've created the files for your imagemap, the only thing left to do is to test it. Even though some map-editing programs let you try the region types within the program, this built-in facility is often imperfect. The programmers have made certain assumptions with the imagemap process. The best way to test the imagemap is to put it on your Web server and act like an average user.

By testing the imagemap in this fashion, you can see different aspects that you might have overlooked. If the imagemap graphic file is too large and takes a long time to download, you'll see it. You'll also be able to see if the imagemap regions are distinct enough for the average person. Finally, you can see if the URLs for each region actually work as they should. If you're using relative links, testing the imagemap on the server is especially important.

TIP Keep your FTP client open and ready. Then, you can quickly change and test your imagemap by flipping back and forth between the text editor, FTP client, and Web browser (don't forget to reload the Web page if you're changing the graphic).

Before releasing your imagemap for everyone's perusal, find someone else to try it. Get a friend with a different Internet service provider to access your new imagemap. He or she can give you a (somewhat) unbiased opinion of the imagemap graphic and region types.

Building Client-Side Imagemaps

Until HTML 3.2, the client-side imagemap was an extension limited to Netscape and Internet Explorer. Now, client-side imagemaps are no longer an extension; they are part of the standard.

Client-side imagemaps are very similar to server-side imagemaps. The only difference is that instead of using an imagemap file and CGI script on the server, you use an imagemap that you store right there in the HTML file. The greatest benefit is in the reduced network traffic. That is, instead of hitting the Web server to look up a URL, the browser handles the imagemap itself.

Defining a Client-Side Imagemap

Remember the formats of the NCSA and CERN imagemap definition files? The HTML format for an imagemap definition contains the same types of information, but it uses HTML tags. Here's what the syntax of an imagemap definition in HTML looks like:

```
<MAP NAME="mapname">
<AREA [SHAPE="shape"] COORDS="x,y,..." [HREF="URL"][NOHREF]>
</MAP>
```

The imagemap definition starts with the <MAP> tag and ends with the </MAP> tag. It's a container. So that you can refer to the imagemap definition later in the IMG, you give it a name by using the NAME attribute.

You define each region, or hot spot, by using the AREA tag. The coordinate system starts from the upper-left corner of the imagemap. Table 12.1 describes each of the AREA tag's attributes:

Part
III

Ch
12

Table 12.1   The *AREA* Tag's Attributes

Attribute	Description
SHAPE	Defines the shape of the region. Just like the server-side, imagemap definition files, you can use rect, poly, circle, default. If this attribute is missing, the browser assumes rect. When two regions overlap, the browser uses the first one in the list.
COORDS	Defines a comma-separated list of coordinates. Note there is a comma between each set of coordinates.

continues

Table 12.1 Continued

Attribute	Description
HREF	Defines the URL of the Internet resource to which the region is linked. All relative links are relative to the document containing the MAP tag, not the one containing the USEMAP attribute, if different. If you use a BASE tag in the HTML file containing the MAP tag, that URL is used.
NOHREF	Specifies the region is a dead area within the imagemap. That is, that area is not linked to any Internet resource. Note HREF and NOHREF are mutually exclusive.

Listing 12.2 shows you a complete example of an imagemap definition in HTML. Figure 12.7 shows the Web page created by this HTML code.

Listing 12.2 A Client-Side Imagemap

```
<MAP NAME=mymap>
<AREA SHAPE=RECT COORDS="0,0,100,100" HREF=item1.html>
<AREA SHAPE=RECT COORDS="101,0,200,100" HREF=item2.html>
<AREA SHAPE=RECT COORDS="201,0,300,100" HREF=item3.html>
</MAP>
<IMG SRC=mymap.gif USEMAP=#mymap>
```

FIG. 12.7
The client-side imagemap produced by the example HTML code.

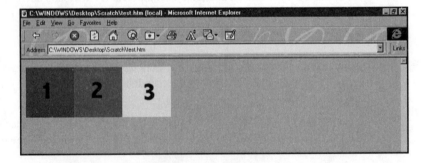

Referencing the Client-Side, Imagemap Definition

The final line of the previous example shows how to reference an imagemap after it's built:

```
<IMG SRC=mymap.gif USEMAP=#mymap>
```

This IMG tag loads the image called MYMAP.GIF. USEMAP is a new HTML 3.2 attribute that specifies the name of the imagemap definition that you define elsewhere in the HTML file by using the MAP tag.

Combining Client-Side and Server-Side Imagemaps

If you want to take care of those folks with browsers that don't support client-side imagemaps, while reducing network traffic for those folks with browsers that do support client-side image-maps, you can combine the best of both worlds. You can define an imagemap that works with both client-side and server-side imagemaps. Combine both definitions within the IMG tag, like this:

```
<A HREF="http://www.myserver.com/cgi-bin/mymap.map">
<IMG SRC=mymap.gif USEMAP=#mymap ISMAP>
</A>
```

If the browser supports client-side imagemaps, it'll use the map from the USEMAP attribute. Otherwise, the browser will use the map on the server.

> **N O T E** If you want to use client-side imagemaps, but don't want to or can't create a server-side imagemap, you can create an alternative. Like this:
>
> `<A HREF=textmenu.html><IMG SRC=mymap.gif USEMAP=mymap></A>`
>
> Whether or not the user's browser supports imagemaps, they'll see the image. If a user clicks the image and their browser doesn't support imagemaps, they'll see a text menu, from which they can choose a URL. ▪

Working with Mapping Programs

As mentioned previously, you can create the imagemap definition file the easy way or the hard way. The easy way is to use one of the many programs that will create the file for you. These programs are called *mapping tools*, and they let you draw various imagemap region types on top of a specified image.

Many map-editing programs are available for both Windows and the Macintosh. Generally speaking, most map-editing programs have the same basic features. They all support the three basic geometric region types, rect, poly, and circle. Some of the more advanced map-editing programs support the point- and default-region types. The only thing you should look for in imagemap-editing programs is how the user interface feels. Because such a wide variety is available, if one doesn't feel right to you, you don't have to use it.

> **T I P** Even though a map-editing program might not support every region type, you can still add other region types by editing the imagemap definition file after you have saved it.

Working with Mapedit

Mapedit is a shareware, no-frills, map-editing program for Windows 95 and UNIX. You can get Mapedit from **http://www.boutell.com/mapedit**. It was written by Thomas Boutell, maintainer of the FAQ (frequently asked questions) for the World Wide Web. This program allows you to create imagemap definition files in either CERN or NCSA format. Mapedit provides support for the basic geometric shapes, although the point-region type isn't supported.

Navigating Mapedit is pretty straightforward. To create a new imagemap definition file for your imagemap graphic, simply choose File and then choose Open/Create. Mapedit's Open dialog box then appears. You must have an existing imagemap graphic, which you can find by using the Browse button under the Image Filename heading. Mapedit supports GIF, JPEG, and the little-used PNG (Portable Network Graphics) image format for imagemap graphics.

N O T E PNG (Portable Network Graphics) is a new graphics file format that's similar to GIF. It's lossless, so you don't lose colors when it's compressed and portable across multiple platforms. The biggest advantage of PNG over GIF is that you're not stepping on anyone's patents when you use it. As well, PNG provides many technological benefits, such as interlaced images that appear on the screen quicker than GIF's interlaced images. Many browsers, including Internet Explorer, don't yet support PNG. ■

To edit an existing imagemap definition file, you can use the Browse button under the Map or HTML File heading (see Figure 12.8). To create a new imagemap definition file, simply type in the file name you want to use. Be sure to also specify whether you want a CERN or NCSA imagemap definition file, using the appropriate option buttons. Mapedit then asks you to confirm that you want to create a new imagemap.

FIG. 12.8

When you want to create or edit an imagemap file with Mapedit, you have to fill in the information for this dialog box.

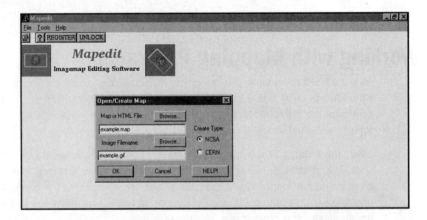

After you click the OK button, the shareware notification appears. After the graphic is loaded, the shareware dialog box is dismissed, and the whole image is loaded into Mapedit. If the image is bigger than the current screen resolution, you can use the scroll bars to see different parts of the picture.

N O T E If the colors on the imagemap graphic you specified look a little weird, don't worry. Mapedit isn't concerned with the way the picture looks; it's more concerned with the imagemap region types. ■

You can create any number of imagemap region types by choosing options from the Tools menu. You can create circle-, polygon-, or rectangle-region types. For people accustomed to many paint programs, or other imagemap creation programs, the region-creation interface is counterintuitive (see Table 12.2). Generally speaking, you can create shapes in other programs by clicking and holding the right mouse button, dragging the shape, and then releasing the mouse button. Unfortunately, in Mapedit, it's a matter of clicking and releasing the mouse button, dragging the shape, then reclicking and rereleasing the mouse button. After you have created a region type on the imagemap graphic, you can't delete it by using Mapedit.

Table 12.2 Creating Region Types by Using Mapedit

Region Type	How to Create
Circle	Click the left mouse button to specify the center of the desired circle. Use the mouse to specify the size of the circle. Click the right mouse button when the circle is the desired size.
Rectangle	Click the left mouse button to specify one corner of the rectangle. Use the mouse to specify the size of the rectangle. Click the right mouse button to specify the diagonally opposite corner of the first corner.
Polygon	Click the left mouse button to specify a corner of the polygon. Move the mouse to the next corner you want to specify. Repeat these steps for each corner of the polygon. When you're back to the first corner, click the right mouse button.

CAUTION

Mapedit works in very distinct "modes." That is, whatever option you last selected from the Tools menu is still active. If, for example, you just specified a URL for a rectangle-region type, the next region type you'll create is a rectangle. If you just selected the Test+Edit menu item, you remain in "Test+Edit" mode until you specify a region type.

Part
III

Ch
12

After you create a region type, the Object URL window opens (see Figure 12.9). Simply type in the URL to associate with the newly created region. You can define the default URL for the entire imagemap graphic by choosing File and then Edit Default URL.

If you can't see the outline of the region type as you're creating it, don't worry. Mapedit doesn't care about the appearance of the image in its window. To change the color of the outlines for each region type, choose File and then Edit Hotspot Color.

TIP If you make a mistake in the location of the region type, you can cancel its creation in two ways. You can either press Escape while you're specifying the size of the region, or you can click the Cancel button in the Object URL dialog box.

FIG. 12.9

After you create a region type, Mapedit asks for the URL to which that region should refer.

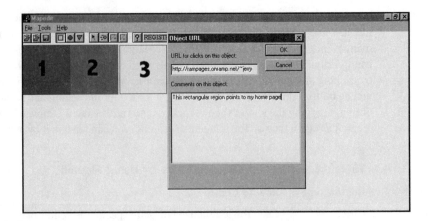

Using Mapedit, you can test the regions you've created. You choose Tools and then Test+Edit. When you press the left mouse button while moving the mouse over an imagemap, the URL for the corresponding region shows up. This testing capability is a function of Mapedit, and doesn't require a Web browser or server to use.

You can save your current imagemap definition file by choosing File and then either Save or Save As.

N O T E   Mapedit doesn't force any file-name extensions on you. As a result, when you're creating a new imagemap definition file, you need to specify the extension yourself. Most imagemap servers look for a file with the MAP extension. ■

Mapedit also allows you to easily change the position of hotspot regions. To move any clickable region, simply select the Tools menu heading, followed by the Move menu item. Next click the region you want to move, and a number of "control points" will show up. By clicking and dragging any of the control points that bound the region, you can reshape or resize it. If you click and drag the control point in the middle of the region, you'll move the entire region itself. Since Mapedit will still be in the Move mode, you can fine-tune the position of the clickable region.

Polygon regions can also be reshaped by adding or removing points in Mapedit. Just click the Tools menu heading, and choose either the Add Points or Remove Points menu items. These two options only work on polygon region types, and do as their name implies. With the Add Points option, click the polygon you want to add a point to, then put your mouse on roughly where you want the new point to appear. Similarly, for Remove Points, you click the polygon from which you want to remove a point, then select the point to remove.

Mapedit can also be used to create client-side imagemaps. Instead of loading in a MAP file, you specify an HTML file. Mapedit will look for any HTML that includes a graphic. Whatever images are found, it'll present a dialog box with the pictures that were found (see Figure 12.10). Select the picture you want to create a client-side imagemap for, and click the OK button. The file name for the image is automatically filled in Mapedit's Select Inline Image dialog box. Once you click the OK button, you'll be taken into Mapedit as usual. After you've created all the shapes you want, saving the changes will cause the HTML file to be updated.

FIG. 12.10

To create client-side imagemaps, just select the picture you want to make an imagemap for.

Using WebMap

WebMap, a capable Macintosh map-editing program, is currently free, until it's released commercially. You can get WebMap from **http://www.city.net/cnx/software/webmap.html**. It lets you create all the geometric region types from rectangles to circles and ellipses to polygons to points. It can create imagemap definition files for CERN, NCSA, or MacHTTP Web servers. It also enables you to easily move and change regions that have already been defined.

With this user-friendly program, you can easily create imagemap definition files. Simply choose File and then New. Then, using the Mac file selector, find the location of your imagemap graphic. This picture can be in either GIF or PICT graphics formats.

You can create as many imagemap region types as you want by using the floating toolbox next to the WebMap window (see Figure 12.11). The interface is similar to drawing programs (see Table 12.3). The only difference between the circle- and ellipse-region type is the circle has a constant radius. If you make a mistake in either the placement, size, or mere existence of a region type, you can fix it.

Part
III

Ch
12

FIG. 12.11

An alternative to creating a transparent GIF is to fill the background with the same color as the Web pages' background color; white in this case.

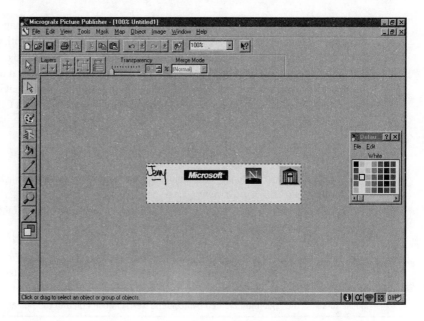

Table 12.3   Creating Region Types by Using WebMap

Region Type	How to Create
Circle	Click and hold the mouse button to specify a corner of the square to contain the circle. Hold down the mouse button and move the mouse to specify the size of the circle. Release the mouse button when the circle is the desired size.
Ellipse	Click and hold the mouse button to indicate a corner of the square in which the ellipse will reside. While holding down the mouse button, move the mouse to size the ellipse. Let go of the mouse button when the ellipse is at the size and shape you want.
Rectangle	Click and hold the mouse button to indicate a corner of the rectangle. Release the mouse button when the rectangle is the size you want.
Polygon	Click the mouse button to specify a corner of the polygon. Release the mouse button. Move the mouse pointer to the next corner you want to indicate. Repeat these steps for each corner of the polygon. After you specify the last corner, move the mouse pointer close to the first vertex and then click the mouse button.

CAUTION

With WebMap, you can't create a smaller region on top of a larger one. However, you can easily place larger region types on top of smaller ones. As a result, you have to plan carefully which regions you place when. You should place the smaller region types first and then work your way up to the largest regions.

After you've created all the regions you want, you can save the imagemap definition file by choosing File and then Save. This saves the imagemap definition file with an .m extension, which is the default extension that MacHTTP looks for in an imagemap definition file. WebMap also automatically saves the file in MacHTTP's custom format, making it unusable for the prevalent Web servers around. To create an imagemap definition file that other Web servers can use, choose File, Export As Text. You can specify to create either a CERN- or NCSA-compatible file.

CAUTION

WebMap assumes your imagemap definition file has the same name as the graphic. When you're editing an existing imagemap definition file, WebMap looks for an .m file based on the imagemap graphic's name. You therefore can't simply rename one of the files; you have to rename both of them. Otherwise, WebMap cannot see the other and will assume you're creating a new imagemap definition file.

 TIP Sometimes the Undo feature doesn't work with WebMap. If you've accidentally created a region and Undo doesn't work, just clear the region. Go to the toolbox and select the Arrow icon. Then use the mouse to select the region you created by accident. Next, choose Edit and then Clear.

Using Alternatives to Imagemaps

For whatever reason, you may not want to use HTML 3.2 imagemaps in your Web page. Maybe your audience is a group of text-only folks. Maybe your service provider doesn't support CGI scripts, and thus doesn't support server-side imagemaps, and you're afraid of abandoning those folks with older browsers. This section presents you with three alternatives to imagemaps:

Chunking images

Scripting

Textual alternatives

Image Chunks

Instead of defining rectangular regions within a larger image, you can divide the image into smaller images by using your favorite paint program. Then, you can insert each image into your Web page, causing it to appear to the user as a single image. Of course, you'll link each image to a different URL.

For example, if you divide a 100×100 image into four square chunks, each 50×50, you can combine them on the Web page like that shown in Listing 12.3.

Listing 12.3   An Imagemap Created from Individual Images

```
<A HREF=item1.html><IMG SRC=item1.gif WIDTH=50 HEIGHT=50 BORDER=0></A>
<A HREF=item2.html><IMG SRC=item2.gif WIDTH=50 HEIGHT=50 BORDER=0></A>
<BR>
<A HREF=item3.html><IMG SRC=item3.gif WIDTH=50 HEIGHT=50 BORDER=0></A>
<A HREF=item4.html><IMG SRC=item4.gif WIDTH=50 HEIGHT=50 BORDER=0></A>
```

Part
III

Ch
12

To the user, these four chunks will appear as one larger image. However, each chunk is linked to a different URL. Note that you must specify the exact height and width of the image and turn off borders.

 TIP   You can also use tables to assemble each portion of the imagemap.

Scripting

Part V, "Programming and Scripting," provides a thorough description of scripting a Web page. You can use VBScript or JavaScript to create client-side imagemaps. That is, you can associate a script with the mouse-click event of an image. Then, when the user clicks the mouse on that image, you can open a different URL depending on the area of the image on which the user clicked. Chapter 29, "VBScript," shows you how to create a client-side imagemap by using a script.

Textual Alternatives

Imagemaps and graphics in general don't translate particularly well into text. In fact, they don't translate at all. For this reason, you should provide some alternatives for people who don't have graphical browsers. Also bear in mind that some people have configured their browsers so they don't automatically load pictures. People who access the Web through UNIX's command-line mode and people with slow modems fall into these categories. Because they are a strong minority, you have to provide some support for them.

You can let nongraphics people access the various points on your imagemap in a number of ways. You can provide a separate home page for these people and mention it in your graphics-heavy page. You also can put in regular hypertext links at the top or bottom of all your home pages. These links can point to the same links accessible through the imagemaps. Whichever approach meets your fancy, you should take one of them. If you ignore the text-only crowd, you're alienating a large group of people.

Example: Building an Imagemap

You've learned a lot of general information about creating imagemaps, but you'll benefit more from walking through an example, beginning to end. The example in this section is a simple imagemap that you can use as a toolbar. The image is straightforward. When creating your own imagemap, however, you can substitute images from your own favorite clip-art library or images you create by hand. The following instructions show you how to create an imagemap:

1. Decide what links you want in your imagemap and how you want to communicate those links to the user. Then, sketch out a rough idea of what you want the imagemap to look like before you start drawing it. In this example, I'm creating regions for the following links: **http://rampages.onramp.net/~jerry**, **http://www.microsoft.com**, **http://www.netscape.com**, and **http://www.mcp.com**.

2. Open your graphics program (Micrografx Picture Publisher) and, in this example, create a new image that's 320 pixels in width and 80 pixels in height.

3. Add each graphic, which represents each link you're putting in the toolbar, to the image. Position the graphics so that they're spread evenly across the imagemap, as shown in Figure 12.12.

4. Add text labels underneath each graphic so the user can easily discern what each image does (see Figure 12.12).

5. Save the image as a GIF file called IMAGEMAP.GIF.

6. Open IMAGEMAP.GIF in Mapedit, or your favorite imagemap editor.

7. Create a rectangular region around each graphic in the toolbar. Don't forget to include the text label that you added underneath each graphic in the region.

8. Save the imagemap definition to a file called IMAGEMAP.MAP. Listing 12.4 shows you what the imagemap definition file for this example looks like:

FIG. 12.12

In imagemaps used as toolbars, text labels help the user understand what each icon represents.

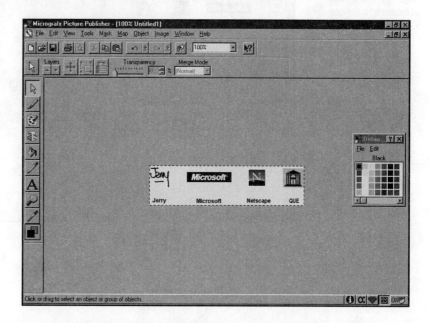

Listing 12.4   Imagemap Definition File: IMAGEMAP.MAP

```
rect http://rampages.onramp.net/~jerry 1,0 39,77
rect http://www.microsoft.com 75,8 169,79
rect http://www.netscape.com 199,4 251,79
rect http://www.mcp.com 273,4 323,82
```

Part
III

Ch
12

9. Add the following line of code to your HTML file. You'll replace *www.myserver.com/cgi-bin* with the path that's appropriate for your Web server. Ask your Web server administrator if you're not sure what path to use. Alternatively, you can create a client-side imagemap by using the Mapedit as described earlier in this chapter. Figure 12.13 shows you what the completed example looks like.

```
<A HREF="http://www.myserver.com/cgi-bin/imagemap.map">
<IMG SRC=imagemap.gif ISMAP></A>
```

FIG. 12.13

You can position the toolbar at the top and bottom of the Web page to make it more accessible to the user.

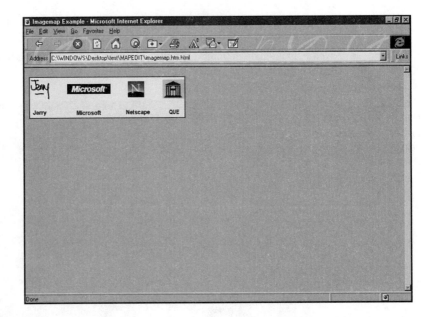

## CHAPTER 13

Layers

by Jerry Honeycutt

In the desktop publishing world, layers are rectangular blocks of text and artwork that you can position anywhere on the page that you like. You can also overlap layers so that one is hidden behind another or so that one bleeds through another. Publishers use layers to create some pretty awesome layouts. Take a look at some print advertisements or brochures, for example. Chances are, the publisher used layers.

While desktop publishers take layers for granted (even the simplest of desktop publishing programs allow you to create and overlap layers); HTML designers don't. They've never had the capability to overlap blocks of text and artwork because HTML is streaming. That is, each preceding HTML element is displayed before the next; in order. HTML has never provided for the positioning of an HTML element, much less for overlapping HTML elements.

Until now.

Netscape Navigator 4.0 introduces the <LAYER> tag. You use this tag to create layers, which you can position anywhere on the HTML document, overlapping the HTML document and other layers. You can use it to create advanced layouts on your HTML document, to create simple animations such as a curtain that unveils the contents of your document, or even to provide simple fly-over help for each link on the HTML document. ■

Easily add layers to your HTML documents

The <LAYER> tag gives you real publishing capabilities. It's easy, too.

Overlap multiple layers

You have complete control over the way overlapped layers appear in your HTML document.

Control your layers with scripts

The real power of layers comes from controlling them with scripts. This chapter shows you how.

Create groups by nesting layers

You can insert one layer within another. The nested layer always moves with the outside layer.

Create fly-over help using layers

The example at the end of this chapter shows you how to create fly-over help for each of your links.

You can put any valid HTML within a layer. You can even put plug-ins within a layer.

Creating a Basic Layer

Listing 13.1 shows the most basic usage of the <LAYER> tag. You simply enclose the contents of the layer within <LAYER> and </LAYER>. No attributes. As shown in Figure 13.1, however, you can hardly tell the difference between this result and streaming HTML.

The sections that follow show you how to really use the <LAYER> tag. You can position a layer anywhere you like, change the size of a layer, or even change the background of the layer. A bit later in this chapter, you also learn how to overlap layers and control layers with scripts.

Listing 13.1   A Simple *<LAYER>* Tag

```
<HTML>
<HEAD>
<TITLE>Layer 1</TITLE>
</HEAD>
<BODY>

<P>This example shows what a basic layer that contains an image.
Note that the layer isn't positioned in any way whatsoever. Thus,
you can hardly tell it from in-line HTML.</P>
<LAYER>
<IMG SRC=init.gif>
</LAYER>

</BODY>
</HTML>
```

CAUTION

<LAYER> is not part of HTML 3.2 and is only supported by Navigator 4.0. Thus, if you're concerned about compatibility with Internet Explorer, you should avoid the <LAYER> tag or provide an alternate HTML document for those users.

N O T E   Internet Explorer does have support for layers through a different technology. You use the HTML Layout Control. See Chapter 23, "ActiveX Control Pad," for more information. ▪

▶ **See** "Controlling Page Layout with the HTML Layout Control," **p. 524**

FIG. 13.1
Without positioning the layer, you can't tell the difference between this result and streaming HTML.

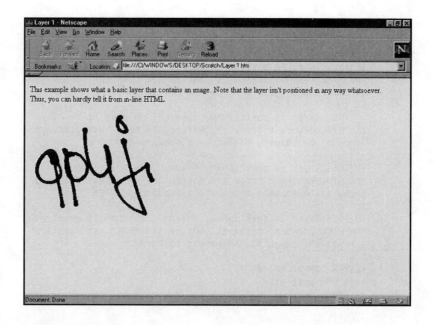

Positioning a Layer

Positioning a layer on your HTML document is real power. You no longer have to struggle to get just the look you want with HTML. Now, you create any look you like by creating individual blocks of HTML and positioning them individually using the LEFT and TOP attributes of the <LAYER> tag, like this:

```
<LAYER TOP=100 LEFT=20>
```

LEFT and TOP are represented in pixels, and are relative to the top-left corner of the containing area within the HTML document. That is, these attributes are relative to the area created if you remove the <LAYER> and </LAYER> tags. For example, to create a layer 10 pixels from the left edge of the browser window and 40 pixels from the top edge, use LEFT=10 and TOP=40. The browser draws the HTML document as though the entire <LAYER> container did not exist, and then the layer is overlapped with the Web page at the given offset.

Listing 13.2 shows an HTML document with a layer positioned at 0, 0. Notice in Figure 13.2 how the contents of the HTML document show through the layer.

Part
III

Ch
13

Listing 13.2 Positioning a Layer

```
<HTML>
<HEAD>
<TITLE>Layer 2</TITLE>
</HEAD>
<BODY>
```

continues

Listing 13.2 Continued

```
<P>This example shows what the same basic layer.</P>
<P>This layer is positioned, however, so that it overlaps
the HTML document below it. Notice how this text displays
through the image's transparent background.</P>

<P>This layer is positioned, however, so that it overlaps
the HTML document below it. Notice how this text displays
through the image's transparent background.</P>

<P>This layer is positioned, however, so that it overlaps
the HTML document below it. Notice how this text displays
through the image's transparent background.</P>

<P>This layer is positioned, however, so that it overlaps
the HTML document below it. Notice how this text displays
through the image's transparent background.</P>

<LAYER TOP=0 LEFT=0>
<IMG SRC=init.gif>
</LAYER>

</BODY>
</HTML>
```

FIG. 13.2

Using a layer positioned at 0, 0, you can write HTML that fits snugly against the left border of the browser window.

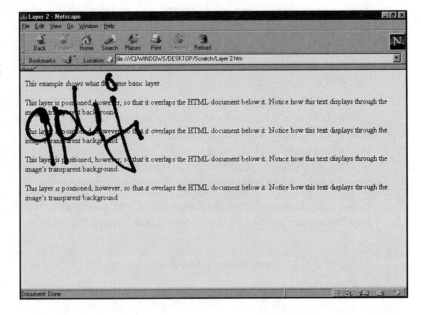

NOTE Positioning a layer at 0,0 isn't the same as omitting the LEFT and TOP attributes from the <LAYER> tag. Positioning a layer at 0, 0 causes the layer to overlap the Web page at the top-left corner. Omitting the LEFT and TOP attributes causes the contents of the layer to appear inline. ■

Listing 13.3 is a similar example that positions the layer in the middle of the Web page. As shown in Figure 13.3, the contents of the HTML document bleed through the contents of the layer.

Listing 13.3   Placing a Layer in the Middle of the Page

```
<HTML>
<HEAD>
<TITLE>Layer 3</TITLE>
</HEAD>
<BODY>

<P>You can position the layer anywhere you like.</P>
<P>This layer is positioned, however, so that it overlaps
the HTML document below it. Notice how this text displays
through the image's transparent background.</P>

<P>This layer is positioned, however, so that it overlaps
the HTML document below it. Notice how this text displays
through the image's transparent background.</P>

<P>This layer is positioned, however, so that it overlaps
the HTML document below it. Notice how this text displays
through the image's transparent background.</P>

<P>This layer is positioned, however, so that it overlaps
the HTML document below it. Notice how this text displays
through the image's transparent background.</P>

<LAYER TOP=40 LEFT=100>
<IMG SRC=init.gif>
</LAYER>

</BODY>
</HTML>
```

Part
III

Ch
13

CAUTION

Careful! If the layer doesn't entirely fit within the browser window, the browser clips the layer.

FIG. 13.3

You can position the
layer wherever you want
on the browser window.

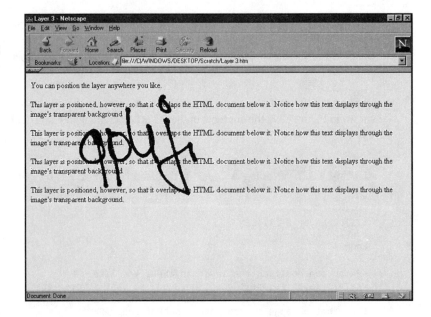

Changing the Size of a Layer

You can't change the height of a layer, because the height is determined by the size of the
layer's content. You can control the width of a layer, however, and let the browser determine
the appropriate height. You use the <LAYER> tag's WIDTH attribute to set the width of the layer in
pixels:

```
<LAYER TOP=5 LEFT=5 WIDTH=300>
```

You don't use the WIDTH attribute to define the absolute width of the layer. What this attribute
does is suggest a width for purposes of wrapping the text contained within the layer. If the text
doesn't completely fill the layer, however, the layer will not actually be as wide as the specified
value. If you're inserting an image (or another element that the browser can't wrap) inside of a
layer, and the image is wider than the suggested width, the actual width of the layer will be
bigger than the suggested value.

Listing 13.4 shows an example of a layer positioned 100 pixels from the top that is 60 pixels
wide. As shown in Figure 13.4, the text wraps within the layer, just as it would wrap within a
table cell that's 60 pixels wide.

Listing 13.4 Specifying the Width of a Layer

```
<HTML>
<HEAD>
<TITLE>Layer 6</TITLE>
```

```
</HEAD>
<BODY>

<LAYER TOP=0>
This text is contained within the first layer. It starts in the
upper, left-hand corner of the browser window. Notice that the
width of this layer isn't controlled.
</LAYER>

<LAYER TOP=100 WIDTH=160>
This text is contained within the first layer. It starts in the
upper, left-hand corner of the browser window. Notice how the width
of this layer is controlled.
</LAYER>

</BODY>
</HTML>
```

FIG. 13.4

You can leave either the TOP or LEFT attributes out, and the browser will position the layer as though the omitted attribute is 0.

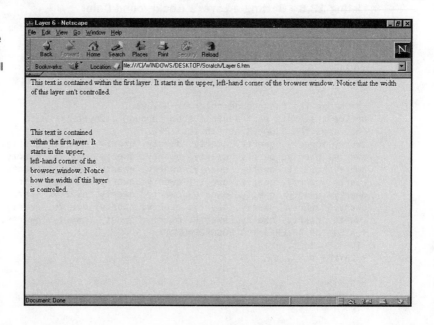

TIP You can use a layer to do many of the same formatting tricks you've learned to do with the <TABLE> tag.

▶ **See** "Using Tables as a Layout Tool," **p. 162**

Part
III

Ch
13

Using a Background Image or Color

By default, the empty space in a layer is transparent. That is, if a pixel in the layer doesn't contain any rendered text or it contains a portion of an image that's transparent, anything underneath the layer shows through at that point. You can use this to create some incredible effects.

However, if a layer contains mostly text and it's overlapped, the content of the layer might be hard to read. Regardless, you might want the layer to be better defined; to occupy a well-defined space on the HTML document. You use a background image or background color with a layer so that what's behind the layer doesn't show through.

Listing 13.5 shows a layer that defines a background color for a layer by using the BGCOLOR attribute. You can set this attribute to any valid color name or color value (#FF0000, for example). As Figure 13.5 shows, the content behind the layer no longer shows through.

Listing 13.5   Setting a Layer's Background Color

```
<HTML>
<HEAD>
<TITLE>Layer 4</TITLE>
</HEAD>
<BODY>

<P>Change the background color of a layer.
Notice that this text doesn't show through a layer
that uses the BGCOLOR attribute.</P>
qwerty. qwerty. qwerty. qwerty. qwerty. qwerty. qwerty. qwerty. qwerty.
qwerty. qwerty. qwerty. qwerty. qwerty. qwerty. qwerty. qwerty. qwerty.
qwerty. qwerty. qwerty. qwerty. qwerty. qwerty. qwerty. qwerty. qwerty.
qwerty. qwerty. qwerty. qwerty. qwerty. qwerty. qwerty. qwerty. qwerty.
qwerty. qwerty. qwerty. qwerty. qwerty. qwerty. qwerty. qwerty. qwerty.
qwerty. qwerty. qwerty. qwerty. qwerty. qwerty. qwerty. qwerty. qwerty.
qwerty. qwerty. qwerty. qwerty. qwerty. qwerty. qwerty. qwerty. qwerty.
<LAYER TOP=40 LEFT=100 BGCOLOR=GRAY>
<IMG SRC=init.gif>
</LAYER>

</BODY>
</HTML>
```

Listing 13.6 shows you a similar example that sets a background image for the layer by using the BACKGROUND attribute. You set the BACKGROUND attribute to the URL (relative or absolute) of the image you want to tile in the background of the layer. Unlike normal tiled backgrounds, if a layer's background image has transparent areas, the content behind the layer shows through them. Figure 13.6 shows what this example looks like in the browser window.

FIG. 13.5

When you use a background color, the content behind the layer doesn't bleed through.

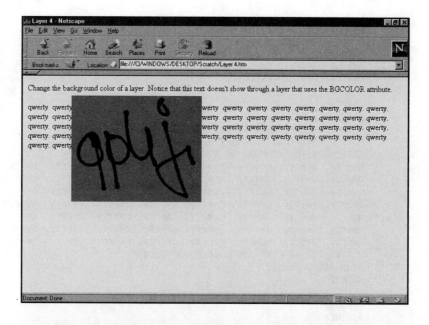

FIG. 13.6

You can create a border for a layer by creating a border in your favorite graphics editor and inserting it into the layer.

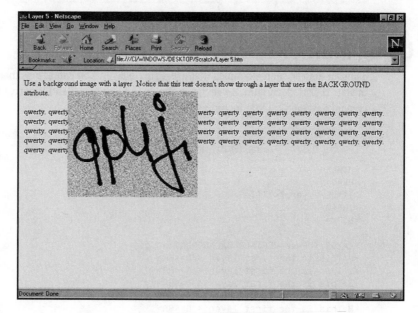

Listing 13.6 Setting a Layer's Background Image

```
<HTML>
<HEAD>
<TITLE>Layer 5</TITLE>
</HEAD>
<BODY>

<P>Use a background image with a layer.
Notice that this text doesn't show through a layer
that uses the BACKGROUND attribute.</P>
qwerty. qwerty. qwerty. qwerty. qwerty. qwerty. qwerty. qwerty. qwerty.
qwerty. qwerty. qwerty. qwerty. qwerty. qwerty. qwerty. qwerty. qwerty.
qwerty. qwerty. qwerty. qwerty. qwerty. qwerty. qwerty. qwerty. qwerty.
qwerty. qwerty. qwerty. qwerty. qwerty. qwerty. qwerty. qwerty. qwerty.
qwerty. qwerty. qwerty. qwerty. qwerty. qwerty. qwerty. qwerty. qwerty.
qwerty. qwerty. qwerty. qwerty. qwerty. qwerty. qwerty. qwerty. qwerty.
qwerty. qwerty. qwerty. qwerty. qwerty. qwerty. qwerty. qwerty. qwerty.
<LAYER TOP=40 LEFT=100 BACKGROUND=bg.gif>
<IMG SRC=init.gif>
</LAYER>

</BODY>
</HTML>
```

Using Multiple Layers

Thus far, you've seen examples that use a single layer. You can add as many layers as you like in your HTML document, however, as shown in Listing 13.7 and Figure 13.7. Each layer can contain any valid HTML, including images, text, and plug-ins.

Listing 13.7 Using Multiple Layers

```
<HTML>
<HEAD>
<TITLE>Layer 7</TITLE>
</HEAD>
<BODY>

<LAYER TOP=40 LEFT=60 BACKGROUND=bg.gif>
<B>This is the first layer.</B><BR>
<B>This is the first layer.</B><BR>
<B>This is the first layer.</B><BR>
<B>This is the first layer.</B><BR>
<B>This is the first layer.</B><BR>
<B>This is the first layer.</B><BR>
<B>This is the first layer.</B><BR>
<B>This is the first layer.</B><BR>
</LAYER>

<LAYER TOP=40 LEFT=220>
```

```
<IMG SRC=init.gif>
</LAYER>

</BODY>
</HTML>
```

FIG. 13.7
You can build your entire HTML document using layers, and then arrange them as you like.

You can also cause layers to overlap by setting each layer's TOP and LEFT attributes so that one layer appears on top of another. Figure 13.8 shows two layers. The first layer contains a handful of text and has a background image. The second layer contains an image with a transparent background. The second layer is positioned so that it overlaps the first layer (see Listing 13.8).

Listing 13.8 Making Two Layers Overlap

```
<HTML>
<HEAD>
<TITLE>Layer 8</TITLE>
</HEAD>
<BODY>

<LAYER TOP=40 LEFT=60 BACKGROUND=bg.gif>
<B>This is the first layer. It's behind the second layer.</B><BR>
<B>This is the first layer. It's behind the second layer.</B><BR>
<B>This is the first layer. It's behind the second layer.</B><BR>
<B>This is the first layer. It's behind the second layer.</B><BR>
<B>This is the first layer. It's behind the second layer.</B><BR>
<B>This is the first layer. It's behind the second layer.</B><BR>
<B>This is the first layer. It's behind the second layer.</B><BR>
<B>This is the first layer. It's behind the second layer.</B><BR>
<B>This is the first layer. It's behind the second layer.</B><BR>
```

Part
III

Ch

13

continues

Listing 13.8 Continued

```
</LAYER>

<LAYER TOP=80 LEFT=200>
<IMG SRC=init.gif>
</LAYER>

</BODY>
</HTML>
```

FIG. 13.8
Since the image in the second layer has transparent areas, the content behind this layer bleeds through.

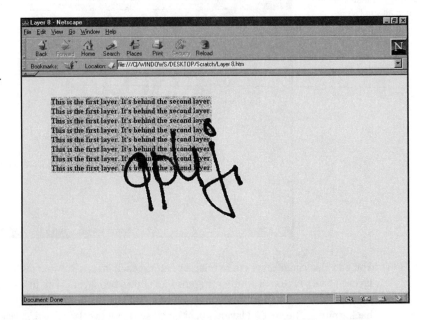

N O T E By default, the browser draws overlapped layers in the order it encounters them. That is, it draws the first layer, overlaps that with the second layer, and so on. ▄

Changing a Layer's *Z-INDEX*

If you don't like the order in which the browser overlaps layers, you can change it. The most straightforward way to change the order in which layers overlap is by using the <LAYER> tag's Z-INDEX attribute, which defines the stacking order for layers:

```
<LAYER Z-INDEX=1>
```

You set this attribute to any positive integer value. A layer with a stacking order larger than another draws over the other layer. For example, a layer with a stacking order of ten overlaps a layer with a stacking order of five. On the other hand, a layer with a stacking order of three is overlapped by a layer with a stacking order of five.

Listing 13.9 is an example of three layers, each of which uses the Z-INDEX attribute to define its stacking order. The first layer has a stacking order of two; the second has a stacking order of one; and the third has a stacking order of three. Thus, the browser draws the second layer first, the first layer second, and the third layer last, as shown in Figure 13.9.

FIG. 13.9
The Z-INDEX attribute essentially defines the order in which each layer is drawn.

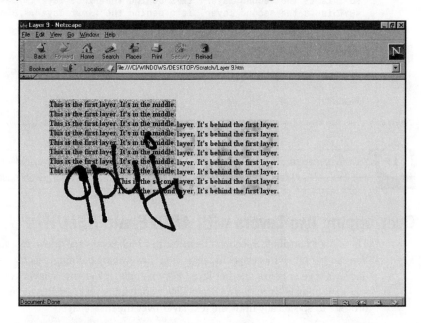

Listing 13.9 Using *Z-INDEX*

```
<HTML>
<HEAD>
<TITLE>Layer 9</TITLE>
</HEAD>
<BODY>

<LAYER TOP=40 LEFT=60 BACKGROUND=bg.gif Z-INDEX=2>
<B>This is the first layer. It's in the middle.</B><BR>
<B>This is the first layer. It's in the middle.</B><BR>
<B>This is the first layer. It's in the middle.</B><BR>
<B>This is the first layer. It's in the middle.</B><BR>
<B>This is the first layer. It's in the middle.</B><BR>
<B>This is the first layer. It's in the middle.</B><BR>
<B>This is the first layer. It's in the middle.</B><BR>
<B>This is the first layer. It's in the middle.</B><BR>
</LAYER>

<LAYER TOP=80 LEFT=200 BACKGROUND=bg2.gif Z-INDEX=1>
<B>This is the second layer. It's behind the first layer.</B><BR>
<B>This is the second layer. It's behind the first layer.</B><BR>
<B>This is the second layer. It's behind the first layer.</B><BR>
<B>This is the second layer. It's behind the first layer.</B><BR>
```

Part
III

Ch
13

continues

Listing 13.9 Continued

```
<B>This is the second layer. It's behind the first layer.</B><BR>
<B>This is the second layer. It's behind the first layer.</B><BR>
<B>This is the second layer. It's behind the first layer.</B><BR>
<B>This is the second layer. It's behind the first layer.</B><BR>
</LAYER>

<LAYER TOP=100 LEFT=80 Z-INDEX=3>
<IMG SRC=init.gif>
</LAYER>

</BODY>
</HTML>
```

 TIP You can overlap several layers at the same position, define each layer's stacking order in sequence, and then peel away the layers one at a time (using a script) to create a simple animation.

Overlapping Two Layers with *ABOVE* and *BELOW*

The Z-INDEX attribute specifies the order in which layers are drawn by ranking each layer. You can get much more specific than that, however, by defining exactly which layer you want to display above or below another layer. For example, if you have a layer containing an image, and you want to make sure that a specific layer containing text is displayed over it, you can tell the browser to specifically draw the text layer over the image layer.

Before you can do that, however, you have to give each layer a name. Use the NAME attribute, like this:

```
<LAYER NAME=MYLAYER>
```

Then, when creating a new layer, you specify which layer you want to draw above or below it. You use the <LAYER> tag's ABOVE attribute to specify which previously defined layer draws above it, or use its BELOW attribute to specify which previously defined layer draws below it. Both of these attributes are mutually exclusive. For example, if you have an existing layer called MYLAYER, and you want to make sure that the browser draws it below a layer, you'd write a <LAYER> tag that looks like this:

```
<LAYER BELOW=MYLAYER>
```

On the other hand, if you want to make sure that the browser draws MYLAYER on top of a new layer, you'd write the new <LAYER> tag that looks like this:

```
<LAYER ABOVE=MYLAYER>
```

Listing 13.10 shows the example from Listing 13.9, using the ABOVE and BELOW attributes. Instead of defining a Z-INDEX for each layer, it specifies that the layer called FIRST is above the layer called SECOND and below the layer called THIRD (see Figure 13.10).

FIG. 13.10
If you specify an order that doesn't make sense, Navigator gets very confused and displays nonsense.

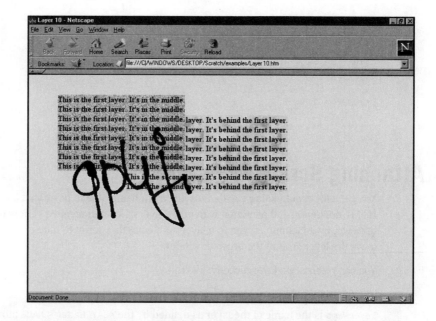

Listing 13.10   Using *ABOVE* and *BELOW* to Specify Order

```
<HTML>
<HEAD>
<TITLE>Layer 10</TITLE>
</HEAD>
<BODY>

<LAYER NAME=FIRST TOP=40 LEFT=60 BACKGROUND=bg.gif>
<B>This is the first layer. It's in the middle.</B><BR>
<B>This is the first layer. It's in the middle.</B><BR>
<B>This is the first layer. It's in the middle.</B><BR>
<B>This is the first layer. It's in the middle.</B><BR>
<B>This is the first layer. It's in the middle.</B><BR>
<B>This is the first layer. It's in the middle.</B><BR>
<B>This is the first layer. It's in the middle.</B><BR>
<B>This is the first layer. It's in the middle.</B><BR>
</LAYER>

<LAYER NAME=SECOND TOP=80 LEFT=200 BACKGROUND=bg2.gif ABOVE=FIRST>
<B>This is the second layer. It's behind the first layer.</B><BR>
<B>This is the second layer. It's behind the first layer.</B><BR>
<B>This is the second layer. It's behind the first layer.</B><BR>
<B>This is the second layer. It's behind the first layer.</B><BR>
<B>This is the second layer. It's behind the first layer.</B><BR>
<B>This is the second layer. It's behind the first layer.</B><BR>
<B>This is the second layer. It's behind the first layer.</B><BR>
<B>This is the second layer. It's behind the first layer.</B><BR>
</LAYER>
```

Part
III

Ch
13

continues

Listing 13.10   Continued

```
<LAYER NAME=THIRD TOP=100 LEFT=80 BELOW=FIRST>
<IMG SRC=init.gif>
</LAYER>

</BODY>
</HTML>
```

Attaching Scripts to Layers

You get a lot of publishing capabilities just from being able to position a layer anywhere on an HTML document and overlap it with other layers. You can create a variety of special effects, however, by attaching a script to a layer and using that script to hide or show the layer; or even move the layer around the browser window.

You can reference a layer directly, like this:

```
Layers.LayerName
```

LayerName is the name of the layer as defined by the `<LAYER>` tag's NAME attribute. You can also reference a layer using the layers array: `document.layers`. You can use an index with the layers array or you can reference a layer in the array by name:

```
document.layers[2]
document.layers["MyLayer"]
```

▶ **See** Chapter 27, "JavaScript/JScript," **p. 599**

Layers have a variety of properties and methods. A reference to a layer's property looks like *LayerName.PropertyName* and a reference to a layer's method looks like *LayerName. MethodName(Parameters)*. For example, to make a layer invisible, you set its `visibility` property to HIDE, like this:

```
layers.MyLayer.visibility = "hide";
```

▶ **See** "Using Functions, Objects, and Properties," **p. 604**

Table 13.1 describes the layer object's properties. These properties roughly correspond to the attributes you've already learned about in this chapter.

Table 13.1   The Layer Object's Properties

Property	Description
name	Contains the name of the layer; you can't change this property.
left	Specifies the left offset of the layer.
top	Specifies the top offset of the layer.
visibility	Contains "hide" or "inherit"; note that these are strings, not keywords.

Property	Description
clip	Defines the region of the layer that's displayed; clip has the subproperties left, top, right, bottom, width, and height.
siblingAbove	Contains the name of the layer displayed immediately above the referenced layer.
siblingBelow	Contains the name of the layer displayed immediately below the referenced layer.
parentLayer	Contains the name of the layer that contains the reference layer if the layer is nested.
layers	An array that contains all of the child layers that are nested within the referenced layer.

Table 13.2 describes the layer object's methods.

Table 13.2   The Layer Object's Methods

Method	Description
offset(x,y)	Offsets the layer by the given axis so that LEFT = LEFT + x and TOP = TOP + y.
moveTo(x,y)	Changes the layer's position so that LEFT = x and TOP = y.
resize(width, height)	Changes the height and width of the layer's clipping rectangle.
moveAbove(layer)	Stacks the referenced layer above the layer called layer.
moveBelow(layer)	Stacks the referenced layer below the layer called layer.

Using a Script to Hide or Show a Layer

You can use a script to hide and show layers on the HTML document. For example, you can create a layer that you want to display only when the user moves the mouse across an image. In that case, you'd set the layer's VISIBILITY attribute to "HIDE" so that it's not displayed initially. Then, in the image's OnMouseOver event, you'd set the layer's visibility property to "SHOW", like this:

```
Layers.MyLayer.visibility = "show";
```

N O T E   As of this writing, Navigator 4.0 doesn't support SHOW. It does support the INHERIT value, which specifies that the layer inherits the visibility property of the parent layer, however. Thus, the examples in this book use the INHERIT value. By the time you get your hands on this book, Navigator will support the SHOW value. ■

Listing 13.11 shows you an example that does something similar. It contains three layers and three buttons. The script associated with each button toggles the visibility of each layer. Click

Part
III

Ch
13

a button associated with a visible layer, and the script makes the layer invisible (see Figure 13.11).

Take a look at the function called ToggleFirst(). It toggles the state of the flag called ShowFirst, which indicates whether or not the layer called FIRST is visible. Then, it sets the layer's visibility property to "HIDE" if ShowFirst is false; otherwise, it sets the property to "INHERIT."

Listing 13.11   Hiding and Showing Layers

```
<HTML>
<HEAD>
<TITLE>Layer 11</TITLE>

<SCRIPT LANGUAGE=JAVASCRIPT>
ShowFirst = true;
ShowSecond=false;
ShowThird=true;
function ToggleFirst()
{
ShowFirst = !ShowFirst;
document.layers["FIRST"].visibility = ShowFirst ? "INHERIT" : "HIDE";
}

function ToggleSecond()
{
ShowSecond = !ShowSecond;
document.layers["SECOND"].visibility = ShowSecond ? "INHERIT" : "HIDE";
}

function ToggleThird()
{
ShowThird = !ShowThird;
document.layers["THIRD"].visibility = ShowThird ? "INHERIT" : "HIDE";
}

</SCRIPT>
</HEAD>
<BODY>
<LAYER NAME=FIRST TOP=80 LEFT=60 BACKGROUND=bg.gif>
<B>This is the first layer. It's in the middle.</B><BR>
<B>This is the first layer. It's in the middle.</B><BR>
<B>This is the first layer. It's in the middle.</B><BR>
<B>This is the first layer. It's in the middle.</B><BR>
<B>This is the first layer. It's in the middle.</B><BR>
<B>This is the first layer. It's in the middle.</B><BR>
<B>This is the first layer. It's in the middle.</B><BR>
<B>This is the first layer. It's in the middle.</B><BR>
</LAYER>

<LAYER NAME=SECOND TOP=120 LEFT=200 BACKGROUND=bg2.gif Z-INDEX=1 BELOW=FIRST
VISIBILITY=HIDE>
<B>This is the second layer. It's behind the first layer.</B><BR>
<B>This is the second layer. It's behind the first layer.</B><BR>
<B>This is the second layer. It's behind the first layer.</B><BR>
```

```
<B>This is the second layer. It's behind the first layer.</B><BR>
<B>This is the second layer. It's behind the first layer.</B><BR>
<B>This is the second layer. It's behind the first layer.</B><BR>
<B>This is the second layer. It's behind the first layer.</B><BR>
<B>This is the second layer. It's behind the first layer.</B><BR>
</LAYER>

<LAYER NAME=THIRD TOP=140 LEFT=80 BELOW=FIRST>
<IMG SRC=init.gif>
</LAYER>

<LAYER TOP=0 LEFT=0>
<FORM NAME=TOGGLE>
<TABLE ALIGN=CENTER>
<TD>
<INPUT NAME=FIRST TYPE=BUTTON VALUE="Toggle First Layer "
➥onclick="ToggleFirst();">
</TD>
<TD>
<INPUT NAME=SECOND TYPE=BUTTON VALUE="Toggle Second Layer"
➥onclick="ToggleSecond();">
</TD>
<TD>
<INPUT NAME=THIRD TYPE=BUTTON VALUE="Toggle Third Layer "
➥onclick="ToggleThird();">
</TD>
</TABLE>
</FORM>
</LAYER>

</BODY>
</HTML>
```

FIG. 13.11

As you click buttons to hide a layer, the browser peels that layer away, unveiling what's underneath.

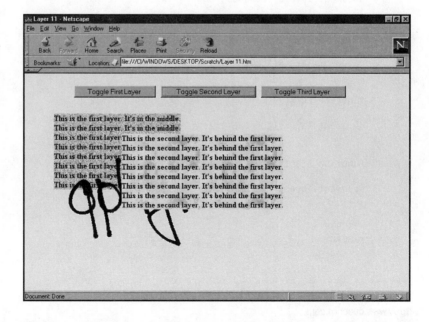

Part
III

Ch
13

TIP In Windows, you've seen dialog boxes that contain a button with the text More>>. When you click that button, additional fields are presented. You can achieve the same effect in an HTML form by attaching a script to a form's button that shows another form hidden within a layer.

Moving a Layer with a Script

Besides showing and hiding a layer, you can also move it around on the Web page. You can use this to create some pretty fancy animations, such as a current that appears to open, unveiling the contents of the page. Moving a layer around is easy. You can either use the offset or moveTo methods; or you can set the value of the left and top properties, which is the approach taken in Listing 13.12 and Figure 13.12.

This example contains two layers. It also contains four buttons, labeled Up, Down, Left, and Right. Each button is associated with a function that moves the second layer in the appropriate direction. For example, the Up function subtracts 10 from the second layer's top property, which has the effect of moving the layer up 10 pixels. The Right function adds 10 to the second layer's left property, which has the effect of moving the layer right 10 pixels.

Listing 13.12   Moving a Layer with a Script

```
<HTML>
<HEAD>
<TITLE>Layer 12</TITLE>

<SCRIPT LANGUAGE=JAVASCRIPT>
function Up()
{
document.layers["SECOND"].top -= 10;
}

function Down()
{
document.layers["SECOND"].top += 10;
}

function Left()
{
document.layers["SECOND"].left -= 10;
}

function Right()
{
document.layers["SECOND"].left += 10;
}

</SCRIPT>
</HEAD>
```

```
<BODY>

<LAYER NAME=FIRST TOP=200 LEFT=300 BACKGROUND=bg.gif>
<B>This is the first layer. It's always on top.</B><BR>
<B>This is the first layer. It's always on top.</B><BR>
<B>This is the first layer. It's always on top.</B><BR>
<B>This is the first layer. It's always on top.</B><BR>
<B>This is the first layer. It's always on top.</B><BR>
<B>This is the first layer. It's always on top.</B><BR>
<B>This is the first layer. It's always on top.</B><BR>
<B>This is the first layer. It's always on top.</B><BR>
<B>This is the first layer. It's always on top.</B><BR>
</LAYER>

<LAYER NAME=SECOND TOP=180 LEFT=0 ABOVE=FIRST>
<IMG SRC=init.gif>
</LAYER>

<LAYER TOP=0 LEFT=0>
<FORM NAME=BUTTONS>
<TABLE>
<TR>
<TD></TD>
<TD ALIGN=CENTER>
<INPUT WIDTH=100% NAME=UP TYPE=BUTTON VALUE="Up" onclick="Up();">
</TD>
<TD></TD>
</TR>

<TR>
<TD ALIGN=CENTER>
<INPUT NAME=LEFT TYPE=BUTTON VALUE="Left " onclick="Left();">
</TD>
<TD></TD>
<TD ALIGN=CENTER>
<INPUT WIDTH=100 NAME=RIGHT TYPE=BUTTON VALUE="Right" onclick="Right();">
</TD>
</TR>

<TR>
<TD></TD>
<TD ALIGN=CENTER>
<INPUT WIDTH=100 NAME=DOWN TYPE=BUTTON VALUE="Down " onclick="Down();">
</TD>
<TD></TD>
</TR>

</TABLE>
</FORM>
</LAYER>

</BODY>
</HTML>
```

Part
III

Ch
13

FIG. 13.12

As you move the second layer by the first layer, it disappears under the first layer, because the second layer's ABOVE property is set to FIRST.

 T I P Resizing the Web browser causes the layers to return to their original position.

Nesting Layers

So far, you've only seen cases where a handful of layers were added to the HTML document. They were siblings in that one was not contained within another. You can insert one layer inside of another layer, however, to create a parent-child relationship. In that case, the child (inside) layer is relative to the parent (outside) layer. Thus, if you create a layer called PARENT and locate it at 10, 10; and nest a layer inside of PARENT called CHILD located at 5, 5; the child layer will actually display at 15, 15 on the HTML document. If you move the parent layer to 20, 20, the child layer will move right along with it to 25, 25.

Listing 13.13 shows you an example of nested layers. The parent layer contains an image of a rough Christmas tree. It contains a number of nested layers that represent bulbs. The coordinates of each nested layer are relative to the upper-left corner of the parent layer. If you moved the Christmas tree to another location on the Web page, the bulbs would move right along with it (see Figure 13.13).

> **N O T E** The empty <LAYER> tag that you see at the top of the listing is a work-around for an anomaly in the current beta version of Navigator that causes the first nested layer to be positioned incorrectly. When you use this example with the release version of Navigator, you should be able to omit the empty layer. ▪

Listing 13.13 Nesting Layers

```
<HTML>
<HEAD>
<TITLE>Layer 13</TITLE>
</HEAD>
<BODY>

<LAYER TOP=0 LEFT=0 CLIP=300,400>
<IMG SRC=xtree.gif>

<LAYER TOP=160 LEFT=60>
</LAYER>

<LAYER TOP=150 LEFT=60>
<IMG SRC=ball1.gif>
</LAYER>

<LAYER TOP=20 LEFT=100>
<IMG SRC=ball2.gif>
</LAYER>

<LAYER TOP=130 LEFT=120>
<IMG SRC=ball1.gif>
</LAYER>

<LAYER TOP=170 LEFT=140>
<IMG SRC=ball2.gif>
</LAYER>

<LAYER TOP=200 LEFT=120>
<IMG SRC=ball2.gif>
</LAYER>

<LAYER TOP=80 LEFT=80>
<IMG SRC=ball3.gif>
</LAYER>

<LAYER TOP=90 LEFT=125>
<IMG SRC=ball3.gif>
</LAYER>

<LAYER TOP=200 LEFT=60>
<IMG SRC=ball3.gif>
</LAYER>

<LAYER TOP=200 LEFT=180>
<IMG SRC=ball3.gif>
</LAYER>

</LAYER>
</BODY>
</HTML>
```

Part

III

Ch

13

FIG. 13.13

By capturing the mouse events for each bulb, you can allow the user to move the bulbs around on the Christmas tree.

Bulbs nested to move as a group

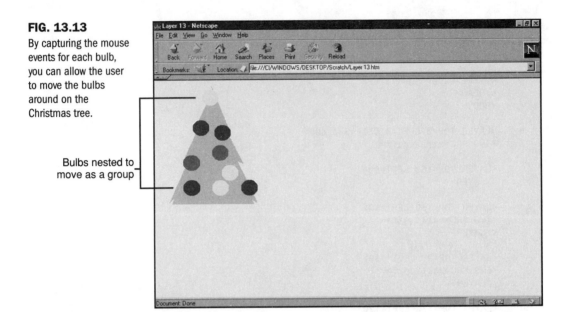

Putting Layers to Practical Use: Fly-Over Tips

One of the practical uses for layers is to create fly-over help or tips for links and objects on the HTML document. For example, you can insert a number of art images on a page and then display more information about the image when the user moves the mouse across the image.

The example shown in Listing 13.14 gives the user additional information about each link on the HTML document. When the user moves the mouse over the second link shown in Figure 13.14, for example, the function associated with that link shows the appropriate layer, which contains additional information about the link. Take a look at the HTML in the listing, and then examine each part.

Listing 13.14   Providing Fly-Over Help for Links

```
<HTML>
<HEAD>
<TITLE>Layer 14</TITLE>
</HEAD>
<BODY>

<SCRIPT LANGUAGE="JAVASCRIPT">
// Hide all of the layers (tips) in this HTML document
function ClearHelp()
{
for( i=0; i < document.layers.length; i++)
document.layers[i].visibility = "HIDE";
}
```

```
// Clear all the displayed layerss; then, display the layer by the
// given name. Set a timer to automatically clear the layers after
// five seconds.

function OnLink( Name )
{
ClearHelp()
document.layers[Name].visibility="INHERIT";
window.window.setTimeout( "ClearHelp()", 5000 );
}
</SCRIPT>
<A OnMouseOver='OnLink("LINK1")' HREF="http://rampages.onramp.net/
➥˜jerry">Jerry's Home Page</A>
<LAYER NAME=LINK1 VISIBILITY=HIDE>
<TABLE BORDER=1 BGCOLOR=YELLOW>
<TD>
Click on this link to jump to Jerry's home page.
</TD>
</TABLE>
</LAYER>

<BR>
<A OnMouseOver='OnLink("LINK2")' HREF="http://www.netscape.com">Netscape's Home
➥Page</A>
<LAYER NAME=LINK2  VISIBILITY=HIDE>
<TABLE BORDER=1 BGCOLOR=YELLOW>
<TD>
Click on this link to jump to Netscape's home page.
</TD>
</TABLE>
</LAYER>

<BR>
<A OnMouseOver='OnLink("LINK3")' HREF="http://www.yahoo.com">Yahoo!</A>
<LAYER NAME=LINK3  VISIBILITY=HIDE>
<TABLE BORDER=1 BGCOLOR=YELLOW>
<TD>
Click on this link to jump to Yahoo!
</TD>
</TABLE>
</LAYER>
</BODY>
</HTML>
```

At the bottom half of the listing, you see three links. Each link uses the OnMouseOver attribute to associate a JavaScript function with that link. In this case, each link is associated with the function called OnLink, and the function is passed the name of the layer to show. The first link calls OnLink like this:

```
OnLink("LINK1")
```

Just under each link, you see a layer. Each layer has a unique name and is hidden. As well, each layer contains the help text associated with the preceding link.

FIG. 13.14
Using a bordered table within a layer helps better set it off from the underlying HTML document.

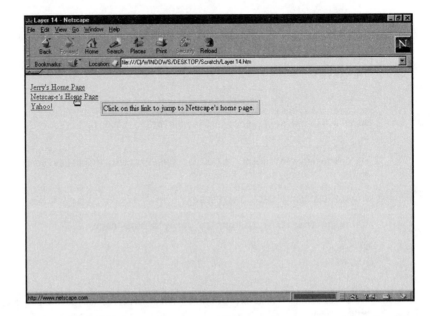

At the top of the listing, you see two functions. Here's a description of each:

OnLink(*Name*)   Hides all of the layers on the HTML document; then, displays the layer called *Name*. Last, it sets a timer to call ClearHelp in five seconds (5,000 milliseconds) so that the browser will hide the layer after a few seconds.

ClearHelp()   Hides all of the layers in the HTML document. It uses the layers array to visit each layer and set its visibility property to "HIDE". Note that you get the size of the layers array by using document.layers.length.

## CHAPTER 14

Style Sheets

by Jerry Honeycutt

Style sheets are a W3C recommendation that defines a standard by which you can format Web pages using desktop publishing concepts. Microsoft Internet Explorer 3.0 is the first (and only at the time of this writing) browser to support style sheets, but Netscape is committed to supporting style sheets in future versions of its browser. You can get more information about W3C's recommendation at its Web site: **http://www.w3.org/pub/WWW/TR/WD-css1.html**. Note that W3C uses the terminology "cascading style sheets level 1." In this chapter, however, I use the simpler language, "style sheet."

Before you go any further, you need to understand what it is that you can do with style sheets. Have you used a word processor lately? Microsoft Word? Most word processors let you specify styles that describe how a block of text will be formatted. For example, you can specify a paragraph style that sets the line spacing to one, font to Courier, and left margin to one inch. Then, you can assign this style to any number of paragraphs in your document. You can use HTML style sheets to do essentially the same thing. Here's a sample of what you'll learn in this chapter:

Attach style sheets to your HTML file

This chapter shows you four ways to associate a style sheet with your HTML document.

Set a variety of properties within a style

Style sheets support a large variety of properties you can set within your style definitions.

Save time and space by grouping properties

You can group the most common properties together to save time and make your HTML file more readable.

Learn about more-advanced topics

In this chapter you learn more-advanced style sheet topics such as classes and inheritance.

What about browsers without style sheet support?

If you follow a few simple rules, folks who don't have browsers with style sheet support will be okay.

- Change the spacing between text lines, individual words, and individual characters.
- Set the left, right, top, and bottom margins for an element (block of text within an HTML container).
- Set the indent for an element.
- Change the font size, style, and other font attributes of the text in an element.
- Create a border around an element, and set the border's width and style.
- Set the background color or background image of an element (kind of like a watermark).

> **CAUTION**
>
> At the time of this writing, W3C's recommendation hasn't been approved and browser support for style sheets is very limited. Thus, there is a possibility that this recommendation will change and invalidate certain portions of this chapter. As well, many portions of the W3C recommendation are optional and are thus not supported by all browsers claiming to support style sheets.

Attaching a Style Sheet to Your HTML Document

The big benefit of using HTML style sheets is in separating the format of your Web pages from the content. You specify how the text will look in a different location then you specify the contents of the text itself. If you later decide that you want all your headings to display using blue characters, you only have to change the style for those headings, instead of changing each heading within the HTML file.

This is great. So, how do you attach a style sheet to an HTML file? It's easy. There are four methods:

Linking	You can link an HTML file to a style sheet contained in a separate file.
Embedding	You can embed the style sheet within the HTML file within the `<STYLE>`container.
Inline	You can define styles on-the-fly within an HTML tag such as `<P>`.
Import	You can use the `@import` keyword to import a style sheet into your HTML file.

Linking a Style Sheet

As noted earlier, you can create a style sheet in a separate file and then apply that style sheet to all of the pages on your Web site. I recommend this method to you only because it makes creating a consistent Web site much easier. In fact, you can create a corporate style sheet and have everyone in your organization use it with their Web sites. (Imagine an intranet with a common look; wow!)

You store a linked style sheet in a text file with the CSS file extension. It's a plain text file that you can create with your favorite text editor (Notepad, for example). The format of the text file is readable by humans and easy to understand. Thus, you won't have any trouble creating your style sheets by hand.

To link to a style sheet stored in a separate file, store all of it in the CSS file and link your HTML files to it using the <LINK> tag, like this:

```
<LINK REL=STYLESHEET HREF="http://www.myserver.com/mysheet.css" TYPE="text/css">
```

Assign the URL of the style sheet to the HREF attribute. Set TYPE to "text/css" so browsers that don't support style sheets can avoid the download.

 Store your corporate style sheets in a common location on the Web server, and then have everyone who is creating Web pages reference that style sheet from their HTML files. Everyone can even use the same <LINK> tag. In this way, you can have a more consistent look across all of the Web pages on the server.

Embedding a Style Sheet

You don't have to store your style sheet in a separate file. You can embed the style sheet inside each HTML file. Note that the styles within an embedded style sheet only affect the HTML within that file. Thus, you can't embed a style sheet in an HTML file and expect to use that across multiple HTML files without copying and pasting it into each file (thus, my earlier recommendation that you use linked style sheets).

You use the <STYLE> container to embed a style sheet in your HTML file. Put this container between the <HTML> and <BODY> tags of your°âle, like this:

```
<HTML>
<HEAD>
</HEAD>
<STYLE TYPE="text/css">
Style definitions go here
</STYLE>
<BODY>
</BODY>
</HTML>
```

The <STYLE> tag has a single attribute, called TYPE, that specifies the MIME type. Set it to "text/css" so browsers that don't support style sheets can ignore this tag.

The following example shows you what a real <STYLE> tag looks like. You can ignore the actual style definitions for now because you haven't learned about those yet.

```
<STYLE TYPE="text/css">
H1 {color: BLUE}
</STYLE>
```

Part
III

Ch
14

Defining Styles Inline

Inline styles are simple styles that you define on-the-fly. You can use inline styles to quickly change the appearance of a single tag—on the run. You can also use inline styles to override a style for a particular tag. For example, if you've defined a style that sets the color of the H1 tag to blue, you can set the color of a specific element by using the H1 tag set to red.

Inline styles affect the individual tag for which they're defined; that is, you define a tag's style within the tag itself. You do this by using the STYLE attribute, which is supported by all the child tags of the BODY tag. To define an inline style, add the STYLE attribute to the tag for which you want to change the style and set its value to the string representing the style definition, like this:

```
<H1 STYLE="color: blue">
```

N O T E   If an inline style conflicts with an embedded or linked style, the inline style wins. For example, if you define the color of an H1 tag in a linked style sheet to be blue, and you also define the color of a particular H1 tag within your HTML file to be red, the browser will display that particular occurrence of the H1 tag using the color red. ■

You can use inline styles with the <DIV> tag to set the style for an entire block of HTML within your document. This works because of the concept of inheritance, which you'll learn about later in this chapter. For example, if you want to change the text color of an entire block of tags to blue, you can put those tags in the DIV container, and define a style for the <DIV> tag that sets the text color to blue. It looks like this:

```
<DIV STYLE="color: blue">
<H1>This is a heading</H1>
<P>This is a paragraph. It will look blue in the user's browser</P>
</DIV>
```

You can also use inline style sheets with the <SPAN> tag to change the formatting for a few words or even just a few letters. For example:

```
This is a <SPAN STYLE="color: blue">simple</SPAN> block of text.
```

> **CAUTION**
>
> Don't rely on inline styles too much. They'll quickly clutter your HTML file so that it's harder to read and much, much harder to maintain. This obviously diminishes the greatest advantage of style sheets: separating format from content.

TIP   If you don't want to take full advantage of style sheets, but you still want to add a bit of special formatting to a few elements in your HTML file, use inline styles.

Importing Style Sheets

You learned about linking to a style sheet earlier in this chapter. You can also use the `@import` keyword to import a style sheet into your HTML file. Remember that you're just importing the text file, thus, you have to insert it in the `<STYLE>` container. In this manner, importing a style sheet works just like embedding a style sheet into your HTML file. For example:

```
<STYLE TYPE="text/css">
@import url(http://www.myserver.com/style.css);
</STYLE>
```

N O T E As of this writing, Internet Explorer doesn't support the `@import` keyword. Thus, you should link to your style sheet if you want to store it in a separate file. ■

Style sheets will help you create a great looking site. There are other style matters, however, that will contribute as greatly, if not more, to the impact your site has on its users:

- Put navigational aids at the top and bottom of each Web page so the user can easily get around.

- Limit your graphics. Many folks are still using slow connections, so keep graphics down to 50K or less.

- Indicate to the user that a particular link leaves your Web site. You can use a special icon next to the link.

- If you're using frames on your site, provide an alternative for the user who has a frameless browser.

- Design your Web pages for 640 by 480 resolution. Yes, people still use monitors at that resolution.

Understanding What Style Sheets Look Like (Syntax)

As noted earlier, style sheets are stored in text files you can easily read and understand. They're also very easy to create by hand. Note that, in the future, you'll be able to create and use styles sheets with the more popular HTML editors such as Microsoft FrontPage.

Linked and embedded style sheets allow you to define styles for one or more individual tags. For example, you can create a style sheet that defines styles for the `<H1>`, `<H2>`, `<P>`, and `<EM>` tags. Each style definition is called a *rule*. A rule contains a selector (the HTML tag), followed by the declaration (the definition of the style). The rule's selector is what ties the style's definition to tags you use in the HTML file. Here's an example of what a rule looks like that defines a style for each occurrence of the `<H1>` tag:

```
H1 {color: blue}
```

The declaration is enclosed in curly braces ({}). Each item in the declaration has two parts: the property name and the value you're assigning to the property, separated by a colon (:). In the previous example, `color` is the property name and `blue` is the value you're assigning to it.

Part

III

Ch

14

HTML predefines dozens of property names (`font-size`, `font-style`, `color`, `margin-right`, and so on), which you'll learn about a bit later in this chapter. Each property also accepts a predefined type and range of values.

Setting Multiple Properties

The examples you've seen so far only set a single property: `color`. You can also set multiple properties within a declaration. You do this by separating each assignment with a semicolon (;), like this:

```
H1 {color: blue; font-size: 12pt; text-line: center}
```

In this example, the browser will display each occurrence of the `<H1>` tag using the color blue, a font size of 12 points, and centered in the browser window. For all other properties, the browser uses its default values. For example, it sets the `font-style` property to `normal`.

Grouping Selectors

If you want to define a similar style for several tags, you can list them individually in your style sheet, like this:

```
P {font-size: 12pt}
UL {font-size: 12pt}
LI {font-size: 12pt}
```

This isn't the most efficient way to do this, however, considering that you can group the selectors together and define a rule for them as a group. The following example groups the selectors in the previous example on one line, and defines a rule that sets the `font-size` property to 12pt:

```
P, UL, LI {font-size: 12pt}
```

Note the comma between each selector in the list. Leaving this comma out means a totally different thing (see "Using Contextual Selectors," later in this chapter).

Adding Comments to Your Style Sheet

If your style sheet gets a bit complicated, or you need to explain why you've made a particular design decision, you can add a comment to the style sheet. Comments only serve to document your style sheet; they don't have any impact on how the browser displays the HTML document.

Enclose your comments between `/*` and `*/`. The following example shows you what a one-line comment looks like:

```
BODY {margin-left: 1in}              /* Create space for sliders */
H1 {font-size: 16; margin-left: -1in}    /* Out one inch */
H2 {font-size: 14; margin-left: -1in}    /* Out one inch */
```

You can also use the `/*` and `*/` characters to create block comments. This is useful to explain an entire portion of your style sheet. Like this:

```
/*----------------------------------------------------------------
   The margin-left property is set to one inch for the BODY tag.
   Since all of its enclosed tags will inherit this setting, the
   entire page will appear to be indented by one inch. The first-
   and second-level headings are indented to the left by one inch
   so that they slide out into the margin.
   -------------------------------------------------------------*/

BODY {margin-left: 1in}            /* Create space for sliders */
H1 {font-size: 16; margin-left: -1in}      /* Out one inch */
H2 {font-size: 14; margin-left: -1in}      /* Out one inch */
```

Exploring the Properties of a Style

HTML style sheets define a wide variety of properties you can use to change how your HTML document looks in the browser. Most of the names contain multiple words, each separated by a hyphen (-). In property names that contain multiple words, the first word usually indicates a category and will also usually have a shorthand property you can use to simplify your style sheet (see "Grouping Properties to Simplify Style Definitions," later in this chapter).

Table 14.1 provides an overview of the properties available in HTML style sheets. The property column contains the name of the property. Each name is explained in much more detail later in this chapter. The shorthand property column indicates whether or not that particular property can be set within a shorthand property. The inherited column indicates whether or not that particular property is inherited by its child tags (you'll learn about inheritance later in this chapter).

Table 14.1   Properties in HTML Style Sheets

Property	Shorthand	Inherited?
background-attachment	background	No
background-color	background	No
background-image	background	No
background-position	background	No
background-repeat	background	No
border-bottom-width	border	No
border-color	border	No
border-left-width	border	No
border-right-width	border	No
border-style	border	No
border-top-width	border	No

Part

III

Ch

14

continues

Table 14.1   Continued

Property	Shorthand	Inherited?
clear		No
color		Yes
float		No
font-family	font	Yes
font-size	font	Yes
font-style	font	Yes
font-variant		Yes
font-weight	font	Yes
height		No
letter-spacing		Yes
line-height		Yes
list-style-image	list-style	Yes
list-style-position	list-style	Yes
list-style-type	list-style	Yes
margin-bottom	margin	No
margin-left	margin	No
margin-right	margin	No
margin-top	margin	No
padding-bottom	padding	No
padding-left	padding	No
padding-right	padding	No
padding-top	padding	No
text-align		Yes
text-decoration		No
text-indent		Yes
text-transform		Yes
vertical-align		No
white-space		Yes
width		No
word-spacing		Yes

Background Properties

HTML style sheets provide you with the ability to decorate the background of an element by using color and images. Note that using the properties described in the following sections doesn't define the background for the Web page as a whole. These properties set the background of an element on the Web page. For example, if you define a background for the <UL> tag, like the following example, then the background only appears within each occurrence of that tag on the Web page.

```
UL {background-image: URL(http://www.myserver.com/images/watermark.gif)}
```

N O T E Internet Explorer 3.0 doesn't match the W3C recommendation with regards to the background properties. It has a single property called background to which you can assign a background color or the URL of a background image. ■

background-attachment The background-attachment property determines whether the background image is fixed in the browser window or scrolls as the user scrolls the window. You can use this to create a watermark behind your Web page that stays put regardless of which portion of the Web page the user is viewing.

You can assign two possible values to background-attachment, as described in Table 14.2.

Table 14.2 *background-attachment* **Values**

Value	Description
fixed	The image is fixed within the browser window.
scroll	The image scrolls as the user scrolls the window.

background-color You can change the background color for an element by using the background-color property. You can assign one of the valid color names to background-color or an RGB value like #808080 (white). For example, if you define a style for the <UL> tag that changes the background color to blue, then all of the unordered lists in your HTML file will be displayed with a blue background.

T I P Changing the background color for certain types of tags is useful to highlight information on the Web page.

background-image You can display a background image in an element by setting the value of the background-image property to the URL of an image. This has the effect of a watermark displayed behind that element on the Web page (the element's content is displayed over the background image).

You set the URL by using the URL(*address*) format, like this:

```
H1 {background-image: URL(http://www.myserver.com/images/heading.gif)}
```

Figure 14.1 shows you what a background image looks like.

Part

III

Ch

14

FIG. 14.1

If you want to use a background image as a watermark, use your favorite paint program to fade the image by filling it with 50 percent white.

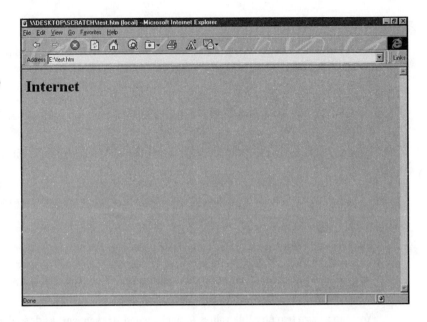

Most of the style sheet properties accept some sort of length. You can use many different units to specify a length, too. HTML supports two types of units: relative and absolute lengths. Table 14.3 describes the relative units.

Table 14.3   Relative Units

Unit	Example	Description
em	0.5em	The height of the element's font.
ex	0.75ex	The height of the letter X.
px	15px	Pixels, relative to the output device.

Whenever possible, you should use relative units so your Web pages will scale better from one device to the next. You can also use the absolute units described in Table 14.4.

Table 14.4   Absolute Units

Unit	Example	Description
in	.5in	Inches
cm	1cm	Centimeters
mm	20mm	Millimeters
pt	12pt	Points (1pt = 1/72 inch)
pc	1pc	Pica (1pc = 12pt)

Aside from relative and absolute lengths, you can also specify most lengths in terms of percentages. With HTML style sheets, percentages are almost always relative to the parent element. For example, if you're specifying a font size of 50 percent, what you're really saying is that you want the element's font size to be half as big as the parent element's font size.

background-position You change the position of the background image by using the background-position property. The position is always relative to the top-left corner of the element in which you're positioning the image. That is, if you're positioning an image for the <UL> tag, the image's position will be relative to the top-left corner of the unordered list.

The background-position property looks like

background-position: *x y*

where *x* is the horizontal position and *y* is the vertical position of the image. *X* and *y* can be a percentage, which is relative to the size of the element; a fixed amount such as 1in; or one of the keywords that indicates a relative position, as described in Table 14.5.

Table 14.5 *background-position* Positions

Keyword	Description
top	Aligns the image with the top of the containing element; only useful when substituted for *y*.
left	Aligns the image with the left side of the containing element; only useful when substituted for *x*.
right	Aligns the image with the right side of the containing element; only useful when substituted for *y*.
bottom	Aligns the image with the bottom of the containing element; only useful when substituted for *y*.
center	Centers the image within the containing element; when substituted for *x*, the image is centered horizontally; when substituted for *y*, the image is centered vertically.

background-repeat You can cause the user's browser to tile the background image so that it fills the entire area of the containing element. The background-repeat property can have four values, as described in Table 14.6.

Table 14.6 *background-repeat* Values

Value	Description
repeat	Repeats the image both vertically and horizontally.
repeat-x	Repeats the image horizontally.
repeat-y	Repeats the image vertically.
no-repeat	Doesn't repeat the image.

Part
III

Ch
14

Box Properties

W3C's style sheet recommendation provides you with the ability to define the borders, margins, and padding for elements on the Web page. You can wrap a border around a heading, for example, or change the margins of the <P> tag so that any occurrences of this tag are indented into the page. Here's an overview of the properties that you can use to change the boxes associated with an element:

border	You use the border properties to set the left, right, top, and bottom borders of an element. You can set the border's width, color, and style.
margin	You use the margin properties to set the left, right, top, and bottom margins of an element. With these properties, you only specify the size of the margin.
padding	You use the padding properties to specify how much space the browser displays between the border and the content of the element. With the padding properties, you only specify the size of the margin.

Figure 14.2 shows you how the border, margin, and padding properties work with the height and width properties to form the boxes around the element. The following list describes these in more detail:

- The height and width properties determine the overall size of the element's containing box.
- The border properties determine the position of the border within the element's margins.
- The margin properties determine the element's margins within its containing box.
- The padding properties determine the amount of space between the element's border and the contents of the element itself.

border-bottom-width You set the width of the bottom border by using the border-bottom-width property. This doesn't affect the other sides of the border. You can assign any of the values described in Table 14.7 to this property.

Table 14.7 *border-bottom-width* Values

Value	Description
thin	Displays the border by using a thin line.
medium	Displays the border by using a medium line.
thick	Displays the border by using a thick line.
length	You can define the exact width of the border by using points (pt), inches (in), centimeters (cm), or pixels (px); (for example, 2in).

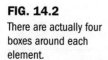

FIG. 14.2

There are actually four boxes around each element.

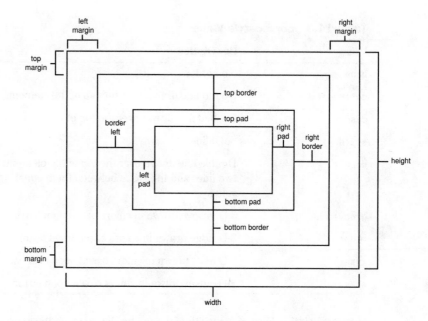

border-color   The border-color property sets the color of the element's border. You can use a named color, such as RED, or you can use an RGB value, such as #FF0000.

border-left-width   You set the width of the left border by using the border-left-width property. This doesn't affect the other sides of the border. You can assign any of the values described in Table 14.7 to this property.

border-right-width   You set the width of the right border by using the border-right-width property. This doesn't affect the other sides of the border. You can assign any of the values described in Table 14.7 to this property.

border-style   The border-style property determines the style of the border that the browser displays. You can specify from one to four values for this property:

One Value	All four borders are set to the style.
Two Values	The top and bottom borders are set to the style in the first value; and the left and right borders are set to the style in the second value.
Three Values	The top border is set to the style in the first value; the right and left borders are set to the style in the second value; and the bottom border is set to the style in the third value.
Four Values	The top border is set to the style in the first value; the right is set to the second value; the bottom is set to the third value; and the left is set to the fourth value.

Table 14.8 describes the values you can use for a border's style.

Part
III

Ch
14

Table 14.8 *border-style* **Values**

Value	Description
none	No border.
dotted	Dotted line drawn over the top of the element.
dashed	Dashed line drawn over the top of the element.
solid	Solid line.
double	Double line drawn over the top of the element; the width of the two lines and the space between them equals the border-width value.
groove	3-D groove drawn in colors based upon color.
ridge	3-D ridge drawn in colors based upon color.
inset	3-D inset drawn in colors based upon color.
outset	3-D outset drawn in colors based upon color.

border-top-width   You set the width of the top border by using the border-top-width property. This doesn't affect the other sides of the border. You can assign any of the values described in Table 14.7 to this property.

TROUBLESHOOTING

I've set the width of my border, but it still doesn't display? Setting the width of the border isn't enough. You also have to set the border style by using the border-style property. This is because the default style for every border is none.

clear   The clear property determines if the browser can display floating elements on the sides of an element. The property's value indicates the sides on which floating elements are not allowed. For example, clear: left means that the browser can't float elements on the left side of the element. Table 14.9 describes the values you can assign to this property.

Table 14.9 *clear* **Values**

Value	Description
none	Floating elements are allowed on all sides.
left	Floating elements are not allowed on the left.
right	Floating elements are not allowed on the right.
both	Floating elements are not allowed on either side.

float The float property specifies that the element is floated to the left or right side, with the surrounding elements flowing around it. Table 14.10 describes the values you can assign to this property.

Table 14.10   *float* Values

Value	Description
none	Displays the element where it is.
left	Move to the left and wrap text around it.
right	Move to the right and wrap text around it.

height You set the total height of the element with the height property. You can set this property for text blocks or images. For example, you can use the height and width properties to create a special warning on the Web page that has a fixed size. height is more useful with images, however. You can set this property to any length, a percentage value, or auto, which lets the browser determine the best size for the element.

margin-bottom You set the bottom margin by using the margin-bottom property. You can specify any valid length, a percentage value (relative to the height and width) of the element, or auto, which lets the browser determine the best margins to use for the element. You can also use a negative margin size to create special effects.

margin-left You set the left margin by using the margin-left property. You can specify any valid length, a percentage value (relative to the height and width) of the element, or auto, which lets the browser determine the best margins to use for the element. You can also use a negative margin size to create special effects.

margin-right You set the right margin by using the margin-right property. You can specify any valid length, a percentage value (relative to the height and width) of the element, or auto, which lets the browser determine the best margins to use for the element. You can also use a negative margin size to create special effects.

margin-top You set the top margin by using the margin-top property. You can specify any valid length, a percentage value (relative to the height and width) of the element, or auto, which lets the browser determine the best margins to use for the element. You can also use a negative margin size to create special effects.

padding-bottom The padding-bottom property specifies the amount of space to display between the element's bottom border and the element's contents. You can set this property to a valid length or a percentage value (relative to the height and width) of the element.

padding-left The padding-left property specifies the amount of space to display between the element's left border and the element's contents. You can set this property to a valid length or a percentage value (relative to the height and width) of the element.

Part

III

Ch

14

padding-right   The padding-right property specifies the amount of space to display between the element's right border and the element's contents. You can set this property to a valid length or a percentage value (relative to the height and width) of the element.

padding-top   The padding-top property specifies the amount of space to display between the element's top border and the element's contents. You can set this property to a valid length or a percentage value (relative to the height and width) of the element.

width   You set the total width of the element with the width property. You can set this property for text blocks or images. You can set this property to any length, a percentage value, or auto, which lets the browser determine the best size for the element.

List Properties

You use the list properties to specify how lists display in the browser window. You can change the position of the marker (list-style-position), and the style or image used for the marker (list-style-type and list-style-image). The sections that follow describe each property in more detail. Enjoy.

The list properties are inherited, so if you define a property for the <UL> tag, all of its enclosed <LI> tags inherit those properties. These tags are only meaningful for HTML list tags.

list-style-image   You use the list-style-image property to specify an image that the browser will display as the marker for a list item. The property's only value is the URL, using the URL(address) format, of the image to use as the marker, like this:

```
list-style-image: url(http://www.myserver.com/images/marker.gif)
```

To affect all of the list items within a list, set this property for the list container, such as <UL> as opposed to the list item <LI>. You can override an individual list item, however, by setting this property in a single occurrence of the <LI> tag.

list-style-position   The list-style-position property determines the relative position of the marker. Table 14.11 describes the possible values you can assign to this property.

Table 14.11   *list-style-position* Values

Value	Description
inside	The list item's text wraps to the next line underneath the marker.
outside	The list item's text wraps to the next line underneath the start of the text on the previous line (hanging indent).

list-style-type   You use the list-style-type property to specify the type of marker the browser will display. Use this instead of a marker image. Table 14.12 describes each of the possible values you can assign to this property.

Table 14.12 *list-style-type* **Values**

Value	Description
disc	Disc
circle	Circle
square	Square
decimal	Numbered (1, 2, 3, …)
lower-roman	Lowercase roman numerals (i, ii, iii, …)
upper-roman	Uppercase roman numerals (I, II, III, …)
lower-alpha	Lowercase alphabet (a, b, c, …)
upper-alpha	Uppercase alphabet (A, B, C, …)
none	No markers

Text Properties

The text properties give you complete control over how the browser displays an element's text. You can change its color, size, font, spacing, and so on. The sections that follow describe each text property you can set. Figure 14.3 shows a combination of these properties.

FIG. 14.3
HTML style sheets
support most of the text
formatting capabilities
that many word
processors do.

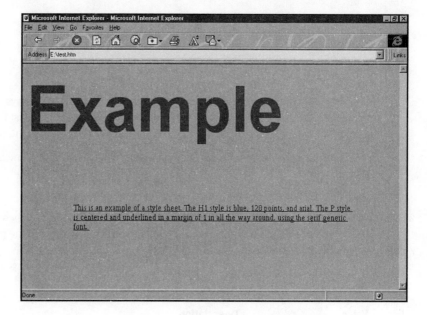

Part

III

Ch

14

color   The `color` property determines the foreground color for the element. Thus, the browser displays the element's text using this color. You can set `color` to a named color or an RGB value. Named colors include those in the following list:

black	silver	gray	white
maroon	red	purple	fuchsia
green	lime	olive	yellow
navy	blue	teal	aqua

font-family   `font-family` is a prioritized list of typefaces for the element. You can specify a single typeface or a list of alternatives, separated by commas, for example:

```
font-family: Courier, Times, Serif
```

You can use a font name you expect to be on the user's computer, such as Courier or Helvetica, or you can use a generic font name. Table 14.13 shows you the generic font names and provides an example of a font that looks similar.

Table 14.13   Generic Fonts

Name	Similar to
serif	Times New Roman
sans-serif	Arial
cursive	Script
fantasy	Comic
monospace	Courier New

In case the user doesn't have the font you've requested, you should always use a generic font name as the last item in the list. In the previous example, `serif` is the last font in the list. If the user doesn't have `courier` or `times`, the browser will use the generic font, instead.

If you're using a font name that has multiple words, enclose the font name in quotes, for example:

```
font-family: "Courier New", serif
```

font-size   `font-size` determines the size of the text in points (`pt`), inches (`in`), centimeters (`cm`), or pixels (`px`). You can also use a percentage, which is relative to the parent element's font size, or one of the values shown in Table 14.14.

Table 14.14   *font-size* Values

Value	Description
xx-small	50 percent smaller than the x-small font.

Value	Description
x-small	50 percent smaller than the small font.
small	50 percent smaller than the medium font.
medium	A medium-sized font, probably 10 points.
large	50 percent larger than the medium font.
x-large	50 percent larger than the large font.
xx-large	50 percent larger than the x-large font.
larger	50 percent larger than the parent element's font.
smaller	50 percent smaller than the parent element's font.

N O T E The W3C recommendation that browsers use a scaling factor of 50 percent is only a recommendation. Browsers are free to use any scaling factor that they wish. Thus, the values in Table 14.14 are only guidelines. ■

font-style You can change the style of the font by using the font-style property. Table 14.15 describes each of the possible values.

Table 14.15 *font-style* Values

Value	Description
normal	Selects a normal face.
oblique	Selects an oblique face.
italic	Selects an italic face.

font-variant You use the font-variant property to display text in small-caps. Setting this property to normal causes the browser to display the text normally. Setting this property to small-caps causes the browser to display the text using small-caps.

font-weight font-weight determines the thickness of the font. You can assign normal, bold, bolder, or lighter to this property. You can also use the series of numbers from 100, 200, … 900 to this property, with each successive number representing a weight that is thicker than the previous number. For example, font-weight: 700 sets a thicker font weight than does font-weight: 400.

 T I P A font weight of 400 is roughly equivalent to a normal font weight.

letter-spacing letter-spacing determines the spacing between each letter in a line of text. You can set this property to normal, and let the browser worry about it, or you can set this property to any valid length, such as 1px.

Part

III

Ch

14

line-height   You use the line-height property to set the leading for an element. An element's leading is the distance between the baselines of two text lines. You can use any valid length, a percentage (which is relative to the parent element's line-height property), or you can set this property to normal. Note that the spacing is added before each line, not after.

> **CAUTION**
>
> This setting doesn't work well on text lines that use multiple font sizes on the same line of text.

text-align   text-align defines how text is aligned in an element. You can set this property to any of the values shown in Table 14.16.

Table 14.16   *text-align* Values

Value	Description
left	Text is left-justified.
right	Text is right-justified.
center	Text is centered within the element.
justify	Text is left- and right-justified.

text-decoration   You can add special decorations, such as underlining, to an element by using the text-decoration property. Table 14.17 describes the values you can assign to this property. You can combine these values, too.

Table 14.17   *text-decoration* Values

Value	Description
none	No decorations
underline	Underlined text
overline	Text with a line over it
line-through	Strike through
blink	Blinking text

text-indent   You use the text-indent property to indent the first line of an element's text. You can set this property to any valid length. For example, here's how to indent the <P> tag's text to the right by one inch

```
P {text-indent: 1in}
```

TIP You can create a hanging indent by setting a tag's style `text-indent` to a negative value and `margin-left` to a positive value.

text-transform   `text-transform` specifies that the text should be changed according to the values in Table 14.18.

Table 14.18   *text-transform* Values

Value	Description
capitalize	Capitalize first letter of each word.
uppercase	Uppercase all letters in the element.
lowercase	Lowercase all letters in the element.
none	No transformation.

vertical-align   You use the `vertical-align` property to change the vertical position of the element's text within the element itself. You can use one of the keywords described in Table 14.19.

Table 14.19   *vertical-align* Values

Value	Description
baseline	Align the baseline of the element with the baseline of the parent.
middle	Align the middle of the element with the middle of the parent.
sub	Subscript the element.
super	Superscript the element.
text-top	Align the top of the element with the top of the parent element's text.
text-bottom	Align the bottom of the element with the bottom of the parent element's text.
top	Align the top of the element with the tallest element on the line.
bottom	Align the bottom of the element with the lowest element on the line.

white-space   The `white-space` property defines how the browser handles white space within the element. You can leave things alone and let the browser collapse all of the white space, or you can specify that the browser treat white space as if you're within a `<PRE>` container. Table 14.20 shows the values you can assign to this property.

Part
III

Ch
14

Table 14.20   *white-space* **Values**

Value	Description
normal	White space is collapsed.
pre	Handle white space like the <PRE> tag.
nowrap	Wrapping is only permitted with .

word-spacing   word-spacing determines the spacing between each word in a line of text. You can set this property to normal and let the browser worry about it, or you can set this property to any valid length, such as 1px.

Grouping Properties to Simplify Style Definitions

Many of the properties described in the previous section can be grouped together. Thus, instead of writing a rule that looks like this:

```
H1 {font-weight: bold; font-style: normal; font-size: 12pt; font-family: serif}
```

you can write a rule that looks like this:

```
H1 {font: bold normal 12pt serif}
```

HTML style sheets provide groups for the border, background, font, list, margin, and padding properties. You'll learn more about each of these in the following sections.

Border Properties

You can group border properties in five different ways. You can specify the properties for a particular side of the element by using border-top, border-right, border-bottom, or border-left. You can also specify all sides of the border at one time by using border.

With any of these attributes, you specify the width, style, and color of the border, for example:

```
border-top: thin dotted black
```

Background Properties

You can group the background properties by using background. You specify the background color, image, repeat, attachment, and position, like this:

```
background: white URL(http://www.myserver.com/images/bg.gif) repeat-x fixed top, left
```

Font Properties

You can group the font properties by using font. You specify the weight, style, size, and family, for example:

```
font: bold normal 12pt times, serif
```

List Properties

You can group the list properties by using `list-style`. You specify the marker type, marker image, and position, like this:

```
list-style: square URL(http://www.myserver.com/images/marker.gif) inside
```

Margin Properties

You can group the margin properties by using `margin`. You specify the top, right, bottom, and left, like this:

```
margin: .5in 1in .5in 1in
```

If you specify only one value, the browser uses that value for all sides. If you leave out one or two values, the browser takes the missing value from the opposite side. For example, if you leave off the last value (left), the browser sets the left margin to the value you specified for the right margin.

Padding Properties

You can group the margin properties by using `padding`. You specify the top, right, bottom, and left padding values, like this:

```
padding: .25in .25in .25in .25in
```

If you specify only one value, the browser uses that value for all sides. If you leave out one or more values, the browser takes the missing value from the opposite side. For example, if you leave off the last value (left), the browser sets the left padding to the value you specified for the right margin.

Using Inheritance

In HTML, tags inherit certain properties from their parents. For example, all of the tags within the `<BODY>` tag (`<P>` and `<UL>`) inherit certain properties from the `<BODY>` tag. Likewise, a `<LI>` tag inherits properties from the `<UL>` tag that contains it.

Consider the following bit of HTML:

```
<STYLE TYPE="text/css">
P {color: blue}
</STYLE>
<BODY>
<P>Hello. This is a paragraph of text. <EM>This text is emphasized</EM></P>
</BODY>
```

The style sheet for this example sets the color for the `<P>` tag to blue. There is no definition for the `<EM>` tag, however. You might expect the text in the `<EM>` tag to suddenly change back to the default color: black. That's not the case. Since the `<EM>` tag is within the container tag `<P>` (it's a child, in other words), the `<EM>` tag inherits the color property from the `<P>` tag.

Table 14.1, earlier in this chapter, indicates which properties are inherited by child tags.

Part
III

Ch

14

Using Contextual Selectors

With HTML style sheets, you can get very specific about when a style is applied to a tag. For example, you may want to define two styles for the <LI>, tag: one that's applied when it's a child of the <UL> tag and another when it's a child of the <OL> tag. You do this with contextual selectors.

Contextual selectors define the exact sequence of tags for which a style will be applied. In other words, you can specify that a style applies to a particular tag, such as <LI>, only if it's a child of the <OL> tag, like this:

```
OL LI {list-style-type: decimal}
```

You can also specify that a particular style applies to the <LI>, tag only if it's a child of the <UL> tag, like this:

```
UL LI {list-style-type: square}
```

Note the list of selectors is not comma-separated. Separating each selector with a comma would cause all of the tags in the list to be assigned the rule.

Understanding the Cascade

W3C refers to style sheets as "cascading style sheets" because you can use multiple styles to control how your Web page looks; the browser follows a certain set of rules to determine the precedence and to resolve conflicts between styles (cascading order). For example, you can define a style sheet for your Web site, and the reader can have their own style sheet. The cascading rules determine who wins if both style sheets define a style for a particular type of text.

So, how does this work? Each rule is assigned a weight by the browser. When the browser is working with the occurrence of a particular tag, it finds all of the rules that apply to it. The browser then sorts those rules by their weight, applying the style with the greatest weight.

In general, there are just a few rules that you need to be aware of when dealing with competing style sheets:

- The author's style sheet overrides the user's style sheet; while the user's style sheet overrides the browser's default values.
- Inline styles take precedence over embedded style sheets; while embedded style sheets take precedence over linked style sheets.

You can also override the precedence for a rule by using the important keyword. In the following example, the assignment of red to the property color and the assignment of sans-serif to the property font-family are marked as important. Thus, the browser will not override these styles. If two competing style sheets mark the same property as important, however, the rules in the previous list apply.

```
H1 {color: red ! important font-weight: bold font-family: sans-serif ! important}
```

Working with Classes in Your Style Sheets

A class defines a variation of style, which you refer to in a specific occurrence of a tag by using the CLASS attribute. For example, you can define three variations of the H1 style and then use each one in the appropriate context. You define a class much like you normally define a style, but you add an arbitrary class name to the end of the tag, separating them with a period, for example:

```
H1.blue {color: blue}
H1.red {color: red}
H1.black {color: black}
```

Then, when adding the <H1> tag to your HTML document, you set the CLASS attribute to indicate exactly which style you're using:

```
<H1 STYLE=red>Red Heading</H1>
```

 TIP You can address all of the tags within a particular class by omitting the tag name from the selector, like this: .red {color: red}. After defining this style, any tag that you associate with the red class, will be displayed using the color red.

Taking Care of Browsers That Don't Support Style Sheets

HTML style sheets are new. Internet Explorer and Netscape will be the first browsers to support them. You still need to worry about all those browsers that don't support style sheets.

Most browsers are designed to simply ignore the tags and attributes they don't understand. Thus, they'll ignore the <STYLE> tag, for example. They won't necessarily ignore what you put in the <STYLE> tag, though, and will display its contents as text on the Web page. To get around this problem, you can use an HTML comment within the <STYLE> tag to hide the style definitions, like this:

```
<STYLE TYPE="text/css">
<!--
H1 {color: red}
-->
</STYLE>
```

Browsers that don't support style sheets will display the HTML files with their default styles. They'll ignore the style definitions.

 TIP Take a look at your HTML documents with the associated style sheets so that you can verify how your Web pages look in browsers that don't support style sheets.

Part

III

Ch

14

## CHAPTER 15

Netscape/Microsoft Extensions

by Bill Bruns

Have you heard about the war? It's going on right now. It's not in Germany, or Korea, or Vietnam this time. It's not about land, or dictators, or personal freedoms. This is a marketing war over who has the best Web browser. It's taking place in cyberspace, and the victor will gain control of your desktop and the way the Internet looks to you for years to come—or until something else better comes along.

The participants are fighting tooth and nail, yet shedding little blood. Netscape claims its is faster. Microsoft denies that. Microsoft is planning to integrate its into its operating system. Netscape screams "antitrust!"

Both want you on their side. Whom will you choose? Do you have to choose? ■

The Browser Wars

This chapter talks about differences between what is considered "standard" HTML, and what is a Microsoft tag and a Netscape tag.

The W3C and the HTML "standard"

Standards are useless if they are ignored. Learn who makes the decisions about what is and isn't considered in the HTML "standard."

HTML tags that work exclusively with Netscape Navigator

Netscape has some tags to which only its browser will respond.

HTML tags that work exclusively with Microsoft Internet Explorer

Microsoft has some of those ideas, too—and only Internet Explorer will display them.

The Browser Wars

Currently, Microsoft and Netscape are battling, release after release, for control of the Internet. Neither company really is selling very many browsers (Internet Explorer is free and Navigator is shareware, which relatively few people are actually registering and paying for). Nevertheless, the company that commands the browser market will be able to enjoy a corresponding increase in sales of its server product. And that's just a bonus. Many people believe that the winner of the browser wars will be able to dictate how the Internet will evolve.

The real prize is the support of the Webmasters. Webmasters, like many technical people, continually try to be on the cutting edge. It's a source of pride to them to have the latest and greatest hardware and software. Since the Web is the most progressive technology available to the most people, it's reasonable to believe that Webmasters will want to have the most current configurations (hardware and software both) available.

Some Webmasters express their loyalty to the companies that supply their hardware and software by publicly aligning themselves and their site with their favorite product by putting a logo on their own page. You may have seen pages declaring that a Web site is powered by a Digital Alpha server, or more commonly, that a Web site is "Designed for Netscape" or "Designed for Internet Explorer" (see Figures 15.1 and 15.2).

Are Differences Good?

I hear you asking, "So what is the difference between Microsoft Internet Explorer and Netscape Navigator?"

Well, Internet Explorer has a snazzier interface and is free. Navigator has a much larger market share and, in my experience, loads pages slightly faster. All in all, they both look relatively the same. They are both pretty user-friendly.

Both browsers support the HTML 3.2 standard, but above and beyond that, both Microsoft and Netscape have enabled their browsers to recognize tags that are not recognized by that standard—and not recognized by the other browser.

N O T E The significant differences that will determine who ultimately wins the Browser Wars are not found in how you interact with the browser, but in how the browser interacts with your favorite Web pages. All in all, people will use the browser that the Webmasters of their favorite sites recommend, not the browser that may be most user-friendly or has the most bells and whistles. After all, if you can't see the Web page correctly with a certain browser, who'll want to use it? ▪

Both Microsoft and Netscape add features to their browser that other browsers don't recognize. So, when you don't use Navigator to look at a site that is "Designed especially for Netscape," it may not look the way the Webmaster intends it to look. It may not, for example, have newspaper-style columns displayed correctly. And when you fail to use Internet Explorer to look at a site that is "Designed especially for Internet Explorer," it may not show you a marquee scrolling across your page.

FIG. 15.1

Some Webmasters design for Netscape.

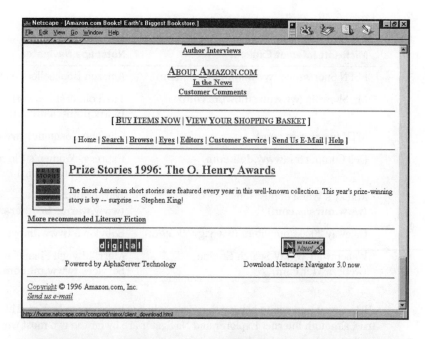

FIG. 15.2

Other Webmasters design for Internet Explorer. The choice, if you choose to make it, is yours.

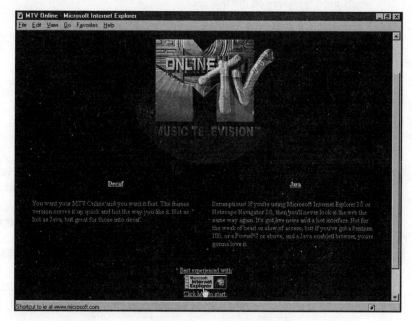

Both companies are recruiting your favorite Web sites to fight the battle on their side. Table 15.1 shows where some sites have enlisted their support.

Table 15.1   Where the Sites Are

Microsoft Internet Explorer	Netscape Navigator
ESPN Sportszone (**www.sportszone.com**)	Amazon Booksellers (**www.amazon.com**)
Mr. Showbiz (**www.mrshowbiz.com**)	The Pointcast Network (**www.pointcast.com**)
MTV (**www.mtv.com**)	Clinique Cosmetics (**www.clinque.com**)
Dell Computers (**www.dell.com**)	Express - Women's Clothing (**express.style.com**)
Mirsky's Worst of the Web (**www.mirsky.com**)	Warner Brothers (**www.warnerbrothers.com**)
Gateway 2000 Computers (**www.gw2k.com**)	Babylon 5 (**www.babylon5.com**)
Webcrawler WWW Search Engine (**webcrawler.com**)	Merrill Lynch Financial Services (**www.ml.com**)

All this may lead you to believe there are only two browsers to be had. This is not completely true, although Internet Explorer and Navigator are by far the two most well-known and prevalently used browsers on the market.

Others are out there, waiting, nay, *begging* to be downloaded.

Table 15.2 is a sampling of other, less popular Web browsers.

Table 15.2   A Few Other Sites

Browser Name	URL	Notes
Lynx	**http://lynx. browser.org/**	Text-only, telnet-based browser
NCSA Mosaic	**http://www. ncsa.uiuc.edu/SDG/ Software/Mosaic/**	The forerunner of all advanced Web browsers
Arena	**http://www.w3.org/ pub/WWW/Arena/**	Developed by W3C (the same organization that approves the HTML standards).
Opera	**http://traviata. nta.no/opera.htm**	It's the fastest graphical browser around.

But let me stress that although these browsers are useful to some people, in hard marketing percentages, they are hardly significant. And not all of them even keep up with the current HTML standard. For example, NCSA Mosaic doesn't support nested tables. Horrors!

Joining the Fracas

There was a time when office workers would literally get into fistfights over which was the "perfect" word processor. Should the company standardize on WordPerfect or WordStar? And when mice were uncommonly used on IBM-compatible PCs, my father would tell me: "You'll take my Mac away from me when you pry my cold, dead fingers off my mouse." Although important at the time, their significance pales when put next to the importance of the Browser Wars.

So, should you join the Browser Wars? Should you once again take that plunge? Are you afraid? Did you go to all the trouble to learn and love WordStar just to see the IS department switch you to WordPerfect the next year? What if you choose wrong?

As a Web surfer, you really don't have to make that choice. You can run both browsers on your Windows 3.x or Windows 95 machine very comfortably. Each will occasionally try to persuade you to make it the default browser, but most times, it really doesn't matter which one you award that title.

However, if you are a Webmaster, your choice is critical. If you choose to design "especially for Netscape," or "especially for Internet Explorer," you are enlisting as a foot soldier in their battalion. When people who like your site see the choice that you have made, they will be more likely to agree with you and take your side by using that browser. The more popular your site becomes, the more people you will be recruiting. Of course, some people promote both (see Figure 15.3).

FIG. 15.3
Some Webmasters, like those of the Illini Union at the University of Illinois, like to straddle the fence.

As a Webmaster, your mission should be to serve as many Web surfers as possible. Does that mean you have to write your pages for the lowest common denominator? Make your graphics so small that your pages can be loaded quickly even by the last person on Earth actively using a 9,600-baud modem? Eschew tables and imagemaps because someone might be trying to load your page with a browser that can't handle them? Limit your background choices to 16 colors because more than a few folks can't afford a super VGA video card?

Well, maybe everyone doesn't have to go that far. You should first profile your customer. Are you an inner-city library that serves a largely poor clientele mostly from the text-only, donated PCs in your reading room? Then maybe you should limit your graphics and shy away from the cutting edge. On the other hand, are you a corporate intranet running on high-speed ethernet and you control the choice of browser? Then, by all means, choose your army, install your browsers, and write especially for them.

However, there is a path that leads away from the battle, and this may be the wisest choice of all. You can stick to the letter of the current HTML standard. You will be bypassing some of the "cooler" capabilities of the advanced browsers, but in the end, you will be able to reach many more people, take no chances at alienating any of them, and still be able to design pages that are creative, informative, and pleasing to the eye.

The HTML "Standard" and the W3C

Standard. You've heard that mentioned a couple of times already. On the battlefield, a standard is an army's flag, and it is raised to inspire that army on to victory. In peacetime, it is a set of rules to which others are compelled to conform. When talking about HTML, does either of these definitions apply?

Well, to tell you the truth, they both apply to the HTML situation. There really are three "standards," and they are very similar. There is the W3C standard, the Microsoft standard, and the Netscape standard.

The W3C (the World Wide Web Consortium) has approved HTML standard 3.2. This is equivalent to saying that it has met to rewrite the rules of how to write a Web page. It may add tags, and it may recommend changes to the way current tags are used. It may also recommend that Webmasters not use certain older tags anymore. So far, it has been very careful about not dropping tags from the standard, thus remaining backwards-compatible.

The W3C defines itself as "an international industry consortium," jointly hosted by the Massachusetts Institute of Technology Laboratory for Computer Science [MIT/LCS] in the United States; the Institut National de Recherche en Informatique et en Automatique [INRIA] in Europe; and the Keio University Shonan Fujisawa Campus in Asia.

All of the major Internet players are members. The membership includes Adobe, Microsoft, Netscape, Apple, IBM, Pointcast, Spyglass, CompuServe, and the Hong Kong Jockey Club.

 TIP You can find out exactly what the W3C is currently considering by looking at **www.w3.org**. Also, the full list of member organizations is at **www.w3.org/pub/WWW/Consortium/Member/List.html**.

You can imagine the politics of these standards meetings. Microsoft and Netscape both want certain tags to be included in the standard because they both have visions for the future of the Internet. These visions certainly include their respective browsers at the center of the Internet. However, as in most committees, everyone must compromise a little. Microsoft doesn't always get what it wants, and neither does Netscape.

Remember when we defined a standard as "a set of rules to which others are compelled to conform"? Well, by that you would think that Microsoft and Netscape would then go back to the drawing board and write their new browsers not for their proposed standards, but for the standards that the W3C has approved, right? Wrong.

Microsoft and Netscape, due to sheer dominance of the market, have successfully been able to take that W3C standard, implement it fully, but then add on their own tags. They've come up with the Microsoft standard and the Netscape standard that they are actively trying to convince the W3C to include in future HTML standards. These are the flags that these respective armies rally around, and are commonly referred to as "extensions to the HTML standard." Critics of this practice have derisively called the extra tags "Microsoftisms" and "Netscapisms."

Netscape Extensions

Nevertheless, if you make a choice to implement some or all of these tags, you will need to know what they are and what they do. Let's start with Netscape.

Blink

Blinking text on a page is probably the most annoying thing that I've ever come across on the Web. First it's there, then it isn't. Then it is, then it isn't. Stylistically, it's not pleasing to any design, either. And it's a Netscape invention. Yuck.

```
<H1><CENTER><ALIGN="CENTER"><BLINK>This </BLINK>is the Headline of My
Page!</CENTER></H1>
```

Newspaper-Style Columns

Netscape has added a nice tag that allows you to show newspaper-style columns on a Web page. To use it, you should use the following HTML:

```
<MULTICOLS COLS=2 GUTTER=20 WIDTH=800>
This would be where you would put your text and graphics.
</MULTICOLS>
```

There are three attributes that you can use with the MULTICOLS tag. Those are COLS, GUTTER, and WIDTH.

COLS is the number of columns you want to have (see Figure 15.4).

GUTTER defines the amount of white space in pixels that you want between your columns.

WIDTH defines the total width in pixels of your browser screen.

FIG. 15.4
Columns can be used to give a newspaper-style feel to your Web page.

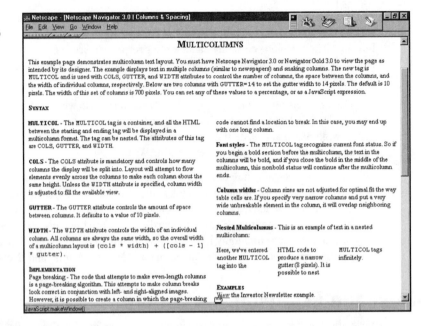

Whitespace

I just hate when I can't control how much space goes between words and lines. Since HTML ignores extra spaces, tab characters, carriage returns, and multiple </P> tags put in a row, it's practically impossible to really control whitespace on a Web page. Sure, to control vertical spacing you could use multiple <BR> tags, but what if I wanted a half line, instead of a full one? For horizontal spacing, I could use a <PRE> tag, but that makes my font take that horrible type-writer quality.

Now Netscape has introduced the <SPACER> container tag to help control both horizontal and vertical spacing.

```
The spacer tag can put whitespace in the
<SPACER TYPE-"HORIZONTAL" SIZE="75">middle of a line.<P>
It can also control how much space until
<SPACER TYPE="VERTICAL" SIZE="100">the next line starts.<P>
```

It also has a more powerful value for the TYPE attribute. You can use TYPE="BLOCK" to create a rectangle or square of whitespace.

```
<SPACER TYPE="BLOCK" HEIGHT="50" WIDTH="30" ALIGN="LEFT">
```

Embedding Technologies

With Netscape, you can use plug-in technologies to turn Navigator into a hotbed of multimedia. Built right into the browser is support for LiveAudio (which can play WAV, AU, AIFF, and MIDI sound formats), Live3D (VRML), LiveVideo (AVI movies), and QuickTime (MOV files that include text and MIDI sound).

All you need to do to incorporate any of these into your Web pages is to use the <EMBED> tag.

N O T E   Although <EMBED> is a Netscape extension, Internet Explorer supports it for most of these technologies through ActiveX controls. ■

▶ For an explanation of the EMBED tag, as well as information about many of these technologies, **see** the section "The <EMBED> Tag," in Chapter 18, "Browser Plug-Ins."

Microsoft Extensions

Let's face it. Internet Explorer 2.0 was a sad excuse for a browser. It had support for practically nothing. But when looking at IE3, you realize that it's incredible what Microsoft can do when it really puts its money and resources behind the cause. Not only did IE3 propel Microsoft into the forefront of the Internet browser competition, but it made the company into a major player in the HTML standards decisions. Yet, it still didn't get everything it wanted. So these are some of the tags that Internet Explorer supports that aren't in the current HTML standards.

 A great place to learn about HTML is the Microsoft Site Builder Workshop at **www.microsoft.com/ workshop**. Make sure you visit the section especially for Web authors—**www.microsoft.com/ workshop/author/**.

Background Music

Microsoft allows you to embed background music right into your pages with a simple tag, <BGSOUND>. BGSOUND takes the attribute LOOP to determine how many times your sound file will play. Your sound file can be a .wav, .au, or MIDI file. An example of this would be:

```
<BGSOUND SRC="chimes.wav" LOOP=5>My, aren't those
pretty chimes playing five times in a row?
```

> **CAUTION**
> Sound files can be rather large, so make sure you don't use files that will slow down your users dialing in from modem connections.

 MIDI files can be used as background sounds, which is advantageous because they can be much smaller than other sound files.

Fixed Backgrounds

This is the same as a normal background, except when your viewers scroll down the screen, it doesn't move with them. This has been called the "watermark" background because of its similarity to the watermark that some companies have on their letterhead.

Just add the attribute BGPROPERTIES=FIXED to your BODY tag:

```
<BODY BACKGROUND="mypattern.gif" BGPROPERTIES=FIXED>
```

Marquees

Microsoft has also included a container tag called MARQUEE that allows you to animate a line of text. The text in the MARQUEE tag will scroll in the direction of your choice. It takes the attributes BEHAVIOR, DIRECTION, SCROLLDELAY, and SCROLLAMOUNT to determine specifically how you will see the marquee.

```
<MARQUEE BEHAVIOR=SCROLL DIRECTION=LEFT SCROLLDELAY=100
SCROLLAMOUNT=40>Now we all want to use Microsoft
Internet Explorer because of this cool scrolling
marquee, right?</MARQUEE>
```

When you use this tag, text will be scrolling from the right to the left, as specified by BEHAVIOR and DIRECTION. SCROLLAMOUNT and SCROLLDELAY specify that the text moves 40 pixels after a delay of 100 milliseconds.

AVI Video

Microsoft has made embedding AVI video into your Web pages rather easy by adding an attribute to the <IMG> tag, as follows:

```
<IMG DYNSRC="VIDEO.AVI">
```

If you want the users to get play, pause, forward, and other buttons so that they can watch the video over and over again, modify your tag as follows:

```
<IMG DYNSRC="VIDEO.AVI" CONTROLS>
```

And if you want to provide a still image for those viewers who still aren't using Internet Explorer to view your site:

```
<IMG DYNSRC="VIDEO.AVI" SRC="STILLPHOTO.JPG CONTROLS">
```

CAUTION

If you thought I was being overly careful when warning you about using large sound files in your Web pages, you should really pay attention now. Video files are almost always huge and may take forever and a day to download. Unless you expect everyone to be logging into your site from a fast ethernet connection, I'd be real careful about alienating my viewers coming in from modem connections.

Style Sheets

Microsoft has taken the lead in bringing a resolution to the W3C Standards committee for Cascading Style Sheets (CSS1). Style Sheets will allow the author to contol properties such as margins, fonts, and colors from within a Web page or from an external document.

Internet Explorer currently supports Cascading Style Sheets. For a full explanation of how to use the <STYLE> tag to implement this feature, see Chapter 14, "Style Sheets."

The <*OBJECT*> Tag

The <OBJECT> tag is a container tag used by authors to implement ActiveX Controls into a Web page. It merely gives the ActiveX Control a name and points to URLs where the actual ActiveX code resides.

▶ For more information about how to implement the <OBJECT> tag, **see** the section, "Inserting Controls with the OBJECT Tag" in Chapter 22, "ActiveX Controls."

## CHAPTER 16

Dynamic HTML

by Rob Falla

The Internet is advancing the way we communicate with each other. Originally, you started by posting hyperlinked documents on the Internet. You could go to a text-only document, read its contents, and follow a link to another document. These early versions of Web sites had very little to offer aside from the ability to connect many documents together with target/anchor tag sets and some control (more like suggestions) over the appearance of the document. At that time it was seen as a major advancement in communications.

Slowly, additions were made to HTML. The ability to initiate an FTP, WAIS, or e-mail session was added. Images and sound capabilities, with all the negative effects on bandwidth, came to be major selling points of the Internet. More recently, additions to the Web include plug-ins, Java, JavaScript, VBScript, and other scripting languages.

The next big wave on the Internet came from the introduction of Cascading Style Sheets (CSS). By including a CSS style sheet on an HTML document, the developer could control with greater certainty the appearance of the document. CSS allows the developer to assign style properties to HTML elements. You can give a table a background color of yellow with a small font size, and assign different variables to an embedded table (see Figure 16.1). Microsoft included support for CSS with Internet Explorer 3. It was the first commercial browser to support CSS and, at the time of this writing, is still the only publicly available browser to support it.

What is Dynamic HTML?

This chapter will teach you how to begin using HTML documents created with Dynamic HTML and how to create your own Dynamic HTML documents.

The Basics of Dynamic HTML

To properly create Dynamic HTML documents, you should understand some of the basics.

Dynamic Multimedia

As well as modifying the basic elements of an HTML document, Dynamic HTML also allows you to create Advanced Multimedia presentations in the HTML document.

Examples

A number of examples will be presented throughout this chapter to facilitate the learning process.

FIG. 16.1
Here's a CSS Example.

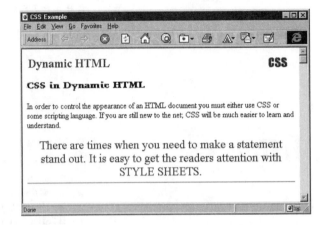

CSS is limited to altering only the appearance: the background, the font data, border, and margins. Although that is a major step in the right direction for HTML document presentation, it merely scratches the surface of what developers want.

With each addition to HTML and the Web family of technologies, Web sites began looking more programmatic. The more programmatic the Web appeared, the more control developers wanted over the HTML document. That is where Dynamic HTML comes into play.

▶ **See** "Attaching a Style Sheet to Your HTML Document," **p. 286**

Introducing Dynamic HTML

Dynamic HTML is best described as an application program interface (API) for manipulating the behavior of HTML tags and elements on an HTML document. The components of the document will do whatever you program them to do.

Think of the HTML document as a static presentation of data. There are many ways to display that data—as part of a table, for example. But, the document remains static. In order to remove the static label from your Web site, you will probably add a Java script that inserts a message into the status area of the browser. You are almost certainly going to use a CGI order form. You may even start using ActiveX scripts. That is a good start, but for a truly interactive document you need to be able to control every HTML element.

Using Dynamic HTML, you override and change the properties of the individual elements dynamically. You are no longer limited to accepting the tags for what they are (working around the limitations they impose on you). You define what they (HTML elements) are, what they do, and how they do it.

If you are familiar with VBScript or JavaScript, learning Dynamic HTML should be fairly easy. With Dynamic HTML, you write Scripts that respond to user actions or timer events. The events will cause the script to run, dynamically altering the appearance of the element almost instantly, without causing the page to refresh.

N O T E The absence of the refresh action is responsible for allowing the content of the page to be altered dynamically. Each time the page is refreshed, it will revert to its original state, not the desired effect for Dynamic content, which requires that the document not automatically refresh. ■

In this section, you will learn the basics of Dynamic HTML, as well as what tools are required to run it. The section will end with an example HTML document.

Reduce Download Time

Dynamic HTML greatly speeds up the loading time for subsequent links within your site, thus eliminating the annoying wait, usually experienced while the document is loaded. This seemingly amazing feat of data transfer is actually performed in the background; the browser shows no outward indication. However, all related documents and any other document inclusions are loaded and cached.

When the first page is completely loaded, the user can begin reading and interacting with that page. While the user is going over the first page, the remainder of the site will be cached to the user system. Any additional pages for the site will appear to the user to upload almost instantly. Audio and video files, as well as animation, images and anything else included within your site will also be cached.

Many Web sites consist of not just one, but a number of HTML documents. Often, those documents also include an audio file, possibly even a movie. Well, it may be true that the first page of a Web site is almost always, as a general design rule, small and easy to load, the linked pages can often take many seconds, or even minutes. Dynamic HTML has the ability to cut that time to a mere fraction by caching the remainder of the site when you load the first page.

Tools of Dynamic HTML

You need an *editor* and a *browser* to create and use Dynamic HTML documents. Unfortunately, there are no WYSIWYG editors that can be used to create Dynamic HTML documents at this time. With the pace of Internet technology development, you will probably see one soon.

Choose an Editor   Any text-based editor, or combination of text and WYSIWYG editor will be sufficient for creating a Dynamic HTML document. In fact, there are many advantages to using the WYSIWYG editor to get the document started, adding the script and CSS later with a text-based editor. The problem with that approach is that once you have added the CSS and scripts, you cannot use the WYSIWYG editor again. It will not be able to handle the under-the-hood CSS and script. There are some editors that are attempting to overcome that barrier. Chapter 35, "WYSIWYG HTML Editors," will probably be helpful on this point.

Which Browser Do You Need?   Dynamic HTML is another creation from Microsoft. The only browser that supports the API at present is Internet Explorer 4.0. With many of the components of Dynamic HTML being before the W3C as proposals, there is a real possibility that Dynamic HTML, like the scripting languages, will be supported by the other browsers (Netscape and Mosaic).

Before you begin creating Dynamic HTML documents, you should make sure your audience knows which browser they should be using, including the version number. Also, you should remember that it will take time for the newest browser to become the standard (which actually never happens; people change browsers faster than any other application). Make sure your site is reverse compatible, or you will lose too many visitors because they haven't yet started using the right browser.

Here's How Dynamic HTML Works

When an HTML document is created with Dynamic HTML, everything on the document is considered an object. If it weren't, there would be no way to dynamically manipulate the document elements (objects).

Every element within the document object is actually a subobject of the main or a super document object. The HTML document includes parts that may be from outside of the HTML file. They are still part of the document and are therefore subobjects of the document object. A CSS style sheet is an example of an external element that takes on the characteristics of being an object of the document object. Each of the CSS elements in the style sheet are children objects of the style sheet object.

Each HTML tag is an object. These objects can be accessed and manipulated by using one of many methods. Dynamic HTML provides the interface methods for direct access of the tag properties. Another method included (as a requirement of CSSOM) under the Dynamic HTML umbrella is CSS.

Each of the collections created by the Dynamic HTML document is an object that can be used to manipulate the document (adding a new element for example).

Scripts and inline scripts are also objects. These objects may include several subobjects of their own. There is a lot of potential in the HTML document development area for creating dynamic documents by using object-oriented programming. When the timer or user event action occurs, the event causes the script to be fired, for example, by placing a mouse over an HTML element.

The Basics of Dynamic HTML

Dynamic HTML provides greater presentation control for the developer. There is also greater support for 2-D layout and data bindings. The basic components of Dynamic HTML, data bindings, and 2-D layout will be briefly introduced here.

Understanding the Components

Dynamic HTML is separated into four components: content, structure, style, and interaction. As understanding these topics is important for the developer, they will be presented here. This is a discussion of concepts which are also common sense.

Content   The major difference between Dynamic HTML and basic HTML is the way the content of the document is presented (dynamically, something happens when the user strikes a key on the keyboard or positions the mouse over the appropriate element).

Structure   The structural hierarchy tree of an HTML document is usually thrown by the browser when the document is painted to the browser window. Dynamic HTML creates collections from the tree, keeping the collections open and ready to respond (by altering the appearance of the document) to timer or user-action events (see Table 16.1).

Table 16.1   Additional Topics Related to the Structure

Topic	Description
Structure	The Structure of the Dynamic HTML document
Events	Using script events
Objects	Containers for HTML elements
Collections	Grouping the HTML elements and Objects for future referencing

As you read this chapter, you should notice that the HTML elements (tags) are treated as objects. These objects, along with other traditional objects, are sorted and placed into collections at runtime (when the document is downloaded). Normally, there would be no collecting of elements and objects; the browser would just throw the document structure as soon as the document was loaded. That is not the case with Dynamic HTML.

As events are fired, the browser opens the collections, allowing the script to alter the properties of the objects or create new objects. When the properties in the collection are edited by the script, the change is immediate.

Style   CSS already provides a mechanism for altering the properties of an HTML element. Dynamic HTML takes that mechanism, throws in the object model, and delivers a mechanism for altering the appearance of an HTML document dynamically. There is at present no mechanism for writing to a linked or imported style sheet; only inline and embedded style sheets can be written to, that is where the CSSOM comes in. The CSS Object Model allows the developer to create style sheet rules for dynamically altering the appearance of the document by writing to a virtual representation of the linked or imported style sheet. There is a more complete discussion on the CSSOM and how to use it later in this chapter.

Interactivity   Dynamic HTML takes interactive Internet communications to the next level, expanding the boundaries of what is interactive far beyond any expectations. Interactive elements with Dynamic HTML include every HTML element. If you have inserted a hidden paragraph in the text of the document, and want the user to be able to make the paragraph appear by clicking the H1 element immediately preceding the hidden paragraph, you need to tell the user the H1 is clickable. You have two choices here—you either insert a line of text near the paragraph that tells the user to click the H1 element, or you can make it more interesting by making the color of the H1 element change when the user moves the mouse over it, for example. There is more on this later in the chapter.

Data Binding

Using a database on an HTML document has traditionally required using a complicated set of procedures. With the HTML extensions Dynamic HTML introduces, it is as easy as creating a table.

Dynamic HTML seeks to minimize the scripting required to make a great-looking Web site. An example of that goal is the work put into creating a simple group of HTML extensions that take many of the tasks of database management out of the realm of the server and make them client-dependent. This switch of responsibilities will greatly improve the bandwidth consumption problems experienced by present Web sites. It is beyond the scope of this chapter to go into a full discussion of this topic.

2-D Layout

In addition to easing the task of using a database on your HTML document, Dynamic HTML helps you to create simple animation effects with HTML. The trick is rather simple; you use a combination of CSS, a scripting language for timing the animation, and HTML.

This is another example of how Dynamic HTML will reduce the amount of bandwidth currently being wasted. How many sites are using animated gifs to present some fairly simple animation? One that could be created with Dynamic HTML by using only a few lines of code and HTML?

Using the Document Structure

The user requests your URL (clicks a link to it from Yahoo! or some other source). Your browser sends the request and waits for a reply. When your site starts loading to the browser, it will read through the document HEAD to look for any handling instructions, such as setting the background and foreground colors, assigning style sheets, meta links, and so on.

Next, it will scan the body of the document and collect all occurrences of HTML elements, scripts, inline elements, and so on. The browser creates the structure array, remembering the location in the document (showing order) of each occurrence of each element. Finally, the browser will display (show) the document in the browser window.

Why Is Structure So Important in Dynamic HTML?

The browser must have some sort of reference point for dynamically altering the appearance of the document. Since you are opting out of having the browser fetch a new, HTML-on-the-fly document from the server, there must be an interface between the browser and the physical layout of the document.

The only way for the browser to maintain control over the appearance of the document is to keep the document display structure open, allowing it to be modified when scripts are fired.

How Collections Work

As the document is loaded, the editable collection is automatically created. This will allow the browser to interpret the various aspects of the Web document in a more organized way than with the present static HTML documents.

This is how it works:

1. The browser creates a collection, similar to an index.
2. Items, tags, and classes are all sorted.
3. The sorted data items are indexed by their showing order on the document.
4. Sorted data is also indexed by the exposed keys. (Objects provide methods for accessing parent and children elements.)

The collection consists of items, tags, and classes, called collecting methods in Dynamic HTML (see Table 16.2). The collecting methods are explained as follow:

Table 16.2 Collecting Methods

Method	Description
Item	Used to search the document specifically for one item. The item is returned as a collection if there is more than one occurrence of the selected item. If the item is only matched once throughout the document, it is returned as an element.
Tags	Used to create a collection of tags. This method will return a collection of the specified tags. This method is not case sensitive.
Classes	Used to return a collection of classes in the document. The method will return a collection of the specified class. This method is not case sensitive.

The collections are dependable; they will always represent the current state of the document. The collections that are created when the document is loaded will automatically be updated if the user manipulates the document.

A structural collection is used to provide an interface for accessing the properties of elements, as well as an index of all elements in the document. Since it is the access to the document structure which makes Dynamic HTML possible, you will see more about it in the following sections. This section was meant to get you thinking about the structure of the document and how each item is related to the other.

cancelBubble versus *returnValue*

cancelBubble is used to prevent an action from being fired on any other element in the hierarchy. A document may contain an image that is nested with an anchor element, which is itself neatly positioned on the document with the assistance of a borderless table. Using Dynamic HTML, you may set the anchor element to flash colors when the mouse enters the element area. To prevent the rest of the document from also flashing colors, you must insert a cancelBubble in the event handler script.

returnValue is the function used to tell the browser if the default value of the element is used. You will only need to use it to prevent the default action of the element from happening. A simple example of using the returnValue function is given in Listing 16.1.

Listing 16.1 Cancel the Bubble

```
<HTML>
<!--
    Listing 1
    TITLE: Bubbling
-->
<HEAD>
<title>canceling the bubbling action</title>
<STYLE>
<!--
BODY {background:white}
A:LINK {text-decoration:none
        font-size:12px;
        color:black;
        weight:bold}
-->
</STYLE>
  <SCRIPT Language=Javascript>
  function thisA(){
event.returnValue=false;
event.cancelBubble=true;
            }
  function inA() {
document.all.thisA.style.color= "green"
        }
function outA() {
document.all.thisA.style.color= ""
        }
  </SCRIPT>
</HEAD>
<BODYonmouseover="setupEffect()" onmouseout="cleanupEffect()">
<TABLE>
<P>Well now, <A HREF="newpage.html" ID=thisA onclick="thisA()"
onmouseover="inA()" onmouseout="outA()">Hello</A> and how are you today?</P>
</TABLE>
</BODY>
</HTML>
```

Using Events with Dynamic HTML

An event must occur for a script to be fired. The event can be a user action or it can be a timer event. In this section, you will learn about some of the Dynamic HTML events, and you will learn how to use them. It would be impossible to present every single event in this chapter, but the most common events are explained.

Using Elements of Events

Each element in the document will expose an interface for editing the element's properties. By exposing the element properties, the Dynamic HTML API allows developers to modify elements of the document dynamically. What that means is the developer can write an event-handler script that will go into the structural hierarchy of the document and make modifications based on actions of the user. Consider Listing 16.2.

Part

III

Ch

16

Listing 16.2   Added Functionality to the *menuH1* Example Element

```
<HTML>
<!--
     Listing 2
     TITLE:
-->
<HEAD>
<STYLE>
<!--
body   {background:white}
H1   {font-size:26px}
-->
</STYLE>
<SCRIPT TYPE="text/javascript">
function menuH1()   {
     // menu box pop-up
     }
</SCRIPT>
<SCRIPT FOR=menuH1 EVENT="onmouseover()" TYPE="text/javascript">
document.menuH1.style.color="blue"
</SCRIPT>
<SCRIPT FOR=menuH1 EVENT="onmouseout()" TYPE="text/javascript">
document.menuH1.style.color = ""
</SCRIPT>
</HEAD>
<BODY onmouseover="setupEffect()" onmouseout="cleanupEffect()">
<H1 ID=menuH1>This H1 element will do more than an average H1.</H1>
</BODY>
</HTML>
```

Inspection of the code reveals the elements that these codes apply to. The first one is `function menuH1()`; to put it in plain English, that script is an inline event-handler script for the element that has `menuH1` included within its name.

```
<H1 ID=menuH1>This H1 element will do more than the average H1.</H1>
```

The two other scripts in Listing 16.3 are also applied to the menuH1 element. They are fired when the required event occurs. These two scripts are supplied to make identifying the interactive portion of the script easier.

When the user puts the mouse into (onmouseover) the selected elements area, the first of the two scripts is fired. This will cause the color of the element to change to black (or whatever other color you choose). This changing of colors has probably attracted the user's attention.

If the firing of the first script failed to attract the user's attention and alert him to the fact that this is more than another H1 header, don't worry; there is still the other script, the final script in the listing. When the user moves the mouse away from the element (onmouseout), the final script of Listing 16.3 would be fired. This script causes the element to return to its original color.

Even if the user only passes over the element with the mouse while reading through the document (using the mouse as a pointer to follow along at the rate of reading), both scripts will be fired. The effect of that type of pass-over will be to make the element flash from its original color to black and back to its original color. That should be enough to alert the reader to the fact that the element has some function other than being a simple header.

The reader will position the mouse on the element again to see if it actually did change colors (or if he should lay off the computer for a while). When he sees the element change colors, he will either click the element to see where it takes him, or he will file the information into memory and continue on with reading the document, returning to the element when he is ready.

The naming rules for Dynamic HTML are similar to those of other languages like JavaScript. The first keyword is lowercased; any other keyword's first letter is capitalized.

The following is an example:

```
exampleKeywords
```

Using the Events

The Dynamic HTML events are specific for the Dynamic HTML API and will not work in a browser that doesn't support the API. Some of the events are generic events that are supported by Internet Explorer 3.0 and Netscape Navigator 3.0. With careful planning, you can create Dynamic HTML documents that still look cool in the older browsers.

The events are given here to help you begin developing Dynamic HTML documents. There are three types of events in Dynamic HTML. Each of these event types will be discussed here.

Standard Events   The first of the three types of Dynamic HTML events are Standard Events. These are events that can be used with any HTML element (in a variety of ways). Table 16.3 identifies the Standard Events that are included as part of the Dynamic HTML API:

Table 16.3   Standard Events

Event	Fired When...
onclick	The user clicks the mouse button (left only) to make a script fire. This event was illustrated in a previous section.
ondblclick	The user must double-click the element.
onmousedown	The mouse button goes down while on an element.
onmousemove	The mouse must be moved over the element. This event is fired when the mouse crosses the element boundaries. No further action from the user is required.
onmouseup	This event will fire the script when the mouse button goes up over the selected element.
onmouseover	When the mouse enters the element, the script is fired. This event was illustrated in Listing 16.3.
onmouseout	When the mouse exits the element. This event was shown in Listing 16.3.
onkeydown	A key on the keyboard went down.
onkeypress	A key is pressed.
onkeyup	A key on the keyboard has gone up.
onscroll	The script is fired only if the event of scrolling the element occurs.

Focusable Element Events   Some elements can receive the focus, which means the browser will turn its attention almost exclusively to that element. These elements have the events in Table 16.4 available to them in addition to the events previously described.

If you use a focusable event, you must use them all for the element. For that reason, the events are displayed here, not in alphabetical order but rather in the order they must appear if used on an element.

Table 16.4   Focusable Events

Event	Fired When...
onenter	The element is being entered.
onfocus	The element is receiving the focus.
onexit	The element is being exited.
onblur	The focus leaves the element.

Element-Specific Events These are events that are only valid events for specific elements. They are for specialty events, such as what the browser should do if the user aborts the loading of an image (see Table 16.5).

Table 16.5 Element-Specific Events

Event	Valid Elements	Fired When...
onabort	`<IMG>`	The user aborts the download of an image.
onchange	`<input type=checkbox>` `<input type=file>` `<input type=password>` `<input type=text>` `<input type=radio>` `<select><textarea>`	The object changes from user input. The element must be focusable for this event.
onload	`<body><image>`	The element is completely loaded.
onreadystatechange	`<applet><embed><frame>` `<iframe><IMG><object>` `<script src=>`	The state of the element has changed.
onreset	`<form>`	The reset button is clicked, which means the user has reset the form.
onselect	`<input type=password>` `<input type=text>` `<textarea>`	The mouse button is released which causes text to be selected.
onsubmit	`<form>`	A form is about to be submitted. It submits the form.
onunload	`<body>`	Just before the document is unloaded.

With your knowledge of JavaScript or VBScript and the data provided in the above three tables, you should have no problem converting your HTML document to a Dynamic HTML document. Consider Listings 16.3 and 16.4. They are for the same document, but one uses Dynamic HTML. If you are using Internet Explorer 4.0, you will be able to evaluate the two listings. If you are using Internet Explorer 3.0 or Netscape Navigator 3.0, they will both look almost the same, the major exception here being that Internet Explorer 3.0 supports CSS and will therefore render the document by using the styles provided in the style sheet.

Listing 16.3 A Simple HTML Document

```
<HTML>
<HEAD>
<STYLE>
```

```
<!--
body {background:white; color:black}
big {font-size:150%; color:blue}
small {font-size:50%; color:blue}
UL {color:red}
H1 {font-size:25px; color:blue; weight:bold}
H2 {font-size:25px; color:blue; font-family:impact}
H3 {color:black}
PRE {font-size:12px; color:brown}
A:LINK {text-decoration:none
        color:black;
        weight:bold}
-->
</STYLE>
<TITLE>Stewart Computerized Service</TITLE>
</HEAD>
<BODY>
<TABLE WIDTH=98% >
<TR><TD ALIGN="LEFT" ><H1>Welcome to</H1></TD>

<TD ALIGN="RIGHT" ><H2>Stewart Computerized Services</H2></TD></TR>
</TABLE>
<TABLE CELLSPACING=20  CELLPADDING=0>
<TR ><TD>
<H3>we specialize in</H3>
<UL>
<LI>reports, transcripts</LI>
<LI>mailings, flyers</LI>
<LI>resumes, portfolios</LI>
<LI>invoicing, statements</LI>
<LI>theses, essays</LI>
<LI>correspondence, contracts</LI>
<LI>Dictaphone</LI>
<LI>spreadsheets, proposals</LI>

</UL>
</TD><TD WIDTH=500  VALIGN="TOP" >
<P>Would you like a fast, economical way to deal with all that tiresome
paperwork???  Just pick up the phone & call Steward Computer Services! We have
several years experience in the computer field and we can take care of all that
paperwork for you!  We have a complete system including Windows '95, a voice/fax
modem, CD ROM and deskjet printer with a colour kit as well as a photocopier
capable of reducing and enlarging.  We can provide all the necessary supplies or
you can supply your own, whichever you wish.</P>
</TD></TR>
</TABLE>
<CENTER>
No job is<BIG> too big</BIG> or <SMALL>too small</SMALL>
</CENTER>


<DIV id=hidden STYLE="text-align:center">
<P>a paragraph describing the item on the list.</P>
</DIV>
<BR>
```

Part
III

Ch
16

continues

Listing 16.3   Continued

```
<P><EM>Rush Job???</EM> <B> No problem</B> - </P><P><CENTER>
Our staff will work nights and /or weekends, if necessary, to ensure <I>your</I>
satisfaction!
</CENTER></P>
<HR>
<P>Please call anytime for a free estimate!<BR>"You won't believe how inexpen-
sive we can be"</P>

<P><PRE>
Stewart Computer Services
Attention:  Vicky Stewart,  President
E-mail: <A HREF="mailto:vstewart@netroute.net"> vstewart@netroute.net</A>
</PRE></P>
<HR>

</BODY>
</HTML>
```

Listing 16.4   The Simple Document—with Dynamic HTML

```
<HTML>
<HEAD>
<STYLE>
<!--
body {background:white; color:black}
big {font-size:25px; color:blue}
small {font-size:10px; color:blue}
UL {color:red}
H1 {font-size:25px; color:blue; weight:bold}
H2 {font-size:25px; color:blue; font-family:impact}
H3 {color:black}
PRE {font-size:12px; color:brown}
A:LINK {text-decoration:none
        color:black;
        weight:bold}
-->
</STYLE>
<TITLE>Stewart Computerized Service</TITLE>
<SCRIPT language=javascript>
function myAddress(){
document.all.myAddress.style.fontSize="16px"
}
function init() {
document.all.myAddress.style.fontSize="12px"
}
</SCRIPT>
</HEAD>
<BODY>
<TABLE WIDTH=98% >
<TR><TD ALIGN="LEFT" ><H1>Welcome to</H1></TD>
```

```
<TD ALIGN="RIGHT" ><H2>Stewart Computerized Services</H2></TD></TR>
</TABLE>
<TABLE CELLSPACING=20  CELLPADDING=0>
<TR ><TD
<H3>we specialize in</H3>
<UL>
<LI onmouseover="document.all.hidden.style.display = ''"
onmouseout="document.all.hidden.style.display='none'">reports, transcripts</LI>
<LI>mailings, flyers</LI>
<LI>resumes, portfolios</LI>
<LI>invoicing, statements</LI>
<LI>theses, essays</LI>
<LI>correspondence, contracts</LI>
<LI>Dictaphone</LI>
<LI>spreadsheets, proposals</LI>

</UL>
</TD><TD WIDTH=500  VALIGN="TOP" >
<P>Would you like a fast, economical way to deal with all that tiresome paper-
work???  Just pick up the phone & call Steward Computer Services! We have
several years experience in the computer field and we can take care of all that
paperwork for you!  We have a complete system including Windows '95, a voice/fax
modem, CD ROM and deskjet printer with a colour kit as well as a photocopier
capable of reducing and enlarging.  We can provide all the necessary supplies or
you can supply your own, whichever you wish.</P>
</TD></TR>
</TABLE>
<CENTER>
No job is<BIG> too big</BIG> or <SMALL>too small</SMALL>
</CENTER>


<DIV id=hidden STYLE="display:none;text-align:center">
<P>This content is hidden using display</P>
<MARQUEE WIDTH=98%>
A paragraph about each item on the list can be used to further describe them
without having to link to another document or having a huge list.
!</MARQUEE>
</DIV>
<BR>

<P><EM>Rush Job???</EM> <B> No problem</B> - </P><P><CENTER>
Our staff will work nights and /or weekends, if necessary, to ensure <I>your</I>
satisfaction!
</CENTER></P>
<HR>
<P>Please call anytime for a free estimate!<BR>"You won't believe how inexpen-
sive we can be"</P>

<P><PRE ID=myAddress onmouseover="myAddress()" onmouseout="init()">
Stewart Computer Services
Attention:  Vicky Stewart,  President
```

continues

Listing 16.4 Continued

```
E-mail: <A HREF="mailto:vstewart@netroute.net"> vstewart@netroute.net</A>
</PRE></P>
<HR>

</BODY>
</HTML>
```

In the preceding example, there are two Dynamic HTML elements; the first reveals text when the mouse is placed over the first item on the list—reports, transcripts. The hidden text is brought to view by the `onmouseover` event occurring on the element. The other Dynamic element is at the bottom of the document, the address. When the user puts the mouse on the address area, the font size increases. Figures 16.2 and 16.3 fall short of displaying the results of the Dynamic HTML code—which is quite impossible in a book—but they show the final outcome. If you try these examples for yourself, you will see the hidden text appear under the list and the address resizing itself.

FIG. 16.2

Hidden text.

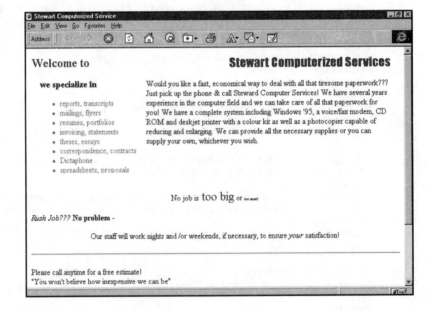

FIG. 16.3

Dynamically resized text.

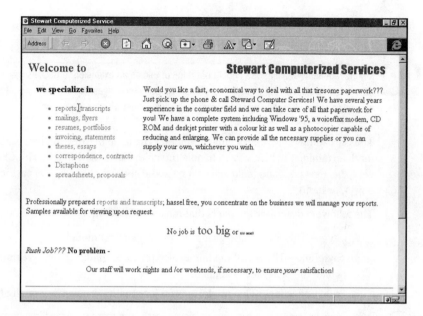

Using the CSSOM

Cascading Style Sheets allow you to modify the appearance of content by defining presentation rules that are rendered by the CSS-compliant browser. CSSOM (CSS Object Model) will allow you to access the presentation rules and properties of the Style Sheet object elements and edit, add, or delete elements of the style sheet.

This means that with Dynamic HTML, it is possible to change the style properties based on interaction with the user. Now, there is the possibility of making a script that tells the browser to change the font family of a particular element when the user enters that element, and to revert to the original font family when the user exits the element.

The structural data array for the document will have the style elements mapped out and cross referenced by the HTML elements they affect. This mapping is in the form of a database of entries organized by their showing order, then further organized by the position of each occurrence of the element.

Simply put, CSSOM gives you the ability to write scripts that dynamically alter the properties of the style sheet. This can be accomplished by the user doing something like moving the mouse onto a particular element. The script can also include a timer event or an ActiveX timer, making simple animation effects with text and CSS.

Containment in HTML

There are three containment types to choose from.

■ Scripts—References to the structure and properties are made from within a script.

- Objects—Any construct that has access to the Object Model.
- Inline scripts—Inline event-handler scripts.

 TIP Anyone familiar with using CSS should not think of this as an extension to CSS. As you can see from the preceding list, CSSOM is an Object Model. Scripting languages like ActiveX or JavaScript are allowed to modify the style rules declared in the style sheet with the object model.

The Cascading Style Sheets Object Model is made up of three distinct parts; each one is used for determining the best way to handle the rule, based on the type. The CSSOM parts perform very specific tasks, and make sure you use the correct object model part for the job (element, object, or item).

The following describes the parts that make up CSSOM:

- Style—This is a "single group" (style properties) model.
- StyleRule—The StyleRule model also provides guidance for determining the context in which the StyleRule is applied.
- Rule Collection—This model is used for creating a collection of all StyleRules.

 TIP Most CSSOM properties are R/W (Read/Write) unless explicitly declared R/O (Read Only).

Style Model

The style (single group) model will be used for adding, editing, or deleting a single (instance occurrence) item. This is useful for changing the style properties based on user interaction. You may recall that this method was already used in Listing 16.4. To reinforce the example, look at the following code:

```
<SCRIPT FOR=menuH1 EVENT="onmouseover()" TYPE="text/javascript">
document.menuH1.style. color = "black"
</SCRIPT>
```

In the preceding script, you have probably noticed that the word style appears. This is a keyword telling the browser that the single item property (color) is to be restyled as indicated.

```
document.menuH1.style.backgroundColor= "black"
```

The code would be read by the browser in the following order. From within the structure of the document. there is an element identified as menuH1.; it should be modified as a single item occurrence style. by using the backgroundColor= property.

Only the color property (in this example) is modified; any other style features will remain the same. Because of the way the Dynamic HTML API uses the structural array, any changes required by the script have been anticipated by the browser. That means immediately after the required event occurs, the element modifications become the element properties.

styleRule Model and styleRule Collections

While being similar to the style model, styleRule is used to modify every occurrence of a style sheet element. The distinction is an important one because if you will be using style sheets regularly, you will probably use the @import method for your style sheet. Using that (or the LINK) method to add style to an HTML document, especially a large Web site, is just common sense. Why put an embedded style sheet on every page of the site when a simple two-line LINK or one-line @import will accomplish the same task?

▶ **See** "Linking a Style sheet," **p. 286**

▶ **See** "Importing Style sheets," **p. 289**

Recall that the style model is for a single occurrence, and styleRule is used to modify every occurrence of a single element. If you are working with a large site, it makes no sense to change the properties from within the style sheet if you only mean to use the new style properties for the single page. When you add new styleRules to the document, an embedded style sheet will be created to contain those rules (you cannot write new rule properties to a read-only style sheet) (see Listing 16.5).

Also, if your intention is to modify the appearance of the element only where it is found within another element (a table), you don't want to modify the properties in the embedded style sheet (that would change EVERY occurrence of the element).

Listing 16.5   Imported Style Sheet (Embedded into Listing 16.6)

```
<style type="text/css">
<!--
BODY        { background:white;
                    color:black
                    font-size:15px
}
P   {color:blue;
     margin:6pt;
     font:13px
}
B {color:darkblue;
      font-size:12px
}
H1   {color:red;
         font-family:impact;
         font-size:30px
}
A:link  { text-decoration:none;
             color:gray;
             font-size: 10pt;
             font-weight: bold
}
A:visited     { color:#00009c; text-decoration:line-through;
                    font-size: 8pt;
         font-weight: bold
```

continues

Listing 16.5   Continued

```
}
TABLE  TABLE  {background:"#F5F9D0";
                  color:blue;
                  font:12px
}
TH { color:brown;
                  font:14px
}
HR {color:red}
-->
</style>
```

The style sheet and the script are given as two separate listings to simplify understanding of the relationship between the two components of the same Dynamic HTML document (see Listing 16.6).

Listing 16.6   Example CSSOM styleRules Model

```
<SCRIPT LANGUAGE=Javascript>
'the first line will turn every B element
'(within the current document) purple
document.styleRules.[2].style.color= "purple"

'instead of brown you want the TH element to
'be purple as well (a theme for the document),
document.styleRules.[7].style.color= "purple"

'now add a new style rule to the structure
var pend_index
pend_index = document.styleRules.add ( "P.end" )

'the following will make any P element with the .end class
'be resized to the specified size
document.styleRules.[ pend_index ].style.fontSize=8px
</SCRIPT>
```

The first line of the script for Listing 16.6 reads as follows:

From the document. tree in the structural array go to the substructure for the styleRules.

Once there, look for the item identified as number [2]. in the tree. This is the location of the style control properties for the B element.

The next keyword, (style.) is used to tell the API to change the style property (color=) being modified for the item ([2].) with the new property information, specified for this example as color="purple".

The items in the document structure are numbered [0 - n]. If there are 30 items in the styleRules structural tree, they are numbered [0 - 29] (the first item is [0] and the last item is

[29] in the tree hierarchy). So, the item numbers [2] and [7] in Listing 16.6 are references to the third and eighth items in the tree.

The next section of the script is a directive to add a new class to the styleRules document subtree. This would prove useful if you are working with a large collection of HTML documents (a large Web site comes to mind, although there are other uses for HTML documents).

```
pend_index = document.styleRules.add ( "P.end" )
```

The preceding line will add a new styleRules item to the pend_index. The new style sheet property is called P.end, a class addition to the Paragraph element.

The key to setting the properties for this new styleRules item is the pend_index, found in the next script as a reference to which styleRule element the script is modifying.

```
document.styleRules.[ pend_index ].style.fontSize=8px
```

N O T E It is possible to specify a requested position to place new styleRules in the collection when you use the add method. If you attempt to force (using a specific index in an external style sheet) the new rules into an R/O (external style sheet) element, the operation will fail.

If no position is requested, the new styleRule will, by default, be placed at the bottom of the styleRules collection. The new rule, if placed at the end of the collection, is given the highest precedence. ▪

You can use any index name you want, but remember the limitations. You cannot write to a read-only style sheet. Any time you add a new rule, it is either added to the embedded style sheet or (when there are no embedded style sheets) a new embedded style sheet is created.

CSSOM Naming Rules

As was previously discussed, Dynamic HTML has its own naming rules. The naming rules that apply specifically to CSSOM are the following:

- Start with the normal CSS name for the property.
- Convert the property name (first word) string to lowercase.
- Convert any characters following nonalphanumeric characters to uppercase.
- Remove all nonalphanumeric characters from the string.

N O T E The two following examples of the same property name represent the problem developers are facing—which is to say that there really is no problem if you remember that in CSS you can use nonalphanumeric characters, while in CSSOM the name must always consist of alphanumeric characters.

```
font-family
```

is the normal CSS property name when used in a style sheet.

```
fontFamily
```

is the name for the property using the CSSOM naming conversion rules. ▪

The naming rules absolutely must be applied when using CSSOM. If you forget, the CSSOM styles simply won't work. The property names are exposed as strings. This will facilitate further expansion in the name values, and make it easy to incorporate any additions into your documents. ●

Incorporating Objects

## CHAPTER 17

Graphics

by Eric Ladd

Without graphics, the World Wide Web would simply be just a souped-up version of Gopher. But thanks to its support for graphics as part of documents, the Web quickly grew to become one of the top sources of Internet traffic.

The same could be said about any document, whether in print or published electronically. Without graphics, the document is flat, stagnant, and less interesting. Thus, a properly placed graphic in a document does two things: It makes the document more visually appealing, and, more importantly, it conveys one of the document's critical ideas.

However, it's possible to reduce a document's impact by using graphics inappropriately. You've probably seen your share of Web pages with distracting animated GIFs, cluttered background images, and graphics that are just plain overused. As you plan your documents, make sure you have a proper reason for using each graphic. Whatever you do, don't throw in graphics just for their own sake!

This chapter examines some of the specifics behind Internet graphics. After a review of the different storage formats available, you'll also learn how to make your images bandwidth-friendly, how to use scanned images in your documents, and how to use several popular graphics software tools. ■

Which storage formats can you use on the Web?

Graphic information can be stored in a number of different ways, but only a few of these are appropriate for Internet graphics.

Special effects with GIFs

CompuServe's Graphic Interchange Format (GIF) is one of the most popular on the Internet today, because of its support for some key special effects.

Full-color support with JPEG

The Joint Photographic Experts Group (JPEG) developed its own storage format that is useful for graphics done in full color.

Users appreciate small graphics files

Keeping your image files small reduces download time and is therefore an important audience service.

Helpful graphics utilities

If you're supporting the graphical side of an Internet publication, there are many useful programs that can help you out. Learn about a few of them here.

How Graphic Information Is Stored

When you see a graphic on your computer screen, what you're really seeing is a collection of colored screen pixels that, taken together, produce a meaningful image. An image file, therefore, has to contain information on how to reproduce that collection of pixels on-screen. This is accomplished by describing the pixels' properties mathematically and storing these descriptions in the file.

The catch in this situation is that there's not a unique way to mathematically describe image data. Given time, you can come up with your own way and, thus, your own storage format. Because you can express image data many ways, there are correspondingly many image file formats—on the order of several dozen!

Fortunately, each of these formats can be classified as one type or another: a bitmapped graphic or a vector graphic. The next two sections examine the specifics of each type.

Bitmapped Graphics

With a bitmapped graphic, information about each pixel is stored as a sequence of bits in the file. Depending on the storage formats, these bits could represent colors, saturation levels, brightness, or some other visual characteristic of the pixel. What's important is that each sequence of bits tells the computer how to paint the pixel on the screen.

Bitmaps are something of a natural format because they store information in exactly the same way the computer displays it on a monitor. This means the program that renders the image has to do very little processing. It just reads in the data and passes that information along to the screen drivers which, in turn, display the pixels.

N O T E   The preceding is not entirely true if the bitmapped image is compressed. Compression reduces the size of an image file by reducing the amount of information needed to replicate the image. A compressed file will download more quickly, owing to its smaller size, but it needs to be decompressed before the image can be displayed. This decompression step means additional processing effort. ■

Vector Graphics

A vector graphic file contains mathematical information that is used to redraw the image on-screen. When a computer displays a vector image file, it reads in the redrawing instructions and follows them. This might sound like a lot of unnecessary processing, but there is an important advantage to this approach: You can rescale the image to new sizes without loss of resolution because there's no fixed relationship between how it's defined in the file and the pixel-by-pixel image on the screen. When you try to resize a bitmapped file, you often get a loss of resolution that detracts from the image.

Vector graphic formats are typically used for images with distinct geometric shapes. Computer Aided Design (CAD) drawings are examples of this type of image.

N O T E Some file formats combine the best of both bitmapped and vector graphics into what's called a metafile format. Windows metafiles (.WMF) are frequently used to store clip-art images that need to be resized often. ◼

Web Graphic Formats

When you focus your attention on Web graphics, the vast field of usable graphic storage formats quickly reduces to two. The Graphics Interchange Format, or GIF, was developed by CompuServe in 1987 to store graphics used over its network. The other format came about more recently and is named for the group that developed it: the *Joint Photographic Experts Group* or *JPEG*. Both formats are bitmapped formats. Currently, there is virtually no support for vector storage formats.

The specifics of each of these formats, and instances when you would want to use one over the other, are discussed in the following sections.

Part

IV

Ch

17

GIF

CompuServe released the GIF standard in 1987 and updated it in 1989 and 1990. The current standard is 89a and it supports 8-bit color. That is, a GIF image can contain up to 2^8 or 256 colors.

How GIF Works Image data in a GIF file is organized into related blocks and subblocks that provide information on how to paint screen pixels to reproduce the image. When transmitting a GIF, a program called an encoder is used to produce a GIF data stream of control and data blocks that are sent along to the destination machine. There, a program called a decoder parses the data stream and assembles the image.

GIF is a compressed format as well. GIF files employ the LZW compression scheme to reduce the amount of information needed to completely describe the image. The LZW scheme is best suited to simple images like line drawings or images with just a few unique colors. As the number of colors grows, LZW compression becomes less efficient, providing compression ratios of 2:1 or less.

N O T E The LZW compression used with GIFs was actually conceived by the Unisys Corporation and not by CompuServe. CompuServe and Unisys were entangled in patent disputes for a while. The end result was CompuServe's licensing of the GIF format—a move that had Internet developers worried that they would have to pay for a license. Fortunately for them, the license agreement pertained only to software that was primarily used for accessing CompuServe. The downside was these developers still had to worry about licensing with Unisys as well. Unisys has yet to pursue this with any vigor, though, and the GIF format continues to be one of the most popular formats on the Internet. ◼

Transparent GIFs GIF supports many effects that are desirable on Web pages. Chief among these is transparency. In a transparent GIF, you can designate one color to be the transparent color. Then, whenever the GIF is rendered on-screen, pixels painted with the transparent color will actually be painted with the color of the page background. This gives the illusion of the pixels being transparent, since they allow what's behind them to show through.

The advantage of transparent GIFs is that they make a graphic appear to float freely on a page. To see what this means, take a look at Figure 17.1. The image at the top is nontransparent. The words you see are sitting inside of a rectangular bounding box, and both the words and the bounding box are visible. The bottom image is a transparent GIF in which the color of the bounding box was designated as the transparent color. The result is that the bounding box disappears and the words seem to sit on the background with no particular boundary around them.

FIG. 17.1

You can make images float on a page by using a transparent GIF.

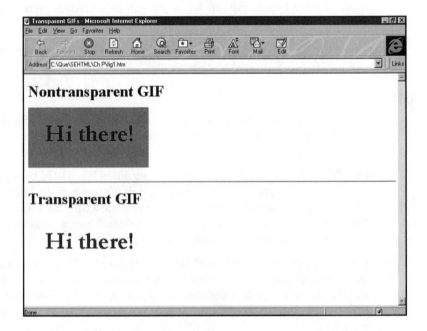

Many graphics programs available today come with support for creating transparent GIFs. LView Pro, a graphic utility discussed later in this chapter, makes it very easy to designate a transparent color in a GIF.

Interlaced GIFs   When you store a GIF in an interlaced format, nonadjacent parts of the image are stored together. As the GIF is decoded, pixels from all over the image are filled in rather than being filled in row by row. The result is that the image appears to "fade on" to the page, as if it were being revealed from behind a set of Venetian blinds. This permits the user to get a sense of the entire image right away instead of having to wait for the whole thing to be read in from top to bottom.

It usually takes several passes for the image to fade in completely. Figure 17.2 shows an interlaced GIF on the Discovery Channel site in the process of being read in. The complete image is shown in Figure 17.3.

FIG. 17.2
An interlaced GIF
appears fuzzy as it
is read in.

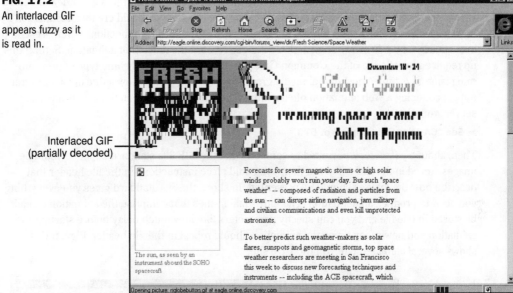

Interlaced GIF
(partially decoded)

FIG. 17.3
As the last pieces of
image data are read
in, the interlaced
GIF comes into
sharper focus.

Interlaced GIF (fully
decoded)

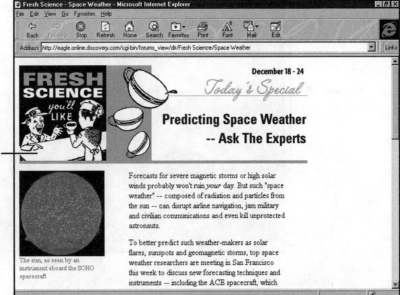

Just as with transparency, most good graphics programs give you the option of saving a GIF as interlaced. All three programs discussed in this chapter support interlaced GIFs.

Animated GIFs   The first animations that appeared on the Web required a great deal of effort. Using an approach introduced by Netscape called *server push*, you could create an animation by having a server literally push several images down an open HTTP connection. When presented in sequence on the browser screen, these images created the illusion of animation. Setting this up required knowledge of the Common Gateway Interface (CGI) and some type of programming language. Since most digital media graphic artists don't have knowledge of CGI programming, producing a Web animation often required collaboration between the artists and the server administrator.

▶ **See** "Creating CGI Scripts," **p. 573**

Then, about a year ago, it occurred to someone that the GIF 89a standard supports multiple images stored in the same file. Further, you could place instructions in the file header that describe how the images should be presented. In short, the 89a standard gives you everything you need to produce an animation! The individual frames that comprise the animation can all be stored in one file and you can specify parameters like how much delay before starting the animation and how many times the animation should repeat in the file header. Figure 17.4 shows several animated GIFs on the 7-Up site.

FIG. 17.4

Animated GIFs let you place animations on a page without knowledge of programming.

Animated GIFs—

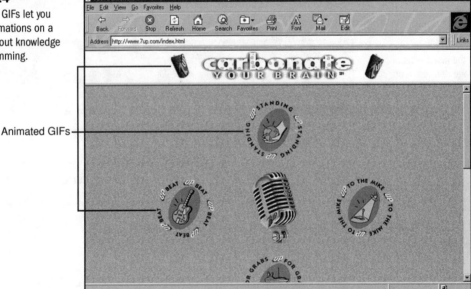

Creating animated GIFs has become fairly easy with the advent of software tools like the GIF Construction Set. In this program, you can specify the individual GIF files that make up the animation and presentation instructions in a set of dialog boxes. When you're finished with the setup, the program will create the animated GIF file using the information you specified.

Part
IV

Ch
17

> **CAUTION**
>
> Like many popular Web page components, a number of animated GIFs have been made publicly available for download at many sites. The result is that these GIFs quickly become overused. Placing such a GIF on your pages does nothing to distinguish them. If you really need an animated GIF on your page, create your own unique animation. Don't put a trite animated GIF on a page just for the sake of having one there.

JPEG

JPEG actually refers to a set of formats that supports full-color and grayscale images and stores them in compressed form. JPEG stores color information at 24 bits per pixel, allowing an image to contain 224 or over 16.7 million colors! This makes it the format of choice for photographs, especially photographs of things in nature, where a continuum of colors is in play (see Figure 17.5).

FIG. 17.5
Photographs of naturally occurring objects are prime candidates for being stored as JPEGs.

JPEG image

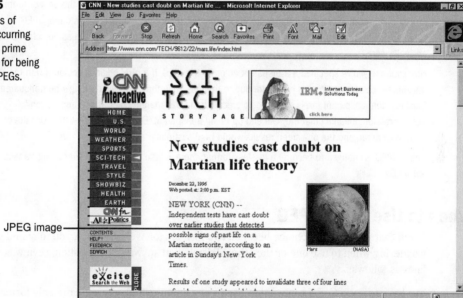

How JPEG Works   JPEG can handle so many colors while still keeping file sizes reasonable because it compresses the image data. You even have some control over how big or small the file ultimately is. You can specify a high level of compression to get a very small file, but the quality of the image on-screen will be reduced.

When you decompress a JPEG image, there is always some amount of loss, meaning that the image will not look the way it did originally. Fortunately, JPEG's compression/decompression scheme is such that the lost image data tends to be in the higher color frequencies, where it is harder for the human eye to detect the differences. In spite of this loss, you can still use JPEG to achieve compression ratios between 10:1 and 20:1 without appreciable change in the image. This means you've essentially reduced the amount of storage space per pixel from 24 bits to 1 or 2 bits—quite a savings! You can take the compression ratios even higher but, as noted previously, the loss will become more detectable and image quality will suffer.

 T I P Always do your conversion to JPEG as your very last step in creating a Web image. Resaving as a JPEG after each change can increase the amount of loss since the image is recompressed each time.

Progressive JPEGs   JPEG isn't as versatile a format as GIF is when it comes to supporting desirable Web page effects. However, a new type of JPEG, called a progressive JPEG or p-JPEG, provides an analogy to the interlaced GIF. A p-JPEG is stored as a series of scans that together comprise the entire image. When the first scan is read in, users see an approximation of the whole image, so they can quickly get an idea of what they're ultimately going to see. As subsequent scans are read in, the image comes into sharper focus.

N O T E   People often ask if there will ever be transparent JPEGs. Unfortunately, the answer to this question is no. To understand why, recall that there is always some loss during JPEG compression/decompression. This means that some pixels are not colored with the same color as they originally were.

Now suppose you've specified a transparent color for the JPEG. If a pixel originally colored with the transparent color is assigned a new color due to the loss, then that pixel will no longer be transparent. Similarly, nontransparent pixels could be colored with the transparent color after compression/ decompression, meaning that they will end up being transparent. Either way, you get the opposite of what you wanted and the on-screen results would be disastrous.

Unless JPEG is changed to become a lossless format, there is little hope of there ever being transparent JPEGs. ■

When to Use GIF or JPEG

Given that you have the choice between two formats for Web graphics, you may find yourself wondering when to use one or the other. To help you answer that question, review some guidelines as follows.

You have to use a GIF if you want transparency or animation, since it's the only format that supports them. Beyond that, you should consider GIF for the following types of images:

- Black-and-white line art and text
- Images with a limited number of distinct colors
- Graphics with sharp or distinct edges (most menus, buttons, and graphs fit this category)
- Graphics that are overlaid with text

JPEG is better suited for the following situations:

- Scanned photographs and ray-traced renderings
- Images that contain a complex mixture of colors
- Any image that requires a palette of more than 256 colors

Because the compression computations work better with a continuum of color, the JPEG format is not well suited to images that have very sharp color changes.

Up and Coming: PNG

GIF and JPEG are the two prominent Web formats currently, but there's a new kid on the block that shows a great deal of promise. The *Portable Network Graphics (PNG)* format is in draft form, and members of the World Wide Web Consortium (W3C) are busy reviewing it and making revisions.

The abstract of the working draft describes PNG as "an extensible file format for the lossless, portable, well-compressed storage of raster [bitmapped] images. PNG provides a patent-free replacement for the GIF format and can also replace many common uses of TIFF format. Indexed-color, grayscale, and true color images are supported. PNG is designed to work well in online viewing applications, such as the World Wide Web, and so it is fully streamable with a progressive display option." Look for PNG graphics to become more prevalent on the Web as the draft specification is refined and eventually adopted.

N O T E   Thomas Boutell maintains a copy of the PNG working draft on his site at: **http://www. boutell.com/boutell/png/**. ■

Part
IV

Ch
17

Making Good Use of Images

While it is true that a properly designed image can enhance a document, a poorly designed image can detract from it. Graphic images certainly have their place in Web documents and, in fact, they are expected in many places by users. The next few sections look at the types of graphics commonly found on the Web and give you some tips on how to maximize the effectiveness of each kind.

Main Page Graphics

If you've visited many Web sites, you very likely noticed the tendency to put a large graphic on the main page of a site that lets a visitor navigate to all of the major sections of the site. Such a graphic is a good idea for many reasons. It lets the user know right away what major content sections are available. Additionally, it lets the site designer establish a visual look for each section, which can be helpful to the users later as they navigate through the site. But there are pitfalls to this type of image. Some things to think about include the following:

- *Keep the file size small.* Forcing the user to wait a long time for a large image to load can prompt him or her to interrupt the loading and move on to another site. Make sure that your main-page graphics are of a reasonable size—somewhere between 50K and 100K, if possible.

- ■ *Be consistent.* Use the graphics elements (colors, icons, headings) that you associate with each content section consistently throughout the site. This gives visitors a better chance of figuring out where they are and how to get to where they want to go.
- ■ *Provide a text-based alternative.* Users with text-only browsers or who have image loading turned off won't be able to see your main-page graphic at all. Be sure to include a set of hypertext links that these users can use to navigate to the major areas of your site.

Your main-page graphic is the first thing users will see when visiting your site and sets the tone for the rest of their time there. The best rule of thumb for this kind of graphics is to make sure it is eye-catching and distinctive, without falling prey to one of the preceding issues.

Icons

Icons are small graphics that are meant to represent a certain content section or piece of information on your site. Commonly used icons include a question mark for Help and Frequently Asked Questions (FAQ) sections or a magnifying glass for a search engine.

Because icons are small, file size is usually not a problem. Icons download quickly and, once they are in a user's cache, can be reused again and again without further downloading. But an icon's smallness can also be a disadvantage because you have to pack a very specific concept into a fairly small part of the screen. For this reason, your chief concern when designing icons is *intuitiveness*. Users should be able to look at an icon and almost immediately discern what it means.

The best way to see if your icons are intuitive is to test them with a group of users as you're designing the site. A commonly used test involves presenting users with a set of potential icons and asking them to write down what they think each icon represents. If you find that most users interpret an icon the same way, you can feel pretty good about using that icon to represent the idea they say it does. If there's no clear interpretation of an icon, you should scrap it or send it back to the drawing board.

Once you have your icons chosen, be sure to use them consistently. This helps to reinforce their meaning with the user and makes navigating your site much less stressful.

N O T E If you expect a global audience to visit your site, you also need to consider how your icons will be interpreted by users from cultures different from your own. This typically requires bouncing your icons off users from those cultures, if at all possible. ■

Navigation Bars

Very large sites have to support the user with some kind of navigation aid. Navigation image maps are frequently found at the top or bottom (and sometimes both) of a document and give the user single-click access to the major content areas of the site and other useful resources like a table of contents or a search engine. You may also include some navigation options that point to places within a given section of a site, particularly if the user has had to drill down several levels to get to a document.

Navigation graphics present some of the same design issues as main page graphics. These include the following:

- *Being consistent.* Consistency is much more important at this level, since the user may have forgotten what the main-page graphic looks like. Be sure to incorporate the visual cues you built into your main-page graphic when you design navigation graphics and also make use of your icons. If you have an iconographic representation of each section of your site, you can line them up in a row to produce a simple navigation bar that the user should be able to use easily.

    Consistency also applies to where you place the navigation graphic in a document. If users see navigation options at the bottom of the first few pages they see, they'll come to expect them to be there on every page.

- *Providing a text-based alternative.* Again, you can't forget about users who can't see graphics or who have shut them off. Make sure there is always a set of hypertext links available that duplicate the links found in the navigation graphic.

Backgrounds

A well-chosen background image can make a page look very distinctive. Many corporate sites have a faded version of the company logo in the background. This approach reinforces the company's corporate identity, while not being so obtrusive that it obscures the primary content of the document.

Another popular approach to background images is to use a very small pattern that is tiled to fill the browser window. Typically, these files are very small and load quickly. However, if the tiling isn't smooth, it can produce seams on the page that can distract a user. Fortunately, more and more graphics programs are including a tessellating function that allows you to produce seamless tiling in all directions when using a tiled background pattern. Both Paint Shop Pro and Adobe Photoshop come with this useful feature.

 TIP Whether you're using a large image or tiling a small image in your background, you can use the BGCOLOR attribute of the <BODY> tag to immediately paint the background with a color that approximates the dominant color of your background image. This smooths over the transition to the image and, if the image fails to load, the user can at least have a sense of what color your background was supposed to be.

The worst thing you can do is use a background image that is so busy that it detracts from content in the foreground. If you're not using a solid color or a pattern, make sure that the visual elements in your background image are sufficiently muted so that they don't interfere with the user's ability to read and understand the content of your document.

Finding Graphics Online

Not everyone is lucky enough to have a team of digital graphic artists on staff to support a Web site. If your role as a Webmaster is "jack-of-all-trades," that most likely means you're

Part
IV

Ch
17

responsible for graphic content as well. Fortunately, there are many sites out on the Web that provide royalty-free graphics that you can download and use on your own site.

One particularly good public repository of graphics is Microsoft's Multimedia Gallery at **http://www.microsoft.com/workshop/design/mmgallry/**. Not only can you find icons, background patterns, and navigation graphics in the Gallery, but you can also download audio clips as well!

One caution about using graphics from a public-download site: Other people might be using them, too. This robs your site of a truly distinctive look and, in cases where the graphics are overused, can make your pages seem trite. Do you remember the little colored balls people used to use as bullets in a bulleted list? This is a classic example of an overused graphic. The colored balls even made a comeback as animated GIFs where the color of the ball cycles through many different colors!

Don't let your pages be common—try to customize the graphics you download to set them apart. One easy way to do this is to repaint the graphics in the color scheme of your site. This makes them seem more like they were designed just for your site.

Bandwidth Issues

As popular as graphics are with users, they can become immensely unpopular when they take forever to download. By keeping file sizes small, you minimize the time your users spend waiting to see your pages. A good rule of thumb is to keep each large image to between 30K and 50K. Icons should be even smaller—between 5K and 10K.

Think of Your Audience

Even with small file sizes, different users may have to wait different lengths of time for an image to download. A 50K image may transfer in just a few seconds over a T1 connection, but dial-up users who are limited to 14.4Kbps or 28.8Kbps may have to wait several minutes. Be sure to remember your users with slower connections when you design your graphics. You may even ask a few of them to test your image files to see if they require a long time to download.

Don't forget to use the ALT attribute in your <IMG> tags so that the user can see a description of your image in case it fails to load.

Corporate intranet designers tend to be a little more fortunate in this department. Most intranet users are on a high-speed connection over the company's wide-area network (WAN). With such a homogeneous group, it's usually possible to design higher-end graphics and still have reasonable download times. You should still have some coworkers test your images, though, especially those who are located a great distance from your server.

Tips for Reducing File Size

If you think you have an image file that's too big, don't despair! There are plenty of techniques for bringing the size down. Depending on the makeup of the image and the format you saved it in, you may want to try one of the following:

- *Resize the image*. Larger images take up more disk space because there are more pixels and, hence, more color information that has to be stored. By shrinking the height and width of an image to the smallest they can be, you take a big step toward making the file as small as it can be.

> **CAUTION**
>
> Always resize an image in a graphics program, keeping the aspect ratio the same. If you try to use the WIDTH and HEIGHT attributes of the <IMG> tag to resize the image, you're relying on the browser to do the resizing and you're likely to be disappointed with the results. Additionally, resizing with the browser doesn't save you download time because the original image file still has to be downloaded.

> ▶ **See** "Adding Inline Images to Your HTML Document," **p. 93**

Part IV
Ch
17

- *Use thumbnails*. Thumbnails are very small versions of an image, usually a photograph. Because they're smaller, their file sizes are smaller, too.

 Thumbnails are typically set up so that a user can click them to see the full image. If you do this, be sure to include the size of the full image file in parentheses next to the thumbnail so that users can make an informed decision about viewing it or not.

- *Store GIFs as JPEGs*. JPEG compression works best on images with lots of color gradation. If you have a GIF file that fits this description, try saving it as a JPEG to see if that makes the file any smaller.
- *Increase the compression ratio*. If you're working with a JPEG, you can resave it at a higher compression ratio to shrink the file size. But don't forget the tradeoff: Higher compression reduces the quality of the image.
- *Reduce the color depth*. Color depth is another way to express how many colors can be stored by a format. A GIF image has a color depth of 8 bits (256 colors)—but what if there are fewer than 256 colors in the image? In this case, you can reduce the color depth to a smaller number of bits per pixel. With less information to store per pixel, the resulting file will be smaller.
- *Adjust contrast levels in the image*. Contrast refers to the brightness of objects in the image relative to one another. Most popular graphics programs offer retouching options like gamma correction and highlight/midtone/shadow that change contrast within an image. By tweaking these values, you can usually bring down your file size.
- *Suppress dithering*. Dithering refers to the use of colors in an existing color palette to approximate colors that are not in the palette. Dithering tends to increase file size in GIFs because the GIF compression scheme is less efficient when adjacent pixels are painted with different colors. Disabling dithering will make more adjacent pixels have the same color so the compression can better shrink the file.

Working with Scanned Images

It's not always necessary to create your own graphics. In fact, it's very often convenient to scan something in (if you have access to a scanner) or use an image that someone else has already scanned in. Either approach is perfectly valid. No one will ever expect you to create all of your own images. When you do use a scanned image, though, you should make sure that it really contributes to the message you're trying to convey in your document, and that you're not just using it for the sake of using it.

> **CAUTION**
>
> Some people will let you use images that they scanned as long as you give them credit in your document. Make sure you acknowledge the sources of your scanned images.

When to Use Them and Where to Get Them

If you do have a flatbed scanner, making your own scanned images is a simple task. You can use the software that came with the scanner, or you can use a program like Photoshop or Paint Shop Pro.

If you're looking for existing scanned images, you can try any of the following sources:

- *Graphics service bureaus.* A graphics service house may have existing images you can use on a royalty basis. It can also probably scan images at a higher quality than you could on a desktop scanner.
- *Stock Photo and ClipArt CD-ROMs.* Many companies sell CD-ROMs with stock photos or simple line art you can use. You usually have to acknowledge the producer of the CD-ROM in your document as the source of the images.

Manipulating Scanned Images

Scanned images invariably need some kind of touch-up done on them so they are a truer representation of the original. By zooming in on the scanned image in an editor, you can usually see imperfections along the edges of objects and in the coloring of pixels. Be sure to give your scan a good "once-over" in this way, so it can look its best in your document.

Useful Graphics Tools

Throughout this chapter, reference has been made to many different manipulations and edits you can make to an image. Now it's time to look at some of the programs you can use to make these modifications. The next five sections introduce you to the following image-editing programs:

- LView Pro
- Paint Shop Pro
- Adobe Photoshop
- Microsoft Image Composer
- GIF Construction Set

Each of these is a great graphics program in its own right. You should consider each one and then select the one that meets your needs and is within your means.

LView Pro

LView Pro is a great shareware program you can use to edit existing graphics or to convert them to GIF or JPEG format. It offers many of the common manipulation features found in most paint programs plus several other options that give you very fine control over image appearance.

N O T E The information on LView Pro presented here is based on the evaluation copy of version 1.D2. You can download the latest version of LView Pro by pointing your browser to **http:// www.lview.com/**. A license costs $30 U.S. plus $5 U.S. for shipping and handling. ■

Figure 17.6 shows the LView Pro window along with its extensive tool palette. Almost every tool in the palette corresponds directly to one of LView Pro's menu options.

FIG. 17.6
LView Pro's tool palette enables you to make modifications to most aspects of an image.

The only LView Pro tool for creating anything is the Add Text tool. It stands to reason that you'll probably have to use a different program to create your graphics. But, what LView Pro

Part
IV

Ch
17

lacks in ability to create, it makes up for with its ability to make very particular changes to an image. These program features are found under the Edit and Retouch menus.

The Edit Menu   LView Pro's Edit menu provides options for many basic manipulations that Paint can perform, including horizontal and vertical flips and rotations by 90 degrees to the right or left. The Add Text option, discussed previously, is also found under the Edit menu.

The Resize and Redimension options can create some confusion for the user who is unfamiliar with them. Resize changes the dimensions of an image, with the option to retain the image's aspect ratio (the ratio of the width and height). When you Resize, you can choose from a standard set of sizes or you can enter your own size. Redimension lets you choose only from the standard set of sizes and doesn't permit you to keep the same aspect ratio.

The Capture option under the Edit menu does a screen capture of either the Desktop, the Window, or the Client Area. When you invoke one of the screen capture options, LView Pro will minimize itself and capture the region that you requested on-screen.

The Retouch Menu   The options under LView Pro's Retouch menu really expand the program beyond a simple graphics manipulator. One option of note is Gamma Correction, a parameter that can impact the contrast in an image (and therefore, the size of the image file). Gamma correction is used to increase or decrease the brightness of pixels in the image. You can set gamma correction values for red, green, and blue color components separately by moving the scrollbar next to each color. A gamma correction value bigger than zero will brighten the color, and values less than zero will darken the color. If you want to adjust the gamma correction for all three colors simultaneously, check the Lock RGB Scrollbars check box. This moves all three scrollbars whenever you move any one of them. To reduce the size of an image file, you can reduce the contrast in the image. This means you want a negative value for gamma correction.

Another useful option under the Retouch menu is Palette Entry. Choosing this option calls up the Select Color Palette Entry dialog box, shown in Figure 17.7. From this dialog box, you can select one of the colors in the current image's palette and change its RGB color specification. You can also select the image's transparent color from this dialog box.

FIG. 17.7

Changing a particular palette color is easy with the Palette Entry option of the Retouch menu.

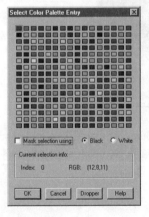

A final Retouch option of interest is Color Depth (see Figure 17.8). This option is used to select a True Color image (24 bits per pixel, 16.7 million colors) or a Palette image (up to 8 bits per pixel and 256 colors). Palette images can be two colors (black and white), 16 colors (like the default Windows palette), 256 colors (as with a GIF image), or a custom number of colors. If you're decreasing your color depth, you may want to activate Floyd-Steinberg dithering, a process that uses combinations of colors in the palette to approximate colors that are not in the palette.

FIG. 17.8

If you need to reduce your color depth to make an image file smaller, you can do it in LView Pro from the Color Depth dialog box.

LView Pro Properties Settings   The Properties dialog box (choose File, Properties) lets you do much more than set up retouch instructions. There are 11 different tabs on the panel that enable you to configure LView Pro to run according to your own image-editing preferences.

Two of the tabs deserve special attention because of their relevance to creating Web graphics. The GIF tab, shown in Figure 17.9, has two check boxes which can be used to instruct LView Pro to save a GIF file as either interlaced or transparent.

FIG. 17.9

LView Pro can make interlaced and transparent GIFs if you tell it to do so.

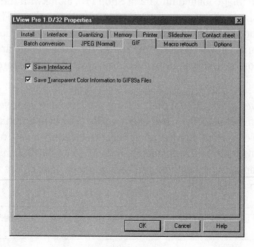

N O T E   To designate the transparent color in LView Pro, choose Retouch, Background Color and select the color you want to be the background color from the palette you see. When you save the image as a transparent GIF, the background color will become the transparent color. ■

The other noteworthy tab is the JPEG tab, shown in Normal mode in Figure 17.10. From this tab, you can choose compression and decompression options, including progressive decompression for making a progressive JPEG.

FIG. 17.10

LView Pro can also make a progressive JPEG once you activate progressive compression.

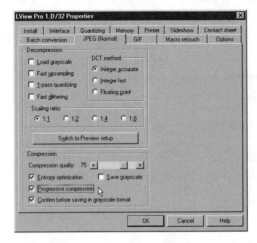

Paint Shop Pro

Another good shareware program for graphics work is Paint Shop Pro from JASC, Inc. Paint Shop Pro handles many types of image storage formats, enables you to do the most common image manipulations, and even comes with a screen capture facility.

Figure 17.11 shows an image loaded into Paint Shop Pro, along with the many available tool panels that give you single-click access to Paint Shop Pro's functions. The Zoom panel lets you zoom in to magnifications as high as 16:1 and out to magnifications as low as 1:16. Tools located on the Select panel allow you to sample colors, move the image around in the window, define a custom area of the image to clone or resize, and change the foreground and background colors.

The Paint panel is a welcome addition that was not available in earlier versions of Paint Shop Pro. It supports 22 different tools you can use to make your own graphics. These tools enable you to create brush, pen, pencil, marker and chalk effects; draw lines, rectangles and circles; fill a closed region with color; add text; and sharpen or soften part of an image. The Histogram window displays a graphic representation of the luminance of all colors in the image, measured with respect to the brightest color.

TIP You can toggle any of the tool panels on or off by using the options found under the View menu.

FIG. 17.11
Paint Shop Pro's tool panels give you easy access to common painting and image manipulation.

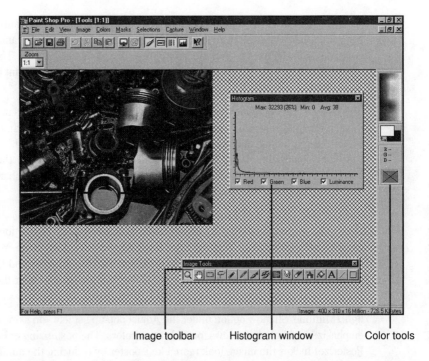

Image toolbar   Histogram window   Color tools

Paint Shop Pro's versatility enables you to open images stored in 25 bitmapped formats, including GIF and JPEG, and 9 meta/vector formats (image components stored as geometric shapes that combine to produce the entire image), including CorelDRAW!, Micrografx, and Ventura. However, it can save in only one of the raster formats. Nevertheless, Paint Shop Pro is still handy for converting to bitmapped formats. The Batch Conversion option under the File menu lets you select any number of files to convert to a new storage format (see Figure 17.12).

FIG. 17.12
Have a bunch of files to convert? Paint Shop Pro can be set up to handle them all at once.

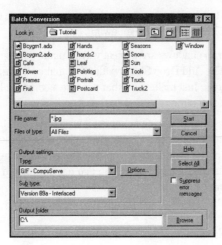

TWAIN refers to a set of industry standards that allow graphics programs to work with image acquisition hardware like scanners. If you have a TWAIN-compliant scanner attached to your computer, you can use the File, Acquire option to scan in a new image. The Select Source option, also under the File menu, lets you choose which device you want to use for the acquisition.

The Image menu includes the options used to do many of the standard manipulations like flipping the image upside down, creating a mirror image of an image, and rotating the images. The Image, Resample option is used to change the size of an image, without the jagged edges caused by standard resizing. You'll also find several effect filters under the Image menu that let you add or remove noise, enhance darker or lighter colors, and blur (sharpen or soften) the image. You can even define effect filters of your own.

The Colors menu is host to many of the advanced image manipulations you read about in the LView Pro section, including adjustment of brightness, gamma correction, RGB values, and conversion to grayscale or photographic negative versions of an image. You can also load, modify, and save color palettes from the Colors menu. The Increase and Decrease Color Depth options allow you to change the number of colors being used to render the image.

Paint Shop Pro adds some color editing functionality that LView Pro doesn't have. The Highlight/Midtone/Shadow option under the Adjust pop-up list lets you skew an image's contrast to emphasize highlights, shadows, or mid-range colors. The posterizing effect (choose Colors, Posterize) makes the image look more like a poster by reducing the number of bits used per RGB color channel. You can also use the Colors, Solarize option to invert colors that are above a luminance level specified by you.

One very useful feature of Paint Shop Pro is its screen and window capture facility. Options in the Capture, Setup dialog box are used to capture the whole screen, a single window on the screen, the client area inside a window, or a user-defined area. You can also choose whether the mouse pointer should be included in the capture and which hotkey will activate the capture.

The current release of Paint Shop Pro comes bundled with many more special effects filters than in previous versions. These include the following:

- *Add Drop Shadow.* Drop shadows are a great way to make your graphics appear to float over the document. The Add Drop Shadow function makes it simple to add drop shadows to your images. Just make sure that you use a common light source for images that will be placed on the same page.

- *Create Seamless Pattern.* Earlier in the chapter, it was noted that background images are often small files that are read in and tiled to fill the browser window. To avoid seams between tiled copies of the same image, you need to tessellate the edges of the image so that they come together smoothly. Paint Shop Pro has automated this procedure with the Create Seamless Pattern function.

- *Cutout.* The Cutout function allows you to remove a section of an image, enabling you to see through it to what lies behind it.

- *Chisel.* Applying the Chisel function to a selected area of an image transforms it to make it appear as if it were chiseled out of stone.

- *Buttonize.* You can use the Buttonize function to apply a three-dimensional border to a selected portion of an image to make it appear raised. This is especially useful in creating clickable buttons that readers can use to select different navigation options.

- *Hot Wax Coating.* Rather than holding a burning candle over an image on your computer monitor, you can avail yourself of the Hot Wax Coating effect to make it look like you did.

Additionally, you can install Adobe Photoshop-compatible plug-ins and define your own effect filters.

When it comes to saving an image as a GIF or JPEG, Paint Shop Pro can handle the basic format, as well as most of the associated effects. About all that Paint Shop Pro won't do is allow you to save a progressive JPEG.

Paint Shop Pro is a very capable image editing program. You can also purchase it bundled with Kai's Power Tools SE for added functionality. To order this combination package, contact JASC sales at 1-800-622-2793. For more information about Kai's Power Tools, consult **http://www.metatools.com/**. To learn more about Paint Shop Pro, direct your browser to **http:// www.jasc.com/**.

Adobe Photoshop

Adobe promotes Photoshop as the "camera for your mind," but it's really much more—it's the premier software package for doing graphical manipulations. You can use Photoshop to create your own original artwork, scan in an image, or make edits to an existing image. Photoshop can read in files stored in over a dozen formats and save them in just as many formats, including GIF and JPEG.

Making Your Own Artwork   Photoshop supports you in graphics creation with an extensive toolbar, located on the left side of the window (see Figure 17.13). You can choose tools for placing text, filling regions, drawing lines, airbrushing, painting, freehand drawing, smudging, blurring, and lightening.

T I P   Many toolbar tools have special options available in the dialog box at the bottom left of the Photoshop window.

Part **IV**

Ch **17**

FIG. 17.13

Many of the drawing options found in other image creation programs are available in Photoshop as well.

Layers and Channels   One of Photoshop's nicest features is image layers—different levels of the image you can overlay to produce the entire image. Figure 17.14 shows an image that uses layers. The sun is on a separate layer from the checkered background, but when the two are superimposed, they produce the desired image.

FIG. 17.14

Layers separate the different components of an image into their own separate entities, so you can work on them individually.

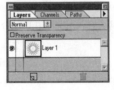

A graphic element in a given layer can be painted with RGB color and Photoshop will provide access to each component color through color channels. Figure 17.15 shows the channels for the sun layer from the graphic in Figure 17.14. The sun is painted yellow, which is formed by a combination of green and blue. Notice in Figure 17.15 that there is no contribution from the red channel—only from the green and blue channels.

FIG. 17.15
Color channels split a color into its individual red, green, and blue components.

Web Graphics Effects   Photoshop can help you apply a number of desirable effects to Web graphics. An important one is *antialiasing*, a process that softens the jagged edges that often occur at a boundary between two different colors. Antialiasing an edge is fairly easy to do. You just select the item with the edge to be antialiased by using the Lasso (freehand region selection) tool, and then check the Anti-aliased box on the Options tab in the dialog box at the bottom-left of the window.

N O T E   Antialiasing is available when using the magic wand, fill, and line tools as well. ■

Embossing is an effect that makes an image look "raised," just as lettering on an engraved invitation is raised. Photoshop has an embossing filter that is easy to apply to an image. You select the part of the image to emboss, then choose Filter, Stylize, and then select the Emboss option from the pop-up list that appears. An image and its embossed equivalent are shown in Figure 17.16.

FIG. 17.16
Embossing "raises up" parts of an image and gives your pages the illusion of depth.

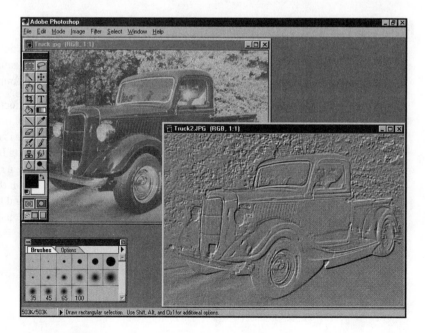

Part
IV

Ch
17

Photoshop also supports saving files in GIF, interlaced GIF, transparent GIF, JPEG, and progressive JPEG formats, although plug-in programs are required to accomplish this. Two of the most popular plug-ins are PhotoGIF and ProJPEG from BoxTop Software, Inc. You can download the latest versions from BoxTop's Web site at **http://www.boxtopsoft.com/**.

So Much More!   Trite as it may sound, Photoshop is much more than what has been noted here. Some of the program's other handy features include:

- Numerous built-in effects filters, and many more available from plug-in programs; Kai's Power Tools is one set of utilities that is particularly well integrated into Photoshop.

- Options for dithering to lower color depths and different color palettes.

- Highly efficient memory management.

- A flawless interface with other Adobe products like Illustrator and PageMaker.

Photoshop is a powerful image creation and modification tool that makes a worthy addition to your software library. For many folks, the limiting factor is often price since Photoshop can cost between $500 and $1,000 per license, depending on which platform you're running it on. Students can obtain a "light" version of Photoshop at a substantial discount. If you're running a highly graphical Web site and you can afford Photoshop, you should seriously consider purchasing it as your graphics tool of choice.

> **N O T E**   For a fuller treatment of Photoshop and its many features, consult Que's *Special Edition Using Photoshop 3 for Macintosh*. The Windows version of Photoshop 3 has the same functionality, although the interface may be different in places. ■

Microsoft Image Composer

Microsoft continues to expand its software offerings that support Internet publishing by producing Microsoft Image Composer (see Figure 17.17), which is a full-featured, image-editing program that works with Microsoft FrontPage and the Microsoft GIF Animator.

Image Composer breaks new ground in developing graphics for Web documents by introducing *sprite technology*. Put simply, a sprite is an image whose shape is not necessarily rectangular (like it would be in any other image program). Instead, a sprite's shape is exactly the shape of the object in the image. Microsoft provides a good example on one of its Image Composer Web pages (see Figure 17.18). The image on the left is a sprite. It does have a rectangular bounding box, but the image's shape is that of the bunch of flowers. The image on the right would be done in a traditional image editor. You could make the black background transparent to achieve the same effect as you get in the sprite, but this would require extra steps that aren't needed with Image Composer.

FIG. 17.17
Microsoft Image Composer comes bundled with either Microsoft FrontPage or Microsoft's Visual InterDev.

FIG. 17.18
A *sprite* is an image that takes on the shape of the object in it, instead of just being rectangular.

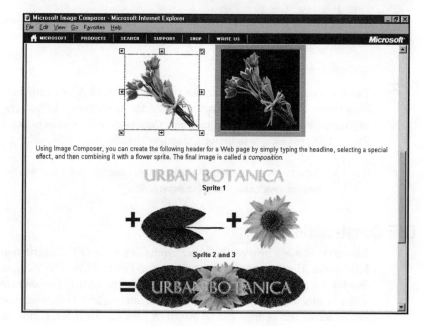

CAUTION

Macromedia Director users should not confuse Image Composer sprites with Director sprites. Although they share the same name, they are not the same thing.

Sprites are made possible by an Image Composer feature called the *alpha channel*. Every sprite has a built-in, 8-bit (256 color) alpha channel that stores transparency information. This means you can have up to 256 levels of transparency—much more flexible than the single transparent color you get in a transparent GIF! You can use the levels of transparency to seamlessly overlay sprites (refer to Figure 17.18) and create eye-catching effects. When you've finished your composition, you can export the whole thing as a GIF and place it in any of your Web documents.

Beyond sprite technology, Image Composer offers many of the things you'd want in a graphics-editing program. It saves images in both the GIF (including transparent GIF) and JPEG formats. You get all of the standard image creation tools like paint, fill, text, and shapes. Further, you get over 500 different special effect filters that include.

- Angled Strokes
- Dry Brush
- Fresco
- Halftone Screen
- Neon Glow
- Pencil Sketch
- Stained Glass

Those are just a few. Image Compose can also work with Adobe-compatible plug-ins such as Kai's Power Tools 3.0, KPT Convolver, and Andromeda Series 1 Photography. The Impressionist plug-in package is shipped with Image Composer and the effects found in Adobe Gallery Effects 1.51 are resident in Image Composer already.

N O T E For more information about Microsoft Image Composer, point your Web browser to **http:// www.microsoft.com/imagecomposer/**. ■

GIF Construction Set

A program that will help you build animated GIFs is the GIF Construction Set from Alchemy Mindworks. The program is shown running in Figure 17.19. The text you see in the window denotes the different blocks that comprise the animated GIF. The animated GIF always begins with a header block and can be followed with images, text, comments, controls, and looping instructions. Each of these can be placed by pressing the Insert button you see in the figure.

FIG. 17.19
Assembling the building blocks of an animated GIF is easy with the GIF Construction Set.

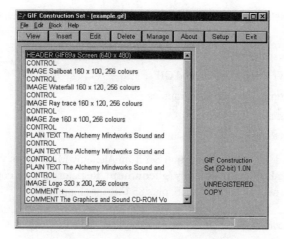

You don't even need to be familiar with the GIF Construction Set's GIF building "language" to use the program. By choosing File, Animation Wizard, you are taken through a series of dialog boxes (see Figure 17.20) that ask whether the animation is for the Web or not, whether it should loop once or indefinitely, whether the frames are line drawings or photorealistic, how much delay there should be between frames, and what files contain the images for the individual frames. The GIF Construction Set uses this information to author the animated GIF file for you automatically.

FIG. 17.20
The Animation Wizard makes preparing an animated GIF as easy as answering a few questions.

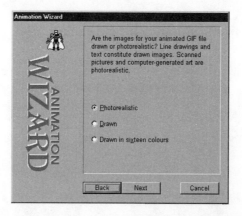

CAUTION
Think twice before letting an animation run indefinitely. An animation that's going constantly can be a distraction from the rest of the content on your page.

The GIF Construction Set is robust enough to support you in other Web graphics endeavors. It can:

- Create transparent GIFs.
- Convert AVI videos to animated GIFs.
- Add transition effects to still graphics.
- Create animated text banners.
- Add words to images as blocks of plain text.

You can download the GIF Construction Set from Alchemy Mindworks Web site at **http://www.mindworkshop.com/alchemy/gifcon.html**. Registering your copy of the GIF Construction Set will set you back $20 U.S. plus $5 U.S. for shipping.

 T I P Macintosh users should check out GifBuilder for creating animated GIFs.

## CHAPTER 18

Browser Plug-Ins

by Mark R. Brown

Although most HTML browser programs are pretty versatile, you'll still encounter many files that they can't display—video files, audio files, odd graphics files, strange document formats, and even compressed files. To display or play these files inline, you need to install the proper plug-ins or helper applications to work alongside your browser client.

Plug-ins extend and complement a browser's native capabilities, expanding and enhancing the type of content that can be delivered in HTML documents. Using plug-ins, a browser can display animation, multimedia, audio, interactive applications, and video inline, right on the page, without launching external helper-application programs.

Unlike a browser's built-in display capabilities, which are limited to generic file formats like GIF and JPEG images, plug-ins offer open-ended expansion that can include just about any content type. Dozens of companies have released plug-ins capable of displaying their own proprietary multimedia, applications, animation, and other data format files in Netscape Navigator, Microsoft Internet Explorer, and other browser clients. Plug-ins now support most of the widely used cross-platform media formats; those that aren't currently supported soon will be.

If you want to include multimedia and other "rich" content in your HTML documents, odds are you'll be relying on browser plug-ins to interpret and display that content. ■

Plug-ins for Multimedia

Browser plug-ins are the delivery system of choice for most developers for playing audio, video, and other multimedia content inline in HTML documents.

Origins in Navigator

Netscape was the first to develop plug-ins for the Navigator browser client, and today there is a wide variety of plug-ins available for Navigator.

Plug-ins for Explorer, too

Microsoft's Internet Explorer can also make use of most "Navigator" plug-ins to deliver inline multimedia content.

The *<EMBED>* Tag

HTML developers use the <EMBED> tag to embed plug-in content inline in their documents.

How Plug-Ins "Plug In"

Because plug-ins were originally created by Netscape Communications Corporation for its Netscape Navigator browser client, plug-ins are often referred to as "Netscape" plug-ins. However, most also work just fine with Microsoft's Internet Explorer client, and there are other browser clients available that can use plug-ins, as well. Because plug-ins are most often associated with Netscape, however, you'll often see Netscape Navigator in this and the following chapters.

N O T E Though Microsoft supports plug-ins in its Internet Explorer browser client, its preferred method of dealing with inline content is via ActiveX controls. There are many ActiveX controls available that mimic the functions of Netscape plug-ins. Ironically, Netscape Navigator can also now support ActiveX controls via—you guessed it—a plug-in from a third-party company called Ncompass Labs. You can find out more about ActiveX controls and how to implement them in your HTML documents in Chapter 22, "ActiveX Controls," and Chapter 23, "ActiveX Control Pad." ◼

N O T E As of this writing, Netscape plans to add functionality to Navigator 4.0 that automatically downloads and installs plug-ins on the user's computer. If Navigator encounters a MIME-type for which it doesn't find an installed plug-in, it asks the user if he or she wants to download and install the plug-in. If the user says "yes," Navigator downloads the plug-in, gives the user a chance to approve the signature of the plug-in, and installs it. ◼

Plug-ins are simply feature add-ons that can understand and interpret files that a browser can't handle itself. They extend the capabilities of your browser in much the same way that plug-in software modules are used to extend the capabilities of other software programs, such as Adobe PhotoShop. They are essentially transparent, appearing as enhancements and supplements to the browser itself. The browser user interface remains relatively constant no matter what plug-ins are installed—if you're displaying an inline QuickTime movie, for example, the parts of the display that handle page navigation, scrolling, and so on aren't affected by the plug-in's presence.

In more technical terms, plug-ins are dynamic code modules that are a part of Netscape's application programming interface (API) for integrating third-party software into Navigator. It's a part of Netscape Communication Corporation's "open systems" philosophy regarding Navigator; this approach allows third-party developers to use Navigator to integrate their products into HTML documents seamlessly.

Plug-ins enable you to customize your browser to interact with third-party products and industry media standards. They are generally meant to supplement and complement, not supplant, other interapplication architectures such as ActiveX and Java. Plug-ins can accomplish the following tasks:

- ◼ Create a window in your browser client for displaying information, as in a Video for Windows movie player.

- ◼ Execute an application such as a Musical Instrument Digital Interface (MIDI) player.

- Generate data for display by a browser or by other plug-ins. For example, a plug-in might create an index on-the-fly.

- Provide interapplication communication. For example, a plug-in might transfer data to a stand-alone spreadsheet program.

- Override a native browser capability and supply its own implementation. For example, a plug-in might provide an improved .GIF viewer.

- Link to and receive data from Uniform Resource Locators (URLs). For example, some plug-ins can download stock quotes.

Because plug-ins are platform-specific (and, occasionally, browser-specific), you must have a different version of each plug-in for every operating system that you use, such as Windows, Windows 95, UNIX, or the Macintosh operating system. Regardless of your platform, however, plug-ins should be functionally equivalent across all platforms.

TIP Several plug-ins may have shipped with the browser that you use. These plug-ins are already designed for your platform. However, if you find other plug-ins that you want either to purchase or download from the Internet, make sure they are intended for use with your specific browser and platform.

For most users, the use of plug-ins is totally transparent. When your browser starts up, it checks to see which plug-ins have been installed; if it encounters a data MIME type for which a plug-in is registered, it launches the plug-in to handle that data. When you leave the page that contains that data, the plug-in unloads, freeing up system resources.

You activate a plug-in only by opening an HTML document that initiates it; usually, you don't even see the plug-in at work. For example, after you install the Crescendo MIDI plug-in in Netscape Navigator, you notice no difference in the way that Navigator functions until you come across a page that features MIDI content (see Figure 18.1).

When your browser client launches, it notes any available plug-ins, but does not load any into your computer's memory. This way, a plug-in resides in memory only when needed; however, you still need to be aware of memory allocation because many plug-ins can be in use at any one time. Plug-ins simply reside on disk until you need them. As soon as you move to another HTML page that doesn't require a plug-in, it is deleted from RAM.

At its most fundamental level, a plug-in can access an URL and retrieve MIME data just like a standard browser client. This data is streamed to the plug-in as it arrives from the network, making it possible to implement viewers and other interfaces that can display information progressively as it arrives from the server. If a plug-in requires more data than a single data stream can supply, the plug-in can request multiple, simultaneous data streams, so long as the user's system supports such data streams.

Plug-ins can also handle data in the old-fashioned way: caching data for display only when it has all been downloaded. For instance, a plug-in can draw a simple frame and introductory graphic while the bulk of the data is streaming off the network into the browser cache.

Part

IV

Ch

18

FIG. 18.1

The Crescendo plug-in in action, playing a MIDI music file inline on a Web page.

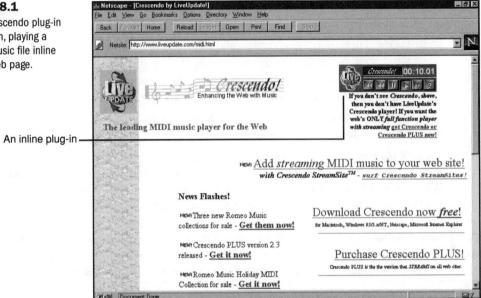

An inline plug-in

If your browser or another plug-in needs data while a plug-in is active, the plug-in can generate the needed data. Therefore, plug-ins not only process data, but also generate it. For example, a plug-in can be a data translator or filter.

The integration of plug-ins with browser clients is quite elegant and flexible, making the most of asynchronous processes and multithreaded data. All plug-ins are associated with a MIME type not native to the client and can be associated with multiple MIME types. The browser can concurrently run multiple instances of the same plug-in if the page contains several plug-in-compatible data files of the same type. Netscape's plug-in API also attempts to address the concerns of programmers, providing a high degree of flexibility and cross-platform support to plug-in developers.

Plug-ins are a godsend for applications developers, who can extend the utility of existing products into the burgeoning Internet market by developing a quick and easy plug-in that reads existing data files instead of developing a whole new product. Not only does this save developers time and effort, it also lets them ride into a huge market on the coattails of Netscape Navigator, the Internet's most popular browser. Applications developers are happy because their market expands quickly and almost for free; HTML content developers are happy because they have new formats that they can provide; Web users are happy because they have new ways in which to use the Web; and even Netscape is happy because its Web browser becomes more powerful and useful without any additional effort on its part. Everybody wins!

CAUTION

You should be keenly aware of the potential system security problems that plug-ins present. Plug-ins have full access to all the data on your computer system. They are written by third parties whom you may or may not know. Plug-ins are delivered by servers over whom you have no control. Each of these factors poses a potential security risk. Make sure that you trust the plug-in developer and the plug-in server before you install a plug-in on a system in which a security breach could cause serious problems.

For example, a plug-in could easily be developed that scans through the Windows 95 Registry looking for passwords, then passes them back to the plug-in developer through the Internet. Although you're unlikely to encounter such an insidious plug-in at a major developer's site, you might want to exercise more caution when downloading a plug-in from an individual's Web site.

Almost worse is the case of a poorly written plug-in that means no harm, but through sloppy programming, manages to reformat your hard drive or trash your system registry. Be careful.

The Three Kinds of Plug-Ins

After you install a plug-in on your machine and an HTML document initiates the plug-in, it manifests itself in three potential ways:

Part IV

Ch

18

- Embedded
- Full-screen
- Hidden

An *embedded* plug-in appears as a visible, rectangular window integrated into a page. This window might not look any different than a window created by a graphic, such as an embedded .GIF or JPEG picture. The main difference between the previous windows supported by most browser clients and those created by plug-ins is that plug-in windows can support a much wider range of interactivity and movement, and thereby remain dynamic rather than static.

Embedded plug-ins can read and note mouse clicks, mouse location, mouse movement, keyboard input, and input from virtually any other input device. In this way, a plug-in can support the full range of user events required to produce sophisticated applications.

Examples of embedded plug-ins include a Moving Picture Expert Group (MPEG) movie player, the QuickTime movie player, the Shockwave for Macromedia Director player, or Video for Windows players like LiveVideo (see Figure 18.2).

A *full-screen* plug-in takes over the entire current browser window to display its own content. This is necessary when a page is designed to display data that HTML does not support. An example of this type of plug-in is the Adobe Acrobat viewer (see Figure 18.3).

If you view an Acrobat page using the Adobe plug-in, the page displays just like an HTML page, but retains the look and functionality of an Acrobat document viewed in Adobe's stand-alone viewer. For instance, if a site uses Acrobat to display an online manual for a product, the site might enable you to scroll, print, and interact with the page just as if the stand-alone Acrobat Reader program were displaying it.

An HTML page designer can invoke some plug-ins in either embedded or full-screen mode, depending on how they create their page.

FIG. 18.2
LiveVideo is an example of an embedded plug-in that can seamlessly integrate a window within an HTML document.

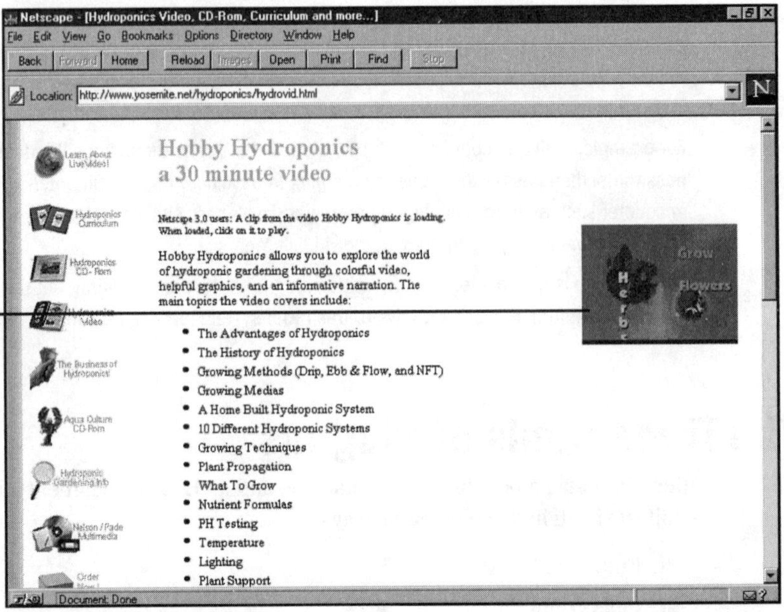

Embedded LiveVideo player plug-in

FIG. 18.3
The Adobe Acrobat viewer is a full-screen plug-in that even incorporates its own control bar.

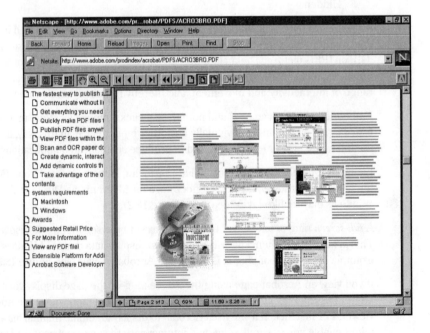

A *hidden* plug-in doesn't have any visible elements, but works strictly behind the scenes to add some feature to the browser that is otherwise not available. Examples of possible hidden plug-ins include MIDI music players or file decompression engines. A MIDI player plug-in could read MIDI data from a page whenever it's encountered and automatically play the data through your local hardware without so much as even displaying a control panel. Similarly, a decompression engine might function much the way that it does on commercial online services—decompressing data in real time in the background—or delaying decompression until the user logs off the Internet.

Regardless of the plug-ins you use, and whether they are embedded, full-screen, or hidden, the rest of the browser's user interface remains relatively constant and available. Therefore, even if the main window is displaying an Acrobat page, you still can access the browser's menus and navigational controls.

N O T E If you're a programmer, you can even write your own plug-ins. Netscape offers software developer's kits (SDKs) for Windows, Macintosh, and UNIX system plug-ins development. These kits are available for free downloading from Netscape's Web site. You can find further information, including a download link, at:

http://home.netscape.com/eng/mozilla/3.0/handbook/plugins/sdk.html

Running a Plug-In

Running a plug-in is simple; in fact, you don't have to run a plug-in at all. Plug-ins run themselves whenever a page or link contains the proper kind of embedded file. You don't have to decide when to run them, and you don't have to figure out how to load the data file.

However, you do have to learn how the controls work. Many of these plug-ins provide on-screen a set of specialized controls for zooming, printing, panning, scrolling, and so on. Each plug-in comes with detailed documentation explaining its specific controls and how they work. (In some cases, you might have to download a separate manual file, or find the plug-in's documentation is online in the form of Web pages. Make sure you get your plug-in's documentation.) Read the documentation so you know all about a plug-in before you encounter any files that it will display. Then you won't have to spend valuable online time trying to figure out your plug-in's behavior.

Using Plug-Ins with Netscape Navigator

Since Netscape Communications Corporation invented browser plug-ins, let's take a quick look at how they implemented them in Netscape Navigator.

Downloading plug-ins couldn't be much easier. Netscape Communications Corporation maintains a page that lists many of the currently available Netscape plug-ins, with links to the pages from which you can download them. You can find the page at the following address:

http://home.netscape.com/comprod/mirror/navcomponents_download.html

The independent Plug-Ins Plaza site seems to be even more consistently up-to-date than Netscape's own site. You can find the Plug-Ins Plaza at the following address:

http://browserwatch.iworld.com/plug-in.html

Before installing a plug-in, you should download the plug-in file into its own temporary directory. You might keep a directory called C:\INSTALL on your hard drive just for this purpose. Then you can download a single plug-in to the INSTALL directory, install the plug-in, then delete the files in C:\INSTALL so that the directory is empty and available for your next installation. (You might make sure the plug-in is actually installed correctly and working properly before you delete the installation files.)

Each plug-in downloads as a single file. Installation involves one of two procedures:

- If the file is called SETUP.EXE, all you have to do is run it. It will automatically install itself as a Navigator plug-in. The installation program might let you specify the directory into which to install the plug-in. Don't change the default unless you already have a directory by that name that contains something else.

- If the file has some obscure name like XX32B4.EXE, it is almost certainly a self-extracting archive. In this case, double-clicking the file in Windows 95 extracts the archive into a whole bunch of files in your INSTALL directory. It may proceed to install the extracted files automatically, or you may have to run the program SETUP.EXE, using the same process described in the preceding procedure.

In any event, the download page for a plug-in should contain complete instructions on downloading and installation. Read and follow these instructions carefully. Different plug-ins might require different instructions, and you don't want to be caught by surprise. (For example, you can optionally download a bare-bones version of the Crescendo MIDI player plug-in without a set-up program. But, if you do, you have to unpack and copy the file into the Navigator plug-ins directory yourself.)

> **CAUTION**
>
> Before you install a browser plug-in, make sure you have a plug-ins-capable browser program properly installed. For example, the plug-ins discussed in this book do not work at all with versions of Netscape Navigator earlier than 2.0, and some require version 3.0 or later.

Identifying Installed Netscape Navigator Plug-Ins

Each Navigator plug-in is assigned one or more file types that it can play or display when it is installed. For example, the LiveAudio plug-in (which is bundled with Navigator) plays four unique sound-file formats.

Navigator is aware of which plug-ins are installed, and which is assigned to each type of file. You can see a list of these file-to-plug-in assignments by selecting Help, About Plug-Ins from the Navigator menu (Figure 18.4). Navigator will display a list of installed plug-ins and their assigned files in the main display window.

FIG. 18.4

You can display a list showing which plug-ins are installed in Navigator by selecting Help, About Plug-Ins from the menu.

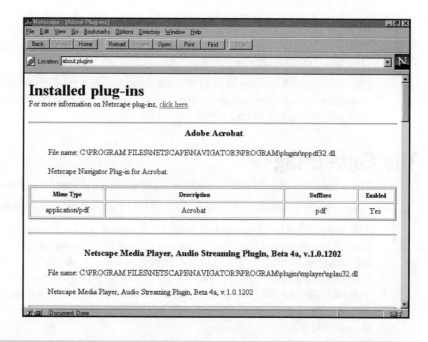

CAUTION

Navigator will display plug-in information only if Java and JavaScript are enabled. (The list is generated by an internal Java applet.) If you don't get a list of installed plug-ins when you select Help, About Plug-Ins from the Navigator menu, select Options, Network Preferences from the Navigator menu, then make sure the Enable Java and Enable JavaScript check boxes are selected on the Languages Tab.

Adding Plug-In Content to Your Pages

Content for delivery using plug-ins is created outside of an HTML document and is saved as an independent file. It is then included in the document with a reference to the URL of the content file.

There is one type of standard Web page element that is created and delivered in almost exactly the same way as plug-in content—inline GIF and JPEG graphics. When you include a graphic on a page, you first create it in a separate stand-alone paint program, then you incorporate it into your HTML code by using the IMG tag.

For example, if you wanted to include some kind of title graphic in an HTML document, you would load a paint program, create the graphic, then save it as a GIF or JPEG file. Let's say you call your image "title.gif"; to display it on your page, you would include this line of HTML code:

```
<IMG SRC="title.gif">
```

Plug-in compatible content works the same way—you first create your content file in a separate stand-alone development program, then incorporate it into your HTML code. However, plug-ins don't use the IMG tag, but the EMBED tag.

The *Embed* Tag

You present live objects inline on a Web page by using the EMBED tag. Here is a typical use:

```
<EMBED SRC="video.avi" WIDTH=100 HEIGHT=200 AUTOSTART=TRUE LOOP=TRUE>
```

This line of HTML code embeds a Video for Windows movie called video.avi in place on the page. When displayed, the plug-in that is configured for playing .avi files launches invisibly in the background. The WIDTH and HEIGHT attributes create a playback area 100 pixels wide and 200 pixels high in the browser window. The AUTOSTART=TRUE command starts the video playing automatically, and the LOOP=TRUE attribute indicates the video should play in a loop until stopped. The EMBED tags AUTOSTART and LOOP attributes in this example have been defined for this specific plug-in.

> **N O T E**   The generic sample plug-in used for this example is available on the Netscape Web site
> at **http://www.netscape.com/comprod/development_partners/plugin_api/**
> **win_avi_sample.html.** ■

Each real-world plug-in has its own attribute syntax for the EMBED tag, which is defined by the plug-in publisher. An EMBED tag line in an HTML document must include the SRC attribute, which specifies the URL of the file to be loaded, as well as the width and height of the window in which the plug-in is to be displayed. You can also optionally specify PALETTE and PLUGINSPAGE values, as well as additional attributes that are specific to individual plug-ins. Here's the syntax for a generic EMBED tag call:

```
<EMBED SRC="URL" WIDTH=n HEIGHT=n [PALETTE=FOREGROUND¦BACKGROUND]
[PLUGINSPAGE="URL"]>
```

SRC="URL" specifies the URL of the data file to be included when the HTML document is viewed. This attribute is required. WIDTH=n and HEIGHT=n determines the width and height of the plug-in display window, where "n" is a value in pixels. This attribute is also required.

PALETTE=FOREGROUND¦BACKGROUND is optional. You should specify either FOREGROUND or BACKGROUND as the value for PALETTE. When there's more than one plug-in on a page that uses a palette, you should use the PALETTE attribute to indicate which plug-in takes palette precedence—that is, which one gets to set the palette for the page. The EMBED tag call for this plug-in should have the attribute PALETTE=FOREGROUND. All other plug-in EMBED calls on the page should define PALETTE=BACKGROUND. If the PALETTE attribute isn't specified, PALETTE=BACKGROUND is assumed.

PLUGINSPAGE="URL" defines the URL of the page from which a plug-in can be downloaded for the current file type. If a user accesses your Web page but hasn't installed a plug-in for the file type you specify in your EMBED tag, the PLUGINSPAGE attribute will allow Netscape to jump right to the page from which the appropriate plug-in can be downloaded and installed. Though optional, the PLUGINSPAGE attribute is a real godsend for users; it means they'll always be able to view your plug-in content relatively hassle free.

Each individual plug-in almost always includes some optional attributes designed specifically for that plug-in. Our example above included AUTOSTART and LOOP attributes, which are appropriate for a Video for Windows movie player. Other plug-ins will include their own optional attributes. The only way to know what these are and how you should use them is to check their documentation or their section in this book.

N O T E Plug-ins and the EMBED tag aren't the last word on inline multimedia. The OBJECT tag allows multiple implementations of the same object as, say, a Java applet, an .avi movie, and an ActiveX object, with the browser able to pick content that matches its capabilities. This goes a long way toward making every HTML document accessible to every browser program, rather than requiring pages to be set up to suit a particular brand of browser. ■

Part
IV

Ch
18

Server Issues

Before you can deliver plug-in compatible content using your HTTP server, you have to configure your server to deliver the proper MIME data type for the content you want to provide. Depending on the type of content you're delivering, you may even have to install a custom server program.

If your Web site is set up through an ISP (Internet Service Provider), you'll have to inform it of your desire to deliver content of a certain type or types, and provide it with the MIME configuration information it needs to set up its Web server files properly, if it hasn't already done so.

If your company or institution runs its own server, you'll have to contact your system administrator to set up the MIME types for you. If you run your own server, you'll have to do it yourself.

Setting MIME Types

HTTP (HyperText Transfer Protocol) is the defined protocol for delivering Web-page content over the Internet. Web-server computers use HTTP to send packets of Web-page data over the Internet to a user's Web-browser program, which then interprets and displays that data as Web pages.

Under HTTP, each separate block of data is invisibly preceded by its MIME type. This MIME type definition is used by the browser program to determine how to interpret the following block of data. If a plug-in has been defined to handle the data type indicated in the MIME type definition, the browser launches the appropriate plug-in before trying to display the data.

This means the server has to be configured to know and send the proper MIME type before it can send plug-in-compatible data. For example, if your pages are going to include MIDI music files, your server has to be set up to send the proper MIME type header before it delivers the actual MIDI file. Otherwise, your viewers' browser programs won't know when to launch their MIDI plug-in.

Here's a typical server setting for delivering MIDI content files:

```
MIME type = audio/midi or audio/x-midi or application/x-midi or audio/x-mid

action = binary

suffix = .mid

type = midi
```

This particular example defines four different MIME types: audio/midi, audio/x-midi, application/x-midi, and audio/x-mid. The file suffix it defines for MIDI files is .mid. Anytime a page delivered by this server EMBEDs a file type with the file name extension of .mid, the server will send a MIME type header containing the four MIME types defined for MIDI files. It's up to the browser on the other end to use this MIME type header to figure out which plug-in it must use to play the data contained in the associated .mid file.

This information needs to be included in your server software's setup file for MIME type information. How to do this varies with the specific server software.

N O T E　So how does the user's browser program know which plug-in is associated with which MIME type? That's done automatically when the plug-in is installed. For example, if you choose Help, About Plug-Ins from the Netscape Navigator menu, you'll see a page that shows you which MIME types are set up to launch plug-ins. ▪

Here's a real-world example of setting up the MIME type in the Netscape Netsite Server to deliver RealAudio files:

First, you edit Netscape Netsite's "MIME.types" file by adding the following line:

```
type=audio/x-pn-realaudio     exts=ra,ram
```

To Netsite's main configuration file (called "magnus.conf" in the examples given in the Netsite documentation), you would add the following line:

```
Init fn=load-types mime-types=mime.types
```

Once both files had been changed, you reinitialize the Web server to activate the changes.

In any case, each plug-in discussed in this book includes documentation that specifies the MIME type definition for the type of content it deals with, and that MIME type must be defined for your server software. The procedure for defining MIME types for any particular server is explained in the documentation for that server—it is beyond the scope of this book to include specific information on the steps involved in setting up MIME types for every available server. Refer to your server documentation for an explanation of how to set up specific MIME types for your particular brand of Web server software.

Installing Content Servers

Once the MIME type is set up, most plug-in-compatible content can be delivered by an HTTP server just as though it were text, GIF graphics, or other standard page content. However, some plug-in content—particularly files that must be sent as continuously streamed data—may require a custom content server program.

Your server already makes use of several custom content server programs. The Web server is an HTTPD, or HyperText Transfer Protocol Daemon—that is, it's a program designed to deliver content that conforms to the HTTP standard (in other words, HTML pages). However, most HTTP server computers hand over control to other server programs for other types of content. For example, if a user calls up their Mail client, the HTTP server switches control to a Mail server program that can handle mail data. If the user invokes a News reader, the HTTP server switches in a News server. Depending on the server setup, the News and Mail server programs may run on the same computer as the HTTP server software, or they may run on different computers connected to the same network.

Though these processes are invisible to the end user, a server computer has to be set up properly to make the switch to a News, Mail, or other content server program smoothly and automatically when needed.

Some plug-ins also require that special data servers be installed and configured on your server computer. RealAudio is a prime example. Because RealAudio files must be delivered in real time, without breaks or interruptions, a server computer must use a special server program to deliver RealAudio content. When a page includes a RealAudio file, the HTTP server program simply switches control to the RealAudio server program. When the RealAudio file is done downloading, control is handed back to the HTTP server program.

Of course, this means that, in order for a site to deliver RealAudio content, you or your system administrator has to install and configure a RealAudio server program on your network. There are a half dozen or more plug-in-compatible data types that require their own specialized server software program.

Part
IV

Ch

18

Issues of Space and Time

Many real-world factors place a practical limit on what kinds of plug-in-compatible content you can use in your HTML documents. File size is certainly a primary consideration because big files can draw out page download times to unreasonable lengths, and they can eat up valuable system storage space.

Bandwidth Limitations

Bandwidth limits how much data can be delivered to your audience in a given amount of time. Though bandwidth is not much of a concern on intranets, it can be a prime limiting factor on the World Wide Web.

Web users with fast, direct, dedicated T1 or T3 landline connections will, under ideal conditions, have no problem using browser plug-ins to view real-time videos or listening to real-time audio broadcasts. Even interactive multimedia presentations can be downloaded and displayed in a reasonable amount of time.

However, those connecting to your Web site via dial-up connections will have problems viewing huge files of any type. Over a standard 14.4 Kbps (kilobit per second) or 28.8 Kbps dial-up connection, even large GIF and JPEG graphics can take several minutes to load. Pages that are extremely graphics-rich can take 15 minutes or more to download over such slow connections.

Multiply the problem by a factor of 10 or even 100 for video and multimedia content, and you'll begin to see that plug-in-compatible content is not generally a realistic option for those who are connecting to the Web via a dial-up connection.

However, remember the real issue is file size, not content type. A MIDI music file might be only a couple of kilobytes in size, and is a good candidate for delivery over even dial-up lines. Videos, and even multimedia presentations, are not totally out of the question, either, as long as your viewers are willing to wait for them to download first—you won't be able to stream them for viewing in real time. The issue here is whether or not the content is worth waiting for.

If you consider who your audience is, it's easy to determine what types of content you can provide. If your viewers are likely to be connecting from university, corporate, or government sites with direct Internet links, then bandwidth is not generally an issue, and almost any type of content can be incorporated into your pages. On the other hand, if most of your viewers are likely to be connecting to the Internet via dial-up lines from home or through online services, your pages should be sparser, with smaller files that can be viewed in a reasonable amount of time over a slow dial-up connection.

A good rule of thumb is to remember that a 14.4 Kbps dial-up can read a maximum of about 1.7K (kilobytes) of data per second from the Internet. Thus, a 25K file will take about 15 seconds to download (if everything goes well). A 250K file will take two and a half minutes. If that 250K file is a 10-second animation, your viewer is likely to feel cheated that he or she had to wait so long for such a short display. Keep this wait/reward ratio in mind whenever you develop any plug-in-compatible content for your pages and you should be able to keep your site under control and your audience happy.

Storage Problems

In these days of 4G hard drives and CD-ROM changers, it's sometimes hard to imagine that storage can be a problem. But it's also the age of multimegabyte multimedia files. While a simple MIDI music file can occupy as little as 10K—an almost insignificant file these days—a full-motion video several minutes in length can easily occupy 250M or more. Four such files will fill today's standard 1G hard drive, and only two will fit on a CD-ROM. Clearly, storage on your server computer can become a real issue very quickly if, for instance, you're planning on delivering training videos over your corporate intranet.

Before planning to use a huge amount of multimedia content in your HTML documents, take a few moments to do the math and make sure you'll have not only the bandwidth for delivery, but the storage space for your files. ●

Part
IV

Ch
18

## CHAPTER 19

Audio

by Mark R. Brown

There are three different kinds of audio files your computer can play: digitized audio, music files, and text-to-speech. Text-to-speech is a technique for converting text files into (somewhat) recognizable speech by replacing the letters with phonemes. Music files are like sheet music—they specify a sequence of notes and the "instruments" to play them. Digitized audio is sound that has been run through an analog-to-digital converter to turn it into data.

Audio plug-ins are available for all varieties of digitized sound files, as well as MIDI music and speech. When you want to add audio to an HTML document, you'll likely rely on one of these plug-ins to play your sounds. This chapter steps through many of the most popular audio plug-ins for browser programs, and tells you how to add plug-in-compatible sounds to your HTML documents. ■

Plug-ins for multimedia

Plug-ins can be used to play digitized audio, MIDI music, and even speech.

LiveAudio is included

The audio player plug-in that ships with Netscape Navigator is LiveAudio, which can play most digitized audio files.

The Mac can talk

The Macintosh's native text-to-speech capabilities give it an edge in speech delivery.

RealAudio is the audio king

Though it requires special server software, RealAudio is one of the most popular programs for playing real-time audio over the World Wide Web.

Audio Hardware—What You Need

Back in the "good old days" of personal computing—when "PC" was always followed by "XT"; processor numbers were only four digits long; and software ran directly off floppy disks— every PC shipped with a tinny little AM-radio-quality speaker that beeped nastily at you any time you did something wrong. Some masochists (the kind who like to scrape their fingernails on blackboards) even wrote a few annoying DOS programs that played what they claimed to be digitized sounds on that little speaker. But no normal human being ever heard a single recognizable sound in the cacophonous din that emanated from a PC when those programs ran.

Now that we're in the high-tech age of multimedia computers—complete with 24-bit true color animations, 16-bit stereo music soundtracks, and digitized CD-ROM voice-overs by the likes of Star Trek's Patrick Stewart—all PCs still ship with that same nasty, tinny little speaker.

Sure, Microsoft has a Windows driver that purportedly plays music and audio by using only the internal PC speaker, but it freezes up your system when it runs, and everything still sounds like it's being fed through a weather-beaten, drive-in movie speaker with a shorted connection.

To get real audio out of your PC, you need a sound card. If you bought your computer recently, or if you've spent a few bucks upgrading, the odds are good you already have a sound card. But if you don't, you can pick one up for anywhere between $30 and $800, depending on what you want it to do.

A good 16-bit stereo Sound Blaster Pro (or compatible) sound card does just about everything the average person needs done audio-wise, and does it for under $100. If you haven't invested in a sound card yet, drop this book right now, scan a few computer magazine reviews and ads, run to your local computer store, buy a sound card, and plug it in. You'll need one for any sound player plug-in you might choose to use.

LiveAudio

Because it ships with Netscape 3.0, the LiveAudio plug-in is essentially the "official" Netscape audio player. Unlike many other audio plug-ins, LiveAudio doesn't use a proprietary sound-file format, but instead plays industry standard AIFF, .AU, MIDI, and .WAV files. LiveAudio features an easy-to-use console with play, pause, stop, and volume controls.

As long as your system is equipped with a sound card, LiveAudio enables you to listen to audio tracks, sound effects, music, and voice files embedded in Web pages. You can also use LiveAudio to listen to stand-alone sound files on the Web, on a local area network, and on your own computer system.

LiveAudio is a huge improvement over the NAPlayer audio helper application that Netscape shipped with versions of Netscape Navigator prior to version 3.0. Where NAPlayer played only Sun/NeXT (.AU and .SND) and Mac/SGI (.AIF and .AIFF) sound files, LiveAudio automatically identifies and plays four of the most popular standard sound formats:

- .AIFF, the Mac/SGI
- .AU, the Sun/NeXT

- MIDI, the Musical Instrument Digital Interface
- .WAV, the Microsoft Windows

.AU files were once the Internet standard file format; .AIFF files are the Macintosh standard; and .WAV files are the Windows standard file; so LiveAudio can play a good percentage of the nonproprietary sound files that you're likely to encounter on the Web. Add in its capability to play MIDI music, and LiveAudio proves itself a very good "Swiss Army Knife" plug-in for Web audio.

LiveAudio Controls

When you encounter a LiveAudio-compatible sound file embedded or linked into a Web page, LiveAudio creates the on-screen control console shown in Figure 19.1.

FIG. 19.1
The LiveAudio plug-in appears as a minimalist inline audioplayer control console, shown here on a Netscape Web site demo page. The LiveAudio player control box features four manual controls and a simple drop-down menu.

Volume slider

Stop button

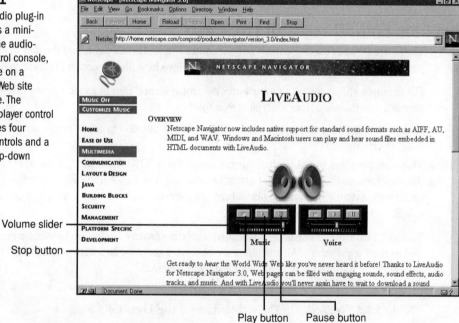

Play button   Pause button

Part
IV

Ch
19

The LiveAudio plug-in works with both embedded sound files, like the two it encountered in Figure 19.1, and with stand-alone sound files. In the case of stand-alone files, a blank Netscape window displays only a LiveAudio console.

The LiveAudio console controls are intuitive and easy to use (see Figure 19.1). The Stop, Play, and Pause buttons work just as they do on a tape or CD player. You click the Play button to play the sound, the Stop button to stop it, and the Pause button to pause audio playback. If you click the Pause button a second time, play resumes from the point at which you paused the sound.

Click to the right or left of the Volume slider knob to increase or decrease volume. The volume can be jumped only in increments of 20 percent—you can't slide the volume smoothly from 0 percent to 100 percent. The light-emitting diode (LED) bar graph below the Volume slider indicates the current volume level. The dark green LEDs are for the 0–40 percent range; light green LEDs take over for 40–100 percent.

Right-clicking the LiveAudio console displays the pop-up menu shown in Figure 19.1. This menu includes selections that duplicate the Play, Stop, and Pause buttons. The menu also provides a selection to display the program's About dialog box and a final nonselectable menu item that tells you the volume level as a percentage of the maximum.

The LiveAudio player has a single keyboard hot key: the spacebar. Pressing the spacebar reactivates whichever button you pressed last (Stop, Play, or Pause). Restopping an already stopped playback is of limited use, but if you last pressed Pause, the spacebar becomes an unpause/repause toggle. If you last pressed Play, the spacebar becomes a handy replay key.

Using the *EMBED* Tag with LiveAudio

The <EMBED> tag is used to embed plug-in content on an HTML page, and the way in which a page designer uses the <EMBED> tag often determines how plug-in content is displayed.

For example, the <EMBED> tag's attributes control several different aspects of the LiveAudio plug-in's functionality. Here's a typical example:

```
<EMBED SRC="audio.aif" WIDTH=144 HEIGHT=60 AUTOSTART=false VOLUME=100
     CONTROLS=Console>
```

This example plays the Macintosh format sound file AUDIO.AIF (SRC="audio.aif") only when the user presses the Play button (AUTOSTART=false). The LiveAudio control window is 144 pixels wide (WIDTH=144) and 60 pixels high (HEIGHT=60) and contains a complete control console (CONTROLS=Console).

Table 19.1 lists all the attributes associated with the <EMBED> tag for the LiveAudio plug-in, as well as their legal values. All attributes are optional except for SRC, WIDTH, and HEIGHT, which are generally required when embedding plug-in content.

Table 19.1   *<EMBED>* Tag Attributes for the LiveAudio Plug-In

Attribute	Values
SRC="*filename*"	A file name with an extension associated with a MIME type assigned to be played by LiveAudio (.AU, .AIFF, .AIF, .WAV, .MIDI, or .MID). Required.
WIDTH=*integer*	The control console width in pixels. Required.
HEIGHT=*integer*	The control console height in pixels. Required.
AUTOSTART=TRUE ¦ FALSE	If True, the sound clip plays automatically. The default is False.

Attribute	Values
AUTOLOAD=TRUE¦FALSE	If False, the sound clip does not automatically load. The default is True.
STARTTIME="*mm:ss*"	The start time in minutes and seconds from the start of the clip. The default is 00:00.
ENDTIME="*mm:ss*"	The end time in minutes and seconds from the start of the clip. The default is the end of the clip.
VOLUME=*percentage*	Playback volume expressed as a percentage of the maximum. The default is the last previously set volume.
ALIGN="*value*"	The point at which to align the control panel with respect to adjoining text. The possible values are CENTER, BASELINE, TOP, LEFT, and RIGHT. BASELINE is the default.
CONTROLS="*value*"	The controls to include on the control panel. The values can be CONSOLE, SMALLCONSOLE, PLAYBUTTON, PAUSEBUTTON, STOPBUTTON, or VOLUMELEVER. The remainder of this table describes the sets of controls associated with each of these values. The default is CONSOLE.
CONSOLE	A full set of controls: Play, Pause, Stop, and Volume.
SMALLCONSOLE	A reduced set of controls consisting of Play, Stop, and Volume. AUTOSTART defaults to True.
PLAYBUTTON	The Play button only.
PAUSEBUTTON	The Pause button only.
STOPBUTTON	The Stop button. Also, the sound file unloads.
VOLUMELEVER	The Volume control only.
CONSOLE="*name*"	A combination of controls that enables you to include multiple sound clips on a page. For example, you could specify CONSOLE="MySetup" as an attribute on two <EMBED> lines on a single HTML page; then each line would use the controls defined by the other as well as its own.

N O T E If you specify the settings CONTROLS="VolumeLever" and CONSOLE="_MASTERVOLUME", the user changes the system's master volume (not just the sound clip's volume) by manipulating the volume slider. ■

If you need to set up a Web server to deliver LiveAudio-compatible content, you first must set up the proper MIME types. How you do so varies with the specific server software; check your server documentation or ask your system administrator to set up the following MIME types, shown in Table 19.2 with associated file-name extensions:

Part
IV

Ch
19

Table 19.2   MIME Types for LiveAudio

MIME Type	Extensions
audio/basic	.AU
audio/x-aiff	.AIF, .AIFF
audio/aiff	.AIF, .AIFF
audio/x-wav	.WAV
audio/wav	.WAV
audio/x-midi	.MID, .MIDI
audio/midi	.MID, .MIDI

The <EMBED> tag works similarly with other plug-ins, though they may specify their own attributes.

Other Audio Plug-Ins

Though LiveAudio is bundled with Netscape Navigator, there are many, many more audio plug-ins available for delivering audio content in your HTML documents. This section takes a quick look at a few of the most popular.

N O T E   The latest version of Macromedia's Shockwave for Director plug-in—originally just for playing multimedia presentations—now includes the ability to play streaming audio in real time. Macromedia is now enthusiastically promoting Shockwave as a viable alternative to an audio-only delivery medium. You might want to check it out, especially if you intend on delivering multimedia content in your documents, as well as audio. Chapter 20, "Video, Animation, and Multimedia," includes a section covering Shockwave on p. 449. Macromedia's Web site is at:

http://www.macromedia.com/ ■

TrueSpeech

If nothing else, TrueSpeech is convenient. If you're using Windows 3.1 or Windows 95, the supplied Sound Recorder program can digitize sound files and convert them to TrueSpeech format. You can then use the TrueSpeech player to listen to them on the Web in real time. Despite its name, TrueSpeech can be used for any type of audio file. You don't need a special server. You can download TrueSpeech players for Windows 3.1, Windows 95, Windows NT, Macintosh, and PowerMac from the DSP Group's home page:

http://www.dspg.com

Crescendo and Crescendo Plus

Most sound cards go a step beyond merely digitizing and playing back sounds. They can also generate their own sounds. If your sound card is MIDI-compatible (as most are), you have more than a passive record-and-playback system—you have a full-fledged music synthesizer. With a MIDI plug-in, you can experience Web sites with a full music soundtrack.

LiveUpdate's Crescendo plug-in enables Navigator to play inline MIDI music embedded in Web pages. With a MIDI-capable browser, you can create Web pages that have their own background music soundtracks. Because MIDI instruments can be sampled sounds, you can also create sound-effects tracks.

Crescendo requires an MPC (MIDI-capable) sound card and Navigator version 2.0 or above. The plug-in launches automatically and invisibly and is a fun addition to Web browsing. Crescendo is available for Windows 95 and Windows NT, Windows 3.1, and Macintosh. You can download Crescendo from the following site:

http://www.liveupdate.com/midi.html

An enhanced version, Crescendo Plus, adds on-screen controls and live streaming. With the live streaming feature, you don't have to wait for a MIDI file to download completely before it starts playing. You can purchase Crescendo Plus also from LiveUpdate's Web site.

ToolVox

If all you need is speech, three kinds of speech plug-ins are available for Navigator:

- Players for digitized audio that is of less-than-music quality.
- Text-to-speech converters, currently available only for the Macintosh.
- Speech recognition plug-ins, which are also for the Macintosh only

ToolVox provides audio compression ratios of up to 53:1, which creates very small files that transfer quickly over the Internet. Speech can be delivered in real time even over 9,600-baud modems. One unique feature is that you can slow down playback to improve comprehension, or speed it up to shorten listening times without changing voice pitch.

Like the higher-fidelity RealAudio, ToolVox streams audio in real time, so you don't have to wait for a file to download before you can listen to it.

ToolVox doesn't need special server software to deliver audio content from your Web server. The player, in the form of a Navigator plug-in, controls buffering and playback. As a result, any standard HTML server can act as a streaming media server. Even the encoder is free. It compresses a speech file from .WAV format to an 8kHz, 2,400 bits-per-second (bps) VOX file.

Netscape Communications Corporation has become part owner of Voxware, the makers of ToolVox, so you can expect to hear much more about the plug-in. Netscape has also licensed key elements of Voxware's digital-voice technology, including the Voxware RT24 compressor/ decompressor (codec) and ToolVox, for incorporation into the Navigator LiveMedia multimedia standard.

Voxware has also announced plans to release ToolVox Gold, an enhanced version of ToolVox. ToolVox Navigator plug-ins are available for Windows 3.1 and Windows 95. Voxware also promises Macintosh and PowerMac versions. You can download these plug-ins from the Voxware site:

http://www.voxware.com/download.htm

EchoSpeech

EchoSpeech compresses speech at a ratio of 18.5:1. Therefore, 16-bit speech sampled at 11,025Hz is compressed to 9,600bps. Even users with 14.4Kbps modems can listen to real-time EchoSpeech audio streams. Because EchoSpeech is designed to code speech sampled at 11,025Hz rather than 8,000Hz, EchoSpeech files sound better than ToolVox.

Real-time decoding of 11kHz speech requires only 30 percent of a 486SX-33 CPU's time. EchoSpeech plug-ins are also small—40–50K when decompressed.

No server software is required to deliver EchoSpeech content; your Internet service provider (ISP) or server administrator need only declare a new MIME type and pay a one-time $99 license fee. To add EchoSpeech files to your Web pages, you compress them with the EchoSpeech Speech Coder (available for evaluation with free downloading) and then use the HTML <EMBED> tag to include the files in your documents.

EchoSpeech is available for Windows 3.1 and Windows 95, and a Macintosh version is promised. You can get EchoSpeech from the following address:

http://www.echospeech.com

Talker and Other Macintosh Speech Plug-Ins

MVP Solutions' Talker plug-in is just for the Macintosh. The plug-in uses the Macintosh's built-in PlainTalk speech-synthesis technology to create text-to-speech voice messages—in other words, Talker reads text files to you out loud. This plug-in uses much less bandwidth than recorded audio, and you can change the words that your Web page speaks by editing a text file.

Speech capability is one area in which Macintosh owners can claim a considerable edge over Windows and Windows 95 Navigator users—this plug-in simply will never work on those platforms because they lack the speech-synthesis technology of the Macintosh. You can find Talker at the following address:

http://www.mvpsolutions.com/PlugInSite/Talker.html

If you haven't yet installed Apple's English Text-to-Speech software on your Macintosh, you can download a copy of the software's installer from Apple's site:

ftp://ftp.info.apple.com/Apple.Support.Area/Apple.Software.
Updates/US/Macintosh/System/Speech/PlainTalk_1.4.1/

William H. Tudor's Speech Plug-In for the Macintosh and PowerMac does essentially the same thing as Talker. You can get Tudor's plug-in at the following address:

http://www.albany.net/~wtudor/

Macintosh plug-ins aren't limited only to talking to you—they can also listen to you and understand what you're saying!

Bill Noon's ListenUp is for the Power Macintosh running System 7.5 or above. The plug-in also requires the PlainTalk Speech Recognition v1.5 program. You can find out all the details and download the plug-in at the following address:

http://snow.cit.cornell.edu/noon/ListenUp.html

Digital Dream's ShockTalk speech recognition plug-in isn't a Navigator plug-in at all; it's a plug-in for the Shockwave for Director plug-in. ShockTalk is available for Macintosh and PowerMac. You can find the plug-in at the following address:

http://www.surftalk.com/

More Sound Plug-Ins

If you can't get enough of listening to sound, this section describes a few more Navigator sound plug-ins.

Arnaud Masson's MIDI plug-in is for the Macintosh and PowerMac only. You can get it from the following site:

http://www.planete.net/~amasson/

Another Macintosh-only plug-in for MIDI files is GRAME's MidiShare. You can find this plug-in at the following address:

http://www.grame.fr/english/MidiShare.html

Do you prefer the sound of the orient? Then Sseyo's Koan might better suit your taste. It plays real-time, computer-generated Japanese Koan music on Windows 3.1 and Windows 95 versions of Navigator. You can find Koan at the following site:

http://www.sseyo.com/

DBA from Delta Beta (**http://www.deltabeta.com**) for Windows 95 is a player for audio files compressed in Delta Beta's .DBA format. (The compressor is freely downloadable.)

DSM Plug-in by Dmitry Boldyrev (**http://www.spilk.org/dsm/**) for Mac Power PC lets you play ScreamTracker 3 (S3M), Oktalyzer, ProTracker, FastTracker (MOD), TakeTracker, MultiTracker (MTM), Farandole Tracker (FAR), Composer 669 (669), MIDI, and other computer music files.

Pixound from Hologramophone Research (**http://www.pixound.com/**) for Mac Power PC, Macintosh, and Windows 95 is truly strange; it translates pictures into sound as you move the mouse cursor over an image on a Pixound-enabled Web page.

Virtual Sound Canvas from Roland (**http://www.rolandcorp.com/vsc/vscd.html**) for Mac Power PC, Macintosh, Windows 95, Windows 3.1, and UNIX, is a software emulation of a Roland SC77 sound module. Ultra-cool. But if you like Yamahas better...

Yamaha XG MIDPlug from Yamaha (**http://www.yamaha.co.jp/english/xg/html/midhm.html**) for Mac Power PC, Windows 95, and Windows 3.1 is a software Yamaha synthesizer.

RealAudio

With any emerging technology, there is a tremendous advantage to being first. RealAudio was the first to deliver real-time streaming audio over the World Wide Web. Because it is being used by so many professionals, it will be your plug-in for stepping through the entire process of adding a specific type of audio to your HTML documents. Other plug-ins may have different requirements—for example, many do not require special server software—but you'll find the process is more similar than it is different for embedding different audio formats into your HTML documents.

Since its introduction, thousands of Web sites have begun to deliver RealAudio content over the Internet. Today, it is undoubtedly the most popular streaming audio application on the Net, with more than 4 million RealAudio Players downloaded from the Progressive Networks Web site.

N O T E Netscape has recently introduced its Netscape Media Server and Netscape Media Player programs, which will compete heartily for the niche currently occupied by RealAudio. In addition to real-time, high-quality streaming audio, these programs will also allow synchronized multimedia content. These programs provide high-quality audio even with 14.4Kbps modem connections, and automatic bandwidth-optimized streaming for the best possible audio quality at various connection speeds. Audio can be synchronized with HTML documents, Java applets, and JavaScript for a multimedia experience. Players are available for Macintosh Power Mac, Windows, and UNIX systems. More information and download files are available at:

http://home.netscape.com/comprod/mirror/media/download_mplayer.html

How RealAudio Works

RealAudio files are digitized audio—that is, they start out as analog sound which is fed through a sound card and digitized into a stream of digital bits.

RealAudio is actually a suite of three programs that work together. The RealAudio Encoder encodes preexisting sound files or live audio streams into the RealAudio format. The RealAudio Server delivers these encoded RealAudio streams over the Internet or your company intranet. (A RealAudio Server and a Web server are usually run simultaneously on the same server computer.) Finally, the RealAudio Player plays these streams when they are received by your computer. Versions of all are available from the Progressive Networks Web site at **http:// www.realaudio.com** (see Figure 19.2).

FIG. 19.2
The Progressive Networks RealAudio site is a treasure trove of downloadable software, technical information, and audio streams.

If you're just planning on listening to RealAudio on the Web or on your company's intranet, all you need is the RealAudio Player. If you want to create RealAudio content for your Web server to deliver, you also need the RealAudio Encoder. If you run your own Web server, you need the RealAudio Server, as well.

N O T E   Progressive Networks supports the LiveMedia Real-time Transport Protocol (RTP) and Microsoft's ActiveMovie Streaming Format (ASF) in all its RealAudio products. ▪

RealAudio streams are compressed and encoded from either a preexisting sound file or live audio. The RealAudio encoder can create files that are optimized for either 14.4 Kbps or 28.8 Kbps modem delivery. (If a file is intended for delivery over a fast direct Internet or intranet connection, the higher-quality 28.8 encoder is used.) The resulting file is always much smaller than the original. For example, a one-minute .wav file (sampled at 22kHz) takes up about 2.6 megabytes; the 14.4 RealAudio encoded version is only 60 kilobytes in size, while the 28.8 version is about twice that size. Those represent compression ratios of about 40:1 and 20:1, respectively. The resulting 14.4 encoded RealAudio file has a quality comparable to an AM radio broadcast and is best for speech only, while the 28.8 file sounds like monophonic FM and is adequate for most music.

The compression routines in the RealAudio Encoder leave out some sound file information—that's the nature of compression. You give up a little quality for a great gain in transmission speed. These omissions appear in the resulting audio stream as a sort of "graininess" or loss of depth and tone quality.

The RealAudio Server delivers audio streams in a unique manner. The Internet can send data in one of two ways. The TCP protocol, upon which the Web is based, emphasizes reliability. TCP ensures accurate data packets are always received, even if that means retransmitting some of them to overcome errors. On the other hand, the UDP protocol emphasizes speed, sometimes at the cost of accuracy. Sacrificing accuracy is a bad thing when you're talking about text or graphics, where every bit counts. But inaccurate or incomplete audio transmissions are interpreted by your ears as just a little noise, like a skip or static in a radio station signal. Much more important to audio is the uninterrupted transmission of the signal, so that large blocks of audio aren't skipped and transmission continues in real time. That's why RealAudio uses a special server program to deliver RealAudio data packets by using the UDP protocol. Though this may mean an occasional skipped "sound byte," it means the data stream continues on, uninterrupted, in real time.

N O T E To get around the problem of occasional packet loss, the RealAudio server incorporates a loss correction system that minimizes the impact of lost packets. This system works well when packet loss is in the two to five percent range, and even works acceptably when packet loss is as high as eight to ten percent. ▪

A RealAudio Server connection is actually a two-channel, two-way communication system—UDP is used for sound-data transmission, and TCP is used to negotiate the proper bandwidth (14.4 or 28.8), as well as to communicate pause, fast forward, play, and rewind commands. Because of this two-channel communication, you can listen to a RealAudio stream just as you would an audio tape. Because the stream is delivered to your computer on demand, in real time, the RealAudio Player's commands to the RealAudio Server can jump you back and forth to different spots in the audio stream. (Of course, this only works for prerecorded audio—live audio broadcasts are like listening to the radio.)

N O T E Progressive Networks developed RealAudio as an open architecture application and encourages RealAudio development by third parties.

The Playback Engine API (Application Programming Interface) provides software developers with direct access to functionality of the RealAudio Player, so that commercial Web authoring tools and other applications can incorporate RealAudio streams.

The Encoder API allows developers to use a variety of audio compression algorithms with RealAudio. For example, using RealAudio Encoder 2.0 Xtra for Macintosh, you can use Macromedia's SoundEdit 16 to save sound files directly into the RealAudio format.

The RealAudio APIs are available as part of the RealAudio Software Development Kit from the Progressive Networks Web site at **http://www.realaudio.com**. ▪

The RealAudio Player

You can download the RealAudio Player for Windows, Windows 95/NT, Macintosh, or UNIX, in either 14.4 or 28.8 versions. (Only those with a 14.4 Kbps dial-up connection should get the 14.4 version—all others should get the 28.8 version.) You get two versions of the RealAudio Player—one is a stand-alone program that can also be used as a browser helper application, and the other is a Netscape-compatible plug-in.

The RealAudio stand-alone application (see Figure 19.3) is a fully functional program that you can use to play RealAudio files from any source, including your own hard drive, a corporate intranet, or the World Wide Web. It's one of a growing number of applications that can access the Web independently of a browser program.

FIG. 19.3
The stand-alone
RealAudio player can
be used as a browser
helper application or
can play sound files
from any source.

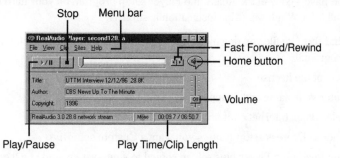

Whether you listen to a prerecorded or live-audio stream, and whether it comes from your own system, network, or the Web, a RealAudio stream will begin playing as soon as the Player has latched onto a few packets. You don't have to wait for the whole stream to load before it starts playing. Because it's a stand-alone application, you can even go on to browse other Web pages and the RealAudio file will continue to play in the background.

The Netscape plug-in is also installed automatically when you install RealAudio. It automatically plays in-line RealAudio files that have been included on Web pages using the <EMBED> tag. It manifests itself as controls that appear inline in the Web page. How many controls you see depends on how the RealAudio file has been embedded. This will be covered in detail later in this chapter.

N O T E If a Web page includes RealAudio content by using a standard link, you'll have to click the link to hear the audio stream, and your browser will launch the stand-alone RealAudio Player as a helper application. You'll then need to close the Player when the clip is done playing.

However, if the RealAudio content is included by using the <EMBED> tag, your browser will automatically use the RealAudio plug-in, and any activated controls will appear inline in the Web page. Depending on the page design, the clip may even begin playing automatically. The plug-in will remain in place until you leave the associated Web page. ∎

Part
IV

Ch
19

Installation and Setup

You can download the latest version of the RealAudio Player setup program from the Progressive Networks Web page at **http://www.realaudio.com/products/welcome/index.html**. Select the proper version from the online form for your computer and its connection speed.

N O T E The RealAudio Player 3.0 Standard Edition CD-ROM (for Windows 95 only) includes the RealAudio Player 3.0, technical support by e-mail, a manual, the RealAudio Encoder 3.0, and the American Recordings Jukebox, which is described as "today's hottest music groups in a RealAudio Synchronized Multimedia presentation." It retails for $29, and can be ordered by calling 1-800-632-8920. ▨

Once you have a copy of the RealAudio Player setup program on your hard drive, here's how you install it for Windows. (Mac installation is similar):

1. Find the .exe file you downloaded to your hard drive. Double-click it to run the setup program.
2. Accept the license.
3. Enter your name and, if applicable, company.
4. Select your Internet connection speed: 14.4, 28.8, ISDN, or T1.
5. Choose Express setup (unless you want a Custom setup).
6. The RealAudio Player files will be copied to your system, and you'll get a Success message.
7. The RealAudio Player will automatically launch and play a welcome message.

N O T E You can get full instructions for setting up the UNIX version of RealAudio from the Progressive Networks site at **http://www6.realaudio.com/help/player/unix2.0/** ▨

If you choose Custom Setup rather than Express Setup in step five, you can change the default directory where the stand-alone RealAudio player will be installed (usually C:\RAPLAYER in all Windows versions). You can also choose whether to install the plug-in version of the RealAudio player into any browsers you have installed on your system.

N O T E In most cases, the default RealAudio Player preferences settings should work just fine. If you have problems, you can find help on setting the Preferences on Progressive Network's Web site at **http://www6.realaudio.com/help/player/win3.0**.

If you're having trouble playing RealAudio streams through your local area network's firewalls, check out the instructions at **http://www.realaudio.com/firewall.html**. ▨

Controls and Menus

The RealAudio Player controls are elementary.

The Toolbar includes Play/Pause, Stop, and a Time Into Clip Indicator. There are also Fast Forward/Rewind buttons, which work in 10-second increments, and a Home Button. The Home Button shows a spinning speaker when the Player is receiving a file, and a lightning bolt when it is encountering a high data loss. Clicking on the Home Button takes you to the RealAudio home page at **http://www.realaudio.com**.

The Volume slider is at the right-hand side of the Player window. Title, author, and copyright information is displayed to the left of the Volume slider in the Clip Info window. The current state of the Player is displayed in the Status Bar at the bottom of the Player window, with the play time and clip length shown in the lower-right corner.

If you're listening to a Web page with embedded RealAudio content, you may see inline versions of any or all of these controls inside the Web page, depending on how the Web page has been set up.

TROUBLESHOOTING

Why don't I hear any sound from very short sound clips? The file may be too short. Current versions of the RealAudio 3.0 Player will not play files shorter than one second.

Play, Pause, and Stop are also available from a right-mouse-button, pop-up shortcut menu. The RealAudio Player menus are also pretty simple. The RealAudio File menu lets you open a RealAudio file from a drive on your system or network, or from a server on an intranet or the World Wide Web. Open File [Ctrl+O] is the option for loading a .ra or .ram file from a disk or a network; Open Location [Ctrl+L] lets you specify the URL of a file located on an intranet or Web site. Open Recent is where you'll find a list of recently played RealAudio files.

N O T E   A RealAudio URL takes this format: **pnm://Server:Port#/pathname**

"pnm://" indicates the file is located on a RealAudio Server system. "Server:Port#" is the address of the RealAudio server. "pathname" is the complete directory path and file name. Here's a real-world example: **pnm://audio.realaudio.com/welcome.ra**

From the View Menu, you can turn on or off the display of the Player Info and Volume window, or Status the Bar. Choosing Preferences [Ctrl+P] brings up the Preferences dialog box, where you can set Network, Proxy, and other advanced options. The Statistics item pops up a dialog containing information about the current connection. (The Preferences and Statistics dialog boxes are also available from the right-mouse-button, pop-up menu.) Finally, Always on Top keeps the RealAudio Player window on top of all other open windows.

The Clip menu (or the right-mouse-button, pop-up menu) lets you choose to play the Previous [PageUp] or Next [PageDown] clip. The Sites menu takes you directly to the RealAudio Home Page, RealAudio Guide, or RealAudio Help Page. Finally, the Help menu has two choices: Contents [F1] or About.

> **N O T E** Want to find some cool RealAudio sound sites? Check out Timecast (Figure 19.4) at
> **http://www.timecast.com**. Continually up-to-date, Timecast is the definitive guide to live
> RealAudio broadcasts and the best prerecorded RealAudio content on the Web. It's all here, from ABC
> News to PBS specials, from live FM radio to real-time sports broadcasts. You can even customize your
> own daily news broadcast with time-sensitive, audio content delivered live. ■

FIG. 19.4
Timecast is the ultimate Web guide to RealAudio sites.

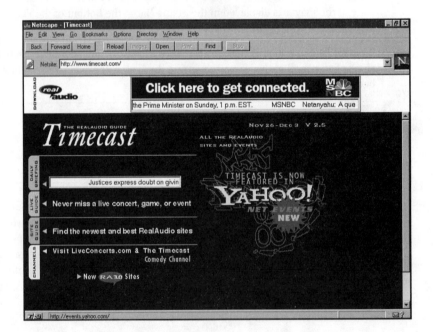

The RealAudio Encoder

You use the RealAudio Encoder (see Figure 19.5) to translate audio-format files into RealAudio files. This encoded RealAudio material can then be played over an intranet or the Internet in real time, using the RealAudio Server to send, and the RealAudio Player to receive.

The RealAudio Encoder 3.0 is available for Microsoft Windows 95/NT, Microsoft Windows 3.1, Macintosh, and UNIX. The RealAudio Encoder supports the input file formats listed in Table 19.3.

FIG. 19.5
The RealAudio Encoder lets you specify a Source file, a Destination file, and set Description elements. You can also choose the Compression Type in the Options window.

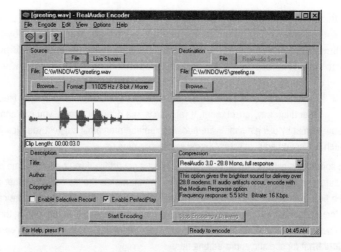

Table 19.3   Input File Formats Supported by RealAudio Encoder

Type	Sampling Rate	Resolution
.wav audio	8,11,22,44kHz	8- or 16-bit, monophonic
.au audio	8,22,44kHz	monophonic
raw .pcm Data	8,11,22,44	8- or 16-bit, monophonic

The RealAudio Encoder does not support stereo or compressed files.

Installing the RealAudio Encoder

The RealAudio Encoder can be downloaded from the Progressive Networks site at **http:// www.realaudio.com/products/encoder/index.html**. Installation and setup are so similar to that of the RealAudio Player that you can simply refer back to the RealAudio Player installation instructions on p. 404.

Because audio encoding is more demanding than simply playing back encoded files, you should be aware that Progressive Networks recommends a minimum of a 486/66 CPU with 8M of RAM and 1M of hard-drive space for installation of the Encoder program, plus an additional 1-2K of hard drive space per second of audio that you plan to encode and store. You'll also need a 16-bit sound card capable of recording an 8kHz signal, like a Sound Blaster Pro or something compatible.

Encoding

You need to start with a sound file in .wav, .au, or .pcm format. The Web is a great source for a wide variety of sound files. I suggest prospecting at **http://www.yahoo.com/ Computers_and_Internet/Multimedia/Sound/Archives**. If you want to record your own sound files, you'll need an audio-digitizing program. Most sound cards come with such a program. You can record audio from tape or other external audio sources by using your sound card's line input, or you can record live audio by using its microphone input. For the specifics of how to record sound with your particular sound card, check your sound-card manual.

N O T E   The RealAudio Encoder does not support stereo or compressed files, or files of a format other than .wav, .au, or .pcm. If your file is in a different format, you can convert it to a compatible format by using a shareware audio-file editing program. I suggest you pick your platform and search for "sound edit" at **http://www.shareware.com/**.

You can sometimes get better results when encoding a sound file if you perform some adjustments to the file before you encode it. Almost any adjustment that makes the file sound cleaner and clearer will make the final encoded version sound better, too. Most audio-digitizing programs are capable of performing at least a few basic adjustments like equalization or noise gating. (Along the way, you can also add cool effects like echo!) Check out **http://www.realaudio.com/help/content/ audiohints.html** for specific audio-editing tips. ■

Follow these steps to encode audio files for RealAudio. (Refer to Figure 19.5.)

1. In the RealAudio Encoder Source panel, select the File tab, then click Browse and choose the source file.

2. A default file name automatically appears in the Destination panel. Either use the default file name or select a different destination.

3. In the Options panel, select the desired Compression Type. RealAudio 28.8 provides higher fidelity and requires a 28.8 Kbps modem, or faster, Internet connection. RealAudio 14.4 compression is optimized for 14.4 Kbps modem connections and also works with RealAudio Player 1.0.

4. In the Description panel, enter the title, author, and copyright information for the clip. These fields may be left blank.

5. If you want to listen to the audio file as it is being encoded, check the Play While Encoding box under Options and choose to play the original audio file or the .ra file that is being created.

6. Choose Start Encoding from the Encode menu or click the left-most toolbar button.

N O T E   The RealAudio Encoder 3.0 can encode live audio input directly from your PC's sound card. However, only the version of the Encoder provided with the RealAudio Server 3.0 can send the RealAudio output directly to the Server for live broadcast on the Internet. A special server utility called the Live Transfer Agent (LTA) acts as a bridge between the RealAudio Live Encoder and the Server. The LTA transfers encoded RealAudio from the Live Encoder to the Server in real time to allow for live cybercasting.

You can encode any sound data delivered to your sound card, including CD audio. The downloadable trial version of the Encoder has this feature disabled. ■

If Show Audio Signal is selected under the Options menu, you'll see amplitude graphs of the source and destination files.

There are a minimal set of controls available via the Encoder menus. All are intuitive, and are explained via the Help, Contents menu selection.

N O T E   The RealAudio Encoder will automatically encode a .wav or .au file when you drag an icon of the file to the RealAudio Encoder shortcut on your desktop. The Encoder can also be run from the command line to automatically encode multiple audio files with options from a setting file. Complete instructions for doing this are located on Progressive Network's Web site at **http://www. realaudio.com/help/encoder/win3.0/settings.html**. ■

Once you have a .ra format file, you need to create an associated .ram metafile. This is just a fancy name for a text file that contains a single line containing the full URL for the .ra file. A typical .ram file might look like this:

```
pnm://audio.realaudio.com/welcome.ra
```

The .ram file containing this line would probably be called welcome.ram to make its association with the encoded RealAudio file it calls, welcome.ra, clear. Why use an intermediary .ram file to play a .ra file? Well, for one thing, .ram files can contain a list of URLs for .ra files, which will be played in sequence. (Just make sure .ram files that contain lists of .ra file URLs don't contain any blank lines!) For another, .ram metafiles can contain timing instructions that will start a .ra file playing at some time into the file, rather than at the beginning.

To do this, you append the starting time to the end of the URL, preceded by a dollar sign, like this:

```
pnm://audio.realaudio.com/welcome.ra$0:30
```

This file would begin playing 30 seconds into the .ra file. The complete format is:

```
$dd:hh:mm:ss.t
```

where dd signifies days, hh hours, mm minutes, ss seconds, and t is tenths of a second (note the decimal point before the t).

Using RealAudio Content on Your Web Pages

If you are content with having viewers of your site launching the stand-alone RealAudio player as a browser helper application, you can use a standard HTML link to play RealAudio files on your Web page, as in this example:

```
<A HREF="pnm://audio.realaudio.com/duck.ram">Duck Quacking</A>
```

Part
IV

Ch
19

This line of HTML code produces a text link labeled Duck Quacking which, when clicked, launches the stand-alone RealAudio Player. The viewer must then click the Play button to hear the "duck.ram" file, then exit the RealAudio Player program.

> **CAUTION**
>
> Remember, you must have the RealAudio Server software installed and properly configured on your Web server computer before you can use RealAudio content on your Web pages.

A more elegant solution is to use the EMBED tag to incorporate an inline RealAudio file, like this:

```
<EMBED SRC=" pnm://audio.realaudio.com/duck.rpm" WIDTH=300 HEIGHT=134>
```

The SRC attribute specifies the URL of the RealAudio file to play. Note that, to avoid backwards-compatibility conflicts with the stand-alone RealAudio Player, URLs for use with the EMBED tag—which invokes the RealAudio plug-in—use an .RPM extension instead of the .RAM extension. In all other ways, however, files with an .RPM extension are identical to .RAM files—they differ only in the file-name extension.

The WIDTH and HEIGHT attributes specify the size of the embedded component. Unlike images, plug-ins do not size automatically. The WIDTH and HEIGHT can be specified in pixels (the default) or percentages of screen width (for instance, WIDTH=100 percent).

Here's the generic syntax for using the EMBED tag with RealAudio files:

```
<EMBED SRC=source_URL WIDTH=width_value HEIGHT=height_value [CONTROLS=option]
[AUTOSTART=True] [CONSOLE=value] [NOLABELS=True]>
```

The CONTROLS, AUTOSTART, CONSOLE, and NOLABELS attributes are unique to RealAudio, and are all optional.

The CONTROLS attribute defines which RealAudio Player controls appear embedded on the Web page. Table 19.4 lists all the valid values for the CONTROLS attribute.

Table 19.4   Values for the *CONTROLS* Attribute

Value	Description
CONTROLS = All	Embeds a full Player view including the ControlPanel, InfoVolumePanel, and StatusBar. (This is the default if CONTROLS is not specified.)
CONTROLS = ControlPanel	Embeds the Play/Pause button, the Stop button, and the Position slider. (Same as the stand-alone Player application with none of the options on the View menu checked).
CONTROLS = InfoVolumePanel	Embeds the information area showing title, author, and copyright with a Volume slider on the right-hand side. (Same as the panel displayed by the stand-alone Player application when the Info and Volume option on the View menu is checked).

Value	Description
CONTROLS = InfoPanel	Similar to InfoVolumePanel, but embeds the information area showing title, author, and copyright without the Volume slider.
CONTROLS = StatusBar	Embeds the Status Bar that shows informational messages, current time position, and clip length. (Same as the panel displayed by the stand-alone Player application when the Status Bar option on the View menu is checked.)
CONTROLS = PlayButton	Embeds the Play/Pause button only.
CONTROLS = StopButton	Embeds the Stop button only.
CONTROLS = VolumeSlider	Embeds the Volume slider only.
CONTROLS = PositionSlider	Embeds the Position slider (scroll bar) only.
CONTROLS = PositionField	Embeds the field of the Status Bar that shows Position and Length.
CONTROLS = StatusField	Embeds the field of the Status Bar that displays message text and progress indicators.

AUTOSTART=TRUE automatically begins playing the RealAudio file when the page is visited. Use this feature to automatically begin a narration or play background music. Since only one RealAudio clip can play at a time, if you specify AUTOSTART for more than one EMBED tag, only the last one to load will play automatically. (The order in which the source files arrive is dependent on the Web server and Netscape's cache.)

The CONSOLE attribute lets you relate any number of clips that appear on the same Web page together. Normally, each is independent; but those that are related by the CONSOLE attribute are controlled by the same controls. To relate two RealAudio clips on the same page, you simply give them each a CONSOLE attribute with the same name. Here's an example:

```
<EMBED SRC="sample1.rpm" WIDTH=30 HEIGHT=33 CONTROLS="PlayButton" CONSOLE="Clip1">
<EMBED SRC="empty1.rpm" WIDTH=300 HEIGHT=33 CONTROLS="PositionSlider" CONSOLE="Clip1">
```

Normally, the first clip would have an associated Play Button, and the second would have a Position slider. However, since these clips both have the attribute CONSOLE="Clip1", the Play Button and Position slider work for both clips.

You can specify a CONSOLE value of "_master" to link one clip to all the others on a Web page. Use this value when you want a control such as a StatusBar to display information for all your audio clips.

If your clip includes controls (such as InfoPanel and InfoVolumePanel) that display the title, author, and copyright information, you can suppress this information by using the attribute NOLABELS=TRUE.

Part

IV

Ch

19

If you're concerned about those who use browsers that don't support the EMBED tag, don't worry—just use the NOEMBED tag to include alternative content! Follow your EMBED line with a line like this:

```
<NOEMBED> Content for non-capable browsers </NOEMBED>
```

For example, it would be nice to include a line that would launch the RealAudio helper application automatically if a browser doesn't support plug-ins, like this:

```
<EMBED SRC="sample1.rpm" WIDTH=300 HEIGHT=134>
<NOEMBED><A SRC="sample1.ram"> Use the RealAudio helper app! </A></NOEMBED>
```

CAUTION

Don't accidentally use an .RPM file when you mean to use a .RAM file to launch the stand-alone RealAudio Player as a helper application! If you do, you'll get a full-screen instance of the RealAudio plug-in instead!

Here's what NOT to do:

```
 <A HREF="sample1.rpm">Play sample clip full-screen!</A>
```

The HTML code in Listing 19.1 implements three instances of RealAudio clips on the same Web page. The results are shown in Figure 19.6.

Listing 19.1   Implementing Three RealAudio Clips on a Page

```
<HTML>
<HEAD>
</HEAD>
<TITLE>RealAudio EMBED Examples</TITLE>
<BODY>
Here are three examples of the RealAudio Plug-in.<P>
Thexe examples require the RealAudio Player 2.0 or greater.<P>
<H3>(1) Play and Stop buttons only</H3>
<EMBED SRC="audio/jazz.rpm" ALIGN=BASELINE WIDTH=40 HEIGHT=20
CONTROLS=PlayButton CONSOLE="jazz2">
<EMBED SRC="audio/jazzs.rpm" ALIGN=BASELINE WIDTH=40 HEIGHT=20
CONTROLS=StopButton CONSOLE="jazz2">
The "CONTROL" command specifies which attributes of the plug-in you want
➥displayed.<P>
The "CONSOLE" command allows the two elements to effect the same music clip.
<H3>(2) Control Panel only</H3>
<EMBED SRC="audio/tchai.rpm" WIDTH=200 HEIGHT=35 CONTROLS=ControlPanel>
<H3>(3) Entire Plugin</H3>
<EMBED SRC="audio/pace.rpm" WIDTH=300 HEIGHT=135 CONTROLS=All>
</BODY>
</HTML>
```

FIG. 19.6
This page uses the RealAudio plug-in in three different ways.

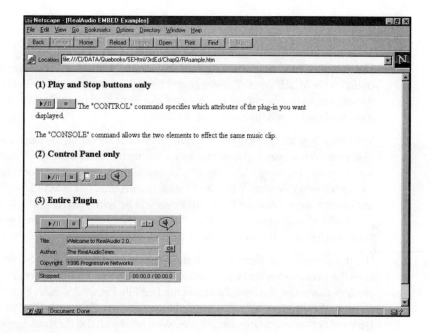

The RealAudio Servers

There are two versions of the RealAudio server: the RealAudio Personal Server: and the RealAudio Server 3.0. Both incarnations send RealAudio audio streams over a TCP/IP network (intranet or Internet) to users of the RealAudio Player. They differ mostly in the number of simultaneous audio streams they support—the Personal Server can handle two, while the 3.0 version can deliver from 5 to over 100 simultaneous audio streams, depending on its configuration.

The RealAudio Personal Server

The RealAudio Personal Server runs on a 486 or Pentium system running Windows 95 or Windows NT, or on Mac OS 7.5.x. The Personal Server is started, stopped, and configured through a user-friendly graphical Windows interface. The RealAudio Personal Server can deliver two simultaneous audio streams. Each stream requires 10 Kbits per second of network bandwidth, which means you'll need a 56Kbaud or T1 leased line to use it effectively. It supports full-random access for each stream and generates a log file containing usage statistics and error information.

The RealAudio Personal Server has been tested with the following Web server software:

- Netscape Netsite
- EMWAC HTTPS 0.96
- NCSA HTTPD (v1.3 or v1.4)

Part
IV

Ch
19

■ CERN HTTPD (v 3.0)

■ O'Reilly Website NT

The Personal Server can generally be set up to work with any Web server that supports configurable MIME types. The suggested retail price for the RealAudio Personal Server is $99, though it is, as this is written, available for free download for evaluation purposes from **http://www.realaudio.com/persserv/apply.html**.

You probably want to install the RealAudio Personal Server on the same computer that's running your Web server. It can be run on a separate machine, but since it takes up so little in the way of resources, there's little need to. To install the server, all you have to do is double-click the server setup file icon. When installation is complete, the RealAudio Personal Server Control Panel will open and the Personal Server will be activated. However, before setting up your RealAudio Web site, you will need to identify the file location where you wish to store your audio and log files. This is done by using the Personal Server Control Panel Setup window.

Use the Setup button, located on the right-hand side of the Personal Server Control Panel, to open the Personal Server Setup window (see Figure 19.7). The Control Panel Setup shows two configurable paths: the Base Path, and the Log File Path. All RealAudio files must reside in, or beneath, the directory specified by the base path. This directory will contain the RealAudio Personal Server executable file. All files associated with the Personal Server, such as audio clips and Server logs, should reside in subdirectories under this directory.

FIG. 19.7

The RealAudio Personal Server incorporates a simple setup window for defining server-directory paths.

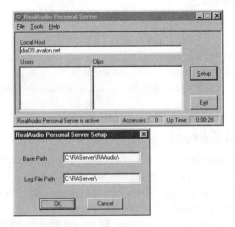

You should enter the full path name of the base directory by using the following format:

```
C:\path\to\rafiles
```

If you specify a directory name that does not currently exist, it will automatically be created when you click OK to exit the setup window.

The Log File Path points to the location of the Personal Server log. The Personal Server log records information about clients who have connected to the Personal Server, and errors generated by the Personal Server. Enter the full path name of this directory by using the following format:

```
C:\path\to\ralogfiles
```

When you have entered all relevant information in the setup window, select OK. You then need to restart your system to activate the Personal Server.

Setting MIME Types

One thing you must do before either version of the RealAudio Server can deliver RealAudio content is to configure your Web server to recognize the MIME types listed in Table 19.5.

Table 19.5	RealAudio MIME Types
Extension	**MIME Type Definition**
.ra, .ram	audio/x-pn-realaudio
.rpm	audio/x-pn-realaudio/plugin

The process for setting MIME types varies from Web server to Web server—check your server documentation for details on how to set MIME types for your particular server. But don't forget to do so. If you don't, viewers will see a screen full of indecipherable text—they won't hear RealAudio sound!

The RealAudio Server 3.0

The RealAudio Server 3.0 is sold in packages that can deliver 5, 20, or 100 streams, and larger servers can be created on a custom basis. This version of the RealAudio server also handles live audio streams as well as prerecorded ones. RealAudio Server 3.0 is available for the following Microsoft Windows NT and UNIX platforms, and is promised soon for the Macintosh:

- DEC Alpha Digital UNIX v3.2
- DEC Alpha Windows NT 3.51
- Hewlett Packard PA/RISC HP/UX 10.01
- 486/Pentium Microsoft Windows NT 3.51
- 486/Pentium BSDI 2.0
- 486/Pentium LINUX 1.x, including ELF
- 486/Pentium FreeBSD 2.x
- IBM Power PC AIX 4.0
- Sun SPARC SunOS 4.1x

- Sun SPARC Solaris 2.x
- Silicon Graphics IRIX version 5.2

The RealAudio Server 3.0 requires a network bandwidth of at least 10Kbps for 14.4 format and 22Kbps for 28.8 format for each client connected to the Internet backbone. Therefore, a 56Kbps leased line can only accommodate approximately five simultaneous 14.4Kbps connections. A T1 line can accommodate over 100 simultaneous 14.4 connections, and is recommended for commercial RealAudio Server applications.

N O T E Bandwidth Negotiation is a feature supported only by the RealAudio Server 3.0. It allows a RealAudio Player to automatically select whether to receive a 14.4 or 28.8 encoded audio stream.

To use this feature, you must use the RealAudio Encoder to create both 14.4 and 28.8 stream files. In the directory you have set up as your source for .ra files, for each sound you want to deliver you create a subdirectory that contains both encoded files. The 14.4 encoded file should be called 14_4.18, while the 28.8 file should be named 28_8.36. The subdirectory—which should be named to include the .ra extension—rather than a specific file, should be referenced in the URL listed in the associated .ram or .rpm file. There is a utility included with the RealAudio Server 3.0 called raconv that automates this process. See the server documentation for full details. ■

The RealAudio Server 3.0 has been tested with the following Web servers:

- Webstar and Webstar PS
- Mac HTTP
- HTTPD4Mac
- Netscape Netsite
- EMWAC HTTPS 0.96
- NCSA HTTPD (v1.3 or v1.4)
- CERN HTTPD (v 3.0)
- O'Reilly Website NT
- Microsoft Internet Information Server

The RealAudio Server can be configured to work with any Web server that supports configurable MIME types.

N O T E Installation and configuration of the RealAudio Server 2.0 varies depending on the platform and operating system. Providing detailed instructions for this process is beyond the scope of this book. Complete documentation comes with the RealAudio Server 3.0 CD-ROM, which is currently priced from $495 to $11,490, depending on configuration. You can purchase the server online at **http://www.realaudio.com/products/server.html**. ■

Synchronized Multimedia

Perhaps the most advanced feature of the RealAudio Server 3.0 is its ability to synchronize RealAudio clips to serve as elements in a multimedia presentation. The process is straightforward, but involves several distinct steps.

First of all, synchronized multimedia "shows" should take place only on pages that include frames. One frame is reserved for the RealAudio plug-in with its associated controls, and at least one frame is needed to display the multimedia content. This is necessary because loading a new page would otherwise replace the page containing the plug-in, which stops the plug-in from playing. By using frames, you keep the plug-in active.

▶ For information on creating frames, **see** Chapter 10, "Frames," on **p. 171**

Second, you create a text file listing the times that the frame content should change, and the URLs that should be loaded at those times. The format is:

```
u[space]starttime[space]endtime[space] &&framename&&URL
```

The starting u is required for each line. The starttime and endtime elements have the format dd:hh:mm:ss.t, where dd is days, hh is hours, mm is minutes, ss is seconds, and t is tenths of a second. (This is the same format used for delayed play in .ram files.) These times refer to the time in the clip at which the frame should begin and end playing. &&framename&& is the ampersand-delimited name of the target frame for the intended content change. URL is the URL of the frame to be displayed at the indicated time. There should be no blank lines between lines in the list. However, the input file may contain comment lines beginning with the # symbol. A real-world example might look like this:

```
u 00:00:10.0 00:00:59.9 http://www.RealAudio.com/
u 00:01:00.0 00:02:00.0 http://www.mysite.com/page2/
```

This input file tells the Player to send the Web browser to the RealAudio home page at 10 seconds into the audio clip. At one minute into the audio clip, the Web browser will display a page from "www.my_site.com."

Once you have created this text file, it must be compiled into a binary by using the *cevents* command-line tool supplied with the RealAudio Server 3.0. The syntax is:

```
cevents source.txt audiofilename.rae
```

The resulting .rae file (which should have the same base name as the associated .ra audio file) is then placed in the same directory as the .ra audio file. This file is then automatically located by the RealAudio Server when the listener opens the associated .ra file. The RealAudio Server streams audio and event information to the Player. As the event information is streamed to the RealAudio Player, the RealAudio Player then sends requests to the Web browser telling it when to update the page's content.

N O T E Detailed information on creating RealAudio Synchronized Multimedia files is available at http://www.realaudio.com/products/ra2.0/features/synchmm.html. ∎

Part

IV

Ch

19

## CHAPTER 20

Video, Animation, and Multimedia

by Mark R. Brown

Video, animation, and interactive multimedia presentations can really liven up your pages. They pull in and involve your audience in a way that simple text and static graphics can't. Of course, presenting inline multimedia elements means creating and delivering a whole new kind of page content that can't be viewed by using browser programs that only understand HTML. Only plug-in-capable browsers can display such a wide variety of multimedia content.

Though plug-in-compatible content integrates almost seamlessly into your pages, developing and delivering that content involves steps that are quite different than those involved in creating straight HTML pages. Each type of content—video, animation, and multimedia—must be created by using a different program specifically designed to create that type of content. Each must then be displayed by using a different browser plug-in. ■

Learn how to create great multimedia content

Creating multimedia content requires a variety of dedicated hardware and software tools, such as a video camera, a multimedia authoring system, or an animation program.

Choose between straight HTML and multimedia content

Some kinds of information are more suitable for multimedia presentation via plug-ins, as opposed to straight HTML.

Work within the user's limited bandwidth

Bandwidth is an important limiting factor when delivering multimedia content in HTML documents, especially over the World Wide Web.

Limitations on Multimedia Content

Many real-world factors place a practical limit on what kinds of plug-in-compatible content you can use on your site. File size (mainly a concern in regards to throughput over dialup connections) and browser compatibility are certainly two primary considerations. There is also the issue of good content versus good looks, and how that helps to determine which plug-ins are best for your site. Finally, there's the issue of the sheer number of plug-ins that are available, and how you quickly run into the problem of pure practicality.

> **N O T E**   Most of the plug-ins that you read about in this chapter work equally well in Internet
> Explorer, as Internet Explorer supports Netscape Plug-ins. On the other hand, you'll likely
> find comparable ActiveX controls for each of the plug-ins in this chapter at the publisher's Web site.
> You can learn more about ActiveX controls in Chapter 22, "ActiveX Controls." ▪

File Size and Dialup Connections

When developing plug-in-compatible content for delivery over the World Wide Web, a prime consideration is *bandwidth*, or how much data can be delivered to your audience in a given amount of time.

Users with fast, direct-dedicated T1 or T3 landline connections will, under ideal conditions, have no problem viewing real-time videos or listening to real-time audio broadcasts. Even interactive multimedia presentations will be up and ready for display in a reasonable amount of time.

Those connecting to your Web site via dialup connections will have problems viewing huge files of any type. Over a standard 14.4Kbps (kilobit per second) or 28.8Kbps dialup connection, even large GIF and JPEG graphics can take several minutes to load. Pages that are extremely graphics-rich can take 15 minutes or more to download over such slow connections.

Multiply the problem by a factor of 10, or even 100, for video and multimedia content, and you begin to see that plug-in-compatible content is not generally a realistic option for those who are connecting to the Web via a dialup connection.

However, remember that the real issue is file size, not content type. A MIDI music file might be only a couple of kilobytes in size and, therefore, is a good candidate for delivery even over dialup lines. Videos and multimedia presentations are not totally out of the question, either, as long as your viewers are willing to wait for them to download first—you won't be able to stream them for viewing in real-time. The issue here is whether or not the content is worth waiting for.

If you consider who your audience is, it's easy to determine what types of content you can provide. If your viewers are likely to be connecting from university, corporate, or government sites with direct Internet links, then bandwidth is not generally an issue and almost any type of content can be incorporated into your pages. On the other hand, if most of your viewers are likely to be connecting to the Internet via dialup lines from home or through online services, your pages should be sparser, with smaller files that can be viewed in a reasonable amount of time over a slow dialup connection.

A good rule of thumb is to remember that a 14.4Kbps dialup can read a maximum of about 1.7K (kilobytes) of data per second from the Internet. Thus, a 25K file will take about 15 seconds to download (if everything goes well). A 250K file will take two and a half minutes. If that 250K file is a 10-second animation, your viewer is likely to feel cheated that she had to wait so long for such a short display. If you keep this wait/reward ratio in mind whenever you develop any plug-in-compatible content for your pages, you should be able to keep your site under control and your audience happy.

Browser Compatibility

There are a lot of companies promoting their own proprietary formats on the Web for everything from video and audio to compressed graphics and animation.

The problem with proprietary formats on the World Wide Web is that they can quickly prevent the Web from being "worldwide" at all. Each new proprietary format leads to further balkanization of the Web—that is, to its division into ever smaller, more proprietary pieces.

Not that innovation is bad. It has become painfully obvious that older technologies—.WAV audio and GIF graphics, for example—just aren't robust enough for future use on the Web. The files are too big for the information they hold. Compression is the key to the future expansion of the Web; it's certainly the key to emerging multimedia and 3-D technology.

How can you reconcile this issue? Clearly, we need to continue to experiment with new formats, but without scattering them throughout the Web willy-nilly. The experiments should be localized. Discussion should be encouraged. Then, new standards should be proposed for adoption Web-wide.

The latest HTML standard incorporates many of Netscape Communication Corporation's and Microsoft's innovative extensions, and we will see many more changes in the future. Graphics, audio, video, and multimedia standards should be pursued as well.

In the meantime, plug-ins provide an excellent way to experiment with new and different types of page content, hopefully without dividing Web users into drastically opposing camps. If you keep your content *optional*, you'll go a long way towards promoting feelings of cooperation and good will among all Web users.

How can you do this? Keep your home page generic. Use only HTML-formatted text and standard GIF and JPEG graphics on your home page, then use links to jump to pages that contain your plug-in-compatible content files. For example, you might use a GIF image of a still from a video on your home page as a link to a separate page that includes the entire video.

It's also good form to include text-only, or at least text-and-GIF-graphics versions of your pages for viewing by those who can't or won't use plug-ins to experience the full thrust of your highly glorified pages. After all, HTML is about communication, and you can't communicate if there are those who can't or won't view your pages.

Listing 20.1 shows the HTML code for a courteous page that provides only text and graphics up front, with a link to both enhanced and unenhanced pages:

Part
IV

Ch
20

Listing 20.1 Linking to Enhanced and Unenhanced Pages

```
<HTML>
<HEAD>
<TITLE>The Wonderful World of Weebles</TITLE>
</HEAD>
<BODY>
<H1>The Wonderful World of Weebles</H1>
<HR>
Weebles are cool! I've been into those rockin', sockin'
little Playschool Weebles since I was a kid, and think
there must be a lot of people out there on the Web who
share my interest. That's why I've created the Wonderful
World of Weebles!<P>
<A HREF="Animated.htm"><IMG SRC="weebles2.gif" ALT="[LINK]"></A>
Click here for Multimedia...
<A HREF="Standard.htm"><IMG SRC="weebles3.gif" ALT="[LINK]"></A>
or here for standard Weebles.<P>
</BODY>
</HTML>
```

This page loads fast even over slow dialup lines, and displays just fine in any graphical browser program (see Figure 20.1). It then provides links to pages both with and without multimedia content. The fancy stuff can come on page two, and if people want to bookmark your fancy page rather than your home page, that's fine.

The key is courtesy—your home page should be generic, with optional, fancy multimedia content. That way, everyone can view your site.

FIG. 20.1

This does what a courteous page should do—it presents its case right up front, it loads fast, and it provides links to more user-friendly pages.

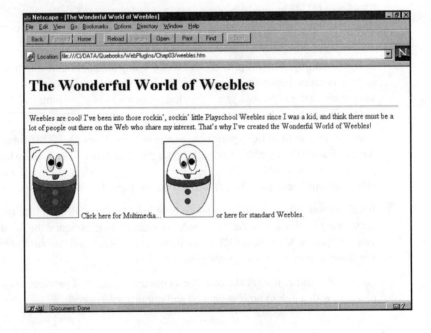

Of course, compatibility is less of an issue over corporate intranets, where everyone is likely to be issued the same browser and plug-ins, and file type standards are likely to be firmly established. Still, there may be situations where staff on the road or at satellite sites dial into the intranet via potentially slow connections, so keep those poor souls in mind when you consider multimedia content.

What Are Plug-Ins Best Used For?

So what use are plug-ins? Plug-ins can deliver content that is more vibrant, interactive, and involving than straight HTML text or GIF graphics. They are best used to deliver content that goes beyond what text and graphics can do.

For example, Figure 20.2 shows an interactive concentration-style game on the Toy Story site. Its purpose is to involve the viewer with the story's characters and make them familiar, but in a fun way. By making the experience interactive and hands-on, the creators of the Toy Story site have done at least three positive things:

- By virtue of its uniqueness (that is, it's a game, not just static text and images), the experience is memorable.

- The game involves memorizing images of the characters from the movie. This makes them familiar and comfortable, which means that Web surfers who play this game will likely want to see more of them.

- Interactivity means the viewer has to hang around long enough to finish the game, which allows time for the message "Toy Story is fun!" to become imprinted.

FIG. 20.2

This Shockwave multimedia game on the Toy Story movie Web site is more than just cool—it involves the viewer with the story's characters and gets her interested in seeing the movie.

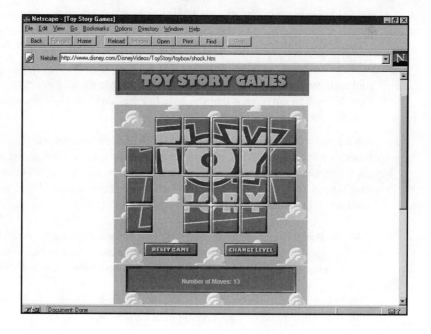

Part

IV

Ch

20

All of these things help the creators of the Toy Story site to achieve their primary goal, which is to increase interest in the movie Toy Story, thus selling more videos and licensed merchandise.

It all sounds rather mercenary when put into these terms, but it's not all that bad—the user was looking for entertainment and enjoyment when she came into the Toy Story site, and this game certainly provides that. It's a classic win-win situation.

If your plug-in content provides the same kind of experience on *your* site, you've done things the right way. Your viewer should go away with a positive impression, a sense of having experienced something good, and a clear idea of what it is you are trying to communicate.

Before you include any plug-in-compatible content on your pages, ask yourself the following questions:

- What is my message?
- How does this content help me deliver my message?
- Will viewing this content be a pleasing experience to my viewers?
- Will my viewers get the message better by interacting with this content than they would without it? Keep in mind the wait/reward ratio you learned about earlier.

If you can answer these questions in the positive, you can justify using at least some plug-in-compatible content on your pages.

Plug-In Content-Creation Programs

Every plug-in delivers content created by its own unique content-creation program. That's a fact of life. Just as you must use a paint program to create GIF graphics, you must use the proper audio-digitizing, video-grabbing, spreadsheet-creating, or other type of program to create each type of plug-in content.

And each content-creation program is unique, with its own user interface, controls, quirks, and capabilities. The sad truth is that you have to install and learn to use a whole new program for each and every type of content you want to create.

From a real-world point of view, this is going to limit the amount and types of content you can provide on your pages. While it might sound appealing to have a site that includes audio, video, multimedia, interactive games, spreadsheets, ad nauseum, the truth is that you simply don't have time to learn how to create and deliver every single kind of plug-in content in existence. You have to be selective.

NOTE Don't forget your audience, too. For every plug-in you use, that's one more plug-in they're going to have to install. If they need to download and install a half dozen plug-ins before they can view your page, the odds are good that they'll just move on to a more user-friendly site!

That means sifting through the chaff to find the kernels of wheat. And, of course, what's chaff to some is wheat to others. Animation might be what you want to present on your personal

Looney Toons Web site, while in your day job as an investment analyst, you might be more interested in putting spreadsheets on the corporate intranet.

Keep It Small

As we've said, for delivery on the World Wide Web, bandwidth is the primary consideration. That makes non-real-time plug-ins most appropriate for Web pages. Video in real-time is a practical impossiblity on dialup connections. It's best to avoid real-time video on your Web pages, but non-real-time (that is, download-then-view) files are okay, as long as you warn your audience that long download times are involved.

In general, try to keep your files as small as possible. Multimedia games are fine if they download quickly. Remember that much of a plug-in-compatible file's capabilities come from the plug-in itself. Data files may be relatively small while incorporating a lot of flashy content. Watch your file sizes and don't worry about how much the file is doing. If it's doing a lot, but doing it very efficiently, that's the key to successful plug-in use over the Internet.

Plug-Ins and Intranets

While plug-ins open up many new possibilities when browsing the World Wide Web, they really shine on intranets. Why? Because organizations can really benefit from the file standardization that intranets impose and intranets don't suffer from the bandwidth problems that can hound sites on the Internet.

As a corporation grows, it sometimes balkanizes—that is, departments and groups drift apart in the way they work, and even in what tools they use to do that work. For example, your company's accounting department might use Lotus 1-2-3 as its spreadsheet program, while engineering uses Microsoft Excel. The secretarial pool might use WordPerfect, while R&D uses Word. Worse, the secretaries might all be on Macs, while engineering uses UNIX workstations. If this is the sort of situation that prevails at your organization, communication among departments might be spotty, at best.

However, a corporate intranet can help smooth over these communication problems. With exceptions, Mac, Windows, and UNIX computers that are running HTML browser programs can all view the same documents. A report created in HTML by the accounting department on a Windows 95 machine can easily be read by engineering on a UNIX workstation or by the HR department on its Macintoshes. Plug-ins are now more widely available across platforms, so they can also be used to view MPEG movies, listen to RealAudio sound clips, and view Word documents that are included in intranet pages. If nothing else, HTML makes it easy to include alternate content for machines that can't read proprietary formats, so everyone can access the same information, regardless of format.

Because corporate intranets run over fast computer networks, streaming video, real-time audio, and other bandwidth-intensive data can also easily be included on intranet sites. This makes video-based in-house training, interactive multimedia, and other data-intensive applications a natural for inclusion on an intranet (see Figure 20.3). Plug-ins that are geared to display multimedia are likely to see much more use on corporate intranets than on the Web.

FIG. 20.3
By publishing multi-media files on its intranet, HBO is saving thousands of dollars previously incurred for printing, duplication of videocassettes, and distribution of marketing campaign materials among 200 to 300 sales representatives.

Video and Animation Plug-Ins

Pictures that move—that's the magic of video and animation. With only sound and graphics, HTML documents are static. But with video and animation, pages come alive with television-like action.

Of course, all this motion comes at a price—even a few seconds of video or animation can come in a package of several megabytes; and with the transmission times involved in transmitting data over the Internet, that can mean sluggish response and jerky images.

When to Use Video Content

You have a stunningly cute VHS video recording of your little niece Gloria spitting up her first mouthful of strained peas, and you have a hunch it would make a wonderful addition to your personal Web page.

Uh…probably not. Unless you have a million relatives out there browsing the Web, the odds are good that nobody is willing to wait the dozens of minutes it takes their dialup connection to download 15 seconds of video that shows dear little Gloria at her worst. Not only that, it's probably going to take you a few hours—or at least a couple of hundred dollars—to get that short video clip onto your site.

Video Speed

As with all HTML document content, while considering when to use video or animation content, it's important to keep in mind the effort/payoff ratio. And with video and animation, that ratio is often very low.

If your audience is mostly connecting to the Internet via a dialup connection, your use of video should be sparse. Not only that, you should give your viewers ample warning. Don't put a video on your home page. Instead, put a link to your video content and include a warning next to the link that states how long to expect the download to take and how long the video clip will be.

A 14.4Kbps connection can deliver, at best, 1,800 bytes of information per second; a 28.8 dialup, twice as much (3,600). Divide the size of your file (in bytes) by these numbers, and put those figures in the warning on your Web page, like this:

> Click here to see the AVI video of Lindberg Landing.
>
> This video is 1M in size. On a 14.4 connection, it will take approximately 9 minutes to download. On a 28.8 connection, it will download in approximately 4 minutes.

If you are delivering information mostly to those who connect directly to the Internet via commercial, university, or government sites, then you can be more generous in your use of video. Users on a 56Kbps direct line will be able to download a 1M video in just a little over two minutes. Still, two minutes is a good chunk of time. If you are using a video plug-in capable of *streaming* its content (so that the video can be viewed as it's coming down the line), you have a lot better chance of keeping your viewers with you. However, you also stand a chance, even on a fast direct line, of having your video content not keep up with real-time. In other words, your viewers may experience skips and jumps.

On a corporate intranet, all such worries vanish. You should be able to deliver video content at will. However, if your corporate intranet includes remote sites connected via the Internet, remember their special needs.

Content Considerations

As always, after the technical details are worked out, your major consideration should be this: does the content add to the value of your site? Is it relevant? Does it fit your theme and topic? If the answer to any of these questions is no, you should probably ask yourself if something else would do the job better.

Videos and animations are especially suited to the following tasks:

- **Training**—Many people learn better by watching someone else do something before trying it out for themselves.
- **Education**—Historical film clips, entertaining animations, and other visual aids can be extremely useful in helping to emphasize and illustrate important concepts.
- **Entertainment**—If your site is devoted mostly to entertaining your viewer, video clips and fun animations are some of the best entertainment around (see Figure 20.4).

Part
IV

Ch
20

■ **News**—People are used to getting their news on TV, and if you are in the business of delivering news to your viewers, clips of important events connote an immediacy and sense of involvement you just can't get from text and still images.

FIG. 20.4

The site promoting the blockbuster film *Independence Day* is the perfect place for a few exciting video clips. Even so, the authors place each clip on its own page and link to them from a menu that warns of large file sizes.

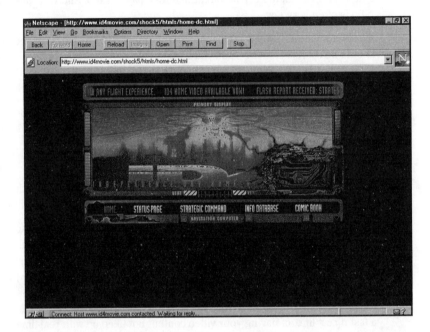

Pages where video and animation should be used sparingly or not at all include the following:

■ **Lengthy Presentations**—If your presentation goes on for many pages, using too many video or animation clips slows down your presentation to the point that only the most dogged viewer will ever get through it all.

■ **Index Pages**—Pages of links should be used as reference points, not sources of entertainment. If your link pages include videos, it's a sure bet that people won't be willing to suffer through the long load times again and again just to use your links. They'll go elsewhere.

■ **Reference Material**—If the main purpose of your site is to serve as a reference source, at least have the courtesy to link to any videos or animations—or big graphics, as far as that goes. If people are going to come back to your site on a regular basis, they will not want to have to load video data every time.

Not only do you need to consider the time your viewers will be putting into downloading and watching your videos and animations, you need to also consider the time you'll invest in creating them.

Creating Video Content

When you get down to it, videos and animations are the same thing—a series of still images presented one after the other to give the illusion of motion. The only real difference is the source. Videos are generally a series of digitized, real-world images, while animations are usually hand-drawn (or at least hand-assembled).

Using a PC to digitize video from a live source is surprisingly complex and expensive. Just as you need a sound card to digitize audio, you need a video digitizer card to digitize video. These aren't cheap. You can buy a card (or external box) to digitize a single image for a couple hundred dollars. But capturing live video streams requires a super-fast card that costs well in excess of a thousand dollars. Not only that, but you also need a fast system with lots of memory and a huge amount of online storage. A computer system set up to do real-time video digitizing will set you back a minimum of $6,000 to $10,000, and we're not even talking VCRs, video mixers, and other esoteric add-ons.

For example, the Salient Video Capture Subsystem model VCS89 (**http://www.salientsys. com/**) offers real-time video digitization, image processing, data compression, high-resolution graphics display, and mass storage of captured images. It comes with 8M of video buffer memory and up to 128M of program memory. It can capture images up to 1280×1024 resolution, and up to 16 million colors by using its on-board Texas Instruments DSP (Digital Signal Processor) chip, the TMS320C80-40. It includes a fast, wide SCSI-2 interface and a PCI format card. The VCS board with 0M of program RAM and 8M display RAM retails for $5,000. Of course, to use this card, you also need a fast Pentium PCI bus computer with lots of RAM of its own, as well as several gigabytes of hard drive storage space.

Other video-capture cards include the Targa 1000, DPS Perception, Quadrant Q-Motion 250, and MiroVideo DC-20. All are high-priced with similar requirements. Popular video-capture software you can use with these cards includes Adobe Premiere 4.0, Ulead Media Studio Pro 2.5, and Asymetrix Digital Video Studio.

If you have the budget to investigate this avenue further, you can find more information by checking out the Yahoo! index for video frame grabbers at **http://www.yahoo.com/ Business_and_Economy/Companies/Computers/Peripherals/Graphics_Cards/ Frame_Grabbers/**.

But there are cheaper solutions. Unfortunately, they involve that annoying equation you seem to run into everywhere in life:

Time = Money

There are always people looking for ways to turn a quick buck with their computers, and the odds are good that living close to you is someone who has already shelled out for one of the mondo-expensive, frame-grabbing systems just described. The odds are also good that he's dying to recoup some of his investment by digitizing video clips for people like you. Check your local phone book for Video Digitizing services. Prices vary greatly, but you can probably get a rate comparable to $40/minute. (That's per minute of video time, not per minute of conversion time.) There are, of course, companies that offer these services over the Web, too.

Part
IV

Ch
20

You'll find some listed at **http://www.yahoo.com/Computers_and_Internet/Multimedia/Video/**.

A less expensive, though more time-consuming, method of creating video clips is to employ an animation technique; digitize individual frames by using an inexpensive frame-capture device; then assemble them by using an animation program.

Video Frame Digitizers

There are a handful of devices on the market that let you digitize a single frame at a time from a video source, which you can then assemble into a video-frame animation. One of the most popular and least expensive of these devices is the Snappy Video Snapshot. If you want to capture single, live video images, you need a device with a built-in camera, like the Connectix QuickCam or WinCam.One.

Snappy

The Snappy video frame-capture device is a self-contained, palm-sized unit that plugs into your computer's printer port. You run a cable from the video-out port of your VCR or other video source into a jack on the Snappy, install the software, and start digitizing.

As you play a video, you preview it on-screen in the Snappy window (see Figure 20.5). Clicking a button instantly freezes and captures a digital image up to 1500×1125 in 16.8 million colors, which can then be enhanced or saved in one of several common file formats. The Snappy software is even Twain-compliant (a standard used for scanning), so you can digitize images from within many software programs that support scanners.

FIG. 20.5
The Snappy video digitizing software lets you adjust brightness, contrast, and other image characteristics.

Fauve Matisse, an image creation and editing program, and Gryphon Morph, a morphing system, are both included in the package, so you can modify images for use on your pages to your heart's content.

For more information on the Snappy, check out Play Incorporated's site at **http://www.play. com**.

Connectix QuickCam

The second way to digitize video images is to use a video camera that is designed to interface directly with a computer. The most famous, inexpensive, computer-interfaced, digital video camera is the Connectix QuickCam (see Figure 20.6). A tiny ball-shaped video camera that connects to your computer's serial and keyboard ports, the $99 fixed-focus QuickCam can digitize gray scale video clips and still images up to 340×240 resolution. It's a great way to get bitmap pictures into your computer, if you can live with digitizing images of things that are close by. A $299 version can do the same thing in color and has a focusable lens. You can get more information at the Connectix site at **http://www.connectix.com**.

FIG. 20.6
The Connectix QuickCam is tiny and easy to hook up and use. This is the black-and-white version, though an almost identical color version is also available.

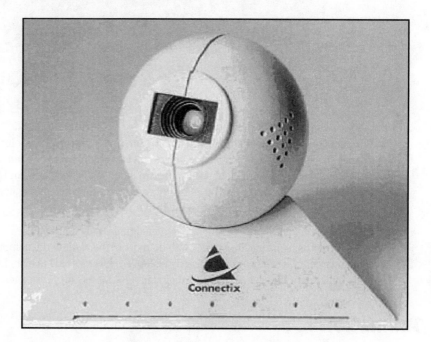

WinCam.One

WinCam.One is a similar (if slightly larger) $199 video still camera. Like the Color QuickCam, WinCam.One uses an inexpensive CCD (Charge Coupled Device) array and a focusable plastic lens in a combination that is the video camera equivalent of an inexpensive film camera. It's a lot like having a nonportable, electronic digital camera like those currently marketed by Nikon,

Canon, Sony, and others. (These also can provide you with the images you need to create animated sequences, by the way.) The digitizing software included with WinCam.One (see Figure 20.7) gives you a great deal of control over brightness and so on, but it's mostly an easy-to-use, point-and-shoot setup.

FIG. 20.7

The WinCam.One digitizing software features a control panel that allows minute control over image quality.

WinCam.One digitizes in high-quality, 24-bit True Color at 640×480 resolution. However, it doesn't do video streams—just single image still capture. It does have one impressive trick up its sleeve though—its serial interface cable can be up to 250 feet long, and WinCam.One can even be run from a remote site by using only a modem and a telephone line! More information can be found online at **http://www.wincam.com**.

Both QuickCam and WinCam.One are totally digital—they deliver their image to the computer without ever using an analog signal. Both do most of the work in the computer software, not camera circuitry, so they are ridiculously cheap. Each is targeted to a slightly different audience, but either can be used to create digital images for use on your pages.

Animation

You can, of course, also draw animations frame by frame. Even at a slow playback rate like 11 frames per second (considered the absolute minimum, even by today's cheap Saturday morning cartoon production houses), you can see that this takes time (see Figure 20.8). It's another great argument for using video and animation sparingly. But if you have talent and all the time in the world, you can use tools like Pixar's RenderMan (a close cousin to the software used by Pixar to create the smash hit movie *Toy Story*) to create your own animation masterpieces.

FIG. 20.8
Even a short, animated cartoon like this one at the official Pinky & the Brain Web site can be composed of hundreds of individual drawings.

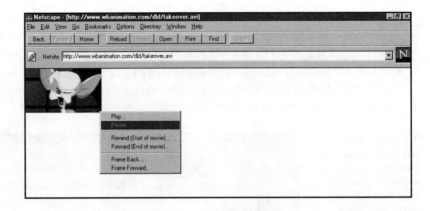

For links to many publishers of animation programs (including Pixar), check Yahoo!'s list of animation links at **http://www.yahoo.com/Computers_and_Internet/Graphics/Computer_Animation/**.

Video for Windows Plug-Ins

There are three standard video formats: Video for Windows, QuickTime, and MPEG. Video for Windows is the standard for PC platforms; QuickTime is used extensively on the Macintosh; and MPEG is the standard for high-end video. We'll discuss plug-ins for each in this chapter.

A Video for Windows driver is built in to the Windows 3.1, Windows 95, and Windows NT operating systems. Windows' Media Player is the system-supplied, stand-alone application for playing Video for Windows movies, which are identified by the file name extension *AVI* (stands for *Audio Video Interleave*). Not surprisingly, AVI format movies have also become popular on the Web. With the right plug-in, you have no problem viewing them inline in HTML pages.

TROUBLESHOOTING

When I try to play an online AVI file using a plug-in, I get a message saying `Cannot find "vids:msvc" decompressor`. What's wrong? Your Windows 95 MS Video 1 video compressor might not be loaded. It's required for playing any AVI file. Go to the Win95 Control Panel, select Add/Remove Programs, Windows Setup, and Multimedia. Scroll down to Video Compression and make sure there is a check mark in the box. If you have to add one, you are prompted to insert your Windows 95 system CD or diskettes.

LiveVideo

Netscape's official plug-in for AVI video is LiveVideo, which is included with the Netscape Navigator distribution. It automatically installs and configures as your Video for Windows player of choice. You click a movie image to play it and click again to stop. Right-clicking an image pops up a complete menu of controls, including Play, Pause, Rewind, Fast Forward,

Frame Back, and Frame Forward. If you didn't get LiveVideo with Netscape, you can download it by following the links from Netscape's home page at **http://www.netscape.com**.

LiveVideo installs automatically side-by-side with Netscape 3.0. You don't have to do anything to install, set up, or configure it. Because it's a plug-in, you don't have to do anything to launch it, either. It sits there, blithely waiting, until you encounter a page with an embedded AVI format video, and then plugs its video player into your browser window, as shown in Figure 20.9.

FIG. 20.9

LiveVideo plays AVI videos inline in the Netscape window. The right mouse button brings up the pop-up menu shown here.

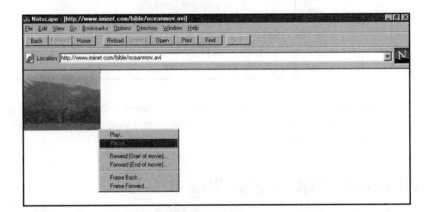

You simply click the embedded video frame to start it playing, click again to pause, then click to resume, and so on.

TIP You can also use LiveVideo to play stand-alone AVI videos, either from the Web, your corporate intranet, or your hard drive—just use File, Open File (Ctrl+O) from the Netscape menu and pick a file of type AVI.

To access the LiveVideo player controls, you right-click the displayed video frame. You get the pop-up menu shown in Figure 20.9.

There are six basic controls available from the LiveVideo pop-up menu. You can Play, Pause, or Rewind to the start of the movie, and Fast Forward to the end. Like a VCR, when you play a video through to the end, you have to rewind it before you can play it again. You can also select Frame Back or Frame Forward to step backwards or forwards through the movie one frame at a time.

LiveVideo is included in the Windows 3.1 and Windows 95 versions of Netscape 3.0. Both require a system with at least a 386 CPU and a compatible sound card. Win 3.1 also requires the Video for Windows driver. (Video for Windows is automatically installed in Win95.)

To embed an AVI format Video for Windows movie in a page, use the EMBED tag, using this generic format:

```
<EMBED SRC=[URL] WIDTH=integer HEIGHT=integer
AUTOSTART=[TRUE¦FALSE] LOOP=[TRUE¦FALSE] CONTROLS=[TRUE¦FALSE]>
```

SRC, WIDTH, and HEIGHT are required attributes. There are also three optional attributes:

AUTOSTART=TRUE¦FALSE	If TRUE, the video starts playing automatically.
LOOP=TRUE¦FALSE	If TRUE, the video plays repeatedly until stopped.
CONTROLS=TRUE¦FALSE	If TRUE, the video appears with a set of player controls.

Remember to set your server's MIME type to associate video/x-msvideo with the file name extension AVI.

N O T E If you're creating an HTML document for Internet Explorer users, you can use the IMG tag with the DYNSRC attribute to insert a video into the document. Set the DYNSRC attribute to the URL of the video clip, like this: <IMG DYNSRC=movie.avi>. ■

VDOLive

Before Netscape came up with its own video plug-in, VDOLive enabled inline Video for Windows clips to be included in HTML pages and played back in real-time.

Unlike the other AVI video plug-ins discussed in this chapter, VDOLive requires a separate VDOLive Personal Server program to deliver video from your server computer. The VDOLive Personal Server and Tools software package enables you to deliver up to two streams of video; capture, compress, and serve up to one minute of video and audio; and will scale up to 256Kbps connections. But the server and plug-in work as a team. You need the server, and your viewers need the plug-in to view your content.

What's the advantage? Well, if your viewers are operating over a slow connection, VDOLive intelligently downloads a video file, skipping over enough information to retain real-time playback. The percentage of actual reception is displayed in the lower-right corner of the VDOLive display window. In cases of severe bandwidth shortage, such as 14.4Kbps connections, you get a low frame rate (approximately one frame every 1–3 seconds) but you are still able to view videos. In other cases, the VDOLive Player and the VDOLive Server try to converge at the best possible bandwidth, which can sometimes result in blurry display and/or low frame rate. While this can result in jerky playback, especially over a slow modem connection, it makes for adequate viewing rather than intolerable viewing.

VDOLive is available for Power Macintosh, Windows 3.1, and Windows 95/NT from VDONet's site at **http://www.vdolive.com/download/**.

Other AVI Video Plug-Ins

There are several more plug-ins available for displaying AVI video in your HTML pages. Iterated Systems' CoolFusion plays inline Video for Windows (AVI) movies. It lets you view videos at any size all the way up to full-screen, and you can stop, replay, and save them using a full set of controls. Using optional EMBED tag attributes, CoolFusion can even play video when the user

Part
IV

Ch
20

drags the mouse pointer over it, or it can provide an alternate audio track (perhaps another language) that plays on a double-click. Like LiveVideo, CoolFusion needs no special server software. A future version will support playback of QuickTime MOV movies as well as AVI movies. For Windows 95 or Windows NT, CoolFusion requires a 256-color graphics card, though a 24-bit or high-color graphics adapter is recommended. You can download CoolFusion at **http://webber.iterated.com/coolfusn/download**.

Vosaic, or Video Mosaic, has been developed as a joint venture between the University of Illinois and Digital Video Communications. Plug-ins are available for both Netscape and Spyglass Mosaic. Video Mosaic's features include embedded hyperlinks within the video stream, and moving objects in the video stream that are clickable and that can lead to other documents. Mac PowerPC and Windows versions can be downloaded from **http://vosaic.com/html/video.html**.

The VivoActive Player is a streaming, AVI video plug-in that uses Video for Windows AVI files that have been compressed up to 250:1 into a new VIV file format, which can be transmitted by using standard HTTP protocol; so you don't need special server software to use them on your pages. The VivoActive Player plug-in is available for Windows 95 and Windows NT from **http://www.vivo.com**.

QuickTime Plug-Ins

QuickTime is the video format used on the Apple Macintosh. However, because it was one of the first movie formats, and because it is so widely used by the art community, which favors the Mac, QuickTime MOV movie files are in ample supply on the Web.

The Apple QuickTime Plug-In

Long-promised and finally shipped as a part of the Navigator 3.0 distribution, Apple's QuickTime plug-in (see Figure 20.10) lets you view QuickTime content directly in the browser window. The QuickTime plug-in works with existing QuickTime movies, as well as with movies prepared to take advantage of the plug-in's fast-start feature. The fast-start feature presents the first frame of the movie almost immediately and can begin playing even before the movie has been completely downloaded.

FIG. 20.10
The Apple QuickTime plug-in features an integral control toolbar and a right mouse button pop-up menu.

If you didn't get it with a copy of Netscape Navigator, you can download the latest versions of the QuickTime plug-in for the Mac, PowerMac, Window 3.1, or Win95/NT from **http://quicktime.apple.com/sw**. After you have it up and running, check out the QuickTime Plug-in Sample Site at **http://www.mediacity.com/~erweb**.

All flavors of the Apple Macintosh ship QuickTime-enabled, but if you want to play QuickTime movies on your Windows computer, you need the proper version of QuickTime for Windows, in addition to the QuickTime plug-in. You can download versions for Windows 3.1 and Win 95/NT from **http://quicktime.apple.com**.

The plug-in can play many kinds of QuickTime movies (MOV files), including movies with text, MIDI, and other kinds of data. The QuickTime plug-in supports a wide set of embedded commands that allow changes in user interface and background playing of content, like music. If you have downloaded and installed the QuickTime VR component, it also lets you interact with QuickTime VR Panoramas and Objects.

QuickTime VR stitches together a series of images into a panorama or scene (see Figure 20.11). To view VR scenes, you also need to get the QuickTime VR Component from the QuickTime Software page and drop it into your Netscape plug-in folder. It's available at **http://quicktime.apple.com/sw**.

FIG. 20.11
To view a QuickTime VR panorama, you just click and drag the mouse.

If you're interested in creating QuickTime movies to play back on your site, you can find tools for Webmasters (like the Internet Movie Tool for the Mac) at **http://quicktime.apple.com/sw**. You can also check into **http://quicktime.apple.com/dev** for more information on how to use QuickTime in HTML documents.

To use QuickTime movies on your site, you have to associate the MIME type video/quicktime with the file name extension MOV on your server. Then you must use the EMBED tag, complete with the required SRC, HEIGHT, and WIDTH attributes.

Part
IV

Ch

20

TIP If you want to display the movie's controller, you need to add 24 pixels to the HEIGHT.

In addition, you can use the following optional attributes:

HIDDEN	Hides the movie. Appropriate only for sound-only QuickTime files.
AUTOPLAY=TRUE¦FALSE	If TRUE, plays the movie automatically. Default is FALSE.
CONTROLLER=TRUE¦FALSE	If TRUE, displays the control toolbar. Default is TRUE. If you display the toolbar, the HEIGHT parameter should be 24 pixels greater than the actual height of the movie to make room for the toolbar. (Do not use CONTROLLER=TRUE with QuickTime VR files.)
LOOP=TRUE¦FALSE¦PALINDROME	Defaults to FALSE. If TRUE, plays the video over and over. PALINDROME plays the movie forward, then backward, then repeats in an infinite loop. (Not used with VR files.)
PLAYEVERYFRAME=TRUE¦FALSE	If TRUE, plays every frame as it is received, even if this means playing at a slow rate. Defaults to FALSE. (Automatically turns off audio.)
HREF="URL"	Provides a link for the movie object.
TARGET="FRAME"	Provides a targeted link for the movie.
PAN=integer	For VR movies only. Specifies initial pan angle, from 0.0 to 360.0 degrees.
TILT=integer	For VR movies only. Specifies initial tilt angle, from –42.5 to 42.5 degrees.
FOV=integer	For VR movies only. Specifies initial field of view angle, from 5.0 to 85.0 degrees.
NODE=integer	For VR movies only. Specifies initial node for a multi-node VR movie.
CORRECTION=NONE¦PARTIAL¦FULL	Optional VR movie parameter.

Other QuickTime Plug-Ins

There are a lot of QuickTime movie plug-ins out there on the Web. Here are a few more you might want to try out.

Knowledge Engineering's MacZilla is a Mac-only plug-in that's a sort of Swiss Army knife of plug-ins. Besides QuickTime movies, it plays or displays: MIDI background music; WAV, AU, and AIFF audio; and MPEG and AVI movies. Using its own plug-in component architecture, MacZilla can extend and update itself over the Internet with the click of a button. You even get a built-in MacZilla game! Download it from Knowledge Engineering at **http://maczilla.com**.

MovieStar by Intelligence at Large is less ambitious—it's only for QuickTime movie playback. Using their MovieStar Maker, a multimedia editing application also available for download, Webmasters can optimize QuickTime movies so that Navigator users can view them while they download. You can also use autoplay, looping, and many other settings. This one is available for Windows, Windows 95, and Macintosh at **http://www.beingthere.com/**.

Need more choices? There are at least three more QuickTime player plug-ins for Netscape: Iván Cavero Belaúnde's ViewMovie for Win95 and Macintosh at **http://www.well.com/ ~ivanski/**; TEC Solutions' TEC Player, also for Win95 and Mac, at **http://www.tecs.com/ TECPlayer_docs**; and Kevin McMurtrie's Mac-only Multimedia Plug-in at **ftp://ftp.wco. com/users/mcmurtri/MySoftware/**.

MPEG Plug-Ins

MPEG is the standard video-compression method developed by the Motion Picture Experts Group. MPEG video delivers excellent quality with better compression than other methods. The MPEG-1 standard is used for computer-based video on the Internet and CD-ROMs, while MPEG-2 is designed for commercial broadcast applications.

MPEG works best with a video board capable of doing hardware decompression. But, even running in software on fast Pentium systems, MPEG works pretty well.

InterVU MPEG Plug-In

InterVU's MPEG plug-in plays streaming MPEG video without specialized MPEG hardware or a proprietary video server. It gives you a first-frame view inline, streams viewing while down-loading, and supports full-speed cached playback off your hard drive. InterVU is available for PowerMac and Windows 95/NT. It can be downloaded from **http://www.intervu.com/ download.html**.

InterVU has no pop-up menu, but it does have an integral control toolbar (see Figure 20.12).

FIG. 20.12
The InterVU MPEG player plug-in has minimalist controls, but offers full streaming playback.

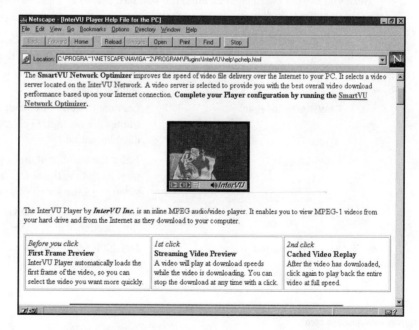

You click the Play button to start a video playing. While a video is playing, the Play button is replaced by a Stop button. Clicking the left mouse button anywhere on the video also starts and stops the video.

As you download the file, a speaker symbol appears if the file has sound, and a crossed-out speaker symbol appears if the file is silent. After the MPEG file has played to completion, a disk button appears on the control bar next to the Play button. If you want to save the file, left-click this disk button, and a Save As dialog box appears. To replay an MPEG video, click the Play button again.

Clicking the InterVU logo in the lower-right corner connects you to the InterVU Web site. To embed MPEG videos into your pages for viewing with InterVU, you first need to make the following MIME type associations in your server software:

video/mpeg	mpg
	*.mpe
	*.mpv
	*.mpeg
	*.mp1
	*.mp2
video/x-mpeg	mpg
	*.mpe
	*.mpv
	*.mpeg
	*.mp1
	*.mp2

Next, you use the EMBED tag, including the standard SRC, WIDTH, and HEIGHT attributes, as well as these optional attributes:

AUTOPLAY=NO¦YES	If YES, the clip is automatically played. NO is the default. (It's unfortunate that this plug-in doesn't use TRUE and FALSE with AUTOSTART, which is the standard usage.)
FRAMERATE=integer	Legitimate values are from 1 to 25, representing frames per second. (This attribute automatically disables sound.)
LOOP=Integer	Enter the number of times you want the video to play. Each time the Start button is pressed, the video plays the specified number of times.
DOUBLESIZE=YES¦NO	Default is NO. If YES, the video is shown at double the encoded size.
HALFSIZE=YES¦NO	Default is NO. If YES, the video is shown at half the encoded size.

CONBAR=YES¦NO	If NO, the control toolbar is not displayed. Default is YES.
FRAMES=YES¦NO	If YES, autoplays the video on a Mac when Netscape Framesets are used.
PALETTE=FOREGROUND¦BACKGROUND	If FOREGROUND, specifies that the video's palette be used as the standard palette on a 256-color screen.

Animation Plug-Ins

Everybody loves a good cartoon. A simple animation can add a lot to your Web page. Though animations are essentially the same as videos, there can be a great difference in scale. Videos take up a lot of memory, storage space, and transfer bandwidth because video images are usually complex, real-world images composed of a lot of pixels in a wide variety of colors.

Animations, on the other hand, are often simple images comprising only a few colors. Because of this, they compress extremely well in comparison to video. If they are put into a proprietary format that is optimized for the delivery of simple animation, they can be even smaller. Compression is one good reason to consider animation when livening up your pages. If you pick a good format, you can deliver animations hundreds of times faster than you can deliver video clips.

Animation always requires at least two proprietary programs: One to create animations and save them in a special format, and a second to play back those special-format files. Because you can't create animations unless you use these companies' animation-creation products, you won't have any material to embed unless you download or buy their programs anyway. These animation-creation programs all contain extensive information on how to include the final result in your pages.

▶ **See** "Animated GIFs," to learn more about how to create simple animations using animated GIFS, **p. 352**

Enliven

The Enliven suite is comprised of three distinct software components: Enliven Viewer, a browser plug-in; Enliven Server, software for Windows NT Web servers to feed multiple streams of animation to browsers; and Enliven Producer, a post-production environment to prepare content for online delivery.

The Enliven product family features patent-pending streaming technologies, including a new multimedia object format and a time-based, scene-description language specifically designed for Internet use. Called Narrative MediaElements and the Narrative Screen Description Language (NSDL), respectively, these technologies stream animation components by separating media-specific components—such as audio, graphics, and animation—and then applying

Part

IV

Ch

20

optimized media-specific compression solutions to each media class. The individual codes used to perform the element compression and decompression are individually upgradable into the various Narrative products, which means they can easily take advantage of any compression technology breakthroughs.

Enliven Producer is a scene-based, drag-and-drop, post-production environment that is used for importing existing digital content from sources such as Macromedia Director or the Microsoft WinToon AVI, and then optimizing that content for delivery via the Enliven Server. This makes it easy to convert animated content you might have already produced, and you can continue to use familiar tools to create future content, as well. Enliven animations can even include interactive hot spots for full interactivity. Enliven Producer runs on Windows 95/NT and a future version is promised for the Macintosh.

The Enliven Server works in conjunction with your server computer to deliver multiple, simultaneous animation streams. The Enliven Server manages real-time streaming of animation sequences with accompanying sound and graphics, while transferring data for subsequent portions of an animation in the background. The Enliven Server currently runs on Windows NT and can reside on the same server as an existing HTTP server or, optionally, on its own server. A UNIX Enliven server is also planned.

The Enliven Viewer plug-in (see Figure 20.13) can also be used as a helper application for a Mosaic browser, or as a stand-alone application, for displaying content in the Enliven format. A beta version of the Enliven viewer plug-in for Win 95/NT can be downloaded from **http://www.narrative.com**.

FIG. 20.13

This sample Enliven animation has been converted from a Macromedia Director file by using Enliven Producer.

A Few More Animation Plug-Ins

GEO Interactive Media Group's Emblaze plug-in is a real-time animation player that plays a proprietary animation format that GEO says needs only 3M to 4M of disk space for approximately 30 minutes of play time. The animations can be displayed at a rate of 12 to 24 frames per second in 256 colors in real-time over a 14.4Kbps connection. Animations are created by using the commercial Emblaze Creator program, which can integrate animation with sound. The end result is an animated cartoon that plays quickly over the Web, even over slow 14.4Kbps dialup connections. Windows 3.1, Macintosh, PowerMac, and Win95 versions of both the player plug-in and the Creator program can be found at **http://www.Geo.Inter.net/ebz/ebz.htm**.

Totally Hip Software's Sizzler plug-in and companion converter program let you create and display small, efficient animations that are among the best I've seen. These animations display like an interlaced GIF or progressive JPEG still image, only *moving*. That is, they start out blocky but animated, and fill in with detail as the data streams in. Sizzler animations are great for spot animation attention-getters, as well as motion illustrations. It's a perfect replacement for those GIF 89a animations that don't always work right. The Sizzler converter (currently available only in a version for the Macintosh) takes Macintosh PICS files or QuickTime movies, and BMP files, AVI videos, or DIB lists for Windows, and converts them into sprite files that can be played in real-time via their plug-in. However, Totally Hip's core technology (called Object Scenario) allows for streamed delivery of several media types including text, animation, video, sound, and interactivity. Totally Hip Software plans to add all of these to Sizzler in the near future. The Sizzler plug-in and Converter are available as free downloads for Windows 95/NT, Macintosh, and PowerPC (only the plug-in is available for Windows 3.1) from **http://www.totallyhip.com/sizzler/sizzler.html**.

Deltapoint's Web Animator, for the Macintosh only (a Windows version is promised), combines animation, sound, and live interaction. The authoring tool for creating animations to add to your own site is also available from its Web site at **http://www.deltapoint.com/animate/index.htm**.

Multimedia Plug-Ins

There are dozens of multimedia authoring systems out there, and it seems like every one of them has a plug-in for delivering its particular brand of multimedia file inline in HTML documents. Is all this really necessary?

Taken in the context of the "Big Picture," probably not. Java and JavaScript are turning out to be the new tools of choice for application, animation, and multimedia applications in HTML documents, mostly because the major browser programs—Netscape Navigator and Microsoft Internet Explorer—support embedded Java applets.

But that means you have to be a programmer to develop multimedia content for your pages, and not all of us are programmers. Thanks to multimedia plug-ins, we don't have to be. If your users are willing to download and install a plug-in, you can use just about any of the multimedia programs discussed in this chapter to bring multimedia content to your site. And you can pick the one that's most appropriate to your requirements.

Over corporate intranets, the solution is even simpler—if you've been using one of these programs to create presentations, training materials, or other multimedia content for your company, you can instantly make that content available to your entire organization by installing the right plug-in on all your desktop systems. You get another advantage from this: anyone can develop multimedia for your intranet by using end-user development programs. You don't have to rely on your programmers to do it for you.

ASAP WebShow

Software Publishing Corporation's ASAP WebShow is a plug-in for viewing, downloading, and printing presentations created with ASAP WordPower. Similar to PowerPoint presentations, WordPower presentations can contain tables, organization charts, bullet lists, and other graphic and text elements in a slide show format. Because the files are compressed, they can be transmitted very quickly.

Presentations and reports can be embedded as icons, live thumbnails, or in a window on a page. Each slide can be viewed in a small live-area window, enlarged to fill the current page, or zoomed to full screen. You can select one slide at a time or watch a continuously running show.

Win95 and Windows 3.1 versions are available (see Figure 20.14), and you can even download a fully functional copy of ASAP WordPower for a free 30-day trial for creating your own WebShow-compatible presentations. All are available at **http://www.spco.com/PRODUCTS/ WSMAIN.htm**.

FIG. 20.14
The ASAP WebShow toolbar and right mouse button pop-up menu give you complete control when viewing its PowerPoint-style slide show presentations with your browser.

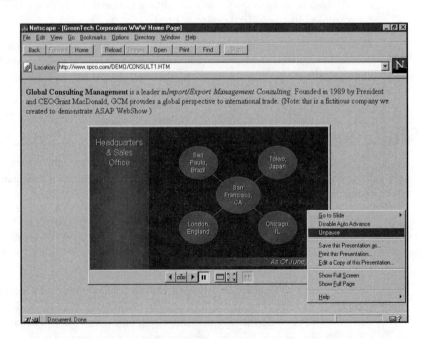

You use ASAP WordPower to create the slide shows for your pages. It can import PowerPoint 7.0 files and convert them to ASAP WordPower format. You can even drag and drop individual slides from the PowerPoint slide viewer into WordPower. ASAP WordPower also imports graphics files in PCX, BMP, WMF, TIF, and GIF formats. Built-in transition effects, dozens of border styles, and a set of startup templates simplify the creation of compelling slide shows. The suggested retail price for ASAP Webshow is $99.

Slide show sound is handled through integration with RealAudio.

The ASAP WebShow Presentation Kit contains everything you need to create, view, and hear a presentation in your HTML documents. For $129, you get both Win95 and Windows 3.1 versions of the ASAP WordPower presentation creation program, the ASAP Viewer plug-in, the ASAP Image Compressor, the RealAudio Player program, a two-stream RealAudio Server (Windows 95/NT only), and the RealAudio Encoder.

The ASAP Image Compressor is an add-on for ASAP WordPower that lets you save presentations in a compact format. The Compressor allows you to adjust the balance of image quality and file size in a compressed presentation. (Only the bitmap images in a presentation are compressed.) The ASAP Image Compressor is also available for download from the ASAP Web site.

To use ASAP WebShow presentations in your own pages, you first have to set the MIME type application/x-asap to the file name extension .ASP on your server. ASAP WebShow content is embedded on HTML pages by using the EMBED tag, along with the required SRC, HEIGHT, and WIDTH parameters.

In addition, WebShow supports a wide range of additional EMBED tag parameters. If you don't use any of the optional parameters, default settings result in a display that puts the presentation in an embedded window, includes a navigation bar, and provides the ability to save, print, and edit the presentation. The following are some of the most important WebShow optional parameters; for a full list, consult the WebShow documentation or refer to the help pages on the ASAP Web site:

`AUTOADVANCE= ON¦OFF`	If ON, automatically advances to each slide. To temporarily stop autoadvance, click the Pause button on the navigation bar or right-click in the ASAP WebShow window and select Pause from the pop-up menu. To completely turn off autoadvance, right-click in the ASAP WebShow window and then click Disable Auto Advance. To turn on autoadvance from the current slide, select Enable Auto Advance from the pop-up menu.
`BORDER= RAISED¦RECESSED¦SLIDE¦` `SHADOWED¦SIMPLE¦NONE`	Changes the border type.

Part
IV

Ch
20

`DELAYTIME= <INTEGER>`	In seconds, delays before advancing to next slide when in autoadvance mode.
`DITHERING= EMBED¦PAGE¦SCREEN¦NONE`	For 256-color screen display only; specifies dithering method.
`EFFECT= <EFFECTNAME, DIRECTION >`	Transition effect between slides. Transitions include:

Effect Name	Direction
BLINDS	LEFT¦RIGHT
BLINDS	UP¦DOWN
CLOSE	HORIZONTAL¦VERTICAL
FADE	
DEFAULT	
IRIS	IN¦OUT
NONE	
OPEN	HORIZONTAL¦VERTICAL
RAIN	UP¦DOWN
REPLACE	
SCROLL	UP¦DOWN
SCROLL	RIGHT¦LEFT
WIPE	UP¦DOWN
WIPE	RIGHT¦LEFT
PEEL	UPPERRIGHT¦LOWERLEFT
PEEL	UPPERLEFT¦LOWERRIGHT

`LOOPBACK= ON¦OFF`	If ON, presentation loops on playback.
`MENU= ON¦OFF`	If ON, enables the right mouse button pop-up menu.
`NAVBAR= ON¦OFF`	If ON, displays the navigation bar.
`NAVBUTTONS= ON¦OFF`	If ON, displays the Next Slide, Previous Slide, and Go to Slide buttons on the navigation bar.
`ORIENTATION= LANDSCAPE¦ PORTRAIT¦N:M¦FREEFORM`	Specifies how the presentation slide page fits in the window. landscape or portrait, maintains the aspect ratio by displaying the slide show in letter-box format. N:M, uses the custom aspect ratio specified, where N and M represent the proportion between width (N) and height (M). freeform (default), the slide fills the available window space.

PALETTE= FOREGROUND¦BACKGROUND	If FOREGROUND, uses the embedded object's palette as the palette for the display window.
PAUSE= ON¦OFF	If ON, autoadvance slide shows pause before playing.
PAUSEBUTTON= ON¦OFF	If ON, includes the Pause button on the navigation bar.
PRINTING= ENABLED¦DISABLED	If ENABLED, the Print This Presentation menu item appears on the pop-up menu.
SAVEAS= ENABLED¦DISABLED	If ENABLED, the Save This Presentation As menu item appears on the pop-up menu.
SOUND= <URL OF A SOUND	Specifies a sound configuration file to play.
ZOOMBUTTONS= ON¦OFF	If ON, Zoom buttons for full page and full screen appear on the navigation bar.

ASAP WebShow supports sound by invoking the RealAudio server. Because RealAudio uses a special server program, WebShow presentations can't embed RealAudio .RA files directly. Instead, the SOUND attribute of the EMBED command is used to specify the URL of a Sound Configuration File, which is simply a text file that contains the URL of the actual RealAudio file.

▶ **See** "RealAudio" for more information on the RealAudio server, **p. 400**

You can create a Sound Configuration file using a text editor. Here's the syntax:

```
<slide#>=<URL of the RealAudio sound file on the RealAudio server>
```

Here's a real-world example:

```
1=pnm://audio20.prognet.com/test/jupiter/slide1.ra
2=pnm://audio20.prognet.com/test/jupiter/slide2.ra
3=pnm://audio20.prognet.com/test/jupiter/slide3.ra
```

You can include as many .RA files in a Sound Configuration file as you want. However, the URL you put in the Sound attribute definition with the EMBED tag must be absolute, not relative. In other words, it must be a complete URL. Here's an example:

```
<EMBED SRC="DEMO2.ASP" Width="300" Height="170" sound="http://www.spco.com/
asap/presents/rasound.txt">
```

ASAP WebShow is a powerful tool for creating business slide show-style presentations, and its EMBED tag attributes let you control most of the plug-in's behavior through HTML.

Part
IV

Ch

20

TIP If you want to publish your Microsoft Power Point presentation on the Web, you can use the Power Point Animation Player that you find at **http://www.microsoft.com/powerpoint/internet/player/default.htm**.

Other Multimedia Plug-Ins

There are at least a dozen more multimedia plug-ins available, with more coming all the time. You can keep up-to-date on multimedia plug-ins development by checking in at the Plug-Ins Plaza Web site at **http://browserwatch.iworld.com/plug-in/plug-in-mm.html**.

Another in the series of Shockwave plug-ins from Macromedia, the Shockwave for Authorware plug-in lets users interact with Authorware interactive multimedia *courses* and *pieces* right in the browser window. Intended for the delivery of large, content-rich multimedia presentations, such as courseware and training materials, Authorware can also write viewer data back to a server computer using FTP; so it's useful for creating market surveys, tests, and quizzes, and customer service applications. Like all Shockwave plug-ins, this one includes an Afterburner module for compressing files for delivery on the Web. Windows 95/NT, Windows 3.1, and Macintosh versions of Shockwave for Authorware and Authorware Aftershock can be downloaded from the Macromedia Web site at **http://www.macromedia.com/Tools/Shockwave/Info/index.html**.

The Astound Web Player plug-in displays multimedia "greeting cards" and other interactive documents created with the Astound or Studio M programs. These presentations can include sound, animation, graphics, video, and even interactive elements. The Astound Web Player is available for Win95 and Windows 3.1. You can even get a stand-alone version for use with browsers that don't support plug-ins. You can choose to download a "slim" version of the player without chart, texture, and animation libraries if you already own Studio M or Astound. If you plan on including movies in your presentations, you need QuickTime for Windows, which is also available from the Astound site at **http://www.astoundinc.com/main.html**.

The mBED plug-in plays multimedia *mbedlets*, small applets that are intended as interesting, interactive, on-the-page components. mBED is not intended for those big, killer multimedia applications. It's intended to create interactive multimedia buttons and spot animations. The .MBD file format and the built-in mBED players are license-free and are available for Windows 95/NT, Windows 3.1, Macintosh, and PowerMac. You can find out more and download these plug-ins from **http://www.mbed.com**.

Asymetrix's ToolBook is one of the top multimedia authoring tools. Now, with its Neuron plug-in, you can deliver ToolBook multimedia titles over the Net. The Neuron plug-in supports external multimedia files, so you can access either complete courseware or multimedia titles, or just the relevant portions of titles, in real-time. Content that is not requested is not downloaded, saving you download time and making the application more responsive. The Neuron plug-in and a 30-day trial version of the ToolBook II program are both available for free download at Asymetrix's Web site at **http://www.asymetrix.com/toolbook/neuron/index.htm**.

RadMedia (**http://www.radmedia.com**) has a plug-in to play back multimedia applications built in RAD PowerMedia. Designed for corporate communicators and Web designers, PowerMedia provides authoring and viewing of interactive content, presentations, training, kiosks, and demos. It's available for Windows 95/NT and several UNIX platforms. The download file for this plug-in is 9M, and the sample PowerMedia applications on the RadMedia site are also in the multi-megabyte range. If your multimedia needs are serious—especially if you are going to be running over a fast T1 or intranet connection—you should check out this solution. Free Demonstration CD-ROMs for PowerMedia are available for qualified users.

The mFactory plug-in promises streamed playback of, and communication between, fully interactive multimedia "worlds" embedded in HTML pages. Here are the supported file formats:

Video:	QuickTime
	QTVR
	Video for Windows (AVI)
Graphic:	PICT
Text:	Dynamic and editable text
Audio/sound:	AIFF
	MIDI
Animation:	PICT
	PICS
	QuickTime

Their cel-based proprietary mToon animation format enables ranges of cels to be defined and played. Check out **http://www.mfactory.com/** for information and download availability.

Finally, the SCREAM inline multimedia player for Windows 3.1, Win95, and Mac, is worth a look. It's at **http://www.savedbytech.com/sbt/Plug_In.html**.

Shockwave for Macromedia Director

Shockwave for Director is a plug-in that lets you play multimedia movies created with the most popular multimedia creation tool available today—Macromedia Director. In the following pages, you'll take a close look at the process involved in using the Shockwave plug-in to deliver Director content on your pages.

Director versus Java and JavaScript

The Shockwave for Director plug-in came before Java; it was introduced at about the same time as Netscape Navigator 2.0, which had just added plug-in capability. Hundreds of developers began using Macromedia Director—literally overnight—to add animation and interactive multimedia content to their Web sites. Many of them already had Director movies on hand that they had created for other applications. All they had to do was run their movies through the new Afterburner Xtra module and then place their converted movies on their Web pages by using the new EMBED tag.

Suddenly, Web pages included inline animations, games, and button-rich interactive multimedia presentations. It was clear the Web would never be the same again. But then Netscape added support for Java and JavaScript. Shockwave didn't go away, but suddenly Java was the new darling of Web site developers. Animations, presentations, and even interactive multimedia sites multiplied by the thousands. Now it seems like all you hear about are Java and JavaScript.

Part
IV

Ch
20

Did Java and JavaScript kill Shockwave? Did they completely take over the multimedia/animation niche that the Shockwave for Director plug-in had created?

Hardly. With a quarter of a million copies of Director in use, Macromedia is still doing quite well. What happened is that Java and JavaScript jumped into a niche that was expanding so rapidly, there was plenty of room for Shockwave to not only hold its own, but to also keep expanding its influence, even as Java and JavaScript carved out their own territories.

In truth, Java and Director appeal to two inherently different types of people. You develop content with Macromedia Director in a friendly, point-and-click environment that uses a stage metaphor. You bring in *casts* composed of *actors*, who strut their stuff on a *stage*. The end result is even referred to as a *movie*. Director includes painting and animation tools with menus, dialog boxes, and buttons. People who are used to creating content with end-user applications like Word and Paint are those who are most comfortable developing multimedia content using Director.

N O T E   Don't confuse Director movies with digitized video movies like Video for Windows or QuickTime files. Though they share a common name, Director movies are much more than a simple sequence of images; they are multimedia scripts. ▪

On the other hand, Java and JavaScript are programming languages. They resemble the C programming language, which is the most popular language for developing applications, so they appeal mostly to programmers. People who think in terms of code and programs are more likely to develop their multimedia content with Java and JavaScript.

N O T E   Actually, though you use a user-friendly program to create Director movies, the end result is a script or set of scripts in a language called Lingo. You can edit these scripts or even write your own from scratch if you want. So Director really offers the best of both worlds. ▪

What You Can Do with Shockwave for Director

The Shockwave for Macromedia Director plug-in (see Figure 20.15) can integrate animation, bitmap, video, and sound, and can bundle all of them up with an interactive interface, complete with control buttons and graphic hot spots. Its playback compatibility with a variety of computer platforms, including Windows, Mac OS, OS/2, and SGI, has helped to make Director the most widely used professional multimedia authoring tool.

Using Shockwave for Director, a Director movie run over the Internet can support the same sort of features as a Director movie run off a CD-ROM, including animated sequences, sophisticated scripted interactivity, user text input, sound playback, and much more. You can even add hot links to URL addresses.

FIG. 20.15

The Shockwave for Director plug-in features no controls or menus of its own. Any such controls must be provided as part of the Director movie being played, like the Click Here to Continue button shown in this science lab animation.

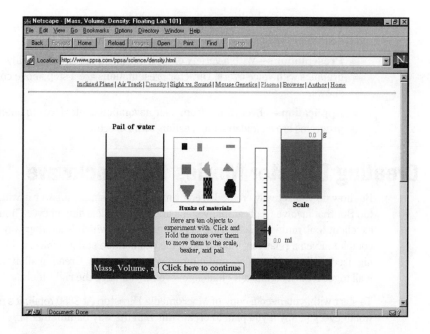

Shockwave for Director consists of two main components, the Shockwave plug-in itself and Shockwave Afterburner, a compressor Xtra program that runs from within Macromedia Director to squeeze a Director movie file by 40 to 50 percent for faster transfer. You can download the Shockwave for Director plug-in and Afterburner from Macromedia's Web site at Shockwave, **http://www.macromedia.com**.

N O T E Don't be confused by the abundance of Shockwave plug-ins at the Macromedia site. Besides Shockwave for Director, you can find a Shockwave plug-in for playing Authorware files, as well as one for viewing Freehand drawings. ■

Before we get too deeply into the mechanics of Director, let's consider what you can do on your site with the Shockwave plug-in for Director. Though you are really only limited by your imagination (and network download times), there are several categories that lend themselves well to Director solutions:

- **Animation**—Director can be used to create frame animations (including audio, if you want) that are second to none.

- **Games**—Director games can be as fast and fun as those written in high-level programming languages.

- **Entertainment**—Video and audio content can be tied together and delivered as a unified package.

- **Training**—Interactivity through on-screen buttons and graphic hot spots means student-guided training is a snap.

- **Education**—The ability to tie together a myriad of components means you can compose educational materials that are second to none.

- **Presentations**—With a variety of built-in transitions and the ability to link text and graphics with voice-overs, Director presentations are a step above conventional slide shows.

- **Applications**—Everything from user navigational interfaces to out-and-out application programs are candidates for creation with Director.

Creating Director Movies for Shockwave

But how do you actually create Director movies? The simple answer is with Macromedia Director. But that involves a great many steps and a bit of a learning curve. Though Director is an excellent tool, multimedia files are very content-rich, which is another way of saying they are complex. Even a relatively unambitious file can include still graphics, animation sequences, digitized audio and/or video, and interactive components. Creating all of that content and tying it all together is a significant challenge, even if you have the right tools.

To start with, you need a copy of Macromedia Director. At $850 retail, it's not cheap; but it's worth every penny if you plan to create much in the way of multimedia.

Director 5.0 (the latest version) is available for the following platforms:

- Windows 95
- Windows NT
- Windows 3.1
- Power Macintosh
- Macintosh

Director is based on a theater metaphor. With this metaphor, you have a Stage where you can view your Director movie. Behind the scene, you have a Cast Window that stores all of your media objects. These media objects can be sounds, 2-D and 3-D graphics, animations, digital video, text, and even database objects. To organize your media elements on the Stage, you use the Score. The Score window allows you to precisely sync your media elements and to provide different layers of elements on the screen. The main Director screen is shown in Figure 20.16.

Director movies are composed of Cast members, which are media elements like images or sounds. These are inserted into the Score window, which sequences all of the file's elements. (Director also includes a full set of Paint and other tools for creating these media elements.) After you create and coordinate all of a movie's elements, you save the result as a Director movie file.

FIG. 20.16
The Director screen consists of many elements that can be called up when needed.

Score window (top left)

Stage (background)

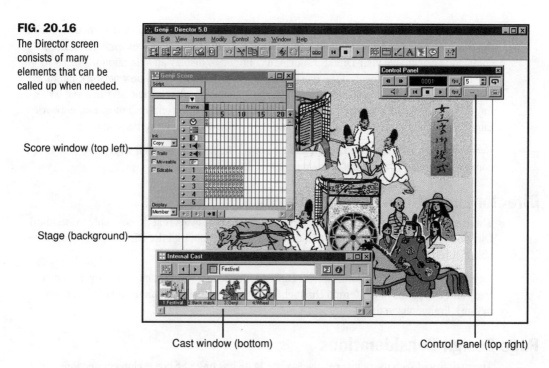

Cast window (bottom)

Control Panel (top right)

To use a Director movie in your HTML documents, you need to first run it through After-burner, a post-processor application that compresses and converts your Director movies for faster playback. The Afterburner application doesn't alter the way a Director movie appears or behaves, but merely preps it by compressing it and changing its file format. Afterburner is available for download from the Macromedia Web site at **Shockwave http://www. macromedia.com**. After you have downloaded and installed it, Afterburner is run by selecting it from the Director Xtras menu. Compressed (or *shocked*) Director movies have the file name extension .DXR, rather than .DIR.

Before serving up Shocked Director movies, your server computer must be configured to recognize and handle them by associating the file name extensions .DIR, .DXR, and .DCR with the MIME type application/x-director.

The final step in the process is, of course, to EMBED your Director movie files on your pages. You use the ubiquitous EMBED tag and the required SRC, WIDTH, and HEIGHT parameters. You can also elect to use the PALETTE attribute. If PALETTE=FOREGROUND is selected, the Director movie's palette is loaded and used as the palette for the entire page. The default is PALETTE=BACKGROUND.

Lingo Network Extensions

Macromedia Director ties together all of its elements with the Lingo scripting language. This is a rich language with a great many complex commands, and it's documented in the Director box with two thick manuals, plus comprehensive online Help.

Part
IV

Ch
20

There are many new extensions to the Lingo language that are specifically designed to work in the context of delivering multimedia content in HTML documents. For example, new Lingo commands can enable your Director movie to continue to display an animation while it's streaming the next segment of the movie from a network. Most of the new network Lingo commands enable you to set some sort of process in motion, check back later to see if it's finished, and then act after the process is complete. This is different from most non-network Lingo commands that execute a process and then immediately give you a result.

Even if you're an old Lingo wrangler, make sure you familiarize yourself with these new Lingo commands before you attempt to create content for plug-in delivery.

Director Limitations on HTML Pages

There are some special limitations for Shocked Director movies that do not apply to standard Director movies. Most of these limitations are due to the fact that the Director movie must be able to interact over a network (either an intranet or the Web).

For example, Shocked Director movies can't use movie-in-a-window, nor can they use any of the Wait For options in the tempo channel. The Director documentation covers all of these network limitations in detail.

Page Design Considerations

The majority of Web users use relatively slow 14.4Kbps or 28.8Kbps dialup connections. At these rates, the user can receive in the neighborhood of about 1K of information a second, so it takes about one minute to transfer a 60K file. Remember this when creating Director files for Web pages. Don't torture your viewers with overly long download times.

Here are some other things to consider when designing HTML pages with Shocked content:

- Although, technically, there's no limit to how many movies you can incorporate into a page, don't include more than three. Remember that when a user leaves a page containing shocked Director movies, the Shockwave plug-in frees the RAM it was using to play them.

- You might encounter technical problems when your browser tries to sort out the sound tracks of two movies playing simultaneously. Use automatically played sound in only one movie per page, and program the others so that the user can play the sound tracks by clicking the mouse.

- Movies programmed to loop indefinitely tie up the processor. It is strongly recommended that you program a movie to stop playing after a given number of loops, or program some way for the user to stop the movie.

Optimizing Director Movies

Here are some tips and techniques that will help you to create effective and efficient Director movies for your site:

- Keep each cast member as small as possible to keep file size down.
- Use small graphics and resize them up to the size you need. Use the Sprite Info dialog box to reset a cast member back to its normal size or any specific size.
- Use Lingo to add interactivity to your application. If possible, use Lingo loops and branches to sections of your movie.
- Use the Transform Bitmap dialog box to dither a graphic down to a lower bit depth.
- To add spectral variety without adding size, set the background or foreground color of a black-and-white bitmap to another color with the Tools window.
- Use scalable text in text fields instead of bitmapped text.
- Use objects from the Tools window whenever possible in place of bitmapped graphics.
- Use ink effects on graphics you already have before creating a new bitmap. Layering graphics with different ink effects can produce some interesting results.
- Use film loops to reuse cast members.
- Tile small bitmaps to produce backgrounds. Create tiles that have heights and widths of 16, 32, 64, or 128 pixels to maintain perfect tiling.
- Use small looping music clips instead of long soundtracks.
- Down sample all sound to 11.025kHz.
- Try capturing and sequencing a few single frames from a video clip in lieu of playing a whole video.
- Render anti-aliased bitmaps to solid system colors, especially black or white.

More Information

The Online ShockWave Developer's Guide at **http://www.macromedia.com/shockwave/director5/contents.html** contains a great deal of detailed information about building sites that use Shocked content.

You might also want to check out the Director 5 Shockwave Movie Lab at **http://www.macromedia.com/shockwave/director5/movielab.html**. This page includes many samples of Shocked Director movies with source code for both Mac and Windows. ●

Part
IV

Ch
20

## CHAPTER 21

VRML

by Jim O'Donnell

For information distribution on the Internet, the next big step beyond HTML might be the Virtual Reality Modeling Language (VRML). HTML's hypertext links, and the Web browsers that make use of them, create a two-dimensional interface to Internet information. VRML expands this by allowing the creation of three-dimensional worlds on the Web, offering a much more intricate way of presenting information. The advent of VRML 2.0 has expanded the use of VRML from static worlds to ones with interactivity, motion, and sound.

The process of creating a VRML world involves several steps, from the creation of VRML objects to their placement and assembly into a complete VRML world. Then, using VRML 2.0 or Java, it is possible to bring that world alive. This chapter discusses the basics of going from the lowest level step in this process, the creation of VRML objects, through assembling them into worlds and bringing them to life. You also find out where on the Web to look for resources, information, software, and other tips that will help you become a proficient VRML world builder. ■

Find out about VRML

The Virtual Reality Modeling Language allows you to add 3-D elements to Web pages, the additional capabilities possible with Netscape's Live3D, and the new VRML 2.0 standard.

Learn basic VRML syntax and create simple VRML objects

VRML worlds are created from ASCII files. Learn the rudiments of the VRML language and create simple VRML objects by hand, using nothing more than a text editor, a VRML browser, and a little imagination.

Learn VRML design issues

Consider some issues that affect the designing of a VRML world, including laying out a world and moving simple VRML objects around to combine into more complex objects and scenes.

Link VRML worlds to the Web

Use basic VRML nodes to include other objects, local or elsewhere on the Web, into your VRML world. Create hypertext links inside VRML objects to link to the rest of the Web.

Learn about available VRML resources

Find information, software, and pre-made VRML objects to help you in producing your own VRML worlds.

The Virtual Reality Modeling Language

The Virtual Reality Modeling Language (VRML) is a language intended for the design and use of three-dimensional, multi-person, distributed interactive simulations. To put it in simpler language, VRML's designers intend it to become the building block of cyberspace.

The World Wide Web is based on HTML (Hypertext Markup Language), which was developed from the SGML (Standard General Markup Language) standard. SGML and HTML are fundamentally designed as two-dimensional text formatting toolsets. Mark D. Pesce, Peter Kennard, and Anthony S. Parisi presented a paper called *Cyberspace* at the First International Conference on the Web in May 1994, in which they argued that, because humans are superb visualizers and live and work in three dimensions, extending the Web with a third dimension would allow for better organization of the masses of data already on the Web. They called this idea the Virtual Reality Markup Language. The concept was welcomed and the participants immediately began searching for a format to use as a data standard. Subsequently, the M in VRML was changed from *Markup* to *Modeling* to accentuate the difference between the text-based nature of the Web and VRML.

N O T E   The paper *Cyberspace* is available over the Web at **http://www.hyperreal.com/~mpesce/ www.html**. ▓

Silicon Graphics' Open Inventor was settled on as the basis for creating the VRML standard. Open Inventor is an object-oriented (C++) developer's toolkit used for rapid development of three-dimensional graphic environments. Open Inventor has provided the basis for a number of standards, including the Keystone Interchange Format used in the entertainment industry and the ANSI/ISO's X3H3 3D Metafile specification.

VRML's design specifications were guided by the following three goals:

- Platform independence
- Extendibility
- The capability to work over low-bandwidth connections

VRML Objects

The building blocks of VRML creations, usually called VRML worlds, are objects created in VRML. The VRML language specification contains a collection of commands, called nodes, for the creation of a variety of simple objects such as spheres, cubes, and cylinders, as well as objects consisting of an arbitrary collection of vertices and faces.

N O T E   For a three-dimensional object, *faces* are the flat surfaces that make up the object, and *vertices* are the points where the faces meet. A cube, for instance, is made up of six square faces, each defined by four vertices. There are eight vertices needed to define a cube, since each vertex is shared by three faces. ▓

VRML allows for the creation of more complex objects through the combination of simple objects. It is a hierarchical language, with *child* objects inheriting the properties of their *parents*. For instance, if a complex object was being defined to create a model of a human body, then by default, any properties defined for the body as a whole (such as color) would also apply to the simple objects that make up the body, such as the head, arms, legs, and so on. The rest of this chapter focuses on the creation of VRML objects.

VRML Worlds

The assemblage of VRML objects into a (hopefully) coherent whole defines a VRML world. There are many example VRML worlds on the Web that use the three-dimensional paradigm for different purposes. To define the placement and relationship of different objects to one another, you need to be able to specify their relative sizes and positions, using VRML's different coordinate systems. Additionally, VRML allows you to define what lighting sources are present in your world and what preset views are included.

Adding Motion and More to VRML

VRML 1.0 worlds are static. The only motion within them is the movement of the viewpoint representing the user as he or she uses a VRML browser to traverse through the VRML world. With the definition of VRML 2.0, VRML's capabilities were extended to allow the creation of dynamic worlds.

VRML 2.0 objects can now be given movement of their own, and three-dimensional sound (audio that sounds different depending on the position of the listener with respect to the source) can be added. Another new capability introduced with VRML 2.0 is the ability to add behaviors to VRML objects. *Behaviors*—which can be scripted or specified in Java applets, for instance—are characteristics of objects that depend on their relationship to other objects on the VRML world, to the viewer, or to other parameters, such as time. For instance, a VRML 2.0 fish in an aquarium might swim away if you get too close to it.

While the VRML 2.0 standard has been finalized, support for it is still hard to come by. Very few VRML browsers and Web browser plug-ins fully support the VRML 2.0 standard. If you want to create VRML worlds with movement and animation, a better choice at the moment is using Netscape's Live3D. Because it is a standard part of Netscape Navigator and also works within Microsoft Internet Explorer, the potential audience for a Live3D-format VRML world is much greater.

Why (and How) Should You Use VRML?

As a Web author interested in VRML, you need to ask yourself what you would like to achieve with it. Unfortunately, there are two important characteristics of VRML that restrict its usefulness at the current time. The first is that VRML worlds tend to be *big*. Specifying three-dimensional objects as a collection of flat surfaces can lead to very large object descriptions, particularly when trying to model a curved surface. The other important characteristic is that the connection speed of the majority of people on the Internet is still limited to no higher than that achieved with a 28.8Kbps modem.

Full-blown VRML worlds can take a long time to be transmitted over the Internet, which very often limits the audience to only those people looking for cool VRML worlds to look at. These worlds can also be extremely complicated to define and set up, requiring a lot more discussion than the space we have here. (Something more along the lines of Que's *Special Edition Using VRML* is needed to adequately cover the subject.)

However, a very good use for VRML (one that doesn't have the problems of requiring huge files to be downloaded) is to add special effects to HTML Web pages. Because Live3D is being distributed with the most popular Web browser on the market (and also works within the second most popular browser), and because you can embed small VRML scenes into HTML Web pages, VRML is an ideal addition to the Web author's bag of tricks.

Because of this, the primary focus of this chapter is to familiarize you with enough VRML that you can create small VRML scenes to achieve specific special effects within your Web pages. In the course of doing so, you will also learn enough of the VRML language and syntax to give you a good grasp on the language fundamentals so that you can move on to the creation of larger VRML worlds, if you want.

Basic VRML Syntax

VRML files are plain ASCII (though they are often gzipped—compressed by using the GNU zip, or gzip, utility—to make them easier to transmit over the Internet), which means that you can create them using ordinary text editors. It is likely that you will decide to use a VRML authoring program if you want to create a very large, complex VRML world—and even smaller worlds, if you have an authoring program available—in which case the details of VRML syntax are hidden from you. It is a good idea to get a basic grasp of the important VRML language elements, though. Later, this knowledge will help you get the results you want.

Listing 21.1 shows a simple VRML file that displays a red cone on a white background (see Figure 21.1).

Listing 21.1   rcone.wrl—Display a Red Cone on a White Background

```
#VRML V1.0 ascii

Separator {
   Info {
      string "Special Edition, Using HTML, 3rd Edition"
   }
   DEF BackgroundColor Info {
      string "1 1 1"
   }
   Separator {
      Material {
         diffuseColor 1 0 0 # the color red
      }
      Cone { }
   }
}
```

FIG. 21.1
Specifying simple objects can be done with just a few lines of VRML code.

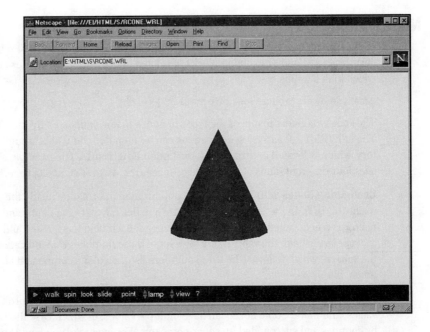

The VRML comment character is the #; everything after a # on any line is a comment (such as the color red). The first line of the file begins with a #, so it is a comment. Unlike other comments in the file, this one is necessary. It identifies the file as being VRML and gives the version number of VRML used. VRML browsers require this information to be located at the start of any VRML file.

The first line of the file shown in Listing 21.1 reads #VRML V1.0 ascii, meaning the file conforms to version 1.0 of the VRML specification. The word ascii means the standard ASCII character set is used in the file. VRML 2.0 files generally have the comment #VRML V2.0 utf8 in their first line, indicating conformance to the VRML 2.0 specification and that an international character set based on ASCII is being used.

Other than ignoring comments, the file format is entirely free form. Anywhere there is white space—tabs, spaces, or carriage returns—you can have as much or as little space as you'd like. For instance, an equivalent listing to the one shown in Listing 21.1 is:

```
#VRML V1.0 ascii
Separator{Info{string "Special Edition, Using HTML, 3rd Edition"}
DEF BackgroundColor Info{string "1 1 1"}Separator{Material{diffuseColor 1 0 0}
Cone{}}}
```

 TIP As with any programming language, you should structure and comment your VRML files well enough that they can be easily read and understood.

Part
IV

Ch
21

Nodes and Fields

If you are familiar with the C, C++, or Java programming languages, you might recognize the curly braces ({ and }) to define blocks of related information. VRML files are made up of *nodes*, which look like this:

```
NodeType { configuration information }
```

The NodeType refers to one of the types of nodes that is supported by the VRML specification. The full VRML 1.0 and 2.0 specifications can be found on the Web, through the VRML Repository, which is located at **http://rosebud.sdsc.edu/vrml/**. The example shown in Listing 21.1 uses four different kinds of nodes: Info, Separator, Material, and Sphere.

Configuring Nodes with Fields   The configuration information inside the braces consists mainly of *fields*. In the example, the two Info nodes have string fields, and the Material node has a field called diffuseColor. In general, each field has a name and a value. For the diffuseColor field, the value is 1 0 0, a set of three numbers that indicate the color to use for the Sphere, which follows (the three numbers list the color's components in the order red, green, blue).

Field values can be simple numbers, groups of numbers, strings, keywords, images, Boolean values, and more. Some fields can have multiple values, in which case the values are separated by commas and surrounded by square brackets. For example, you could specify three colors for the diffuseColor field of the Material node as:

```
Material { diffuseColor [1 0 0,0.5 0.5 0,0 1 0] }
```

In this case, three colors would be defined that could be assigned to different faces of objects.

Naming Nodes   Any node can be assigned a name by which it can be referred to later. This is done with the DEF prefix, as shown in Listing 21.1:

```
DEF BackgroundColor Info { string "1 0 0" }
```

In this case, BackgroundColor is a special, predefined node name used to specify a background color. In general, though, you can assign any name to any node.

CAUTION

Specifying a background color, as shown in the preceding, is not a standard part of VRML 1.0—it is an extension to the specification supported by some VRML browsers. If you are using a VRML browser that does not support this extension, the node is ignored and the background remains the default color used by the browser (usually black). This background color node is used in the examples shown in this book because there is no official way in VRML 1.0 to set a background color, and it is necessary to do so to enable the examples shown to be clearly reproduced in printed form.

Objects, Hierarchies, Separators

A VRML world can be thought of as a hierarchy of simple VRML objects. In VRML, the `Separator` node is used as the container for an object. Not all `Separator` nodes contain any geometry (vertices and faces of VRML objects); some are used for grouping other objects together into a more complex object. This is how object hierarchies are specified in VRML. The attachment information is specified by placing objects within other objects, using the `Separator` node. In other words, the `Separator` node can contain *children* nodes to describe objects that are attached to it.

Simple VRML Objects

The VRML 1.0 specification includes eight nodes that let you specify geometric shapes. All VRML 1.0 objects are made up of one or more of these nodes. These nodes consist of four geometric shapes, one for ASCII text, and three for the creation of general sets of two- and three-dimensional objects.

Geometric Shapes

You already saw an example of the `Cone` node, in Listing 21.1. Along with the `Cone` node, VRML allows you to directly create spheres, cubes, and cylinders. The syntax for each of these nodes is shown in the following:

■ **Cone**: The syntax for this node is:

```
Cone {
        bottomRadius      radius
        height            height
        parts             [ALL¦SIDES¦BOTTOM]
}
```

■ **Cube**: The syntax for this node is:

```
Cube {
        depth             depth
        height            height
        width             width
}
```

■ **Cylinder**: The syntax for this node is:

```
Cylinder {
        radius            radius
        height            height
        parts             [ALL¦BOTTOM¦SIDES¦TOP]
}
```

■ **Sphere**: The syntax for this node is:

```
Sphere {
        radius            radius
}
```

Each of these nodes has default values for each of its fields. So, if you specify a sphere by simply using Sphere{}, you will get a sphere with a radius of one.

N O T E   While the Sphere, Cone, and Cylinder nodes seem to specify curved surfaces in VRML, when the VRML file is parsed by a VRML browser, the objects are converted into vertices and faces through a process called *tessellation*. To see this for yourself, load a VRML example showing one of these curved surfaces into a VRML browser and switch the browser into flat-shading mode (in Live3D, you do this by right-clicking in the VRML scene, and selecting Lights, Flat Shading) to see the individual faces. ■

ASCII Text

The AsciiText node allows you to create flat-text objects in VRML. Because the resulting text is flat, it is possible that it might not be visible when viewed, if looked at edge on. The AsciiText node has four fields: string, spacing, justification, and width, and its syntax is as follows:

```
AsciiText {
    justification        [CENTER¦LEFT¦RIGHT]
    spacing              vertical spacing
    string               ["ASCII string(s)",...]
    width                [horizonatal spacing of each string,...]
}
```

Listing 21.2 shows an example of the use of the AsciiText field, with the results shown in Figure 21.2.

Listing 21.2   ascii2d.wrl—Two-Dimensional ASCII Text in VRML

```
#VRML V1.0 ascii

Separator {
   Info {
      string "Special Edition, Using HTML, 3rd Edition"
   }
   DEF BackgroundColor Info {
      string "1 1 1"
   }
   AsciiText {
      string ["This Is","A Test","Of AsciiText"]
      spacing 2
      justification CENTER
      width [0,0,0]
   }
}
```

FIG. 21.2
VRML ASCII is two-dimensional; if you rotate it so that you view it edge on, it is not visible.

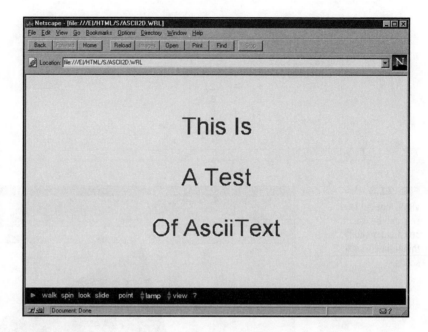

General VRML Shapes

The nodes discussed so far are useful to start, especially if you're building simple worlds by hand. Most VRML files, however, make extensive use of another node, `IndexedFaceSet`. An `IndexedFaceSet` node is a way of describing an object using a set of vertices that are joined together by faces. Listing 21.3 shows an example of this, which creates a pyramid using five vertices and five faces to create the four sides and the base (see Figure 21.3).

Listing 21.3 pyrface.wrl—Building General Shapes Using IndexedFaceSet

```
#VRML V1.0 ascii

DEF Pyramid Separator {
    Info {
        string "Special Edition, Using HTML, 3rd Edition"
    }
    DEF BackgroundColor Info {
        string "1 1 1"
    }
    Coordinate3 {
        point [-1  0 -1,
                1  0 -1,
                1  0  1,
               -1  0  1,
                0  2  0]
```

Part
IV

Ch

21

continues

Listing 21.3 Continued

```
    }
    IndexedFaceSet {
       coordIndex [0,   4,   1,  -1,
                   1,   4,   2,  -1,
                   2,   4,   3,  -1,
                   3,   4,   0,  -1,
                   0,   1,   2,   3,  -1]
    }
}
```

FIG. 21.3

VRML indexed face sets can be used to construct arbitrary three-dimensional solids.

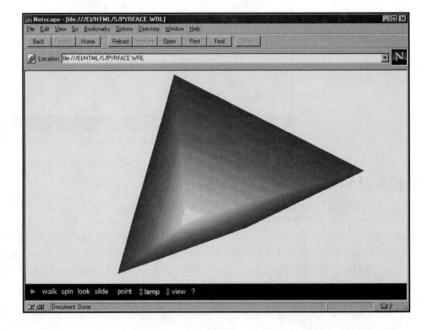

The array of vertex coordinates is specified by using the Coordinate3 node and its own field, point. The point field takes multiple values, each of which is a triplet of numbers giving the X, Y, and Z coordinates of one vertex. There can be as many vertices as you need. Keep in mind, though, that each vertex only needs to be specified once, no matter how many faces it is used in, because vertices define single points that may be shared by multiple faces.

The actual IndexedFaceSet node contains a field called coordIndex that stores a list of faces, as specified by the indices of vertices in the order they are used for each face. For instance, the sequence 0, 4, 1, -1 is used to create one face from the 0th, 4th, and 1st vertices (vertices are numbered from 0). The -1 signifies the end of the current face; the next face begins with the next number.

N O T E Although IndexedFaceSet is a very powerful tool, there are some things to watch out for when you are using it.

Make sure all the vertices in a given face are *coplanar*, meaning that the face is flat (this is true if either the X, Y, or Z component of each vertex in the face is equal). If one or more of the vertices are not in the same plane, then the object will look very strange when viewed from certain angles.

Avoid T-intersections. Two faces should always meet at a shared edge. If you have a face that touches another face without sharing common vertices, the round-off errors in the VRML browser will cause viewing problems.

Avoid using too many faces, when possible, because that will slow down rendering more than any other factor. ■

VRML includes two other nodes that work much the same as IndexedFaceSet, called IndexedLineSet and PointSet. Each is used similarly to IndexedFaceSet, except that IndexedLineSet is used to construct a general set of lines between a set of vertices, and PointSet creates a field of dots at the vertices.

Adding Color and Texture to VRML Objects

VRML offers several different ways of changing the appearance of its objects. One of these, the Material node, is shown previously in Listing 21.1, and is used to create a red cone. Two nodes in particular can be used to affect the color, texture, and general appearance of VRML objects: the Material and Texture2 nodes.

Material

The most common use of the Material node is that shown in Listing 21.1—using its diffuseColor field to specify the color of an object. The Material node supports other fields for achieving different effects, many of which are not supported by most VRML browsers. In general, you usually want to stick to using the diffuseColor field.

Texture2

With the Texture2 node, it is possible to achieve a much wider variety of effects. The Texture2 node maps an image file to a VRML object. Listing 21.4 shows an example with my picture mapped onto a VRML cube (see Figure 21.4).

Listing 21.4   cubejod.wrl—Map Images to VRML Objects Using *Texture2*

```
#VRML V1.0 ascii

Separator {
  Info {
      string "Special Edition, Using HTML, 3rd Edition"
```

Part
IV

Ch

21

continues

Listing 21.4 Continued

```
    }
    DEF BackgroundColor Info {
        string "1 1 1"
    }
    Texture2 {
        filename "jod.jpg"
    }
    Cube { }
}
```

FIG. 21.4

Images can be mapped to the faces of VRML objects.

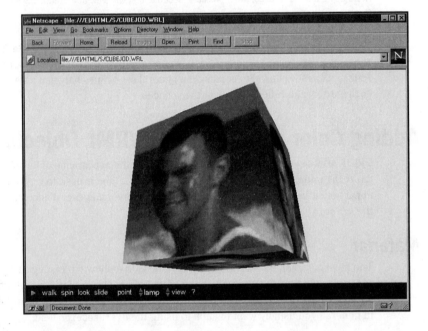

Because the faces are all flat in the preceding example, the image used isn't noticeably distorted. That isn't the case when images are mapped to curved surfaces, such as those created by Sphere, Cone, or Cylinder nodes. In these nodes, images are distorted as they are mapped to the curved surfaces. Note that different graphics formats can be used as textures; which formats are supported is VRML browser-specific.

Creating VRML Worlds and Inline VRML Scenes

In the context of this discussion, a VRML world refers to a VRML file that is designed to be stand-alone, and will be loaded into a VRML-compatible Web browser on its own, without being embedded in an HTML-based Web page. Though there is no lower or upper limit on the size and complexity of a VRML world, these worlds tend to be fairly large. The three-dimensional VRML paradigm is often used to allow the user to "move through" the VRML world, visiting the parts of interest to him.

One example of good use of VRML worlds is demonstrated through sites that model an actual three-dimensional object, building, or geographic location, allowing remote users from all over the world to actually "see" what that object looks like, perhaps even to travel through it. The University of Essex in Britain maintains such a site at **http://esewww.essex.ac.uk/campus-model.wrl**. This VRML world consists of a three-dimensional model of its campus. Users can move around the campus and see it from any conceivable angle. In addition, each building on the campus contains a hypertext link to an HTML Web page with information about that building.

Inline VRML scenes are best used to achieve a given special effect within an HTML Web page. By creating a very small, very specialized VRML scene and displaying it inline, you can achieve a variety of special effects. This is particularly true if you add some of the animation and movement extensions possible with Live3D, as discussed later in this chapter. An inline VRML scene can be used to achieve a similar effect to an animated GIF; depending on the desired effect, this can be done with a VRML file smaller than the GIF.

Design Considerations

After you come up with an idea for your VRML environment, you need to consider a number of other factors that influence the final design. As well as deciding what objects you want to put in the VRML environment and where they are with respect to each other, there are other factors that might limit what you can achieve. How big of a VRML environment should you create? How detailed should it be? How should it be shaped? How should everything be laid out? How should you create it?

Size and Detail

The first thing you should consider before drafting your environment is size—not in terms of the space it takes up in the virtual world, but the final size of your .WRL file. In a perfect world, everyone has a high-powered graphics workstation and a T1 line connecting them to the Internet, and you don't have to worry about how big your VRML file is, how long it takes to transmit over the Internet, or how long it takes to render after it arrives at the client machine.

In reality, however, things are quite different. Most people are running 486 and Pentium PCs over 14.4 and 28.8Kbps modems. If you come up with a VRML world that is 10M, you severely limit your audience because of the hour and a half download time and the time it takes for the client computer to render it. No matter why you are interested in providing VRML environments on the Web, no one will look at it if it takes that long.

Therefore, you need to consider how big you are going to make your VRML environment, and how detailed it should be. It is a question of compromise. You can have a very large environment, but then you cannot add a great amount of small details. Or, if you only have a few objects in your environment, they can probably be displayed with a great deal of detail. It becomes a trade-off between size and detail.

That is why it is important to start the process with a purpose for your VRML environment. If you are trying to sell something and you want your customers to understand what they are

Part
IV

Ch
21

getting, you should probably opt for multiple VRML environments, each of which displays a few objects—or even just one—in great detail. However, if you want to give your users a sense of what it's like to stand next to the Pyramids in Egypt, texturing each pyramid brick by brick isn't necessary. If you want to let your users tour a model of your entire electronics workshop, you might not need to include every oscilloscope and soldering iron. But, if you want them to see the tools used, you can limit your environment to a single workbench.

Design and Layout

After you have decided how big your environment will be and what to include in it, the next step becomes deciding how it will look. A VRML environment is like any other space, virtual or not. If it looks cluttered and unkempt, people won't want to look at it. You need to decide how you want things to be laid out, and how you want people to navigate through your environment. Is it a scene that they will be looking at from a distance? Or do you want them to jump in and poke around?

Again, the important factor in answering these questions is your environment's purpose. For example, if you are creating a VRML world that requires users to follow a particular sequence, then you need to find ways to direct their travels through your world. On the other hand, if you want people to be able to freely explore through your VRML world, you might want to have a more open environment. Even if you are re-creating a space that exists in the "real world," you need to consider what is necessary and not necessary.

VRML World Design Steps

We will now go through the steps required to design a very simple VRML world. First, we go through the process of initial layout, building VRML objects together into compound objects, and placing them in our world. Then, we find out about some of the ways to add realism to our VRML world, through the use of textures, lighting, and the addition of multiple camera viewpoints. Finally, we find out how to link our VRML world to other VRML worlds, HTML pages, or anything with an URL.

While the process of building this VRML world might be easier with a VRML authoring or three-dimensional modeling software package, this chapter instead shows how it is done by hand. By performing the steps of VRML world-building manually, you get a much better grasp of the fundamentals of the VRML language; and if you subsequently want to use a VRML authoring tool, this foundation makes it much easier.

Mapping Your VRML Environment

Rather than charging off and starting to throw together VRML objects that you might need in your world, the first step in the design process should be to sketch out what you want your world to look like. An important tool at this point of the design process is a simple sheet of graph paper. By using graph paper, including both a top view and a side view of what you would like to put in your world, you get a very good first idea of the following important points:

- What simple VRML objects do you need?
- What compound objects do you need, and how should they be created from the simple ones?
- How much space do you need in your environment?
- Where should the VRML objects be placed in that environment?
- Where can you add lighting and camera views for the best effects?

VRML Coordinate Systems   While it is important to have a visual way of thinking to design your VRML environment, the way that it is stored is as a set of coordinates and mathematical transformations. You need to convert your visual design into these coordinates and transformations—this is one of the reasons that sketching out your world on graph paper is a good idea. To fully understand how to accomplish this, you need to know a bit about the coordinate systems that VRML uses, as well as the vectors and matrices it employs.

Cartesian coordinates, those used in VRML, are named after the geometry developed by René Descartes. They are basically the standard way of describing the two- or three-dimensional geometry of something. By default, when you begin looking at a VRML scene, the positive direction of the x-axis goes from left to right, the positive direction of the y-axis goes from down to up, and the positive direction of the z-axis goes from the back of the environment towards the front. This is called a right-handed coordinate system, because if you curl the fingers of your right hand from the x- towards the y-axis, your thumb will point along the z-axis.

The right-handedness of the coordinate system also comes into play when you discuss rotations. The direction of a positive rotation about an axis is determined by the *right-hand rule*. For instance, to determine the direction of a positive rotation about the z-axis, point your right thumb along the z-axis in its positive direction. The way your fingers curl defines a positive rotation. Figure 21.5 shows the Cartesian coordinate system used within VRML.

FIG. 21.5
VRML uses the Cartesian coordinate system shown to create objects and define where objects are placed with respect to one another.

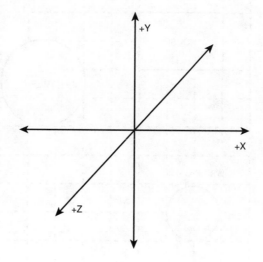

Vectors   A point in the Cartesian coordinate system is called a *vertex*. A vertex is simply a location in space represented by three numbers, *x*, *y*, and *z*. A *vector* is related to a vertex, in that it is also represented by x, y, and z coordinates. Whereas a vertex represents a point in space, a vector represents a direction. So, the vertex (1,0,1) represents the point x=1, y=0, and z=1. The vector (1,0,1) represents the direction you would be traveling in going from the origin, the point (0,0,0), to the vertex (1,0,1).

VRML Units   When specifying coordinates and rotation angles in VRML, you need to remember the default measure of distance is a *meter*, and the default measure of rotation angle is a *radian*.

> **N O T E**   A *radian* is a unit used to measure angles and rotations. There are 2π radians in 360, so you can determine the number of radians from a given number of degrees by multiplying by $\pi/180$, about 57.3. ■

Putting Your Design on Paper

The first step in the design of a VRML world is to sketch out what you want it to look like. By putting this down on graph paper, you are already a long way towards defining the coordinates, size, and position of the things in the world.

Figures 21.6 and 21.7 show a top and side view of the VRML world we will try to put together throughout the rest of this chapter. Figure 20.6 shows a "front" view of the world, with the z-axis pointing straight out of the paper. The two drawings define what the world should look like pretty well; you might find it helpful to include another side view, however, looking down the x-axis, for example.

FIG. 21.6

Top view of our planned VRML world.

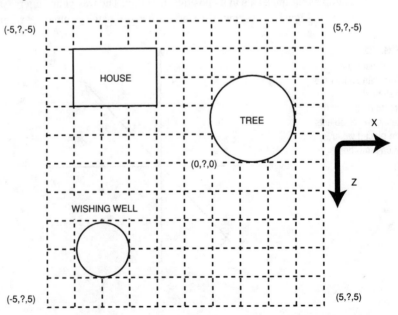

FIG. 21.7
Side view of our
planned VRML world.

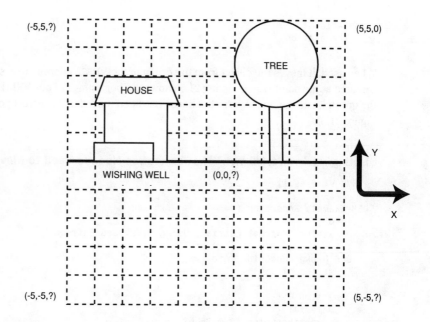

Now that we have our VRML world sketched out, let's go back and see if these sketches answer the questions we asked before about the design:

- What simple VRML objects do you need?

  It looks like we need a flat plane for the ground, a cube and a solid made from an indexed face set for the house, an oblate sphere and a cylinder for the tree, a cylinder or two for the wishing well, and another indexed face set (this one two-dimensional) for the walkway.

- What compound objects do you need, and how should they be created from the simple ones?

  The compound objects that need to be formed are the addition of the house and its roof, the treetop and its trunk, and the parts of the wishing well.

- How much space do you need in your environment?

  The virtual environment needs to be a 10-meter cube.

- Where should the VRML objects be placed in that environment?

  The coordinates shown on the graph paper sketches define exactly where each object needs to go in three-dimensional space (three-space).

Moving Things Around

Creating the objects needed for our example shouldn't be very difficult. However, we now need to be able to move them around within the VRML environment. Without the capability to do this, all created objects will be lumped together at the origin of the VRML coordinate system. This is done using VRML's Translation node, whose syntax is:

```
Translation {
     translation          x y z
}
```

When used, it moves the object from the origin of the VRML coordinate system so that it is centered at the point (*x,y,z*). Listing 21.5 shows the beginnings of our VRML world, showing the ground, and the house, after the house has been moved to its correct position (see Figure 21.8).

Listing 21.5   world1.wrl—The Translation Node Is Used to Move Objects

```
#VRML V1.0 ascii

DEF Example Separator {
    Info {
        string "Special Edition, Using HTML, 3rd Edition"
    }
    DEF BackgroundColor Info {
        string "1 1 1"
    }
    Separator {
      Material {
          diffuseColor [0 0.75 0]
      }
      Coordinate3 {
          point [-5 0 -5,
                  5 0 -5,
                  5 0  5,
                 -5 0  5]
      }
      IndexedFaceSet {
          coordIndex [0,1,2,3,-1]
      }
    }
    Separator {
      Material {
          diffuseColor [0 0 0]
      }
      Translation {
          translation -2.5 1 -3
      }
      Cube {
         width  2.3333
         depth  1.3333
         height 2
      }
    }
  }
}
```

FIG. 21.8
The Translation node allows simple and compound VRML objects to be moved around the VRML environment.

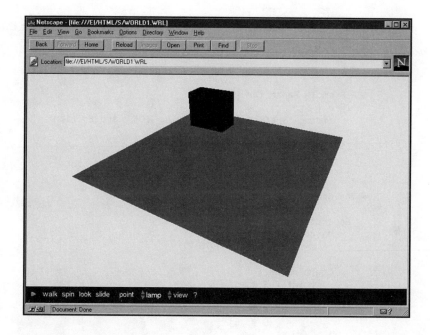

Creating Object Hierarchies

Unless your VRML world is very simple—even simpler than our example—you might find yourself very often building up more complex VRML objects from simpler ones. While it is possible to treat each of the objects separately—and move and scale each individually—it's a lot easier to create the compound object from the individual ones and then manipulate that object with one operation. The VRML Separator node is used to create compound objects by enclosing other nodes. An object hierarchy is created by defining simpler objects, specifying their positions with respect to one another, and then enclosing this information within a Separator node. Then, the entire hierarchy can be manipulated at once.

Listing 21.6 shows the next addition to our VRML world, the addition of the roof to our house. Note that the roof is created with an IndexedFaceSet and positioned on top of the bottom part of the house within a Separator node. Then, the compound object representing the complete house is moved into the correct position within the VRML environment (see Figure 21.9).

N O T E In this listing, differences between it and the previous one are shown in italics. For further listings, as we build up this example, we will only show the new elements. ■

Part
IV

Ch
21

Listing 21.6 world2.wrl—Creating Compound Objects with the *Separator* Node

```
#VRML V1.0 ascii

DEF Example Separator {
    Info {
        string "Special Edition, Using HTML, 3rd Edition"
    }
    DEF BackgroundColor Info {
        string "1 1 1"
    }
#
# The Ground
#
    Separator {
        Material {
            diffuseColor [0 0.75 0]
        }
        Coordinate3 {
            point [-5 0 -5,
                    5 0 -5,
                    5 0  5,
                   -5 0  5]
        }
        IndexedFaceSet {
            coordIndex [0,1,2,3,-1]
        }
    }
#
# The House
#
    Separator {
        Material {
            diffuseColor [0 0 0]
        }
        Translation {
            translation -2.5 1 -3
        }
        DEF House Separator {
            Cube {
                width   2.3333
                depth   1.3333
                height  2
            }
            Material {
                diffuseColor [0 0 1]
            }
            Translation {
                translation 0 1 0
            }
            Coordinate3 {                          # Vertex Indices:
                point [-1.5 0 -1,-1.1667 1 -0.6667, #   0----2
                        1.5 0 -1, 1.1667 1 -0.6667, #   ¦1--3¦
                        1.5 0  1, 1.1667 1  0.6667, #   ¦7--5¦
                       -1.5 0  1,-1.1667 1  0.6667] #   6----4
```

```
        }
    IndexedFaceSet {
        coordIndex [0,2,4,6,-1,
                    1,3,5,7,-1,
                    0,2,3,1,-1,
                    2,4,5,3,-1,
                    4,6,7,5,-1,
                    6,0,1,7,-1]
        }
    }
  }
}
```

FIG. 21.9
Creating compound objects in VRML makes it much easier to create and manipulate complex scenes.

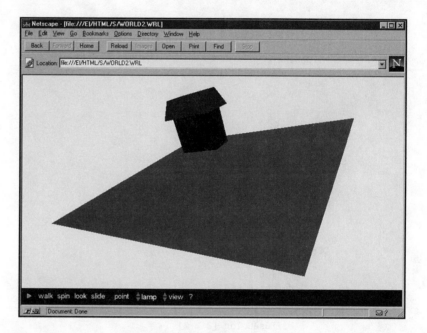

With the ability to create compound objects, we can add the rest of the elements to our VRML world—a tree made up of a sphere and a cylinder, and the wishing well made up of two cylinders. Listing 21.7 shows the new VRML code to produce these objects, and the resulting scene is shown in Figure 21.10.

Listing 21.7 world3.wrl (excerpt)—Completing the VRML World

```
#
# The Tree
#
    Separator {
        Translation {
            translation 2.5 1.5 -1.5
```

Part
IV

Ch
21

continues

Listing 21.7   Continued

```
        }
      DEF Tree Separator {
         Material {
            diffuseColor [0.5 0.25 0]
         }
         Cylinder {
            radius 0.1667
            height 3
         }
         Material {
            diffuseColor [0 1 0]
         }
         Translation {
            translation 0 1.5 0
         }
         Sphere {
            radius 1.5
         }
      }
   }
#
# The Wishing Well
#
   Separator {
      Material {
         diffuseColor [1 1 1]
      }
      Translation {
         translation -3 0.3333 3
      }
      DEF WishingWell Separator {
         Cylinder {
            radius 1
            height 0.6667
         }
         Material {
            diffuseColor [0 0 0]
         }
         Cylinder {
            radius 0.8
            height 0.6667
         }
      }
   }
```

FIG. 21.10
All of our objects have
been placed in the
VRML world.

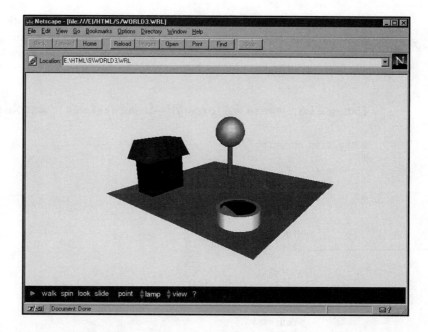

Adding Realism with Textures

Earlier you learned a little about how to use the Texture2 node to add realism to an object
through the addition of image file textures. By default, VRML maps the image file specified by
Texture2 to each entire face of the solid in question—the six faces of a cube or the top, bottom,
and curved surface of a cylinder, for instance. When mapping a texture to a surface to make it
more realistic, it is best to tile small images repeatedly over the different faces. This can be
done by using the Texture2Transform node. Its syntax is:

```
Texture2Transform {
    translation    x y
    rotation       angle
    scaleFactor    x y
    center         x y
}
```

These fields allow you to move, rotate, scale, and center the image on the solid to determine
how it is applied. To make a tiled texture more realistic looking, the most important field is
the scaleFactor field, which determines how many times the image will be tiled. Note that
scaleFactor refers to how the coordinates of the object to which the texture is being mapped
will be scaled, so scale factors greater than one result in the image appearing smaller on the
object and tiled more times.

Listing 21.8 shows an example of the texturing applied to our VRML world (the full listing on the CD shows the textures applied to all of the objects). In this case, a rocky appearance is given to the wishing well, and other, more realistic appearances are given to the other objects in the VRML world (see Figure 21.11).

Listing 21.8   world4.wrl (excerpt)—Using Textures to Add Realism

```
#
# The Wishing Well
#
   Separator {
      Translation {
         translation -3 0.3333 3
      }
      DEF WishingWell Separator {
         Texture2Transform {
            scaleFactor 8 1
         }
         Texture2 {
            filename "rock.jpg"
         }
         Cylinder {
            radius 1
            height 0.6667
         }
         Texture2 {
            filename ""
         }
         Material {
            diffuseColor [0 0 0]
         }
         Cylinder {
            radius 0.8
            height 0.6667
         }
      }
   }
```

FIG. 21.11
While textures certainly lend a more realistic appearance to a VRML world, they do slow down the file transmission and rendering, so use them only when needed.

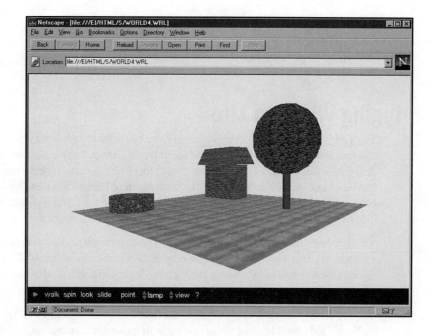

Linking to the Web

VRML, like HTML, is a language meant to be used on the Internet and the Web. An essential element for this is the hypertext link. This allows VRML worlds to be linked to other VRML worlds. And, if the VRML browser supports it, URLs can also be followed to HTML Web pages and other Internet resources.

WWWInline   One use of VRML's capability to link to the Web is through the WWWInline node. This node allows you to include VRML objects in your VRML worlds from any local VRML file or any VRML world on the Web. The syntax of the WWWInline node is:

```
WWWInline {
    name "path of local file or URL"
}
```

The VRML object, objects, and/or VRML world defined by that file or URL is placed into your VRML world as if the code for it was entered in the same place in your VRML code. This means that any colors, translations, or scaling in effect will also affect the *inlined* VRML.

WWWAnchor   Hypertext links are implemented in VRML by using the WWWAnchor node. The important fields for this node are the name field, which is used to specify the URL hypertext link, and the description field, which gives a text description of the link. Objects that are defined within the WWWAnchor node are the objects to which the hypertext link is attached. Like the Separator, WWWAnchor is a container node; the other VRML nodes that it contains become the anchors for the hypertext link defined by the node. The syntax of the WWWAnchor node is:

Part
IV

Ch

21

```
WWWAnchor {
    name "http://www.rpi.edu/~odonnj"
    description "JOD's Home Page"
    other VRML node(s)...
}
```

Bringing VRML to Life

The VRML 1.0 standard provides a means for the creation and display of static, three-dimensional worlds over the Web and the Internet. It supplies a collection of language elements—called *nodes*—for creating simple three-dimensional objects and assembling them into more complex objects and VRML environments. These VRML environments are generally either smaller, special purpose applications meant to be used (via the <EMBED> HTML tag) as inline VRML scenes or larger ones used as full-blown VRML worlds.

VRML 1.0 environments are static, though. The objects within them do not move and do not interact very much with the user. The only motion is the navigation of the user through the world. The only real interaction is through the inclusion and use of hypertext links within the VRML world.

The VRML 2.0 standard was created to alleviate this shortcoming of VRML 1.0 worlds. Objects within a VRML world can be programmed with movement, animation, and behaviors that allow them to interact with the user and with one another. Three-dimensional sound can be included to add further realism to the VRML world.

However, the VRML 2.0 standard is a new one. At the time of this writing, there are no VRML browsers or plug-ins that support the final VRML 2.0 standard, and it will probably be some time before VRML 2.0-compatible browsers become widespread. Netscape has released a version of its Live3D VRML plug-in that supports much of the VRML 2.0 standard, and Microsoft has announced plans to add VRML 2.0-compatibility to its Internet Explorer. In the meantime, before these VRML 2.0 capabilities become more commonplace, an attractive alternative for creating dynamic VRML worlds are the VRML extensions that are a long-standing part of Live3D. These extensions give it some of the dynamic capabilities of the full VRML 2.0 standard, and are available to many more people now. This allows Web authors to create dynamite VRML worlds for Live3D that will have a much greater potential audience than those made for VRML 2.0. (The Live3D plug-in also works within Microsoft's Internet Explorer 3 and higher.)

For the remainder of this chapter, we concentrate on Live3D. At the end, a summary of the capabilities of VRML 2.0 is given.

Live3D Extensions for Dynamic Worlds

Through Netscape's Live3D Web site, much information and documentation about Live3D's capabilities and language elements can be found. The Live3D Web site is located at **http://home.netscape.com/comprod/products/navigator/version_3.0/**.

For more complete information about the syntax and language elements of Live3D, you can check out the Live3D: Creating Content Web site.

N O T E **http://home.netscape.com/eng/live3d/live3d_content.html** This Web site gives information about how to create content for the Web by using VRML and Netscape's Live3D. ■

This site contains a beginner's guide to VRML and the Live3D extensions and pointers to some cool VRML worlds that use Live3D.

Some of the Live3D VRML nodes and node extensions are as follows:

- `MotionBlur`: Motion blur is activated through this node or through one of the commands available through the Live3D plug-in Options, Motion Blur menu item. This feature creates a viewing mode where all objects that are moving with respect to the viewer blur as they move, giving a greater appearance of movement. This effect can be quite distracting when there are moving objects in the VRML world. It works best when the world is static and the effect arises from motion of the viewer.

- `Animator Node`: The `Animator` node is used to add animation to a VRML model. Currently, this can only be done by linking an Autodesk 3DStudio .VUE animation file to the VRML model.

- `SpinGroup`: This node is a grouping node, like the `Separator` node, that is used to spin the object or objects within it. The objects can be spun about a specified axis, either about the object itself or about the center of the VRML world. An example showing the use of this node is shown in the next section.

- `WWWAnchor Node` with Target Frames: Live3D adds the `target` field to the `WWWAnchor` node to allow target frames to be specified in a VRML hypertext link. For example, to create a hypertext link inside a VRML cube to a frame named `IndexFrame` in an HTML document, the following can be used:

```
WWWAnchor {
    name   "http://www.company.com/example.html"
    target "IndexFrame"
    Cube {}
}
```

- `DirectedSound Node`: This node implements a directional sound source within Live3D VRML worlds. The sound is described in terms of two regions: an inner ellipse, where the sound volume is constant and at its maximum intensity, and an outer ellipse, outside of which no sound is heard. Between the two ellipses, the sound drops off in intensity, depending on where the viewer is located with respect to distance away from the source and away from the direction in which the sound is pointed.

- `PointSound Node`: This node implements a sound that is omni-directional and drops off in intensity uniformly, from the minimum to the maximum range.

- `Texture2` with Animated Textures: Animated textures provide animation of any supported file format in the `Texture2` node. The image must consist of multiple images

Part
IV

Ch
21

stacked vertically—the height of the image must be an even multiple of the width, which should be a power of two. For instance, to cycle through eight images on one of your VRML objects—where each image is 64×128 pixels—you need to create one image that ends up being 64×1024 pixels long.

■ Texture2 with Environment Mapping: This added capability of the Texture2 node is provided with the envmap field. It is used to shift the coordinates of the affected texture in response to the movement of the user's viewpoint. One use of this field is to create an object with a polished surface that reflects its surrounding environment. The envmap field is implemented with the following:

```
Texture2 {
    filename "surface.gif"
    envmap    TRUE
}
```

■ AxisAlignment Node: The AxisAlignment node forces objects to stay aligned with the specified axes. This can be used, for instance, to force objects to always face the camera. In this usage, it is particularly effective in conjunction with AsciiText nodes to create text tags that can be viewed from any angle. An example showing the use of this node is shown in the next section.

■ Info Nodes BackgroundColor and BackgroundImage: These Live3D VRML extensions add support for two named Info nodes that allow you to specify a color or background image to be used in your VRML world. Examples of their use are:

```
DEF BackgroundColor Info {
    string "1 0 0"   # red background
}
DEF BackgroundImage Info {
    string "sky.jpg" # image URL
}
```

■ CollideStyle Node: The CollideStyle node enables cube-based collision detection to your VRML world (this can also be enabled using the Live3D plug-in's Navigation, Collision Detection menu item). Collision detection is enabled by including the following in your VRML world:

```
CollideStyle {
    collide TRUE
}
```

Example Live3D VRML World

Listing 21.9 shows an example VRML world, using Live3D to set it in motion (see Figure 21.12).

Listing 21.9   jod.wrl—Dynamic VRML World Using Live3D

```
#VRML V1.0 ascii

#
# Add info and background, JOD
```

```
#
Separator {
     Info {
          string "Special Edition, Using HTML, 3rd Edition"
     }
     DEF BackgroundColor Info {
          string "1 1 1"
     }
}
#
# Add ground
#
DEF GROUND Separator {
     Material {
          diffuseColor [1 0.5 0]
     }
     Coordinate3 {
          point [-6 0 -2,
                 6 0 -2,
                 6 0  2,
                -5 0  2]
     }
     IndexedFaceSet {
          coordIndex [0,1,2,3,-1]
     }
}
#
# Add cube #1
#
Separator {
     Translation { translation -5 1.1 0 }
     Material {
          diffuseColor     [1 0    0,
                            1 0.5 0,
                            1 1    0,
                            0 1    0,
                            0 0    1,
                            1 0    1]
     }
     MaterialBinding {
          value     PER_FACE
     }
     DEF JCUBE1 SpinGroup {
          rotation -1 1 -1 0.1
          local      TRUE
          Cube {
               height 1.5
               width  1.5
               depth  1.5
          }
     }
}
#
# Add cube #2
```

continues

Part

IV

Ch

21

Listing 21.9 Continued

```
#
Separator {
    Translation { translation  5 1.1 0 }
    Material {
        diffuseColor       [1 0   0,
                  1 0.5 0,
                  1 1   0,
                  0 1   0,
                  0 0   1,
                  1 0   1]
    }
    MaterialBinding {
        value    PER_FACE
    }
    DEF JCUBE2 SpinGroup {
        rotation  1 1 -1 0.2
        local     TRUE
        Cube {
            height 1.5
            width  1.5
            depth  1.5
        }
    }
}
#
# Hypertext Links
#
WWWAnchor {
    name "http://www.rpi.edu/~odonnj"
    description "JOD's Home Page"
    AxisAlignment {
        alignment ALIGNAXISXYZ
    }
    Translation { translation 0 0.5 0 }
    Separator {
        FontStyle {
            size  3.0
        }
        AsciiText {
            string "JOD"
            justification CENTER
        }
    }
}
#
# Cameras
#
DEF Cameras Switch {
    whichChild 0
    DEF Entry PerspectiveCamera {
        position   0 3 10
        orientation -1 0  0 0.2
    }
```

```
DEF "Step Back" PerspectiveCamera {
        position     0  6  14
        orientation -1  0  0  0.2
}
DEF Above PerspectiveCamera {
        position     0  11  0
        orientation  1  0  0  -1.5708
}
}
```

FIG. 21.12
Simple dynamic VRML
scenes can be crafted
to be viewed with
Netscape's Live3D
plug-in, using Netscape
Navigator or Microsoft
Internet Explorer.

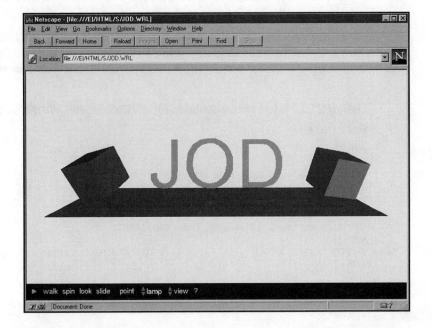

Some of the Live3D nodes (and a few VRML 1.0 nodes that we didn't discuss earlier) used in this example are:

- SpinGroup: This node is used to set the two cubes spinning. The rotation field determines the *x y z* vector about which the object spins, and the *rate* of rotation in radians per second. The local field is set to true, indicating that the objects spin about their origin, not the origin of the VRML world.

- MaterialBinding: This is a VRML 1.0 node that determines how the information in the Material node is attached to the subsequent objects. In this case, the diffuseColor field of the Material node defines six different colors. The MaterialBinding node value field setting of PER_FACE means that each face of the cube will be assigned one of these colors.

Part

IV

Ch

21

■ `AxisAlignment`: This node is used to align the `AsciiText` node (the "JOD" text in the VRML world), so that it is always facing the viewer. Note that, as a result, it is possible because of this to have the text partially or totally obscured by the ground.

■ `Switch` and `Camera`: These two VRML 1.0 nodes are used to set up multiple VRML "cameras." These just predefine views of the VRML world. In Live3D, these views are accessed by right-clicking in the VRML world and selecting Viewpoints from the pop-up menu.

■ `WWWAnchor`: An example of the VRML 1.0 `WWWAnchor` node, described in the preceding "Linking to the Web" section, is shown.

Listing 21.10 shows how this VRML scene would be embedded in an HTML document, which is then shown in Figure 21.13. Note that this looks a bit like an animated GIF when loaded, except that the viewer can actually proceed to navigate around within the scene.

Listing 21.10   jod.html—Embedding a VRML Scene Within an HTML Document

```
<HTML>
<HEAD>
<TITLE>JOD's VRML Home Page</TITLE>
</HEAD>
<BODY BGCOLOR=#FFFFFF>
<CENTER>
<H1>Welcome to... JOD's VRML Home Page!</H1>
<HR>
<EMBED NAME=JODWORLD SRC="jod.wrl" WIDTH=400 HEIGHT=150>
</CENTER>
<HR>
<ADDRESS>
Jim O'Donnell, <A HREF="mailto:odonnj@rpi.edu">odonnj@rpi.edu</A>
</ADDRESS>
</BODY>
</HTML>
```

FIG. 21.13
Embedded VRML
scenes can make ideal
special effects within
HTML documents.

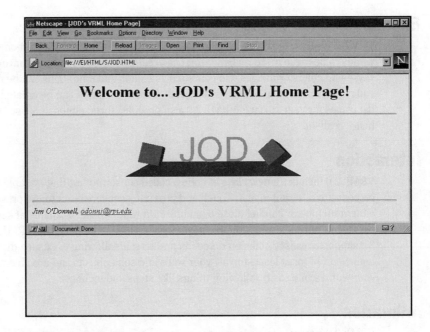

Features of VRML 2.0

The VRML 1.0 language specification allows for the creation, presentation, and viewing of static three-dimensional scenes and worlds. VRML 2.0 has been designed to build on that standard to provide a lot more. The goal of the VRML 2.0 standard is to provide the tools to create three-dimensional worlds that include movement and sound and allow the objects within the world to be programmed with behaviors that allow them to react to your presence and the presence of other objects. VRML fish can be programmed to swim away from you if you get too close, for instance.

A second goal of VRML 2.0 is to create a foundation for Web-based three-dimensional content that can continue to evolve and grow. As computers continue to grow more and more powerful, the Internet continues to develop, and high-bandwidth, high-speed connections become more commonplace, the VRML standard will continue to be developed to take advantage of the new capabilities.

The new capabilities of VRML 2.0 over VRML 1.0 fall into the five general categories of static world enhancements, interaction, animation, scripting, and prototyping. These are discussed in the VRML 2.0 specification, available at **http://vrml.sgi.com/moving-worlds/**. They are summarized in the following sections.

Part
IV

Ch
21

Enhanced Static Worlds

VRML 2.0 supports several new nodes and fields that allow the static geometry of VRML worlds to be made more realistic. You can create separate backdrops for the ground and the sky, using colors or images. Objects such as clouds and mountains can be put in the distance, and fog can be used to blur distant objects. Irregular terrain can be created, rather than using flat planes for your surface. VRML 2.0 also provides three-dimensional sound to further enhance realism.

Interaction

VRML 2.0 includes a new class of nodes, called sensor nodes, that are able to set off events in response to different inputs. Touch and proximity sensors react to the presence of the viewer either touching or coming close to an object. A time sensor is capable of keeping track of the passage of time, allowing time-correlated events to be added to your VRML world. And VRML 2.0 supports realistic collision detection and terrain following to ensure that your viewers bounce off of (or at least stop at) your walls and solid objects and are able to travel through your world while easily following things like steps and inclines.

Animation

VRML 2.0 interpolator nodes allow you to create predefined animations for any of the objects in your VRML world. These animations can be programmed to occur automatically or in response to some other factor, either an action of your viewer or at a given time. With these interpolators, you can create moving objects, objects such as the sun or the moon that change color as they move, or objects that change shape. The viewpoint can also be animated to create an automatic guided tour of your VRML world.

Scripting

The key to many of VRML 2.0's other features—particularly the movement of VRML 2.0 objects—is its support of scripting. Scripting is used to program objects' behaviors, not only allowing them to move but also giving them the capability to react realistically to objects around them. A script is the link that is used to take an event—generated by a sensor node, for instance—and generate the appropriate action.

Prototyping

The final category of enhancement to VRML 2.0 is the capability for prototyping. What this allows you to do is to create your own nodes. By grouping a set of nodes together to achieve a specific purpose within a new prototype node, that node becomes available for reuse.

N O T E   For more information, tutorials, and examples of VRML 2.0, as well as VRML 1.0 and other VRML implementations, take a look at the excellent Web site provided by Vijay Mukhi at **http://www.neca.com/~vmis/vrml.htm**. ■

VRML Resources

Probably the central clearinghouse of all things VRML, appropriately called the VRML Repository, is located at **http://rosebud.sdsc.edu/vrml/**. This Web site contains a vast array of information about VRML, links to sites containing VRML browser and authoring software, and just about anything else you can think of that has to do with VRML.

VRML Software

A wide range of software is available on the Web, most of it listed on the VRML Repository. The general categories of software available include:

- VRML browsers and plug-ins
- VRML and other 3-D authoring programs
- VRML server software

VRML Object Libraries

If you are interested in creating VRML objects for use in a VRML world or with an embedded VRML special effect in a Web page, you should probably take a look around on the Web before starting from scratch. There are many places to get three-dimensional objects that you can use for your purposes, both in VRML files and in other formats that can be converted to VRML.

The best place to start, predictably, is the VRML Repository. This site maintains a library of example applications, categorized by topic, that can be examined through the Web page at **http://rosebud.sdsc.edu/vrml/worlds.html**.

Among the many other sites featuring VRML examples, applications, and objects, one is the VRML Models site located at **http://www.ocnus.com/models/models.html**. This site, like the VRML Repository library, features an indexed list of VRML objects and worlds. A unique feature of the VRML Models site is its VRML Mall, which is an actual three-dimensional gallery through which you can view all of their VRML objects.

Finally, the Mesh Mart, located at **http://cedar.cic.net/~rtilmann/mm/**, was set up as a source of three-dimensional objects. While most of these objects are not in VRML format, they are available in formats that can be easily converted to VRML. Through the Mesh Mart, a program called wcvt2pov.exe is available that can convert between many different three-dimensional formats. It can read in files with the following formats:

- AOFF (*.geo) files
- AutoCAD (*.dxf) files
- 3D Studio (*.3ds) files
- Neutral File Format (*.nff)
- RAW (*.raw) files
- TPOLY (*.tpoly) files

Part
IV

Ch
21

- TrueType fonts (*.ttf) files
- Wavefront (*.obj) files

In addition, it can write out files in the following formats:

- AutoCAD (*.dxf)
- 3D Studio (*.asc)
- Neutral File Format (*.nff)
- OpenGL (*.c)
- POVRay V2.2 (*.pov, *.inc)
- PovSB (*.psb)
- RAW (*.raw)
- TPOLY (*.tpoly)
- VRML V1.0 (*.wrl)
- Wavefront (*.obj)

## CHAPTER 22

ActiveX Controls

by Jerry Honeycutt

You use ActiveX controls (the objects formerly known as OLE controls or OCXs) to add a variety of features to your Web page. For example, you can add a Timer control to your Web page that periodically updates the page's content, or you can use a Popup Window control to display tooltip-style help when the user holds the mouse pointer over a link. Considering there are over a thousand ActiveX controls available for you to use, the possibilities are just about endless.

Simply dropping ActiveX controls onto your Web page isn't enough, if you want to build a dynamic and exciting Web page. You have to make all those controls work together. That's where scripting comes in. You associate scripts with the events and values of the controls you put on a Web page so that you can make them interact. You can update the contents of a TextBox control when the user clicks a button, for example, or you can open a Web page in a frame when the user chooses an item from a Popup Menu control.

What is an ActiveX control?

ActiveX controls provided by Microsoft for Internet Explorer 3.0, and how you use them.

Inserting controls in your Web page is easy

How to insert ActiveX Controls in your Web pages by using the OBJECT tag and how to set properties by using the PARAM tag.

Interact with ActiveX controls by using scripts

You can make controls interact with each other with scripting. This chapter shows you how to connect scripts to controls.

An example of ActiveX controls

You'll learn more about ActiveX controls by trying out the real-world example at the end of this chapter. Enjoy.

This chapter does describe how to connect scripts to controls, but this book isn't about scripting languages. It's about using ActiveX controls and plug-ins with Internet Explorer. Even though, this book is a perfect companion to Que's other books about scripting languages, such as these:

> *Visual Basic Script by Example*
>
> *JavaScript by Example*
>
> *Special Edition Using Visual Basic Script*
>
> *Special Edition Using JavaScript* ■

The Evolution of ActiveX Controls

In the Nov. 1, 1996 edition of *Windows Magazine*, Fred Langa traces the lineage of ActiveX controls all the way back to the early days of cut and paste. Do you remember how cool that seemed back then? Cut and paste was touted as one of the major benefits of Windows because you could now share data between different applications.

OLE

Next was OLE (object linking and embedding). This technology allowed objects to be inserted into containers. In laymen's terms, OLE allowed a document from one application to be embedded within a document in another application. When you insert an Excel spreadsheet into a Word document, you're using OLE. You're also using OLE when you insert a picture into a Word document.

The first step was OLE 1.0. OLE 1.0 only provided the ability to share documents, but it didn't provide the ability to actually work with a document that's embedded within another. OLE 2.0 came along, however, and allowed you to actually work with a document while it's embedded within another. That is, if you embed a spreadsheet in a Word document, as shown in Figure 22.1, you can work with that spreadsheet within the Word document. For that matter, you can even use Excel's toolbars and menus while you're working with the spreadsheet in the Word document.

Following OLE 2.0 is OLE 2.5, or Distributed OLE. Distributed OLE lets you work with documents and links across a network.

FIG. 22.1
Choose Insert, Object from Word's main menu to see the types of objects you can insert into a Word document.

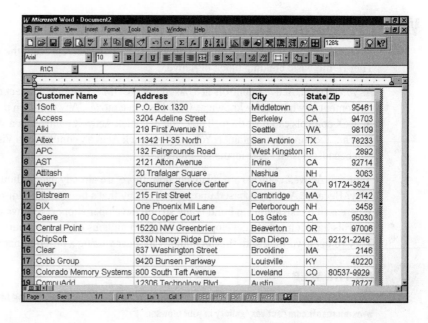

	Customer Name	Address	City	State	Zip
3	1Soft	P.O. Box 1320	Middletown	CA	95461
4	Access	3204 Adeline Street	Berkeley	CA	94703
5	Alki	219 First Avenue N.	Seattle	WA	98109
6	Altex	11342 IH-35 North	San Antonio	TX	78233
7	APC	132 Fairgrounds Road	West Kingston	RI	2892
8	AST	2121 Alton Avenue	Irvine	CA	92714
9	Attitash	20 Trafalgar Square	Nashua	NH	3063
10	Avery	Consumer Service Center	Covina	CA	91724-3624
11	Bitstream	215 First Street	Cambridge	MA	2142
12	BIX	One Phoenix Mill Lane	Peterborough	NH	3458
13	Caere	100 Cooper Court	Los Gatos	CA	95030
14	Central Point	15220 NW Greenbrier	Beaverton	OR	97006
15	ChipSoft	6330 Nancy Ridge Drive	San Diego	CA	92121-2246
16	Clear	637 Washington Street	Brookline	MA	2146
17	Cobb Group	9420 Bunsen Parkway	Louisville	KY	40220
18	Colorado Memory Systems	800 South Taft Avenue	Loveland	CO	80537-9929
19	CompuAdd	12306 Technology Blvd	Austin	TX	78727

ActiveX Controls

Now, Microsoft has breathed new life into OLE and called it ActiveX Controls. In reality, both OLE and ActiveX controls are based upon COM (component object model). OLE is still alive and kicking. You use it all the time in the applications you know and love. ActiveX controls, on the other hand, is a trimmer version of OLE that's built for distribution on the Internet. That is, ActiveX controls are optimized for size and speed. You can insert an ActiveX control into any ActiveX container, such as Internet Explorer, Microsoft Office 97, and even the Windows desktop (with the help of Internet Explorer 4.0).

N O T E On the Internet, the availability of technology across all platforms is a key to that technology's success. As a Web developer, it doesn't make sense for you to rely on technology which is only available for the Mac, does it? Likewise, Microsoft knows that if UNIX and Mac users don't have support for VBScript and ActiveX objects, no one will develop Web pages with it because they can't reach the largest possible audience; all those UNIX and Mac users will be left out in the cold. Thus, Microsoft intends to make ActiveX available across all of the popular platforms you find on the Internet. ■

What ActiveX Controls Mean to You

If ActiveX is a technological umbrella, then ActiveX controls represent the umbrella's handle. They're the basic building block of ActiveX.

As you've read, ActiveX controls are based upon COM (component object model). They're a refinement of what you've known as OLE custom controls. Any program that is a container for ActiveX controls can host them. Thus, you can stick ActiveX controls in a Web page, because Internet Explorer is a container. You can also stick ActiveX controls in a Visual Basic application because Visual Basic forms are containers.

Although ActiveX controls are relatively new, there are already over a thousand available. Why? Because ActiveX is based upon a technology that's been around for quite awhile—OLE. Whereas, it'll take awhile to build really strong developer support for Java or plug-ins, ActiveX controls have immediate developer support from millions of programmers all over the world. They've been working with this technology for years, using a different name.

ON THE WEB

You can get a good idea as to what types of ActiveX controls are available by opening **http://www.microsoft.com/activex/gallery** in your browser.

Working with Data

Do you remember what Web pages were like a few years ago? No? I'll remind you. They were static. The Web browser basically displayed what it was given: a fancy text file that contained information (HTML) about how the browser should display it. Once the browser had displayed the Web page, nothing changed. It just sat there. Great for reading the Unabombers Manifesto, but not very useful or productive.

ActiveX controls let the content developer build Web pages that actually work with data they're given. The Web page is not static. It changes depending on the data the controls are working with and input from the user. That's starting to sound like what a program does, work with input and provide output, huh? In fact, you can actually distribute programs, as ActiveX controls, via the Web page.

Here are a few examples of the types of things an ActiveX control can do with data:

- Allow the user to input information on the Web page by using a wide variety of metaphors (lists, buttons, outlines, and so on.).
- Query a database on the server and display the results of the query on the Web page.
- Work with a spreadsheet or grid right there in the Web page. Figure 22.2 shows you an example of the ProtoView DataTable Grid.

FIG. 22.2

You can get more information about the ProtoView DataTable Grid at its Web site: **http://www. protoview.com**.

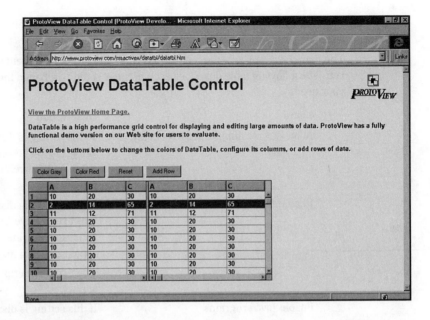

Integrating with Windows

Since ActiveX controls are fully conversant in COM, they can work closely with the other COM objects on the user's computer. For example, an ActiveX control can manipulate a document in Microsoft Word or it can work with the user's Windows 95 desktop (a container).

> **CAUTION**
>
> ActiveX controls are not limited like Java applets. That is, they have full access to your computer, including your file system, when they run. Make sure you install only those controls that come from vendors you trust.

N O T E Publisher certificates (a.k.a. authenticode, code-signing) identify component vendors to your browser. As of this writing, Internet Explorer is the only browser to support publisher certificates. When you install a publisher certificate in your browser, you're telling the browser that anything published by the company listed in the certificate is A-OK. The browser can trust that company. It's similar to buying shrink-wrapped software at the computer store. You know the computer store and you know the publisher. You trust them. So, you run home and install the program without worrying too much about the damage it might cause to your computer.

Certificates are given by a certifying authority, and they're validated when your browser tries to download and install a program from the Internet. If the browser doesn't find a certificate for the program, it'll either dump the program into a bit bucket or ask you if you want to go ahead and install it, anyway. This is totally under your control, too. ∎

1. From Internet Explorer's main menu, choose <u>V</u>iew, <u>O</u>ptions. Then, click the Security tab. The part you're interested in is the bottom area.

2. The four check boxes at the bottom determine what type of content you'll let the browser run. The following table describes each of these settings. Change the settings to suit your needs.

Name	Description
Allow <u>d</u>ownloading of active content	If this setting is disabled, your browser won't even attempt to download ActiveX controls or Java programs.
Enable Active<u>X</u> controls and plug-ins	If this setting is disabled, the browser won't run ActiveX controls or Netscape plug-ins.
R<u>u</u>n ActiveX scripts	If this setting is disabled, the browser won't run VBScript or JavaScript scripts.
Enable <u>J</u>ava programs	If this setting is disabled, the browser won't run Java programs at all.

3. Click the Safety <u>L</u>evel button.

4. These three check boxes determine what the browser does when it downloads a program that could be a security problem. Select <u>H</u>igh if you want it to avoid any control that doesn't have a certificate, select <u>M</u>edium if you want the browser to give you a choice, or select <u>N</u>one if you want the browser to install all programs no matter what.

5. Click OK to save your changes to the safety level. Then, click OK again to save your Security settings.

CAUTION

You should note that just because an ActiveX control has a publisher certificate, that doesn't mean it can do no harm to your computer. For example, awhile back there was a control called Exploder that would shut down your system when it was installed. This control was indeed digitally signed. It demonstrated that publisher certificates aren't foolproof.

Provide Building Blocks

You should think of ActiveX controls as building blocks. That is, you can assemble a bunch of small building blocks into a much larger structure, and you can combine a variety of ActiveX controls to build a solution that you distribute on the Web page. Here are some ideas of the types of things you can build with ActiveX controls:

- You can use a combination of controls, such as the Popup Menu and Popup Window controls, to provide advance navigation and help on your Web site. The user can jump to another Web page by choosing it from a menu, or she can find more information about a link by letting her mouse linger over it for a few seconds. Figure 22.3 shows you such an example.

FIG. 22.3
Microsoft's NT Web pages use the Popup Menu control to provide navigational tools.

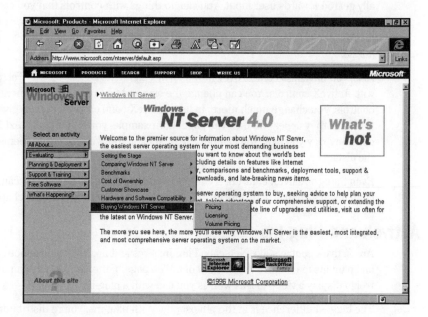

■ You can build and distribute on a Web page a mean game of checkers by using ActiveX controls. Each piece may be a control, while the board is a container such as the HTML Layout control.

■ You can build a complete interface to a corporate database by using ActiveX controls for the user interface and the database access.

ActiveX versus Everything Else

From time to time, you'll hear a bit of confusion about what ActiveX is and what it isn't. You'll hear questions like, why do I need ActiveX when I can use Java? What's so great about ActiveX controls when compared to Netscape Plug-Ins? The following sections will answer many of these questions for you.

ActiveX and Forms

ActiveX controls do not supplant forms. Forms have their lot in life. They collect basic data from the user, in the form of text boxes, check boxes, lists, and so on, and submit that information to the server. Scripts on the server pretty much do as they see fit with the information. The script can add the information to a database, for example, or verify a user's logon to a Web site. Like forms, ActiveX controls do let you collect information from the user, but they do so much more than forms.

There is a limited number of elements you can put on a form. You can use text boxes, lists, text areas, and so on. And they're all geared towards collecting information from the user. There are currently over a thousand ActiveX controls, however, and only a handful of them are actually geared towards user input. You can do things with controls that you can't with forms. For example, you can insert a control on the Web page that queries a database on the server and displays the results of the query. You can insert a control that lets the user play a crossword puzzle.

Also, you have less control over how a form's elements appear on the Web page than you do with ActiveX controls. You can change the size and font of a form's elements, but, with ActiveX controls, you change much more. In fact, ActiveX controls pretty much give you total control over how they appear on the Web page. For example, you can rotate a text label and change its color any way you like. You can put a text label on the Web page that seems to disappear into the distance.

Even though ActiveX controls are not necessarily related to forms, you can still submit the contents of a control with a form. You learn how to do this later in this chapter.

ActiveX and Plug-Ins

Are ActiveX controls like Netscape Plug-Ins? Yes and no. You can use both ActiveX controls and plug-ins to enhance the content of a Web page. For example, you can use an ActiveX control to display a video just as well as you can with a plug-in.

The biggest difference is in the philosophy. With plug-ins, you're distributing data. That is, you embed a data file in a Web page, and the plug-in behaves like a browser extension, displaying or otherwise doing something with the data. Thus, the primary purpose of a plug-in is to handle data embedded in the Web page. With ActiveX controls, on the other hand, you're actually distributing smallish programs or those which have a specific purpose. You can associate some data with the program, but the primary purpose of an ActiveX control is to add some sort of functionality to the Web page, such as inputting a bit of information from the user or displaying a menu from which the user can make a choice.

ActiveX controls install themselves automatically. They don't require the user to stop right in the middle of a Web page, download an installation program, and run it. The user does have to install plug-ins manually, however. In fact, many times the user has to shut down the browser altogether in order to install a plug-in.

Another difference is plug-ins are not based upon COM (component object model). ActiveX controls are based upon COM, however. Thus, ActiveX controls can be used outside of the Web page, in other applications such as those built with Visual Basic.

ActiveX and Java

Microsoft contends ActiveX and Java are not competing technologies—they're complimentary. You don't have any reason to disbelieve them, either. Here's some of the bigger differences between ActiveX controls and Java applets:

- Java is an Internet language that's great for distributing simple applications on the Internet. ActiveX is a much larger base of technology, however, that integrates a variety of objects from a variety of sources.

- ActiveX controls have a life outside of the Web page. That is, since ActiveX controls are based on COM, they can also be used in things such as Visual Basic applications.

- Java applets are secure because they have no access to the world outside of the Web page and, thus, have no direct access to the user's computer. ActiveX controls, however, do have direct access to the user's computer and are therefore not as secure.

- The biggest difference between ActiveX controls and Java applets is how they behave on the user's computer. Java applets run in a Java Virtual Machine (JVM). They're interpreted, so they run slower than ActiveX controls. ActiveX controls, on the other hand, are compiled into native code that is not interpreted. They run much faster.

Getting Microsoft's ActiveX Controls

Microsoft provides a collection of ActiveX controls with Internet Explorer 3.0. You don't have to do anything other than install Internet Explorer 3.0 to get them. Microsoft does package some controls only with the complete installation of Internet Explorer 3.0, though, and Microsoft provides other controls through its ActiveX Gallery Web site at **http://www.microsoft. com/ activex/gallery**. Table 22.1 briefly describes each control and how you get it. The sections that follow show you real, live examples of some of these controls.

Table 22.1   Microsoft's ActiveX Controls

Name	Description
Provided by the Minimum, Typical, and Complete Installs of Internet Explorer 3.0	
Web Browser	Displays HTML files, ActiveX Controls, and ActiveX documents.
Timer	Triggers an event at specific intervals.
Marquee	Scrolls an HTML file horizontally or vertically.
Provided by the Complete Install of Internet Explorer 3.0	
ActiveMovie	Displays streaming and nonstreaming video and audio.
HTML Layout	Displays 2-D HTML regions created with the ActiveX Control Pad.
Forms 2.0 Label	Displays a text label.
Forms 2.0 Textbox	Prompts the user for text.
Forms 2.0 Combo Box	Displays a drop-down list of options.
Forms 2.0 List Box	Displays a scrollable list of options.

continues

Table 22.1 Continued

Name	Description
Provided by the Complete Install of Internet Explorer 3.0	
Forms 2.0 CheckBox	Displays a check box option.
Forms 2.0 Option Button	Displays an option button.
Forms 2.0 Toggle Button	Displays a button which the user can toggle on and off.
Forms 2.0 Command Button	Displays a basic button.
Forms 2.0 Tabstrip	Displays multiple pages of controls which the user selects by clicking a tab.
Forms 2.0 ScrollBar	Displays vertical and hortizontal scrollbars.
Forms 2.0 Spin Button	Displays a spin button that can be pushed up or down.
Image	Displays a progressive image from a JPG, GIF, or BMP file.
Hotspot	Adds a transparent hotspot to a layout
Provided at http://www.microsoft.com/activex/gallery	
Animated Button	Displays an AVI file on a button.
Chart	Draws various types of charts.
Gradient	Shares an area with a range of colors.
Label	Displays a text label with a given angle, color, and font.
Menu	Displays a button that pops up a standard menu which fires an event when the user chooses an item.
Popup Menu	Displays a pop-up menu that fires an event when the user chooses an item.
Popup Window	Displays an HTML file in a pop-up window.
Preloader	Downloads the file at the given URL into the user's cache.
Stock Ticker	Displays data from a text file at regular intervals.
View Tracker	Fires events when the control enters or leaves the browser's viewing area.

N O T E Many of the ActiveX controls you find on the Internet aren't digitally signed. By default, Internet Explorer 3.0 won't install unsigned controls—it doesn't even give you the chance to override it. Thus, Internet Explorer will ignore many of the controls the Web page authors are using. Check your security configuration to make sure you have a choice: choose View, Options from the main menu; click the Security tab; click the Safety Level button; and make sure you select Medium. Then, Internet Explorer 3.0 will ask you before installing an unsigned control. If you choose not to install the control, the Web page may not work as the author intends. On the other hand, if you do install the control, you open yourself up to troubles that come from running controls from unknown sources, such as bugs that cause the browser to crash or, worse, controls that damage your system. ■

Label Control

The ActiveX Gallery shows an example of the use of the ActiveX Label control, shown in Figure 22.4. Using this control, you can display text within a Web page by using any installed font, with any style, color, and at an arbitrary angle you choose. In this example, the two regions change—either color, text, or orientation—whenever you click them.

FIG. 22.4
The Label control gives you the ability to place text on the Web page without resorting to graphics.

Preloader Control

The ActiveX Preloader control makes your Web site seem faster than all the rest. You use it to make your Web site seem to work faster than normal. It's a slight-of-hand, because the Preloader control quietly caches files (graphics, video, audio, and HTML files) from the Web site while the user is reading the current Web page. You can see an example of the Preloader control at Microsoft's ActiveX Gallery.

Timer Control

The Timer control lets you periodically run a script which you can use to change the content of a Web page or perform some other task. Figure 22.5 shows a Web page that uses a timer to change the size and color of the two labels (each implemented with the Label control) over time. Both labels change at different intervals because this Web page uses two different Timer controls.

 T I P To see how these controls are inserted into the HTML file, right-click the Web page and choose View Source.

FIG. 22.5

You use the Timer control to execute a script at preset intervals, such as every second or every 10 seconds.

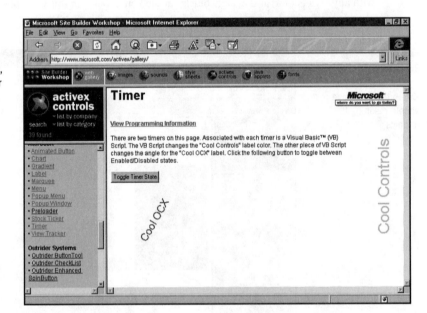

Menu Control

You use the Menu control to put a button on your Web page that, when clicked by the user, displays a menu. When the user chooses a menu item, the control fires an event which you can handle with a script. Figure 20.6 shows you the example from Microsoft's ActiveX Gallery. It contains two Menu controls; each one displays a different submenu.

FIG. 22.6
You can use the Menu control to add menu-driven navigation to your Web site, like Microsoft's Site Builder Workshop.

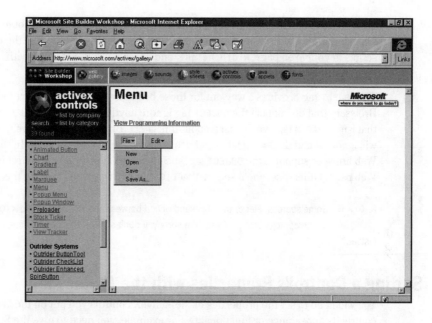

Inserting Controls with the *OBJECT* Tag

You've seen the controls, now you need to know how to insert them into your Web pages. You use the OBJECT tag to do just that. With regard to ActiveX controls, the OBJECT tag identifies the control you're using. That is, the OBJECT tag identifies which control on the user's computer you want to use and gives that instance of the control a name, which you can use in scripts. That's all.

In the following sections, you'll learn much more about each of the OBJECT tag's attributes. Before doing that, however, take a look at how you use the OBJECT tag in a Web page. In its simplest form, the OBJECT tag looks something like this:

```
<OBJECT
        classid="clsid:1A771020-A28E-11CF-8510-00AA003B6C7E"
        id=Track1
        width=400
        height=2
        align=left>
<IMG SRC="noobject.gif">
<PARAM NAME="Image" VALUE="image.gif">
</OBJECT>
```

The classid attribute uniquely identifies, on the computer, the control you're using. Every control installed on the user's computer is installed in the Registry. The control's CLASSID is the number that Windows uses to identify that control. You can think of the CLASSID as a name that is guaranteed to be unique. You'll learn more about this attribute later. In this case, I'm using the View Tracker control. You use the id attribute to identify the control to the scripts in your Web page. width, height, and align work the same as with other types of tags; they specify the size and location of the control on the Web page.

The OBJECT tag provides a way out for those browsers that don't support the OBJECT tag. Browsers that do support the OBJECT tag ignore anything between <OBJECT> and </OBJECT> that isn't a PARAM tag (you'll learn about this later). Browsers that don't support the OBJECT tag will ignore it and the PARAM tags, and use the sandwiched tags instead. In this case, if the user's Web browser supports the OBJECT tag, she'll see the View Tracker control inserted into her Web page. Otherwise, she'll see an IMAGE.GIF image inserted by using the IMG tag.

N O T E   Some sources refer to the tags sandwiched between the <OBJECT> and </OBJECT> tags
as the apology section. As in: "I'm sorry you don't support this object; here, try these tags
instead." ■

Setting a Control's Properties with the *PARAM* Tag

You will need to set the properties of the ActiveX controls you put on the Web page in order to control its appearance or functionality. For example, you need to give the Stock Ticker control the URL of the text file it should use for data. You need to provide the Label control with the text it should display. The only way to know for sure which properties each control requires is to check in the control's documentation. You can also use the ActiveX Control Pad to set a control's properties, as described in Chapter 23, "ActiveX Control Pad."

So, how do you set these properties? You use the PARAM tag to assign a value to a named property within the control. This works very much like Visual Basic property sheets. Note the PARAM tag has no closing </PARAM> tag. Table 22.2 describes the attributes you use with the PARAM tag. You frequently need to use only the NAME and VALUE attributes.

Table 22.2   Attributes of the *PARAM* Tag

Attribute	Description
NAME	Defines the name of the property. An ActiveX control can treat the name as case-sensitive.
VALUE	Specifies the value of the property identified in NAME.
VALUETYPE	Can be one of REF, OBJECT, or DATA.
TYPE	Refers to Internet Media Type (RFC 1590) of the item referred to in the VALUE field when VALUETYPE = REF.

NAME, VALUE, and TYPE are self-explanatory. Table 22.3 describes the settings you can use with VALUETYPE.

Table 22.3   Values for *VALUETYPE* Attribute

Value	Meaning
REF	VALUE contains an URL.
OBJECT	VALUE contains URL of another OBJECT.
DATA	VALUE contains string data.

The following is an example of inserting an ActiveX control by using the OBJECT tag. The CLASSID attribute specifies the Popup Menu control, and each PARAM tag adds a menu item to the menu.

```
<OBJECT
        id=iemenu1
        classid="clsid:0482B100-739C-11CF-A3A9-00A0C9034920"
        width=1
        height=1
        align=left
        hspace=0
        vspace=0
   >
   <PARAM NAME="Menuitem[0]" VALUE="First Choice">
   <PARAM NAME="Menuitem[1]" VALUE="Second Choice">
   <PARAM NAME="Menuitem[2]" VALUE="Third Choice">
   <PARAM NAME="Menuitem[3]" VALUE="Fourth Choice">
   <PARAM NAME="Menuitem[4]" VALUE="Fifth Choice">
</OBJECT>
```

More About the *OBJECT* Tag

The OBJECT tag has a number of attributes you can use. The sections that follow describe each attribute. In reality, however, you'll find yourself using only a few: classid, id, height, width, align, and, possibly, codebase.

ALIGN   You use the ALIGN attribute to specify where to place the object. You can position an object relative to the text line or on its own on the left, right, or center of the page. Table 22.4 describes the settings you can use to align the object with the text line. Table 22.5 also describes the settings you can use to align the object with the page.

Table 22.4   Aligning the Object with the Text Line

Setting	Description
TEXTTOP	The top of the object is aligned with the top of the current font.
MIDDLE	The middle of the object is aligned with the baseline of the text line.
TEXTMIDDLE	The middle of the object is aligned with the middle of the text line.
BASELINE	The bottom of the object is aligned with the baseline of the text line.
TEXTBOTTOM	The bottom of the object is aligned with the bottom of the current font.

Table 22.5 Aligning the Object with the Web Page

Setting	Description
LEFT	The object is aligned with the left side of the Web page and text flows around the right side of the object.
CENTER	The object is aligned in the center of the Web page and the text starts on the line following the object.
RIGHT	The object is aligned with the right side of the Web page and text flows around the left side of the object.

BORDER   When you use an object as part of a hypertext link, you can specify whether or not the object has a border. The BORDER attribute specifies the width of the border around the object. If you don't want a border around the object, set this attribute to 0, like this: BORDER=0.

CLASSID and CODEBASE   You use CLASSID to refer to the ActiveX control to be placed within the object's borders. There are several different ways to indicate the object to be inserted here. ActiveX uses the clsid: URL scheme to specify the ActiveX class identifier.

ON THE WEB

For further information on the clsid: URL scheme see **http://www.w3.org/pub/WWW/ Addressing/clsid-scheme**.

The best way to obtain the CLSID for an ActiveX control is to look at the control's documentation. You can look up Microsoft's ActiveX controls at Microsoft's ActiveX Gallery. Alternatively, use the ActiveX Control Pad to insert an ActiveX control in your Web page so you don't have to worry about the CLSID (see Chapter 23, "ActiveX Control Pad"). If the CLASSID attribute is missing, ActiveX data streams will include a class identifier that can be used by the ActiveX loader to find the appropriate control.

The CODEBASE attribute can be used to provide an URL from which the control can be obtained. If the control is already installed on the user's computer, the browser will do nothing with this attribute. If the control isn't installed on the user's computer, however, the browser will try to download the control from the URL in CODEBASE and install it.

N O T E   You can also get the CLASSID for an ActiveX control from the Windows Registry, like this:

1. Open the Registry Editor. Choose <u>R</u>un from the Start menu, type **regedit**, and press Enter.

2. Locate a control under HKEY_CLASSES_ROOT, such as Internet.Gradient or Internet.Label.

3. Note the default value of the CLSID subkey for that control. This is the string you use in the CLASSID attribute.

You can learn more about CLSIDs in *Special Edition Using the Windows 95 Registry* or *Windows 95 Registry and Customization Handbook* by Que. ■

CODETYPE The CODETYPE attribute is used to specify the Internet Media Type for the code pointed to by the CLASSID attribute. Browsers use this value to check the type of code before downloading it from the server. Thus, the browser can avoid a lengthy download for those objects which it doesn't support.

Currently, the CODETYPE attribute is supported in a limited fashion in Internet Explorer 3.0. Microsoft has indicated that TYPE will be implemented for all relevant MIME types.

DATA The DATA attribute contains an URL that points to data required by the object, for instance, a GIF file for an image. Internet Explorer 3.0 currently supports the DATA attribute.

DECLARE You'll use the DECLARE attribute to tell the browser whether to instantiate the object or not. If the DECLARE attribute is present, it indicates the object should not be instantiated until something references it. That is, the browser will note the declaration of the object, but won't actually load it until you reference it.

HEIGHT The HEIGHT attribute defines the height, in pixels, to make available to the ActiveX control when rendered by the browser. The Web browser may (or may not) use this value to scale an object to the requested height.

HSPACE The HSPACE attribute defines the amount of space, in pixels, to keep as white space on the left and right as a buffer between the ActiveX control and surrounding page elements. The Web browser may (or may not) use this value to allocate white space.

ID The ID attribute defines a document-wide identifier. This can be used for naming positions within documents. You also use the control's ID to reference it in scripts.

NAME You use the NAME attribute to indicate whether an object wrapped in a FORM tag will be submitted as part of the form. If you specify NAME, the Web browser submits the VALUE property of the object to the host. If you don't specify NAME, the ActiveX control is assumed to be decorative and not functional in the form.

STANDBY STANDBY is a short string of text the browser displays while it loads the ActiveX control.

TYPE The TYPE attribute is used to specify the Internet Media Type for the data specified by the DATA attribute.

ON THE WEB

You can learn more about Internet Media Types by referring to RFC 1590. You can get RFC 1590 from the Internet at **ftp://ds.internic.net/rfc/rfc1590.txt**.

USEMAP The value in USEMAP specifies an URL for a client-side imagemap.

VSPACE The VSPACE attribute defines the amount of space in pixels to keep as white space on the top and bottom as a buffer between the ActiveX control and surrounding page elements. The Web browser may (or may not) use this value to allocate the requested white space.

WIDTH The WIDTH attribute defines the width, in pixels, to make available to the ActiveX control when rendered by the browser. The Web browser may (or may not) use this value to scale an object to the requested width.

Using ActiveX Controls in Netscape (NCompass)

NCompass Labs provides a Netscape Plug-In called ScriptActive that makes ActiveX controls work in Netscape. It requires Netscape Navigator 3.0 or greater. Here's how to install the ScriptActive plug-in:

1. Download ScriptActive from **http://www.ncompasslabs.com**, saving it into a temporary folder.
2. In Windows Explorer, double-click on the file that you downloaded to start the setup program. Follow the instructions you see on the screen.

N O T E As of this writing, the Netscape Navigator 4.0 beta doesn't yet support ActiveX controls. Netscape has publicly stated that, by the time you get your hands on the final release, Navigator 4.0 will directly support ActiveX controls. ■

As always, there are a few caveats that make the ScriptActive plug-in a wary choice. For example, you won't have much luck using Microsoft's new development tools with ScriptActive, because ScriptActive doesn't support ActiveX Controls with the OBJECT tag. Here's more information about these caveats:

ScriptActive only supports VBScript if it's stored in a separate file. Thus, if you want both Internet Explorer and Netscape users to be able to use your Web page, you must store your scripts in files with the ALX extension and refer to that script by using the EMBED tag, like this:

```
<EMBED SRC="myscript.alx" WIDTH=1 HEIGHT=1 LANGUAGE="VBScript">
```

ScriptActive doesn't directly support the OBJECT tag. It only supports the EMBED tag. Thus, if you're authoring a Web page that you want to be compatible with both Internet Explorer and Netscape, you must insert a comparable EMBED tag inside of each OBJECT tag. Otherwise, Netscape users won't be able to use your Web page, regardless of whether or not they have ScriptActive. Internet Explorer will use the OBJECT tag, ignoring the EMBED tag, and Netscape will use the EMBED tag, ignoring the OBJECT tag. Note that ScriptActive does come with a program that you can use to convert HTML documents into compatible forms. It adds an <EMBED> tag for each <OBJECT> tag.

N O T E For more information, and more caveats, about using ScriptActive with Netscape, I recommend that you read NCompass Lab's FAQ. It's at **http://www.ncompasslabs.com/faq_main.htm**. ■

Connecting Controls to Scripts

Now, we're getting to the meat of the matter. You've learned how to insert ActiveX controls into your Web page by using the OBJECT tag. Now, you need to learn how to interact with those controls by using a scripting language. In the sections that follow, you'll learn how to handle the events that are fired by a control. You'll also learn how to get and set a control's properties from your scripts. Incidentally, my scripting language of choice is VBScript, so that's what I'm using in these examples. The JavaScript versions of these examples aren't much different, however.

▶ **See** "Picking the Best Tool," to learn more about VBScript and JavaScript, **p. 540**

ActiveX controls act like and quack like the elements on a form. That is, you interact with each ActiveX control's properties, methods, and events in exactly the same way in which you interact with a form's element. You handle a control's events when the control needs attention; you call a control's methods; and you get and set the control's properties.

Handling an Event

You can use a couple of different methods of handling events for forms and elements (event-procedures, inline event-handlers, and so on). One such method is to use the FOR/EVENT attributes of the SCRIPT tag.

▶ **See** "Understanding Event-Driven Programming," to learn how events work within an HTML document, **p. 541**

The FOR and EVENT attributes let you associate a script with any named object in the HTML file and any event for that object. Take a look at the following:

```
<SCRIPT LANGUAGE="VBScript" FOR="btnButton" EVENT="Click">
<!--
 window.alert( "Ouch! You clicked on me." )
-->
</SCRIPT>
<OBJECT ID="btnButton" WIDTH=96 HEIGHT=32
        CLASSID="CLSID:D7053240-CE69-11CD-A777-00DD01143C57">
        <PARAM NAME="Caption" VALUE="Click Me">
        <PARAM NAME="Size" VALUE="2540;847">
</OBJECT>
```

You can add this code to an HTML file, and you'll see a button (with an ID of btnButton) that executes the script when you click it. Take a look at the <SCRIPT> tag. It contains the FOR and EVENT attributes which define the object and event associated with that script. FOR="btnButton" EVENT="Click" says that when an object named btnButton fires the Click event, every statement in this script is executed.

Some events pass arguments to the event handlers. How do you handle arguments when you're handling the event by using the FOR/EVENT syntax? Like the following:

```
<SCRIPT LANGUAGE="JavaScript" FOR="btnButton" EVENT=
"MouseMove(shift, button, x, y)">
```

The enclosed script can then use any of the parameters passed to it by the MouseMove event.

Once you've specified a language in your HTML file, you don't need to do it again. Your browser defaults to the most recently used language in the HTML file. You can put `<SCRIPT LANGUAGE="VBScript">` `</SCRIPT>` at the very beginning of your HTML file one time and forget about it. The rest of the scripts in your file will use VBScript.

You just saw the `Click` event. ActiveX controls support a wide variety of other events. The best way to know for sure which events a control supports is to consult the control's documentation or the ActiveX Control Pad's documentation. For your convenience, however, the following list describes the most prevalent and useful events:

- **BeforeUpdate** occurs before data in a control changes.
- **Change** occurs when the value property in a control changes.
- **Click** occurs when the user either clicks the control with the left mouse button or selects a single value from a list of possible values.
- **DblClick** occurs when the user clicks twice with the left mouse button rapidly.
- **DropButtonClick** occurs when a drop-down list appears or disappears.
- **KeyDown** occurs when a user presses a key.
- **KeyUp** occurs when a user releases a key.
- **KeyPress** occurs when the user presses an ANSI key.
- **MouseDown** occurs when the user holds down a mouse button.
- **MouseUp** occurs when the user releases a mouse button.
- **MouseMove** occurs when the user moves the mouse pointer over a control.
- **Scroll** occurs when the user changes a scroll bar.

N O T E Often, the easiest way to see the events, properties, and methods that an ActiveX control supports is to insert it into a Web page by using the ActiveX Control Pad, and pop open the Script Wizard. The Script Wizard lists all of the control's events in the left-hand pane. It lists all of the control's properties and methods in the right-hand pane. See Chapter 23, "ActiveX Control Pad," for more information. ■

Changing an Object's Properties

Many objects let the user input data. For example, the user can choose an item from a list, type text into an edit box, or click a check box. What good are those objects if you can't get and set their value? Not much. You read the value of most elements by using the object's `value` property in an assignment or logical expression. The following example assigns the text the user typed into the `txtTextBox` control to a variable called `str`. The next example compares the text the user typed into the `txtTextBox` with the word "Howdy."

```
str = txtTextBox.value
If txtTextBox.value = "Howdy" Then
```

You can also set the value of an element from within a script by assigning a string to the element's value, as follows:

```
txtTextBox.value = "New Contents of the Text Box"
```

The value property is the default property for most ActiveX controls which accept user input. Thus, you can use them in an expression without explicitly using the value property, like this:

```
alert txtTextBox
txtTextBox = "New Contents of the Text Box"
```

Tying It All Together with an Example

You've learned a lot in this chapter. You learned about the variety of ActiveX controls you can put in your Web page. You learned about using the OBJECT and PARAM tags to insert controls in your Web page. You also learned how to associate scripts with controls.

A full example might make things clearer for you, so that's exactly what you'll do in this section: work through a quick example. This example in particular is a simple Web page that contains a button. When the user clicks the button, she sees a pop-up menu that displays a list of Web sites which she can visit. As well, if the user doesn't click the button after 30 seconds, she sees a message telling her what to do. You can use the <OBJECT> tags and scripts in this example to add some slick navigational tools to your own Web site. Use these steps to create this example:

1. Start with an empty HTML file. All you really need in this file are the <HTML> and </HTML> tags.

2. Insert a Microsoft IE30 Button-Menu control called mnu into your Web page by using the following OBJECT tag. This is where the user will type his name. Set the Caption property to the text you want to display in the button (From Here in this case). Set each Menuitem[0], Menuitem[1], and Menuitem[2] to the text you want to display for each menu entry.

   ```
   <OBJECT ID="mnu" WIDTH=83 HEIGHT=39
     CLASSID="CLSID:52DFAE60-CEBF-11CF-A3A9-00A0C9034920">
     <PARAM NAME="Caption" VALUE="From Here...">
     <PARAM NAME="Menuitem[0]" VALUE="Jerry's Web Site">
     <PARAM NAME="Menuitem[1]" VALUE="Microsoft's Web Site">
     <PARAM NAME="Menuitem[2]" VALUE="MacMillan's Web Site">
   </OBJECT>
   ```

   N O T E You can add as many Menuitem[] properties to a Microsoft ActiveX menu as you require. You must number each Menuitem[] property consecutively, however, starting from zero. ■

3. Insert a Microsoft IE30 Timer control named clk into your Web page by using the following OBJECT tag. The only property you need to set is the Interval property, which determines the amount of time in milliseconds before the control fires the timer event.

```
<OBJECT ID="clk" WIDTH=39 HEIGHT=39
  CLASSID="CLSID:59CCB4A0-727D-11CF-AC36-00AA00A47DD2">
  <PARAM NAME="Interval" VALUE="30000">
</OBJECT>
```

4. Add the following script to the HTML file. This script handles the user's menu choice. When the user clicks the button and makes a choice, the browser calls the associated event-procedure and passes it the index of the menu choice, start from one (not zero). The `If ... Then ... Else` statement determines what the user chose and opens the appropriate Web page by assigning its address to `Window.location.href`.

```
<SCRIPT LANGUAGE="VBScript">
<!--
 Sub mnu_Select(item)
   If item = 1 then
     Window.location.href ="http://rampages.onramp.net/~jerry"
   elseif item = 2 then
     Window.location.href ="http://www.microsoft.com"
   elseif item = 3 then
     Window.location.href ="http://www.mcp.com"
   end if
 end sub
-->
</SCRIPT>
```

5. Add the following script to the HTML file. This script handles the timer when it goes off. It displays a message that tells the user how to use the button. It also resets the timer so that it doesn't go off again.

```
<SCRIPT LANGUAGE="VBScript">
<!--
 Sub IeTimer1_Timer()
   call window.alert("Choose a destination by clicking on 'From Here'")
   clk.Enabled = 0
 end sub
-->
</SCRIPT>
```

6. Save the HTML file and open it in Internet Explorer 3.0. Click the button, choose a menu option (see Figure 22.7), and the browser will open the Web page in the browser. Listing 22.1 shows you what the completed listing looks like.

Listing 22.1   The Whole Thing

```
<HTML>
<HEAD>
<TITLE>Menu</TITLE>
</HEAD>

<BODY>
<SCRIPT LANGUAGE="VBScript">
<!--
```

```
Sub IeTimer1_Timer()
  call window.alert("Choose a destination by clicking on 'From Here'")
  clk.Enabled = 0
end sub

Sub mnu_Select(item)
  If item = 1 then
    Window.location.href ="http://rampages.onramp.net/~jerry"
  elseif item = 2 then
    Window.location.href ="http://www.microsoft.com"
  elseif item = 3 then
    Window.location.href ="http://www.mcp.com"
  end if
end sub
-->
</SCRIPT>

<OBJECT ID="mnu" WIDTH=83 HEIGHT=39
  CLASSID="CLSID:52DFAE60-CEBF-11CF-A3A9-00A0C9034920">
  <PARAM NAME="Caption" VALUE="From Here...">
  <PARAM NAME="Menuitem[0]" VALUE="Jerry's Web Site">
  <PARAM NAME="Menuitem[1]" VALUE="Microsoft's Web Site">
  <PARAM NAME="Menuitem[2]" VALUE="MacMillan's Web Site">
</OBJECT>
<OBJECT ID="clk" WIDTH=39 HEIGHT=39
  CLASSID="CLSID:59CCB4A0-727D-11CF-AC36-00AA00A47DD2">
  <PARAM NAME="Interval" VALUE="30000">
</OBJECT>
</BODY>
</HTML>
```

FIG. 22.7

The user can't interact with Internet Explorer 3.0 as long as the message box is displayed.

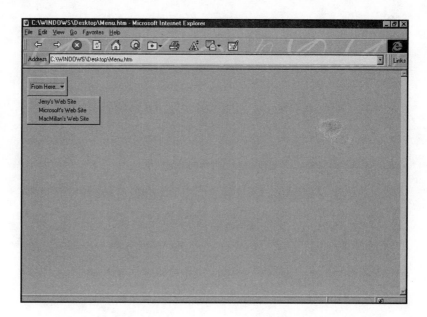

N O T E   You've punished yourself enough—you've inserted a few ActiveX controls into a Web page by hand. Although you can continue to work with ActiveX controls by hand, I don't recommend you do so. Microsoft's ActiveX Control Pad makes inserting ActiveX controls into a Web page far too simple for you to continue whacking yourself with the OBJECT tag. See Chapter 23, "ActiveX Control Pad," for more information. ■

N O T E   No doubt, you've seen the Netscape logo on just about every page on the Web. Did you know that you can also put the Internet Explorer logo on your Web page? Microsoft has a few more requirements than Netscape, however, and they're different for each of the logos you can use:

 This is a static logo. It doesn't contain any animation. If you use any of Internet Explorer's HTML extensions, such as background sounds, frames, and tables, you qualify to use this logo on your site. Microsoft also recommends, but doesn't require, that you showcase some of the more advanced HTML features like ratings and style sheets.

 This is the animated logo that you frequently see on Microsoft's Web site. All you have to do to use this logo is use one or more ActiveX controls on your Web site. Since you bought this book for that purpose, you shouldn't have any problems qualifying, right?

You can apply for and download the logo at **http://www.microsoft.com/powered/pbbo.htm**. There is a short questionnaire that you must complete in order to use the logo. After you've answered the questions, click Accept & Register at the bottom of the page, to download the file. ■

## CHAPTER 23

ActiveX Control Pad

by Jerry Honeycutt

In Chapter 22, "ActiveX Controls," you learned how to insert ActiveX controls into your Web pages by using the OBJECT and PARAM tags, but doing this by hand is nasty. First, you have to find the control's CLSID. Then, you have to type the OBJECT by hand and, worse yet, set all those properties by using those PARAM tags. If you're inserting more than a few ActiveX controls in your Web page, you'll quickly become frustrated.

The ActiveX Control Pad (from Microsoft, of course) makes the process a whole lot easier. It has three primary features, as follows:

- The control pad lets you easily insert ActiveX objects into your HTML files by using a graphical user interface. This means you don't have to mess around with those <OBJECT> tags at all. Point the control pad at a control, fill in the property sheet, and the control pad inserts all the required HTML into your Web page.

- The control pad provides the Script Wizard, which lets you create event handlers by associating events with actions. You make these associations by using a graphical user interface, too.

Download and install the ActiveX Control Pad

Microsoft provides the ActiveX Control Pad free of charge. This chapter shows you how to download and install it onto your computer.

Easily insert ActiveX controls into your Web page

There is no easier way to insert ActiveX controls in your Web page than by using the control pad. You'll learn how to insert controls automatically and set their properties.

Use the Script Wizard to create your scripts

The Script Wizard takes the drudgery out of writing scripts (JScript or VBScript). You'll learn how to point and click your way to a dynamic Web page.

Take complete control of your Web page's layout

You can take complete two-dimensional control of your Web page with the HTML Layout Control. Learn how to use it in this chapter.

■ The control pad lets you graphically edit layout controls. That means you can take full control of where objects are placed on your Web page. You can actually place and edit controls just like the form editor in Visual Basic. ■

The ActiveX Control Pad contains the complete VBScript reference and a complete HTML reference. It also contains a reference for all of Microsoft's ActiveX controls and the Internet Explorer Object Model. Unfortunately, it doesn't include a JScript reference. To access these references, choose Help from the control pad's main menu. Choose either VB Script Reference, HTML Reference, or Control Pad Help Topics.

Downloading and Installing the ActiveX Control Pad

Before you can take advantage of all this wonderment, you need to download the ActiveX Control Pad onto your computer. It's a free download available through Microsoft's Site Builder Workshop at **http://www.microsoft.com/workshop/author/cpad/download-f.htm**.

Click "Download" (in the middle of the Web page) to download the self-extracting, self-installing file that contains the ActiveX Control Pad, SETUPPAD.EXE, into a temporary directory on your hard drive. Then run SETUPPAD.EXE and follow the instructions you see on the screen.

The control pad uses VBScript by default. If you want to use JScript (Microsoft's version of JavaScript), you need to set it up to do so. Run the control pad. Then, choose Tools, Options, Script from the main menu. Select JavaScript, and click OK to save your changes. The Script Wizard (described later in this chapter) will now generate JScript language scripts instead of VBScript language scripts.

Getting Acquainted with the HTML Editor

Figure 23.1 shows you the control pad's HTML editor with an HTML file in it. You can open many HTML files in control pad because it's an MDI (Multiple Document Interface) application. You switch between each open HTML file by using the Window menu.

The control pad isn't the best program to use to edit files that contain a lot of HTML. In these cases, you can cut the OBJECT tags and scripts that it generates and paste them into your favorite HTML editor.

FIG. 23.1
The Editor window shows you only the contents of your HTML. Open the HTML file in your Web browser to preview what the Web page looks like.

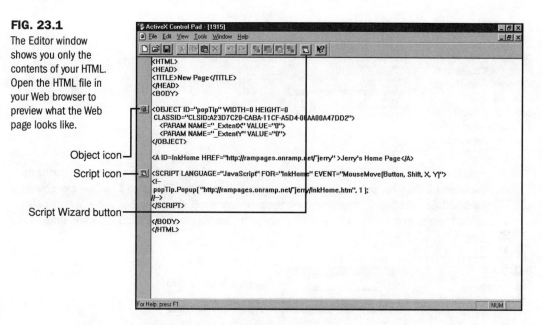

Object icon

Script icon

Script Wizard button

Part
IV

Ch
23

The HTML file you see in Figure 23.2 contains an object. You see an <OBJECT> tag. You also see the object icon in the margin of the Editor window. Click this icon to change the object next to it in the Editor window. Just below the object, you see a script. You can also see the script icon in the margin of the Editor window. You can edit the script using the Script Wizard by clicking this icon.

You can type any text you like in the Editor window. You can add forms to the file, for example. You can also add everyday text and tags such as headings, lists, and so on. If you're really into punishment, you can add objects to your HTML by typing them in the Editor window. Considering the features you learn in the next section, however, I strongly discourage you from doing that.

Placing Objects into Your HTML File

Inserting an object into an HTML file is easy. Position your mouse pointer to the point at which you want to insert an object, and right-click. Choose Insert ActiveX Control, and you'll see a dialog box similar to the one shown in Figure 23.2. The Insert ActiveX Control dialog box lets you pick one of the many controls that are available on your computer.

FIG. 23.2

The usable ActiveX controls are called things like `Microsoft ActiveX` *something* or `Forms 2.0 Something`. Don't use the objects whose names end with `Ctl`.

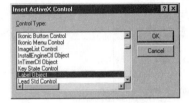

Select one of the controls, such as the `Label Object`, and click OK. The control pad opens up the Object Editor and property sheet for the control, as shown in Figure 23.3. You can change each of the control's properties by using the property sheet shown in the figure. You can also adjust the size of the control by grabbing one of its handles in the Object Editor and dragging it.

FIG. 23.3

Select a property, change it at the top of the property sheet, and click Apply to save your changes.

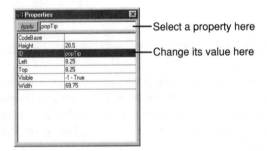

— Select a property here

— Change its value here

Using a control in this manner is called using it at *design time*. You're designing how the control is going to look on your Web page. The user uses the control at *runtime*, however, because all she is doing is using a page built with that control. Many controls require that you have a license to use it at design time. The controls you see in this chapter don't require a license, however, because they all come with Internet Explorer.

After you've made your changes to the control's property sheet, close both windows. After you close both windows, the control pad inserts the <OBJECT> and <PARAM> tags into your HTML file, which match how you filled in the property sheet. The control pad even fills in the CLSID for you.

You can change the properties in the HTML by using the control pad's text editor. The next time you open that control's property sheet, the property sheet will reflect any changes you made.

TIP The control pad has its own way to format the <OBJECT> and <PARAM> tags. You might as well make all of your tags consistent with the way the control pad formats them, as shown in this chapter's figures, so your scripts will be easier to read.

N O T E The control pad automatically recognizes any control that's installed on your system. Thus, if you've downloaded and installed controls as described in Chapter 22, "ActiveX Controls," you can insert them into your HTML file by using the control pad. ■

Editing Scripts with the Control Pad's Script Wizard

The Visual Basic and Visual C++ integrated development environments make the process of writing code as pleasant as possible. They provide text editors, graphical editors, and other tools to make managing objects much easier. The control pad is a lot like these environments. Whether or not you've ever used them, you'll appreciate the control pad's features that make editing scripts easier.

The control pad's Script Wizard helps you point and click your way to some terrific scripts. The best part about it is you don't have to know anything about the browser's object model; a control's properties, methods, and events; or even the runtime functions the browser provides. The Script Wizard displays them for you, so you can automatically insert statements in your scripts that use them. Point and click—literally.

To call it a wizard is a bit misleading, however, because it doesn't act or quack like other wizards in Windows 95. It does give you a smooth interface for editing the events of each object in your HTML file, though. In fact, it lets you edit an object's events in two different ways, as follows:

■ The List view lets you associate an event with a list of actions. You give arguments for those actions by answering questions in the Script Wizard.

■ The Code view is more of a traditional programming approach. You select an object's event, and edit the code in the window.

The following sections show you how to use both methods for editing event handlers in your HTML file. You can't use the Script Wizard to edit other types of scripts, though, such as support functions and subprocedures. That is, you can't use the Script Wizard to edit a function that's not an event handler. You can create event handlers that call your JScript or VBScript functions, however.

 T I P Are you unsure which properties, methods, and events a particular object in your HTML file supports? Click the Script Wizard button in the toolbar, and select that object in the left pane to see its events. Select the object in the right pane to see its properties and methods.

List View

The Script Wizard's List view lets you edit an event handler with the greatest of ease. Click the Script Wizard button in the toolbar to open the Script Wizard. Then click the List View button at the bottom of the window. You see the window shown in Figure 23.4.

FIG. 23.4

In most cases, the
List view is all you
ever need to create
exciting Web pages.

Events

Properties and Methods

Actions associated
with the selected
event

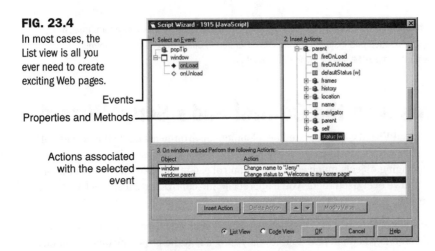

Here's how it works. You associate an object's event with another object's methods and properties by taking the following steps:

1. Expose the events for an object in the left pane by clicking the plus sign (+) next to the object. Select an event you want to handle. You can select the window object's onLoad event, for example.

2. Expose the methods and properties for an object in the right pane by clicking the plus sign (+) next to the object. Select a method or property that you want to associate with the event you selected in the left pane.

3. Click the Insert Action button below the bottom pane. If you select a property, control pad prompts you for the value you want to assign to that property in the event handler. If you pick a method that has arguments, control pad prompts you for the arguments you want to use. If you pick a method that doesn't have arguments, control pad doesn't prompt you for anything at all. After you've answered any questions that control pad asks, it inserts the association in the bottom pane.

4. You can rearrange the order of the actions in the bottom pane by selecting an action, and clicking the up and down arrow buttons to move it around in the list. You can also remove an action by selecting it and clicking the Delete Action button.

5. When you're happy with the way you're handling that particular event, you can move onto another object and another event, or close the Script Wizard by clicking OK.

N O T E The control pad creates a script block with an event-procedure or with the FOR and EVENT tags for each event that you handle. Alternatively, you can write a VBScript or JScript function that handles an event the way you want, and then associate an event with the function by using the Script Wizard. ■

Code View

If you're more comfortable with the traditional programmer view of life (optimistic about everything), you can use the Script Wizard's Code view. This works just like the List view, except you don't see a list of associated events and actions in the bottom pane. You see the actual code the Script Wizard creates, instead. You can also work with the full feature set of VBScript, JavaScript, and the object model using code view.

Click the Script Wizard button in the toolbar to open the Script Wizard. If you created the original script by using Code view, you won't be able to edit it by using List view. Then click the Code View button at the bottom of the window. You see the window shown in Figure 23.5.

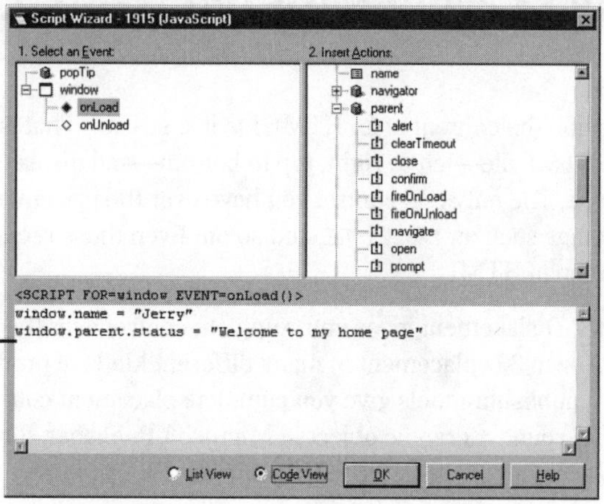

FIG. 23.5

You have to use the Code view if you want to use compound statements such as `If` and `For` in your scripts.

Code associated with the select event

You can insert actions into the bottom pane of the Code view just as you do in the List view. That is, you select an event in the left pane and select an action in the right pane. This view doesn't have an Insert Action button, however, so you double-click the action in the right pane to add it to the bottom pane.

After you've added a few actions to the event handler by double-clicking them in the right pane, you can edit the code any way you like. You can add or change the arguments for each method, add conditional and looping statements, or whatever you want. For that matter, you can use Code view's script editor to create your entire script, while only using the list of events and actions as a reference.

When you're happy with the way you're handling that particular event, you can move on to another event, or close the Script Wizard by clicking OK.

> **TIP** Code view's script editor supports cut, copy, and paste. Thus, you can edit scripts in Notepad and paste them back into the script editor.

If you'd rather edit your scripts by using the control pad's HTML editor, use Code view to insert all of the statements you think you'll use. Then, edit the templates that the Script Wizard put in the file using the HTML editor.

 Keep your Web browser running with the Web page you're working on open in it. Then, you can save the HTML file from control pad, flip to the browser, and refresh the Web page to see your changes while you're working in control pad.

Controlling Page Layout with the HTML Layout Control

Web browsers position the content of an HTML file in a stream. That is, the Web browser reads the contents of an HTML file—left to right, top to bottom—and displays its contents in the order it encounters it. The only real control you have over the placement of an HTML file's content is through tags such as TABLE, PRE, and so on. Even these require that you understand the stream orientation of HTML.

On the other hand, 2-D placement gives you complete control over the positioning of objects on a Web page. You've seen 2-D placement in many different kinds of products; Visio, Micrografx Designer, and most publishing tools give you complete placement control. You can position text so that it wraps around a graphic object in Microsoft Publisher, for example. In fact, the exception to 2-D placement seems to be HTML and the Web browsers that display it.

Microsoft created the ActiveX Layout Control expressly for this purpose. It gives you complete control over how you place objects on a Web page. You can place an object at a specific coordinate, for example. You can also overlap objects and make parts of some objects transparent so that objects in the background show through.

The layout control is similar to all the other objects you've seen in this book. You insert the layout control into your Web page by using the OBJECT tag. It's a container, however, that can host other objects. You'll learn more about this later in this chapter.

N O T E In the meantime, W3C (World Wide Web Consortium) is developing a standard for HTML that will give you compete control over how you position objects in a Web page. That is, you will be able to specify the exact horizontal (x) and vertical (y) positions (coordinates) of each object on a Web page. The problem is they haven't finished their work yet. So, you need to use the layout control for now.

You should know the layout control is a temporary solution. It goes away eventually. Thus, when the W3C defines its standard, and browsers such as Internet Explorer and Netscape support it, you won't need to use the layout control to have 2-D placement of objects.

Microsoft has committed to providing a utility you can use to convert your ActiveX Layout Control layouts to the new HTML standard for 2-D layouts when that standard becomes available. You can get more information about this standard at **http://www.w3.org/pub/WWW/TR/WD-layout.html**. ■

Understanding the Layout Control

The layout control is a container. This is the primary concept you need to understand about this object. It's an object you put in your Web page that can contain other objects. If you think of your Web page as a grocery bag, the controls you put in it are the groceries. With a layout control, you're going to put your groceries inside plastic bags (the layout control); then you drop the plastic bag into your grocery bag. Bet you didn't think of the layout control as produce, did you?

Another way to think of the layout control is as a form. It works just like forms you create in Visual Basic or in Visual C++. You drop a layout control on the Web page, and then you can arrange objects within it in any way you like. You can, in fact, use the layout control to create virtually any form using the Visual Basic form editor.

The following are some of the other things the layout control brings to the party:

■ You can overlap the objects you put on a layout control. Try that in HTML and you'll be very frustrated.

■ You can control the Z-order of each object you overlap. That is, you can control which objects are in front and which objects are in back.

■ You can make parts of some objects transparent so the objects in the background show through.

■ You can use a WYSIWYG environment to place and arrange objects on a layout control.

N O T E If you don't really need to control the exact location of the objects you're putting on a Web page, don't use the layout control. It comes with a heavy price (download time, compatibility with other browsers, and so on) that's hard to justify when you're just trying to be cute. ■

Inserting the Layout Control into an HTML File

A layout has two components. First, you insert the actual layout control into your Web page by using the <OBJECT> and <PARAM> tags. This tag looks very much like this:

```
<OBJECT CLASSID="CLSID:812AE312-8B8E-11CF-93C8-00AA00C08FDF"
ID="example" STYLE="LEFT:0;TOP:0">
<PARAM NAME="ALXPATH" REF VALUE="file:example.alx">
</OBJECT>
```

The other component is the layout itself. You store a layout in a separate text file that has the .ALX file extension. The ALXPATH property that you see in the previous example tells the layout control where to find this file. You can set this property to any valid URL, including a Web server. You'll learn more about the contents of the ALX file later in this chapter.

You don't have to insert the OBJECT tag or create the ALX file by hand, however, because the ActiveX Control Pad does it automatically. This tag simply loads an ActiveX object into your Web page that defines a region in which you can place other ActiveX objects or a layout. You don't use the Insert ActiveX Object menu item; you do use the Insert HTML Layout menu item—by taking the following steps:

1. Position your mouse pointer where you want to use a layout control, right-click, and choose Insert HTML Layout.

2. When the control pad asks you for a file name, type the name of the file in which you want to store the layout, and click Open. If the file doesn't exist, the control pad will ask you if you want to create it.

 TIP Before uploading your HTML and ALX files onto the Web server, double-check the paths in each OBJECT tag to make sure that they're valid for the server and directory structure that you're using.

As a result, the control pad inserts an OBJECT tag in your HTML file. Take a look at Figure 23.6—it shows what the tag looks like.

FIG. 23.6

Insert the layout control by using a plain old OBJECT tag.

Layout button

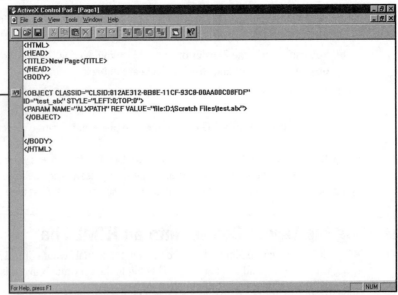

Editing the Layout

After you have inserted a layout control into your Web page, you can open it for editing. This allows you to place other ActiveX objects inside the layout control. Remember the layout button in Figure 23.6? Click this button, and the control pad opens the layout in the layout editor, as shown in Figure 23.7.

FIG. 23.7
The layout editor is very similar to VB's form editor.

Layout ——

Toolbox——

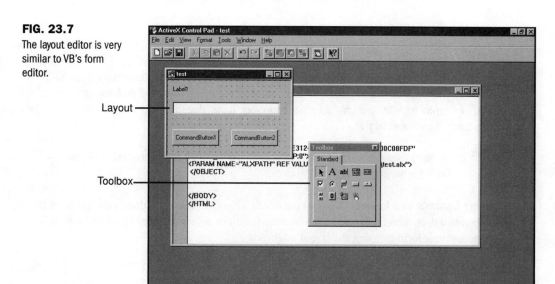

The layout editor lets you drag controls from the toolbox to the layout. Then you can rearrange the controls, write event handlers for controls, and so on.

Understanding What's in the ALX File As you've seen, the control pad stores layouts in separate files with the .ALX file extension. It gives the name of a layout file to the layout control by using the ALXPATH property.

The contents of the layout file aren't too mysterious. Each layout region begins and ends with the DIV and /DIV tags. You can give a region a name by using the ID attribute, and you specify the style of the region by using the STYLE attribute. The following is what the tag looks like:

```
<DIV STYLE="LAYOUT:FIXED;WIDTH:240pt;HEIGHT:180pt;">
</DIV>
```

What you do between the DIV tags is your business. You can insert objects into the layout by putting an OBJECT tag inside the layout's DIV tag. Inserting an object into a layout is not very different from inserting an object directly into your HTML file. The only difference is that you can specify the location of the object by using the properties inherited from the layout control. The following is what a label control looks like in a layout file:

```
<DIV STYLE="LAYOUT:FIXED;WIDTH:423pt;HEIGHT:265pt;">
    <OBJECT ID="MyLabel" CLASSID=
"CLSID:978C9E23-D4B0-11CE-BF2D-00AA003F40D0"
STYLE="TOP:83pt;LEFT:74pt;WIDTH:72pt;HEIGHT:18pt;ZINDEX:0;">
        <PARAM NAME="Caption" VALUE="MyLabel">
        <PARAM NAME="Size" VALUE="2540;635">
        <PARAM NAME="FontCharSet" VALUE="0">
        <PARAM NAME="FontPitchAndFamily" VALUE="2">
```

```
        <PARAM NAME="FontWeight" VALUE="0">
    </OBJECT>
</DIV>
```

You don't need to worry about understanding or setting the DIV tag's attributes (or the at-tributes of the objects you put in the layout control), because the control pad does it for you. I don't recommend editing a layout by hand anyway. It just doesn't make sense considering the tools that are available to you.

N O T E   You can also put scripts in an ALX file. You can put them before or after the <DIV> tag, but not inside the tag, however. ■

Adding Controls to a Layout   Adding controls to a layout is easy. You drag a control from the toolbox and drop it on the layout in the layout editor. The following steps show you how to create a simple form by using the layout editor:

1. Insert an HTML layout control into an HTML file and click the layout button next to it. You'll see the layout editor, as shown in Figure 23.8.

FIG. 23.8

You now have two files: an HTML file and an ALX file.

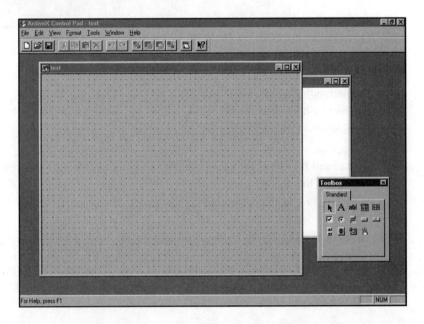

2. Drag a control from the toolbar and drop it onto the layout. Change the control's ID and any other properties which make sense for how you're using the control. If the control's property sheet isn't open, you can open it quickly by double-clicking the control. This property sheet is the same one you learned about earlier in this chapter. In this example, drag the TabStrip control to the layout and use the control's handles to resize it.

3. Repeat Step 2 for each control you want to add to your layout. In this example, add a label with its caption set to `Type your name:`; a text box; and a button with its caption set to `Display`.

4. Save the layout by clicking the Save button. Then, open the Web page in your browser by double-clicking the HTML file in Explorer. Figure 23.9 shows what the layout looks like in Internet Explorer.

FIG. 23.9

It works! It works!

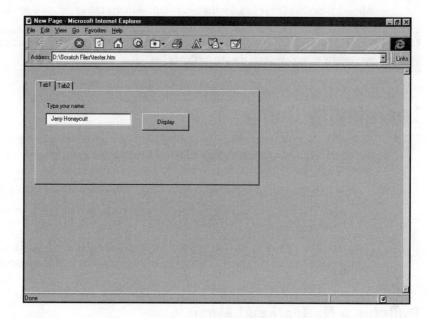

 You can create control templates in the layout editor. Create a new page in the toolbox, right-click a tab, and choose New Page. Drag a control from your layout onto the new page. You can then use this template at any time by dragging it onto a layout.

Adding Scripts to Your Layout You can add scripts to a layout just as you would add scripts to an HTML file. You use these scripts to handle the events fired by the objects in the layout. You can validate that the user has entered valid text in each field, for example. Click the Script Wizard button in the control pad's toolbar. In this case, the Script Wizard works exactly as you learned it would in the previous chapter.

N O T E In many cases, ActiveX controls that you put on a layout control have many more events, properties, and methods than the ActiveX controls you use directly on the Web page. For example, the label control you insert in a layout contains a `Picture` property, whereas the Microsoft IE30 Label control doesn't. Also, when you open the Script Wizard in an HTML layout control, you don't see the events, properties, and methods for ActiveX controls on your Web page or the browser's object model. ▪

Changing a Layout's Tab Order   When you create a form using the HTML layout control, the user can't tab between each field. That's because you haven't set up the tab behavior for each tab box.

To set up the tab behavior, first, double-click each control in the layout, and set the `TabStop` property to `True` and `TabKeyBehavior` to `False` (if the control supports it). Then, change the `TabIndex` property for each control in the layout. Set `TabIndex` to 0 for the first control in the tab order. Set `TabIndex` to 1 for the next control in the tab order, and so on.

 TIP   You can leave the property sheet open all the time. When you select a different object on the layout, the property sheet changes to the one for that object.

Learning by Doing

As always, the best way to learn something like the control pad is to try an example. This section contains a few examples that'll help you become an expert at using the control pad to create classy Web pages. Here are the examples you find in this section:

- You'll re-create the example from Chapter 22, "ActiveX Controls," by using the control pad. This will give you a whole new appreciation for how much trouble the control pad saves you.

- You'll learn how to add tooltips to your Web pages. That is, you'll learn how to add scripts to your Web page that pop up a little Help window when the user hovers over a link.

Building a Navigational Menu

Remember the example in Chapter 22? You'll create this same example by using the ActiveX Control Pad. In this example, when the user clicks a button, she sees a pop-up menu that displays a list of Web sites which they can visit. If the user doesn't click the button after 30 seconds, she sees a message telling her what to do. In Chapter 22, you had to insert the `OBJECT` and `PARAM` tags into the HTML file yourself—kind of a pain in the browser. Creating this Web page by using the control pad is a snap, however, with the following steps:

1. Open the ActiveX Control Pad and create a new HTML: click the New button, choose Internet Document (HTML) from the list, and click OK.

2. Position the cursor inside the `BODY` tags, and insert a Microsoft IE30 Button-Menu control. That is, right-click in the area inside the `BODY` tags, choose Insert ActiveX Control, choose Microsoft IE30 Button-Menu from the list, and click OK. You'll see the control editor, as shown in Figure 23.10.

FIG. 23.10
You learned about the control editor in "Placing Objects into Your HTML File" earlier in this chapter.

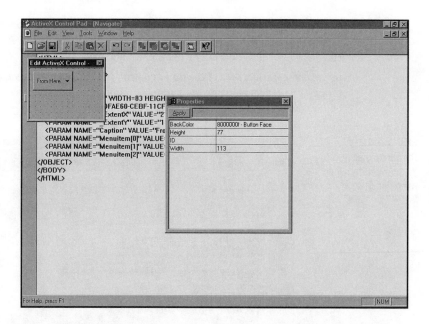

3. In the control editor, select the Microsoft IE30 Button-Menu control and stretch it, by dragging the control's handles, so that it's an appropriate size for a button. In the property sheet, change the ID property of the Button-Menu control to **mnu**, and change the Caption property to **From Here....** Then close the control editor. Your HTML file should look similar to Figure 23.11.

FIG. 23.11
Get used to the way the control pad formats OBJECT and PARAM tags, because you can't change it.

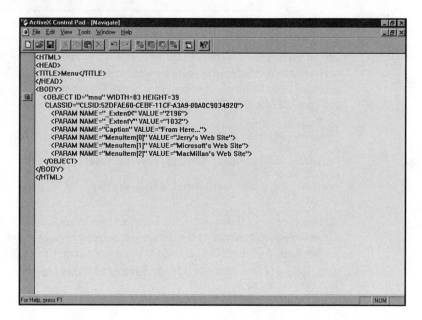

4. Position the cursor inside the BODY tags again, and insert a Microsoft IE30 Timer control. That is, right-click in the area inside the BODY tags, choose Insert ActiveX Control, choose Microsoft IE30 Timer from the list, and click OK.

5. In the control editor, select the timer control. In the property sheet, change the ID property to **clk** and change the **Interval** property to **30000**. Then close the control editor. Your HTML file should look similar to Figure 23.12

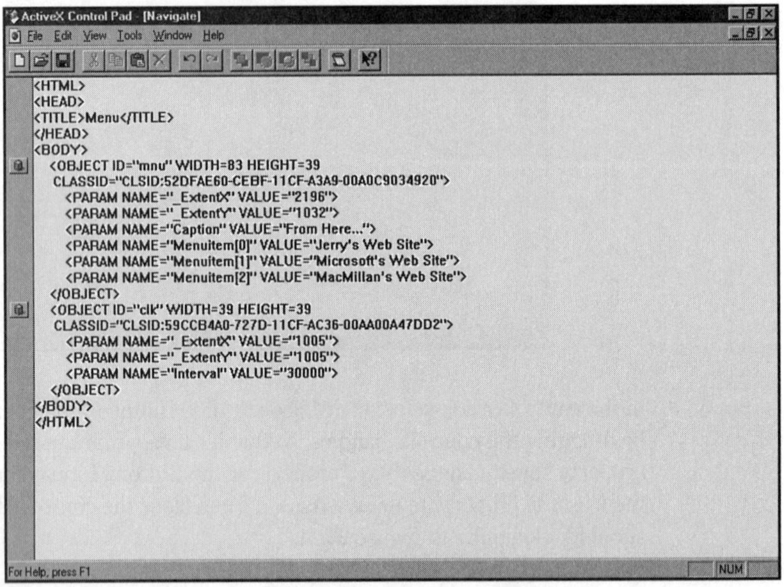

FIG. 23.12

The control pad inserts more PARAM tags than you did in Chapter 22, "ActiveX Controls."

```
ActiveX Control Pad - [Navigate]
File  Edit  View  Tools  Window  Help

<HTML>
<HEAD>
<TITLE>Menu</TITLE>
</HEAD>
<BODY>
   <OBJECT ID="mnu" WIDTH=83 HEIGHT=39
   CLASSID="CLSID:52DFAE60-CEBF-11CF-A3A9-00A0C9034920">
      <PARAM NAME="_ExtentX" VALUE="2196">
      <PARAM NAME="_ExtentY" VALUE="1032">
      <PARAM NAME="Caption" VALUE="From Here...">
      <PARAM NAME="Menuitem[0]" VALUE="Jerry's Web Site">
      <PARAM NAME="Menuitem[1]" VALUE="Microsoft's Web Site">
      <PARAM NAME="Menuitem[2]" VALUE="MacMillan's Web Site">
   </OBJECT>
   <OBJECT ID="clk" WIDTH=39 HEIGHT=39
   CLASSID="CLSID:59CCB4A0-727D-11CF-AC36-00AA00A47DD2">
      <PARAM NAME="_ExtentX" VALUE="1005">
      <PARAM NAME="_ExtentY" VALUE="1005">
      <PARAM NAME="Interval" VALUE="30000">
   </OBJECT>
</BODY>
</HTML>

For Help, press F1                                    NUM
```

6. Add a script that handles the Button-Menu's Select event, opening the appropriate Web site for each menu selection. Click the Script Wizard button in the toolbar, and change to the Code view. Select the Select event for the mnu object in the left pane. Add the following code to the script editor. Your Script Wizard window should look very similar to Figure 23.13. Click OK to save your changes.

```
If item = 1 then
  Window.location.href ="http://rampages.onramp.net/~jerry"
elseif item = 2 then
  Window.location.href ="http://www.microsoft.com"
elseif item = 3 then
  Window.location.href ="http://www.mcp.com"
end if
```

7. Add another script that handles the Timer's Timer event. Click the Script Wizard button in the toolbar, and change to the Code view. Select the Timer event for the clk object in the left pane. Add the following code to the script editor. Click OK to save your changes.

```
call window.alert("Choose a destination by clicking on 'From Here'")
IeTimer1.Enabled = 0
```

FIG. 23.13
After you've edited an
event by using the
Script Wizard's Code
view, you can't go back
to the List view.

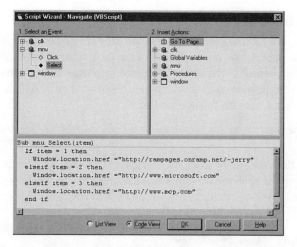

N O T E In the Script Wizard, the only way to see absolutely all of the methods and properties for a control is to change to the Code view. The List view hides many methods and properties of most controls. ▪

8. Save your HTML file, and open it in Internet Explorer 3.0. Your Web page should look something like Figure 23.14.

FIG. 23.14
You can insert these
navigational buttons at
the top, middle, and
bottom of your Web
page to make it easy
for the user to get
around.

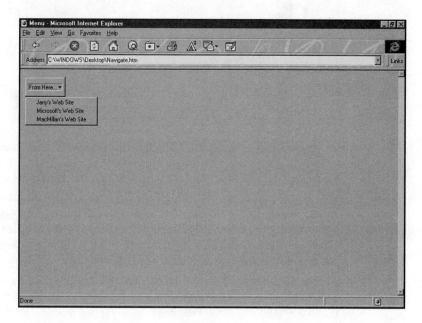

Pop-Up Help (Tooltips)

If you're not sure what tooltips are, try this little experiment: pop open Internet Explorer and hold the mouse pointer over one of the buttons in the toolbar. What do you see? A little window that displays the purpose of the button. Microsoft calls these *tooltips*. You can use tooltips on your Web pages to provide additional help to users when they hold their mouse pointer over a link. To add tooltips, take the following steps:

1. Open the control pad and create a new HTML file. Add a link to the body of the HTML file.

2. Add an ID to the link by using the ID attribute for anchors. That is, add ID=Name to the A tag. Figure 23.15 shows what this example looks like with a link that contains an ID of lnkHome.

FIG. 23.15

The Popup Window control only works with files using HTTP. That is, you can't use it with local files.

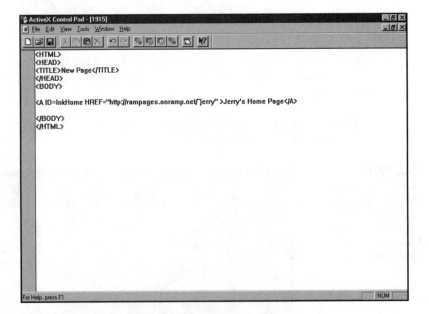

3. Insert the Microsoft IE30 Popup Windows Control to your HTML file (if you don't have this control, see Chapter 2, "HTML Page Design and Implementation," to learn how to get it). That is, right-click above the link you added in Step 2, choose Insert ActiveX Control, select Microsoft IE30 Popup Windows control from the list, and click OK. Change its ID to popTip by using the control's property sheet. Change its size so that it has no height and no width. Close the control editor.

4. Add the following script to your HTML file. This handles the MouseMove event for the link called lnkHome. In this case, it pops up the Popup Window with the contents of LNKHOME.HTM found on my Web site. You can replace this with an HTML file on your Web site as described in the next step.

```
<SCRIPT LANGUAGE="VBScript" FOR="lnkHome" EVENT=
"MouseMove(Button, Shift, X, Y)">
<!--
 popTip.Popup( "http://rampages.onramp.net/~jerry/lnkHome.htm", 1 );
//-->
</SCRIPT>
```

5. Create a file called LNKHOME.HTM that contains the formatting and text you want to display in the tooltip. You need to provide only the HTML and BODY tags, as well as the text you want to display in the Window. You can use the BODY tag's TOPMARGIN, LEFTMARGIN, BGCOLOR, and TEXT attributes to change the size of the tooltip window and its colors. Here's what the file I created looks like:

```
<HTML>
<BODY TOPMARGIN=0 LEFTMARGIN=0 BGCOLOR=YELLOW TEXT=BLACK>
Click this link to go to Jerry's home page
</BODY>
</HTML>
```

6. Save your new HTML file and load it in Internet Explorer 3.0. Move the mouse pointer over the link, and you should see a small window pop up that contains the words "Click this link to go to Jerry's home page," as shown in Figure 23.16. When you click the mouse pointer outside the pop-up window, the pop-up window goes away.

Part
IV

Ch
23

FIG. 23.16

You can also add tooltips for images, objects, and forms.

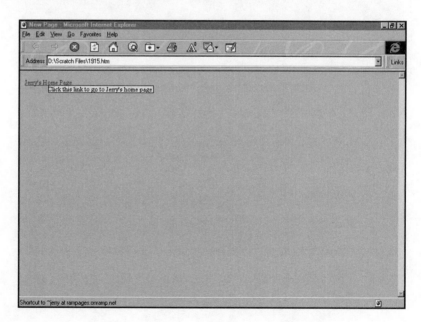

NOTE Microsoft's HTML Wizard is a very simple tool that enables you to use a folder's context menu to create brand-new HTML files using a template that you choose, without opening an HTML or text editor. You can get your own copy from Microsoft's Web site at **http://www.microsoft.com/intdev/download.htm**. ■

Programming and Scripting

## CHAPTER 24

Overview of Programming and Scripting

by Jerry Honeycutt

One of the recent and more exciting advances for Web developers, such as yourself, is the ability to script the Web page. You can liven up a Web page by adding animated decorations, for example. You can make your site more interactive or even completely dynamic, based upon a user's preferences. If you can dream it up, you can do it with HTML scripting.

Scripting also lets you push back work where it belongs, on the client, instead of bogging down your Web server with scripts and other server-side processes. For example, you can validate an HTML form before submitting the form to the server for processing. This cuts down on a tremendous amount of waste because you're sure the data is good before tying up your Web server's bandwidth.

The only problem is that you have to make decisions: Write a script or create a Java applet? Use JavaScript or VBScript? A combination of both? The candy store is open, so to speak. The following section will help you nail down how you want to approach this topic. ■

Know your options

You have many programming (Java, CGI) and scripting (VBScript, JavaScript) options available to you.

Work with your scripts in HTML files

HTML can get messy; it can get even messier if you don't carefully organize your scripts.

Learn the basics and script like a professional

Scripting isn't difficult. You'll learn the basic concepts such as events, Boolean logic, and more.

Use the scripting object model to the fullest

The scripting object model is somewhat skimpy, but you'll get a good overview in this chapter.

Picking the Best Tool

You can pick from a countless number of tools to program or script a Web page. You can go to the extreme and create an ActiveX object or Netscape Plug-In. In most cases, that's unnecessary. On the other side of the extreme, you can write a simple script that satisfies your requirements. Somewhere in the middle lies Java, CGI scripting, and so on.

Programming and Scripting Options

The list that follows describes each of the options you learn about in this book. Armed with this information, you can choose the appropriate scripting or programming tool for your situation:

- **CGI**   CGI is a server-side scripting language that generally handles form processing on the server. Many fear that CGI is going away, but they can relax—it'll be around for quite a while yet. You learn all about CGI scripting in Chapter 25, "All About CGI Scripts."

- **Java**   Java is a programming language based upon C++. It's different from C++, however, because it's built to distribute on a Web page. Like C++, you can use Java to create full-blown applications, even word processors. Whereas scripting will feel very natural to you if you're used to writing HTML code, Java is an intense language that requires significant programming skills. You can learn more about Java in Chapter 26, "Java."

- **JavaScript**   JavaScript (JScript for all the Microsoft folks) is a scripting language based on C++ that has gained worldwide acceptance on the Internet. You can use JavaScript to handle events on the Web page, glue objects together, and script the content of the page itself. Both Netscape Navigator and Internet Explorer support JavaScript. Learn about JavaScript in Chapter 27, "JavaScript/JScript."

- **VBScript**   VBScript is a scripting language that's based upon Visual Basic created by Microsoft. You also use it to create client-side scripts that handle events on the Web page, glue objects on the Web page together, create dynamic content, and more. Its biggest advantage is that you can leverage your existing knowledge about Visual Basic onto the Web page. Its biggest weakness? Internet Explorer is currently the only Web browser that directly supports VBScript. You can learn more about VBScript in Chapter 29, "VBScript."

Scripting Advantages

Scripting is the easiest way to add excitement to your Web pages. It takes little time to learn and the payoff is tremendous. Here's a taste of the advantages you'll find with scripting:

- You can associate a script with the events (click, mouse move, and so on) of just about any object you put on a Web page, even anchors. Then you can handle those events any way you like.

- You can generate HTML on-the-fly. That is, you can write a script that generates HTML as the browser loads the Web page. Variables affecting the HTML you generate can be things like cookies or the type of browser being used.

- You can implement many of the features that once required server-side processing by using a script. For example, you can create client-side image maps by using a script that handles an image's mouse-click event. You can validate forms before sending them to the server for processing.

- Scripts are embedded in the file with all of your HTML. Thus, working with, implementing, and distributing scripts is very easy. Unlike Java and ActiveX controls, you don't have to worry about getting the code onto the user's computer and you don't have to worry about correctly inserting the <OBJECT> tag into the Web page. All you need is your favorite text editor and a small bit of know-how.

Scripting Disadvantages

Scripting has its limitations. Here's a brief look at some of the most notable limitations:

- Everyone in the world can see your code. There are few secrets on the Internet. If you've written a nifty bit of script, there isn't anything stopping other folks from ripping-off your code. Likewise, there's nothing stopping you from lifting someone else's code, either.

- VBScript and JavaScript are just scripting languages. By themselves, you're limited to working within the Web page. You also have a limited set of keywords and runtime functions. You can get around a lot of scripting's limited feature set by creating your own ActiveX objects or Java applets, however.

- The designers of VBScript and JavaScript left out just about every keyword that could cause a security problem for your computer. You don't have to worry about viewing a Web page that uses scripts. The worse thing that could happen is that a poorly written script could cause the browser to crash. On the other hand, ActiveX objects and Netscape Plug-ins could be a problem. For example, Microsoft removed a function called CreateObject from VBScript due to security concerns. It didn't take long for some clever programmer to develop an ActiveX object that simulates the CreateObject keyword, however.

Part
V

Ch
24

Understanding Event-Driven Programming

Freud or Pavlov can do a much better job of explaining why people do certain things, but here's a stab at it. An event by any other name is still an event. Thus, you can easily understand how event-driven programming works because you handle events in your own life every day.

You deal with a variety of objects, such as a phone, a child, or a traffic light. These are all objects in your world. Each of these objects absorbs information about its environment, and responds based upon what it finds. The phone rings when someone calls. The child cries when she's hungry. The traffic light changes to yellow when its time is up. Each response is an event.

You're likely to handle each of these events in the same manner as most people. When the phone rings, you answer it, for example. When the child cries, you feed her. And when the traffic light changes to yellow, you drive faster. In this manner, you are an event handler. Here are some other events you possibly encounter and how you might handle them:

Object	Event	Your Response
Car	Dies	Kick the tires.
Cat	Meows	Pet the cat.
Microwave	Dings	Open and eat frozen din-
ner.		
Plant	Wilts	Water the plant.
TV	Plays Commercial	Go to the refrigerator.

What Are Events?

I'm moving on from reality to computers, now. Where do events come from? You. Events are mostly a result of something you do. You click the mouse on a button, for example, or you press the Tab key in a dialog box. You're not the only source of events, however. Windows also causes events such as a timer event, which occurs each time Windows' internal clock ticks. The Web browser creates events, too, such as an event that occurs each time it loads a Web page.

Take another look at the table you saw earlier and put the object and event names together in a sentence. The car dies. The cat meows. The plant wilts. Notice a pattern here? An event comes from an object. That is, objects cause events in response to something you do. In Windows, click a button and it causes a click event. Type a character in an edit box and it causes a change event. You can think of it like Pavlov's dog—ring a bell and the dog salivates.

Events have a lot of benefits over the old style of programming. The biggest benefit is the fact that you stay in control of your computer. Here are the highlights:

- Events let you determine the order in which a program executes.

  Clicking different parts of the screen, such as buttons, menus, and windows, causes different bits of code to execute. Contrast that to a procedural application that determines the order in which it executes: starts at the beginning, expects to see certain inputs at certain times, and stops when it hits the last line of code.

- When an event-driven program is waiting for an event, it's not using much of the computer's resources.

  This lets you do other tasks, such as run other programs. How does this work? Event-driven programs have a message loop that checks for messages; if no messages are waiting, they return control back to the operating system to give another program a shot.

- Events simplify programming.

  Instead of a program constantly checking each input device, it sits back and waits for the operating system to send it an event. The program doesn't miss out on input when it's not looking, either, because every input event is queued and waiting for the program until it gets around to it.

■ Events allow programs to work with objects that define their own behavior.

The operating system simply forwards events to an object, and the object's event handlers determine how to handle it. The program doesn't need to know how the object works internally, it just needs to know how to talk to it. For instance, you don't need to know how your car works to drive it, do you? You just send it events by using the gas pedal and steering wheel. Oh yeah, and the brake pedal!

How Events Work in Windows (and Other GUIs)

When you click an object, Windows sends messages to the object, letting it know what you've done. It also sends along any data the object needs to better understand the message, such as the mouse's position when you clicked a window. The object's message loop dispatches that message to the bit of code that handles the message. Objects that can receive these messages include windows, dialog boxes, icons, buttons, text boxes, and so on.

An object doesn't always know how to handle every message, either. A window may not understand what to do with a message telling it that the user is moving it. In these cases, the object gives the message back to Windows and tells it to handle the message. In essence, the object is saying "I'm too dumb to handle this, you figure it out."

Did you notice that you didn't see the term "event" once in the preceding paragraphs? That's because Windows doesn't do events, per se. It does messages. Remember that objects cause events in response to something you do to them. In VBScript, a button object causes a click event when it receives a mouse click message from Windows. Likewise, an edit box causes a change event when it receives keyboard messages from Windows that change the contents of the field.

How Events Work on a Web Page (Scripting)

In the previous section, you read that Windows sends messages to an object to let it know you've done something horrible, such as clicked it with the mouse. You don't have any way to receive messages, however. Even if you could receive messages, the object would get the message before you ever get a crack at it. So how is your script going to know that something has happened to the object?

In a script, an object causes events in response to the messages the object receives. When you click inside an object, Windows sends a message to the object telling it that you clicked the mouse. In turn, the object causes a click event and the browser looks for a special script, called an event handler, to address that event.

How does the browser know which event handler is the right one? In VBScript, the browser looks for a procedure whose name begins with the name of the object, followed by an underscore (_), and ending with the name of the event—Button_OnClick, for example. You specify the name of each object in your HTML file, and each type of object has a predefined set of event names, which you'll learn about later in this chapter. In JavaScript, you use an inline event handler (*scriptlet*) to execute a function. You'll learn more about handling VBScript events in Chapter 29, "VBScript," and handling JavaScript events in Chapter 27, "JavaScript/JScript."

Learning to Program: An Overview

Before you can venture off and start writing scripts, you need to understand a few concepts about programming. If you're already familiar with the basic programming skills, you can skip the rest of this section. You might consider visiting your bookstore to purchase one of Que's many programming books.

If you're an HTML developer, however, you probably need a quick tutorial on programming concepts such as loops and Boolean logic. The sections that follow provide you with an overview of these topics. Note that you can't possibly learn everything you need to know about programming in these few pages. This will introduce you to the concepts, though.

Variables

Variables are really just names for a small chunk of memory in which you store a value. Variables can store any number or any bit of text. You don't need to worry about where in the computer's memory the script stores the variable's value because you use the variable's name to change or read its value.

Mathematical Expressions

It takes two things to make a mathematical expression: values (numbers or strings) and operators. You understand values; you called them operands in school. You probably already understand the idea of an *operator*, too. When you add two numbers by using a calculator, you enter the first number, press the plus sign (+), enter the second number, and press the Enter key. The plus sign is an operator. It performs an operation on two numbers. Likewise, the minus (–), multiplication (*), and division signs (/) are operators.

Boolean Expressions

Where mathematical expressions let you evaluate complex calculations, Boolean expressions let you make decisions. Mathematical expressions evaluate to a number. Any number. The result depends entirely on the expression. Boolean expressions, on the other hand, evaluate to one of two values: True or False. Always. They never evaluate to 10, 56, or the string "Hello," for example.

You'll learn about two types of Boolean operators. Comparison operators are the heart and soul of Boolean expressions. They let you compare two values any way you like. Logical operators let you combine multiple comparison operators in a single expression. These are very similar to writing complex mathematical expressions.

Comparison Operators   Comparison operators compare two expressions and return True if the comparison is true or False if the comparison is false. That's it. For example, 1 < 2 returns True because one is, indeed, less than two. On the other hand, 1 > 2 returns False because one is never greater than 2. Table 24.1 describes the most common comparison operators you find in most programming languages.

Table 24.1   VBScript Operators

Symbol	Description	Syntax
=	Equal	*Expression1 = Expression2*
<> (!=)	Unequal	*Expression1 <> Expression2*
<	Less than	*Expression1 < Expression2*
>	Greater than	*Expression1 > Expression2*
<=	Less than or equal	*Expression1 <= Expression2*
>=	Greater than or equal	*Expression1 >= Expression2*

Logical Operators   *Boolean logic* is one of the most difficult concepts to teach someone who is logically challenged. Boolean logic is very easy, however, because it's one of those things into which you can plug a couple of values and get a predictable result in return. For example, A And B is always True if both values are True. It's always False if either value is False. It's a cookie-cutter approach to logic:

Not	The Not operator negates a Boolean value. Not True returns False, for example, and Not False returns True.
And	The And operator compares two Boolean values and returns True if both values are True. Otherwise, it returns False. Table 24.2 shows the result for each combination of *Boolean1* and *Boolean2*.
Or	The Or operator compares two Boolean values and returns True if either value is True. Otherwise, it returns False. Table 24.3 shows the result for each combination of *Boolean1* and *Boolean2*.
Xor	The Xor operator compares two Boolean values and returns True if both values are different. Otherwise, it returns False. Table 24.4 shows the result for each combination of *Boolean1* and *Boolean2*.

Part
V

Ch

24

Table 24.2   *And* Operator

Boolean1	*Boolean2*	Result
True	True	True
True	False	False
False	True	False
False	False	False

Table 24.3 *Or* Operator		
Boolean1	**Boolean2**	**Result**
True	True	True
True	False	True
False	True	True
False	False	False

Table 24.4 *Xor* Operator		
Boolean1	**Boolean2**	**Result**
True	True	False
True	False	True
False	True	True
False	False	False

Decisions

VBScript and JavaScript contain a variety of statements that you can use to control how your script flows. The syntax is different in each language, but they have roughly the same form.

The most basic type of decision-making statement you'll use is the `If...Then...Else` statement. This statement evaluates a decision and conditionally executes a block of statements depending on the result. It has many different forms, but in general it looks like this:

```
If Condition Then
    Statements
Else
    Statements
End If
```

The first line is the heart of the `If...Then...Else` statement. It begins with the keyword `If` and ends with the keyword `Then`. `Condition`, the middle part, is the criteria. This is a Boolean expression that evaluates to either `True` or `False`. You learned to write Boolean expressions earlier in this chapter. If the condition is `True`, the script executes the first block of statements; otherwise, the script executes the second block of statements.

Loops

You can write a script that executes the same statements over and over again until you've had enough. You call this *looping*. The primary reason to write a loop is so you don't have to repeat a bunch of statements, like this:

```
Add the first number to sum
Add the second number to sum
Add the third number to sum
Add the fourth number to sum
Add the fifth number to sum
```

N O T E Pseudo-code is a tool that programmers use to plan how their program is going to flow. It's really nothing more than plain English statements that closely resembles the programming constructs. ▪

You can put these statements in a loop, instead, and let the script repeat them for you:

```
repeat the following line five times
    assign the next number to sum
```

Both VBScript and JavaScript support a variety of looping mechanisms, but the For loop is the most straightforward. Its form is similar in both scripting languages. The syntax of the For loop is very simple:

```
For Counter = Start To End
    Statements
```

Statements is called the *body* of the loop. *Counter* is any numeric value. This is the *loop control variable* that contains the current count. The loop starts counting at the value in *Start* and ends at the value in *Counter*.

N O T E In JavaScript, For loops work differently than in VBScript. JavaScript For loops are more than just counters. A loop will execute until any arbitrary condition becomes false, such as the loop-control variable equaling the square root of your age. As well, you can use more than a numeric variable in a loop. ▪

Functions and Subprocedures

Functions and procedures let you divide your scripts into chunks that you can call from any other script. Invoking a procedure in your scripts is called *calling* a function or procedure.

You give a function a name and a list of arguments. You call the function by its name and pass arguments by their position. A function can return a value to the calling script; thus, you can use a function on the right side of an equal sign, like this:

```
Result = MyFunction( Variable1, Variable2 )
```

Here's what a function looks like:

```
Function Name( Argument-List )
     Statements
End Function
```

Subprocedures are unique to VBScript. The only difference between a subprocedure and a function is that a subprocedure can't return a value. Thus, you can't use a function on the right side of an equal sign (=).

Understanding the Scripting Object Model

The scripting object model (object model, from now on) exposes a variety of Web-related objects (windows, links, documents, etc.) to your scripts. You can manipulate the Web browser and Web page, for example, because the object model makes much of the internal data and functions available to your scripts. Both VBScript and JavaScript use the same object model.

This section gives you a brief overview of the object model as shown in Figure 24.1. It describes the objects you see in the model, the relationship between each object, and how to access the properties, methods, and events in each object. The next two chapters describe how to use these objects in your scripts.

FIG. 24.1
A shaded box indicates that one or more of that particular object can exist. You can have multiple frames in a window, for example.

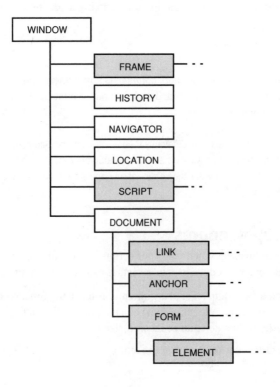

TIP The best way to see all of the object model's properties, methods, and events is to browse them in the ActiveX Control Pad. See Chapter 23, "ActiveX Control Pad," for more information. You can also access Microsoft's object model document at **http://www.microsoft.com/intdev/sdk/docs/scriptom**.

window

A window object is always at the top level. This is easier to understand if you relate the model to what you actually see on your desktop. You see the browser window first. Then, you see a document inside of the browser window, forms inside a document, and so on. A window object contains a variety of properties, methods, and events. Table 24.5 gives you a brief overview.

Table 24.5   *window* Properties, Methods, and Events

Properties	Methods	Events
name	alert	onLoad
parent	confirm	onUnload
self	prompt	
top	open	
location	close	
defaultStatus	setTimeout	
status	clearTimeout	
frames	navigator	
history		
navigator		
document		

Every window contains a handful of other objects, including a history, a navigator, a location, scripts, and a document. A window can also contain one or more frames. You access each of these objects by using the corresponding properties as shown in Table 24.6.

Table 24.6   Accessing a Window's Objects

To access this:	Use this property:
Frame	frames
History	history
Navigator	navigator
Location	location
Script	*procedure*
Document	document

As a general rule, you access properties that have plural names, such as `frames`, by using an array. You can tell how many objects are in the array by using the `length` property, like this:

```
window.frames.length
```

Each element of that array represents a single object of that type. To access the second frame in a window, for example, use the following syntax (start counting from 0):

```
window.frames(1)
```

> **TIP**
> You don't have to use the `window.`*name* form to access a window's properties or methods because the window object is always in scope. You can just use the *name* instead. That means that the window object's property and method names are reserved words, though, so you can't use them for variable names.

Frame A window can optionally contain one or more frames. It depends on whether or not you use the `<FRAMESET>` tag in your Web page. If you do use it, the `frames` array contains an element for each frame you define—starting from 0. The following VBScript script gets the name of each frame in the window, for example:

```
For intI = 0 to frames.length - 1
    strName = frames(intI).name
Next
```

You can also use a frame by name if you give it a name in the `<FRAME>` tag. Consider this frame:

```
<FRAME NAME="Body" SRC="http://www.myserver.com/body.html">
```

You can access it by using its name, like this:

```
strName = Body.name
```

The `frame` object doesn't introduce any new properties, methods, or events. That's because each `frame` object is really just a `window` object. You use the same properties, methods, and events you saw in Table 24.6 in the previous section.

The important thing to note here is how you get around frames. That is, if you define a frame called `Body` that contains a frame called `TopBody` inside it, that also contains a frame called `ReallySmallFrame`, you can access the properties of `ReallySmallFrame` like this:

```
Top.Body.TopBody.ReallySmallFrame.name
```

What's going on here? Think of a frame as a window for a moment and it should become clear. You have a window called `Top`, that contains a window called `Body`, that contains a window called `TopBody`, that contains a window called `ReallySmallFrame`.

You can also access each frame by using the `frames` array (numbered list of frames) of each window (frame). Assuming that each of the frames you saw earlier is the first frame defined in each HTML file, you can access them like this:

```
Top.frames(0).frames(0).frames(0).name
```

If `ReallySmallFrame` was actually the second frame in `TopBody`, you'd access it like this, instead:

```
Top.frames(0).frames(0).frames(1).name
```

history   Each window contains a `history` object that contains the window's history. That is, it contains a list of every Web page it has displayed in that window. Table 24.7 shows you its properties.

Table 24.7   *history* **Properties and Methods**

Properties	Methods
length	forward
	back
	go

navigator   Each window contains a `navigator` object that contains information about the Web browser. Table 24.8 shows you its properties.

Table 24.8   *navigator* **Properties**

Properties
appCodeName
appName
AppVersion
userAgent

location   Each window contains a `location` object that defines the URL of the Web page it contains. Table 24.9 shows you its properties.

Table 24.9   *location* **Properties**

Properties
href
protocol
host
hostname
pathname
port
search
hash

Script   Scripts live within the window object. Never mind that you define scripts within the document object. The model stores them under the window object. Each scripting object is actually the name of a procedure, subprocedure, or function.

If you're working with scripts inside of frames, you can get quick-and-easy access to a window's procedures by using the window's name in conjunction with the procedure's name. For example, if you're writing a script in a deeply embedded frame, you can access a script in the top-level window like this:

```
top.MyProcedure()
```

You can access scripts within other frames by using the frame name or the parent keyword, instead. To access a script in the second frame below the current window, use this statement:

```
frame(1).MyProcedure()
```

To access a script in the parent frame, use this statement:

```
parent.MyProcedure()
```

document

The next major object in the model is the document object. This represents the actual Web page that you see in the window, including the text, links, forms, and so on that you see on the page. A document object contains a variety of properties and methods. Table 24.10 gives you a brief overview.

Table 24.10   *document* Properties and Methods

Properties	Methods
linkColor	write
aLinkColor	writeLn
vLinkColor	close
bgColor	clear
fgColor	open
anchors	
links	
forms	
location	
lastModified	
title	
cookie	
referrer	

Every document contains a handful of other objects, including links, anchors, and forms. You access each of these objects by using the corresponding properties, as shown in Table 24.11.

Table 24.11   Accessing a Document's Objects

To access this:	Use this property:
Link	links
Anchor	anchors
Form	forms

As you've learned, you access properties that have plural names, such as `forms`, using an array. You can tell how many objects are in the array by using the `length` property, like this:

```
document.forms.length
```

Each element of that array represents a single object of that type. To access the first link in a document, for example, use the following syntax (start counting from 0):

```
document.forms(0)
```

Since scripts are owned by the window, not by the document, you have to reference a document's properties and methods by name, like this:

```
document.name
```

You can't drop off the `document.` portion like you can drop off the `window.` portion of a `window` object's properties and methods. You can access forms and objects without using document, though.

link   The document's `links` property is a read-only array of `link` objects—you know, links on the Web page that you define with the `<A HREF=URL>` and `</A>` tags. You access it like other object arrays, except that you can't refer to a link by name. The following example is the third link on the document:

```
document.links(2)
```

Table 24.12 describes the `link` object's properties and events.

Table 24.12   *link* Properties and Events

Properties	Events
href	mouseMove
protocol	onMouseOver
host	onClick
hostname	

Part
V

Ch
24

continues

Table 24.12   Continued

Properties	Events
port	
pathname	
search	
hash	
target	

anchor   The document's `anchor` property is a read-only array of `anchor` objects. You create anchors on the Web page by using the `<A NAME="`*`NAME`*`">` and `</A>` tags. You access it like other object arrays, except that you can't refer to an anchor by name. The following example is the third anchor on the document:

```
document.anchors(2)
```

Table 24.13 describes the `anchor` object's properties.

Table 24.13   *anchor* Properties

Properties
name

form   A `document` object can contain one or more `form` objects. It depends on whether or not you've used the `<FORM>` tag in your Web page. If you've used forms in your Web page, `document.forms.length` indicates the number of forms on the page. The following script gets the name of each form in the window:

```
For intI = 0 to document.forms.length - 1
    strName = frames(intI).name
Next
```

You can also use a form by name if you give it a name in the `<FORM>` tag. You see plenty of examples of both methods in the next two chapters. For now, consider this form:

```
<FORM NAME="MyForm">
```

You can access it by using its name, like this:

```
strName = document.MyForm.name
```

Table 24.14 describes the `form` object's properties, methods, and events.

Table 24.14 *form* **Properties, Methods, and Events**

Properties	Methods	Events
action	submit	onSubmit
encoding		
method		
target		
elements		
hidden		

The form object contains one additional object: the element object. You access it by using the elements array. You have to explicitly use the document.*form* way to access a form because the form and document objects aren't in the same scope. Remember that scripts belong to the window and forms belong to the document.

You can put scripts inside of a form object, however. In that case, you don't have to use the document. method for accessing the form in your script. You can just use the form name. Here's an example of a script embedded inside of a form object:

```
<FORM NAME="MyForm">
<INPUT NAME="txtName" TYPE="TEXT" SIZE="40">
<INPUT NAME="btnFill" TYPE="BUTTON" VALUE="Fill">
<SCRIPT FOR="btnFill" EVENT="onClick">
<!--
 txtName.value = "Jerry"

</SCRIPT>
</FORM>-->
```

If you want to access a form's elements outside of the <FORM> tag, you have to fully qualify the property, like this:

```
document.MyForm.txtName.value
```

element A form contains one or more elements, or controls as you probably know them. These include buttons, text boxes, and list boxes. You access each element by using the elements array. The following example script gets the name of each element in a form:

```
For intI = 0 to document.MyForm.elements.length - 1
    strName = document.MyForm.elements(intI)
Next
```

You can also reach an element by using its name if you give it a name in the <INPUT> tag. You see plenty of examples of both methods in the chapters that follow. For now, consider this frame:

```
<INPUT NAME="btnDone" TYPE="BUTTON" VALUE="Done">
```

You can access its current value by using its name, like this:

```
strCaption = document.MyForm.btnDone.value
```

Table 24.15 describes the `element` object's properties, methods, and events.

Table 24.15 *element* **Properties, Methods, and Events**

Properties	Methods	Events
form	click	onClick
name	focus	onFocus
value	blur	onBlur
defaultValue	select	onChange
checked	removeItem	onSelect
defaultChecked	addItem	
enabled	clear	
listCount		
multiSelect		
listIndex		
length		
options		
selectedIndex		

Working with Scripts

Before you learn how to write scripts, there are a few basic things you need to know about scripting. Scripting is interpretive. That is, it's not a compiled language. The browser downloads an HTML file and, at the appropriate moment, interprets the script line by line.

As such, you're actually embedding these scripts within your HTML file. That is, your JavaScript or VBScript code will sit right alongside your HTML. There are a few rules you should follow, then, when placing scripts in your HTML files. The sections that follow cover these rules, which will make your job much easier.

Embedding Scripts in Your Web Pages

You embed scripts in an HTML file by using tags, much like any other content you put in a Web page. Scripts are put between the <SCRIPT> and </SCRIPT> container tags, as shown in Listing 24.1.

Listing 24.1   What the Browser Does at Parse Time

```
<SCRIPT LANGUAGE="VBSCRIPT">
<!--
    Alert "Howdy from Texas" ' Evaluated & executed when the page is loaded

    Sub Pause ' Evaluated and stashed away for later use
        MsgBox "Click on OK to Continue"
    End Sub
-->
</SCRIPT>
```

Use the HTML comment tags to hide scripts from those browsers that don't support them.

What all this means isn't important right now. What is important is what your browser does with the script. When your browser loads a Web page that includes scripts (*parse time*), it immediately evaluates each <SCRIPT> block it encounters. It grabs everything in this block and passes it off to the scripting engine.

The scripting engine takes a look at the <script> block the browser gave it and looks for any subprocedures and variables outside a subprocedure (global variables). It compiles these and stashes their names in an internal table for later use. If you had a subprocedure called DisplayName, for example, the scripting engine compiles that subprocedure's code, saves it, and puts the name of the subprocedure in a table. Later, when you call the subprocedure called DisplayName, the scripting engine looks up that procedure in the table and executes the code associated with it.

You may have noticed in Listing 24.1 that you can include statements outside of a subprocedure or function. The scripting engine immediately executes statements it finds outside of a subprocedure. This is called *immediate execution*. You refer to scripts that the browser executes immediately as *inline scripts*.

Just remember the browser executes inline scripts as it loads the Web page. It saves variables and subprocedures in a symbol table for later use.

Managing a VBScript Project

As a Web developer and a script writer, you have to do without a lot of creature comforts. You don't have a full-blown VBScript or JavaScript script-development environment like Visual Basic or Visual C++'s integrated development environment (IDE). You don't have a form editor that lets you visually create forms and write code for them. You don't have a sophisticated object browser.

Microsoft has recently released a script debugger that you can use to debug VBScript and JavaScript scripts. You can download your own copy at **http://www.microsoft.com/vbscript**.

What you do have is a small collection of tools that you can cobble together to create the next best thing to a development environment. You'll use your favorite text editor (Visual Notepad) in conjunction with the ActiveX Control Pad to edit your scripts, for example. Chapter 23, "ActiveX Control Pad," shows you some tools you can create that help you debug scripts. You can even do some visual editing with the ActiveX Layout Control and Control Pad.

You're free from most of the rules that encumber Visual Basic or Visual C++ developers, though. This means that you can do pretty much as you see fit—as long as the browser can understand the contents of each <SCRIPT> block. The rest of this section suggests a few rules you can impose on yourself to make your job just a bit easier. It suggests how you can store scripts in HTML files. It also recommends a file structure to use for organizing ActiveX Web pages.

Organizing Inline Scripts   You'll add a lot of inline scripts in your Web pages. Inline scripts are blocks of statements that you write outside of a normal procedure or function. The browser executes them in the order it encounters them as it opens the Web page. This is a great way to do work as the browser opens the Web page or to even change the contents of the HTML file itself.

Put an inline script anywhere in an HTML file where you feel it's appropriate. If you want to dynamically add content to the HTML file, for example, put a script in the exact location where you want to add the content. Listing 24.2 is an example of such a script. It prompts you for your name and adds a greeting to the HTML file as the browser opens it.

Listing 24.2   Organizing Inline Scripts in an HTML File

```
<HTML>
This is static content on the Web page.<BR>

<SCRIPT LANGUAGE="VBScript">
<!--
 strName = InputBox( "What is your name?" )
 Document.Write "Howdy " & strName &
". This is dynamic content on the Web page.<BR>"
-->
</SCRIPT>

This is more static content on the Web page.
</HTML>
```

Figure 24.2 shows you what this HTML file looks like in Internet Explorer.

FIG. 24.2

The first and last lines of text are static text contained in the HTML file. The middle line is dynamic text created by a script.

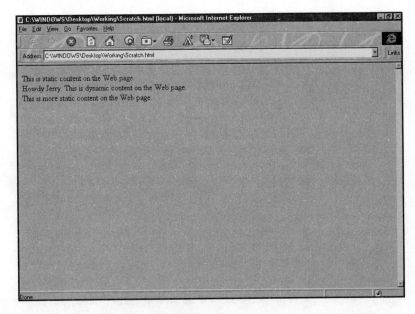

Organizing Scripts in the *<HEAD>* Block Many scripts you create contain procedures that have a supporting role. If you're creating a Web page that displays the average sale for each of four territories, for example, you'll probably create a function called GetAverageSale and then invoke it once for each territory's numbers. Also, if you have a handful of statements you can use in many different places, you'll put those in a procedure and invoke it by name from each place.

You should put most of your scripts containing procedures in the <HEAD> block of your HTML file as shown in Listing 24.3. Why? Two reasons. First, organizing most of your scripts at the beginning of your HTML file separates the scripts from the content of your page. You can find scripts faster this way.

Secondly, scripts are evaluated as the browser loads the Web page—top to bottom. The browser doesn't actually stash away a procedure's name until the browser sees the <SCRIPT> block and passes it to the scripting engine. Thus, if you reference a procedure's name in an inline script that isn't defined until later in the HTML file, your script may not work properly. The easiest way to get around this problem is to make sure all of your general procedures are defined before any of your inline scripts.

Listing 24.3   Organizing Procedures in an HTML File

```
<HTML>
<HEAD>

<SCRIPT LANGUAGE="VBScript">
<!--
 Dim sstrUserName

 Function GetAverageSale( sngTotalSales, intSalesQty )
      GetAverageSale = sngTotalSales / intSalesQty
 End Function
-->
</SCRIPT>

</HEAD>

<BODY>

<SCRIPT LANGUAGE="VBScript">
<!--
 MsgBox "Hello " & sstrUserName
 MsgBox "Average sale is " & GetAverageSale( 1000, 20 )
-->
</SCRIPT>

</BODY>
</HTML>
```

Organizing Event Handlers   If you followed the arguments in the previous section, you'd put event handlers for forms in the <HEAD> section of your HTML file. In fact, you might put all of a form's event handlers inside of a single <SCRIPT> block so they're all together as one big blob of script.

You can make life easier on yourself if you don't, however. Put event handlers within the <FORM> block for two reasons:

- You'll have an easier time maintaining a form's event handlers if you organize them near the actual form. You don't want to have to flip back and forth between the form and the top of the HTML file.

- Putting a form's event handlers inside of the <FORM> block prevents you from having to specify the form's name when accessing an element's properties and methods. Normally, you access the value of a text box element with a statement such as *form*.*element*.value. If you put the scripts inside the <FORM> block, however, you can access the value of the same text box with a statement like *element*.value. This cuts down on the typing.

Listing 24.4 shows you an example of an HTML file that contains a form. You'll notice a script that contains an event handler for the Hello button within the <FORM> block. Not only does this example show you the merits of keeping your event handlers near the forms they service, it shows you that you don't have to use a form's name to access its elements.

Listing 24.4   Organizing Event Procedures for a Form

```
<HTML>
<FORM NAME="Myform">
Name:
<INPUT NAME="MyName" TYPE="TEXT" >
<INPUT NAME="Hello" TYPE="BUTTON" VALUE="Hello">

<SCRIPT LANGUAGE="VBScript">
<!--
 Sub Hello_OnClick
     MsgBox "Hello " & MyName.Value
 End Sub
-->
</SCRIPT>
</FORM>
</HTML>
```

N O T E   You can't put scripts within an <OBJECT> block, so you can't use this method to keep event procedures near the objects to which they tend. Therefore, put event procedures for ActiveX objects in the <HEAD> section of your Web page or below the </OBJECT> tag. You can keep an object's event procedures together in a single <SCRIPT> block to make them easier to deal with, though. ■

Organizing Scripts Within Frames   As you've learned, you can divide the browser window into smaller sections called frames. The entire browser window contains a single HTML file, and each frame contains yet another HTML file. Consider this HTML file, for example:

```
<HTML>
<FRAMESET COLS="10%,90%">
    <FRAME NAME="Left" SRC="left.html">
    <FRAME NAME="Right" SRC="right.html">
</FRAMESET>
</HTML>
```

This example is a Web page that contains two frames. The left frame contains the HTML file called left.html, and the right frame contains the HTML file called right.html. So, in this arrangement, where do you put your scripts? It depends. The important considerations are that the top-level HTML file is always available, and the HTML files in each frame may or may not always be available.

Thus, if you want to have access to a script (procedures or global variables) all the time, from any frame, you should put them in your top-level HTML file, like this:

```
<HTML>
<SCRIPT LANGUAGE="VBScript">
<!--
 Dim strYourName
 Sub DisplayName
     MsgBox strYourName
 End Sub
-->
</SCRIPT>
<FRAMESET COLS="10%,90%">
    <FRAME NAME="Left" SRC="left.html">
    <FRAME NAME="Right" SRC="right.html">
```

```
</FRAMESET>
</HTML>
```

In this case, you can get access to the global variable `strYourName` from any frame's HTML file. You can also invoke `DisplayName` from any frame's HTML file. You do so by prefixing each name with `top.` to indicate to VBScript that you're referring to the top-level HTML file. Here's an example of setting `strYourName` to `Jerry` from `left.html`:

```
top.strYourName = "Jerry"
```

On the other hand, put scripts that you only need to access from within a frame inside the HTML file you display in that frame. You don't need to do anything differently to access the script because it's already within the scope of that HTML file.

Organizing Your Script Project Files   If your Web site has many pages, it'll eventually look quite messy. This is particularly true if you're guilty of storing all your Web pages in a single folder. You'll have a long list of Web pages that link together in some bizarre fashion with a structure that isn't always obvious.

Simplify your life a bit by using the hierarchical nature of your computer's file system to organize your Web pages. Your computer's file system has structure. Your Web pages have structure. It seems reasonable that you can store your Web pages in a structured set of folders resembling the structure of your Web site.

N O T E   If you're using Microsoft FrontPage to visually organize and edit Web pages, you don't need to worry about organizing your Web pages into folders. FrontPage does it for you automatically. You use the FrontPage Explorer to manage the organization of your Web site, instead. ■

Creating a Source of Reusable Scripts   You don't reinvent the block letter every time you write a business letter. You use a style sheet to get you started. Likewise, don't reinvent every script you put in your Web pages. Reuse them. For that matter, reuse the scripts you find in this book and on the Web.

To reuse scripts effectively, you need a painless way to do it. You need to be able to organize scripts individually and as a group. You need to be able to find the right script quickly. You also need to be able to insert the script into your HTML file quickly. Here's how to do it:

1. Create a folder in which you can store scripts. Put each <SCRIPT> block in its own file, and give the file a descriptive name such as Debugging Scripts.txt.

2. In cases where you want to reuse a single procedure, make that procedure the only contents of the file's <SCRIPT> block. If you have a number of related scripts you want to reuse, put all of them in a single <SCRIPT> block.

3. You can also create a file that contains a reusable form and event procedures.

T I P   Put reusable scripts in a TXT file so you can open them quickly in Notepad. You can use any file extension you want, except for HTM or HTML because you'll easily confuse Web pages with reusable scripts.

## CHAPTER 25

All About CGI Scripts

by Robert Niles

In previous chapters you learned how to mark up content for your Web site by using the HTML standard. Now, we will begin our exploration of the CGI (Common Gateway Interface), which will greatly enhance the level of inter-activity on your site. With the use of CGI scripts, you can make your Web presentations more responsive to your users' needs by allowing them to have a more powerful means of interaction with your material. ■

How the CGI works

When someone visits your site, and decides to fill out a form that you have provided, what happens to that information? You'll cover the basics of CGI, and how you can use CGI to your advantage.

Seeing if you can write CGI scripts

Whether you're administering your own Web server, or if your pages are being hosted by someone else, you will have to check and see if you can use CGI scripts.

Common CGI scripting languages

One of the most frequent questions is whether or not a specific language can be used. You'll cover some of the more popular languages that are used for CGI scripting. You'll also get an idea of which one you can use.

CGI scripts in action

There are millions of CGI scripts available on the Net. Some have been customized for specific needs, others are for more general use. You'll receive a few of the more frequently requested scripts.

What Is CGI?

Here is the answer to the $100 question. What is the CGI anyway? Well, in order to answer that, you are going to need a little background information first.

Each time you sit down in your favorite chair (I *hope* it is anyway) and start surfing the WWW, you are a client from the Internet's point of view. Each time you click a link to request a new Web document, you are sending a request to the document's server. The server then receives the request, gets the document, and sends it back to your browser for you to view.

The client/server relationship that is set up between your browser and a Web server works very well for serving up HTML and image files from the server's Web directories. Unfortunately, there is a large flaw with this simple system. The Web server is still not equipped to handle information from your favorite database program or from other applications that require more work than simply transmitting a static document.

One option the designers of the first Web server could have chosen was to build in an interface for each external application from which a client may want to get information. It is hard to imagine trying to program a server to interact with every known application and then trying to keep the server current on each new application as it is developed. Needless to say, it would be impossible. So they developed a better way.

These wizened developers anticipated this problem and solved it by designing the Common Gateway Interface or CGI. This gateway provides a common environment and a set of protocols for external applications to use while interfacing with the Web server. Thus, any application engineer (including yourself) can use the CGI to allow an application to interface with the server. This extends the range of functions the Web server has—including features provided by a potentially limitless number of external applications.

How the CGI Works

Now that you have read a little background, you should have a basic idea of what the CGI is, and why it is needed. The next step in furthering your understanding of the CGI is to learn the basics of how it works. To help you achieve this goal, I will break down this material into the following sections:

- Process
- Characteristics
- Output Header and MIME types
- Environment variables

The Process

The CGI is the common gateway or door that is used by the server to interface—or communicate—with applications other than the browser. Thus, CGI scripts act as a link between whatever application is needed and the server while the server is responsible for receiving information from, and sending data back to, the browser.

N O T E   On a technical note, you should be aware that some people like to use the term program
to refer to longer, usually compiled, code and applications written in languages like C and
C++. When this is the case, the term script is then used to indicate shorter, noncompiled code
written with languages like SH and PERL. However, for the purpose of this and the following chapter, the
terms "program" and "script" will be used interchangeably as the divisions between them are being
rapidly broken down. ■

For example, when you enter a search request at your favorite search engine, a request is
made by the browser to the server to execute a CGI script. At this time, the browser passes the
information that was contained in the online form plus the current environment to the server.
From here, the server passes the information to the script. This script provides an interface
with the database archive and finds the information that you have requested. Once this information is retrieved, the script processes the information entered by the visitor and sends the
result to the server which feeds it back to the visitor's browser as a list of matches to your
query.

There are two popular methods of sending information to your scripts. The first is with the
GET method which is the default method used. If no method is specified, then the browser
assumes that you are using the GET method. If you are creating a form, then you can use this
method by specifying it when you insert the <FORM> tag within your document. An example
would be:

```
<FORM ACTION="mail.pl" METHOD="GET">
```

When using the GET method, the information entered by the visitor is sent to the server within
the environmental variable, QUERY_STRING. And in the case of any environmental variable, you
are limited to 255 characters. This includes any white spaces.

The other method commonly used is the method, POST. Using the method POST, information
entered by the visitor is sent directly to your script through the server's STDOUT and your
script's STDIN. The advantage of using the method POST is that you aren't limited to 255
characters as you are when using the GET method. Here's an example of a form that uses the
method, POST:

```
<FORM ACTION="mail.pl" METHOD="POST">
```

T I P   There is a very nice online description of the CGI at the Common Gateway Interface:

URL address: http://hoohoo.ncsa.uiuc.edu/cgi/

Characteristics of the CGI

Another way of looking at the CGI is to see it as a socket that attaches an extra arm on your
server. This new arm, the CGI script, adds new features and abilities to the server that it was
previously lacking.

The most common use for these new features is to give the server the ability to dynamically
respond to the client. One of the most-often seen examples of this is allowing the client to send

a search query to a CGI script which then queries a database and returns a list of matching topics from the database. Besides information retrieval, another common theme for using CGI scripts is to customize the user interface on the Web site. This commonly takes the form of counters and animations.

As you read earlier, there are two basic methods of sending information to your script. Those methods mentioned were GET and POST. Depending on which method is used, your script will parse the information differently. While this difference is small, it can create havoc if your script doesn't parse the information coming from the visitor correctly. Listing 25.1 checks which method is being used and parses the information coming from the visitor based on the method used.

Listing 25.1   Perl Script That Parses the Information Coming in Depending on the Method Used

```perl
#! /usr/bin/perl

if ($ENV{'REQUEST_METHOD'} eq 'POST')
{
        read(STDIN, $buffer, $ENV{'CONTENT_LENGTH'});
        @pairs = split(/&/, $buffer);
        foreach $pair (@pairs)
        {
                ($name, $value) = split(/=/, $pair);
                $value =~ tr/+/ /;
                $value =~ s/%([a-fA-F0-9][a-fA-F0-9])/pack("C", hex($1))/eg;
                $contents{$name} = $value;

        }
}

if ($ENV{'REQUEST_METHOD'} eq 'GET')
{
        @pairs = split(/&/, $ENV{'QUERY_STRING'});
        foreach $pair (@pairs)
        {
                ($name, $value) = split(/=/, $pair);
                $value =~ tr/+/ /;
                $value =~ s/%([a-fA-F0-9][a-fA-F0-9])/pack("C", hex($1))/eg;
                $contents{$name} = $value;

        }
}
```

Using this basic header for all your CGI scripts written in Perl will save you a lot of headaches. The information is parsed and split automatically, with each item sent by the visitor placed into the array, @contents. Each individual item in the array can be called by using $contents{'name'}, where the name is the name assigned to the variable when you created your form.

The MIME Content-Type Output Header

It won't be long into your CGI programming career when you will want to write a script that sends information to the server for it to process. Each file that is sent to the server must contain an output header. This header contains the information the server and other applications need to transmit and handle the file properly.

The use of output headers in CGI scripts is an expansion of a system of protocols called MIME (Multipurpose Internet Mail Extensions). Its use for e-mail began in 1992 when the Network Working Group published RFC (Request For Comments) 1341, which defined this new type of e-mail system. This system greatly expanded the ability of Internet e-mail to send and receive various nontext file formats.

N O T E Since the release of RFC 1341, a series of improvements has been made to the MIME conventions. You can find some additional information about this by looking at RFC 1521 and RFC 1522. A list of all the RFC documents can be found online at **http://ds0.internic.net/rfc/**. These documents contain a lot of useful information published by the Network Working Group relating to the function and structure of the Internet backbone. ■

Each time you, as a client, send a request to the server, it is sent in the form of a MIME message with a specially formatted header. Most of the information in the header is part of the client's protocol for interfacing with the browser. This includes the request method, a URI (Universal Resource Identifier), the protocol version, and then a MIME message. The server then responds to this request with its own message, which usually includes the server's protocol version, a status code, and a different MIME message.

The bulk of this client/server communication process is handled automatically by the WWW client application—usually your Web browser—and the server. This makes it easier for everyone, since you don't have to know how to format each message in order to access the server and get information. You just need a WWW client. However, to write your own CGI scripts, you will need to know how to format the Content-type line of the MIME header in order for the server to know what type of document your script is sending. Also, you will need to know how to access the server's environment variables so you can use that information in your CGI scripts. In the following sections, you will learn everything necessary to accomplish both of these tasks.

N O T E If you decide to write your own WWW client, then you will need to understand the client/ server communication process before you can begin. A good place to start your search for more information about this is the W3C Reference Library at **http://www.w3.org/pub/WWW/ Library/**. ■

Part
V

Ch
25

Using a Content-Type Output Header

Each document that is sent via a CGI script to the server, whether it was created on-the-fly or is simply being opened by the script, must contain a Content-type output header as the first part of the document, so the server can process it accordingly. In Table 25.1 you will see examples of a few of the more commonly used MIME Content-types and their associated extensions.

Table 25.1   Examples of MIME Types and Extensions

Content-type	Extensions
application/octet-stream	bin exe
text/html	html htm
text/plain	txt
text/richtext	rtx
video/mpeg	mpeg mpg mpe
video/quicktime	qt mov
video/x-msvideo	avi

To help you better understand how to properly use Content-types within a CGI script, let's work through an example. Suppose you have decided to write a CGI script that will display a GIF each time it is executed by a browser.

The first line of code you need is a special comment that contains the path to the scripting language that you are using to write the program. In this case it is PERL. The comment symbol # must be followed by an exclamation point ! then the path. This special combination of #! on the first line of the file is the standard format for letting the server know which interpreter to use to execute the script. The reason that this special comment is used is that while UNIX servers use this line of code to locate the script's interpreter, other types of server systems have alternate methods of specifying the interpreter's location. However, since this line of code starts with a # symbol, it is still a valid PERL comment and does not cause problems on non-UNIX servers.

TIP   You should double-check to make sure you include the correct pathname to your language's interpreter.

```
#!/usr/local/bin/perl
```

The next line you will need simply sets the variable $gif to the full pathname of the image you want to display.

```
$gif = "/file/path/your.gif";
```

Now, it is time to let the server know that it will be receiving an image file from this script to display on the client's browser. This is done by using the MIME Content-type line. The print statement prints the information between the quotation marks to the server. Each set of "\n" characters that you see on this line adds a carriage return with a line feed. This gives you the required blank line that must occur after the Content-type information. A blank line lets the server know where the MIME header stops and where the body of information, in this case the gif, starts.

```
print "Content-type: image/gif\n\n";
```

The next line creates a file handle named IMAGE that forms a link from this script to the file contained in the variable $gif which we set earlier.

```
open(IMAGE,$gif);
```

Now, we create a loop that sends the entire contents of the gif to the server as the body of the MIME message we began with the Content-type line.

```
while(<IMAGE>) { print $_; }
```

To avoid being sloppy, we will close the file handle to the gif now that we are done sending the image.

```
close(IMAGE);
```

Finally, we let the PERL interpreter know that the CGI script is finished running and can be stopped.

```
exit;
```

This type of script can be modified into something a little more useful. For example, you could turn it into a random image viewer. Each time someone clicks the link to the script, it executes and feeds a random gif to the client's browser.

Environment Variables

Hopefully, you now have a little better understanding of what is involved as the client and server communicate with each other. Along with the information that I discussed earlier, a host of environment variables is sent during the client/server communications. Although each server can have its own set of environment variables, for the most part they are all subsets of a large set of standard variables described by the Internet community to help promote uniform standards (see Figure 25.1).

If you have bin access on a UNIX server, then you can use the following script to easily determine which environment variables your server supports. In addition, this script should also work on other server types, such as Microsoft Windows NT server, if you properly configure the server to recognize and execute PERL scripts.

Once again, this is the magic line that lets the server know which type of CGI script this is so it can launch the appropriate interpreter.

```
#!/usr/local/bin/perl
```

This next line, as was described above, is the MIME output header that lets the server know to expect an HTML document to follow.

```
print "Content-type: text/html\n\n";
```

Now that the server is expecting to receive an HTML document, we will send it a list of each environment variable's name and current value by using a `foreach` loop.

```
foreach $key (keys(%ENV)){
        print "\$ENV{$key} = \"$ENV{$key}\"<br>\n";
}
```

Finally, we need to tell the interpreter that the script is finished.

```
exit;
```

FIG. 25.1

Using the CGI script environment.pl from a browser will generate a screen similar to this one.

  If the browser you use doesn't support an environment variable, the value of the variable is set to null and is left empty.

As you can see from the example, most of the variables contain protocol version information and location information, such as the client's IP address and the server's domain. However, if you are creative, you can put some of these variables to good use in your CGI scripts.

The best example I have seen so far is the use of the environment variable HTTP_USER_AGENT. This contains the name and version number of the client application, which is usually a Web browser. As you can see from Figure 25.1, the Netscape 4.0 browser used when running this script has an HTTP_USER_AGENT value of Mozilla/4.0 (Win95; I).

Once you know what the values are for various browsers, it is possible to write a CGI script to serve different Web documents based on browser type. Thus, a text-only browser might receive a text version of your Web page, while image-capable browsers will receive the full version.

Can You Write CGI Scripts?

Hopefully, you now have a good idea of some of the more common uses for CGI scripts. As you can see, many of them provide helpful tools that you can incorporate into your personal Web site. If you would like to use some of these tools to make your site more dynamic, then you will need to consider a few things before you start.

- Can you write CGI scripts?
- Which language should you use?

Can You Write CGI Scripts?

Before you can get started writing your own CGI scripts, you need to find out if your server is specially configured to allow you to use them. The best thing to do is contact your system administrator and find out if you are allowed to run CGI scripts on the server. If you can, you also need to ask what you need to do to use them, and where you should put the scripts once they are written.

In some cases, system administrators do not allow clients to use CGI scripts because they feel they cannot afford the added security risks. In that case, you will have to find another means of making your site more interactive.

If you find that you can use CGI scripts and are using a UNIX server, you will probably have to put your scripts into a specially configured directory which is usually called `cgibin` or `cgi-bin`. If you are using Microsoft's Internet Server, then you will probably put your CGI programs in a directory called `scripts`. This allows the system administrator to configure the server to recognize that the files placed in that directory are executable. If you are using a NCSA version of HTTPD on a UNIX system then this is done by adding a ScriptAlias line to the conf/srm.conf file on the server.

N O T E It is important to remember that although CGI scripts are not necessarily complex, you need to have some basic understanding of the programming language you want to use and the server you plan to run the scripts on. Poorly written scripts can easily become more trouble than they are worth. For example, you could delete entire directories of information or shut down your server if your script were to start forking off new processes in a geometric fashion.

Before starting down the road to becoming a CGI scripter, you should do the following:

- Get a programming book on the scripting language you plan to learn.
- Notify the network administrator of your local server to find out how to run scripts on your system and what security features she wants you to implement in them.

continues

Part
V

Ch
25

continued

- Subscribe to a listserv and read the appropriate newsgroups on the language you plan to use. These are wonderful resources for programming information and good places to ask for help if you are stuck.

- Find a friend who has experience programming in your scripting language and who can help you smoothly overcome some of the early hurdles you will face. ▓

Which Language Should You Use?

Now that you know what a CGI script is, how it works, and what it can do, the next thing you need to consider is which language you should use. You can write a CGI script in almost any language. So, if you can program in a language already, there is a good chance you can use it to write your scripts. This is usually the best way to start learning how to write CGI scripts, since you are already familiar with the basic syntax of the language. However, you still need to know which languages your Web server is configured to support.

UNIX-based Apache and CERN Web servers are the most common. These platforms are easily configured to support most of the major scripting languages, including C, C++, PERL, and the basic shell scripting languages like SH. On the other hand, if your Web server is using the Mac server, then you might be limited to using AppleScript as your scripting language. Likewise, if you are using Windows NT server, you might need to use Visual Basic as your scripting language. However, it is possible to configure both these systems to support other scripting languages like C and PERL, or even Pascal.

N O T E If you are interested in finding out which scripting languages your server is configured to support, you should ask your system administrator to give you a listing of what is available on your server.

Also, if you have access to a UNIX-based server and can log into a shell account, then you can find out which languages your system supports by using the UNIX command "which."

If you are using the SH shell, you should see the following

```
$ which sh
/usr/bin/sh
$ which perl5
/usr/local/bin/perl5
```

Many scripting languages are freely distributed and fairly easy for an experienced administrator to install. As a last resort, you can always request that a new language be considered for addition to your local system. ▓

If you are lucky, you may find that your server is already configured to support several CGI scripting languages. In this case, you just need to compare the strengths and weaknesses of each language you have available with the programming tasks you anticipate writing. Once you do this, you should have a good idea of which programming language is best-suited to your needs.

Common CGI Scripting Languages

When it comes to the CGI, anything goes. Of the vast numbers of programming languages out there, many more than you could possibly learn in a lifetime, most can work with the CGI. So, you will have to spend a little time sifting through the long list to find the one that will work best for you. For some, which language used will completely depend on what you are most familiar with, or what languages are available for use.

Even though there are a lot of different languages available, they tend to fall into several categories based on the way they are processed—compiled, interpreted, and compiled/interpreted—and on the logic behind how the source is written—procedural and object-oriented. A listing of the more prevalent languages is found in Table 25.2.

Table 25.2   Various Languages Used to Create CGI Applications

Language	System	Type
Shell	UNIX	Interpreted (Command Line Interface)
Perl	UNIX, Windows, MacIntosh, Amiga	Interpreted
C	UNIX, Windows	Compiled
C++	UNIX, Windows	Compiled
Visual Basic	Windows	Compiled
AppleScript	Macintosh	Interpreted
TCL	UNIX	Interpreted
REXX (AREXX)	OS2, Amiga	Interpreted (some versions can be compiled)

Creating CGI Scripts

Once you have decided on a language to use, you will find that various applications can be developed using CGI. By far, e-mail, guestbook, redirection, counters, and advertisement banners are the most widely used scripts found to add interactivity to your Web pages, or to simply spice up a Web page. These scripts are covered in this section in more detail.

An E-Mail Script

E-mail scripts are just about the oldest, and most used script on the World Wide Web. Interfacing the Web with e-mail just seems like a good idea. By doing so, you can give someone visiting your site the ability to communicate with you whether or not he or she has an e-mail account. All their browser needs to be able to do is allow the visitor to use forms.

Another benefit of an e-mail script is that you can create scripts that notify you if, let's say, a visitor enters information into a guestbook. You can also provide online ordering. A visitor selects items to be purchased. When he or she is done, the items requested can be e-mailed to you or someone in your company for processing.

Listing 25.2 is a form a user can fill out. The fields entered are: name, an e-mail address, a subject line, and comments—just about the same items most people fill out when sending e-mail via conventional means.

Listing 25.2   mail.html—A Simple Form Which Allows the Visitor to Send E-Mail

```
<HTML>
<HEAD><TITLE>EMAIL ME!</TITLE></HEAD>
<BODY BGCOLOR=#FFFFFF>
<H1>EMAIL ME!</H1>
Please fill out the form to send me email!<P>
<FORM ACTION="mail.pl" METHOD="POST">
Realname:<INPUT TYPE="TEXT" NAME="realname"><br>
Email address:<INPUT TYPE="TEXT" NAME="email"><br>
Subject: <SELECT NAME="subject">
<OPTION>Hello!
<OPTION>Help!!
<OPTION>Reply please
</SELECT>
<P>
Enter your comments:<br>
<TEXTAREA NAME=comments ROWS=10 COLS=60>
</TEXTAREA>
<P>
<INPUT TYPE="SUBMIT">
</FORM>
</BODY>
</HTML>
```

Once the form is filled out by the visitor, the information entered is sent to the server, which in turn sends that information to the CGI script indicated by using the ACTION attribute. In this case, the information entered by the visitor is sent to the script, mail.pl.

If you take a look at Listing 25.3, you can see the full version of our mail.pl script. The first line tells the system this is a Perl script and the full path is given to Perl, which is the program that will interpret the script.

Next, two variables are set. The first variable is the path to the sendmail program, which will handle the mail and actually send the e-mail to its destination. The second variable is the recipient. That is, the e-mail address which will receive the e-mail. We define this here so that the person visiting the site can't save a copy of our form and change the e-mail address to which this message is being sent.

Next, the script breaks the input stream coming from the server and places the value of each entry into the array named *contents*. This allows us to easily manipulate the information entered by the visitor.

Lastly, the e-mail is sent, and a thank-you page is displayed back to the visitors, letting them know that their comments were successfully sent.

Listing 25.3   mail.pl—The Visitor's Comments Are Processed and Sent to the Recipient

```perl
#!/usr/bin/perl
$mailprog = "/usr/lib/sendmail";
$recipient = "user\@foo.bar.com";


if ($ENV{'REQUEST_METHOD'} eq 'POST')
{
        read(STDIN, $buffer, $ENV{'CONTENT_LENGTH'});
        @pairs = split(/&/, $buffer);
        foreach $pair (@pairs)
        {
                ($name, $value) = split(/=/, $pair);
                $value =~ tr/+/ /;
                $value =~ s/%([a-fA-F0-9][a-fA-F0-9])/pack("C", hex($1))/eg;
                $contents{$name} = $value;

        }
}

# Open The Mail
open(MAIL, "¦$mailprog -t") ¦¦ die "Can't open $mailprog!\n";
print MAIL "To: $recipient\n";
print MAIL "From: $contents{'email'} <$contents'realname'}>\n";
print MAIL "Subject: $contents{'subject'}\n\n";
print MAIL "$contents{'comments'}\n\n";
close(MAIL);

print <<"HTML";
<HTML>
<HEAD><TITLE>Thank you!</TITLE></HEAD>
<BODY BGCOLOR=#FFFFFF>
<H1>Thank you!</H1>
Thank you for your comments!
<P>
<HR>
<CENTER>
<A HREF="http://www.selah.net/cgi.html">[Return to the main page]</A>
</CENTER>
</BODY>
</HTML>
HTML
exit;
```

By convention, one of the most important parts of a CGI script is to return something to the visitor. In the previous example, you simply thanked the visitors for their comments. To send something back to visitors is one of the basic rules of CGI scripting. Doing so tells visitors that the information they entered was processed correctly, or the information returned will be results to a query that they entered. Using search engines is a good example of returning information to visitors. If a header is sent to visitors without any content, then your browser will simply sit there or, in the case of Netscape, a dialog box will appear stating that the document contains no data.

A Simple Guestbook Script

Guestbook scripts are another popular script. I'm sure you have seen some sort of guestbook script on someone's personal home page, and even on commercial sites.

Guestbook scripts allow visitors to not only interact with you, but with other individuals that visit that site. By using a guestbook script you expand upon how those visiting your site can interact. Guestbook scripts are used to allow visitors to simply say "Hello," or to allow visitors to ask questions, in hopes that someone visiting the site at a later date can answer that question.

The guestbook script, written by Jeffry Dwight, can be found on the CD-ROM named SGB1.EXE. It contains both the HTML code that is initially provided to allow visitors to enter comments, as well as the guestbook itself, allowing visitors to read what others have entered. This script was written in C to run on Windows NT, and Windows 95 (tested with WebSite and MS's Personal Web Server on Windows 95). The compiled binary has been provided as well as the source code and makefile.

The script is fairly simple, and heavily commented with explanations on how the CGI script works. If you take a look at Figure 25.2, you can get an idea of how it works as it stands. If you have a C compiler (a must if you are going to create CGI scripts in C), you can edit the script so that the script is customized to the look and feel of your specific site.

For those of you who would like to use a guestbook script that was written in Perl, Matt Wright provides a nice guestbook script which can be found at:

http://www.worldwidemart.com/scripts/guestbook.shtml

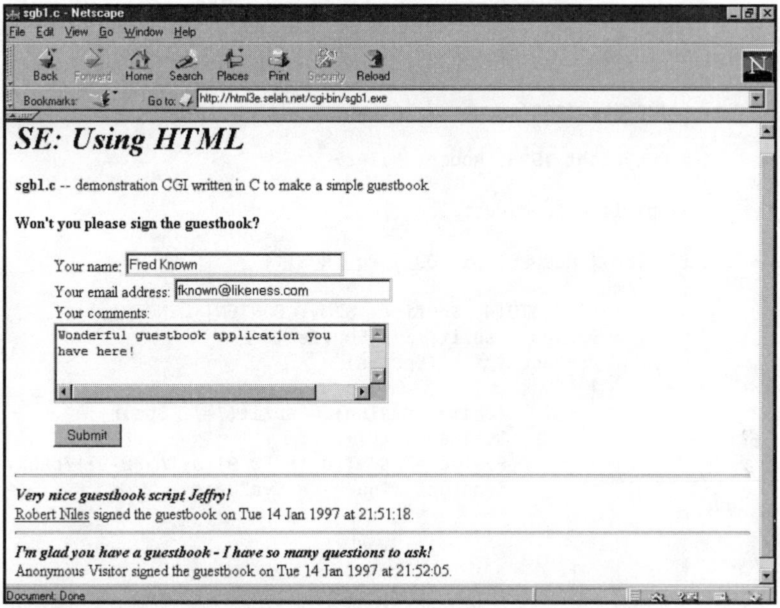

FIG. 25.2
SGB1 is a simple CGI
script written in C, that
allows your visitors to
communicate with each
other.

A Redirection Script

Another commonly requested script is the redirection script. A redirection script allows the visitor to select an item from a list and automatically be sent to the site chosen.

OK, so this is basically how links on Web pages work in the first place. Very true, but as you might or might not be aware, you can only log where a visitor came from; the server doesn't have the ability to log where you go to. Redirection scripts resolve this problem.

No longer are advertisers interested solely in how often their banner is displayed to the public. Advertisers want to know if their banner is having an effect on those visiting your site. Redirection scripts help you log how many times a link has been clicked.

The script redirect.pl, shown in Listing 25.4, performs this function by taking the URL that the visitor requested to go to, logging it, and then by using the Location header, redirecting them to the site in question.

When the script is called, three buttons are provided for the visitor to click. Once clicked, the script logs the request to the log file specified in the variable, `logfile`. In this instance, the log file is called `redirect.log`. The log file contains the date, and which place the visitor wanted to visit.

Part
V

Ch
25

Listing 25.4   redirect.pl—A Simple Script That Logs the URL the Visitor Clicks

```perl
#!/usr/bin/perl

# Copyright 1996, Robert Niles

$logfile = "redirect.log";

if ($ENV{'REQUEST_METHOD'} eq 'POST')
{
        read(STDIN, $buffer, $ENV{'CONTENT_LENGTH'});
        @pairs = split(/&/, $buffer);
        foreach $pair (@pairs)
        {
                ($name, $value) = split(/=/, $pair);
                $value =~ tr/+/ /;
                $value =~ s/%([a-fA-F0-9][a-fA-F0-9])/pack("C", hex($1))/eg;
                $contents{$name} = $value;

        }
}

chop($date = 'date');
&logit if $contents{'location'};
print "Content-type: text/html\n\n";
print <<"HTML";
<HTML>
<HEAD><TITLE>Whatever</TITLE></HEAD>
<BODY>
<H1>Whatever</H1>
<form action="/cgi-bin/redirect.pl" method="POST">
<input type="submit" name="location" value="Infoseek"><br>
<input type="submit" name="location" value="AltaVista"><br>
<input type="submit" name="location" value="WebCrawler"><br>
</form>
</body>
</html>
HTML

exit;


sub logit {

if ($contents{'location'} eq "Infoseek")
   {
   $location = "http://www.infoseek.com";
   }
if ($contents{'location'} eq "AltaVista")
   {
   $location = "http://www.altavista.com";
   }
if ($contents{'location'} eq "WebCrawler")
   {
```

```
        $location = "http://www.webcrawler.com";
    }

open(LOG, ">>$logfile");
print LOG "$date User clicked on: $contents{'location'}\n";
close(LOG);
print "Location: $location\n\n";
exit;
}
```

Simple Count

Counters allow you to find out how many people have been visiting your page. A page with a low count could tell you the page might not be worth keeping. A page with a large count might indicate that it could use some expansion.

Counters are on just about every other page on the Net. In some instances they have been used as some sort of testosterone-created method of bragging that "My dad is tougher than your dad." Some counters seem quite irritating in that they are heavily loaded with graphic images and seem to take forever just to display. Others, though, are simple counters created to not only inform the administrator of the site of how busy a site might be, but are also used to inform those visiting your site how often your page is visited—a very handy tool if you are attempting to attract potential advertisers.

Part

V

Ch

25

The script, count.pl, shown in Listing 25.5, demonstrates how you can keep track of how often your site is being visited. The script is simple, and displays only a small line with the number of times your page has been accessed. The script can also be configured so the access count is not displayed to those visiting your site. This allows you to know what your hit rate is without divulging the count to everyone visiting your page.

The script is accessed by using Server Side Includes (SSI). By using SSI to execute a script, you don't have to access the script directly or with a form. What SSI does is return the result of a script directly within the HTML document that called the script.

Whether you can use Server Side Includes depends on your Web administrator. Some sites, for security reasons, do not allow normal users to utilize SSI. Also, some of the older Web servers don't have the ability to use SSI. If in doubt, check with your administrator.

How SSI is used varies, but with count.pl, you will want to use the SSI command,

```
<!--#exec cgi="count.pl"-->
```

wherever you want the page to display the count. For example, if you would like to have the access count displayed at the bottom of your page, you would have an HTML document that looks like:

```
<HTML>
<HEAD><TITLE>Counting!</TITLE></HEAD>
<BODY>
<H1>HI!</H1>
Hello visitor!<p>
You are visitor number: <!--#exec cgi="count.pl"-->
```

```
</BODY>
</HTML>
```

The count.pl script can also be used to keep track of several pages by using one script. Just make sure you ensure the path is pointing to where the script resides. In this example, the script resides in the same directory in which the script was called. If the script resides in the /cgi-bin/ directory, then the SSI command will need to reflect this.

Also ensure the countfile exists. This script is quite simple, and although it functions well, it doesn't create the countfile automatically.

Last, not all versions of Perl use the `flock()` function. If your version of Perl doesn't support `flock()`, then you will want to rewrite the script to use `fcntl()`.

Listing 25.5   count.pl—A Simple Counter That Tracks the Number of Times Your Page Has Been Accessed

```perl
#!/usr/bin/perl
# simplecount 1.0
# count.pl

$uri = $ENV{'DOCUMENT_URI'};

$countfile = "count";

print "Content-type: text/html\n\n";

open(COUNT, "+<$countfile") || do{
print "Can't open count file";
die; };
flock(COUNT, 2);

while (<COUNT>) {
        chop;
        ($file, $count) = split(/:/, $_);
        $counts{$file} = $count;
}

$counts{$uri}++;

seek(COUNT, 0, 0);


foreach $file (keys %counts) {
        print COUNT $file, ":", $counts{$file}, "\n";
    }

flock(COUNT, 8);
close(COUNT);

print $counts{$uri};

exit;
```

An Advertisement Banner

We mentioned in the last two sections about using advertisement banners like those seen on the more popular Web pages. Advertisement banners allow a company to place a small ad on your page, which is usually linked to its site. The nice thing about allowing advertisement banners is that companies are quite willing to pay large sums of money for you to display their banner, especially if you have a site that is heavily accessed. In fact, the busier your site, the more money you can make with advertising!

The script randpic.pl randomly picks and displays a banner like the banner shown in Figure 25.3. Each banner displayed contains the path to the banner image, the URL visitors will be sent to if they click the banner, a short line used as the graphic alternative, and a line in which a short slogan is displayed.

FIG. 25.3

Randpic.pl is a simple script that randomly picks and displays an advertisement on your page.

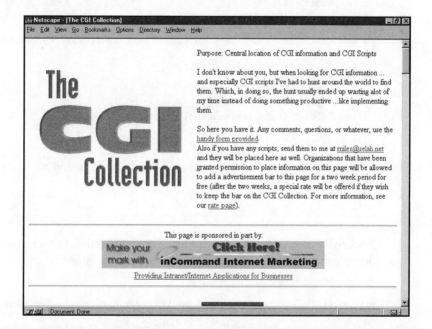

If you take a look at Listing 25.6, there are four arrays used to provide information about each banner. The first section of the script defines each array. The next section selects a random number using the current time as the seed. Once done, HTML is created which is placed in the HTML document calling the randpic.pl script.

Listing 25.6   randpic.pl—Allows You to Place Advertisement Banners on Your Web Pages

```
#!/usr/bin/perl
# randpic.pl
```

continues

Listing 25.6   Continued

```
@pics= ("pics/cgiad.gif",
        "pics/img2.gif");

@url= ("www.selah.net/rate.html",
        "www.in-command.com/");

@alt= ("The CGI Collection",
        "InCommand Internet Marketing");

@comment= ("Advertise on the Web with The CGI Collection",
            "Providing Intranet\/Internet Applications for Businesses");

# Now we pick a random number and assign it to $picnum
srand(time ^ $$);
$picnum = rand(@pics);

# Now we display it. I've used tables here to format the output nicely.

print "Content-type: text/html\n\n";
print "<table border=0>";
print "<tr><td align=center>";
print "<a href=\"http://$url[$picnum]\">";
print "<IMG SRC=\"$pics[$picnum]\" alt=\"$alt[$picnum]\" border=0>";
print "</A>";
print "</td></tr>";
print "<tr><td align=center>";
print "<a href=\"http://$url[$picnum]\">$comment[$picnum]</a>";
print "</td></tr>";
print "</table>";
exit;
```

Just like the count.pl script discussed in the previous section, this script requires the use of Server Side Includes. In this example, you would place the line

```
<!--#exec cgi="randpic.pl"-->
```

in your HTML document where you would like the banner to be displayed.

Now that you have been introduced to CGI scripting, it's time you write your own scripts (or simply edit the scripts provided to suit your needs), which can be used to spice up your pages, and provide a little more interactivity between you and those visiting your site. After all, allowing those visiting your site to interact with you, and others, is the main reason why the World Wide Web has become so popular.

If you would like more information on CGI scripts, and various CGI scripts available for use, visit:

**http://www.yahoo.com/Computers_and_Internet/Internet/
World_Wide_Web/CGI__Common_Gateway_Interface/**

## CHAPTER 26

Java

by Jerry Honeycutt and Stephen R. Pietrowicz

Sun Microsystems's object-oriented programming language Java™ is creating a lot of interest on the Web. You can use Java to create dynamic, interactive Web pages. This chapter gives you a brief introduction to Java and explains how you can use this technology in your own Web pages.

Java's sister scripting language, JavaScript, is a necessity if you're going to work with Java applets on the Web page. Chapter 27, "JavaScript/JScript," shows you how to create and implement these scripts in your Web pages. ■

Java is taking the Internet by storm

In this chapter, you learn about the brief history of Java and where it's going.

Add Java applets to your Web pages

Adding a Java applet to your HTML file is easy; you use the APPLET tag to point the browser to it.

How does Java protect the user's computer?

Java works in a sandbox and, as such, doesn't allow any malicious activity that can harm the user's computer.

Find Java applets and other Java resources

This chapter helps you locate Java applets that you can use in your own Web page.

How Java Got Started

In 1991, Sun started the "Green" project to create intelligent consumer electronics devices. James Gosling, an engineer at Sun, created a new object-oriented language, called Oak, to support the project. He intended to create a language that could be used to write programs for devices like cellular phones and television remote controls. Instead of preprogramming the devices before they left the factory, Oak programs could be downloaded as they were needed. When new features were added, the customer would be able to take advantage of them right away without having to send the device back to the factory. In 1993, Sun built prototypes of remote controls using this technology, and although it was promising, they were having problems gathering support from other vendors. On top of everything else, they found that "Oak" was already in use as a trademark.

In 1994, the Internet and the World Wide Web experienced explosive growth. The Oak team began to realize its downloadable technology could be applied to the Web. It decided to begin work on a new Web browser that would showcase its work. It also renamed the language "Java," a slang word for coffee, a beverage that many engineers drink every day.

Up until that point, Web pages consisted of static images and text. A few interesting examples of complex server-side imagemaps and CGI scripts did show up on the Web to create simple paint programs, for instance, but they weren't really interactive. Requests still had to be sent back to the server, and these requests created additional load on the machine serving the documents.

A browser with the ability to download programs and run them on the client machine would offload the server, allowing it to serve more documents. That's exactly the sort of browser the Java team decided to build.

The Java team's browser, HotJava, was the first program capable of automatically loading and running Java programs. HotJava created quite a bit of interest in Java on the Web, and many companies have licensed Java from Sun so they can incorporate the technology into their own products. Some of the same consumer electronics companies Sun tried to interest with the Green project are now contacting them to license Java.

Java has proven to be so popular that on January 9, 1996, Sun spun off a new business unit called JavaSoft that will concentrate on Java development.

Getting Started with Java

The Java language is object-oriented and very similar to C++. It was designed to take many of the best features of C++ while simplifying it to make writing programs easier.

Programs are normally created to run on only one type of operating system. Windows 95 programs have been specifically created to run on systems running the Windows 95 operating system, and will not run on the Macintosh or on a UNIX system. Java programs, however, are intended to be platform independent. Java programs are compiled into a series of *bytecodes* that are interpreted by a Java interpreter. After a Java program has been compiled, it can run on any system with a Java interpreter. You do not need to recompile it.

This capability makes Java an ideal language for programs on the Web. With so many different systems on the Web, creating programs that will work with all of them is very difficult. Because Java programs are platform independent, programs are no longer restricted to running on one platform. They can run on any platform to which Java has been ported.

Java has been ported to many different platforms. Sun has ported Java to Solaris, Windows NT, Windows 95, and the Macintosh. Other companies have ported Java to Silicon Graphics IRIX, IBM OS/2, IBM AIX, and Linux.

Using Java Applets in Web Pages

Java programs that can be embedded into WWW pages are called Java *applets*. To run applets from Web pages, you must have a browser that supports Java, such as HotJava, Netscape, or Internet Explorer.

If you want to write your own Java applets, you should download the Java Development Kit from Javasoft or purchase Microsoft's Visual J++. Javasoft is available for free on the Web. You can download it from the Javasoft home page:

http://www.javasoft.com

Microsoft Visual J++ is relatively inexpensive. You can purchase it at most computer retailers such as CompUSA or Computer City.

Now take a look at a few examples. Listing 26.1 shows the code for a simple Java applet.

Listing 26.1   A HelloWorld Java Applet

```
import java.applet.*;
import java.awt.*;

class HelloWorld extends Applet {
    public void paint(Graphics g) {
        g.drawString("Hello World!",20,20);
    }
}
```

When you place this applet into a page and run it, it prints Hello World!. But before you can use it in a page, you must compile the applet using javac, the Java compiler. The files that Javac creates are called Java class files. A class file is the platform independent object file that the browser retrieves when downloading a Java applet.

To use this applet on an HTML page, you have to describe it using the APPLET tag. Listing 26.2 shows an HTML page that loads this example applet.

Listing 26.2   HTML for HelloWorld Applet

```
<HTML>
<HEAD>
<TITLE>HelloWorld Applet</TITLE>
<BODY>
<APPLET CODE=HelloWorld HEIGHT=100 WIDTH=150>
</APPLET>
</BODY>
</HTML>
```

The <APPLET> and </APPLET> tags act as a container for the Java applet definition. They indicate to the browser that a Java applet should be loaded. The CODE attribute tells the browser which Java applet should be downloaded. The browser reserves space in the page by using the WIDTH and HEIGHT attributes, just as it reserves space for the IMG element. Then the browser downloads the Java class specified in the CODE attribute and begins running the applet.

In this case, the applet being downloaded is HelloWorld, and it reserves a space 150 pixels high and 200 pixels wide in the page. Figure 26.1 shows what the page looks like when the browser loads it.

FIG. 26.1

A simple Java applet.

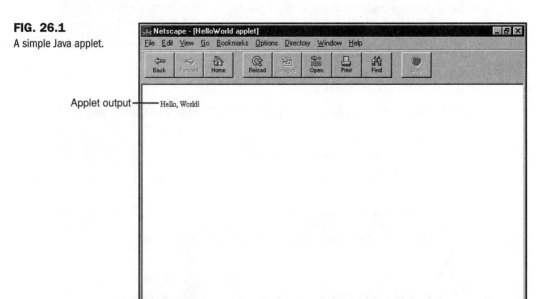

Browsers that can't display Java applets don't display anything when this page is loaded. To prevent this situation from happening, you can place HTML markup or text between the <APPLET> and </APPLET> tags. Browsers that can't display Java applets display the HTML markup instead. You can use this approach to tell visitors to your pages what they would have seen if the applet had loaded.

Browsers that can display applets don't display any of this HTML markup. Listing 26.3 shows an HTML page with alternative HTML markup.

Listing 26.3 HTML for HelloWorld Applet

```
<HTML>
<HEAD>
<TITLE>HelloWorld Applet</TITLE>
<BODY>
<APPLET CODE=HelloWorld HEIGHT=100 WIDTH=150>
<H1>WARNING!</H1>
The browser you are using is unable to load Java Applets!
</APPLET>
</BODY>
</HTML>
```

Figure 26.2 shows how this page looks in a browser that doesn't support Java applets.

FIG. 26.2

Instead of showing the Java applet, the HTML text is displayed. This way, you can alert visitors to your page about what they're missing.

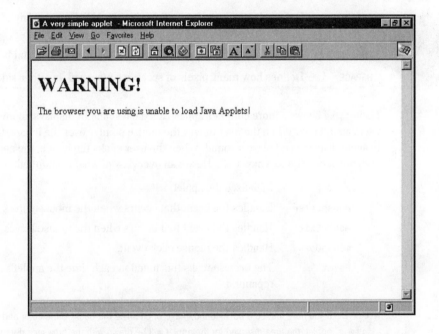

Part
V

Ch
26

 TIP You aren't restricted to writing Web applets with Java. You can write full applications with it as well. The HotJava browser and the Java compiler are both written in Java.

The CODE, WIDTH, and HEIGHT attributes of the APPLET tag are all required. You also can use other attributes in the APPLET tag. Table 26.1 shows the attributes available and their functions.

Table 26.1 *APPLET* Attributes and Their Functions

Attribute	Function
CODE	Defines the applet class to load (required).
WIDTH	Defines the width in pixels of the area in the HTML page to reserve for the applet (required).
HEIGHT	Defines the height in pixels of the area in the HTML page to reserve for the applet (required).
ALT	Defines the alternate text to display if the applet tag is understood, but applet loading is turned off or not supported.
CODEBASE	Defines the directory where the classes for the applet are stored. If this attribute is not specified, the directory of the HTML page is searched.
NAME	Defines the name of this instance of an applet. This attribute can be used by an applet to find another applet on the same page.
ALIGN	Defines how this applet is aligned in the HTML page. Any of the ALIGN options discussed in previous chapters are legal here.
VSPACE	Defines how many pixels of space are reserved above and below the applet.
HSPACE	Defines how many pixels of space are reserved on either side of the applet.

Listing 26.4 shows a more complex applet called URLsound. It displays an image with which a user can interact. When the user moves the mouse pointer over the image, this applet changes to another image and plays a sound. When the user clicks the image, the applet causes the Web browser to go to a new URL. Here's an overview of what each function in this listing does:

init	Initializes the applet.
mouseEnter	Handles the event that occurs when the mouse enters the applet's area.
mouseExit	Handles the event that occurs when the mouse leaves the applet's area.
mouseDown	Handles the mouse click event.
Paint	The browser calls this function each time the applet's canvas needs to be repainted.

N O T E If you have loaded a background image or changed the background color and used an applet, the area reserved for the applet will be drawn with the browser's default gray color. ▪

Listing 26.4 The URLsound Java Applet

```
import java.awt.*;
import java.applet.*;
import java.net.*;
```

```
/**
 * URLSound - This applet displays an image in a page. If the mouse cursor
 * moves over the image, it changes to an alternative image, and
 *      a sound is played. If the image is clicked, the browser
 * changes to another page. The images, sound and new page are
 * all user definable.
 */
public class URLsound extends Applet {
    String sound;
    String href;
    Image image1, image2, current;

    public void init() {
        /*
         * retrieve parameters given to the applet on the HTML page
         */
        String pic1 = getParameter("picture1");
        String pic2 = getParameter("picture2");
        sound = getParameter("sound");
        href = getParameter("href");


        /*
         * The MediaTracker class is used to ensure the images
         * have been loaded before we attempt to use them.
         */
        MediaTracker tracker = new MediaTracker(this);

        try {
            image1 = getImage(getDocumentBase(), pic1);
            tracker.addImage(image1, 0);

            image2 = getImage(getDocumentBase(), pic2);
            tracker.addImage(image2, 0);
        } catch (Exception e) {
        }

        try {
            tracker.waitForID(0);
        } catch (Exception e) {
        }

        current = image1;

    }

    /*
     * This routine is called each time the mouse enters the
     * applet area. It plays a sound and changes the displayed
     * image.
     */
    public boolean mouseEnter(Event evt, int x, int y) {

        /*
         * Try to play the sound
         */
```

Part

V

Ch

26

continues

Listing 26.4   Continued

```java
        try {
            play(getDocumentBase(), sound);
        } catch (Exception e) {
            System.out.println("Unable to play Sound");
        }

        /*
         * Change "current" to the alternate image and force a repaint
         */
        current = image2;
        repaint();
        return true;
    }

    /*
     * This routine is called each time the mouse leaves the
     * applet area. It restores the initial image and forces
     * a repaint.
     */
    public boolean mouseExit(Event evt, int x, int y) {
        current = image1;
        repaint();
        return true;
    }

    /*
     * This routine is called each time the mouse is clicked in the
     * applet area. It causes the browser to jump to the specified
     * URL.
     */
    public boolean mouseDown(Event evt, int x, int y) {
        URL hrefURL = null;

        try {
            hrefURL = new URL(href);
            getAppletContext().showDocument(hrefURL);

        } catch (Exception e) {
            System.out.println("Couldn't go to URL");
        }

        return true;
    }

    /*
     * The paint method is what actually displays the image.
     */
    public void paint(Graphics g) {
        g.drawImage(current, 0, 0, this);
    }
}
```

You can customize URLsound which allows you to specify which images to display, which sound to play, and which URL to jump to. You do so by using the PARAM element inside the APPLET container.

N O T E Version 1.1 of the Java Development Kit, a toolkit that programmers use to write Java programs, supports sound files only in Sun's AU format. If you want to use sound in your Java HTML pages, you must convert the sounds to the AU format. ■

Figure 26.3 shows an HTML page that uses URLsound twice, with different parameters.

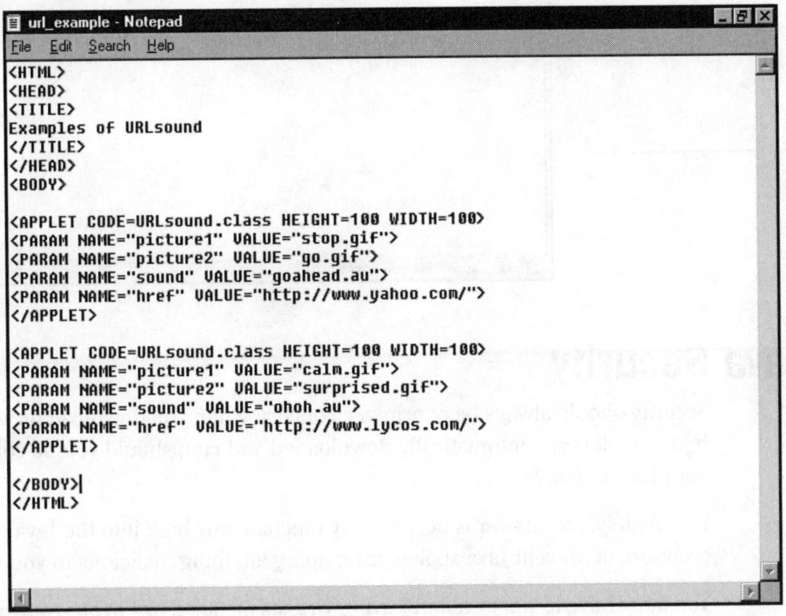

FIG. 26.3

You can change parameters in the URLsound applet to customize it.

```
url_example - Notepad                                    _ 8 X
File   Edit   Search   Help
<HTML>
<HEAD>
<TITLE>
Examples of URLsound
</TITLE>
</HEAD>
<BODY>

<APPLET CODE=URLsound.class HEIGHT=100 WIDTH=100>
<PARAM NAME="picture1" VALUE="stop.gif">
<PARAM NAME="picture2" VALUE="go.gif">
<PARAM NAME="sound" VALUE="goahead.au">
<PARAM NAME="href" VALUE="http://www.yahoo.com/">
</APPLET>

<APPLET CODE=URLsound.class HEIGHT=100 WIDTH=100>
<PARAM NAME="picture1" VALUE="calm.gif">
<PARAM NAME="picture2" VALUE="surprised.gif">
<PARAM NAME="sound" VALUE="ohoh.au">
<PARAM NAME="href" VALUE="http://www.lycos.com/">
</APPLET>

</BODY>
</HTML>
```

Part **V**

Ch **26**

The <PARAM> tag has two required attributes: NAME and VALUE. When an applet initializes, it requests the parameters it's expecting by using the specified NAME, and it receives the VALUE. More than one parameter can be passed to an applet if you put more than one <PARAM> tag in the APPLET container. Parameters that the applet does not recognize are ignored.

In Figure 26.3, the URLsound applet takes four parameters: picture1, picture2, sound, and href. picture1 names the picture in its inactive state. picture2 is revealed when the mouse pointer moves over the picture area, and the audio file specified by sound is played. When the user clicks the mouse on the picture, the browser jumps to the URL specified by href. In Figure 26.4, a browser shows this page.

TIP Special server software is not needed to serve Java applets. You can use your Internet server provider's current Web server to serve Java applets.

FIG. 26.4
Two copies of URLsound
in one page.

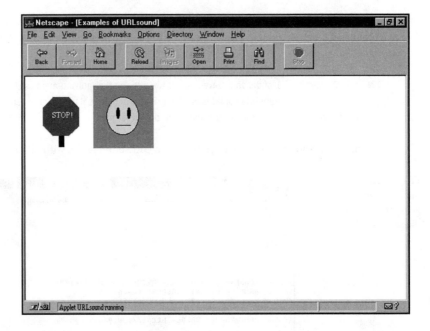

Java Security

Security should always be of primary concern when you download programs into your system. If Java applets are automatically downloaded and run, should you be concerned that you might download a virus?

Fortunately, the answer is no. Security mechanisms built into the Java class structure allow browsers to prevent Java applets from doing anything malicious to your system.

You don't have to worry about having viruses installed or having your private financial files stolen through Java because Java applets that your browser loads from the Web can't read or write files on your hard drive—the security policy in the browser prevents it.

Because files can't be read, Java applets can't start other programs you may already have installed on your system. No need to worry about a rogue applet coming in and wiping out your hard disk.

Java applets can create their own windows outside the browser, however. This could be a problem, too. What if the applet you download looks exactly like another program you already have on your system? What's to prevent you from entering data, like a password, into the applet that you're trying to protect?

Java takes care of this situation, too. To prevent you from thinking that these windows were created by your own system, an applet's window is labeled so that you know a Java applet has created the window. This label cannot be overridden by the Java applet, so you know it is always displayed. Figure 26.5 shows a labeled applet window.

FIG. 26.5

Windows outside the browser contain the words Untrusted Java Applet Window at the bottom of the window.

N O T E If you ever see an unexpected window on your screen with the words "Untrusted Java Applet Window" asking for your password, DO NOT type your password. It's likely that someone is trying to use a Java applet to get your password to break into your system. Report the break-in attempt to your local system administrator or your Internet service provider. ■

Java applets are also incapable of searching through your system's memory to obtain information. The Java language itself doesn't have access to random memory locations in your system, which is a method some criminals use to steal passwords and other confidential information.

Notable Java Applets

The following are just a couple of the most notable Java applets on the Web. They're both great examples of what is possible with Java.

The Impressionist, by Paul Haeberli of Silicon Graphics, is one of the most remarkable applets available (see Figure 26.6). It applies Haeberli's patented computer painting techniques to allow you to draw in the style of an impressionist painter. You select one of the nine pictures available on the page or use one of your own, and start with a blank canvas. As you move your mouse pointer over the canvas, the picture is drawn in the impressionist style. The Impressionist is available from **http://reality.sgi.com/grafica/impression/**.

BulletProof has created the first site on the Internet that uses Java to display stock quotes and stock histories (see Figure 26.7). This subscription service allows you to keep your stock portfolio up-to-date and to search thousands of different securities. Look for it at **http://www.bulletproof.com/WallStreetWeb**.

Part
V

Ch
26

FIG. 26.6

The Impressionist.

FIG. 26.7

The WallStreetWeb Java applet by BulletProof.

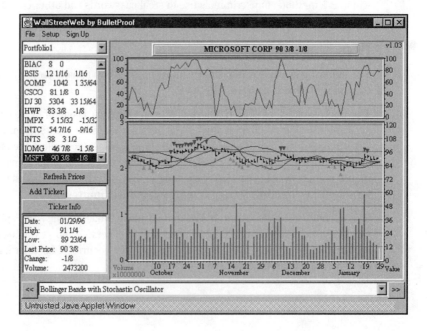

Java Resources

Creating Java applets and JavaScript programs can be a bit difficult, especially for the novice programmer. If you're interested in writing Java applets or JavaScript programs, there are a number of development tools and informational resources available to you.

Development Tools

Since Sun's announcement, many companies have licensed Java and have created Java development tools. Some free development tools are also available. Here are a few:

Symantec (**http://www.symantec.com**) has created an integrated development environment (IDE) for Java called Symantec Cafe. Symantec Cafe is available for Windows 95, Windows NT, and Power Macintosh. You can read more about it at **http://www.symantec.com/lit/dev/javaindex.html**.

Borland International (**http://www.borland.com**) has a new debugger for Java. This graphical debugger is available on the Windows 95, Windows NT, and Solaris platforms.

Silicon Graphics (**http://www.sgi.com**) has ported Java to its IRIX operating system and has created a development environment called Cosmo Code. Cosmo Code provides an extensive set of utilities for Java programming, including a source-level debugger. It is available only for Silicon Graphics machines.

Javamaker is a free IDE from Korea. It contains an editor and has buttons to compile your Java programs automatically. It's simple but very effective. Javamaker is available from **http://net.info.samsung.co.kr/~hcchoi/javamaker.html**.

Diva, another IDE available on the Internet, is a more sophisticated utility than Javamaker. It provides graphical class representations, the ability to write HTML documents, an integrated editor, and more. It is available from **http://www.qoi.com**.

Microsoft has thrown its hat into the Java ring with Visual J++. This is Microsoft's first-rate development environment for Java Developers. Visual J++ is a comprehensive development tool you can use to build software components for the Internet. It compiles over 10,000 lines of code per second and includes a very good debugger that you can use to disassemble bytecode; and it provides a class viewer and a set of wizards which automatically generate the basic code for you. You can purchase Visual J++ at most computer stores. You can also learn more about Microsoft Visual J++ at its Web site. Open **http://www.microsoft.com/visualj** in your Web browser.

Web Resources

Javasoft has a special WWW site set up especially for Java (see Figure 26.8). You can reach it at **http://www.javasoft.com**. You can find the latest version of the HotJava browser and the Java Development Kit (JDK) at **http://www.javasoft.com/download.html**.

T I P The Java Web site has a "What's New" page that's updated frequently with news from Sun. It can be accessed from the Java home page or from **http://www.javasoft.com/new.html**.

The Gamelan home page (**http://www.gamelan.com**) keeps an extensive list of Java applets and other Java resources.

FIG. 26.8

The Java home page.

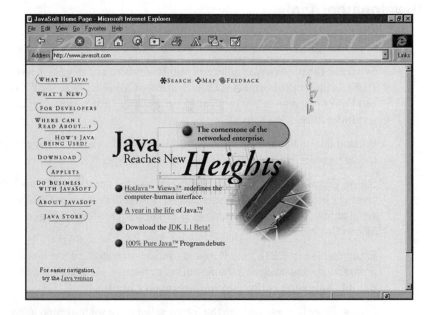

You can learn more about JavaScript by going to Netscape's Authoring Guide page:

> **http://home.netscape.com/comprod/products/navigator**
> **version_2.0/script/script_info/index.html**

The JavaScript Index (**http://www.c2.org/~andreww/javascript**) contains a list of JavaScript links with many examples.

Internet Newsgroups and Mailing Lists

The Internet newsgroups for Java are shown in Table 26.2.

Table 26.2   Internet Java Newsgroups

Group	Purpose
comp.lang.java	General Java language discussions
comp.lang.javascript	General JavaScript discussions
alt.www.hotjava	HotJava browser discussions

Reading these newsgroups is a great way to keep up-to-date with the most current Java information, and a great way to meet other people who are also interested in Java.

Many mailing lists also support Java. Sun maintains several of these Java mailing lists. You should be aware that some of these mailing lists have a tremendous amount of traffic, so be prepared to receive a lot of e-mail if you subscribe to them.

Here's a description of each list:

- The **java-announce** list, a moderated mailing list, distributes press releases and announces new software releases. Subscribe to this mailing list by sending e-mail with the word "Subscribe" in the message to **java-announce-request@java.sun.com**.

- The **java-porting** list discusses porting Java to different platforms. If you're interested in porting Java to a new architecture, this is the list for you. Subscribe to this mailing list by sending e-mail with the word "Subscribe" in the message to **java-porting-request@java. sun.com**.

- The **java-interest** list is an unmoderated forum for discussing Java programming issues that aren't covered by the other lists. The traffic on this list is also sent to **comp.lang.java**. If you already read that newsgroup, you don't need to subscribe to this list. Subscribe to this mailing list by sending e-mail with the word "Subscribe" in the message to **java-interest-request@java.sun.com**.

Part

V

Ch

26

## CHAPTER 27

JavaScript/JScript

by Jerry Honeycutt, David Gunter, Scott J. Walter, and Andrew Wooldridge

JavaScript is a scripting language that's loosely based on Java. Netscape created this language to allow Web developers to "glue" together objects (Java applets) on the Web page. That is, JavaScript allows two objects to cooperate.

Microsoft has recently released Internet Explorer 3.0 (it will be shipping 4.0 soon, too). In the latest version, Microsoft supports JavaScript. They call it JScript, however, the JScript that comes with Internet Explorer 3.0 isn't completely compatible with Netscape's JavaScript. Internet Explorer 4.0 makes it compatible, though.

This chapter teaches you how to use JavaScript to power up your Web pages. ■

Get your first taste of JavaScript

Learn how JavaScript fits into the Web today, what it looks like, and how you include it in your HTML documents.

Learn what JavaScript is all about

As with other high-level languages, JavaScript is built on the concept of objects, methods, and properties.

Use JavaScript with the browser object model

You'll learn about the various built-in objects that give JavaScript access to both the browser and HTML tags, what they do, and how to use them.

Learn how to program in the JavaScript language

How the various operators, expressions, and command statements work together.

Try out the example in this chapter

You'll find a collection of simple functions and programming examples, including data validation, link table construction, manipulating forms, and constructing a calculator.

Introduction to JavaScript

JavaScript allows you to embed commands in an HTML page; when a Navigator user downloads the page, your JavaScript commands will be evaluated. These commands can be triggered when the user clicks page items, manipulates gadgets and fields in an HTML form, or moves through the page history list.

> **N O T E** You've probably heard JavaScript called by its earlier-version name: *LiveScript*; at the time of this writing most of JavaScript's capabilities are based on the functionality of LiveScript. As more and more HTML page designers and enterprise application developers create scripts that define the behavior of objects to run on both clients and servers, you'll continue to see improvements and changes for the better in JavaScript. Just as Java (and any other software, for that matter) becomes better in response to its programmers' and developers' imaginations, so will JavaScript. If you're interested in following up on the latest revisions and additions, keep Netscape's home page (**http://home.netscape.com/**) at the top of your bookmarks list. ■

Some computer languages are compiled; you run your program through a compiler, which performs a one-time translation of the human-readable program into a binary language that the computer can execute. JavaScript is an interpreted language; the computer must evaluate the program every time it's run. You embed your JavaScript commands within an HTML page, and any browser that supports JavaScript can interpret the commands and act on them.

Don't let all these programming terms frighten you off—JavaScript is powerful and simple. If you've ever programmed in dBASE or Visual Basic, you'll find JavaScript easy to pick up. If not, don't worry; this chapter will have you JavaScripting in no time!

> **N O T E** Java offers a number of C++-like capabilities that were purposefully omitted from JavaScript. For example, you can only access the limited set of objects defined by the browser and its Java applets, and you can't extend those objects yourself. For more details on Java, see Chapter 26, "Java." ■

Why Use a Scripting Language?

HTML provides a good deal of flexibility to page authors, but HTML by itself is static; once written, HTML documents can't interact with the user other than by presenting hyperlinks. Creative use of CGI scripts (which run on Web servers) have made it possible to create more interesting and effective interactive sites, but some applications really demand client-side scripting.

JavaScript was developed to provide page authors a way to write small scripts that execute on the users' browsers instead of on the server. For example, an application that collects data from a form and then POSTs it to the server can validate the data for completeness and correctness before sending it to the server. This can greatly improve the performance of the browsing session, since users don't have to send data to the server until it has been verified as correct. The following are some other potential applications for JavaScript:

- JavaScript can verify forms for completeness, like a mailing list registration form that checks to make sure the user has entered a name and e-mail address before the form is posted.

- Pages can display content derived from information stored on the user's computer—without sending the data to the server. For example, a bank can embed JavaScript commands in their pages that look up account data from a Quicken file and display it as part of the bank's page.

- Because JavaScript can modify settings for applets written in Java and ActiveX controls, page authors can control the size, appearance, and behavior of Navigator plug-ins, as well as other Java applets and controls. A page that contains an embedded Director animation might use a JavaScript to set the Director plug-in's window size and position before triggering the animation.

What Can JavaScript Do?

JavaScript provides a rich set of built-in functions and commands. Your JavaScripts can display HTML in the browser, do math calculations (like figuring the sales tax or shipping for an order form), play sounds, open new URLs, and even click buttons in forms.

 TIP A function is just a small program that does something, and a method is a function that belongs to an object. For more lingo, see Chapter 26, "Java."

Code to perform these actions can be embedded in a page and executed when the page is loaded; you can also write methods that contain code that's triggered by events you specify. For example, you can write a JavaScript method that is called when the user clicks the Submit button of a form, or one that is activated when the user clicks a hyperlink on the active page.

JavaScript can also set the attributes, or properties, of Java applets running in the browser. This makes it easy for you to change the behavior of plug-ins or other objects without having to delve into their innards. For example, your JavaScript code could automatically start playing an embedded QuickTime or .AVI file when the user clicks a button.

What Does JavaScript Look Like?

JavaScript commands are embedded in your HTML documents, either directly or via an URL that tells the browser which scripts to load. Embedding JavaScript in your pages only requires one new HTML element: <SCRIPT>...</SCRIPT>.

The <SCRIPT> element takes two attributes: LANGUAGE, which specifies the scripting language to use when evaluating the scripts, and SRC, which specifies an URL from which the script can be loaded. The LANGUAGE attribute is always required, unless the SRC attribute's URL specifies a language. LANGUAGE and SRC can both be used, too. Here are some examples:

Part
V

Ch
27

```
<SCRIPT LANGAUGE="JavaScript">...</SCRIPT>

<SCRIPT SRC="http://www.fairgate.com/scripts/common.js">
...
</SCRIPT>
```

N O T E For security reasons, the SRC attribute was never implemented in the earlier releases of Navigator. As of Navigator 3.0, it is now available (but is not yet supported by Internet Explorer). Keep in mind, however, that if you implement the SRC attribute, your site will only work for those people using Navigator 3.0 or greater. ■

JavaScript itself resembles many other computer languages; if you're familiar with C, C++, Pascal, HyperTalk, Visual Basic, or dBASE, you'll recognize the similarities. If not, don't worry; the following are some simple rules that will help you understand how the language is structured:

■ JavaScript is pretty flexible about statements. A single statement can cover multiple lines, and you can put multiple short statements on a single line—just make sure to add a semicolon at the end of each statement.

■ Curly braces ({}) group statements into *blocks*; a block may be the body of a function or a section of code that gets executed in a loop or as part of a conditional test.

Figure 27.1 shows a small piece of JavaScript code embedded in an HTML page; the front window shows the original HTML file, and the Navigator window shows its output.

FIG. 27.1

The foremost window shows a small piece of JavaScript code embedded in a simple HTML file; the Navigator window shows the result of loading that page (which executes the JavaScript).

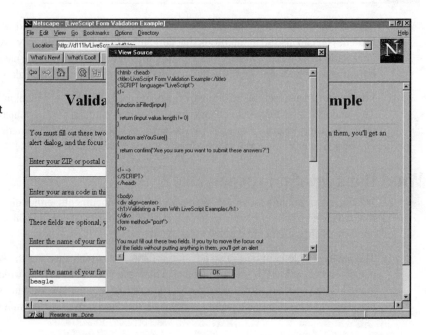

JavaScript Programming Conventions

Even though JavaScript is a simple language, it's quite expressive. In this section, we'll cover a small number of simple rules and conventions that will ease your learning process and speed up your JavaScripting.

Hiding Your Scripts   You'll probably be designing pages that may be seen by browsers that don't support JavaScript. To keep those browsers from interpreting your JavaScript commands as HTML—and displaying them—wrap your scripts as demonstrated in Listing 27.1.

Listing 27.1   Hiding Your Scripts from NonJavaScript Browsers

```
<SCRIPT LANGUAGE="JavaScript">
<!-- this line opens an HTML comment
document.write("You can see this script's output, " +
               "but not it's source.");
// this line closes the HTML comment -->
</SCRIPT>
```

The opening `<!--` comment causes browsers to disregard all text they encounter until they find a matching `-->`, so they won't display your script. You do have to be careful with the `<SCRIPT>` tag, though; if you put your `<SCRIPT>...</SCRIPT>` block inside the comments, even Navigator will ignore it (and all your JavaScript code as well)!

N O T E   You may notice that the closing comment line in Listing 27.1 starts with a double slash (`//`), the JavaScript comment identifier. This is necessary, because once JavaScript starts processing lines within a `<SCRIPT>` tag, it assumes that all lines are JavaScript code until the closing `</SCRIPT>` tag. The double slash effectively hides the closing comment tag from JavaScript, which would otherwise try to evaluate the line. ■

Comments   It's usually good practice to include comments in your programs to explain what they do; JavaScript is no exception. The JavaScript interpreter will ignore any text marked as a comment, so don't be shy about including them. There are two types of comments: *single-line* and *multiple-line*.

Single-line comments start with two slashes (`//`) and are limited to one line. *Multiple-line* comments start with `/*` on the first line, and end with `*/` on the last line. Listing 27.2 demonstrates several examples.

Part
V

Ch
27

Listing 27.2   Examples of JavaScript Comments

```
// this is a legal comment
/ illegal -- comments start with two slashes
/* multiple-line comments can
be spread across more than one line, as long as
they end. */
/* illegal -- this comment doesn't have an end!
// this is OK...as extra slashes are ignored //
```

The JavaScript Language

JavaScript was designed to resemble Java, which in turn looks much like C and C++. The difference is that Java was built as a general-purpose object language, while JavaScript is intended to provide a quicker and simpler language for enhancing Web pages and servers. In this section, you learn the building blocks of JavaScript and how to combine them into legal JavaScript programs.

Using Identifiers

An identifier is just a unique name that JavaScript uses to identify a variable, method, or object in your program. As with other programming languages, JavaScript imposes some rules on what names you can use. All JavaScript names must start with a letter or the underscore character (_), and they can contain both upper- and lowercase letters and the digits 0–9.

JavaScript supports two different ways for you to represent values in your scripts: literals and variables. As their names imply, literals are fixed values that don't change while the script is executing, while variables hold data that can change at any time.

Literals and variables have several different types; the type is determined by the kind of data that the literal or variable contains. The following is a list of the types supported in JavaScript:

- *Integers* or whole numbers—Integer literals are made up of a sequence of digits only; integer variables can contain any whole number value from 0 to more than 2 billion.

- *Floating-point* or decimal numbers—10 is an integer, but 10.5 is a floating-point number. Floating-point literals can be positive or negative, and they can contain either positive or negative exponents (which are indicated by an *e* in the number). For example, 3.14159265 is a floating-point literal, as is 6.02E24 (6.02×10^{24} or Avogadro's Number).

- *Strings* or sequences of characters—Strings can represent words, phrases, or data, and they're set off by either double (") or single (') quotes. If you start a string with one type of quote, you must close it with the same type.

- *Booleans* or true/false values—Boolean literals can only have the values of either true or false; other statements in the JavaScript language can return Boolean values.

Using Functions, Objects, and Properties

Before we go any further, let's talk about functions, objects, and properties. A *function* is just a piece of code that does something; it might play a sound, calculate an equation, or send a piece of e-mail. An *object* is a collection of data and functions that have been grouped together. The object's functions are called *methods*, and its data values are called *properties*. The JavaScript programs you write will have properties and methods, which will interact with objects provided by the browser and its plug-ins (as well as any other Java applets you may supply to your users).

 TIP A simple guideline: An object's properties are things it knows, and its methods are things it can do.

Using Built-In Objects and Functions   Individual JavaScript elements are *objects*; for example, string literals are string objects, and they have methods that you can use to do things, such as change their case. JavaScript also provides a set of useful objects to represent the browser, the currently displayed page, and other elements of the browsing session.

You access objects by specifying their name. For example, the active document object is named document. To use document's properties or methods, you add a period and the name of the method or property you want. For example, document.title is the title property of the document object, and Navigator.length accesses the length property of the string object named Navigator (remember literals are objects, too!).

Using Properties   Every object has properties—even literals. To access a property, just use the object name followed by a period and the property name. To get the length of a string object named address, you can write

```
address.length
```

and you'll get back an integer which equals the number of characters in the string. If the object you're using has properties that can be modified, you can change them in the same way. To set the bgColor (background color) property of a document object, just write

```
document.bgColor = "blue";
```

You can also add new properties to an object just by naming them. For example, let's say you define an object called customer for one of your pages. You can add new properties to the customer object with the following:

```
customer.name = "Scott Walter";
customer.address = "Somewhere out there";
customer.zip = "55122";
```

Finally, it's important to know that an object's methods are just properties, so you can easily add new properties to an object by writing your own function and creating a new object property using your own function name. If you wanted to add a Bill() method to your customer object, you could do so by writing a function named BillCustomer() and setting the object's property with the following:

```
customer.Bill = BillCustomer;
```

To call the new method, you'd just write

```
customer.Bill();
```

Array and Object Properties   JavaScript objects store their properties in an internal table that you can access in two ways. You've already seen the first method—just use the properties' name. The second method, *arrays*, allows you to access all of an object's properties in sequence. The code shown in Listing 27.3 prints out all the properties of the specified object.

Listing 27.3   Displaying an Object's Properties

```
function DumpProperties(obj, objName) {
    var result = "";

    // Look at each element in the object
    // Concatenate object name, element, and value

    for (i in obj) {
        result += objName + "." + i + " = " + obj[i] + "\n";
    }

    return result;
}
```

N O T E   You'll see this code again in the "Sample JavaScript Code" section, and we'll explain in detail what it does. For now, it's enough to know that there are two different, but related, ways to access an object's properties. ■

HTML Elements Have Properties, Too   JavaScript provides objects for accessing HTML forms and form fields and is especially valuable for writing scripts that check or change data in forms. JavaScript's properties allow you to get and set the form elements' data, as well as specify actions to be taken when something happens to the form element (as when the user clicks in a text field or moves to another field).

JavaScript and the Browser

Now that you understand how JavaScript works, let's talk about how the browser supports JavaScript.

When Scripts Get Executed

When you put JavaScript code in a page, the JavaScript interpreter built into the browser evaluates the code as soon as it's encountered. As the interpreter evaluates the code, it converts it into a more efficient internal format so that it can be executed later. When you think about it, this is similar to how HTML is processed; browsers parse and display HTML as they encounter it in the page, not all at once.

However, functions don't get executed when they're evaluated; they just get stored for later use. You still have to explicitly call functions to make them work. Some functions are attached to the object, like buttons or text fields on forms, and they are called when some event happens on the button or field. You might also have functions that you want to execute during page evaluation; you can do this by putting a call to the function at the appropriate place in the page, like this:

```
<SCRIPT LANGUAGE="JavaScript">
<!--
```

```
myFunction();
// -->
</SCRIPT>
```

Where to Put Your Scripts

You can put scripts anywhere within your HTML page, as long as they're surrounded with the
`<SCRIPT>...</SCRIPT>` tag pair. Many JavaScript programmers choose to put functions that
will be executed more than once into the `<HEAD>` element of their pages; this provides a convenient storage place. Since the `<HEAD>` element is at the beginning of the file, functions and
JavaScript code that you put there will be evaluated before the rest of the document is loaded.

Sometimes, though, you have code that shouldn't be evaluated or executed until after all of the
page's HTML has been parsed and displayed. An example is the DumpURL() function described
later in this chapter; it prints out all the URLs referenced in the page. If the function is evaluated before all the HTML on the page has been loaded, it'll miss some URLs, so the call to the
function should come at the page's end.

> **N O T E** For more information on the DumpURL() function, see the section, "Building a Link Table,"
> later in this chapter. ■

Objects and Events

In addition to recognizing JavaScript when it's embedded inside a `<SCRIPT>...</SCRIPT>` tag,
the browser also exposes some objects (and their methods and properties) that you can use in
your JavaScript programs. Also, methods can be triggered when the user takes certain actions
in the browser (called *events*).

The *location* Object   The location object holds the current URL, including the hostname,
path, CGI script arguments, and even the protocol. Table 27.1 shows the properties and methods of the location object.

Table 27.1   Properties of the *location* Object

Property/ Method	Type	What It Does
href	String	Contains the entire URL, including all the subparts; for example, **http://home.netscape.com:80/index.html**.
protocol	String	Contains the protocol field of the URL, including the first colon; for example, **http:**.
hostname	String	Contains only the domain name; for example, **home.netscape.com**.

continues

Table 27.1 Continued

Property/ Method	Type	What It Does
port	String	Contains the port (if specified), such as **80**. If no port is specified, this property is empty.
host	String	Contains the hostname and port number; for example **home.netscape. com:80**.
path	String	Contains the (directory) path to the actual document; for example, / for the root directory.
hash	String	Contains any CGI arguments after the first # in the URL.
search	String	Contains any CGI arguments after the first **?** in the URL.
toString()	Method	Returns the location.href; you can use this function to easily get the entire URL.
assign()	Method	Sets location.href to the value you specify.

The *document* Object   The document object, as you might expect, exposes useful properties and methods of the active document. Table 27.2 shows document properties and methods.

Table 27.2 Properties of the *document* Object

Property/ Method	Type	What It Does
title	String	Contains the title of the current page (from the HTML <TITLE> tag), or Untitled if there's no title.
location	String	A location object that identifies the location of the current page.
lastModified	String	Contains the date the page was last modified (changed).
forms[]	Array	Contains all the forms in the current page.
links[]	Array	Contains all hyperlinks in the current page.

Property/Method	Type	What It Does
write()	Method	Writes HTML to the current document in the order in which the script occurs on the page.

The *history* Object   The list of pages you've visited since starting the browser is called the *history list* and is accessible via the history object. Your JavaScript programs can move through pages in the list by using the properties and functions shown in Table 27.3.

Table 27.3   The *history* Object

Property/Method	Type	What It Does
back()	Method	Contains the URL of the previous history stack entry (that is, the one before the active page).
forward()	Method	Contains the URL of the next history stack entry (that is, the one after the active page) or is empty if the current page is at the top of the stack.
go(x)	Method	Moves *x* entries forward (if $x > 0$) or backward (if $x < 0$) in the history stack.

The *window* Object   The window object is associated with the window in which a document is displayed. Think of the window object as an actual Windows or Macintosh window, and the document object as the content that appears in the window. JavaScript provides the following methods for doing things in the window:

- alert(*strMessage*)—Puts up an alert dialog box and displays the message specified by *strMessage*. Users must dismiss the dialog box by clicking the OK button before they can do anything else (within the browser).

- confirm(*strMessage*)—Puts up a confirmation dialog box with two buttons (OK and Cancel) and displays the message specified by *strMessage*. Users may dismiss the dialog box by clicking Cancel or OK; the confirm() function returns true when users click OK and false when they click Cancel.

- prompt(*strMessage*)—Puts up an input dialog box with a text-entry field and two buttons (OK and Cancel) and displays the message specified by *strMessage*. Users may dismiss the dialog box by clicking either button and can type data into the field (if the dialog is closed by clicking OK) can be passed back to JavaScript for processing (such as entry into a form).

■ open(...)—Allows you to open a second complete browser window and load a document into it. You can also control whether the new window has menus, a status bar, a toolbar, and other gadgets (for creating your own custom dialog boxes).

■ close()—Allows you to close a particular window (that you created earlier with open()) or shut down the browser itself.

HTML Objects and Events

JavaScript also provides access to individual HTML elements as objects, each with their own properties and methods. You can use these objects to customize your pages' behavior.

Properties Common to All Objects   The methods and properties in this section apply to several HTML tags; note that there are other methods and properties, discussed after the following table, for anchors and form elements. Table 27.4 shows the features that these generic HTML objects provide.

Table 27.4   Properties and Methods Common to Most HTML-Oriented JavaScript Objects

Property/ Method	Type	What It Does
onFocus	Event	Called when the user moves the input focus to the field, either via the Tab key or a mouse click.
onBlur	Event	Called when the user moves the input focus out of this field.
onSelect	Event	Called when the user selects text in the field.
onChange	Event	Called only when the field loses focus and the user has modified the data held within; use this function to trigger a validation test.
onSubmit	Event	Called when the user clicks the Submit button of a form.
onClick	Event	Called when a button (on a form) is clicked.
focus()	Method	Moves the input focus to the associated object.
blur()	Method	Moves the input focus away from the associated object (and onto the next object in sequence).

Property/ Method	Type	What It Does
select()	Method	Selects the specified object.
click()	Method	Simulates the pressing of the associated button.
enable()	Method	Enables (ungrays) the associated object.
disable()	Method	Disables (grays) the associated object.

N O T E Note that the focus(), blur(), select(), click(), enable(), and disable() functions are object methods; to call them use the name of the object you want to affect. For example, to turn off the button named Search, you'd use form.search.disable(); ■

Anchor Objects Hypertext anchors don't have all the properties listed in Table 27.4; they only have the onFocus, onBlur, and onClick methods. You modify and set these methods just like others. Remember that no matter what code you attach, Navigator's still going to follow the clicked link—after executing your code.

N O T E With the release of Navigator 3.0, the onClick event can now be told not to activate the hyperlink that was just clicked (by returning a value of false). For example, if you defined a link as follows:

```
<A HREF=http://home.netscape.com/

    ONCLICK=return confirm('Are you sure?');>
```

Clicking the link will display a confirmation dialog box and, if the user clicks the No button, the link won't be followed.

This is currently only available with Navigator 3.0. ■

Form Objects Table 27.5 lists the properties associated with HTML form objects; the later "HTML Events" section also presents several methods that you can override to call JavaScript routines when something happens to an object on the page.

Part

V

Ch

27

Table 27.5   Form Object Properties

Property/ Method	Type	What It Does
name	String	Contains the value of the form's NAME attribute.
length	Integer	Contains the number of elements in the form (and, therefore, in the elements[] array).

continues

Table 27.5   Continued

Property/ Method	Type	What It Does
method	Integer	Contains the value of the form's METHOD attribute (0 for GET, 1 for POST).
action	String	Contains the value of the form's ACTION attribute.
encoding	String	Contains the value of the form's ENCTYPE attribute.
target	Window	Window targeted after submit for form response.
elements[]	Array	Contains all the objects that make up the form.
onSubmit	Event	Called when the user clicks the Submit button of a form. If a value of false is returned from this event, form submission is stopped.
submit()	Method	Forces the submission of the associated form.

Objects in a Form   One of the best places to use JavaScript is in forms, since you can write scripts that process, check, and perform calculations with the data the user enters. JavaScript provides a useful set or properties and methods for text INPUT elements and buttons.

You use INPUT elements in a form to let the user enter text data; JavaScript provides properties to get string objects that hold the element's contents, as well as methods for doing something when the user moves into or out of a field. Table 27.6 shows the properties and methods which are defined for text INPUT elements.

Table 27.6   HTML *INPUT* Object Properties

Property/ Method	Type	What It Does
name	String	Contains the value of the field's NAME attribute.
value	String	Contains the field's contents.
default	String	Contains the initial contents of the field (as specified by the VALUE attribute).

Property/ Method	Type	What It Does
onFocus	Event	Called when the user moves the input focus to the field, either via the Tab key or a mouse click.
onBlur	Event	Called when the user moves the input focus out of this field.
onSelect	Event	Called when the user selects text in the field.
onChange	Event	Called only when the field loses focus and the user has modified the data held within; use this function to trigger a validation test.

Individual buttons and check boxes have properties, too; JavaScript provides properties to get string objects containing the button's data, as well as methods for doing something when the user selects or deselects a particular button. Table 27.7 shows the properties and methods that are defined for button elements.

Table 27.7 Button Object Properties

Property/ Method	Type	What It Does
name	String	Contains the value of the button's NAME attribute.
value	String	Contains the button's VALUE attribute.
onClick	Event	Called when the user clicks the associated button.
click()	Method	Simulates the user's clicking the associated button.

Option buttons are grouped so that only one button in a group can be selected at a time. Because all option buttons in a group have the same name, JavaScript has a special property, index, for use in distinguishing option buttons. Querying the index property of an option button object returns a number (starting with 0 for the first button), indicating which button in the group was triggered.

For example, you might want to automatically put the user's cursor into the first text field in a form, instead of making the user manually click the field. If your first text field is named UserName, you can write the following:

```
form.UserName.focus()
```

in your document's script to get the desired behavior.

Programming with JavaScript

As you've seen in the preceding sections, JavaScript has a lot to offer page authors. It's not as flexible as C or C++, but it's quick and simple. Most importantly, it's easily embedded in your Web pages, so you can maximize their impact with a little JavaScript seasoning. This section covers the gritty details of JavaScript programming, including a detailed explanation of the language's features.

Expressions

An *expression* is anything that can be evaluated to get a single value. Expressions can contain string or numeric literals, variables, operators, and other expressions, and they can range from simple to quite complex. For example,

```
x = 7;
```

is an expression which uses the assignment operator (more on operators in the next section) to assign the result 7 to the variable x. By contrast,

```
(quitFlag == true) && (formComplete == false)
```

is a more complex expression whose final value (a Boolean) depends on the values of the quitFlag and formComplete variables.

Operators

Operators do just what their name implies: they operate on variables and literals. The items that an operator acts on are called its operands. Operators come in the following types:

- *Binary operators* need two operands. The four math operators you learned in elementary school (+ for addition, - for subtraction, * for multiplication, and / for division) are all binary operators, as is the assignment operator (=) seen earlier.

- *Unary operators* only require one operand. The operator can come before or after the operand. The - - operator, which subtracts one from the operand, is a good example. Either count - - or - -count will subtract 1 from the variable count.

Assignment Operators   *Assignment operators* take the result of an expression and assign it to a variable (you can't assign the result of an expression to a literal). One feature that JavaScript has that most other programming languages don't is the ability to change a variable's type on-the-fly, as demonstrated in Listing 27.4.

Listing 27.4   Changing a Variable's Type

```
function TypeDemo() {
    // first, pi is a floating-point
    var pi = 3.1415926;
    document.write("Pi is " + pi + "\n");

    // now, pi is changed to a Boolean
    pi = false;
```

```
    document.write("Pi is now " + pi + "\n");
}
```

This short function first prints the value of pi. In most other languages, though, trying to set a floating-point variable to a Boolean value would either generate a compiler error or a runtime error (with the exception of C, which will valiantly try to set the variable to *some* value...though not necessarily what you want). JavaScript happily accepts the change and prints pi's new value: false.

The most common assignment operator, =, simply assigns the value of an expression's right side to its left side. In Listing 27.4, the variable pi got the floating-point value 3.1415926 after the first expression was evaluated. For convenience, JavaScript also defines some other operators that combine common math operations with assignment (see Table 27.8).

Table 27.8 JavaScript Shorthand Operators

Operator	Example...	...Is Equivalent To...
+=	x += y	x = x + y
-=	x -= y	x = x - y
*=	x *= y	x = x * y
/=	x /= y	x = x / y
++	x++	x = x + 1
--	x--	x = x - 1

Math Operators   The previous sections gave you a sneak preview of the math operators that JavaScript furnishes. You can either combine math operations with assignments, as shown in Table 27.8, or use them individually. As you would expect, the standard four math functions (addition, subtraction, multiplication, and division) work just as they do on an ordinary calculator.

The negation operator (-) is a unary operator that negates the sign of its operand. To use the negation operator, you must place it before the operand.

JavaScript also adds two useful unary operators: -- and ++, called (respectively) the *decrement* and *increment* operators. These two operators do two things: They modify the value of their operand and return the new value. They also share a unique property: They can be used either before or after their operand. If you put the operator after the operand, JavaScript will return the operand's value and *then* modify it. If the operator is placed before the operand, JavaScript will modify the operand *first* and then return the modified value. The following short example might help clarify this seemingly odd behavior:

```
x = 7;      // x set to 7
a = --x;    // x set to 6, THEN a set to 6
b = a++;    // b set to 6, THEN a set to 7
x++;        // x set to 7
```

Comparison Operators   It's often necessary to compare the value of two expressions to see whether one is larger, smaller, or equal to another. JavaScript supplies several comparison operators that take two operands and return `true` if the comparison's `true` and `false` if it's not. (Remember, you can use literals, variables, or expressions with operators that require expressions.) Table 27.9 shows the JavaScript comparison operators.

Table 27.9   Comparison Operators

Operator	Returns *TRUE* When:
==	The two operands are equal.
!=	The two operands are not equal.
<	The left operand is less than the right operand.
<=	The left operand is less than or equal to the right operand.
>	The left operand is greater than the right operand.
>=	The left operand is greater than or equal to the right operand.

T I P   The comparison operators can be used on strings, too; the results depend on standard lexicographic ordering.

It may be helpful to think of the comparison operators as questions; when you write

```
(x >= 10)
```

you're really saying, "Is the value of variable x greater than or equal to 10?"

Logical Operators   Comparison operators compare quantity or content for numeric and string expressions, but sometimes you need to test a logical value—like whether a comparison operator returned `true` or `false`. JavaScript's logical operators allow you to compare expressions that return logical values. The following are JavaScript's logical operators:

- && (read as "and"). A binary operator, && returns `true` only if both operands are `true`. If the first operand evaluates to `false`, && returns `false` immediately (without evaluating the second operand).

- ¦¦ (read as "or"). A binary operator, ¦¦ returns `true` if either operand is `true`.

- ! (read as "not"). A unary operator, ! returns `true` if its operand is `false` and vice versa.

N O T E   Note that && and ¦¦ won't evaluate the second operand if the first operand provides enough information for the operator to return a value. This process, called *short-circuit evaluation*, can be significant when the second operand is a function call. For example,

```
keepGoing = userQuit && theForm.Submit();
```

If `userQuit` is `false`, the second operand—which submits the active form—won't be evaluated (meaning the method won't be executed, in this case). ■

Controlling Your JavaScripts

Some scripts you write will be simple; they'll execute the same way every time, once per page. For example, if you add a JavaScript to play a sound when users visit your home page, it won't need to evaluate any conditions or do anything more than once. More sophisticated scripts might require that you take different actions under different circumstances; you might also want to repeat the execution of a block of code—perhaps by a set number of times or as long as some condition is `true`. JavaScript provides constructs for controlling the execution flow of your script based on conditions, as well as repeating a sequence of operations.

Testing Conditions   JavaScript provides a single type of control statement for making decisions: the `if...else` statement. To make a decision, you supply an expression which evaluates to `true` or `false`; which code is executed depends on what your expression evaluates to.

The simplest form of `if...else` uses only the `if` part. If the specified condition is `true`, the code following the condition is executed; if not, it's skipped. For example, in the following code fragment:

```
if(document.lastModified.year < 1995)
    document.write("Danger!  This is a mighty old document.");
```

The message will only appear if the condition (that the document's `lastModified` property says it was modified before 1995) is `true`. You can use any expression as the condition; since expressions can be nested and combined with the logical operators, your tests can be pretty sophisticated:

```
if((document.lastModified.year == 1996) &&
   (document.lastModified.month >= 10)) {
    document.write("This document is reasonably current.");
}
```

The `else` clause allows you to specify a set of statements to execute when the condition is `false`.

Repeating Actions   If you want to repeat an action more than once, you're in luck! JavaScript provides two different loop constructs that you can use to repeat a set of operations.

The first, called a `for` loop, will execute a set of statements some number of times. You specify three expressions: an initial expression that sets the values of any variables you need to use, a condition that tells the loop how to determine when it's done, and an increment expression that modifies any variables that need it. Here's a simple example:

```
for(count=0; count<100; count++)
    document.write("Count is " + count);
```

This loop will execute 100 times and print out a number each time. The initial expression sets our counter, `count`, to zero; the condition test to see whether `count` is less than `100`, and the increment expression increments `count`.

You can use several statements for any of these expressions, like the following:

```
for (i=0, numFound=0; (i<100 && (numFound<3); i++) {
    if(someObject.found())
        numFound++;
}
```

This loop will either loop 100 times or as many times as it takes to "find" three items—the loop condition terminates when i >= 100 or when numFound >= 3.

The second form of loop is the while loop. It executes statements as long as its condition is true. For example, you could rewrite the first for loop about like the following:

```
count = 0;
while(count < 100) {
    document.write("Count is " + count);
    count++;
}
```

Which form you prefer depends on what you're doing; for loops are useful when you want to perform an action a set number of times (and you know how many times you wish to loop), and while loops are best when you want to keep doing something as long as a particular condition remains true.

JavaScript Reserved Words

JavaScript reserves some keywords for its own use. You may not define your own methods or properties with the same name as any of these keywords; if you do, the JavaScript interpreter will complain. Table 27.10 lists the current reserved words.

Table 27.10   JavaScript Reserved Words

abstract	extends	int	super
boolean	false	interface	switch
break	final	long	synchronized
byte	finally	native	this
case	float	new	throw
catch	for	null	throws
char	function	package	transient
class	goto	private	true
const	if	protected	try
continue	implements	public	var
default	import	return	void
do	in	short	while
double	instanceof	static	with
else			

TIP Some of these keywords are reserved for future use. JavaScript might allow you to use them, but your scripts may break in the future if you do so.

Command Reference

This section provides a quick reference to the JavaScript commands that are implemented as of Navigator 3.0 and Internet Explorer 3.0. The commands are listed in alphabetical order; many have examples. Before we dive in, here's what the formatting of these entries means:

- All JavaScript keywords are in monospaced font.
- Words in *italics* represent user-defined names or statements.
- Any portions enclosed in square brackets ([]) are optional.
- *{statements}* indicates a block of statements, which can consist of a single statement or multiple statements enclosed by braces ({})

break   The break statement terminates the current while or for loop and transfers program control to the statement following the terminated loop.

Syntax

```
break
```

Example

The following function scans the list of URLs in the current document and stops when it has seen all URLs or when it finds an URL that matches the input parameter searchName.

```
function findURL(searchName) {
  var i=0;

  for(i=0; i<document.links.length; i++) {
    if(document.links[i] == searchName)
      break;
  }

  if(i < document.links.length) {
    alert("Found " + searchName + " in position " + i);
  } else {
    alert("" + searchName + " not found!");
  }
}
```

continue   The continue statement stops executing the statements in a while or for loop, and skips to the next iteration of the loop. It doesn't stop the loop altogether like the break statement; instead, in a while loop it jumps back to the condition, and in a for loop it jumps to the update expression.

Syntax

```
continue
```

Part
V

Ch
27

Example

The following function prints the odd numbers between 1 and x; it has a `continue` statement that goes to the next iteration when i is equal to y; thus, it skips y.

```
function printOddNumbers(x, y) {
   var i=0;

   while(i < x) {
      if(i == y)
         continue;

      if((++I % 2) != 0)
         document.write("" + i + "\n");
   }
}
```

for   A `for` loop consists of three optional expressions, enclosed in parentheses and separated by semicolons, followed by a block of statements executed in the loop. These parts do the following:

- The starting expression, `initialExpr`, is evaluated before the loop starts. It's most often used to initialize loop counter variables, and you're free to use the `var` keyword here to declare new variables.

- A `condition` is evaluated on each pass through the loop. If the condition evaluates to `true`, the statements in the loop body are executed. You can leave the condition out, and it will always evaluate to `true`. If you do this, make sure to use `break` in your loop when it's time to exit.

- An update expression, `updateExpr`, is usually used to update or increment the counter variable or other variables used in the `condition`. This expression is optional; you can update variables as needed within the body of the loop if you prefer.

- A block of statements is executed as long as the `condition` is `true`. This block can have one or multiple statements in it.

Syntax

```
for ([initialExpr ;] [condition ;] [updateExpr]) {
   statements
}
```

Example

This simple statement prints out the numbers from 0 to 9. It starts by declaring a loop counter variable, i, and initializing it to zero. As long as i is less than 10, the update expression will increment i, and the statements in the loop body will be executed.

```
for (var i=0; i<10; i++) {
   document.write("" + i + "\n");
}
```

for...in   This is a special form of the `for` loop that iterates the `variableName` variable over all the properties of the `objectName` object. For each distinct property, it executes the statements in the loop body.

Syntax

```
for (variableName in objectName) {
    statements
}
```

Example

The following function takes as its arguments an object and the object's name. It then uses the for...in loop to iterate through all the object's properties; when done, it returns a string that lists the property names and their values.

```
function dumpProps(obj, objName) {
    var result = "";

    for (i in obj) {
        results += objName + "." + i + " = " + obj[i] + "\n";

    return result;
}
```

function   The function statement declares a JavaScript function; the function may optionally accept one or more parameters. To return a value, the function must have a return statement that specifies the value to return. All parameters are passed to functions by value—the function gets the value of the parameter, but cannot change the original value in the caller.

Syntax

```
function name([param] [, param [..., param]]) {
    statements
}
```

Example

```
// This function returns true if the active document has the title
// specified in the theString parameter and false otherwise.
//
function PageNameMatches(theString) {
    return (document.title == theString);
}
```

if...else   The if...else statement is a conditional statement that executes the statements in statementsBlock1 if condition is true. In the option else clause, it executes the statements in statementsBlock2 if condition is false. The blocks of statements may contain any JavaScript statements, including further nested if...else statements.

Syntax

```
if (condition) {
    statementsBlock1
} [else {
    statementsBlock2
}]
```

Example

```
if (Message.IsEncrypted()) {
    Message.Decrypt(SecretKey);
} else {
    Message.Display();
}
```

Part
V

Ch
27

return The `return` statement specifies the value to be returned by a function.

Syntax

```
return expression;
```

Example

The following simple function returns the square of its argument, x, where x is any number.

```
function square(x) {
   return x * x;
}
```

this Use `this` to access methods or properties of an object from within that object's methods. The special word `this` always refers to the current object.

Syntax

```
this.property
```

Example

If `setSize()` is a method of the `document` object, then `this` refers to the specific object whose `setSize()` method is called.

```
function setSize(x, y) {
   this.horzSize = x;
   this.vertSize  = y;
}
```

This method will set the size for an object when called as follows:

```
document.setSize(640, 480);
```

var The `var` statement declares a `varName` variable, optionally initializing it to have a value `val`. The variable name `varName` can be any JavaScript identifier, and `val` can be any legal expression (including literals).

Syntax

```
var varName [= val] [, varName [= val] [..., varName [= val]]];
```

Example

```
var numHits = 0, custName = "Scotty";
```

while The `while` statement contains a condition and a block of statements. If `condition` is true, the body is executed, then the condition is reevaluated and the body is executed again (if `condition` is true). This process repeats until `condition` evaluates to `false`, at which time program execution continues with the next statement after the loop.

Syntax

```
while (condition) {
   statements
}
```

Example

The following simple `while` loop iterates until it finds a `form` in the current `document` object whose name is `OrderForm` or until it runs out of forms in the document.

```
var x = 0;
while ((x < document.forms.length) &&
       (document.forms[x].name != "OrderForm")) {
    x++;
}
```

with   The `with` statement establishes `object` as the default object for the statements in the block. Any property references without an object explicitly identified are assumed to be associated to `object`.

Syntax

```
with (object) {
    statements
}
```

Example

```
with (document) {
    write("Inside a with block, you don't need to " +
          "specify the object.");
    bgColor = "gray";
}
```

Sample JavaScript Code

It can be difficult to pick up a new programming language from scratch—even for experienced programmers. To make it easy for you to master JavaScript, this section presents some examples of JavaScript code and functions that you can use in your own pages. Each of them demonstrates a practical concept.

Dumping an Object's Properties

In the earlier section, "Array and Object Properties," you saw a small function, `DumpProperties()`, that gets all the property names and their values. Let's look at that function again now to see it in light of what you've learned.

```
function DumpProperties(obj, objName) {
    var result = ""; // set the result string to blank

    for (i in obj)
        result += objName + "." + i + " = " + obj[i] + "\n";

    return result;
}
```

As all JavaScript functions should, this one starts by defining its variables by using the `var` keyword; it supplies an initial value, too, which is a good habit to start. The meat of the function is the `for...in` loop, which iterates over all the properties of the specified object. For each property, the loop body collects the object name, the property name (provided by the loop counter in the `for...in` loop), and the property's value. We access the properties as an indexed array instead of by name, so we can get them all.

Note that this function doesn't print anything out. If you want to see its output, put it in a page (remember to surround it with `<SCRIPT>...</SCRIPT>`!); then at the page's bottom, use

```
document.writeln(DumpProperties(obj, objName));
```

where *obj* is the object of interest and *objName* is its name.

Building a Link Table

You might want to have a way to automatically generate a list of all the links in a page, perhaps to display them in a separate section at the end of the page, as shown in Figure 27.2. `DumpURL()`, shown in Listing 27.5, does just that; it prints out a nicely formatted numbered list showing the hostname of each link in the page.

FIG. 27.2

The DumpURL() function adds a numbered list of all the links in a page at the end of the page.

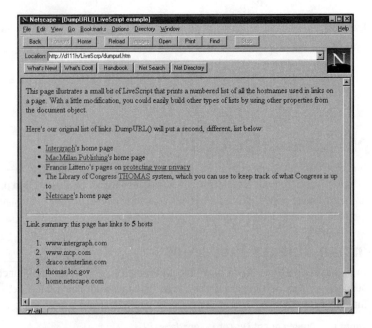

Listing 27.5   *DumpURL()* Displays a Numbered List of All the URLs on a Page

```
<HTML>
<TITLE>DumpURL</TITLE>
<BODY>
<SCRIPT LANGUAGE=JAVASCRIPT>
<!--
    function DumpURL() {
        // declare the variables we'll use
        var linkCount = document.links.length;
```

```
        var result = "";

        // build our summary line
        result = "Link summary: this page has links to " +
                linkCount + " hosts\n";

        result += "\n";

        // for each link in the document, print a list item with it's hostmane
        for(var i=0; i<linkCount; i++)
            result += document.links[i].hostname + "\n";

        return result;
    }
</SCRIPT>

<FORM>
<INPUT TYPE=BUTTON NAME=Dump VALUE="Dump URLS" OnClick="alert(DumpURL())">
</FORM>
<A HREF=http://rampages.onramp.net/~jerry>Jerry's Home Page</A>
</BODY>
</HTML>
```

This function starts by declaring the variables used in the function. JavaScript requires that you declare most variables before using them, and good programming practice dictates doing so even when JavaScript doesn't require it. Next, you build the summary line for your table by assigning a string literal full of HTML to the result variable. You use a for loop to iterate through all the links in the current document and add a list item for each to the result variable. When you finish, add the closing HTML for your list to result and return it.

Updating Data in Form Fields

There have been several mentions of the benefits of using JavaScript to check and modify data in HTML forms. Let's look at an example that dynamically updates the value of a text field based on the user's selection from one of several buttons.

To make this work, you need two pieces; the first is a simple bit of JavaScript that updates the value property of an object to whatever you pass in. Here's what it looks like:

```
function change(input, newValue) {
   input.value = newValue;
}
```

Then, each button you want to include needs to have its onClick method changed so that it calls your change() function. Here's a sample button definition:

```
<input type=button value="Mac"
       onClick="change(this.form.display, 'Macintosh')">
```

When the button is clicked, JavaScript calls the onClick method, which happens to point to your function. The this.form.display object points to a text field named display; this refers to the active document, form refers to the form in the active document, and display refers to the form field named display. Of course, this requires that you have a form INPUT gadget named display!

Validating Data in Form Fields

Often when you create a form to get data from the user, you need to check that data to see if it's correct and complete before sending mail or making a database entry or whatever you collected the data for. Without JavaScript, you have to POST the data and let a CGI script on the server decide if all the fields were correctly filled out. You can do better, though, by writing JavaScript functions that check the data in your form on the client; by the time the data gets posted, you know it's correct.

For this example, let's require that the user fill out two fields on our form: ZIP code and area code. We'll also present some other fields that are optional. First, you need a function that will return true if there's something in a field and false if it's empty:

```
function isFilled(input) {
    return (input.value.length != 0);
}
```

For each field you want to make the user complete, you'll hook to its onBlur event handler. onBlur is triggered when the user moves the focus out of the specified field. Here's what your buttons look like:

```
<input name="zipcode" value=""
        onBlur="if(!isFilled(form.zipcode)) {
                    alert('You must put your zipcode here!');
                    form.zipcode.focus();
                }">
```

When the user tries to move the focus out of the zipcode field, the code attached to the onBlur event is called. That code in turn checks to see if the field is complete; if not, it nags the user and puts the focus back into the zipcode field.

Of course, you could also implement a more gentle validation scheme by attaching a JavaScript to the form's Submit button, like the following:

```
<script language="JavaScript">
<!--
function areYouSure() {
    return confirm("Are you sure you want to submit " +
                "these answers?");
}
// -->
</script>
...
<form method=post action="..." onSubmit="return areYouSure();">
```

A Pseudo-Scientific Calculator

If you ask any engineer under a certain age what kind of calculator he or she used in college, the answer is likely to be "a Hewlett Packard." HP calculators are somewhat different from the ordinary calculators; you use *reverse Polish notation*, or *RPN*, to do calculations.

With a regular calculator, you put the operator in between operands. To add 3 and 7, you push 3, then the + key, then 7, and finally = to print the answer. With an RPN calculator, you put the operator *after* both operands. To add 3 and 7 on an HP-15C, you have to push 3, then Enter (which puts the first operand on the internal stack), then 7, then +, at which time you would see the correct answer. This oddity takes a bit of getting used to, but it makes complex calculations go much faster, since intermediate results get saved on the stack (for quick use as operands in further calculations).

Here's a simple RPN example. To compute

$((1024 * 768) / 3.14159)^2$

you'd enter

1024, Enter, 768, *, 3.14159, /, x^2

to get the correct answer: 6.266475×10^{10}, or about 6.3 billion.

Netscape provides an RPN calculator as an example of JavaScript's expressive power. Let's take a detailed look at how it works. Listing 27.2 shows the JavaScript itself (note that these are really in the same file; we've just split them for convenience). Figure 27.3 shows the calculator as it's displayed in Navigator.

FIG. 27.3

Navigator displays the RPN calculator as a table of buttons, with the accumulator (the answer) and the stack at the top.

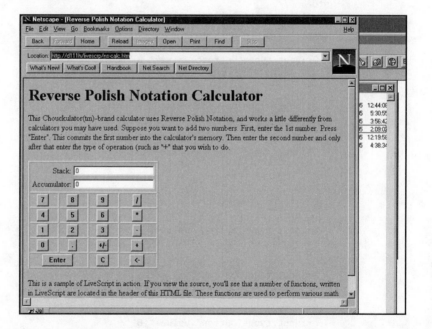

The HTML Page Listing 27.6 shows the HTML for our calculator's page. For precise alignment, all the buttons are grouped into a table; the accumulator (where the answer is displayed) and the stack (where operands can be stored) are at the top.

Listing 27.6   The HTML Definition of the RPN Calculator Example

```
<form method="post">
<table border=1 align=center>
```

continues

Part
V

Ch
27

Listing 27.6 Continued

```html
<tr align=center>
<td colspan=4>

    <table border=0>
       <tr>
          <td align=right>Stack:</td>
          <td><input name="stack" value="0"></td>
       </tr>
       <tr>
          <td align=right>Acc:</td>
          <td><input name="display" value="0"></td>
       </tr>
    </table>

</td>
</tr>

<tr align=center>
    <td>
       <input type="button" value=" 7 "
          onClick="addChar(this.form.display, '7')">
    </td>
    <td>
       <input type="button" value=" 8 "
          onClick="addChar(this.form.display, '8')">
    </td>
    <td>
       <input type="button" value=" 9 "
          onClick="addChar(this.form.display, '9')">
    </td>
    <td>
       <input type="button" value=" / "
          onClick="divide(this.form)">
    </td>
</tr>

<tr align=center>
    <td>
       <input type="button" value=" 4 "
          onClick="addChar(this.form.display, '4')">
    </td>
    <td>
       <input type="button" value=" 5 "
          onClick="addChar(this.form.display, '5')">
    </td>
    <td>
       <input type="button" value=" 6 "
          onClick="addChar(this.form.display, '6')">
    </td>
    <td>
       <input type="button" value=" * "
          onClick="multiply(this.form)">
    </td>
</tr>

<tr align=center>
    <td>
       <input type="button" value=" 1 "
          onClick="addChar(this.form.display, '1')">
```

```html
        </td>
        <td>
            <input type="button" value=" 2 "
                onClick="addChar(this.form.display, '2')">
        </td>
        <td>
            <input type="button" value=" 3 "
                onClick="addChar(this.form.display, '3')">
        </td>
        <td>
            <input type="button" value=" - "
                onClick="subtract(this.form)">
        </td>
    </tr>

    <tr align=center>
        <td>
            <input type="button" value=" 0 "
                onClick="addChar(this.form.display, '0')">
        </td>
        <td>
            <input type="button" value=" . "
                onClick="addChar(this.form.display, '.')">
        </td>
        <td>
            <input type="button" value="+/-"
                onClick="changeSign(this.form.display)">
        </td>
        <td>
            <input type="button" value=" + "
                onClick="add(this.form)">
        </td>
    </tr>

    <tr align=center>
        <td colspan="2">
            <input type="button" value=" Enter " name="enter"
                onClick="pushStack(this.form)">
        </td>
        <td>
            <input type="button" value=" C "
                onClick="this.form.display.value = 0 ">
        </td>
        <td>
            <input type="button" value=" <- "
                onClick="deleteChar(this.form.display)">
        </td>
    </tr>

</table>
</form>
```

Notice that each button has an onClick event handler associated with it. The digits 0 through 9 all call the addChar() JavaScript function; the editing buttons (C for *clear* and <- for *backspace*) call functions that change the value of the accumulator. The Enter button stores the current value on the stack, and the +/- buttons change the accumulator's sign.

Of course, the operators themselves call JavaScript functions, too; for example, the * button's definition calls the Multiply() function. The definitions aren't functions themselves; they include function calls (as in the digit buttons) or individual statements (as in the *clear* button).

The JavaScript   All the onClick events shown in the previous section need to have JavaScript routines to call. Listing 27.7 shows the JavaScript functions that implement the actual calculator.

Listing 27.7   The JavaScript Code That Makes Up the RPN Calculator

```
<script language="JavaScript">
<!-- hide from non-JavaScript browsers

// keep track of whether we just computed display.value
//
var computed = false

// push the the accumulator (display) onto the stack
//
function pushStack(form) {
   form.stack.value   = form.display.value;
   form.display.value = 0;
}

// add a new character to the display
//
function addChar(input, character) {
   // auto-push the stack if the last value was computed
   //
   if(computed) {
      pushStack(input.form);
      computed = false;
   }

   // make sure input.value is a string
   //
   if(input.value == null || input.value == "0")
      input.value = character;
   else
      input.value += character;
}

function deleteChar(input) {
   input.value = input.value.substring(0,
                 input.value.length - 1);
}

function add(form) {
   form.display.value = parseFloat(form.stack.value)
                      + parseFloat(form.display.value);
   computed = true;
}

function subtract(form) {
   form.display.value = form.stack.value
                      - form.display.value;
   computed = true;
}

function multiply(form) {
   form.display.value = form.stack.value
                      * form.display.value;
   computed = true;
}
```

```
function divide(form) {
   var divisor = parseFloat(form.display.value);

   if(divisor == 0) {
      alert("Don't divide by zero, pal…");
      return;
   }

   form.display.value = form.stack.value / divisor;
   computed = true;
}

function changeSign(input) {
   if(input.value.substring(0, 1) == "-")
      input.value = input.value.substring(1, input.value.length)
   else
      input.value = "-" + input.value
}

// done hiding from old browsers -->
</script>
```

As you saw in the previous HTML listing, every button is connected to some function. The `addChar()` and `deleteChar()` functions directly modify the contents of the form field named `display`—the accumulator—as do the operators (`add()`, `subtract()`, `multiply()`, and `divide()`).

This code shows off some subtle but cool benefits of JavaScript that would be difficult or impossible to do with CGI scripts (or, if possible, at least incredibly slow—each update of the form would have to be sent to the server for processing, and a new form sent back to the browser). First, notice that the `divide()` function checks for division by zero and presents a warning dialog box to the user. More importantly, in this example, all the processing is done on the client—imagine an application like an interactive tax form, where all the calculations are done on the browser and only the completed, verified data gets POSTed to the server.

JavaScript Style Sheets (JSSS)

With the introduction of JSSS—or JavaScript Style Sheets—Netscape is helping to automate and simplify the process of adding style to your pages. Just as JavaScript can be used in place of complicated CGI programs, JSSS can be used to build style sheets. (To read more about style sheets, point your Web browser to: **http://www.w3.org/pub/WWW/TR/WD-style.html**.).

> **Part**
>
> **V**
>
> **Ch**
>
> **27**

> **CAUTION**
>
> As of this writing, JSSS has just been released in it's nascent form to the Web. Most likely by the time you read this, the specification will probably have been expanded and modified. The core functionality will most likely stay intact, though.

▶ **See** "Attaching a Style Sheet to Your HTML Document" to learn how to attach a cascading style sheet to your HTML document, **p. 286**

Including Style in HTML

Just as there is more than one way to add traditional JavaScript code in your HTML files, there are—as of this writing—three ways to add style to your pages via JSSS. You can use the LINK element in your head statement to link to an outside JSSS as in the following example:

```
<HTML>
<HEAD>
<title>My Wow Page</title>
<LINK REL=STYLESHEET TYPE="text/javascript" HREF="http://foo.bar.com/styles/wow"
TITLE="Neato">
</HEAD>
```

Notice the MIME type of "text/javascript". If you use style sheets of this kind, make sure your Web server can serve files of this type. You can also use the <STYLE></STYLE> container tags in the heading:

```
<HTML>
<HEAD>
<TITLE>Another Cool Page</TITLE>
<STYLE TYPE="text/javascript"><!--
tags.EM.color="green"
--></STYLE>
</HEAD>
```

Notice here that the <STYLE></STYLE> tags also had to include the HTML comments. This is due to the fact that older browsers may ignore the <STYLE> and </STYLE> but the content in between would have been interpreted as HTML (thus giving an error message). Adding the comments allows the style to be read in by newer browsers.

The final way to add style is the least recommended one—at least by the developers of this specification. You may include the STYLE attribute within any tag. For instance,

```
<DIV STYLE="fontsize='12pt'">
<H1 STYLE="wordSpacing=60">
```

Notice that if you use quotes within the style value, you must use alternating quotes just like you might if you were using onClick or alert(). This is the least recommended way of adding style, simply because it is altering the HTML code itself, instead of being abstracted from that code and placed in a separate file. When you add style directly to the HTML code, you are counteracting the modularity of your style. You might want to later change all of your pages to a new style—but if you used styles within the HTML, you will have to go into each one and change it—whereas if you used a separate file for your style settings, all you have to do is change that one file.

Here is a shortcut to setting multiple attributes of a tag within JavaScript. You may remember seeing this with the Math object:

```
<STYLE><!--
with (tags.DIV) {
color="green"; align='left';
textTransform="uppercase";
}
--></STYLE>
```

Remember to place your <STYLE></STYLE> in the <HEAD> area to ensure that it is loaded before anything is drawn to the browser window.

The Contextual Function

JSSS also adds a new base-level function called contextual. This function allows you to specify style attributes based on the position of other tags. What this means is that you can set default styles—say "all level one headers (H1) are green with 12pt font"—across your page but override this for special cases. The contextual function allows you to add exceptions, like "except the level one headers that are enclosed by <DIV> tags of class rad which are red." The two prevoius statements are translated into the following JSSS:

```
<style type="text/javascript">
with (tags){
h1.color="green";
h1.fontSize="12pt";
}
contextual(classes.rad.div, tags.h1).color="red"
</style>
```

The *Tags* Object

JSSS introduces some new objects to JavaScript. Most notable is the document.tags object. All of the tags on a page are reflected in this object, as well as all of the style attributes for those tags. For instance, to specify that you want all bold text to be red, you could use

```
document.tags.b.color = "red"
```

The *Classes* Object

Another object introduced in JSSS is classes. This object does not pertain to Java classes but instead to the new HTML 3 proposal that allows you to assign a class to a set of elements (tags) within an HTML document. Suppose you had created a class called cool and had assigned to that class a number of tags, as illustrated below:

```
<HTML>
<HEAD>
<TITLE>My Cool Page</TITLE>
</HEAD>
<BODY BGCOLOR="green">
<H1 class=cool>Welcome to my cool page</H1>
<DIV ALIGN=left class=cool>
Too bad it's just an example page.
</DIV>
<P>
More text <B>here</B>.
</BODY>
</HTML>
```

You could add a style element to just the tags that you have set as `cool` or to any subset—like just the `<DIV>` tags that have the class of `cool`. To set this style in the header you could use `classes.cool.div.color="blue"`.

If you wanted all the tags assigned to the class to be blue, you could use `classes.cool.all="blue"`.

The *ids* object

HTML 3 adds another attribute to tags called `ids`. This attribute complements the `class` attribute because instead of grouping together tags, it uniquely identifies each tag that contains the `ids` attribute. Another way of looking at `class` versus `ids` is this: German Shepherds, Dobermans, and Poodles are all in the `class` Dog. Your Poodle has the name—or ID of "Poopsie." Just as you would not name two dogs you own the same name, you must give each tag that uses the `ids` attribute a unique name. For example,

```
<em id=br549>Emphasized Text</em>
```

To use the `ids` object, you might say: `ids.br549.paddingTop=auto`.

The *Tags.___.apply* Property

You will often find yourself setting numerous style functions to a tag—since there are many attributes that can be modified to suit any particular style. Instead of manually setting each of these functions (like `tags.b.color="purple"`) you can define a function to the `apply` property of that tag. Essentially, the `apply` property is a style constructor in a way similar to building objects with a function that returns an object. For example,

```
function setStyle(){
if (textDecoration == "blink") {
textDecoration == "none";
color="blue";
}
else {
textDecoration = "underline";
color = "green";
}
}
tags.h1.textDecoration="blink";
tags.all.apply = setStyle();
```

What happens here is that you define a function that sets attributes to all the tags. You then set one of the tags to have the `textDecoration` style of `blink`. The function will convert all blinking headers to normal and change their color to blue. All other tags will now present green underlined text. ●

## CHAPTER 28

Developing with LiveWire Pro

Netscape Communications got its start, of course, developing browsers and servers. As a company, it has as much experience as anybody using their products to develop Web sites. In 1995, as it began to extend its line of servers, Netscape also decided to develop application development tools. These tools are now marketed under the name LiveWire.

The very use of the term application development as it applies to the Web recognizes Netscape's observation that the static HTML files of 1995 Web sites are now insufficient to sustain the growth of the Web. More and more developers were moving to CGI in order to add capabilities to their sites, but the complexity of CGI and the talent required to develop a new script limited the number of sites that could take advantage of this technology.

Netscape's current direction enables Webmasters who do not have extensive programming skills to reuse components built into Java and to integrate applications with JavaScript. LiveWire Pro includes the tools necessary to allow the Webmaster to integrate a database that understands the Structured Query Language (SQL) into the Web site. ■

How LiveWire works with the HTTP server

It supports server-side JavaScript by intercepting selected URLs.

About HTTP, the protocol of the Web

How knowledge of that protocol enables the Webmaster to extend HTML with CGI, LiveWire, and LiveWire Pro.

The essentials of SQL

Learn about the language of databases.

About the relational database model

The standard for client-server architectures.

The Database Connectivity Library

Netscape's application program interface (API) that enables applications to talk to relational databases by using SQL.

How to build client-server applications

Distribute the computing task between the user's machine and a database server.

The "Pro" in LiveWire Pro

Increasingly, the intranet marketplace is shaping up to a battle between Netscape Communications and Microsoft. Microsoft has nearly two decades of experience marketing personal computer applications. Bill Gates has succeeded in building an impressive group of analysts, programmers, and managers who produce and maintain software products quickly. Microsoft's Windows 95 is particularly strong among corporate users, and thus is commonly used on intranets. By offering its second generation servers and LiveWire on both UNIX and Windows NT, Netscape has ensured that the corporation's choice of server machine will not prevent the Webmaster from choosing a Netscape solution.

Netscape Communications, by contrast, was founded in 1994 and has a fraction of the resources of Microsoft. Unlike Microsoft, however, Netscape was born for the Net; its understanding of what works on the Net, and specifically on the Web, is its greatest asset.

During the explosive growth years of personal computers, Microsoft and others made money selling interpreters for the computer language BASIC—enabling millions of people who were not professional programmers to nevertheless write applications. In the battle for intranet marketshare, both Microsoft and Netscape understand that the winner will be the company that markets the best visual programming environment, enabling Webmasters who are not professional programmers to develop sophisticated applications for the Web.

Microsoft is promoting Visual Basic Script and ActiveX Objects as its entries in this market, whereas Netscape is offering LiveWire and LiveWire Pro. Netscape's initial LiveWire package includes four components:

- Netscape Navigator Gold—a Netscape Navigator client with integrated word processing capabilities that enable users to develop and edit live online documents in a WYSIWYG environment.
- LiveWire Site Manager—a visual tool that enables the Webmaster to see the entire site at a glance, and to manage pages, links, and files using drag-and-drop.
- LiveWire JavaScript Compiler—an extension to Netscape servers that enables the Webmaster to build distributed applications in server-side JavaScript, with some of the functionality remaining on the client computer and some running on the server.
- LiveWire Application Manager—a graphical tool that enables the Webmaster to install and monitor LiveWire applications through Netscape Navigator.
- Database Connectivity Library—a set of software that provides an Application Programmer Interface (API) between JavaScript and any of several commercial relational databases.

LiveWire Pro includes all the components of LiveWire. In addition, it includes a single-user developer version of Informix, one of the more popular database management systems. Using only the components of LiveWire Pro, the Webmaster can develop an application that accesses and integrates data in an Informix database and serves it up as dynamic Web pages or as a datastream to a client-based application.

N O T E The Windows NT version of LiveWire Pro also includes Crystal Reports, a sophisticated report generator from the Seagate Software Information Management Group. More information about Crystal Reports is available online at **http://www.crystalinc.com/**. ■

N O T E Netscape's initial release of LiveWire Pro includes support for database managers from Informix, Oracle, and Sybase, as well as support for the Microsoft ODBC standard. Through ODBC, a LiveWire application can access databases built using dBASE, Visual FoxPro, and even such "standards" as text files.

LiveWire Pro implements its interface to the Informix, Oracle, and Sybase libraries through the vendor's API, rather than through ODBC drivers. This design makes it easier to configure the database and gives higher performance than an ODBC-based approach. ■

LiveWire Pro is available as part of Netscape's *SuiteSpot* tool. SuiteSpot is a collection of tools sold as one integrated package. This package consists of:

- *The Enterprise Server*—Netscape's high-end Web server.
- *The Catalog Server*—a search tool that can be used to build and maintain databases of all the resources on a site.
- *The Proxy Server*—a tool for maintaining copies of frequently used files on a local machine.
- *The Mail Server*—which supports the Simple Mail Transfer Protocol (SMTP) for server-to-server communications, and the Post Office Protocol (POP) for communications with mail clients.
- *LiveWire Pro*—the application-development and database-connectivity tool described in this chapter.

The SuiteSpot architecture is illustrated in Figure 28.1.

 T I P Netscape's pricing is structured so that SuiteSpot costs the same as the four servers (Enterprise, Catalog, Proxy, and Mail). If you're going to buy the four servers anyway, buy SuiteSpot and get LiveWire Pro for free.

How LiveWire Works

While a Webmaster can build LiveWire applications without understanding how LiveWire works, such an understanding will help during the debugging process, and also leads to a more efficient distribution of the work between the various computers available.

All Webmasters understand that the user accesses a Web site using a Web browser such as Netscape Navigator. This software, known as the client, asks the Web server for entities such as HTML pages. The address for each such entity is known as a Uniform Resource Locator, or URL. The protocol by which requests are made and answered is the Hypertext Transport Protocol, or HTTP.

FIG. 28.1
SuiteSpot is designed
to insulate the
Webmaster from the
differences between
various operating
systems and
hardware.

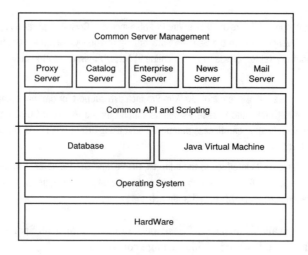

➤ Live Wire Pro adds database connectivity
to the Suitespot Architecture.

Most Webmasters also know that, in addition to offering static pages of HTML (which are rendered
into Web pages by the browser), they can write programs that run on the server. These programs
follow the Common Gateway Interface protocol, or CGI, which enables them to get information from
the user and process it in ways that go well beyond the capabilities of HTTP. Typically, a CGI script
will finish by returning some HTML to the client, so the user sees a new page.

A Brief HTTP Tutorial

Most HTTP requests ask for a specific entity (typically an HTML page) to be sent back from the
server to the client. These requests contain the keyword GET. If the server is properly configured,
some URLs can point to programs that are run (instead of being sent back to the client) and the
output of the program is returned. Such URLs correspond to CGI scripts that are accessed using the
GET method.

Other CGI scripts require more input, such as the output of an HTML form. Such scripts are written
to use a different method, called POST. When the server recognizes a POST request, it starts the CGI
script and then takes the datastream coming in from the client and passes it to the "standard input"
file handle (also known as STDIN) of the CGI script.

CGI is a useful general-purpose mechanism—many sites use CGI successfully to e-mail the results of
an HTML form to the site owner, search the site for key information requested by the user, or even
query a database. So why is Netscape offering alternatives to CGI? There are many reasons:

- Every time a CGI program is activated, it starts, runs, and exits. The process of starting,
  called *forking* on many operating systems, is computationally expensive. If the CGI script is
  busy, the server can spend much of its time forking the same script over and over.

- Communication between the server and the CGI script is limited to streams of data in STDIN
  or perhaps a few characters in environment variables. The CGI script cannot ask the server
  any questions, so the server has to package up everything that any script might want to know
  and store it for every script.

- CGI scripts are generally written in Perl, Tcl, or even C and C++—general-purpose languages that have no built-in mechanisms for dealing with the CGI protocol. Many Webmasters are not comfortable writing the code necessary to implement CGI in such a language.

- CGI scripts directly call the features of the operating system, so they are not particularly portable between UNIX and Windows NT servers.

- CGI scripts can be used by infiltrators to compromise the security of a site. While there are ways of "hardening" a CGI script to make it resistant to most of these attacks, many Webmasters are not aware of these techniques or choose not to use them. Consequently, some system administrators do not allow CGI scripts on their machines, or require that the script be inspected before it is installed. These restrictions add cost and delay to the mainte-nance of the site, and may rule out CGI enhancements altogether.

- CGI scripts, by definition, are run on the server, but many functions (such as validating the input of a form) require less bandwidth and return results faster if they are run on the client's machine.

A Webmaster can add CGI or Netscape's server-side alternative, LiveWire, to a corporate intranet server, just as he might to an Internet server. CGI scripts require special configuration of the server. The LiveWire application must be installed using the Application Manager.

 TIP Even in the relatively benign environment of an intranet, do not ignore the security concerns about CGI. Many scripts provide access to critical corporate resources, and should be hardened against infiltrators from *inside* the company.

What Options Does Netscape Offer?

Netscape offers two kinds of choices to the Webmaster who wants to extend the capabilities of the site beyond the capabilities of HTTP: choice of the language in which the application is written, and choice of which machine on which the application runs.

A Webmaster using the high-end Enterprise server can serve applications (called *applets*) written in Java, an object-oriented language developed specifically for the Web by Sun Microsystems. He can also write programs in JavaScript, a simplified language loosely based on Java. JavaScript is designed to be embedded in an HTML file and run on the client machine. The Netscape browsers understand JavaScript and can execute these programs.

Java applets are stored on the server but are downloaded and run on the client machine. JavaScript scripts are usually run on the client. If LiveWire is installed on the server, they can be compiled and run on that machine as well.

NOTE While client-side JavaScript and server-side JavaScript (i.e., LiveWire applications) use the same language, LiveWire provides several runtime objects on the server that are crucial in building a LiveWire application. These objects are described in more detail later in this chapter, in the section entitled "Server-Side JavaScript." ▓

A programmer can also write an application for a specific platform (such as a Windows computer or a Macintosh) that integrates with the Netscape browser. These applications, called *plug-ins*, are acti-vated when the server sends a specific MIME media type that the plug-in is designed to handle. Plug-ins are usually written in C++.

The predecessors of plug-ins, called *helper applications*, are available on all browsers, while plug-ins work on just a few browsers besides Netscape Navigator. Helper applications open a separate window and run as a separate process, while plug-ins are integrated into the client and can send messages back and forth to the Netscape browser. This tight integration allows programmers to do more with plug-ins than they can with helper applications.

N O T E JavaScript was once called "LiveScript." That name still appears in some literature, and is still supported by the JavaScript compilers and interpreters. Only the name has changed—there is only one language. ■

Many people find JavaScript to be an easier language in which to program than Java—particularly if they are not professional programmers. Using LiveWire, a Webmaster can embed JavaScript on a page but have it run on the server. Then the results of that script are sent to the client software.

What Does LiveWire Do with a Request?

To understand the role LiveWire plays, it is necessary to first understand how LiveWire handles JavaScript on the server. The LiveWire Server Extension Engine includes a script compiler for JavaScript. When the developer finishes writing a page that includes server-side JavaScript, she submits it to the compiler. The compiler attaches the compiled image (a set of bytecodes) to the page.

Recall that a Web server usually handles a GET request by finding the requested entity and sending it back to the client. When LiveWire is installed on a Netscape server, an extra step is inserted in this process. LiveWire registers an interest in certain URLs, and when one of those URLs is requested, the server turns control over to the JavaScript runtime interpreter in the LiveWire Server Extensions. That interpreter runs the code represented by the bytecodes attached to the page. The finished result, which includes both static HTML and dynamic program output, is sent back to the client.

N O T E Netscape likes to use the term "live" in its literature. As it uses the term, it is a synonym for "dynamic" as it is used by most Webmasters. Thus, "live online document" and "dynamic Web page" mean the same thing. ■

Understanding SQL

Recall that the single difference between LiveWire and LiveWire Pro is that LiveWire Pro provides access to relational databases. This section describes Relational Database Management Systems (RDBMS) and their language, SQL.

Some Webmasters with a background in PC applications are more comfortable with database managers such as dBASE than they are with newer programs such as Visual FoxPro or Microsoft SQL Server. Many of the newer or more powerful programs use the Structured Query Language, or SQL (pronounced see-quel). SQL was one of the languages that emerged from early work on relational database management systems. Among RDBMSs, SQL has emerged as the clear winner. Non-relational databases, such as Object Design's object-oriented database, ObjectStore, often offer a SQL interface in addition to any native data manipulation language they may support.

The Relational Model

Most industrial-strength database managers use what is called the *relational model* of data. The relational model is characterized by one or more "relations," more commonly known as *tables*, as illustrated in Figure 28.2. LiveWire provides direct access to tables through the Database Connectivity Library.

FIG. 28.2

A single table is defined by its columns and keys, and holds the data in rows.

ISBN	Title	Publication Year	Retail Price	Publisher ID
0-7897-0801-9	Webmaster Expert Solutions	1996	59.99	7897
1-57521-070-3	Creating Web Applets with Java	1996	39.99	57521
0-7897-0790-X	Enhancing Webscape Web Pages	1996	34.99	7897
1-56205-473-2	Webmasters' Professional Reference	1996	55.00	56205
1-57576-354-0	An Interactive Guide to the Internet	1996	75.00	57576
1-57521-016-9	Bots & Other Internet Beasties	1996	49.99	57521
1-56205-573-9	Building Internet Database Servers/CGI	1996	45.00	56205
1-57521-049-5	Java Unleashed	1996	49.99	57521
0-7897-0758-6	Special Edition Using HTML, Second Edition	1996	49.99	7897
0-7897-0604-0	Special Edition Using Java	1996	49.99	7897
1-57521-073-8	Teach Yourself JavaScript in a Week	1996	39.99	57521
0-7897-0753-5	The Big Basic Book of the Internet	1996	19.99	7897
1-56205-521-6	Flying Through the Web: VRML	1996	30.00	56205

In a well-defined database, each table represents a single concept. For example, a book wholesaler might need to model the concept of a book. Each row holds one record—information about a single title. The columns represent the fields of the record—things that the application needs to know about the book, such as the title, the publication year, and the retail price. Every table must have some combination of columns (typically just one) that uniquely identifies each row; this set of columns is called the *primary key*. For the book table, this column could be the book's ISBN.

Each table may also contain "pointers"—called *foreign keys*—to other tables by storing the primary key from the other table in its own columns. For example, each book is associated with a publisher by storing the publisher's key in the book record, as shown in Figure 28.3. In the book table, the publisher ID is a foreign key. In the publisher table, the publisher ID is the primary key.

FIG. 28.3

A foreign key links two relations.

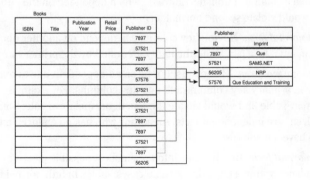

Part
V

Ch

28

Database design is a specialty area in computer science. If you are setting up a new database and do not have experience in database design, consider hiring a specialist to help. Relational databases are pulled in two competing directions. If there is redundancy between the tables, there is always a possibility that the tables may become inconsistent. For example, if the books table were to include the address of the publisher as well as the publisher ID, it would be possible for the application to update the publisher's address in the publisher table but fail to update the address in the book table.

If a database is divided into many small tables so there is no redundancy, it is easy to ensure consistency. But if the database is large, a design with many small tables may require many queries to search through tables looking for foreign keys. Large databases with little or no redundancy can be inefficient both in terms of space and performance.

Database designers talk about five levels of *normalization*—standards to ensure database consistency. The normal forms are hierarchical; a database in third normal form satisfies the guidelines for first, second, and third normal forms. Here are the guidelines that define the five normal forms:

1. *First normal form.* At each row-column intersection, there must be one and only one value. For example, a database in which all of the books published by a given publisher in 1996 are stored in a single row-column intersection violates the rule for first normal form.

2. *Second normal form.* Every non-key column must depend on the entire primary key. If the primary key is *composite*—made up of more than one component—no non-key column can be a fact about a subset of the primary key. As a practical matter, second normal form is commonly achieved by requiring that each primary key span just one column.

   For example, an ISBN is a number that uniquely identifies a book. (There's one on the back cover of this book: 0-7897-1097-8.) The ISBN contains several internal fields. The number "7897" identifies the fact that the book is published by Que. The number 1097 identifies the book itself. If a table included the ISBN as a composite primary key (e.g., one column for the publisher ID, and another for the book ID), and the table also included a column "PublisherAddress" which depended on the publisher ID *only*, that table would violate second normal form.

3. *Third normal form.* No non-key column can depend on another non-key field. Each column must be a fact about the entity identified by the primary key.

4. *Fourth normal form.* There must not be any independent one-to-many relationships between primary key columns and non-key columns. For example, a table like the one shown in Table 28.1 would violate the fourth normal form rule: "cities toured" and "children" are independent facts. An author who has no children and has toured no cities could have a blank row.

5. *Fifth normal form.* Break tables into the smallest possible pieces in order to eliminate all redundancy within a table. In extreme cases, tables in fifth normal form may consist of a primary key and a single non-key column.

Table 28.1   Tables That Are Not in Fourth Normal Form Are Characterized by Numerous Blanks

Author	Children	Cities Toured
Brady	Greg	Seattle
Brady	Cindy	Los Angeles
Brady	Bobby	
Clinton	Chelsea	Washington
Clinton		Los Angeles
Clinton		St. Louis

Databases should not be indiscriminately put into fifth normal form. Such databases are likely to have high integrity, but may take up too much space on the disk (because many tables will have many foreign keys). They are also likely to have poor performance, because even simple queries require searches (called *joins*) across many tables. The best design is a trade-off between consistency and efficiency.

An empty row-column intersection is called a *null*. The specification of each table shows which columns are allowed to have null values.

A SQL Primer

A typical life cycle of a database proceeds like this:

1. The database is created with the SQL CREATE DATABASE command:

   ```
   CREATE DATABASE bookWholesale
   ```

2. Tables are created with the CREATE TABLE command:

   ```
   CREATE TABLE books
   (isbn char(10) not null,
   title char(20) not null,
   publicationYear datetime null,
   retailPrice money null))
   ```

3. One or more indexes is created:

   ```
   CREATE INDEX booksByYear ON books (publicationYear)
   ```

   Many RDBMSs support *clustered* indexes. In a clustered index, the data is physically stored on the disk sorted in accordance with the index. A clustered index incurs some overhead when items are added or removed, but can give exceptional performance if the number of reads is large compared to the number of updates. Because there is only one physical arrangement on the disk, there can be at most one clustered index on each table.

   SQL also supports the UNIQUE keyword, in which the RDBMS enforces a rule that says that no two rows can have the same index value.

4. Data is inserted into the tables.

   ```
   INSERT INTO books VALUES ('0789708019', 'Webmasters Expert Solutions', 1996,
   69.95)
   ```

   Depending upon the application, new rows may be inserted often, or the database, once set up, may stay fairly stable.

Part
V

Ch
28

5. Queries are run against the database.

```
SELECT title, publicationYear WHERE retailPrice < 40.00
```

- For most applications, queries are the principal reason for the existence of the application.

- Data may be changed.

```
UPDATE books
SET retailPrice = 59.99
WHERE ISBN='0789708019'
```

6. Data may be deleted from the tables.

```
DELETE FROM books
WHERE publicationYear < 1990
```

7. Finally, the tables and even the database itself may be deleted when the Webmaster no longer has a need for them.

```
DROP TABLE books
DROP DATABASE bookWholesale
```

 If the number of queries is high compared to the number of inserts, deletes, and updates, indexes are likely to improve performance. As the rate of database changes climbs, the overhead of maintaining the indexes begins to dominate the application.

 When a table is created, the designer specifies the data type of each column. All RDBMSs provide character and integer types. Most commercial RDBMSs also support a variety of character types, floating point (also known as decimal type), money, a variety of date and time types, and even special binary types for storing sounds, images, and other large binary objects.

The Database Connectivity Library of LiveWire provides mappings from a vendor-neutral set of data types to the vendor-specific data types of the RDBMS.

Understanding Transactions

In many applications, the user needs a way to group several commands into a single unit of work. This unit is called a *transaction*. Here's an example that shows why transactions are necessary:

1. Suppose you call the airline and ask for a ticket to Honolulu. The ticket agent queries the database, looking for available seats, and finds one on tonight's flight. It's the last available seat. You take a minute to decide whether you want to go tonight.

2. While you are thinking, another customer calls the airline, asks the same question, and gets the same answer. Now, two customers have been offered the same seat.

3. You make your decision—you'll fly tonight. Your ticket agent updates the database to reflect the fact that the last seat has been sold.

4. The other customer now decides to take the seat. That ticket agent updates the database, selling the ticket to the other customer. The record showing that the seat was sold to you is overwritten and lost.

5. You arrive at the airport and find that no one has ever heard of you. The other customer is flying in your seat.

The above sequence is a classic database problem, called the lost update problem. A skilled SQL programmer would solve this problem by beginning a transaction before processing the query. The database gives the ticket agent a "read lock" on the data, but the ticket agent cannot update the database with only a read lock. When the ticket agent starts to sell the seat, the application requests an exclusive write lock. As long as that agent has the write lock, no one else can read or write that data. After the agent gets the write lock, the application queries the database to verify that the seat is still available. If the seat is open, the application updates the database, marking the seat as sold. Then the transaction ends, committing the changes to the database. Here's what the lost update scenario looks like when transactions are used:

1. You call the airline and ask for a ticket to Honolulu. The ticket agent gets a read lock and queries the database, looking for available seats. One is available on tonight's flight. It's the last available seat. You take a minute to decide whether you want to go tonight.

2. While you are thinking, another customer calls the airline, asks the same question, and gets the same answer. Now, two customers have been offered the same seat.

3. You make your decision—you'll fly tonight. Your ticket agent gets an exclusive write lock on the data, rereads the database to verify that the seat is still available, updates the database, and releases the lock.

4. The other customer now decides to take the seat. That ticket agent gets a write lock and reruns the query. The database reports that the seat is no longer available. The ticket agent informs the customer, and they work to find a different seat for that customer.

5. You arrive at the airport and take your seat on the airplane. Aloha.

Transactions are also useful in system recovery. Because writing to the hard drive, often over a network, is time-consuming, many databases are implemented so that updates are stored in local buffers for a while. If the system fails before the RDBMS can actually update the database, the system could lose some of those updates. The solution used in most commercial products is to write a record of every change to the database in a special place on the hard drive called the transaction log. If a failure occurs before the update is actually made in the database, the transaction log can be replayed during recovery to complete the update.

Understanding Cursors

Webmasters whose experience is mostly with PC-based database engines are used to queries that return a single record. For example, dBASE III had the concept of a "pointer." The programmer could say

```
GOTO 3
DISPLAY
```

and dBASE would return all of the fields of the third record. The programmer could next enter

```
DISPLAY NEXT 1
```

and the program would advance the pointer and display record 4.

Many SQL programmers find this single-record notation a bit awkward. In SQL, one is more likely to say

```
SELECT * WHERE publicationYear = 1996
```

This query may return zero records, or one, or many. Even if the programmer "knows" that exactly one record will be returned, such as a query on the key field like

```
SELECT * WHERE ISBN='0789708019'
```

the nature of the language is such that the program still "thinks" it got back a set of records.

Many commercial SQL implementations support the concept of a *cursor*. A cursor is like the dBASE pointer—it indicates one record at a time, and can be moved back and forth across a set of records. LiveWire Pro supports a cursor-based construct to retrieve data. To set up a cursor, the Webmaster says

```
myCursor = database.cursor (selectStatement, updateFlag);
```

where *selectStatement* is an ANSI 89-compliant SQL SELECT statement, and updateFlag (which takes on values TRUE and FALSE) controls whether the database may be updated through this cursor.

> **N O T E** In the object-oriented language C++, an object's methods are accessed using dot notation. If the programmer has allocated a new aircraft object and wants it to climb to 10,000 feet, he might say
>
> ```
> theAircraft.climb(10000);
> ```
>
> It is more common in C++ to have a variable that holds the address of the aircraft object. Such a variable is called a pointer (no relation to the pointers in dBASE). To call an object's method through a pointer, the programmer uses an arrow notation, like this:
>
> ```
> theAircraftPointer->climb(10000);
> ```
>
> Pointers (in the C and C++ sense) are powerful tools, but the ability to directly access memory locations presents a security risk that the designers of Java and JavaScript were not willing to take. Unlike C++, Java and JavaScript allocate new objects, not pointers to objects, so the programmer uses the dot notation rather than the arrow notation. ■

After the cursor exists, the programmer can move it around the rows that were retrieved by the SELECT statement. For example,

```
myCursor.next()
```

loads the cursor with the next retrieved row.

Introduction to Crystal Reports

Many Webmasters find the day-to-day task of building *ad hoc* SQL queries time-consuming and even a bit daunting. If they run LiveWire on a Windows NT server, they can use Crystal Reports, bundled with LiveWire, to prepare *ad hoc* queries. Crystal Reports offers five major capabilities:

- ■ *Multiple-detail section reports and subreports*—a single report can contain multiple sections. Alternatively, the developer can write complete stand-alone reports, then embed them as subreports in a master document.

- ■ *Conditional reports*—sections of a multiple-detail section report, or text objects, may be set to vary depending on data conditions. For example, a customer record may have a language flag, allowing a report to print out in English or Spanish, depending upon their preference.

■ *Distribution of reports over the Web*—by exporting the report to HTML.

■ *Form-style reports*—text and objects may be placed on the page with the help of grids, guidelines, and rulers.

■ *Cross-tab reports*—which present summary information in a concise two-dimensional format.

In the latest version of Crystal Reports, all fields, texts, and other elements are objects, which can be placed graphically by the user on the page in the Crystal Reports "Report Designer" application.

The Database Connectivity Library

Earlier, this chapter (in the section entitled "A SQL Primer") showed the typical steps in the life of a database. Most Web sites that are integrated with databases enable the Web user to query the database and possibly to insert or delete data. Seldom would a Web user add or drop tables or indexes or create or delete databases.

On those occasions when the built-in Application Programmer Interface (API) is not powerful enough to handle the application, the programmer can use passthrough SQL—a mechanism for sending any SQL to the target database. For example, the programmer could use:

```
database.execute ("CREATE TABLE books
  (isbn char(10) not null,
  title char(20) not null,
  publicationYear datetime null,
  retailPrice money null)");
```

> **CAUTION**
>
> As its name implies, passthrough SQL does not attempt to interpret the SQL—it sends it straight to the target RDBMS. This fact means that the programmer may have to write slightly different code depending on whether the site has Informix, Oracle, Sybase, or one of the other supported databases installed.
>
> Passthrough SQL is often used to build new databases. It cannot be used to bypass the cursor mechanism and return rows as a set. When retrieving data, the built-in cursor mechanism should be used rather than a native call via passthrough SQL.

Opening and Closing the Connection

Recall that CGI scripts are started (forked) for every HTTP request. This process is computationally expensive. Unlike CGI scripts, LiveWire applications remain running until the Webmaster explicitly shuts them down. A side benefit to this design approach is that a LiveWire Pro application can open a connection to the database when it is started and leave that connection open almost forever.

One of the first things a LiveWire Pro application usually does when it is installed is open a connection to the database. The syntax is

```
database.connect(dbType, servername, username, password, databaseName);
```

where `dbType` is one of

- ORACLE
- SYBASE
- INFORMIX
- ILLUSTRA
- ODBC

and *servername*, *username*, *password*, and *databaseName* are the usual pieces of information needed to access a database.

Other requests to this application—whether from the same client but for different pages or from other clients—use the same connection to the database. Figure 28.4 shows several applications and clients interacting with databases. Not having to relaunch the application for each request improves performance on subsequent requests to the application.

FIG. 28.4

When the system reaches steady state, no time is wasted starting applications or establishing database connections.

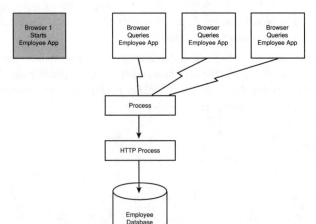

An application can test its connection with the `connected()` method. The following code shows how to start a connection and verify that the database was found and the login was successful:

```
database.connect (INFORMIX, theServer, mmorgan, mySecretWord, demoDB);
if (!database.connected())
  write("Error in connecting to database.");
else
...
```

Information about the connections between applications and databases is kept on the server in shared memory. Over time, the connection spreads to the various copies of the Netscape Server process, a mechanism known as diffusion. Diffusion is illustrated in Figure 28.5. At any time the programmer can have the application disconnect from the database—this disconnect causes all copies of the server to disconnect from the database. A programmer might call for a disconnect for two reasons:

- An application can have only one connection open at a time—the programmer may want to switch the application to a different database.

- RDBMSs are usually licensed for some maximum number of concurrent connections. Disconnecting an application that no longer needs a connection frees that connection for use by another application.

Whatever the reason for calling for disconnection, it is easy to do. The programmer calls:

```
database.disconnect();
```

and all application processes disconnect from the database.

FIG. 28.5

Database connections spread throughout the server until every serve process is connected to the database.

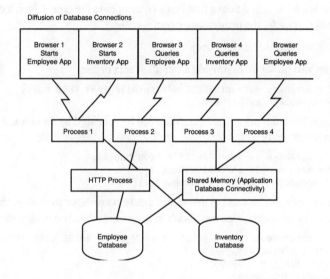

Diffusion of Database Connections

 The copy of the Informix RDBMS bundled with LiveWire Pro is limited to a single connection. While this database engine is entirely satisfactory for development, most Webmasters will want to license a database with more connections for live use.

Inserting Data into Tables

All updates must be done through updatable cursors. Here's a fragment of JavaScript that makes a new, updatable cursor and inserts a new row.

```
myCursor = database.cursor("SELECT isbn, title, publicationYear, retailPrice FROM
books", TRUE);
myCursor.isbn= "078970255x9";
myCursor.title = "Running a Perfect Netscape Site";
myCursor.publicationYear = 1996;
myCursor.retailPrice = 49.99;
myCursor.insertRow (books);
```

Deleting Rows

Deleting rows is easy. Start with an updatable cursor and point it to the row to be deleted. Now call the cursor's deleteRow method. For example, to delete a row that corresponds to a discontinued book, the programmer might write:

Part
V

Ch

28

```
myCursor = database.cursor ("SELECT * FROM books WHERE isbn =
request.discontinuedBookISBN", TRUE);
myCursor.deleteRow(books);
```

Accessing Data a Row at a Time

Data is available one row at a time in LiveWire Pro by using cursors. Cursors can be used to get to the value stored at a row-column intersection. For example, in the `bookWholesale` database, there is a table called `books` that has a column `retailPrice`. Given a cursor that points to some row of that table, the programmer could write:

```
thePrice = myCursor.retailPrice;
```

Cursors can also be set up to provide an implicit sort order:

```
myCursor = database.cursor(SELECT MAX(retailPrice) FROM books);
mostExpensiveBook = myCursor[0];
```

The names of the columns in the SELECT list can be accessed by an index. For example, the programmer can write:

```
myCursor = database.cursor( SELECT * FROM books);
firstColumnName = myCursor.columnName(0);
secondColumnName = myCursor.columnName(1);
```

Updatable cursors can be used to insert and delete records, or to change the fields of a record. For example, to set a new price for a book in the `books` table, the programmer could write:

```
myCursor = database.cursor ("SELECT * FROM books WHERE isbn =
'0789708019',updatable);
myCursor.retailPrice = 59.95;
myCursor.updateRow(books);
```

Accessing Data as a Set

Sometimes, the programmer needs to show all the data in a table as a list. The programmer could make a cursor and loop through all the rows in the retrieved data. As a convenience, however, LiveWire Pro offers the `SQLTable` function.

When the programmer calls

```
database.SQLTable(selectStatement);
```

the Database Connectivity Library displays the result of the SELECT statement in an HTML table, along with column names in the header.

Often, the application design calls for a list of records such as the one shown in Figure 28.6, with each record being hyperlinked to a more detailed single-record page such as the one in Figure 28.7. Cursors cannot span HTML pages of an application, so the best way to satisfy this requirement is to build one cursor on the list page to select all the relevant records and format each field into HTML. The single-record page would take a primary key and use it to make a new cursor, whose select statement looks up all of the fields of the record associated with that key.

FIG. 28.6
The designer intends for the user to choose a record from this list.

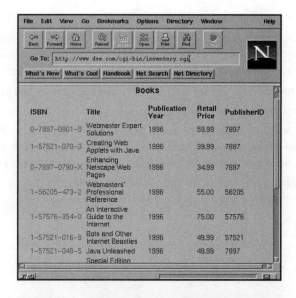

FIG. 28.7
Each selection on the list brings the user to a single-record page like this one.

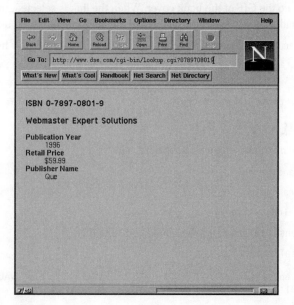

Using BLObs

In the content-oriented applications characteristic of the Web, the Webmaster often wants to store images, software, or audio or video clips in the database. A new database type, called the *Binary Large Object (BLOb)*, was introduced into SQL by commercial vendors to meet these kinds of needs. For example, suppose the book wholesaler wants to store an image of the cover of the book in the database. The general syntax for retrieving an image from a BLOb and outputting it with an HTML image tag is:

```
myCursor.blobFieldName.blobImage (imageFormat, ALTstring, ALIGNstring, ISMAP);
```

ALTstring, ALIGNstring, and ISMAP are optional fields. If they are supplied, they are used in the HTML image tag. Thus, the programmer of the book Wholesale application could say:

```
myCursor.cover.blobImage("gif", "The cover of the book", "Left", ISMAP);
```

BLObs can be hyperlinked, so they are read by helper applications and plug-ins like this:

```
blobFieldName.blobLink(mimeType, linkText);
```

This construct is most commonly used with large BLObs, such as an audio clip. The Netscape server keeps the BLOb in memory until the user clicks on another link or until a 60-second timer runs out, whichever comes first. Here's an example of how to send a BLOb to the client:

```
myCursor = database.cursor ("SELECT * FROM blobbedBooks");
while (myCursor.next())
{
  write (myCursor.isbn);
  write (myCursor.cover.blobImage("gif"));
  write (myCursor.authorReading.blobLink("audio/x-wav", "Selected highlights
  ➥from" + myCursor.title);
  write ("<BR>");
}
```

This code puts up the GIF of the book cover. When the link is selected, the client downloads and plays the audio selection—a few seconds of the author naming the highlights of the book.

BLObs are inserted into records in much the same way as other data is inserted:

```
myCursor = database.cursor("SELECT * FROM blobbedBooks, TRUE);
myCursor.isbn="X0789708019";
myCursor.cover = blob("CoverOfWebmasters.gif");
myCursor.insertRow("blobbedBooks");
```

Transactions in LiveWire Pro

Three database methods support transaction control:

- beginTransaction()
- commitTransaction()
- rollbackTransaction()

These three constructs can be used to build code like this:

```
database.BeginTransaction();
int db_error = 0;
dbError = database.execute ("INSERT INTO books(isbn, title) VALUES (request.isbn,
request.title);
if (!dbError)
{
dbError = database.execute ("INSERT INTO authors VALUES (request.isbn,
➥request.author1));
if (dbError)
  database.rollbackTransaction();
else
  database.commitTransaction();
}
```

```
    else
    // Error occurred while processing book itself
    database.rollbackTransaction();
```

Error Handling

LiveWire Pro provides a degree of insulation between the programmer and the RDBMS. However, if something goes wrong, most programmers want to get the most specific error messages available—the ones generated by the RDBMS itself. To satisfy this need, the Database Connectivity Library returns two different levels of error message.

Every API call returns an error code. The programmer can test the return code—if it is false, no error occurred. TRUE returns codes that indicate the type of error (e.g., server error, library error, lost connection, no memory).

If the error comes from the server or the library, the programmer can call four functions to get more specific information:

- `database.majorErrorCode` returns the SQL error code.
- `database.majorErrorMessage` returns the text message that corresponds to the major error code.
- `database.minorErrorCode` returns any secondary code sent by the RDBMS vendor's library, such as a severity level.
- `database.minorErrorMessage` returns any secondary message returned by the vendor library.

When the programmer is running the JavaScript trace utility, all error codes and messages are displayed.

JavaScript and the Second Generation Netscape Servers

Java and JavaScript play a key role in the new FastTrack and Enterprise servers, and even in the non-HTTP servers such as Mail, News, Catalog, and Proxy. Each server implements a virtual Java machine and understands JavaScript. Furthermore, each server has hooks into the Database Connectivity Library. All of this means that a programmer can tell the server to store information about itself and its work in a database, and can then serve that information to the Net via LiveWire Pro.

Understanding Java and JavaScript

Java is a Web-oriented language. Like traditional languages such as C and C++, it must be compiled before the program will run. Like C++, it is object-oriented. The programmer builds objects at runtime based on object descriptions written by the programmer or inherited from the language's class libraries.

Unlike traditional languages, Java is not compiled into the target machine's native instruction set. It is instead compiled into hardware-independent bytecodes. Netscape implements an interpreter for these bytecodes in its products, such as Netscape Navigator.

Part V
Ch
28

When the programmer completes an application (called an applet), an HTML page designer can embed the applet in his page. At runtime, the applet is downloaded and executed and runs on the server.

JavaScript is an interpreted language loosely based on Java. JavaScript programs are stored in source form in the HTML page. At runtime, the page, with its JavaScript, is downloaded to the Netscape client and the JavaScript is interpreted and run.

Server-Side JavaScript

If LiveWire is installed on the server, the programmer can invoke the LiveWire compiler like this:

```
lwcomp [-cvd] -o binaryFile file
```

where `binaryFile` is the name of the output file (which typically has a file suffix of `.web`) and `file` is the name of the input file. If the input file consists of a mix of HTML and JavaScript, it has a suffix of `.html` (or `.htm` in a DOS/Windows environment). If the input file is pure JavaScript, it has a suffix of `.js`.

Table 28.2 shows the five command-line options available with the LiveWire compiler.

Table 28.2   The Programmer Uses Command-line Options to Issue Broad Directives to the Compiler

Option	Meaning
-c	Check only; do not generate binary file
-v	Verbose output; provide details during compilation
-d	Debug output; the resulting file output shows the generated JavaScript
-o	`binaryFile` name; give the output file this name
-h	Help; display this help message

T I P   The -v (verbose) option provides so much useful information that it is almost always worth including. Get in the habit of always calling the compiler with the -v option set.

The programmer can run the resulting binary file under the `trace` utility (to see each function call and its result codes). In `trace`, calls to the `debug` function in the code are activated. Some programmers prefer to insert calls to the `write` function in their code to check the value of variables or verify the program logic.

When JavaScript is run under LiveWire, several objects are created by the run-time environment and are available to the programmer. The `request` object contains access methods to the components of the HTTP request, including members that, in CGI programming, are passed by environment variables. Examples include `request.ip` and `request.agent`. The `request` object also includes fields for each of a form's fields and from URLs.

The predefined object `server` contains other members that replace CGI environment variables, such as `hostname`, `host`, and `port`.

LiveWire uses the `client` object to maintain user state between requests. The application can be written to preserve user choices across requests using Netscape cookies or other state preservation mechanisms. LiveWire offers the method `client.expiration(seconds)` to tell the system to destroy the client after a certain number of seconds of inactivity.

The Virtual Java Machine

In order to provide cross-platform portability, each of the new Netscape servers includes a virtual Java machine in its architecture. Instead of writing CGI for, say, a UNIX machine, and later having to port it to NT, the Netscape design allows the programmer to write just one version of the program—in JavaScript. That program will run on the virtual Java machine regardless of whether the underlying hardware and operating system is UNIX, Windows NT, or Windows 95.

Putting It All Together—a Database Example

This section shows a simple example application using LiveWire Pro. The application is intended to be set up with start.htm (in Listing 28.1) as its initial page, and home.htm (in Listing 28.2) as the default page.

Listing 28.1 JavaScript Connects to the Database

```
<html>
<head>
   <title> Start Book Wholesalers Application </title>
</head>
<body>
<server>
if(!database.connected())
   database.connect("INFORMIX", "myserver",
           "mmorgan", "ASecretWord", "booksDemo")
if (!database.connected())
   write("Error: Unable to connect to database.")
else {
   redirect("home.htm")
}
</server>
</body>
</html>
```

Listing 28.2 A Central Point Giving the User Access to the Application's Functions

```
<html>
<head>
   <title>Book Wholesalers Application</title>
   <meta name="GENERATOR" content="Mozilla/2.01Gold (Win32)">
</head>
<body>
<hr>
<h1>Administrative Functions</h1>
```

Part
V

Ch
28

continues

Listing 28.2 Continued

```
<ul>
<li><a href="invent.htm">Show Inventory</a> </li>

<li><a href="addTitle.htm">Add a Title</a></li>

<li><a href="delTitle.htm">Delete a Title</a></li>

<li><a href="sales.htm">Make a Sale </a></li>
</ul>

</body>
</html>
```

Figure 28.8 shows the application's home page.

FIG. 28.8

The Book Wholesalers application allows the merchant to add and delete titles, list the inventory, and sell books.

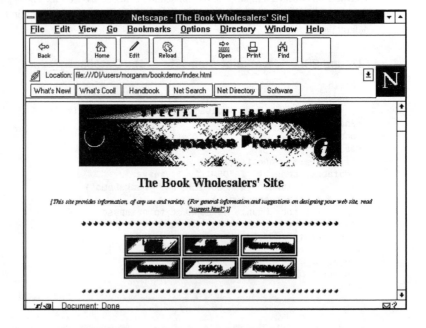

One option given to the user is to list the titles in the database. Listing 28.3 shows how this is done.

Listing 28.3 Show the Active Inventory

```
<html>
<head>
   <title> Inventory List </title>
   <meta name="GENERATOR" content="Mozilla/2.01Gold (Win32)">
</head>
<body>
```

```
<server>
database.SQLTable("SELECT isbn,title, author,publishers.pubName,quantity On Hand
➥FROM books, publishers WHERE books.publisherID = publishers.publisherID");
</server>
<p>
<a href="home.htm">Home</a>
</p>
</body>
</html>
```

The user selects the Addtitle.htm page, shown in Listing 28.4, and fills out the form to enter a new title. Note that this page builds a <SELECT> list on-the-fly from the database, as shown in Figure 28.9.

Listing 28.4   Add a New Title to the Inventory

```
<html>
<head>
    <title> Add New Title </title>
    <meta name="GENERATOR" content="Mozilla/2.01Gold (Win32)">
</head>
<body>
<h1>Add a New Title</h1>
<p>Note: <b>All</b> fields are required for the new title to be accepted.
<form method="post" action="add.htm"></p>
<br>Title:
<br><input type="text" name="title" size="50">
<br>ISBN:
<br><input type="text" name="isbn" size="10">
<br>Retail Price:
<br><INPUT TYPE="text" name="retailPrice" size="6">
<br>Publisher
<SELECT NAME="publisherID">
<SERVER>
publisherCursor = database.cursor("SELECT id, name FROM publishers ORDER BY
➥name");
while (publisherCursor.next())
{
  write ("<OPTION Value="+publisherCursor.id+">"+publisherCursor.name);
}
</SERVER>
</SELECT>
<BR>
<input type="submit" value="Enter">
<input type="reset" value="Clear">
</form>
<p><a href="home.htm">Home</a> </p>
</body>
</html>
```

Part
V

Ch

28

When the user submits Addtitle.htm, control passes to Add.htm (shown in Listing 28.5), which actually does the insert into the database. Control then returns to Addtitle.htm.

Listing 28.5   Complete the Process of Adding a Title

```
<html>
<head>
    <title> Title Added </title>
    <meta name="GENERATOR" content="Mozilla/2.01Gold (Win32)">
</head>
<body>
<server>
 cursor = database.cursor("SELECT * FROM books",TRUE);
 cursor.isbn = request.isbn;
 cursor.title = request.title;
 cursor.retailPrice = request.retailPrice;
 cursor.publisherID = request.publisherID;
 cursor.quantity_on_hand = 0;
 cursor.updateRow(books);
  redirect("addTitle.htm")
</server>
</body>
</html>
```

FIG. 28.9
Addtitle.htm asks the
user about the new title.

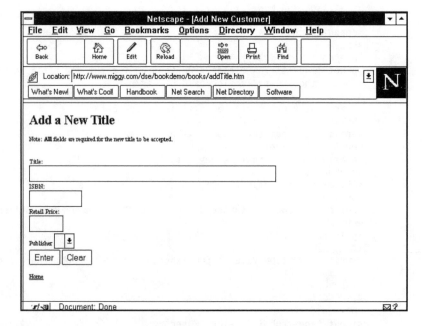

When the user follows the link to Deltitle.htm, he sees a list (generated from the database at runtime) of all the available titles. They click on an ISBN to remove that book from the database. Listing 28.6 shows the page—Figure 28.10 shows what the user sees.

Listing 28.6   The User Prepares to Delete a Title

```
<html>
<head>
    <title> Delete A Title</title>
```

```
</head>
<body>
<server>
cursor = database.cursor("SELECT isbn, title, retailPrice, publishers.name FROM
➥books, publishers WHERE books.publisherID = publishers.ID ORDER BY isbn");
</server>
<table border>
<caption>
<center><p><b><font SIZE=+1>Titles by ISBN</font></b></p></center>
<center><p><b><font SIZE=+1>Click on ISBN to remove the title</font></b></p></
➥center>
</caption>
<tr>
<th>ISBN</th>
<th>Title</th>
<th>Retail Price</th>
<th>Publisher</th>
</tr>
<caption>
<center><p>
<server>
while(cursor.next())
{
  write("<TR><TD><A HREF='remove.htm?isbn='"+cursor.isbn+"</A></
  ➥TD><TD>"+cursor.title+
    "</TD><TD>"+cursor.retailPrice+"</TD><TD>"+
    cursor.name+"</TD></TR>");
}
</table>
</body>
</html>
```

FIG. 28.10
The user selects a title from this list to delete, generated in server-side JavaScript from the database.

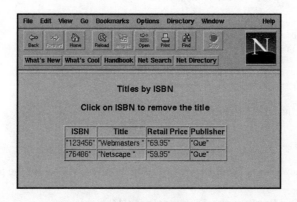

The remove.htm page actually updates the database. Code for this page is shown in Listing 28.7.

Listing 28.7 Actually Does the Work of Removing the Title

```
<html>
<head>
<title> Customer Removal </title>
</head>
<server>
if(request.isbn != null)
{
    cursor = database.cursor ("SELECT * FROM books WHERE isbn =" +
    ➥request.isbn,TRUE);
    cursor.deleteRow(books)
}
redirect("delTitle.htm");
</server>
</body>
</html>
```

To sell books from inventory, the user goes to Sales.htm. Listing 28.8 shows the code for the
page, which is displayed in Figure 28.11.

Listing 28.8 Allows the User to Sell Books

```
<html>
<head>
    <title> Sell Copies </title>
</head>
<body>
<h1>Sell Copies</h1>
<p>Note: <b>All</b> fields are required for the title to be sold.
<form method="post" action="sell.htm"></p>
<br>ISBN:
<br><input type="text" name="isbn" size="10">
<br>Number of Copies:
<br><INPUT TYPE="text" name="copies" size="6">
<BR>
<input type="submit" value="Enter">
<input type="reset" value="Clear">
</form>
<p><a href="home.htm">Home</a> </p>
</body>
</html>
```

Listing 28.9 shows how to confirm a transaction. Figure 28.12 shows the page.

Listing 28.9 Confirm the Transaction *<HTML>*

```
<HEAD>
<TITLE>Selling Copies</TITLE>
</HEAD>
<BODY>
cursor = database.cursor("SELECT title, isbn, retailPrice,
          publishers.name, quantityOnHand FROM books, publishers
```

```
                    WHERE isbn=" + request.isbn +" AND
                    publishers.ID = books.publisherID");
        if (cursor.next())
        {
          if (cursor.quantityOnHand > request.quantity)
          {
            write ("<FORM ACTION=sold.htm METHOD=GET>");
            write ("<P>Confirm sale of <STRONG>" + request.copies +
                "</STRONG> of<BR>" + cursor.title + "<BR>ISBN " +
                cursor.isbn + "<BR>Retail Price " +
                cursor.retailPrice + "<BR>Publisher " +
                cursor.name</P>");
            write ("<INPUT TYPE=submit NAME=submit VALUE=Yes>");
            write ("<INPUT TYPE=button NAME=home VALUE=No
                    onClick='redirect("home.htm");'>");
            write ("<INPUT TYPE=hidden NAME=isbn VALUE=" +
                    request.isbn + ">");
            write ("<INPUT TYPE=hidden NAME=quantity VALUE=" +
                    request.quantity + ">");
            write ("</FORM>");
          }
          else
            write ("<P>There are only " + cursor.quantityOnHand +
                    " copies on hand.</P>");
        }
        else
        {
          write ("<P>ISBN " + request.isbn + " not on file.</P>");
        </BODY>
        </HTML>
```

FIG. 28.11

Use this page to sell books from inventory.

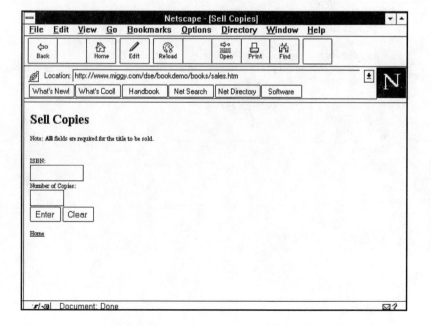

FIG. 28.12

It is a good idea to confirm user-initiated changes in the database.

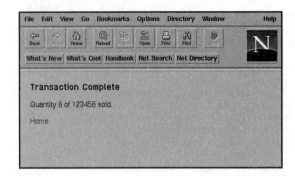

The page actually does the database update. Its code is shown in Listing 28.10.

Listing 28.10   Complete the Sale

```
<HTML>
<HEAD>
<TITLE>Sold Copies</TITLE>
</HEAD>
<BODY>
<SERVER>
cursor = database.cursor("SELECT * FROM BOOKS WHERE isbn=" + request.isbn,TRUE);

// move onto selected row
cursor.next();
cursor.quantityOnHand = cursor.quantityOnHand - request.quantity;
cursor.updateRow(books);
</SERVER>
<P>
<H1>Transaction Complete</H1>
<P>
<server>
write ("Quantity " + request.quantity + " of " + request.isbn + " sold.");
<server>
</P>
<A HREF="home.htm">Home</A>
</BODY>
</HTML>
```

## CHAPTER 29

VBScript

by Jerry Honeycutt

You can use VBScript to create extraordinary Web pages. You can glue together the elements of a form, move processing from the server to the client, and create applications that you distribute on a Web page. You can also control a variety of objects that you put on a Web page.

You can create your own innovative Web pages, too. The only obstacle is coming up with the great ideas. Don't approach a Web page by asking yourself what you can do with the technology that's available. You're far beyond that now. First ask yourself, what you want to accomplish. Period. If nothing were impossible, what would you do? Then, figure out how to make technology such as VBScript and ActiveX do the job. In short, very little is impossible.

You know the old story. Power and flexibility come at a price, and that price is usually time, cost, or difficulty. Not so with VBScript. It's very easy to use. It contains a limited set of keywords. It doesn't have a monolithic development environment. And you deploy it within HTML files.

Learn about the evolution of VBScript

Microsoft cleverly leverages a well established technology—Visual Basic—onto the Internet.

Write VBScript code like a professional

The overview of the VBScript language you find in this chapter will help get you started.

Create three different types of event handlers

You have three alternative types of event-handlers: event-procedures, the <SCRIPT> tag, and inline.

Connect your VBScript scripts to forms

One of the most exciting uses of scripts is making HTML forms more interactive and foolproof.

Use the coding conventions to simplify your scripts

Coding conventions will help make your scripts more readable and much more maintainable.

VBScript has been available for a short time, but I've already seen some incredible examples on the Web, such as these:

- An order form that provides help for each form element in the browser's status line
- A Web site that uses scripts to provide tight control of frames and navigation
- A Web site that uses VBScript and Comboboxes to provide very efficient navigational tools ■

Visual Basic Meets the Internet

The Internet is used by millions of people. It's a great success—sans-VBScript. Visual Basic is also a great success with over three million loyal developers. Combine both technologies, and you have a winner: a huge installed base of users, and a huge installed base of developers. That is, more folks to develop exciting Web pages, and more folks than ever to view those pages.

Visual Basic

Visual Basic (Standard, Professional, or Enterprise edition) is the corporate world's workhorse development environment. You can develop advanced client/server solutions. You can develop the run-of-the-mill Windows application with Visual Basic, too. It's a robust language, which has the support of thousands of tools and control vendors all over the world. It also contains an integrated development environment and a debugger, which you'll learn to live without.

Visual Basic for Applications (VBA) is a subset of Visual Basic, which is available in Microsoft's Office product line. You use it to create task-oriented, document-centric applications with OLE. For example, you can create a VBA application to automatically generate a mass mailing by using Microsoft Word and Access. While VBA is currently available only in Microsoft Office, you'll soon see it in many other product lines because Microsoft has made it available for licensing by third-party vendors.

The Internet

The growth of the Internet during the last 10 years is astonishing. It started as a simple means to share information. You've used or heard of UseNet, e-mail, FTP, and Gopher, for example. And, given that you purchased a book about HTML, you know a bit about the Web, too.

The Web's beginning was very meager. It did text. It did graphics. It did a few other Internet services such as UseNet, FTP, and Gopher, too. Contrast that to what's happening now. Corporate America saw the light. It started throwing an incredible amount of money at the Web and every developer that wanted to create software for it. The result is a technical playground where every idea and every innovation gets a fair shot at the big time.

You already reap the benefits of this technological feast every day on the Web. Take a look:

- Most Web pages contain amazing graphics, including animated GIFs that let you create a Web page which looks like a billboard on acid. You can set up a picture as an imagemap so the users can jump to different Web pages depending on which object in the picture they click.

- High-bandwidth users probably encounter plenty of movies such as AVI, MOV, and QuickTime (low-bandwidth users avoid video like the plague). These let you embed full-motion video clips in your Web pages. Examples? How about Web pages containing movie previews, advertisements, or even personal messages from an individual's Web page—not to mention more questionable entertainment.

- Frames are huge. They let you divide the user's Web browser into separate sections (frames) so you can display a different Web page in each frame. You can create cool navigational aids by using frames. If you're not sure about frames, see Chapter 10, "Frames."

VBScript

VBScript and ActiveX are what happen when you bring a big company with a huge investment in developer technology together with the Internet. Microsoft leveraged most of its existing technology (Visual Basic and OLE Controls, for example) on the Internet. These are the same technologies developers use to create applications for Windows. You don't have to create static Web pages anymore. You can create Web pages with all the features and excitement of a real Windows application, instead. Folks can interact with and *use* your Web page, not just look at it. This is an important step for the Internet and the Web.

Quoting Microsoft, VBScript is a "lightweight" subset of Visual Basic and Visual Basic for Applications. Don't let the term lightweight fool you, however, because VBScript isn't wimpy. In this case, read lightweight as sleek, fleet-of-foot, packing one major punch.

It contains a limited number of VBA's keywords for very good reasons, though:

Security	How would you feel if you loaded a Web page containing a script that deleted files from your computer? What if a script could drop a virus on your computer? No good? Microsoft makes VBScript more secure by eliminating the ability for it to do certain things such as read and write files or make system calls.
Portability	Microsoft removed any keyword that makes VBScript less portable to other environments, including the Mac and UNIX. VBScript would be doomed to failure if it only supported the Windows environment, because no one wants to develop Web pages that leave out a whole portion of the Internet community.
Performance	The pipes that make the Internet work are pretty thin. You're probably using a 28.8K modem, or, if you're lucky, an ISDN connection to connect to the Internet. You don't want to have to wait any longer than necessary for the VBScript engine to load, compile, and run a script. Thus, Microsoft omitted keywords that negatively impacted VBScript's performance.

▶ **See** "Integrating with Windows," to learn about security and ActiveX, **p. 497**

CAUTION

Just because VBScript is secure doesn't mean ActiveX objects are secure. Programmers can put anything they like into an ActiveX object, including a potential virus. If you download a renegade object to your computer and run it, it could do serious harm. That's why Microsoft provides *code signing*, which verifies that the object comes from a known, trusted source and nobody has tampered with it. When Internet Explorer tries to use an object it can't identify as known and trusted, it displays a warning, which gives you the choice of running the object or not.

N O T E NCompass Labs provides a Netscape Plug-In called ScriptActive that allows Netscape Navigator to run VBScript scripts. You find information about downloading, installing, and using ScriptActive in Chapter 22, "ActiveX Controls." ∎

Learning the VBScript Language

VBScript is a very simple scripting language to learn and use. In Chapter 24, you learned how to embed a script in your HTML file by using the <SCRIPT> container tag, like this:

```
<SCRIPT LANGUAGE="VBSCRIPT">
<!--
...
-->
</SCRIPT>
```

That's the HTML code, but it doesn't help you with the VBScript code. That's what you learn to do in this section. You learn about VBScript variable names, operators, keywords, and the runtime library.

TIP The <SCRIPT> container tag supports the SRC attribute which lets you store your scripts in files, separate from your HTML. To use it, put your scripts in a text file with the VBS file extension and assign the URL of this file to the SRC attribute.

N O T E If you're a programmer, or you're already familiar with Visual Basic, this chapter presents enough information to you so that you can start writing scripts immediately. If you've never written a single line of code, however, you'll need additional information provided by books such as *VBScript by Example* or *Special Edition Using VBScript*. ∎

VBScript Variables

You learned what variables are in Chapter 24, "Overview of Programming and Scripting." VBScript has a few limitations for how you should name variables. Here's what they are:

- All variable names must begin with a letter.
- Variable names can't contain periods.

- Variable names can't be longer than 255 characters. In practicality, you should keep variable names shorter than 32 characters in order to make typing easier.

- All variable names must be unique within their scope. That is, if you declare a variable called `intMyAge` in a procedure, you can't declare another variable with the same name in the same procedure. You can declare a variable with the same name in a different procedure, however.

Microsoft has created conventions that you should use while naming variables in your scripts. You learn more about those conventions in "Using the Naming Convention" later in this chapter.

Declaring Variables   If you don't explicitly declare a variable, VBScript will do it for you each time it encounters a new variable name. This can be a problem, however, if you accidentally enter the wrong variable name—you'll get a new variable instead of the value of a variable you thought contained a particular value. You can explicitly declare variables in your scripts so this doesn't happen. Make this the first line in your `<SCRIPT>` block:

```
Option Explicit
```

This causes VBScript to check for previously declared variables. If you try to use a variable that you haven't already declared, you'll get an error message. So how do you declare a variable? You use the `Dim` statement, like this:

```
Dim intHeight
```

This is called *dimensioning* a variable. It causes VBScript to set aside space for the variable and take note of the name.

Understanding Variable Scope   A variable's scope is the visibility and lifetime of a variable. A VBScript variable can have *script-level* or *procedure-level* scope. You declare a variable with *script-level* scope outside of a procedure; and it's visible to every script in the HTML file. You declare a variable with *procedure-level* scope inside of a procedure, and it's visible only to the statements inside that procedure.

The lifetime of a variable is the length of time the variable exists. A procedure-level variable only exists while the procedure in which you declare it is running. A script-level variable exists as long as the Web page is open.

N O T E   Professional programmers consider global variables to be a very bad practice. Script-level (global variables) aren't taboo in VBScript, though. Use them at will. If they help you get the job done faster or easier, go for it. You're not building defense systems or operating systems. You're scripting a Web page. A little sloppiness is a small price to pay for getting the job done. ■

Understanding Variants   Unlike most programming languages, including Visual Basic, VBScript only supports one type of variable. It's called a *variant*. A variant variable can store any type of data you want to put in it. VBScript interprets the data depending on the context in which you use it. For example, if you use a variable where VBScript expects a string, it makes a string out of the variable's value. If you use a variable where VBScript expects a number, it makes a number out of the variable's data.

VBScript does distinguish between the different types of strings and numbers you put in a variant variable. This distinction is called a *subtype*. Table 29.1 shows you the different subtypes you can put in a variant variable.

Table 29.1 Variant Subtypes

Subtype	Description
Empty	Uninitialized—it's a 0 in a numeric context and an empty string in a string context.
Null	No data at all.
Boolean	True (-1) or False (0).
Byte	Number between 0 and 255.
Integer	Number between -32,768 and 32,767.
Long	Number between -2,147,483,648 and 2,147,483,647.
Single	Real number between -3.402823E38 and -1.401298E-45 for negative numbers; and 1.401298E-45 to 3.402823E38 for positive values.
Double	Real number between -1.79769313486232E308 to -4.94065645841247E-324 for negative values; and -4.94065645841247E-324 to 1.79769313486232E308 for positive values.
Date/Time	Number that represents a date between 1/1/100 and 12/31/9999.
String	Variable length string of characters up to 2 billion characters long.
Object	OLE Automation object.
Error	Error number.

 TIP In general, you don't need to worry about the subtype of a variant variable. Just stash a string or a number in a variable and let VBScript figure out how to use it appropriately in each context.

VBScript Operators

In Chapter 24, "Overview of Programming and Scripting," you learned what operators do. The sections that follow describe those operators as VBScript implements them. You learn about mathematical, comparison, and Boolean operators.

Mathematical Operators Table 29.2 shows you each mathematical operator VBScript supports, including each operator's syntax. You can use literal values or expressions with each operator. That is, each of the following statements is an appropriate use of VBScript's operators:

```
intResult = 5 + 1
intResult = intNumber / 2
intResult = 3 * intNumber
intResult = intNumber1 - intNumber2
intResult = intNumber1 + 3 * intNumber2
```

Table 29.2   VBScript Operators

Symbol	Description	Syntax
^	Exponentiation	`Number1 ^ Number2`
–	Unary negation	`– Number`
*	Multiplication	`Number1 * Number2`
/	Division	`Number1 / Number2`
\	Integer division	`Number1 \ Number2`
Mod	Modulo arithmetic	`Number1 Mod Number2`
+	Addition	`Number1 + Number2`
–	Subtraction	`Number1 – Number2`
&	String concatenation	`Expression1 & Expression2`

The order of this table's rows may seem a bit strange (why is the exponentiation operator first?), but it reflects VBScript's order of precedence. Take a look at the following expression. If you evaluate this expression left to right, as you do with some calculators, you get 20. How's that? `100 + 100` is 200. `200 * .1` is 20.

```
sngTotal = 100 + 100 * .1
```

But that's not how VBScript evaluates this expression. VBScript looks at the operators in this expression and decides which one is more important (*order of precedence*). In this case, the multiplication operator has a higher precedence, so it evaluates it first: `100 * .1` is 10. Then it goes back to the addition operator and does that: `100 + 10` is 110. Putting parentheses around the parts of the expression VBScript evaluates first makes it clearer:

```
sngTotal = 100 + (100 * .1)
```

TIP You can override VBScript's order of precedence by group expressions with parentheses, like this:

```
(100 + 100) * .1
```

Comparison Operators   Table 29.3 shows you each VBScript comparison operator. You can use a literal value or an expression with each comparison operator. Unlike mathematical operators, comparison operators have no order of precedence. VBScript evaluates each operator as it encounters it—left to right.

Table 29.3 VBScript Operators

Symbol	Description	Syntax
=	Equality	`Expression1 = Expression2`
<>	Inequality	`Expression1 <> Expression2`
<	Less than	`Expression1 < Expression2`
>	Greater than	`Expression1 > Expression2`
<=	Less than or equal	`Expression1 <= Expression2`
>=	Greater than or equal	`Expression1 >= Expression2`
is	Object equivalence	`Object1 is Object2`

N O T E The assignment operator (=) works as the equality comparison operator when you put it in a place where VBScript expects a comparison. This includes control statements such as `If...Then...Else.` ■

Boolean Operators The Boolean operators (which you learned about in Chapter 24, "Overview of Programming and Scripting") shown in Table 29.4 require one of two values on either side of the operator: `True` or `False`. This is different than the mathematical or comparison operators, which can use any value on either side of the operator.

Table 29.4 VBScript Logical Operators

Symbol	Description	Syntax
Not	Logical negation	`Not Boolean`
And	Logical conjunction	`Boolean1 And Boolean2`
Or	Logical disjunction	`Boolean1 Or Boolean2`
Xor	Logical exclusion	`Boolean1 Xor Boolean2`
Eqv	Logical equivalence	`Boolean1 Eqv Boolean2`
Imp	Logical implication	`Boolean1 Imp Boolean2`

VBScript's logical operators have an order of precedence just like its mathematical operators. VBScript evaluates each `And` in an expression before it evaluates any `Or` statements. Also similar to mathematical operators, you can override the order of precedence by using parentheses. Table 29.4 is arranged in order of precedence. The operators at the top of the table are more important than the operators at the bottom of the table.

VBScript Keywords

VBScript has a very limited set of statements. Each of these is described in the following sections:

```
If ... Then ... Else
Select Case
For ... Next
Do ... Loop
Sub
Function
```

If...Then...Else If you want to express a choice in a script, you'd use the `If...Then...Else` statement. This statement evaluates a decision and conditionally
executes a block of statements depending on the result. It looks like this:

```
If Condition Then
    Statements
Else
    Statements
End If
```

A fully formed `If...Then...Else` statement might look like this:

```
strUserName = InputBox( "Type your name?" )
If strUserName = "Jerry" Then
    MsgBox "Your name is the same as mine!"
Else
    MsgBox "Hello " & strUserName
End If
```

N O T E You don't always need the `Else` clause. In this case, you can use the `If...Then`, which
looks almost exactly like the `If...Then...Else` statement except that it doesn't have
the `Else`. It looks like this:

```
If Condition Then

    Statements

End If
```

Also, you won't always need to write a complete `If...Then` statement. If you have a single statement
you want to execute in a `True` condition, you can write it with a one line `If...Then` statement. This is
kind of a shorthand version of the `If...Then` statement. Here's what it looks like:

If *Condition* Then *Statement* ■

N O T E You can *nest* `If...Then...Else` statements. That is, you can put one If statement within
another If statement. Here's what a nested `If...Then...Else` statement looks like:

```
If Condition Then

    Statements

    If Condition Then

        Statements

    Else

        Statements

    End If
```

continues

continued

```
Else

    If Condition Then

        Statements

    Else

        Statements

    End If

End If
```

Select Case You can use the Select Case statement to match the results of an expression to a block of VBScript statements. Here's what that syntax looks like:

```
Select Case Expression
    Case Expression-List
        Statements
    Case Expression-List
        Statements
    Case Else
        Statements
End Select
```

Here's an example that assigns the textual equivalent of a number to strNumber depending on the value in intNumber with the Select Case statement:

```
Select Case intNumber
    Case 1
        strNumber = "One"
    Case 2
        strNumber = "Two"
    Case 3
        strNumber = "Three"
    Case 4
        strNumber = "Four"
    Case 5
        strNumber = "Five"
    Case Else
        strNumber = "Out of Range"
End If
```

N O T E An alternative to using the Select...Case statement is using the ElseIf keyword in an If...Then...Else statement. You can think of the ElseIf keyword as a way to separate a decision into buckets, like this:

```
If intNumber < 10 Then

    MsgBox "You picked a number less than 10"

ElseIf intNumber < 20 Then

    MsgBox "You picked a number between 10 and 19"

ElseIf intNumber < 30 Then

    MsgBox "You picked a number between 20 and 29"

Else

    MsgBox "You picked a number greater than or equal to 30"

End If
```

For...Next The `For...Next` loop is the most straightforward looping statement in VBScript. Remember when you first learned to count: 1, 2, 3, 4...100? That's exactly what the `For...Next` loop does. It doesn't always have to start with 1 and end with 100, though. It can start and end with any number that suits your needs. The syntax of the `For...Next` loop is very simple:

```
For Counter = Start To End
    Statements
Next
```

The following example is a simple `For...Next` loop that counts from 1 to 10 and displays each number in a message box as it goes along. Here's what it looks like:

```
For intCounter = 1 To 10
    MsgBox "The current number is " & intCounter
Next
```

 You can use the `Step` keyword to change the value by which VBScript increments the loop control variable, like this:

```
For intCounter = 10 to 100 Step 5

    MsgBox intCounter

Next
```

 You can jump out of a `For` loop before it's finished by using the `Exit For` statement.

Do...Loop You can use the `Do...Loop` to execute a block of statements while a condition remains true. You can also use the `Do...Loop` to execute a block of statements until a condition becomes true, or, as long as a condition is false. Thus, the VBScript has two different forms of the `Do...Loop`. First, you can repeat a block of statements while a condition is true, like this:

```
Do While Condition
    Statements
Loop
```

The other syntax executes *Statements* as long as *Condition* is *False*. Here's what it looks like:

```
Do Until Condition
    Statements
Loop
```

Here's an example of what the `Do...Loop` looks like in practice:

```
intIndex = 1
Do While intIndex <= 10
    MsgBox intIndex
    intIndex = intIndex + 1
Loop
```

Sub The most common type of procedure is called a *subprocedure*. A subprocedure begins with the `Sub` keyword and ends with the `End Sub` keyword. The simplest form of a subprocedure looks like this:

```
Sub Name
    Statements
End Sub
```

Subprocedures can also take arguments. *Arguments* are values you pass from the calling script to the subprocedure. This way, you can tell the subprocedure how to behave or you can let the subprocedure change the values for you. Here's what a subprocedure looks like that uses arguments:

```
Sub Name( Argument-List )
    Statements
End Sub
```

Here's an example:

```
Sub DisplayGreetingAndName( strGreeting, strName )
    MsgBox strGreeting & " " & strName
End Sub
```

You call a subprocedure using the `Call` keyword. Here's what it looks like:

```
Call Name( Argument-List )
```

The following examples call the subprocedure you saw earlier called `DisplayGreetingAndName`:

```
Call DisplayGreetingAndName( "Hello", "Jerry" )
Call DisplayGreetingAndName( strMyGreeting, strYourName )
Call DisplayGreetingAndName( "Howdy", strYourName )
```

You can also call a subprocedure without the `Call` keyword. Leave off the parentheses, like this:

```
DisplayGreetingAndName "Hello", "Jerry"
DisplayGreetingAndName strMyGreeting, strYourName
DisplayGreetingAndName "Howdy", strYourName
```

 TIP   You can exit a subprocedure early by using the `Exit Sub` keyword.

Function   Functions are very similar to subprocedures. You give them a name and an argument list. You call them by their name and pass arguments by their position. You find one key difference, though. A function can return a value to the calling script; a subprocedure can't. That is, you can use a function on the right side of the assignment operator (=). Here's what the syntax of a function looks like:

```
Function Name( Argument-List )
    Statements
    Name = Expression
End Function
```

This simple example returns the value a user inputs:

```
Function strGetName()
    strGetName = InputBox( "What is your name?" )
End Function
```

You call a function just like a subprocedure. You use it only on the right side of the assignment operator (=), though, and you always have to use the parentheses. The following example calls the GetName function and assigns its return value to the variable called strUserName:

```
strUserName = strGetName()
```

VBScript Runtime Library

VBScript provides you a lot of functions you can't write yourself. These functions are part of the VBScript *runtime*. Without these functions, you can't manipulate strings or variant subtypes. You can't prompt the user for input or display a message box, either. You could write your own mathematical library, though, but that would take so much effort that it's not worth it.

The sections that follow cover most of the VBScript runtime functions. Each of the following sections describes a broad category of functions in a table.

Math   VBScript provides a healthy amount of mathematical operators, as you learned earlier in this chapter. These operators include multiplication (*), division (/), addition (+), subtraction (–), and so on.

The VBScript runtime provides additional mathematical functions you can use. Table 29.5 shows you each function. All of the mathematical functions in this table take a single number as an argument and return a number from the function.

Table 29.5   VBScript Mathematical Functions

Syntax	Description
Trigonometry Functions	
Atn(*Number*)	Returns the arc-tangent of *Number*.
Cos(*Number*)	Returns the cosine of *Number*.
Sin(*Number*)	Returns the sine of *Number*.
Tan(*Number*)	Returns the tangent of *Number*.
Other Functions	
Abs(*Number*)	Returns absolute value of *Number*.
Exp(*Number*)	Returns *e* raised to *Number*.
Log(*Number*)	Returns the natural log of *Number*.
Rnd(*Number*)	Returns a random number.
Sgn(*Number*)	Returns the sign of *Number*.
Sqr(*Number*)	Returns the square root of *Number*.

Conversion   In most cases, you can put a value in a string and forget about it. In some special cases, such as with dates, you have to explicitly convert a variant from one subtype to another. For example, you can't compare the string version of a date to the date version, like this:

```
If strDate = Date() Then MsgBox "Dates are equal"
```

This won't work. Instead, you have to convert the string date to the variant date subtype; then do the comparison:

```
dtmDate = CDate(strDate)
```

Table 29.6 shows you some other conversion functions in the VBScript runtime. Using these functions, you can convert a variant to any of the subtypes available. Before converting a subtype, though, make sure the subtype can be converted by using one of the functions described in "Variant Type," later in this chapter.

Table 29.6   VBScript Conversion Functions

Syntax	Description
CBool(*Expr*)	Converts *Expr* to Boolean subtype.
CByte(*Expr*)	Converts *Expr* to byte subtype.
CDate(*Expr*)	Converts *Expr* to date subtype.
CDbl(*Expr*)	Converts *Expr* to double subtype.
Chr(*Code*)	Converts *Code* to a character.
CInt(*Expr*)	Converts *Expr* to integer subtype.
CLng(*Expr*)	Converts *Expr* to long subtype.
CSng(*Expr*)	Converts *Expr* to single subtype.
CStr(*Expr*)	Converts *Expr* to string subtype.
Hex(*Number*)	Converts *Number* to a hex string.
Int(*Number*)	Returns integer portion of *Number*.
Fix(*Number*)	Returns integer portion of *Number*.
Oct(*Number*)	Converts *Number* to an octal string.
Val(*Expr*)	Converts *Expr* to a number.

Date/Time   The VBScript runtime provides three types of date and time functions as shown in Table 29.7. It provides functions that return the current date or time. It provides functions that allow you to tear apart the date or time into their components. It also provides functions that allow you to recombine the parts of a date or time.

Table 29.7 VBScript Date/Time Functions

Syntax	Description
Date()	Returns current system date.
DateSerial(*Yr,mo,dy*)	Returns date subtype.
DateValue(*String*)	Returns date subtype.
Day(*Date*)	Returns day of the month.
Hour(*Time*)	Returns the hour.
Minute(*Time*)	Returns the minute.
Month(*Date*)	Returns the month number.
Now()	Returns current date and time.
Second(*Time*)	Returns the seconds.
Time()	Returns current system time.
TimeSerial(*hr,min,sec*)	Returns time subtype.
TimeValue(*String*)	Returns time subtype.
Weekday(*Date*)	Returns day of the week.
Year(*Date*)	Returns year.

Input and Output   VBScript provides two runtime functions you can use to interact with the user, as shown in Table 29.8. You can use InputBox to prompt the user for a string. You can use MsgBox to display a string to the user. You've seen examples of both of these functions all over this chapter.

Table 29.8 VBScript Date/Time Functions

Syntax	Description
InputBox(*Prompt*)	Prompts the user for a string.
MsgBox(*Message*)	Displays *Message* to the user.

String Handling   You can never rely on strings you get from the user to look exactly the way you want. That's one reason VBScript provides an extensive group of string functions as shown in Table 29.9. You can use these functions to change the case of a string, remove spaces from a string, retrieve a portion of string, and so on. The syntax statements in Table 29.9 show the simplest form of these functions.

Table 29.9 VBScript Date/Time Functions

Syntax	Description
Asc(*String*)	Returns ANSI code of first character.
InStr(*str1,str2*)	Returns position of first *str1* in *str2*.
Lcase(*String*)	Converts *String* to lowercase letters.
Left(*Str,Len*)	Returns *Len* characters from left of *Str*.
Len(*String*)	Returns the length of *String*.
Ltrim(*String*)	Trims leading spaces from *String*.
Mid(*Str,Start,Len*)	Returns middle portion of *Str*.
Right(*Str,Len*)	Returns *Len* characters from right of *Str*.
Str(*Number*)	Returns string representation of *Number*.
Rtrim(*String*)	Trims the trailing spaces from *String*.
StrComp(*Str1,Str2*)	Compares *Str1* and *Str2*.
String(*Len,Char*)	Creates string with *Len Chars*.
Trim(*String*)	Trims leading and trailing spaces.
Ucase(*String*)	Coverts *String* to uppercase.

Variant Subtype   VBScript's runtime provides a handful of functions you can use to determine the subtype of a variant variable (see Table 29.10). You'll find these functions handy when you need to verify that a string can be converted from one subtype to another, such as from a string to a date. Each function returns True if the variable can be converted to that particular type. For example, if a strDate contains 7/1/96, IsDate(strDate) returns True. On the other hand, if strDate contains Hello, IsDate(strDate) returns False.

Table 29.10 VBScript Date/Time Functions

Syntax	Description
IsArray(*Variable*)	Returns true if *Variable* is an array.
IsDate(*Variable*)	Returns true if *Variable* is a date.
IsEmpty(*Variable*)	Returns true if *Variable* is empty.
IsNull(*Variable*)	Returns true if *Variable* is Null.
IsNumeric(*Variable*)	Returns true if *Variable* is numeric.
IsObject(*Variable*)	Returns true if *Variable* is an object.
VarType(*Variable*)	Returns type of *Variable* as number.

Array Handling LBound and UBound let you determine the actual lower and upper bounds of an array (see Table 29.11). Note that an array's lower bound is always zero. Thus, you don't have much reason for using LBound (LBound was used in Visual Basic, however) in your scripts.

Table 29.11 VBScript Array Functions

Syntax	Description
LBound(*Array*)	Returns the lower bound of *Array*.
UBound(*Array*)	Returns the upper bound of *Array*.

VBScript Event Handlers

In Chapter 24, "Overview of Programming and Scripting," you learned about events. You learned that events are responses to something the user does (clicking a button, for example) or is a response to something that happens within the system (a timer going off). You can associate scripts with these events to handle them in any manner you like.

In VBScript, you have three methods available to handle events, each of which is appropriate under different circumstances. For normal usage, you should use the event procedure. It's the most straightforward way to create an event handler. There are times (sometimes it's just personal preference) when you'll want to use the FOR/EVENT attributes of the <SCRIPT> tag or inline event handlers, though, as you learn in the following sections.

VBScript Event Procedures

Take a look at the following HTML. The <SCRIPT> tag in the head contains a procedure called btnButton_onClick. Based upon the naming convention you learned in Chapter 24, "Overview of Programming and Scripting," you gather this is an event procedure (In VBScript, event handlers are called *event procedures*) for an object called Button that handles the onClick event. All it does is display Ouch! You clicked me. in a message box. Take a look at the form in the body of the HTML. It contains a single element called Button that's named by using the <INPUT> tag's NAME attribute. The combination of this name and the name of the event is how the browser knows to execute the event procedure called btnButton_onClick each time you click the button, as shown in Figure 29.1.

```
<HTML>
<SCRIPT LANGUAGE="VBScript">
<!--
 Sub btnButton_onClick
      MsgBox "Ouch! You clicked on me."
 End Sub
-->
</SCRIPT>

<FORM><INPUT NAME="btnButton" TYPE="BUTTON" VALUE="Click Me"></FORM>
</HTML>
```

FIG. 29.1

Click the button, and the browser executes the event procedure associated with the button's onClick event.

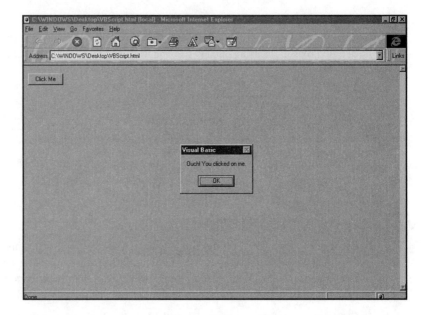

Inline Event Handler (Scriptlet)

HTML cripts are very flexible. You just learned how to handle an event using a VBScript event procedure. You can handle events in other ways, too. For example, you don't have to create a separate procedure for an event at all. You can handle it as an attribute in the element's tag as shown here:

```
<HTML>
<FORM>
<INPUT NAME="btnButton" TYPE="BUTTON" VALUE="Click Me"
onClick='MsgBox "Ouch! You clicked on me."' LANGUAGE="VBScript">
</FORM>
</HTML>
```

Notice this example doesn't have a <SCRIPT> tag anywhere in it. Look at the <INPUT> tag closely, though. It contains an attribute, which is a script. Its name is the name of the onClick event. When the button fires the onClick event, it executes everything between the single quotes ('). Take note here, as this is one of those exceptions. The value of an event's attribute is surrounded by single quotes, unlike other attributes, which use double quotes ("). You can put multiple statements in the event's attribute by separating them with colons (:), like this:

```
onClick='MsgBox "Hello World" : MsgBox "Hello Again"'
```

The LANGUAGE attribute specifies which language you're using for the inline script. You could just as easily use JavaScript as VBScript. If you don't specify a language anywhere in your HTML file, the browser defaults to JavaScript.

T I P Once you've specified a language in your HTML file, you don't need to do it again. Your browser defaults to the most recently used language used in the HTML file. You can put `<SCRIPT LANGUAGE="JavaScript"></SCRIPT>` at the very beginning of your HTML file one time and forget about it. The rest of the scripts in your file will use JavaScript.

Some events pass arguments to the event-handlers. How do you handle arguments when you're handling the event inline? Like this:

```
MouseMove(shift, button, x, y)='window.status="The mouse is at " & x & "," & y'
```

FOR/EVENT Attributes

Yes, VBScript provides one more way to handle events. If you don't want to use an event procedure, and you don't want to use an inline event handler, you can use the `<SCRIPT>` tag itself. This involves using the FOR and EVENT attributes of the `<SCRIPT>` tag. These attributes allow you to associate a script with any named object in the HTML file and any event for that object. Take a look at this code:

```
<HTML>
<SCRIPT LANGUAGE="JavaScript" FOR="btnButton" EVENT="onClick">
<!--
 MsgBox( "Ouch! You clicked on me." );
-->
</SCRIPT>
<FORM><INPUT NAME="btnButton" TYPE="BUTTON" VALUE="Click Me"></FORM>
</HTML>
```

This code defines a button just like the one you saw earlier. The difference is that you won't find an event procedure in this HTML file. Take a look at the `<SCRIPT>` tag, though. It contains the FOR and EVENT attributes which define the object and event associated with that script. `FOR="btnButton" EVENT="onClick"` says that when an object named Button fires the onClick event, execute every statement in this script.

Some events pass arguments to the event handlers. How do you handle arguments when you're handling the event using the FOR/EVENT syntax? Like this:

```
<SCRIPT LANGUAGE="VBScript" FOR="btnButton"
EVENT="MouseMove(shift, button, x, y)">
```

The enclosed script can then use any of the parameters passed it by the MouseMove event.

Handling Common Events

If you're a Visual Basic programmer, you'll be surprised by the limited number of events available for each object you find on a Web page. You just don't need to handle events such as DblClick, DragDrop, DragOver, MouseDown, MouseUp, and so on. They don't make sense in this context. That leaves you with a handful of events such as onClick, mouseMove, onMouseOver, and so forth. Note that you won't find any keyboard events at all.

Each and every intrinsic or ActiveX object defines its own events. You have to look at that object's documentation to find information about the exact events it provides. I describe many of these objects in this book, however. Also, many of the browser's objects, such as the Window or Document object, support events such as onLoad. Look at those objects' documentation for more information about the events they fire.

> **TIP** The best reference for the events that an intrinsic or ActiveX object defines is the ActiveX Control Pad's Script Wizard. See Chapter 22, "ActiveX Controls" for more information.

Mouse Events   Almost all objects you put on a Web page fire a few mouse events. Here are the common ones (most objects have even more events):

MouseMove	Fires as the mouse moves over an object. This event reports the mouse's position as it moves. You can use it to implement fly-over help.
OnMouseOver	Fires each time the mouse moves over an object. The difference between this event and MouseMove is it only fires once each time the mouse crosses the object, and it doesn't report its position.
onClick	Fires each time you click the left mouse button over an object. You can use this event to implement your own image maps or validate a form before you submit it to the server.

State Events   Many elements, such as a text box or buttons, support events that tell you when their state changes. This includes when they get or lose focus, when their data changes, and when the user selects something from a list.

OnBlur	Fires when an object loses the keyboard focus. You can use this event to validate the contents of a text box before the user moves on to another object.
OnFocus	Fires when an object gets keyboard focus. An object has focus when what you type or do with the keyboard affects that object. You can change focus by pressing the Tab key or clicking another object with the mouse.
OnChange	Fires each time the user changes data in the object and the object loses focus. For example, when the user moves the cursor out of a text box in which they've changed data, the text box fires this event.
OnSelect	Fires each time the user selects an item in a list or combo box.

> **CAUTION**
> Be careful not to create cascading events. This occurs when your event-procedure causes the same event to fire over and over again. If your event handler for the OnClick event causes the OnClick event to fire again, your script will eventually crash.

Connecting Scripts to Forms

HTML forms generate events in response to the things the user does. For example, if the user types text in a text box, the browser generates an event that lets you know the text box has changed. If the user selects an item from a list, the browser generates an event that lets you know about it. You can handle a variety of events that a form generates, including events that occur when the user changes a value in a field, picks an item from a list, or moves from field to field.

 TIP Connecting your scripts to ActiveX objects works just like connecting scripts to forms. You learn more about this in Chapter 22, "ActiveX Controls."

Handling an Element's Events

You learned earlier in this chapter that objects on the Web page fire events when they need your attention. A button fires the onClick event when the user clicks the button. A text box fires the onChange event when the user changes the contents of the text box and they move the cursor off of it.

Most, if not all, of the scripts you write are attached to events. They're event handlers. Events are pretty much the only way your scripts get a chance to run after the Web page loads. They're the only way you can interact with the objects on a page, including a form's elements.

Handling the *onClick* Event   Most of the elements you can add to a form support the onClick event. These include the button, check box, and text fields. An element fires the onClick event any time the user clicks the mouse on the element. In some cases, notably the select element, an element fires the onClick event when the user selects an item in a list.

The following code contains a form that displays the contents of txtName when the user clicks the button btnDisplay. The event-procedure is called btnDisplay_onClick because it's handling the onClick event for the object named btnDisplay. This example also shows you how to read the value of an element. BtnDisplay_onClick reads the value from the text field called txtName. Did you notice the .value bit? You have to explicitly use the property name containing the value. If you're a Visual Basic programmer, this may take some getting used to, because you're using to using an object's default property, which is usually the value.

```
<HTML>
<SCRIPT LANGUAGE="VBScript">
<!--
 Sub btnDisplay_onClick
     alert "Hi " & MyForm.txtName.value
 End Sub
-->
</SCRIPT>
<FORM NAME="MyForm">
    <INPUT TYPE=TEXT VALUE="Jerry" SIZE=40 NAME="txtName">
    <INPUT TYPE=BUTTON VALUE="Display" NAME="btnDisplay">
</FORM>
</HTML>
```

Handling the *onFocus* Event The following script shows you how to handle the onFocus event for an element. An element fires the onFocus event any time the user gives focus to a control. The user can give focus to a control by pressing the Tab key until it becomes the current control, or by clicking the control with the mouse.

```
<HTML>
<TITLE>Howdy</TITLE>
<SCRIPT LANGUAGE="VBScript">
<!--
 Sub txtName_onFocus
     status = "Type your first name in this field"
 End Sub
-->
</SCRIPT>

<FORM NAME="MyForm">
    <INPUT TYPE=TEXT VALUE="Jerry" SIZE=40 NAME="txtName">
    <INPUT TYPE=BUTTON VALUE="Display" NAME="btnDisplay" onClick="alert 'Hi ' &
    ➥txtName.value">
</FORM>
</HTML>
```

Handling the *onBlur* Event An element fires the onBlur event when the element loses focus. An element can lose focus because the user pressed the Tab key to select a different element, or the user clicked a different element with the mouse.

The following script shows you an example of handling the onBlur event. This example just clears the status line. You can use the onBlur event to do any last minute processing before the element loses focus, though.

```
<HTML>
<SCRIPT LANGUAGE="VBScript">
<!--
 Sub txtName_onFocus
     status = "Type your first name in this field"
 End Sub

 Sub txtName_onBlur
     status = ""
 End Sub
-->
</SCRIPT>

<FORM NAME="MyForm">
    <INPUT TYPE=TEXT VALUE="Jerry" SIZE=40 NAME="txtName">
    <INPUT TYPE=BUTTON VALUE="Display" NAME="btnDisplay" onClick="alert 'Hi ' &
    ➥txtName.value">
</FORM>
</HTML>
```

Handling the *onChange* Event The following script shows you how to handle the onChange event. An element fires this event when the user leaves a field that he or she changes.

```
<HTML>
<SCRIPT LANGUAGE="VBScript">
<!--
  Sub txtName_onChange
      alert "You changed the field"
  End Sub
-->
</SCRIPT>

<FORM NAME="MyForm">
    <INPUT TYPE=TEXT VALUE="Jerry" SIZE=40 NAME="txtName">
    <INPUT TYPE=BUTTON VALUE="Display" NAME="btnDisplay" onClick="alert 'Hi ' &
txtName.value">
</FORM>
</HTML>
```

Setting and Getting an Element's Value

What good is a form if you can't get and set the values of the elements on it? You read the value of most elements using the element's value property, like this:

```
alert MyForm.txtName.Value
```

You can also set the value of an element by assigning a string to the element's value, like this:

```
MyForm.txtName.value = "jerry"
```

The examples in this section show you how to get at the values of other types of elements, including list boxes. It also shows you how to do other things with fields—such as disable them.

Getting a Radio Selection *Radio buttons* give the user a number of choices. They can choose one from the available items. Figure 29.2 shows a form with radio buttons on it.

The following example shows you the script that created Figure 29.2. MyForm in the following code shows you how to add radio buttons to your own forms. Note that each button has the same name: chkRadio. This is how the browser knows that each of these buttons belongs to the same group. When the user selects one of the radio buttons, the button fires the onClick event.

```
<HTML>
<SCRIPT LANGUAGE="VBscript"></SCRIPT>

<FORM NAME="MyForm">
What type of pet do you prefer:
    <INPUT TYPE=RADIO VALUE="Cats" NAME="chkRadio" OnClick='alert "Cats"'>Cats
    <INPUT TYPE=RADIO VALUE="Dogs" NAME="chkRadio" OnClick='alert "Dogs"'>Dogs
    <INPUT TYPE=RADIO VALUE="Birds" NAME="chkRadio" OnClick='alert "Birds"'>Birds
    <INPUT TYPE=RADIO VALUE="Fish" NAME="chkRadio" OnClick='alert "Fish"'>Fish
</FORM>
</HTML>
```

FIG. 29.2
Radio buttons are a
great way to limit the
user's choices.

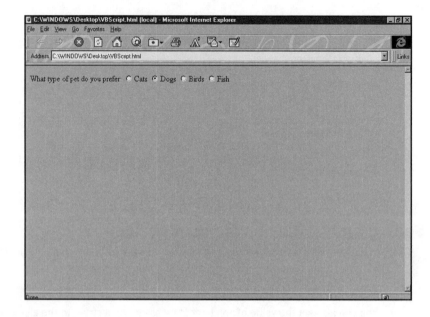

Getting a List Box's Selection The following example shows you how to add a drop-down list box to your form. You do it with the <SELECT> and <OPTION> tags. When the user picks an item from the list, the list fires the onChange event. You can see the value of the name the user picked with the select element's options.Text property, which you must index with the number of the user's selection.

```
<HTML>
<SCRIPT LANGUAGE="VBScript">
<!--
 Sub lst_onChange
     intI = MyForm.lst.selectedIndex
     alert "So, you like " & MyForm.lst.options(intI).Text
 End Sub
-->
</SCRIPT>
<FORM NAME="MyForm">
What type of pet do you prefer:
    <SELECT NAME="lst">
        <OPTION NAME="Cats">Cats
        <OPTION NAME="Dogs">Dogs
        <OPTION NAME="Birds">Birds
        <OPTION NAME="Fish">Fish
    </SELECT>
</FORM>
</HTML>
```

Element Properties, Methods, and Events

Each element you can put in a form supports a variety of properties, methods, and events. Describing every single part of each element is beyond the scope of this book. Table 29.12

gives you a brief summary, however. The examples in this book do show you how to use most of these elements.

Table 29.12 Element Properties, Methods, and Events

Properties	Methods	Events
Button		
form	click	onClick
name	focus	onFocus
value		
enabled		
Reset		
form	click	onClick
name	focus	onFocus
value		
enabled		
Submit		
form	click	onClick
name	focus	onFocus
value		
enabled		
Check Box		
form	click	onClick
name	focus	onFocus
value		
checked		
defaultChecked		
enabled		
Radio		
form	click	onClick
name	focus	onFocus
value		

continues

Table 29.12 Continued

Properties	Methods	Events
Radio		
checked		
enabled		
Combo		
form	click	onClick
name	focus	onFocus
value	removeItem	
enabled	addItem	
listCount	clear	
list	focus	
multiSelect	blur	
listIndex	select	
Password		
form	focus	onFocus
name	blur	onBlue
value	select	
defaultValue		
enabled		
Text		
form	focus	onFocus
name	blur	onBlur
value	select	onChange
defaultValue		onSelect
enabled		
Text Area		
form	focus	onFocus
name	blur	onBlur
value	select	onChange
defaultValue		onSelect
enabled		

Properties	Methods	Events
Select		
name	focus	onFocus
length	blur	onBlur
options		onChange
selectedIndex	onSelect	
Hidden		
name		
value		

Using the Coding Conventions

VBScript is an easy language to understand after you've been exposed to it for awhile. It's much easier, however, if you follow some coding conventions that make scripts significantly easier to understand and debug.

This section describes the conventions used in this book which are those recommended by Microsoft. These conventions are simple methods for writing a script so other people can easily read it.

N O T E The conventions in this chapter are Microsoft's recommendations. You can learn more about Microsoft's coding conventions at **http://www.microsoft.com/vbscript/us/ vbstutor/vbscodingconventions.htm**. ■

N O T E If you don't agree with a particular convention in this chapter, replace it with whatever works better for you. If you do deviate from a particular convention, note the deviation at the beginning of the HTML file containing your script. That way, other people will still be able to read it easily. The most important thing is to be consistent. That is, if you do deviate from a convention, do it throughout your scripts, not just hit or miss. ■

Using the Naming Convention

Naming conventions describe how to name constants, variables, objects, and procedures. The sole purpose for using these conventions is to make precisely clear what a constant represents, what type of data you're storing in a variable, what an object is used for, or what a procedure does. You should use naming conventions because they enable you to see what something is or does by looking at its name, instead of finding the object's declaration elsewhere in your script.

Naming conventions have been around a long time. They're used in COBOL programs, they're used in database tables, and they're used in most Windows programs. The VBScript naming conventions are loosely modeled after the Hungarian naming conventions, so that's where you start.

All Hungarian names have the same *syntax* (form):

`[prefixes]tag[name[suffixes]]`

The parts contained in square brackets are optional. That is, `prefixes`, `name`, and `suffixes` are not required. If you're using a suffix, however, you must also use a name. Only `tag` is required. Here's what each part of a Hungarian name is:

- *Prefixes* are one or more prefixes that further describe the tag. They're always lower-case letters and are typically predefined. The VBScript coding conventions use a single prefix that indicates the scope of a variable.

- *Tag* is two or three characters that indicate the type of the item. A tag is always lowercase and is typically one of a predefined list of tags such as `int` for integer or `str` for string. The VBScript coding conventions provide a list of tags for each variable subtype.

- *Name* is a short name that describes what the item is. The first letter of each word in the name is capitalized, with each subsequent letter in lowercase such as `strMyVariable`.

- *Suffixes* are one or more suffixes that further describe the name. The first letter of each word in the suffix is capitalized, and each subsequent letter is lowercase. The VBScript coding conventions don't use suffixes.

Naming Constants   Constants are variables that contain an unchanging value. The speed of light is a constant, as are pi and the boiling point of water.

Use all uppercase letters for constant names. Separate words in a constant name with an under-score (_). For example, `MAX_TRIES` is a constant that defines a maximum number of attempts at something and `DAYS_OF_WEEK` is a constant that defines the number of days in a week.

Naming Variables   These naming conventions allow you to express precisely why you created a particular variable and what type of data you're storing in the variable. Remember these conventions use a prefix, tag, and name for each variable to precisely define what you're putting in the variable. The only part of a variable that's actually required is the tag. This describes the type of data you're storing in that variable. Table 29.13 shows the tags you use for VBScript.

Table 29.13   Variable Name Tags

Subtype	Prefix	Example
Boolean	bln	blnFinished
Byte	byt	bytLetter
Date (Time)	dtm	dtmBirthday
Double	dbl	dblResult
Error	err	errBadInput
Integer	int	intBeans
Long	lng	lngDistance

Subtype	Prefix	Example
Object	obj	objFirst
Single	sng	sngBalance
String	str	strName

It's okay to use the tag by itself for temporary variables such as loop control variables or flags. For example:

```
Dim int
For int = 1 to 10
    ' Block of code
End For
```

More often than not, you'll add a name to the tag. You might name a variable you're using to store a person's age; intAge, for example. Use names that completely describe the purpose of the variable. strFirstName and strLastName are better than fn and ln. Don't make your variable names so long, however, as to make them difficult and error-prone to type. objSupercalifragilisticexpialidocious, for example. A good guideline is to keep them shorter than 32 characters and consistently use abbreviations where necessary.

> **CAUTION**
>
> Variable names can quickly get out of hand. After staring at your script for hours on end, it's easy to make a mistake typing a name. The worst part is that you won't even know it, because VBScript doesn't consider it an error; it just creates a new variable for you.
>
> To avoid this problem, put the Option Explicit statement (described earlier in this chapter) in a script right after the <SCRIPT> tag. That is, Option Explicit must be the first line after the <SCRIPT> tag. This causes VBScript to require that every variable used in your script be declared before you use it so you don't accidentally define a new variable when you didn't intend to.

Script-level (global) variables also need a prefix. The letter s helps point out variables that are visible to every procedure in your script. Note that you should always try to declare variables with the smallest scope possible (*procedure-level*). If you can't get around a script-level variable, however, prefixing it with the letter s helps identify these troublesome variables to you and other people reading your script.

 Put all script-level variables in a script within the <HEAD> tags of your HTML file. This way, you can easily keep track of all those global variables.

Naming Objects   Just like variables, objects have tags that indicate the type of object with which you're working. The definition of the control is seldom visible while you're editing the procedure associated with the control. Using these conventions helps you remember what type of control you're using. In some cases, you use the tag alone. In most cases, however, you add a name that fully describes for what you're using the object. Table 29.14 describes the tags you use in VBScript.

Table 29.14 Object Name Tags

Object Type	Prefix	Example
3-D Panel	pnl	pnlUserInfo
Animated Button	ani	aniNextPage
Check Box	chk	chkSubscribe
Combo Box, Drop-down List Box	cbo	cboLanguages
Command Button	cmd	cmdSubmit
Common Dialog	dlg	dlgFileOpen
Frame	fra	fraGroup
Horizontal Scroll Bar	hsb	hsbSize
Image	img	imgPicture
Label	lbl	lblDescription
Line	lin	linDivider
List Box	lst	lstCodes
Spin	spn	spnAmount
Text Box	txt	txtName
Vertical Scroll Bar	vsb	vsbAmount
Slider	sld	sldVolume

Naming Subprocedures and Functions   Most subprocedures do something. Otherwise, they'd be useless, right? These coding conventions recommend that you name your sub-procedures accordingly. Use an action verb such as Get, Prompt, or Count to name a sub-procedure. In most cases, you also add a noun to the name of your subprocedure so that you know what the subprocedure is acting upon, such as GetFirstName, which gets the user's first name, PromptForAge, which prompts the users for their ages, and CountLinks, which counts the links on a Web page. Think of subprocedure names as commands you're giving to the computer: "Do this to that." In each case, the name begins with a verb and ends with the name of the object to which the action is being applied.

Functions are different from subprocedures in that they can return a value. In order to ad-equately describe the return value of a function, use a tag in addition to the function name. A function that prompts the users for their names and returns a string might have a name like strGetLastName(), for example, which indicates a function that gets the user's last name and returns it as a string value. A function that returns the day of the week for a given date might have a name like `intDayOfWeek()` that indicates a function that returns the day of the week as an integer value.

 TIP This convention enables you to easily match variable types to the function's return value type. If you declare a variable called `intAge` and you assign the result of a call to `strGetName()` to it, for example, you should immediately notice that you're assigning a string (`str`) value to a variable you intended to hold integers (`int`). Likewise, if you assign the value returned by `intGetNumber` to a variable called `intAge`, you're making an assignment that you intended.

Formatting Conventions

Here are two important things to remember when formatting your script:

- People tend to think in hierarchies (presidents, vice presidents, directors, and so on). It brings order to chaos, structure to complex problems. Indenting your script at appropriate places helps people see its organization.

- Many people reading your script (including yourself) may only have a 640×480 resolution screen. That doesn't leave much space for viewing an entire line of your script.

With that in mind, use the following guidelines when formatting your code. Figure 29.3 shows what a properly formatted script looks like in Notepad.

- Indent each procedure's *comment block* (a comment above the procedure that describes what it does) one space.

- Indent the highest level of code within a script four spaces.

- Indent each nested block of code (`If...Then...Else`) statements four spaces.

> **CAUTION**
> Don't use tabs to indent blocks of code within your script—use spaces. How a tab looks depends on the particular editor that you're using. Tabs won't look the same on everyone's computer, and in many cases will look quite messy. Spaces will look the same on everyone's computer.

N O T E Microsoft recommends putting all of your procedures in the <HEAD> section of your HTML file. This way, all your code is in one place. Alternatively, you can keep event-procedures near the objects that they tend. This requires putting scripts in the <BODY> section of your HTML file. ■

FIG. 29.3

Notepad is good for editing scripts.

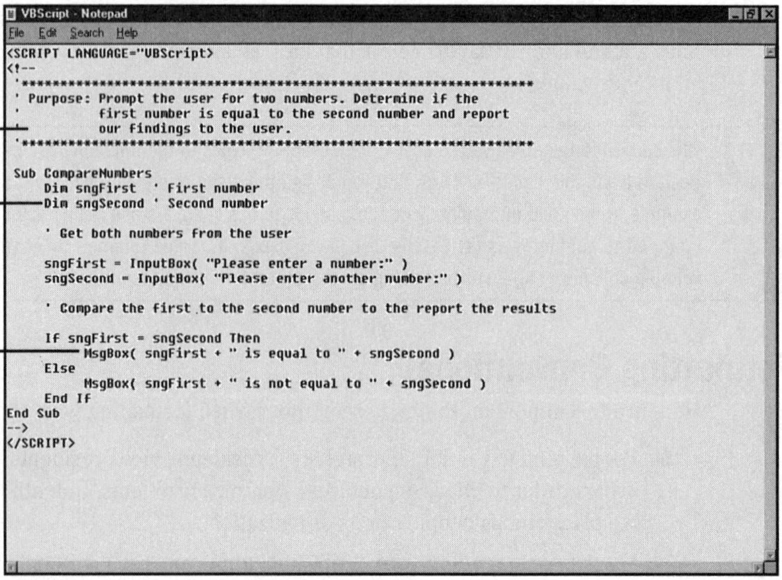

Comment block indented one space

Highest level of code indented four spaces

Nested block of code indented four spaces

```
VBScript - Notepad
File  Edit  Search  Help
<SCRIPT LANGUAGE="VBScript">
<!--
'****************************************************************
' Purpose: Prompt the user for two numbers. Determine if the
'          first number is equal to the second number and report
'          our findings to the user.
'****************************************************************

Sub CompareNumbers
    Dim sngFirst   ' First number
    Dim sngSecond  ' Second number

    ' Get both numbers from the user

    sngFirst = InputBox( "Please enter a number:" )
    sngSecond = InputBox( "Please enter another number:" )

    ' Compare the first to the second number to the report the results

    If sngFirst = sngSecond Then
        MsgBox( sngFirst + " is equal to " + sngSecond )
    Else
        MsgBox( sngFirst + " is not equal to " + sngSecond )
    End If
End Sub
-->
</SCRIPT>
```

Commenting Conventions

A *comment* is text that doesn't do anything that you add to your script. It's only purpose in life is to document your intentions or to explain a section of code that's not intuitively obvious. Every comment starts with an apostrophe ('). VBScript ignores everything from the apostrophe to the end of the line. It starts interpreting again at the beginning of the next line. You can use a comment on a line by itself, or at the end of a line that contains code. Here are a couple of comment examples:

```
' The following code does this, that, and the other
```

```
intAge = 29 ' My wife's perpetual age
```

Start each procedure with a brief comment (comment block) that describes what it does. Don't describe the details (how it works) because the details change frequently. That will make it difficult to keep your comments updated. Instead, describe what it does. In other words, while writing your comment, think of the procedure as a black box. You provide input to the black box and it provides a result or changes the state of the Web page. You don't care how it happens; all you want to write about is the results.

Table 29.15 shows what sections you should include in each procedure's comment block. Assumptions, Effects, Inputs, and Return Values are optional headings. If you're tempted to write the word **none** next to these headings, just leave them out. Always include the purpose, however.

Table 29.15   Comment Headings

Heading	Description
Purpose	A brief description of what the procedure does—not how it works.
Assumptions	A list of external variables, controls, or other elements whose state affects this procedure.
Effects	A list that describes the procedure's effect on external variables, controls, or other elements.
Inputs	A list that describes each argument passed to the procedure.
Return Values	A list that describes the function's return value.

Examples

On this book's CD-ROM, you find a few examples that show what you can do with VBScript. The first example shows you how to validate a form by using VBScript. The second shows you how to use a timer to create a scrolling message in the status line. The last example shows you how to use VBScript to create client-side imagemaps, with a twist.

Validating a Form

The first example (FEEDBACK.HTM) shows you how to validate a form before submitting it to the server. This doesn't work the way Microsoft documents it. Instead of using a SUBMIT button, you create your own button and then attach a subprocedure to its onClick event. Then, if the form is valid, you use the forms Submit method to submit the form. Listing 29.1 shows you what the subprocedure looks like.

Listing 29.1   FEEDBACK.HTML: Validating a Form in VBScript

```
Sub Submit_onClick()
   If Feedback.Comments.Value = "" Then
     alert "You have not typed any comments. Please try again."
   ElseIf Feedback.Name.Value = "" Then
     alert "You must provide your name. Please try again."
   ElseIf Feedback.Email.Value = "" Then
     alert "You must provide your e-mail address. Please try again."
   Else
     Call Feedback.Submit()
   End If
End Sub
```

Scrolling a Message Across the Status Line

The second example (TIMER.HTM) shows you how to use the ActiveX Timer control to update the status line periodically. As shown in the example, you can use this to create a scrolling message in the status line. This example also shows you how to use some of the runtime libraries string functions, such as Len, Right, Left, and String.

Creating Enhanced Client-Side Imagemaps

Remember Chapter 12, "Imagemaps"? I promised to show you how to create a client-side imagemap with VBScript. Well, here it is. The last example on the CD-ROM for this chapter (IMAGEMAP.HTM) shows you how to track the mouse pointer across an image that is inserted by using the following HTML:

```
<A ID="ImageMap" HREF=""><IMG SRC="imagemap.gif"
ALT="Clickable imagemap"></A>
```

Instead of associating event-procedures with the image itself, you enclose the image in the <A> tag and associate event-procedures with that. You use the empty HREF attribute because the script will determine which Web pages to open.

The script puts a bit of context-sensitive help text in the status line based upon the current mouse location. Then, when the user clicks the mouse, the script opens the indicated Web page. This script contains four routines:

Help	This subprocedure displays the given text in the status line of the browser.
InRect	Compares the given x and y coordinates to the given rectangle and returns True if the coordinates are within the rectangle. Otherwise, it returns False.
ImageMap_onClick	This is the event-procedure for the imagemap's onClick event. It determines which region the mouse is in when the user clicks, and opens the indicated Web page.
ImageMap_MouseMove	This is the event-procedure for the imagemap's MouseMove event. It determines which region the mouse is in as the user moves the mouse across the imagemap. Then, it displays the appropriate help text in the status line.

Web Site Management

## CHAPTER 30

Putting Your Pages Online

by Rob Falla

Once your Web site is completed, it has to be published in a way that allows others to access it. There are presently two methods for publishing a Web site; uploading to your Web directory on an ISP or running your own Web server. This chapter will discuss both methods. After reading this chapter, you should be able to determine which method is best suited to your needs. ■

Publish your site

You'll be introduced to the different Internet publishing options presently available.

Hosting your Web

The most common method of publishing a Web site is having it hosted on another system. You will learn the steps required to have your Web site hosted on someone else's server.

Running your own server

This section discusses the steps involved in running your own server.

What Are Your Options?

Before you publish your Web site to the Internet you should consider the options available; your choice will depend on your individual situation. Read this section to gain a better understanding of the two Web-site publishing options—your own server versus having your site hosted by an ISP—and select the one that best suits your needs.

The more common choice, considering the initial cash outlay required to set up and run your own server, is to let someone else worry about the equipment upkeep. Unless you're developing a complete Internet solution for a large company, one that will make use of other Internet features such as FTP, e-mail, and possibly a database, you probably do not require your own server. Make a few phone calls, do a price and service comparison, and have your site hosted by one of your local ISPs.

The focus of this chapter is getting your Web site published on someone else's system. Considering the differences between the policies of the various ISPs, you should look for certain features before signing on with any particular ISP. In addition to a standard dial-up account with e-mail, you will need a shell and an FTP account. It is only common sense that you have easy access to your Web files.

Uploading Files to an ISP

This is the easiest method if you can find an ISP that offers shell accounts and FTP (not a requirement but makes it much easier). If you plan to make frequent modifications to the content of your site, having shell and FTP access means you can quickly add and remove files, add new subdirectories, and include server-side scripts (depending on the ISP) amongst other benefits like using the UNIX mail to sort your e-mail.

Run Your Own Server

This option needs to be considered very carefully. The initial cash layout for the appropriate telephone line service and modem is in excess of $1,000, not a commitment to be taken lightly. In addition to purchasing the digital telephone line service and the digital modems, you will also have to have a computer to act as the server. You do not want your accounting files and sales strategy on the same machine the world is connected to.

Both options achieve the same goal of making the data on the Web site available to anyone on the Internet with a Web-client application (browser). The delivery methods are the same as well. The only difference is you are burdened with maintenance of the networked system—which can become an enormous task if any major problems arise.

Running your own server means you will have total control over who sees your Web site and what kinds of content you can include with your Web site. You can make sections of the site available to anyone with a browser and restrict other parts of your Web site so only authorized users can access it. You own the Web site, and you own the space on the Internet that the Web site is occupying. This option is usually only available if you have a direct connection to the Internet.

You can run a server off your hard drive through a dial-up account, but the Web site would only be available when you are logged on. Also, you would have to make arrangements with your ISP to make sure you had the same IP address each time you log on.

Uploading to an ISP is actually like renting space to store your Web site files. Along with the many benefits, saving money being the biggest, there are a few drawbacks. For one, you have very little control over who can actually use or even see the site. You can't include server-side script files unless arrangements have been made with the administrator (often requiring no more than a call to the ISP).

Part VI

Ch 30

 Talk to your ISP if you want to use CGI or server-side Java and JavaScript.

The benefits to using someone else's system are: You don't have to put out the cash to upgrade to a server-grade computer, you are not responsible for ensuring the system is always operating, and you don't have the monthly bill for having dedicated Internet access.

Choosing an Option

It is important to determine the resources available to you (see Table 30.1).

Table 30.1 Examine the Requirements

Requirement	Own Server	ISP
Dedicated access	✓	
Dial-up access		✓
System Monitoring	✓	
System Maintenance	✓	

It's not all that difficult to choose the appropriate publishing method once you have determined the resources available to you. Answer the following questions about your operation and Web site:

- Do you or your firm have dedicated Internet access or the resources to set it up?
- Do you or your firm have the resources/manpower to maintain a server?
- Is the site a large Web application-type site, using Java applets, server-side scripts, movies, and audio files?
- Do you require a secure server?

If you answered "yes" to the above questions, you will probably want to run your own server. You are not required to, but it would be to your benefit. If you answered "no" to the first two questions and "yes" to the other questions, you may want to have a discussion with your ISP about your needs. It may have a reasonably priced solution for someone in your situation;

if it can't help you, shop around. Many ISPs will try to accommodate your needs; be prepared to pay.

Do you already have the money, the equipment, and the dedicated access to the Internet? Your choice is obvious. You will look over the information about servers in another section of this chapter and go with the one that best matches your requirements. Not much of a decision if you're already set up for it.

N O T E Still think you need the power of running your own server, but you do not have the resources or the dedicated account? There is still a chance that you can run a server (like Microsoft's Personal Web Server) from your local computer.

Your Web site would only be accessible while you were online. The rest of the time the user would get a "file not found" error.

It is beyond the scope of this book to get into the particulars of this option. If you want to find out more, talk to your ISP. ▪

Everyone else will be uploading to the ISP. This choice still offers a range of options for dynamic content inclusions. Many ISPs will put your CGI script on their system to work with your order form, guestbook, or whatever else you may need a CGI script for.

T I P There will most likely be a fee for putting your custom CGI script on the system. The ISP will have to test the script first, to make sure it isn't going to mess up the system by inadvertently allowing someone access to the system. If it passes the test, it will be put on the system. If it poses a security threat, it isn't likely that it will be on the system until the threat is eliminated.

Obvious to all is the benefit that you don't have to worry about monitoring the system. If there are any problems, the administrator will fix them. You can concentrate on producing the Web site and let someone else worry about keeping the system alive.

Carefully consider the next two sections when deciding which option to go with. The first, "Uploading to an ISP," takes you through the steps to publish your Web site on someone else's server. The section following that discusses running your own server and talks about the requirements of running it.

Uploading to an ISP

Uploading to the ISP is relatively easy. Follow the steps outlined in this section. This section is a generic set of instructions based on a UNIX account. Check with your ISP to see if there is any special procedure that must be followed on that system.

Some ISPs require you to e-mail the HTML files to them. They will place the files in a directory area designated for your Web site.

These ISPs charge a fee for putting the files on, and they charge a fee for any updates to your Web site. If the ISP you are dealing with works like that, shop around. It could quickly become very expensive to keep your content fresh in a situation like that.

Part VI

Ch

30

As you progress through this section, notice the following steps:

- Preparing your UNIX shell account for a Web site.
- Setting the permissions in the Web site directory.
- Making any subdirectories that your site requires.
- Uploading the HTML files.
- Uploading any other files that are related to your site.
- Preparing the files for presentation on the Internet.

Make yourself a checklist of all the required steps. When it's time to put your files online refer to the checklist to ensure you do not make any mistakes or forget any steps.

Preparing Your Site

The first thing you must do when putting a new Web site on the Internet is prepare the home on the networked computer in which the files will reside while they are on the Internet.

 Check with your ISP before you attempt to put a Web site on its network. It may not allow UNIX telnet sessions or may complete the following steps for you.

NOTE As was stated at the beginning of this chapter, you should have an account with an ISP that offers shell account access. This section assumes you have the shell account. ▉

You have to be online first. Once you are online, initiate a telnet session. The telnet client will communicate with the remote system requesting telnet access. The telnet session will go like this:

1. Enter the host address in the telnet client. Telnet will establish a connection.
2. Enter your logon ID and password when prompted.
3. Type **pwd** at the prompt to see which directory you are in. You should be in your own area on the system. The reply message should look something like this: /user/home/ userid/, which is your directory on the system.

NOTE Microsoft Windows 95 includes a telnet client. To use the telnet client, click the MS-DOS prompt icon. At the DOS prompt, type **telnet *host address***. ▉

Now you have initiated a telnet session. The default directory when you telnet into the ISP system is always your user directory.

Figure 30.1 shows you what the screen looks like when you log on. If you are having trouble establishing a telnet session, call your ISP.

FIG. 30.1

Here's a new telnet connection.

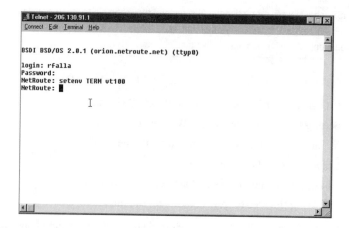

On your first telnet session you should take a few minutes to familiarize yourself with your surroundings. The following are a few commands that will become useful during this and any future telnet session:

`ls`	List. Shows files and directories stored in the current directory that are not hidden.
`la`	List All. An alias for `ls -a`. Shows you all the files (including hidden files) and directories stored in the current directory (see Figure 30.2).
`mkdir`	Make Directory. Creates directories and subdirectories in the current directory.
`rm`	Remove. Deletes files stored in the current directory.
`rmdir`	Remove Directory. Deletes directories and subdirectories stored in the current directory.
`man topic`	UNIX manual. Displays the help files on the topic. `man mail` will provide the help files on the UNIX mail program.
`cd directory`	Change Directory. Changes the current directory to another directory. To go up in the directory tree simply type **cd ...**

TIP If you want more information on the UNIX online manuals type **man man**.

FIG. 30.2
la will list all the contents of the current directory, including hidden system files, which have a dot as the first character.

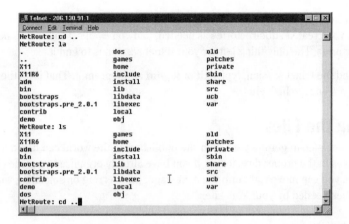

Preparing the UNIX Directory

The Web site files must be placed in a subdirectory of your home directory, specified by the ISP and usually called public_html. The public_html subdirectory is the default location the browser will look in, for all Web files, when it attempts to retrieve a Web page from your account. If there is no public_html subdirectory, the complete path for the Web site files must be supplied.

Also, the access permission level for the public_html subdirectory must be set to allow read-only access for everyone. Once the access permission for the public_html subdirectory is set, all subdirectories of public_html will share the same permissions as the public_html parent directory.

Not every BSD UNIX operating system (BSDOS) is the same. The steps outlined in the following list are based on the BSDI 2.0.1 operating system. Some of the other BSDOS systems will not inherit the permissions set for the directory. The best way to determine the requirements for any system is to ask your ISP.

Follow these steps to create the public_html subdirectory and set the appropriate access permissions.

1. Type **pwd** to make sure you are in your home directory.
2. Type **mkdir public_html**. This will create the public_html subdirectory in your home directory.
3. Type **cd public_html** to make it the current directory.

T I P Steps three and four can be combined into a single step by typing **chmod 755 public_html** or **chmod 644 public_html** from the user directory.

4. Type **chmod 755** to set the access permissions of the directory to read and execute. All subdirectories of public_html will have the same access permissions unless you explicitly change them. If you would prefer to set the permission to read only, type **chmod 644**.

The directory is now ready for your Web files. You have created the directory to store the Web files, you created subdirectories as needed, and you even set the access permissions for all directories. The only thing left for your telnet session is to end it.

To end the telnet session, type **exit** or **logout** at the prompt. That is all there is to the telnet session—not so bad, eh?

Uploading the Files

The next step to getting your Web site published so the world can begin to access it is to put the files in the proper directories. If you have already organized your files by type on your hard drive, you can move right into the next stage, transferring or uploading with an FTP client all the files needed by your Web site.

N O T E There are some ISPs who have accounts that do not have shell access, and everything (including creating subdirectories and giving them the correct permission) will be done via FTP. ∎

Open your FTP client and follow these instructions to connect to your ISP. As with the telnet client, your home directory is the default directory you will be taken to with the FTP client.

N O T E The following is based on using the shareware FTP client application WS_FTP (included on the CD-ROM). If you are using another FTP client application, the steps may be slightly different. ∎

1. Create a new Profile (see Figure 30.3) in the Profile Name area. (Or choose the preset profile for your home directory if one exists.)

2. Enter the host name **ftp.yourhost.net** (or com, org, whatever).

3. Select Automatic Detect in the Host Type area.

4. Enter your logon name in the User ID area.

5. Enter your password.

6. Mark the Save Password check box and click the Save button to save the new profile so that it's still there the next time you have to log on (for modifications to the Web site).

7. Leave the rest of the text areas blank and click the OK button. The FTP client will now connect to the host specified in the profile (your ISP.)

8. Type the full path to and including your public_html directory in Remote Host under Initial Directories.

FIG. 30.3
Setting up a new profile
with WS_FTP.

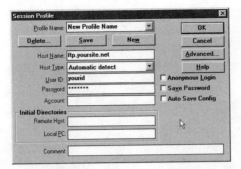

Once you are connected to the remote host, you will see a split directory window. On the left side is the local (your computer) directory tree; on the right you will see the directory tree of the remote host.

Both directory trees are broken up into three sections. The section nearest the top contains the path of the current directory. There is a separate path on both sides, the left representing your local system, the right representing the remote host.

The midsection contains the directory tree. The current directory is the highest on the tree and any subdirectories are placed under the current directory.

The bottom section contains the files that can be found in the current directory. The one on the left will show (by default) the files in the wsftp directory on your system. The right panel should show any files present in the current directory of the remote host.

Use the following instructions listed to upload your Web site files to your public_html directory and the pics subdirectory on your ISP's system:

1. In the local system side, select the directory your Web site files are located in. (Or you can click the ChgDir button and enter the exact path to the directory that contains the Web site files.)

2. In the remote host side, double-click the appropriate directory you want to be in. In this case it is public_html. You will notice that the directory presently contains no files.

3. Using your mouse, highlight all the files that are to be transferred to the remote directory (see Figure 30.4).

 Make sure the Binary option button is selected. Although you can use ASCII for transferring text files, it is much faster to just leave the setting at Binary and transfer files of all types at the same time (bulk transfer).

4. Click the right-arrow button to begin the transmission. A status box will appear which indicates the progress of the transfer.

5. On the local system, go to any additional directories and transfer any relevant files to the appropriate remote directory.

FIG. 30.4
Select the files you want to transfer and then the button indicating which direction (remote-to-host or host-to-remote) you want them to go.

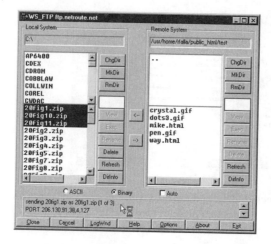

While still in the FTP client you can perform any file management tasks that are required. Depending on how you coded your files you may want to change the extensions of all your files to .html.

Remember, there must be an index.html file for the Web site. If there is not, the user must specify the exact name of your home page in the URL, **www.yourco.com/~yourid/pageone.html**. If there is an index.html, the user can simply put your Web server's domain and your user name such as **www.yourco.com/~yourid**.

You're finished! Using your favorite browser, test the URL for your Web site. If it comes up properly, you can begin testing all the links on your pages to make sure your visitors will not end up clicking a dead-end link.

Now go out and announce your new site by using an announce service like Yahoo!. Good luck!

Running Your Own Server

If you are in the situation where you need to run your own server, and you have the resources to do it, then you need to choose the right server for your operating system. You should also take your unique situation into consideration.

The Right Server

Selecting the right server for your corporate or organizational Web is extremely important. You do not want one that is too complicated or one that doesn't perform to your requirements.

Take a few minutes to draw up a requirements outline. It should contain information about capacity and speed expectations, whether or not you need a secure server, script language requirements, and so on.

You should visit the Web sites of the various server manufacturers and read all the relevant Web pages to determine if the server meets the minimum set of requirements you have outlined. Change the outline as often as is required until it describes your server requirements in a clear and concise manner. As you read the product information pages, you may come across something that you hadn't thought of. You should most definitely add those items to your requirements outline.

Once you have narrowed the candidates to two or three possible servers, find out if you can download a trial version to test evaluate. Run each server through a vigorous evaluation procedure to see how well it performs in certain areas. Your evaluation should include, in addition to anything you consider important for your circumstances, the following:

- Installation procedures—How easy or difficult are the installation procedures for the server?

- Technical support—What kind of technical support package is offered with the purchase of the server?

- HTML tools—Does the server come with HTML authoring tools?

- Speed test—How well does the server handle at different speed benchmarks?

- Your own requirements.

If you invest the time finding the right server, you will avoid many of the problems associated with getting the wrong server. A few days to a week of time spent investigating servers is worth many days or even weeks of headaches in the future.

N O T E For more information about server software, refer to any of the following books: *Running a Perfect Netscape Site*, *Special Edition Using Microsoft Internet Information Server 2*, and *Special Edition Using Netscape LiveWire* (all published by Que). ■

Putting Your Site Online

When you are running your own Web server, the steps for publishing the Web site are slightly different. The biggest difference is you don't make a telnet or an FTP connection because the server is the local host. The following will take you through the steps of publishing your Web site on your own UNIX server.

There are many other servers to choose from, depending on your operating system. If you are not using the UNIX or Windows NT operating systems, you should purchase a book that is more specifically directed to the operating system you have chosen.

1. The first step is to create a root directory on your hard drive.

2. From the root directory create the directory user/home/, which will allow you to add as many Web accounts as you want or need.

3. Create a Web account for your site in the user/home/subdirectory. Typically, your user ID is the account name.

4. Create the public_html directory in the Web account directory.

5. Assign the proper permissions (see previous for details). For more information on permissions, see "Preparing the UNIX Directory" earlier in this chapter.

6. Move the Web site files to the appropriate directories.

7. Change file names if required.

8. Test the links. Once again, you are in the position where you must test the links on your site to ensure that the user will have a nice, unobstructed visit. Test the links at least once a month to find and fix broken links.

When you are running your own server, you have a few additional options to consider.

- Should access to the site be restricted?
- Will it be a secure server site?
- What Web applications (if any) do I want to include?

Each of the three items in the preceding bulleted list consists of many additional steps and procedures that must be followed. Don't be fooled by the brevity of the steps in publishing a Web site on your own server.

The list fails to mention the monthly maintenance procedures that are required on a Web server. It also says nothing about the many other (log report analysis, visitor count analysis, and so on) functions a server administrator must perform.

In the next section, you'll take a look at some of the Web servers that are presently available. This will give you a good starting point for finding and running the server that most meets your individual requirements.

Web Servers

Use the following section to help narrow your search for an appropriate Web server. Each Web server is presented with an introductory paragraph.

Microsoft Internet Information Server

Microsoft IIS is the Web server that comes bundled with the Windows NT operating system (see Table 30.2). IIS has been reviewed favorably by many Internet trade magazines. If Windows NT is your operating system, then you should give this server serious consideration. It's free anyway.

Table 30.2 Microsoft Internet Information Server

Description	
Company	Microsoft Internet Information Server
Web Address	**http://www.msn.com/** or **http://www.microsoft.com/**
Platform	Windows NT
Address	One Microsoft Way, Redmond, WA 98052-6399
Telephone	(206) 882-8080

Part

VI

Ch

30

 TIP   Microsoft IIS is free with Windows NT version 4.0.

Microsoft Internet Information Server (MIIS) is a fairly complete Web server suite. There are no installation problems with this server, in part because it is automatically installed when you install Windows NT 4.0.

Although it performs superbly on the Windows NT platform, that is the only platform it is available on at present. This platform limitation automatically eliminates many potential customers for Microsoft. Look to Microsoft to release a fully interoperable, multiplatform server in early 1997 with the release of the Active Platform.

MIIS comes bundled with an FTP server, WWW server, Gopher server, and the WAIS server. In addition, MIIS also includes an HTML editor to assist authoring of HTML documents, a slew of APIs, and SSL security support.

Another feature of the MIIS package is the inclusion of the FrontPage HTML authoring application. FrontPage is an excellent authoring application for all Web developers—new to the Net or veteran Web developers. Using FrontPage you will have a Web site up and running in only a few short hours.

Luckman Web Commander

The people from Luckman (see Table 30.3) are not new to the Internet. In fact, they have developed many other Intenet-related applications, many of which are included in this package.

Table 30.3 Web Commander Server

Description	
Company	Luckman Interactive
Web Address	**http://www.luckman.com**
Platform	Windows NT and Windows 95
Address	1055 W. 7th Street, Suite 2580, Los Angeles, CA 90017
Telephone	(213) 614-0966

Web Commander provides a complete Internet server solution package. From the time you remove the shrink-wrap to having the package fully installed on your system takes about an hour. There is helpful documentation included with the package to help you get everything running without a hitch.

The server software is only one component of the Web Commander package. Also included in the package are HTML authoring tools, secure-server applications, ODBC database support, WAIS Toolkit, Netscape Navigator, and Perl 5.

Where MIIS is limited to operating only on Windows NT, Web Commander will work with both Windows NT and Windows 95, making it accessible to a wider group of information providers than MIIS. In addition to working on both operating systems, Web Commander has a much better monitoring and logging program than MIIS.

WebSite Professional

In keeping with its reputation for providing high-quality products, O'Reilly has produced the WebSite Professional (see Table 30.4).

Table 30.4 WebSite Professional Server	
Description	
Company	O'Reilly & Associates
Web Address	**http://www.ora.com**
Platform	Windows NT & Windows 95
Address	101 Morris Street, Sebastopol, CA 95472
Telephone	(707)829-0515
Fax	(707)829-0104

Is security important to you? How about database connectivity? WebSite Professional provides excellent support for both, as well as a complete, GUI-based diagnostics application.

The documentation and manuals included with WebSite Professional are well written and easy to use, making installation and administration of your new server as easy as possible. There are no quick solutions to the problem of not understanding the technology. A few good books will go a long way toward improving your understanding of the technology.

Like MIIS and Web Commander, WebSite Professional is also loaded with additional components. HTML authoring tools include SSIs, Hot Dog, WSAPI, and the Netscape Gold browser/editor. ●

## CHAPTER 31

Verification and File Management

by Jerry Honeycutt

I've got a challenge for you. Create a large HTML file by hand that doesn't have a single error in it. Can't do it? Neither can I. You'll leave a bracket off of at least one tag or even mistype an URL in a link—guaranteed. HTML isn't necessarily a complicated language, but the files are large and somewhat monotonous. Errors are bound to creep into them.

Syntax errors aren't the only problem you'll run into, either. As the number of files on your site grows (some sites have thousands of files), managing those files becomes much harder. Imagine a directory that contains several hundred HTML and graphics files. Try to sort out the relationship between each file. You can't.

This chapter describes tools that help you with both situations. It describes verification services you can use to double-check the syntax of your HTML. It also describes tools you can use to manage the files on your Web site or to manage your HTML documents on your own computer. ■

Validate the HTML in your files

You'll find several tools on the Web that you can use to verify the syntax of your HTML documents.

Verify your links

This chapter shows you a handful of tools that will verify each link in your HTML documents.

Store your HTML files by using version control

Version control helps you keep control of the files on your Web site and allows multiple developers to work together.

Create a library of reusable components

WebGal is a tool you can use to create a gallery of HTML, pictures, sounds, and controls for use on your Web site.

Manage the files on your Web site

This chapter describes a couple of products you can use to manage the organization of your Web site. You can also manage your files manually.

Validating Your HTML Documents

In the world of software development, programs are built in essentially three phases: design, programming, and testing. The purpose of each phase is self-explanatory.

When building HTML documents, you probably work with the same sort of phases. You design your HTML document, even if you just make a mental note of the document's general layout before you begin working on it. Then you implement the HTML document by writing individual lines of HTML code. Last, you test your Web pages to make sure they work as you planned and that they're syntactically correct.

Using tools that make that last phase, testing and verification, more productive is what this section is all about. You'll find a variety of tools on the Internet that will help you test your HTML files. Some of the tools you learn about in this section verify the syntax (form) of your HTML files. Other tools in this section just verify the links in your HTML files. Regardless, they help make sure that Web browsers can understand your HTML files and that your HTML files provide a positive experience to the user.

Doctor HTML

Doctor HTML is a verification service that analyzes the contents of a Web page. For example, you can use it to spell-check a Web page, verify the syntax of the HTML in a Web page, or even check a Web page for broken links. You can also use Doctor HTML to verify your entire Web site, but site verification is a commercial service to which you must subscribe.

Doctor HTML isn't a program that you download onto your computer before using. It's a service (implemented as a CGI script) that you access on the Web at **http://www2.imagiware. com/RxHTML/**. Click Single Page Analysis in the left frame and you'll see the Web page shown in Figure 31.1. Table 31.1 describes each test shown in the figure.

Table 31.1 Doctor HTML Tests

Test	Description
Spelling	Removes the tags and accented text from the HTML file and scans it for spelling errors.
Image Analysis	Loads all the images to which the HTML files are linked. It then determines the bandwidth required by each image and reports any images that require excessive download time. As well, Doctor HTML reports the size of and number of colors in each image.
Document Structure	Tests the structure of the HTML file, including unclosed HTML tags.
Image Syntax	Makes sure you're using the HEIGHT, WIDTH, and ALT attributes within the IMG tag. These attributes give the browser hints that help it load the HTML document faster.

Test	Description
Table Structure	Checks the structure of each table in the HTML document. It looks for any unclosed TR, TH, and TD tags.
Verify Hyperlinks	Reports each invalid link contained in your HTML file. Just because Doctor HTML reports a link as being "dead" doesn't mean that the link is invalid; the server may be running slow.
Form Structure	Verifies the structure of each form in the HTML file. It only looks at INPUT tags.
Show commands	Displays an indented list of HTML commands that shows the structure of your HTML document.

Part

VI

Ch

31

FIG. 31.1
You can order all tests by selecting Do All Tests or order individual tests by selecting Select from list below.

Select the tests you want to order

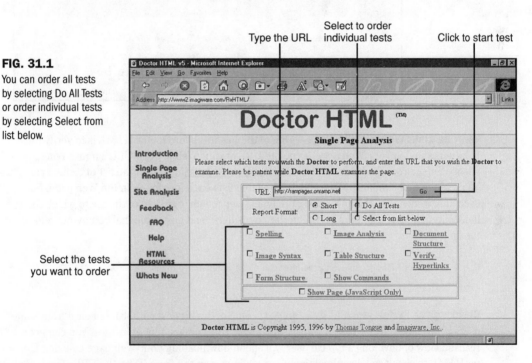

Type the URL Select to order individual tests Click to start test

Using Doctor HTML is straightforward. Type the URL of the Web page you want to verify in the URL field. If you want to specify the individual tests you want to run, choose Select from list below and then select each test you want to run; then click Go. Figure 31.2 shows the results of the tests that I performed on my home page.

N O T E Doctor HTML only looks at Web pages. You provide Doctor HTML the URL of a Web page or site and it analyzes the files it finds. You can't use Doctor HTML to verify small bits of HTML that you type in a form or HTML files that are contained in your local file system. ■

FIG. 31.2

Doctor HTML's output is easy to read.

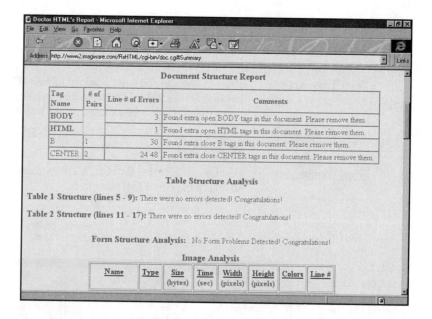

Document Structure Report

Tag Name	# of Pairs	Line # of Errors	Comments
BODY		3	Found extra open BODY tags in this document. Please remove them.
HTML		1	Found extra open HTML tags in this document. Please remove them.
B	1	30	Found extra close B tags in this document. Please remove them.
CENTER	2	24 48	Found extra close CENTER tags in this document. Please remove them.

Table Structure Analysis

Table 1 Structure (lines 5 - 9): There were no errors detected! Congratulations!

Table 2 Structure (lines 11 - 17): There were no errors detected! Congratulations!

Form Structure Analysis: No Form Problems Detected! Congratulations!

Image Analysis

Name	Type	Size (bytes)	Time (sec)	Width (pixels)	Height (pixels)	Colors	Line #

Verifying Links Within a Web Page   One of the best uses for Doctor HTML is to verify the links contained in your Web page. Type the URL of your Web page in URL; choose Long; choose Select from list below; and then select <u>Verify Hyperlinks</u> from the list of tests to run. You'll see output similar to Figure 31.3. The table lists each link found in the Web page. For each link, it identifies the link's URL; the type, size, and change date of the file to which the link points; the line numbers on which the link is used; and any additional comments regarding the link.

N O T E   Doctor HTML doesn't verify the links contained within image maps.

Checking the Performance of Your Images   One of the biggest complaints heard from some users is the time required to download Web pages that contain a lot of images. You can get a realistic view of how long a typical user will spend downloading your Web page by using Doctor HTML to check the download time for each image on the page. Type the URL of your Web page in URL; choose Long; choose Select from list below; and then select <u>Image Analysis</u> from the list of tests to run. You'll see results similar to Figure 31.4. The most important column to note is the <u>Time</u> column, which indicates how long the image takes to download when using a 14.4K modem.

FIG. 31.3
Doctor HTML only lists
those links for which
it finds warnings or
errors.

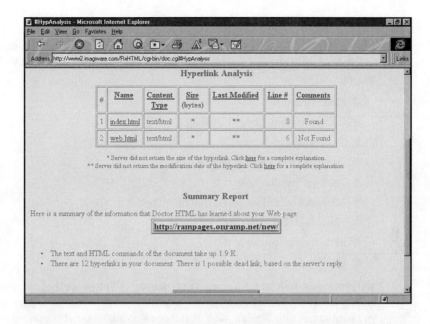

FIG. 31.4
The summary, at the
bottom of the results,
indicates the total
download time for all of
the images on the Web
page.

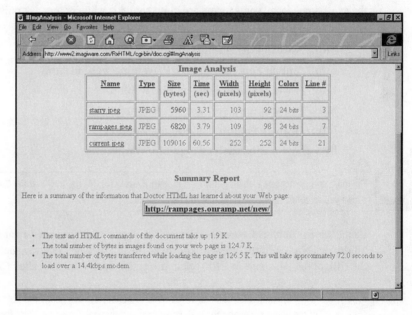

Weblint

Like Doctor HTML, Weblint is a Web-based HTML verification service. It checks the syntax and style of the Web page to which you point it. Some of the things that Weblint checks include:

- Basic structure
- Unknown elements and attributes
- Tag context
- Overlapped or illegally nested tags
- IMG tags that don't use ALT
- Mismatched and unclosed container tags
- Obsolete HTML tags
- Here used as anchor text
- Unclosed comments

You can access Weblint from a variety of gateways (Web pages that provide access to Weblint). Each gateway provides a form you use to point Weblint to your Web page and to set the options you want to use with Weblint. Note that there's no guarantee that every gateway will provide the exact same form; some forms are quite complex while others ask only for the Web page's URL. Here's a list of Weblint gateways you can use:

> **http://www.fal.de/cgi-bin/WeblintGateway**
>
> **http://online.anu.edu.au/CNIP/weblint/weblint.html**
>
> **http://www.cen.uiuc.edu/cgi-bin/weblint**
>
> **http://www.ts.umu.se/~grape/weblint.html**
>
> **http://www.netspot.unisa.edu.au/weblint/**
>
> **http://www.unipress.com/cgi-bin/WWWeblint**

TIP The most comprehensive Weblint gateway is at **http://www.fal.de/cgi-bin/WeblintGateway**. This site allows you to completely configure how you use Weblint.

Using the Fal Weblint Gateway   Figure 31.5 shows what the gateway at **http://www.fal.de/cgi-bin/WeblintGateway**, known as the Fal Weblint Gateway, looks like. Type the URL of the Web page in URL, select the options you want, and click Check HTML.

N O T E   When opening a home page in your Web browser, you can specify the path to the root of the home page, and the Web server will automatically open an HTML file named INDEX.HTM. When using any of the validation services, you have to explicitly specify the file name, however, as it won't look for INDEX.HTM on its own. ▪

FIG. 31.5

Click Simple if you want to use a version of the Fal Weblint Gateway that doesn't provide as many options.

Type the URL ⌐

Click to start test ⌐

Options ⌐

Warnings ⌐

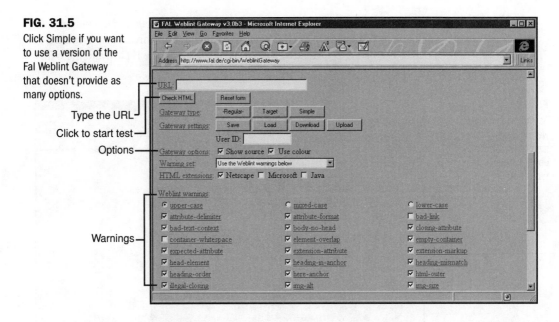

Using UniPress' WWWeblint Gateway   Figure 31.6 shows a much simpler gateway. UniPress' WWWeblint gateway (the authors of Weblint), at **http://www.unipress.com/cgi-bin/ WWWeblint**, is a very simple form that collects the URL of the Web page—and that's about it. After providing the URL, click Check it to verify the Web page.

FIG. 31.6

UniPress' WWWeblint gateway doesn't support Internet Explorer extensions like the Fal Weblint Gateway does.

Type the URL ⌐

Click to start test ⌐

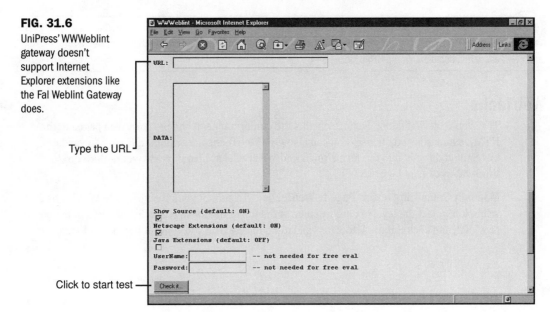

Part
VI

Ch
31

Figure 31.7 shows what the output from Weblint looks like. The top portion of the output lists any warnings and errors Weblint found in the Web page. The bottom portion is a formatted listing of the HTML. The listing is formatted so that the structure of the HTML and the URLs in the HTML are easy to identify.

FIG. 31.7

As well as listing warnings and errors separately, Weblint embeds them within the formatted listing.

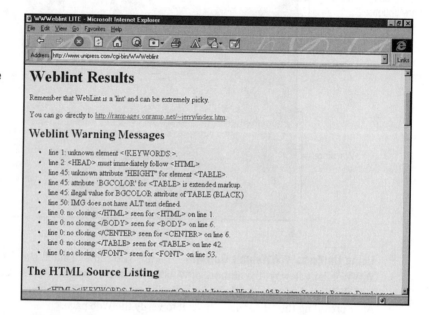

 TIP You can use Netscape's source viewer to more easily see the format of an HTML document. Choose View, Source from Netscape's main menu. The viewer will highlight the tags and attributes, as well as each URL, contained in the HTML file.

WebTechs

The WebTechs Validation Service checks the conformance of one or more Web pages to the HTML standards you choose. You can also give WebTechs a fragment of HTML to validate by typing it directly into the form. You'll find WebTechs at **http://www.webtechs.com/html-val-svc/** (see Figure 31.8).

Manually Submitting a Web Page to WebTechs To submit your Web pages to WebTechs for validation, select the level of conformance at the top of the form, type a list of URLs in the space provided, and click Submit URLs for validation. Figure 31.9 shows what the output looks like.

FIG. 31.8
While visiting this site, check out the *Web Apps Magazine*, an online magazine for Web professionals.

Select conformance level

Select types of output

Type list of URLs to submit

Click to start test

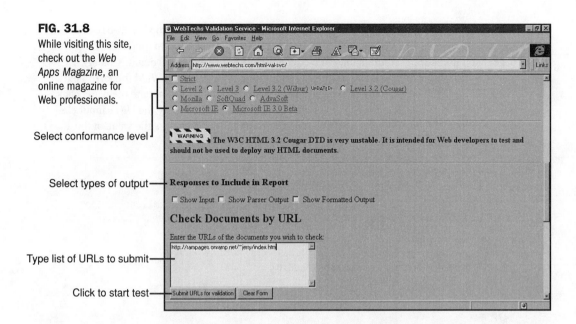

FIG. 31.9
To better understand WebTech's output, see the FAQ at **http://www.cs.duke.edu/~dsb/wt-faq.html**.

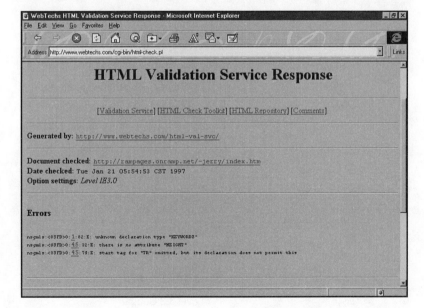

Part
VI

Ch
31

Automatically Submitting a Web Page to WebTechs   You don't have to visit WebTech's Web site in order to submit a Web page for validation. You can add a button to the bottom of a Web page that automatically submits that Web page for validation. This is particularly handy if you're working on a Web site and frequently submitting it for validation. Add the form (see Listing 31.1) to the end of your Web page. Then, anytime you want to validate the page, click Submit for Validation. Note that you must change the URL pointed to by the URLs input element so it points to the Web page that contains it. You might also change the value of the `level` field to that of your browser.

Listing 31.1   Form to Automatically Submit an URL to WebTechs

```
<FORM METHOD=POST ACTION="http://www.webtechs.com/cgi-bin/html-check.pl">
<INPUT TYPE=HIDDEN NAME="recommended" VALUE=0>
<INPUT TYPE=HIDDEN NAME="level" VALUE="IE3.0">
<INPUT TYPE=HIDDEN NAME="input" VALUE=1>
<INPUT TYPE=HIDDEN NAME="esis" VALUE=0>
<INPUT TYPE=HIDDEN NAME="render" VALUE=0>
<INPUT TYPE=HIDDEN NAME="URLs"
VALUE="http://rampages.onramp.net/~jerry/index.htm">
<INPUT TYPE=SUBMIT VALUE="Validate this URL">
</FORM>
```

Here's what each input value contains:

recommended	0=standard, 1=strict
level	See Table 31.2
input	1=show input, 0=don't show input
esis	1=show parser input, 0=don't show parser output
render	1=render HTML, 0=don't render HTML
URLs	URL to submit for verification

Table 31.2   Values for the Level Input Element

Value	Description
2	Level 2
3	Level 3
Wilbur	Level 3.2 Wilbur
Cougar	Level 3.2 Cougar
Mozilla	Mozilla (Netscape)
SQ	SoftQuad

Value	Description
AdvaSoft	AdvaSoft
IE	Microsoft IE
IE3.0	Microsoft IE 3.0 Beta

Other Verification Services

You'll find a handful of other useful verification services on the Web. None of the services described in this section are as comprehensive as the services you learned about earlier. Regardless, each provides some sort of unique or useful verification service.

For example, you can use URL-Minder to catch changes to URLs that your Web page references. Also, the Slovenian HTML check is a decent alternative to the other validation services if you're having trouble connecting to them.

Slovenian HTML check   HTML check is a verification service created at the University of Texas at Austin. The online version is offered on the Web at **http://www.ijs.si/cgi-bin/htmlchek** (see Figure 31.10). HTML check does just about the same thing as Weblint, but its output is considerably harder to read and understand.

FIG. 31.10
HTML check hasn't been updated in a while as it doesn't provide support for HTML 3.2 or other browser extensions.

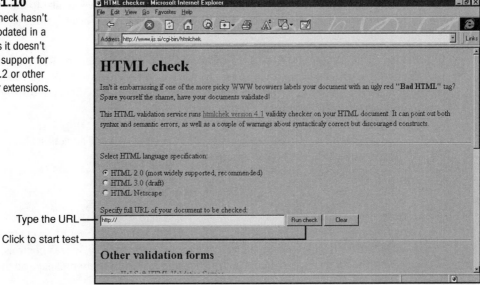

Type the URL

Click to start test

U.S.M.A. (West Point)   Figure 31.11 shows the U.S. Military Academy's verification service, called HTMLverify (**http://cgi.usma.edu/cgi-bin/HTMLverify**). You can specify an URL that you want HTMLverify to test, or you can type some HTML in HTML Source. Click Verify to start the test.

FIG. 31.11
HTMLverify is a modified
version of Weblint.

Type URL to verify

Click to start test

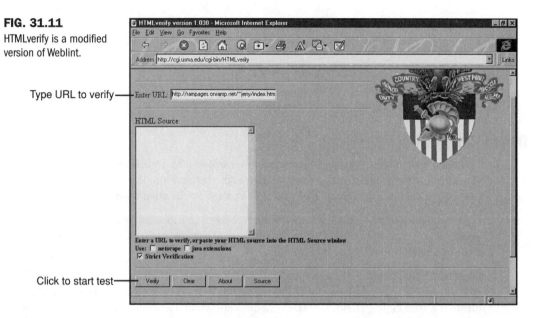

Harbinger Harbinger is a Web site that contains the WebTechs' verification service. You'll find it at **http://www.harbinger.net/html-val-svc**. The interface is very similar to the WebTechs interface you learned about earlier. If you can't access WebTechs, try this site instead.

URL-Minder URL-Minder is a Web-based service that notifies you when the Web page at an URL changes. You give it your e-mail address and a list of URLs. It then notifies you when the contents of one of the URLs you specified has changed. You'll find URL-Minder at **http:// www.netmind.com/URL-minder/example.html**.

N O T E You can embed a form in your Web page that users can use to get e-mail notification when your Web site changes. See the URL-Minder Web site for an example. ■

Managing Your Source Files

If you're working with a fairly complex Web site, you might start pulling your hair out trying to manage all those HTML files—not to mention graphics, sounds, videos, ActiveX controls, Plug-Ins, and so on. The tools you learn about in this section will help you better manage all those files.

■ **Visual SourceSafe**—Visual SourceSafe is Microsoft's version control system. Originally designed to manage programming source files (C++, and so on), Visual SourceSafe is a natural tool to use for managing your Web site's source files.

- **SpiderSoft's WebGal**—WebGallery is a tool that manages small bits of HTML, scripts, and so on. You don't use it to manage your entire Web site, but you use it to manage reusable bits of HTML code.

- **Microsoft FrontPage**—FrontPage is Microsoft's graphical HTML editor. You can use FrontPage Explorer to graphically manage all of the files in your Web site.

- **NetObject's Fusion**—Fusion is similar to Microsoft FrontPage in that you can use it to graphically manage the files in your Web site.

- **Other Techniques**—This section shows you additional techniques you can use to manage your source files, such as organizing them into a logical directory structure.

Visual SourceSafe

Microsoft Visual SourceSafe (see Figure 31.12) is a product that developers traditionally use for version control. It allows a developer to maintain each version of a file as the developer makes changes to it. For example, a developer might create a source file and check it into the SourceSafe. Then, when the developer is ready to make changes to the file, he or she checks it out of SourceSafe, makes any required changes, and checks it back into SourceSafe. SourceSafe keeps both versions of the file so that the developer can back-track if necessary. Not only that, SourceSafe makes it easy to report on the history of a file, merge changes from multiple developers, and so on.

Part
VI

Ch
31

FIG. 31.12
Visual SourceSafe
organizes your projects
like file folders.

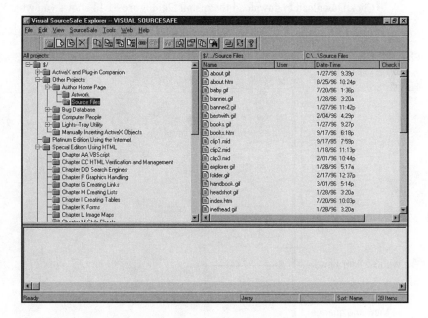

Visual SourceSafe has features that a Web developer will find useful, too. Since you work with many source files on a daily basis, SourceSafe is an ideal solution to help you keep track of the changes you make. You can organize all of your HTML and graphics files into projects that represent a Web site. Then, the Visual SourceSafe Administrator can designate your project as a Web site project. Once that's done, you can use three special features that SourceSafe provides to help you manage your site:

- **Check hyperlinks**—Double-checks the links stored in your HTML files.
- **Create a site map**—Creates a map of the HTML files stored in your project.
- **Deploy**—Deploys the files stored in the project to your Web server.

For more information about how you can use Visual SourceSafe to manage your Web site, take a look at Microsoft's Visual SourceSafe Web site. It's at **http://www.microsoft.com/ssafe**.

Spidersoft WebGal

As your Web site becomes more complex and more people work on your Web site, reusable code will become much more valuable. You'll want to reuse and share style sheets, for example. You'll also want to reuse small bits of HTML that generate forms, frames, and tables. What about scripts? Scripts are a perfect thing to reuse in your Web site.

You can't find a better tool to manage reusable HTML than Spidersoft's WebGal. First, WebGal is a well-built, world-class program. Its quality rivals many products that Microsoft builds. You can get your own copy of WebGal at Spidersoft's Web site (**http://www.spidersoft.com**). Click Download to download the install file. Figure 31.13 shows you what WebGal looks like with the sample gallery file loaded.

FIG. 31.13
WebGal has an Explorer-like interface.

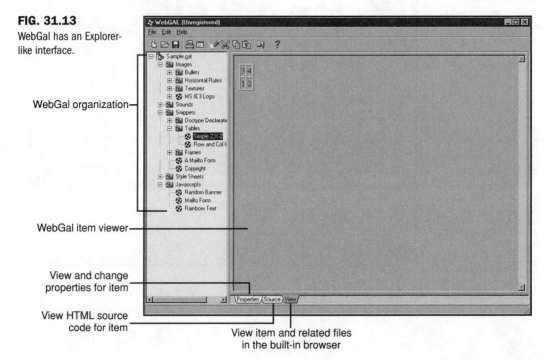

WebGal organization

WebGal item viewer

View and change
properties for item

View HTML source
code for item

View item and related files
in the built-in browser

WebGal has features that are especially designed for managing reusable bits of HTML and other objects. For example:

- **Store and organize any text resource**—You can use WebGal to store and organize bits of HTML such as forms, scripts, and style sheets.

- **Copy and paste text resources into your favorite HTML editor**—You can easily copy any item in the gallery to your favorite HTML editor.

- **Viewer Web related files**—WebGal includes viewers that let you view a variety of files, including GIF, JPEG, PNG, WAV, MID, HTML, OCX, CLASS, JAVA, and so on.

- **Preview resources by using the built-in browser**—WebGal includes a built-in browser (Internet Explorer) you can use to preview reusable resources, including controls, HTML, sounds, Java applets, pictures, and so on. When you've found just the right resource, you paste it into your HTML document.

- **Store file dependencies along with HTML fragments**—Frequently, a reusable bit of HTML will refer to images, sounds, controls, and so on. You store the HTML along with all of the files it uses as a single object.

Part
VI

Ch
31

Using Microsoft FrontPage

Microsoft FrontPage is one of the hottest HTML editors on the market. If the only thing that FrontPage provided was a WYSIWYG HTML editor, that would be enough. But FrontPage also provides a graphical tool you can use to manage the organization of all the files on your Web site. Take a look at Figure 31.14. Chapter 35, "WYSIWYG HTML Editors" shows you how to install and use FrontPage.

FIG. 31.14
You must let FrontPage manage the directory structure itself. You view the organization of your files through FrontPage Explorer.

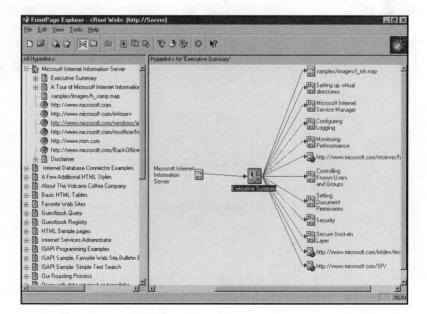

With FrontPage, you don't have to worry about how the files are organized within your Web site. FrontPage Explorer manages the organization of your files behind the scenes. That is, instead of dealing with directories and files, you work with documents in FrontPage Explorer. So what else does FrontPage Explorer do for you? Plenty, as noted here:

- **Use wizards to quickly create an entire Web site**—FrontPage Explorer comes with several wizards you can use to create a complete Web site in minutes. All you have to do is answer a few simple questions.

- **View the relationships between Web pages**—FrontPage Explorer displays the relationship between each Web page graphically. You can easily see how all the Web pages are linked together.

- **Maintain your links**—FrontPage Explorer automatically notifies you when a link goes bad. Not only that, if you rename a file, FrontPage Explorer automatically fixes each reference to that file.

▶ **See** Chapter 35, "WYSIWYG HTML Editors," to learn more about using Microsoft FrontPage to manage your Web site, **p. 801**

Using NetObjects Fusion

NetObjects Fusion is a product with very similar features to Microsoft FrontPage. It's a complete Web site manager and HTML editor rolled into a single product. Whereas FrontPage Explorer displays a Web site as a group of pages with lines connecting them (a directed graph), Fusion displays a Web site as a strict hierarchy that you can view as a structure chart (see Figure 31.15) or an outline.

FIG. 31.15
Double-click one of the boxes representing a Web page to open it in Fusion's HTML editor.

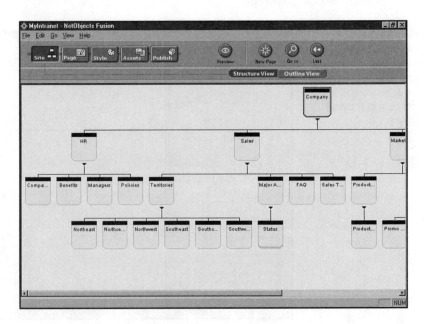

You can download an evaluation copy of NetObjects Fusion from its Web site at **http://www. netobjects.com**. Click Software Download and follow the instructions you see on the Web page.

TIP Since FrontPage's site management features are a bit stronger than Fusion's, and Fusion's site wizards are stronger than FrontPage's, many folks start their Web site using Fusion and then manage it using FrontPage.

▶ **See** Chapter 35, "WYSIWYG HTML Editors," to learn more about using NetObjects Fusion to manage your Web site, **p. 801**

Working Directly with Files

Microsoft FrontPage and NetObjects Fusion are tools that automatically manage your HTML files for you. You're not actually aware of how those files are stored on the disk. If you're still hand editing and organizing HTML files, however, you need to come up with a scheme that helps you keep everything straight.

The following sections describe the things you should consider when organizing your Web site in this manner.

Using the Structure of the File System   Use the hierarchical structure of the file system. If you think about your Web site for a moment, you'll realize that it probably has a very hierarchical structure, like an outline. Create a directory structure on your disk that reflects this organization.

For example, if your Web site is organized similar to Figure 31.16, you might create a directory structure that looks like Figure 31.17. Note how the home page is in the root directory, while each Web page to which the home page is linked has a directory directly underneath the home page. All of the files required by a Web page (graphics, sounds, controls, and so on) are stored in the directory with the home page so you can keep an accurate inventory of the files on which the Web page is dependent.

FIG. 31.16
Keep your Web pages simple and organized hierarchically so that users can more easily navigate your Web site.

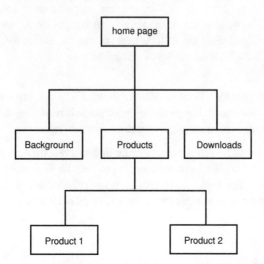

FIG. 31.17

If you link to a Web page from multiple places, don't duplicate the directory for that Web page; just refer to the first occurrence of it.

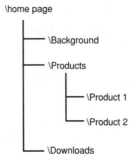

\home page

— \Background

— \Products

    — \Product 1

    — \Product 2

— \Downloads

Mirroring Your Web Site Locally

If you're not using one of the Web site management programs, such as Microsoft FrontPage or Visual SourceSafe, you'll want to keep a copy of your Web site on your local hard drive—regardless of your Web site's directory structure. In fact, you should edit those files locally, and then upload them to the Web site when they're ready. Doing so, you always know that the files on your local disk are the one-and-only master copy of your Web site.

When working with the files on your local disk, you can use one of the Windows built-in file utilities to organize them:

Explorer   Windows 95 and Windows NT provide Explorer, which is very similar to File Manager but works more closely with the files on your disk.

File Manager   All versions of Windows, including Windows 95, provide File Manager. In Windows 95, choose <u>R</u>un from the Start menu, type **FILEMAN.EXE**, and press Enter.

> **CAUTION**
>
> In order to mirror your Web site locally, you must use directory and file names that are valid on both your workstation and the Web server. Note that you can use WS_FTP to automatically convert file extensions from one form to another when you upload your HTML files. For example, WS_FTP will automatically convert files with the HTM extension to the HTML extension when you upload them.

Creating Relative References   Relative references are URLs that are relative to the URL of the containing HTML document. For example, **next/page.htm** is a relative reference, whereas **http://www.myserver.com/next/page.htm** is an absolute reference.

You should always use relative references when linking to a resource on your own Web site. The reason is simple. If you change servers, or you move your Web site to another directory, you have to change all of the absolute references. If you're using a tool such as FrontPage, these would be fixed for you automatically. Since you're managing your files manually, you have to actually change each reference within each file. Relative references assure that if you simply move the entire directory structure of your Web site from one location to another, you don't have to change each reference.

▶ **See** "Understanding Links," to learn more about absolute and relative references, **p. 106**

Launching Related Files   Make sure you have the appropriate programs associated with the files to which a Web page is dependent. By doing so, you can easily launch those files while you're exploring the Web site's files. For example, if you're exploring your Web site, you might want to take a look at a graphics file or play a sound file.

Windows 95 users have it made. You can view most graphics formats using QuickView, which is provided with Windows 95. You can also launch most video and sound files using the Media Player.

If you don't have a program associated with a particular type of file, such as JPG, you can probably view that type of file in your Web browser.

## CHAPTER 32

Search Engines and Advertising

by Jerry Honeycutt and Robert Meegan

Current estimates show that the Web has more than 20 million pages. Even using the fastest connection and taking just seconds to glance at each page would take a reader the better part of a decade to see them all, by which time perhaps 10 times as many new pages would have appeared. Because of the Web's scale, it is very unlikely that many people will find your page by pure chance. In fact, if your page has no links leading to it from other pages, it is very likely that no one will ever find it.

Because the reason to create a Web page in the first place is to publish information, you want to encourage other people to visit your page. The best way to bring people to your page is to make the job of finding it as easy as possible. That's what this chapter is all about—you learn how to list your site with the best search tools on the Internet. You also learn other methods you can use to get your site noticed. ■

How are all those Web users going to find my site?

By using search engines, of course; this chapter shows you how to list with the best around.

Get yourself at the top of the list

There's no sure-fire way to get yourself at the top every time; but check out these tips for doing so.

Target the search tools in this chapter

Target the tools in this chapter, and you'll reach most of the users on the Web.

Learn other methods for getting noticed

Aside from learning how to list with the popular search tools, you also learn other ways to get noticed.

Understanding What Kind of Advertising You Need

The type of advertising that you do depends greatly on the nature of your page. If you are doing a page as a hobby, paying a thousand dollars to get a week's worth of exposure on one of the popular sites probably isn't worth the cost to you. On the other hand, if your site is the home page of a major multinational corporation, the attention that a professionally designed advertisement can bring more than justifies the expense.

N O T E Although I use the term *advertising* extensively in this chapter, most of the methods listed here are free. A better term might be *Web page promotion*. ■

With this point in mind, you should take the first step toward advertising on the Web, which is to answer the following questions about your site:

- How much traffic do I want at my site?
- Does my site have a broad appeal, or is it for a more specialized audience?
- How much of a budget do I have to advertise my site?
- How much time can I devote to advertising my site?
- How important is it to the success of my business (or hobby or organization) that my site become well known?

If your page is just a hobby, where you simply share information with others who share your interests, you can mount a low-key advertising campaign. Most of the people who find your page will do so through links with other pages that cover the same topics. Think hard about the sites that you like to visit, and you'll probably find that most of your visitors like the same sites.

N O T E Even if you are starting a page just as a hobby, it doesn't need to end there. Many of the most successful aspects of the Web began as part-time activities. ■

Nonprofit organizations can achieve tremendous exposure on the Web, far out of proportion to the amount of money invested. These organizations often have enough manpower to find a large number of free locations to advertise the site.

For a small business, the Web can be an excellent place to advertise. On the Web, unlike most other forms of advertising, even a small company can produce a presence that is equally impressive as is that of a huge conglomerate. Unlike the print world, the Web allows anyone access to full-color images and advertising, regardless of budget. In the democratic world of the Web, all addresses are equally impressive, giving your company real estate that is just as valuable as that of your larger competitors.

If your company is a mail-order or service business that can support customers around the country, or even the world, investing a greater proportion of money and energy in Web advertising may well be worthwhile. If you work at one of these companies, you may want to consider using a commercial marketing service.

Listing with WWW Search Engines

Most people find what they're looking for on the Web by using one of the many available search tools. These systems are huge databases containing as many as 20 million Web pages, coupled with powerful indexing software that allows for quick searches. Many of the search engines are run on mainframe computers or large parallel processors that can handle hundreds of searches simultaneously. Other search engines run on arrays of Windows NT servers.

In the beginning of the Web, the first search servers were run by universities, but now most of these early efforts have been taken over by private companies. What benefit do these companies find in providing free searches on these expensive computers? Advertising! The index sites are some of the most frequently visited on the Web, and the maintainers of these sites can charge high rates to the companies that advertise on these pages. That doesn't mean that they charge you to list your site. Many of these companies have become so successful that they're now publicly traded on the stock exchange.

N O T E In WebTrack's study of Web advertising, they discovered that five of the top 10 sites in terms of revenues from advertising were search tools. ■

In addition to the older sites, more than a hundred newer indexes are available. Some of them are restricted to a specific topic, and others are still very small, but all offer the opportunity to get your site noticed.

As you explore the Web, you soon discover that it possesses its own collection of fauna. The wildlife of the Web consists of autonomous programs that work their way across the millions of links that connect the sites, gathering information along the way.

These programs are known by such colorful names as robots, crawlers, walkers, spiders (a generic term), worms, and (in the case of one Australian program) wombats. What do these spiders do? Almost without exception, they arrive at a page, index it, and search it for any links to other pages. These new links are recorded and followed in turn. When all the links on a particular chain have been followed, the next path is restored from the database, and the process continues. Examples of these engines are Lycos and WebCrawler, which you learn more about later in this chapter. A large number of special-purpose spiders are also used to generate statistics regarding the Web. These programs, however, do not generate databases that can be used for text searching.

N O T E Most spiders index the title and content of each Web page they visit. In some cases—AltaVista and infoseek—they also index the <META> tag if it's included on the page (you learn about the <META> tag later in this chapter). ■

The alternative to these spiders are the *structured systems*. Whereas spiders don't organize links hierarchically, structured systems store Web pages indexed against a series of categories and subcategories. You browse or search through the categories looking for entries. The hierarchical nature of these systems appeals to many people who are more comfortable using an

Part
VI

Ch

32

index where they can see all the categories. For example, Yahoo! is a very popular index that almost looks more like an online service than a search tool.

The type of system on which you perform your searches is entirely up to your personal preferences. From the standpoint of advertising your site, you need to be aware of the differences. Some of the structured systems restrict you to a limited number of index entries. This limitation can mean that people who are looking for just the things that you offer may not find you because they are looking in the wrong place.

The Major Search Engines

A complete listing of indexes would be out of date as soon as it was finished. New sites are added monthly, and even sites that are maintained by large corporations have disappeared. I have listed a few of the main sites in this section, but you should take the time to do some of your own searching when you decide to publish your pages.

In the big league, a handful of sites can claim to have indexed a sizable portion of the Web. These sites are the most popular systems, used by the majority of Web surfers. You need to register with these servers first to maximize your exposure. Table 32.1 lists the major search engines on which I recommend you list your Web site. The sections that follow describe each search tool in more detail.

Table 32.1   Major Search Engines

Name	URL
AltaVista	http://www.altavista.digital.com
Excite	http://www.excite.com
infoseek	http://www.infoseek.com
Lycos	http://www.lycos.com
WebCrawler	http://www.webcrawler.com
Yahoo!	http://www.yahoo.com

All of the sites in Table 32.1 are free to the user. They're sponsored by advertisers. Your listings are also free.

CAUTION

Some of the earliest robots were poorly written and could swamp a server with hundreds of requests within seconds of each other. Fortunately, most recent robots are courteous enough not to overload their hosts. If your server does crash, check the logs for a single site that retrieved many documents within a short period of time. If such a site exists, try to contact the postmaster at the site that made the requests and let him or her know about the problems that you saw.

N O T E In the September 1996 issue of *PC World* magazine, each of the search tools was given a grade: A+ to F, with A+ being the best. For your own amusement, here is how *PC World* graded the engines I've discussed in this chapter:

Search Engine	Grade
Excite	A+
Lycos	A
infoseek	A-
Yahoo!	A+
AltaVista	C-
WebCrawler	F ■

AltaVista AltaVista (see Figure 32.1) is a search engine that's owned and operated by Digital. It started indexing the Web in the summer of 1995 and went public with 16 million indexed pages in December of 1995. Now, AltaVista gets about 30 million hits per day.

FIG. 32.1
Click Add URL to add your site to AltaVista.

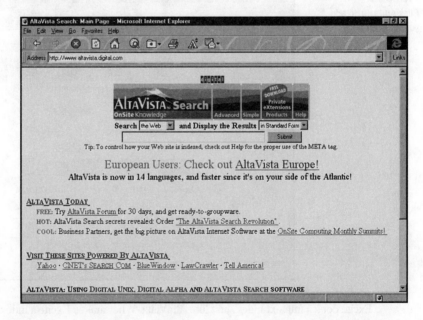

AltaVista scours the Web looking for sites to index. When it finds a site, it indexes the site three levels deep. That is, it indexes the home page, any pages to which the home page is linked, and any pages to which the second level pages are linked. When AltaVista indexes a page, it indexes the full text of the page. It stores the results in its database, on which a user's search is performed.

N O T E   If your Web site changes, you don't need to relist it with AltaVista or most of the other
search engines. AltaVista will visit your site periodically, reindexing the contents of the site
that have changed. AltaVista is unique in that it notes how often your site changes, and will adjust the
frequency of its visits to your site based upon the frequency of your changes. ■

To list your site with AltaVista, open AltaVista (**http://www.altavista.digital.com**) in your
Web browser and click the Add URL link at the bottom of the page. Follow the instructions you
see on the next page. To remove your site from AltaVista, follow the instructions you find at
this Web site.

Excite   Excite (see Figure 32.2) was started in 1993. It currently indexes over 50 million Web
pages, making it one of the largest databases on the Web. What makes Excite unique among
the search engines is that it also contains over 60,000 reviews of individual Web sites. Thus,
you can get a third-party perspective on the type and quality of information at a particular Web
site before you visit the site.

FIG. 32.2

Click Add URL to add
your site to Excite.

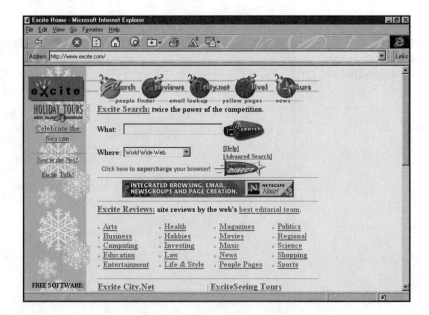

Excite does a full text index, just like AltaVista. What makes Excite's indexing unique, however, is that it also does a concept-based index. That is, if Excite finds the words Dog and Food
on your Web site, those words will match a user's search if they use the terms Pet and Food.
The user is more likely to find your site on Excite, because you don't have to be nearly as careful about picking just the right words.

Like AltaVista, Excite will index your site three levels deep: the home page, its links, and the
next level of links. Excite will reindex your site about every two weeks.

To list your site with Excite, open Excite in your Web browser (**http://www.excite.com**), and click Add URL link at the bottom of the page. Follow the instructions on the subsequent Web page. To remove your site from Excite, follow the instructions you find at this Web site.

N O T E If a spider wants to visit your site, there's really nothing you can do to prevent it. Your site is on the Internet and the pages are available for the spider to access. On the other hand, if you want to keep spiders off your Web site so that they don't affect its performance, most spiders will honor your request if you add a file called ROBOTS.TXT to the root directory of your Web server.

Creating this file is easy. Create a new text file in your root directory called ROBOTS.TXT. Add a line that begins with the field name **User-agent:**. This field must then contain the name of the robot that you want to restrain. You can have multiple User-agent fields, or if you want to exclude all agents not specifically mentioned in a User-agent field, you can use a field value of *. The line following each User-agent field should begin with the field name **Disallow:**. This field should contain a URL path. Any URL that begins with the path specified in the Disallow field will be ignored by the robot named in the User-agent field.

Here are some examples you can use:

```
# Any text that begins with a pound-sign is treated as a comment
User-agent: Webcrawler # Applies to the robot named Webcrawler
Disallow: /webpages/data/ # Webcrawler will skip URLs in this path

# This example is the universal "do not disturb" sign
User-agent: * # All robots
Disallow: / # Every URL begins with a / in the path
```

infoseek   infoseek started as a very meager search tool. It's all grown up now, however (see Figure 32.3). That is, it's a real contender for the best search tool on the Internet. It started in January of 1994 and has grown to the point that it indexes over 50 million Web pages.

Like the other tools, infoseek does a full text index. It only indexes your site two levels deep, however. In addition, infoseek will only visit your site every three weeks, instead of every two weeks.

To list your site with infoseek, open infoseek (**http://www.infoseek.com**) in your Web browser. Then, click the Add Site link at the bottom of the page. Follow the instructions you see on the next page. To remove your site from infoseek, follow the instructions you find at this Web site.

T I P   When submitting your Web site to a spider, only submit the top-level page (home page). The spider will traverse your site to find other pages linked to the home page.

Lycos   Lycos (see Figure 32.4) is one of the granddaddies of the Internet. Its been around for a while, and has gone through some huge changes. Its user interface is greatly improved. Its index is larger. And its hierarchical database is better organized.

Part
VI

Ch

FIG. 32.3
Click Add Site to add
your site to infoseek.

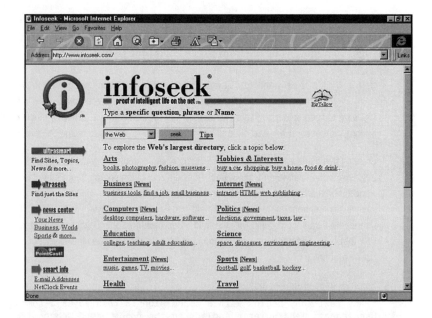

FIG. 32.4
Click Add Your Site to
Lycos to add your site to
Lycos.

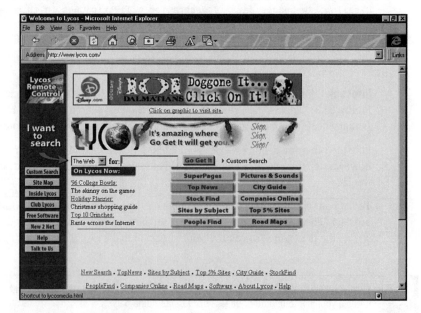

Lycos doesn't do a full text index like the other search tools. Instead, it creates an abstract from your home page that describes the contents of your site. Lycos will index your site three levels deep, and it'll revisit your site about every two weeks.

To list your site with Lycos, open Lycos (**http://www.lycos.com**), and click Add Your Site to Lycos at the bottom of the page. Follow the instructions you see on the subsequent Web page.

N O T E   When you submit your Web site to one of the search engines, don't expect immediate
results. While the spider may index your site immediately, it can take from two to four weeks
before your site actually shows up in the search database. ■

WebCrawler   WebCrawler (see Figure 32.5) started as an educational project in 1994. In 1995,
America Online purchased it. Today, WebCrawler gets about three million hits per day.

FIG. 32.5
Click Add URL to add
your site to WebCrawler.

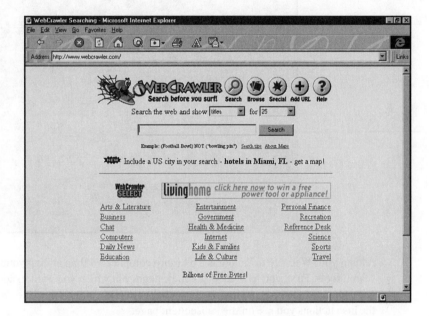

Part

VI

Ch

32

WebCrawler does a full-text index. It only indexes your site one level deep, however, so the
only information it's going to get is off your home page. In addition, WebCrawler will only visit
about once a month. Because of these factors, WebCrawler has taken a beating in the press.
PC Magazine recently gave WebCrawler a failing grade. You should not ignore WebCrawler,
however, because it has a very large following given that it's owned by America Online.

To list your site with WebCrawler, open WebCrawler (**http://www.webcrawler.com**) in your
browser, and click Add URL at the top of the page. Follow the instructions you see on the next
page.

Yahoo!   Yahoo! (started in 1994 as a hobby of its creators) is my favorite search tool. It's not a
worm like the other tools. It categorizes Web sites that users submit into a hierarchical index.
You find what you're looking for by either searching the hierarchy or traversing down each
category until you find a Web site in which you're interested.

Yahoo! (see Figure 32.6) is one of the best-organized hierarchical indexes on the Internet.
Beyond indexing Web sites, however, Yahoo! provides dozens of other services. For example,
Yahoo! categorizes Web sites by their regional areas, such as my hometown of Frisco, Texas.
It also provides telephone books (white and yellow pages) in which you can look up a phone

number and maps so that you can find a restaurant near you or get directions to your favorite computer store.

FIG. 32.6
You'll find Yahoo! on the Internet at **http://www.yahoo.com**.

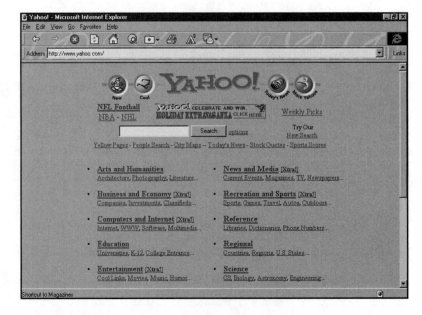

Adding your Web site to Yahoo! is a bit more complicated than adding your site to the other search tools. First, you have to locate the category in which you want to add your site. When you've located the appropriate category, click Add URL, at the top of the Web page, and follow the instructions you see on the subsequent page.

Using Submission Services

You do not always have to do all the work yourself. Several good services submit your pages to the major search systems for you. Many of these services have a charge for this function, but a few services are available free.

Submit It! is a nice forms-based system that allows you to enter all the relevant data for your page, after which it registers you with your choices of more than a dozen popular search tools (see Figure 32.7). This service is provided for free and can help you to hit most of the major search sites. You can find it at **http://www.submit-it.com**.

There are a number of other submission services available on the Web. Table 32.2 shows you a few to get you started.

FIG. 32.7
Submit It! is a powerful tool for registering with multiple search engines quickly.

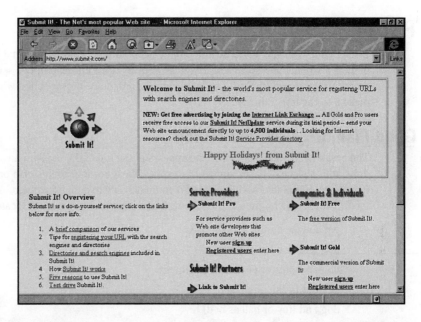

Table 32.2	Submission Services	
Name	**Free?**	**URL**
AAA Internet Promotions	No	**http://www.websitepromote.com**
Ace Basic	No	**http://sffa/acebase.html**
Papparazi	Yes	**http://www.papparazi.com**

Just as with the search tools, any list of services on the Web is obsolete almost as fast as it is generated. Your best bet is to do a little checking on your own to see what else is out there. A good place to start looking is at the Web Announcements topic on Yahoo!.

The big advantage of a submission service is that it cuts down on the amount of work that you have to do. The disadvantage is that your submissions are made automatically, using the same categories and keywords for each database. This is probably sufficient if your page is personal or intended for a specific audience.

If your page is the Web presence for your company or your organization, spending the time to learn about each of the databases yourself is probably better, so that you can ensure that your listing ends up under the right headings. After all, the time required to submit your page is nothing compared to the hard work that you've put into making it as good as it is.

Part
VI

Ch
32

Putting Your Site at the Top of the List

Listing your Web site with a search engine is one thing. Making sure that it appears at the top of the list when a user does a search is an entirely different matter. I've seen a lot of folks try their hardest to pick the right set of keywords, only to be disappointed when their site doesn't make it to the top of the list.

Good Planning Gets You on Top

The best way to make sure your site appears at the top of the list is to do a bit of planning. Sit down with a piece of paper and a few of your colleagues and brainstorm on all the types of queries you think users will use to find your site. Try to anticipate them. Are you selling pet food? If so, people might use the following combination of queries to locate your site:

> pet and grooming and supplies
>
> dog and (food or supplies)
>
> dog and (flea or pest) and treatment
>
> pet and (leash or collar)
>
> dog and (toy or ball or bed)

The list can go on and on. Don't stop until you're absolutely out of ideas and have covered every possible query you can think of. Then, make your Web site responsive to those queries:

1. Make a list of all the words in the queries you created.

2. Beside each word, write down the number of times that word appeared in your list.

3. Sort the list, putting the words with the most number of occurrences at the top of the list.

4. Going down the list from top to bottom, make sure that each word appears in the homepage of your site at least one time. As well, you can use the <META> tag to list those keywords for the search engines that catalog the <META> tag.

Other Tips for Getting on Top

Here are some additional ideas to make sure people find your site:

- *Use good keywords in your Web page.* Make sure that you use words that your perspective audience would choose to use, not words your technical staff would use. For example, your engineers may call it a super-duper widget, but your customers will probably call it a thingy.

- *Use the <META> tag to imbed keywords into your home page.* This doesn't work with all of the search engines, however, as only AltaVista and infoseek use the <META> tag. The next section describes how to use the <META> tag.

- *Don't rely solely on graphics in your HTML file.* In particular, a home page that contains nothing more than an imagemap is disastrous when it comes to listing with the search engines because you're given the searching engine nothing to index.

- *Keep your scripts—VBScript or JavaScript—away from the top portion of your Web page.* The search engines that create abstracts will display your scripts instead of a good abstract of your Web site.

- *Keep each Web page on your site focused on a particular topic.* That is, don't include information about pets on the same Web page that contains information about Windows NT Server. This will severely confuse concept-based search engines such as Excite. If each Web page is narrowly focused on particular topic, you have a better chance of that page bubbling to the top of the list.

> **CAUTION**
>
> Some folks will tell you that the way to get your site to the top of the list is to fill it with the appropriate keywords repeated over and over again. For example, if you want users to find your site when they search for the keywords **Windows 95**, then you might fill an HTML comment tag with those keywords over and over again. Don't do this. Many of the search engines are now catching on to this little trick and will knock your listing out of the index.

Categorize Your Site with the *<META>* Tag

You can use the HTML <META> tag to tell the search engine a bit more about how to categorize your site. This doesn't work with all the search engines, however, as the concept and abstract-based search engines don't necessarily use keywords to categorize a Web site.

The <META> tag is simple. It allows you to create pseudo-tags within your HTML file. Here's what it looks like:

```
<META NAME=name CONTENT=content>
```

You set the NAME attribute to the name of the tag you are creating and the CONTENT attribute to the content of that tag. This is only useful if something on the Internet, be it client, search tool, or whatever, is expecting to find a <META> tag by a certain name.

To help along some of the search engines that do look for the <META> tag, you can create two tags called KEYWORDS and DESCRIPTION. The KEYWORDS <META> tag provides a list of keywords separated by commas to the search engine. You can use this to specify keywords that aren't found within the text of your HTML file. The DESCRIPTION <META> tag contains a description of your Web site that the search engine will display to the user when the search engine displays your site in the list. Here's what both tags look like:

```
<META NAME="KEYWORDS" CONTENT="pet, dog, cat, food, toys, grooming">
<META NAME="DESCRIPTION" CONTENT="My online pet store provides all of your pet
supplies."
```

TIP If your home page uses an imagemap with little text, at least use a <META> tag for those search engines that parse the <META> tag.

Getting Noticed by Using Other Ways

On the Web, there are many other ways to get noticed. You're not limited to the search tools. The sections that follow describe a variety of them. Some require a bit of work or expense on your part, others are free.

Best of the Web Listings

One of the more amazing things to come out of the Web has been the tremendous proliferation of "Best of the Web" sites. These systems generate listings under a variety of names, such as What's Cool, What's Hot, Top 5%, Best of the Web, Hot Picks, and so on (see Figure 32.8). In practice, of course, the selection of pages for these lists is completely arbitrary. For example, with the rapid growth of the Web, it is unlikely that anyone has ever even visited 5 percent of the sites currently available, let alone enough to make a reasonable judgment of which are the very best.

FIG. 32.8

Several organizations present "Best of the Web" awards.

So how are these lists maintained? In most cases, you can submit your site's URL to the administrator of the list, and he or she visits your site and reviews it. If your site meets whatever selection criteria the list is based on, you get added to the list.

Some of these lists provide you with a small graphic that you can display on your page to indicate that you have been awarded the honor, and virtually all the lists include links to your page after you have been accepted.

What is the real value of these lists? In the cosmic scheme of things, very little. But some of these lists are well known, and many people use them as launching points for random surfing.

If you have a general interest site, getting it listed on a couple of these pages can really boost your traffic.

Some examples of these sites are:

- *Cool Site of the Day.* A strange and quirky site located at **http://cool.infi.net**.

- *Macmillan Winner's Circle.* A site that recognizes excellence in personal home pages at **http://www.mcp.com/general/workshop/winner**.

- *What's Cool.* If you can manage to get yourself onto Netscape's What's Cool Page, you'll have to beat back the visitors with a stick. You can find this index of pages at **http://home.netscape.com/home/whats-cool.html**.

Links from Other Web Sites

Even more than the Web crawlers and structured systems, the primary method for traversing the Web is by using links found on other pages (see Figure 32.9). To expose your page to the maximum number of potential visitors, you should make an effort to get as many sites as possible to include links to your site.

FIG. 32.9
Many sites have long lists of links to other related sites.

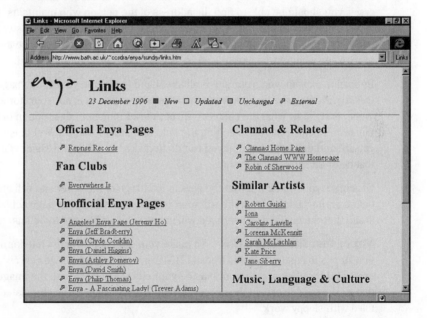

Most sites that cover a specific topic are more than pleased to include links to other sites that cover the same topic. By including as many links as possible, they make themselves more useful and, hence, more popular. To encourage people to link to your page, you need to identify sites that might be interested in linking to yours and then contact the site administrator.

Finding Sites from Which to Link The best way to find sites with information about linking to your site is to surf the Web. Find sites that are of interest to you, and you'll probably find the

Part **VI**

Ch **32**

sites that are of interest to people who would visit your site. Where should you start surfing? The same places that your visitors would.

Start with the indexes and see what's out there. Try several of the more popular ones, and be sure to try both structured systems and Web crawlers. If one of the indexes is particularly useful, you know that it is a good place to register your site. The indexes that aren't useful can wait before you submit to them.

After you find some sites, visit them and see what they have to offer. You're looking for sites that have a theme that is similar to yours, without being identical. For example, if your page contains links to everything that a person might ever want to know about hog farming, pages that might make good links to your page include general farming pages, pages that cover animal husbandry, and pages for companies that do business with hog farmers, including both suppliers and consumers. Other pages that also cover aspects of hog farming but are not duplicates of yours would also be worth linking to.

Convincing Sites to Link to Your Site   The best way to get a link to your Web page is to simply contact the owner of the page that you'd like to be linked from and ask him or her to create the link. You can most easily accomplish this task by sending e-mail to the page author. In most cases, you should be able to find the address of the person who maintains the link on one of the pages at the site. Failing this, try sending e-mail to the address Webmaster at the site that interests you. Finally, if all else fails, you can examine the HTML source for the site's main page to see whether the author's address is included in a comment field.

Be sure to explain what your site is all about and to include your home page's URL in your message. If the page that you want the other site to link to is not your home page, let the Webmaster know what the correct URL is. A brief (one-line) description of your page can save him or her some time when adding the link. Remember that the Webmaster is just as busy as you are and that anything that you can do to make his or her life easier will increase the chance that he or she links to your page.

Of course, you can expect that the person in charge of the other site will check out your page before adding a link. He or she will want to make sure that your page actually is what you say it is and that the quality is such that it will improve his or her site to be linked to yours.

Making Your Site Worth a Link   To make your site more worthwhile for others to link to, the first step is to ensure that it is free of HTML errors and that it loads correctly. Have your site examined by other people from outside your site to check that all the images are available and that all the tags display in the proper format. No one wants to be associated with a site that is filled with sloppy work.

Second, include useful, current, and interesting information and images. No one wants to spend time downloading a site just to find that it contains a mess of outdated or boring gibberish. Links to shareware programs can also make your page more popular.

Finally, make it attractive. Ask yourself if the page makes you want to read it; then get the opinions of some people you can trust.

An important step toward making your site successful is to include a number of links to other sites that might be of interest to visitors to your site. The entire concept of the Web revolves around the interconnection of millions of sites. Don't make your page a dead end.

 TIP Check occasionally that all the links on your page still lead somewhere. Pages maintained by other people may disappear, often without notice. See Chapter 31, "Verification and File Management," for more information.

If your site is a personal page, include connections to pages of your friends and colleagues. A hobby site should include as many links to other sites with similar interests as you can find. Check the links to make sure that they point to pages that you want to be associated with; then include them.

> **NOTE** Although you can certainly add a link to a page without the prior consent of the owner of the page, contacting the maintainer of the page to let him or her know of the new link is courteous. He or she may also have a preference as to which page you establish the link. ■

Business and organization pages can include links to other sources of information related to your site. Including links to your competitors is not necessary, but having links that point to your suppliers and customers might be very effective. Encourage them to include reciprocal links back to your page. Remember that the most effective form of advertising is networking and that a link to your page is an implicit recommendation.

Specialized Index Pages

If your pages are focused on a specific topic, registering with any specialized index pages that cover your area of interest is well worth the time.

At present, you can find many sites for business-related topics. This fact isn't surprising, but what is amazing is the incredible variety of index pages available for other interests as well. A search of the Web turns up many specialized pages that contain dozens of links. The following are a few examples of these pages:

- *Art Planet*. A professionally run site that allows searches based on companies, keywords, or artists (see Figure 32.10). It is located at **http://www.artplanet.com/index.html**.

Part
VI

Ch
32

FIG. 32.10

You can use specialized search tools such as Art Planet to locate your page successfully.

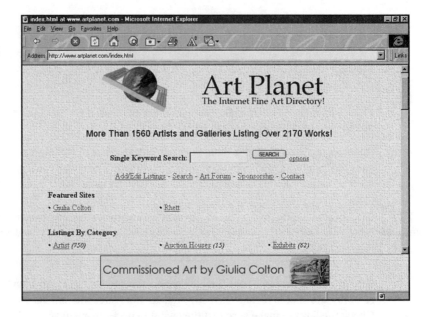

- *The Hamster Page.* This is the definitive hamster resource page, and you can find it at **http://www.tela.bc.ca/hamster**.

- *Special Needs Education Network.* A site that provides a number of links to resources for people with special needs and parents of children with special needs. You can find it at **http://schoolnet2.carleton.ca/~kwellar/snewww.html**.

- *Chess Space.* A comprehensive index to everything in the chess world. It is located at **http://www.redweb.com/chess**.

- *Points of Pediatric Interest.* More than 650 links dedicated to pediatric medicine and child care. You can find it at **http://www.med.jhu.edu/peds/neonatology/poi.html**.

- *Church Online.* A worldwide list of Christian churches. It is located at **http://www.churchonline.com/index.html**.

In the business world, pages exist for many different types of companies. You can see some of the tremendous variety in the following pages:

- *TruckNet.* A site specializing in just about everything that you might ever want to know about the trucking industry. It is located at **http://www.truck.net**.

- *Petro-Links.* This site has links to oil companies, suppliers, petroleum industry magazines, and applicable government agencies. It is located at **http://www.findlinks.com/petrolinks.html**.

- *Fashion Net.* A service with hundreds of links to companies that are involved in the fashion and clothing industries. Not all these companies have Web sites, but many do. You can find Fashion Net at **http://www.fashion.net**.

■ *Thomas Register.* A site run by the company that publishes the famous Thomas Register of Manufacturers. If you work for a manufacturing company or if you supply manufacturing companies, you really should submit your site at **http://www.thomasregister.com**.

Using Newsgroups Effectively

A Web site is very difficult to find in the vast reaches of the Internet. Fortunately, you can use public bulletin boards to broadcast information to a number of people at the same time. These public areas are known as newsgroups, and they serve as public forums for communications and debate.

Much like everything else on the Internet, these groups have their own rules and customs. Very broadly, they fall into two categories: open and moderated groups. Open groups are pretty much what they sound like, in that anyone can post a message. Unfortunately, this freedom often leads to a very low signal-to-noise ratio. Moderated groups require that all postings are passed through a moderator (or group of moderators) who screens the messages and removes off-topic messages. This process greatly improves the proportion of postings that are relevant to the subject of the newsgroup.

Regardless of the type of newsgroup, proper use can greatly increase the traffic at your Web site. By the same token, however, improper use can cause ill feelings and will not attract the visitors for which you are looking.

The Announcement Groups The first newsgroups to use when spreading the word about your new Web site are the announcement groups. These groups are dedicated to the purpose of broadcasting messages dealing with new sites and services (see Figure 32.11). Most of these groups are moderated and do an excellent job of keeping messages on topic.

Part
VI

Ch
32

FIG. 32.11
comp.infosystems.
www.announce is the
number one site for
posting new sites.

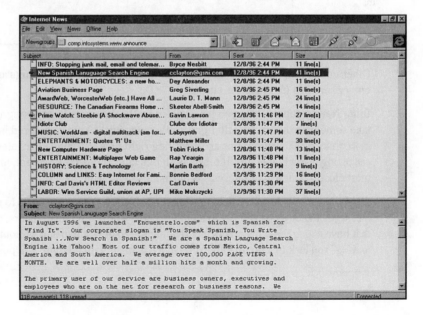

comp.infosystems.www.announce lists virtually every site that is submitted to it. The rules of this group are standard for many of the announcement groups. Postings should be relevant to the purpose of the group and should not have a commercial purpose other than the announcement of a Web site that provides further information about a commercial product or service. The message announcing the site should have the page's URL clearly listed in the message, preferably on a separate line. The message should also include a clear but brief description of the nature of the site. Finally, the subject of the message should be clear and precise. It is recommended that the subject begin with a word or two that clearly defines your site. See the example shown in Figure 32.12.

FIG. 32.12

This announcement is clear and concise, and it lets potential visitors know what they can expect.

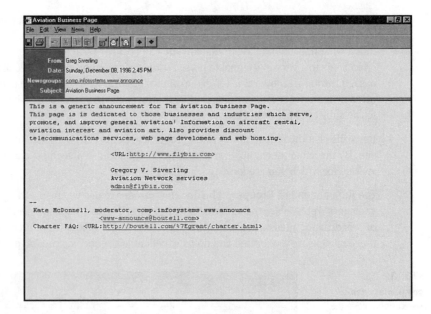

Other good groups to announce in are **comp.internet.net-happenings** and **misc. entrepreneurs** (for business sites).

Other Newsgroups   After you have posted on the announcement newsgroups, you should take some time to find any other groups that may involve topics covered in your Web site. Far more than 20,000 newsgroups are operating right now, although your Internet provider may cache only a fraction of this number. With this kind of diversity present, finding the groups that most closely match your interests is normally not difficult.

After you narrow down the field to a handful of groups, the next step is to read the various messages that are posted. Try to identify people who are regular posters, and look for threads that have a long life. This practice of reading messages on a group without posting is known as *lurking*. You lurk in a group to become more familiar with it before you post.

One of the features many groups possess is the occasional posting of what is called a FAQ. This message is a list of Frequently Asked Questions, and reading it carefully can help you avoid asking any questions that might have been answered repeatedly in the past.

The primary benefit to lurking is that when you are ready to post messages, you can do so in a manner that is perceived as highly competent and professional.

After you start posting, you should make a special effort to ensure that your posts are well written and on topic. Remember that you are not just carrying on a friendly conversation, but rather you are advertising your page. Avoid mentioning your Web site in the body of your posting, but include your signature at the end of the message. If your postings are worth reading, people will make an effort to visit your pages, too.

One form of message posting is not recommended: Sending large numbers of messages to post on many different newsgroups, regardless of the group's topic is known as *spamming* (see Figure 32.13). This kind of posting is a tremendous waste of bandwidth, and many people, particularly those who pay for their access based on time spent logged in, do not appreciate your postings.

FIG. 32.13

The message about saving on long-distance charges is off-topic for this group and is an example of spamming.

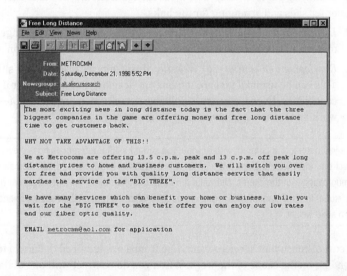

An unfortunate side effect of spamming is that it tends to attract retaliation from residents of the Internet. This retaliation can begin at the annoyance level and rapidly escalate. To avoid any unpleasantness, you should follow the rules and act in a responsible manner.

N O T E The primary offense caused by spamming is the waste of huge amounts of storage space on computers around the world. To help curb the problem, many newsgroups have programs that can excise spamming messages automatically from the group, often before most people even see the message. One side effect of spamming is that you may become blacklisted, which can expose you to remarkable levels of harassment from cybervigilantes. ■

Using a Publicity Consultant

As you may have noticed, developing an effective Web advertising campaign can be a lot of work. For someone working on a page for a hobby, all this work might not matter much, but for a busy professional who is trying to build up business through the Web, the time required may be more than he or she can afford. One solution to this problem is to use a publicity consultant. This person is an agent who handles the details necessary for getting your site noticed.

Some of the functions that a publicity consultant should perform are as follow:

- *Submitting your site to all the major search engines* and to any others that may be appropriate. This submission should be followed up to make certain that the database actually added your site and that it can be located under the correct headings.

- *Locating appropriate newsgroups.* Some agents also identify threads that are relevant to your site and then post messages that subtly promote your site. This task is rather delicate, so you should ask to see examples of the agent's work before hiring him or her for this job.

- *Identifying pages for reciprocal links.* An agent should also take care of contacting the other sites and arranging for the links.

- *Locating and purchasing advertising space* on commercial Web pages. An agent with many contacts and clients may be able to arrange lower rates than you could by yourself.

- *Developing and editing your Web site.* Most agencies also do Web site development work. This can be useful if you are too busy to develop your own site or if you have no artistic capabilities. Even if you are a skilled artist or writer, having a professional critique your work and make suggestions may be productive.

 Before you enter into a contract with anyone, you should ask for references from previous clients. Contact the references and ask if the agent was aggressive in promoting their sites and prompt in communicating with the clients. Also take the time to look at the client sites themselves. Are they professional in appearance? Well-designed pages indicate that the client's recommendation should carry a solid weight.

The cost of consultant services can range from a few hundred dollars to tens of thousands, depending on the scope of the work. When you do contract with one of these consultants, consider the possibility of basing his or her fee on the amount of traffic that is received at your site. This approach requires that the agent put his or her money on the line and increases the incentive to provide good service. Be aware that this tactic may increase the cost of services to you because the consultant is now sharing some of the risk.

Advertise Your Site in Print

In this chapter, you've examined a number of ways that you can advertise your site on the Internet. This certainly does not mean that you can't increase your exposure through other methods. Indeed, if you don't use these other techniques, you may miss out on many opportunities.

The simplest of all of these methods is to include your site's URL in the signature on all your e-mail. Including your URL costs nothing and has the advantage of appearing before an audience that is (or at least should be) receptive to your message already.

You should also add your Web site URL to your business cards and stationery. In effect, your Web site is your office in cyberspace, and you should include its address alongside your physical office. Before you do so, however, remember to walk through your site carefully to check for a professional and finished appearance. You wouldn't invite potential clients into a half-finished office covered with graffiti, and you shouldn't show them your work in progress on the Web, either.

Finally, include your URL on any ads that you might place in magazines, newspapers, or trade journals. For many people, the discovery of a Web site in an advertisement is an illicit thrill. It's a way of letting people with access to the Web feel that they're an exclusive group and that you're catering especially to them. Take advantage of the cachet that comes with being on the Web whenever you can. ●

Part
VI

Ch
32

## CHAPTER 33

Security

by David Wall

On the network, as in real life, bad things happen. Thanks to both the work of mean-spirited people and happenstance, any information you transmit over the Internet is subject to a litany of hazards.

There are people out there who will secretly contract your company's competitors to break into your system and steal critical proprietary information without you ever being aware of its theft. There are Yahoo teenagers, twisted children of the Information Age, who will vandalize your site for fun. There are disgruntled employees, eager to exact revenge on the organization that just downsized them out the door. And there are the cosmic rays, electromagnetic fields, viruses, Trojan horses, and mysterious data-eating failures that come with network territory. It's a harsh network, and it will eat you for lunch if you're not careful.

Fortunately, many means of protecting data traversing the Internet are available to the resourceful site manager. This chapter describes those means in some degree of detail, and refers you to other resources you can use to keep current on what's threatening your system. As with many potential pitfalls, foreknowledge is your most valuable asset in preventing network disaster.

This chapter is designed to give you an overview of security risks and the precautions you should take. However, if you find yourself under attack or require further information, get a book dedicated to the large and complex issues of computer and network security. ▪

Viruses

This section deals with computer viruses—malicious programs that can cripple a system or an entire network.

General security precautions

Find out how to improve security on your networked systems by spending no money and very little time.

Scripting, programming, and security

The network daily becomes more interactive than it was the day before.

Secure transactions

This section addresses transaction security, including ways for people to send credit card information across the network.

Firewalls

One of the most popular ways to protect a local network while maintaining Internet connectivity is to install a firewall.

Checking your site's security

Learn about tools you can use to analyze your network for security weaknesses.

Security on the Internet

Even the big boys get their noses tweaked now and then. In the summer of 1996, both the U.S. Central Intelligence Agency and the U.S. Department of Justice—organizations that one would think would have pretty tight security—had their Web sites vandalized. The CIA became the "Central Stupidity Agency" and the DOJ became the "Department of Injustice." Both sites had their pages populated with diatribes against the Communications Decency Act, as well as Nazi images and pornographic pictures. Check the pages out, if you want, at **http://ww.3rdplanet. com/~evan/gov/hacked/**. Both organizations lost much face over the incidents.

Certain aspects of your Web site cannot be protected. Your HTML will always be publicly viewable—and stealable. Any graphics you have embedded in Web pages will be stealable, as will any VBScript and JavaScript code. Java source code can be kept secure, but compiled .class files are stealable.

The fact is, no one is immune to Internet treachery. You need to be aware of the risks, and the ways in which you can protect your network resources.

Play at Your Own Risk

If you play football, you may get hurt. If you fly somewhere in an airplane, the plane may crash and you may die. If you're going to connect a computer to a network, you're going to expose that computer and the data it contains to security threats. That is the unavoidable truth.

Recall the 1996 movie *Mission: Impossible*. In that movie, the Impossible Missions squad had to steal information from a super-secure computer at CIA headquarters. Why was that computer so secure? Because it was kept in a locked room and connected to no network. To steal data from the machine, the squad had to break into the room and copy information onto a disk. Though they succeeded (naturally, for the sake of the plot), their efforts were far beyond what most wired evildoers are willing to undertake.

Some companies really do isolate their important data from the network. Rumor has it that Microsoft Corporation, attacked by malicious network experts with greater frequency than most any other entity, has actually issued two machines to each of its employees—one for day-to-day sensitive work and the other for Internet connectivity. This way, sensitive data is protected from all attacks that originate on the Internet.

The advantages of having Internet-connected employees far outweigh the risks associated with exposing private information to unwelcome, prying eyes. Similarly, for most people who enjoy football, the fun of playing football outweighs the risk of injury. You shouldn't shun Internet connectivity because you fear security breaks. But sometimes, the bad guys win. You can't beat them all the time. It's part of doing business online. You need to protect yourself as much as possible.

Safe Serving

When you start connecting computers to a network—particularly the Internet—you should be aware of the bad things that can befall your system and the data it holds. Security breaches fall into four general categories:

- Theft of data that's making its way along the data pathways of the Internet.
- Theft of private data stored on a networked computer.
- Modification of public data, including Web page vandalism.
- Hijacking of a server so that server can be used as a base for other attacks, hiding the true identity of the responsible people.

In planning your protection, you should decide what level of security you want to achieve. This should depend upon several factors, including:

- *The sensitivity and value of what you have to protect*. No one cares about your e-mail to your mother. No one cares about your contributions to the JavaScript mailing list or your recipe file. People do, however, want information with money value. If you have plans and reports on your machine that your competitors would pay money to see, those plans and reports merit protection.

- *The attractiveness of you or your organization as a target*. If you run the network presence of some small-time software developer, you probably don't have to worry too much about vandalism-motivated attacks. On the other hand, if you run a site for a prominent organization (Microsoft, say, or an abortion-rights group), people may break into your site just to mess it up.

- *The amount of money you want to spend on security*. Security requires time, expertise, and equipment, all of which come with price tags. You have to decide how much you're willing to spend on protecting data. Clearly, you should spend less on protecting a given piece of data than the data itself is worth.

- *The amount of time you have to build and maintain a security system*. Organizations usually don't hire security experts. Most of the time, they dump responsibility for network security on the network administrator or Webmaster, who most likely already is pretty overworked. Organizations have to decide how to budget the technical people's time to achieve the best results.

Once you've decided what you have to protect and the resources available for protecting things, you have to decide upon a target degree of security—again keeping in mind that you can't win all the battles all the time.

Most people are content to keep their sensitive information isolated from the Internet through the use of a firewall (covered later in this chapter), some password protection, and intelligent use of their server's standard security software. Others take a more extreme approach—by using multiple layers of cryptography and advanced protection schemes like proxy servers. Still others rely on the good nature of human beings and take practically no precautions. The decision is up to you.

Part
VI
Ch
33

Viruses

Since the Michaelangelo scare of 1993, computer viruses have been the subjects of popular and technical news reports. They sound terrifying—malicious little programs replicating themselves all over the place, wreaking havoc on hard drives and playing hob with Windows. The Internet has provided viruses with a whole new way to spread.

In truth, viruses are scary and they really can shut down a system in a hurry, destroying critical data in the process. But they're not as widespread as the popular and industry media might lead you to believe. Like any other security threat, you need to be informed about what viruses are and how they work in order to protect your data from them.

What Are They?

Viruses are computer programs gone wrong. Usually, they perform some kind of malicious deed, such as deleting files or displaying an annoying message, without anyone's assistance and without the knowledge of the victim, until it is too late.

There are several kinds of viruses:

- *Viruses with their own files*. These viruses have their own executable files that copy themselves onto a target computer's hard disk. Viruses of this kind are easiest to detect.

- *Viruses that attach themselves to other files*. These viruses cling to other files as a form of camouflage. Frequently, viruses of this kind will attach themselves to operating system files.

- *Trojan horses*. Just like the Trojan horse of mythology, Trojan horse viruses pretend to be one thing when in fact they're something else. Typically, Trojan horses take the form of a game that deletes files while the user plays.

How to Protect Your System

Viruses are bad news, but they're not an insurmountable problem. There are a couple of things you can do to protect yourself from them, and neither of these preventatives is especially difficult to implement.

Common Sense   Protecting your computer from viruses is like protecting yourself from colds. A little bit of common sense goes a long way toward limiting your machine's exposure. Just like you shouldn't shake hands with someone who is sneezing frequently, don't install unknown software on your computer, and particularly not on your Web server. Try to limit the software you install to shrink-wrapped programs straight from a software retailer (though once in a while, they, too, will carry viruses). Freeware and shareware often carry viruses, so be sure to scan such programs with anti-virus programs before putting them to work.

This goes double for games and other entertainment software packages, which sometimes are fronts for Trojan horses and other malicious software.

Anti-Virus Software   The virus-protection industry is a huge one. Equip your server with one of the commercially available virus-protection software packages (Symantec Norton Anti-Virus is the top seller) and keep your chosen package updated by installing the manufacturer's update modules regularly (usually once every quarter).

General Security Precautions

Much of what you can do to prevent unwanted intrusions into your system is quite simple. In just an hour or two, you can implement these changes and make your system significantly less attractive to casual electronic vandals.

Taking these security precautions is like putting a security system on your car. Sure, an enterprising criminal could defeat your computer security precautions, just as an ambitious thief could break into your car despite your security system. It's an issue of the ease with which a bad guy could get at your stuff—an electronic vandal might move on to easier targets if he or she saw your site was protected, even a little bit. The following are some of the most cost- and time-effective security precautions you can take.

If It's Not There, They Can't Steal It

Don't make a stupid mistake and leave sensitive files in locations where they might be happened upon by the wrong people. Don't laugh—it happens.

Keep all your sensitive files in private directories, preferably on a computer protected by a firewall. You learn more about firewalls later in this chapter.

Get Rid of Guest Accounts

Many server operating systems, including Windows NT 4.0 Server, come from the factory with a preconfigured Guest account. That is, they have a username defined as Guest (often with no password) that gives certain access to anyone who wants it. Though Guest privileges usually are extremely limited, they sometimes are enough to provide a toehold for people looking to get other privileges for nefarious purposes.

Lose your server's Guest account. If someone wants limited access for a short time, make them contact you and ask for a special account. If you must have a generic account for all temporary users, at least make the username something other than "Guest." That way, you'll keep the bad guys guessing and maybe inspire them to move on to easier targets.

Figure 33.1 shows the warning you get when you delete the Guest account on a Windows NT 4.0 system.

Rename the Administrator Account

Similarly, most operating systems for networked computers include a preconfigured account for the person in charge of maintaining that system. Almost without variation, this account has the username "Administrator."

This is bad, because when a bad guy is breaking into a system, he or she is supposed to have to guess at least two things: a username and a password. By leaving your computer configured with the all-powerful username "Administrator," you're giving away half the secret.

So, you should rename your "Administrator" account. Make it "SallyTheAdmin" or some name that only you know. Just don't make it something obvious (your name or your electronic mail address) and don't leave it as "Administrator." Changing the account name in any operating system takes five minutes, if that long.

Figure 33.2 shows the dialog box you use to configure usernames and passwords in Windows NT 4.0.

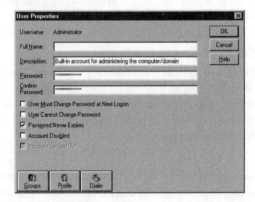

Choose Passwords Intelligently

You've probably heard this advice before, but its importance is magnified on a Web server and it bears repeating. Do not allow users to have obvious passwords. Don't let them use any of the following as their passwords:

- Their names
- The names of anyone in their family
- Their Social Security or employee numbers
- Their car's license plate sequence
- Their ZIP code
- Their telephone number
- Passwords they use on other systems
- Anything else that is either public information or easily guessable

It's also a good idea to disallow any standard word—in any language—as a password. Doing this prevents potential intruders from running through a dictionary (automatically, very fast) in search of a password.

A better way to choose a password is to choose a sequence of letters, numbers, and symbols that appears random but in fact is easily memorable. Don't forget to mix upper- and lowercase letters, too. For example, a password might be based on the sentence, "My second child, Judy, weighs 40 pounds." That could be translated into the seemingly inscrutable password, "m2cJw40#." No one would ever guess that, and it would take a long time to figure it out by brute force.

Also, make sure passwords get changed frequently—every month at least, and more frequently if you suspect that someone is trying to intrude. Many systems have a "Force User to Change Password" option that you should use.

Disable Unneeded Protocols

You can't break into a computer via Telnet if that computer doesn't support the Telnet protocols. If you have no use for a particular Internet service on a particular machine, disable that service. You can reenable it if you ever need to use it, and meanwhile, you're preventing intruders from using that service to their advantage.

Keep track of which services people are using on which computers and disable the unused services promptly.

Be Miserly with Write Privileges

System administrators have the ability to define which users can do what with the system. Among the most valuable privileges is the write privilege—the ability to save information on the hard disk. Any user lacking this privilege may be able to read information (look at Web documents, for example) but is not able to write anything.

This prevents several problems, including:

- People copying viruses onto your server's hard drive
- People deleting, replacing, or modifying Web pages (as happened at the CIA and DOJ sites)
- People creating illegal usernames and passwords for their own future use

Figure 33.3 shows an administrator configuring access privileges in Windows NT 4.0.

Part
VI

Ch
33

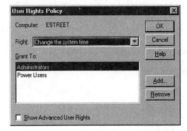

FIG. 33.3
Configuring access
privileges in Windows
NT 4.0.

Disable Your Server's Directory Browsing Feature

Most Web server software packages allow you, the administrator, to enable and disable a feature that allows Web surfers to browse through directories on your server's hard disk, as if your Web server were an FTP server. When this feature is disabled, surfers are limited to viewing pages, and cannot see the contents of directories.

Always keep your server software's directory browsing feature turned off. Doing so makes it that much harder for outsiders to see things you don't want them to see.

Also, your system's root directory and the root URL of your Web site should never be the same. Keep all private files in nonpublic server directories.

Watch Your System Logs

Every operating system suitable for use on a server keeps a log of system events. Usually, system logs make note of who logs on and when, who tries to log on and fails, and who tries to access which pieces of data on the system. System logs also record errors and other technical failures.

You should review your system log regularly—every other day at least. Look for indications that someone is trying to gain access or privileges illegally. You'll often have time to pick up on these goings-on because the process of breaking into a computer is a time-consuming one, and may require efforts spread over several days. Figure 33.4 shows a typical system log, this one from Windows NT 4.0.

N O T E You can always tell from where your pages and images are being accessed by looking at the referrer log of your Web server. If there are requests for images that didn't come from your domain, it usually means that someone at the requesting domain has an URL link to one of your images on their Web page. ■

If you recognize a pattern that indicates someone is trying to do something they shouldn't be doing (look for repeated login failures and overly long Telnet sessions), you need to take pre-emptive action. Block all access from the offending domain, if the attacks are coming from outside. Send the user a note that says you're aware of what's going on and that you'll revoke privileges if the misbehavior continues, if he or she is from your system. Lots of administrators will pull the plug on a user first, then tell him or her why. Disabling the user's account prevents damage from occurring after you reprimand the user. It also illustrates a certain willingness to play hardball.

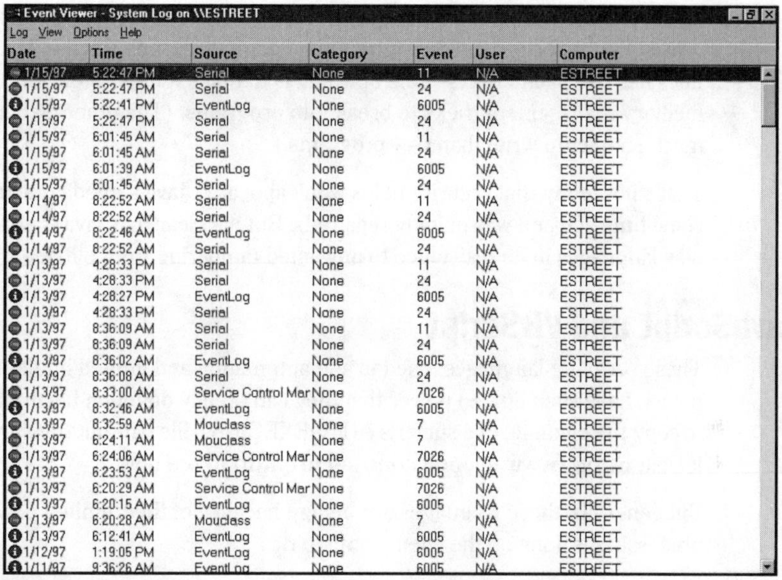

FIG. 33.4
A Windows NT 4.0
event log.

Date	Time	Source	Category	Event	User	Computer
1/15/97	5:22:47 PM	Serial	None	11	N/A	ESTREET
1/15/97	5:22:47 PM	Serial	None	24	N/A	ESTREET
1/15/97	5:22:41 PM	EventLog	None	6005	N/A	ESTREET
1/15/97	5:22:47 PM	Serial	None	24	N/A	ESTREET
1/15/97	6:01:45 AM	Serial	None	11	N/A	ESTREET
1/15/97	6:01:45 AM	Serial	None	24	N/A	ESTREET
1/15/97	6:01:39 AM	EventLog	None	6005	N/A	ESTREET
1/15/97	6:01:45 AM	Serial	None	24	N/A	ESTREET
1/14/97	8:22:52 AM	Serial	None	11	N/A	ESTREET
1/14/97	8:22:52 AM	Serial	None	24	N/A	ESTREET
1/14/97	8:22:46 AM	EventLog	None	6005	N/A	ESTREET
1/14/97	8:22:52 AM	Serial	None	24	N/A	ESTREET
1/13/97	4:28:33 PM	Serial	None	11	N/A	ESTREET
1/13/97	4:28:33 PM	Serial	None	24	N/A	ESTREET
1/13/97	4:28:27 PM	EventLog	None	6005	N/A	ESTREET
1/13/97	4:28:33 PM	Serial	None	24	N/A	ESTREET
1/13/97	8:36:09 AM	Serial	None	11	N/A	ESTREET
1/13/97	8:36:09 AM	Serial	None	24	N/A	ESTREET
1/13/97	8:36:02 AM	EventLog	None	6005	N/A	ESTREET
1/13/97	8:36:08 AM	Serial	None	24	N/A	ESTREET
1/13/97	8:33:00 AM	Service Control Mar	None	7026	N/A	ESTREET
1/13/97	8:32:46 AM	EventLog	None	6005	N/A	ESTREET
1/13/97	8:32:59 AM	Mouclass	None	7	N/A	ESTREET
1/13/97	6:24:11 AM	Mouclass	None	7	N/A	ESTREET
1/13/97	6:24:06 AM	Service Control Mar	None	7026	N/A	ESTREET
1/13/97	6:23:53 AM	EventLog	None	6005	N/A	ESTREET
1/13/97	6:20:29 AM	Service Control Mar	None	7026	N/A	ESTREET
1/13/97	6:20:15 AM	EventLog	None	6005	N/A	ESTREET
1/13/97	6:20:28 AM	Mouclass	None	7	N/A	ESTREET
1/13/97	6:12:41 AM	EventLog	None	6005	N/A	ESTREET
1/12/97	1:19:05 PM	EventLog	None	6005	N/A	ESTREET
1/11/97	9:36:26 AM	EventLog	None	6005	N/A	ESTREET

Scripting, Programming, and Security

As interactivity grows in the online world, the goings-on of our networks are becoming increasingly complex. As a rule, it's tougher to secure a complex system than a simple one. So, as the Web gets more complex with the addition of programming and scripting languages, the opportunities for ne'er-do-wells to take advantage of flaws in the system proliferate.

Generally, language designers have done an excellent job of putting together network-aware languages with security in mind. Java, the most popular programming language for Internet applications, is apparently bulletproof. JavaScript and VBScript are limited in their vulnerability to security breaches by their limited scope of operation.

Other network programming languages, however, present some real opportunities for dastardly deeds to be done. ActiveX Controls are so complex as to be only minimally secure. Common Gateway Interface (CGI) routines have been around a while, but since they offer access to the server's processor, they have the potential to do harm.

This section gives you an overview of the security inherent in several of the most popular network programming and scripting languages.

Java

The people who designed Java at Sun Microsystems did so with security in mind. They wanted to make it impossible to write a virus in Java, and impossible for any Java program to do harmful things to a computer on which it was running.

Part
VI

Ch
33

They succeeded. Java lacks many of the low-level memory-management routines that characterize other object-oriented programming languages, such as C++. The absence of these routines has two main effects—one of which is to make it impossible for bad guys to use low-level memory-management tricks to break into programs. (The other is that Java programs are much simpler to write than C++ programs.)

That's not to say that security holes won't appear in Java someday (actually, one was found some time ago and was quickly repaired). But it's clear that Java is years ahead of other complex languages in its resistance to unwanted tampering from outside.

JavaScript and VBScript

These scripting languages, used to add automation and limited intelligence to HTML documents, have such limited power that they can't really do much harm. JavaScript has been used to copy the contents of a surfer's AUTOEXEC.BAT file without the surfer's knowlege. Take a look at **http://www.scoopy.com/secure.htm** to see how.

But generally, these languages are benign because of their limited power and because all their processing is done on the client computer.

CGI

Common Gateway Interface (CGI) routines are programs that run on the server to provide interactivity and intelligence to Web surfers. Because they use the server's CPU to perform operations, there is the possibility that a person could fool the CPU into thinking that a certain stream of data was a CGI request, when in fact it was a virus or other unauthorized program being sent in for processing.

The easiest and most popular way to defeat CGI attacks is to configure your processor to terminate all CGI activity that continues for more than three seconds or so. This way, legitimate users have CGI access to the processor, while the people trying to break in, whose routines likely will require extra time, will be cut off. You may also want to keep CGI scripts in non-public directories, or use CGI wrappers (programs that encrypt CGI data streams) to protect against intrusions.

Plug-Ins and ActiveX Controls

Plug-ins and ActiveX controls do most of their stuff on the client side, so any harm they do likely will be there.

But the concern for client-side harm is real, since plug-ins—and especially ActiveX Controls—are very complicated and very difficult to secure.

The best way to protect against plug-in and ActiveX Control harm on the client side is to remind people to use the same precautions in selecting ActiveX Controls and plug-ins that they would use in selecting other software. Remind them to only use plug-ins and ActiveX Controls from reputable sources, and to always use anti-virus software.

Secure Transactions

Encryption in and of itself is interesting, but its application to Internet transactions makes it relevant to this discussion. There are two leading protocols for conducting secure transactions on the Internet, both of which can use RSA encryption. They are Secure Sockets Layer (SSL), developed by Netscape, and Secure HTTP (SHTTP), developed by Enterprise Integration Technology (EIT). These two protocols are usually referenced with respect to online commerce, but they are really just mechanisms for secure communication, and could also be put to use for transmitting other sensitive information. SSL is a separate protocol from HTTP, the communications protocol of the Web, while SHTTP is an extension of the HTTP protocol. Let's look at the two in turn and see what they do and how they work.

Secure Sockets Layer (SSL)

SSL is the most common Web security protocol. It was developed by Netscape and it is supported by all major browsers, including Netscape Navigator and Microsoft Internet Explorer. SSL allows for various methods of encryption to be used, with various levels of strength. The encryption algorithm used is negotiated by a client and server at the time of a transaction.

Currently, Netscape Navigator implements several types of SSL encryption with several encryption key sizes, from a relatively weak 40-bit encryption key to a practically unbreakable 192-bit encryption key.

Most commercial Web server software supports SSL. Check your server documentation for information on how it works in your setup. Most noticeably, URLs for accessing a document securely begin with https://, rather than http://.

Secure HTTP (SHTTP)

Secure HTTP (SHTTP) is identical to SSL from the surfer's standpoint. The browser and server establish the encryption algorithms that they will use to make the transaction and information is transmitted securely using those algorithms.

SHTTP differs from SSL in that it is an extension of the HTTP protocol, as opposed to an entirely separate protocol running concurrently with HTTP.

SHTTP isn't used a lot, since SSL technology was out first and thereby collected a large share of the transaction-security market. Though many servers and browsers support SHTTP, its popularity is steadily dwindling.

> **N O T E** Yes, once, a man in Europe decrypted a single message that had been encoded with 40-bit SSL (the weakest kind of SSL) as part of a contest sponsored by Netscape Communications. Here are some facts about what he pulled off:
>
> - He had 120 workstations and two parallel supercomputers running nonstop for eight days. The computer time he used cost about $10,000.

Part

VI

Ch

33

- He did not crack SSL itself, only the one message. Since SSL uses a different encryption algorithm for every encrypted message, theoretically one would need another eight days with 120 workstations and two parallel supercomputers to crack just one more message.

If this had been real life and not a contest, the information he decrypted would have had to have been worth more than $10,000 in order for the decryption process to have been cost-effective. I don't know what your credit limit is, but it's clear from this example that going through the hassle of decrypting an SSL transmission is just not worth it to get a credit card number.

Remember, the encryption that was broken in the contest was 40-bit SSL. It would have taken over 1,000,000,000,000 (one trillion) times more computing power to solve a message encrypted with 128-bit SSL. ▓

Certificates

Authentication, which is essential to secure transactions, is the process of making sure people really are who they claim to be. Usernames and passwords serve authentication purposes for system-access purposes, but certificates serve to ensure authentication when two machines or sites try to communicate with one another. That's important when online transactions are going on.

Certificates are electronic documents that contain digitally signed pieces of information that authenticate a secure server by verifying the connection between a server's encryption scheme and the server's identification. Cryptographic checks, using digital signatures, ensure that the validity of certificates can be absolutely trusted.

Certificates are issued by third parties called certificate authorities. To obtain a certificate for your site, you must contact a certificate authority and register with it. The authority will verify that you are who you claim to be and then will create a digital certificate that is unique to you. There is usually a fee associated with this for businesses. For more information on certificates, check out the VeriSign Web site at **http://www.verisign.com**.

Pretty Good Privacy (PGP)

A public-domain encryption scheme developed by Phil Zimmerman of the Massachusetts Institute of Technology, Pretty Good Privacy is, as the name implies, good enough for most personal online data-encryption needs, including encrypted electronic mail. To date, PGP has been used mainly for encrypted electronic mail, but its use may expand now that a conflict between the U.S. government and Zimmerman (the government claimed that PGP is so powerful, it could be used by subversive foreign powers without the knowledge of the U.S. authorities) has finally been straightened out.

You can get more information and PGP software at **http://www.pgp.com/**.

Firewalls

Like the carpet-defending mother who made you take your shoes off outside after playing in the mud, firewalls protect your network from the dangers of tracked-in data. Named for the fireproof barrier between the engine compartment and passenger cabin of an automobile or airplane, network firewalls form a barrier that's supposed to be (and is, if you do it right) impervious to attempts to get through it.

How Firewalls Work

A firewall is a computer through which all data entering or leaving a local area network (LAN) en route to or from the Internet must pass. In their role as gatekeepers, firewalls work like two-way filters, allowing certain data to pass out of the local-area network and allowing other data (usually much more restricted) to pass from the Internet into the LAN.

For example, a firewall might be set up to protect an intranet. People logged on to the intranet could do whatever they wanted on the Internet—their Web requests would pass out through the firewall and data could come into the intranet in response to those requests. Users could send Internet electronic mail out through the firewall. They also could send out Gopher, Telnet, and FTP requests through the firewall and receive data in response to those requests.

But the firewall's filter is much less porous in the other direction. In most cases, firewalls are configured to allow nothing but electronic mail to come inside the firewall unsolicited. Everything else, such as Telnet and Web data, must enter in response to a request that went out from a legitimate user inside the network.

In cases in which an organization's public Web server is protected by a firewall, the firewall needs to be configured to allow Web data requests to pass from the Internet to the public Web server.

N O T E For more information about firewalls, look on the Web at Marcus Ranum's Internet Firewalls FAQ, at **http://www.v-one.com/newpages/faq.htm**, or at Kathy Fulmer's list of firewall tools developers, at **http://www.greatcircle.com/firewalls/vendors.html**. ■

Part
VI

Ch
33

Implementing a Firewall

The key to implementing a firewall lies in the configuration files of the computer (usually a packet router) that functions as the physical firewall.

So, to set up a firewall, you need to install a dedicated router between the network you're protecting and the potentially hostile network (the Internet, most often) so all data passing between the two networks must pass through the router. This is a physical process—make sure all the wires coming into your network bearing Internet data pass through the router first.

Second, you need to set the router's configuration files to correspond to the rules you've set up for data exchange. A typical set of data-exchange rules looks like this:

- Don't allow any source-routed packets into the protected network. Spoofers like to use source-routed packets to bluff their way onto protected networks.

- Drop any packets from the outside that claim to be from the local network. These clearly aren't up to anything beneficial.

- Allow all packets that are part of established connections (such as those involved in a Web-document exchange) to pass unmolested. This allows you to place your Web server behind the firewall and allows the users of the defended network to use the Web without hassle.

- Block connections to low port numbers, except for those associated with DNS requests and SMTP mail transfers.

Checking Your Security

Forewarned is forearmed—an old saw that holds true for computer networks more than in any other field. Once you've installed a security system, don't sit back and assume your information is safe. The bad guys aren't getting any dumber. Instead, constantly test and refine your security system to make sure it will stand up against the latest break-in techniques.

There are several techniques for testing the security of a site. Some of the most popular are described in this section.

SATAN

On the logic that the best way to get site administrators to improve their sites' security is to make their security weaknesses blindingly obvious to everyone, SATAN (Security Administrator's Tool for Analyzing Networks) was released to the public.

SATAN looks at any UNIX-based network site and points out ways in which evil-minded people could circumvent security and illegally exploit system resources. SATAN derives its knowledge from publicized information of bugs in systems, and so will refer you to fixes for any troubles it detects, if any fixes are available to you. SATAN features a friendly interface, giving output as HTML documents that are viewable with practically any Web browser.

Incidentally, Dan Farmer, the author of SATAN, did an informal security survey of about 2,200 Web sites in January 1997. He found that about three quarters of the surveyed sites—many of them bank sites and other high-profile sites—had "serious security flaws."

N O T E   You can read more about SATAN at **http://www.interaus.net/1995/6/satan.html**. ■

Cracking Consultants

SATAN is a useful tool for administrators trying to flush out security weaknesses, but it detects only fairly well-known security flaws. What happens when your site is crackable, but only by a very skilled operator with highly specialized and current information? Generally, you won't find out about a security breach until it's too late.

That's why many organizations, mainly those with lots of valuable information to protect, hire people to try to break into their systems and, when they succeed (and they usually do), tell the organizations how to head off similar attacks in the future. The "Tiger Teams"—ultra-secret, cracking squads employed by the National Security Agency and Department of Defense— regularly challenge Pentagon computers.

If you have sufficiently valuable information on your network, there's no more certain way to test its safety than with a trained break-in artist. ●

Web Site Tools

## CHAPTER 34

HTML Tag Editors

by Jim O'Donnell

At the advent of Web page and other HTML document programming, the majority of HTML authors simply used their favorite text editor and programmed directly in HTML, adding the necessary markup tags to format their documents. As time has gone by, special purpose HTML editors have been created that make the task of HTML authoring easier and more efficient.

The editors generally fall into two categories. So-called WYSIWYG (What You See Is What You Get) editors, such as Netscape Composer (formerly Netscape Navigator Gold) and Microsoft FrontPage, allow you to set up a Web page the way you want it to look, and the HTML code to create the page is created automatically. The other type of program, called HTML tag editors, involves programming directly in HTML, but has tools and special-purpose functions built-in to make this task much easier. ■

Find out what you can do with HTML tag editors

An HTML tag editor is a special-purpose text editor that lets you easily work with HTML documents, supporting the special markup needs required by the Hypertext Markup Language (HTML).

Learn how HTML tag editors bridge the gap between NotePad and WYSIWYG HTML editors

While WYSIWYG (What You See Is What You Get) HTML editors are becoming more popular, many people still prefer the control afforded by working directly with HTML. Tag editors make the process of working with HTML much easier.

Learn about the capabilities of some popular HTML tag editors

You'll see a quick rundown of three of the most popular HTML tag editors: HotDog by Sausage Software, HoTMetaL by SoftQuad, and HomeSite by Nick Bradbury.

Find out where on the Web to find out more

Compilations and archives of shareware, freeware, and commercial demo software abound on the Web and the Internet. You'll see some of the best places to find the HTML tag editors.

What Is an HTML Tag Editor?

As you know, HTML, the basic language of Web pages and other HTML documents, stands for the Hypertext Markup Language. In order to format text, graphics, and other information within an HTML document, HTML language elements, called tags, are embedded within it. These tags *mark up* the basic text to add formatting and include hypertext information—multimedia graphics, sounds, and other elements.

HTML documents can be created in any editor, and lots of folks still rely on the NotePad or WordPad to create theirs. However, a growing number of editors are being created that understand HTML tags and allow you to create HTML documents more productively, spending more time including the information and less time worrying about the tags themselves.

Tag Editor Features

For this discussion, an HTML tag editor is a special-purpose text editor designed to work with HTML documents. Generally, these editors understand the most commonly used tags in HTML programming—HTML 2, HTML 3, HTML 3.2, Netscape extensions, and Microsoft extensions are generally supported—and provide you with menus, toolbars, or other mechanisms to easily include these tags within your document.

Additionally, the later versions of the most popular tag editors include even more special-purpose tools for creating certain HTML elements. These include wizards and other procedures to ease the creation of HTML tables, forms, frames, and lists. Some editors are even starting to provide the ability to embed and more easily configure such objects as Java applets, ActiveX Controls, and plug-in content into your HTML documents.

Regardless of their specific features and capabilities, each HTML tag editor understands the place of the HTML tags within the documents they are used to edit. When you spell check your document—as many of these editors allow you to do—HTML tags are understood as correct words (and incorrect, unsupported, or mistyped tags are flagged). Some of the HTML tag editors provide syntax and verification to help ensure that your HTML formatting is correct before the document is published.

Why Use a Tag Editor?

With the increasing number of WYSIWYG editors for HTML documents, you might wonder why someone would want to use a tag editor (let alone still program in NotePad). The reason is that, while WYSIWYG editors allow you to create HTML documents without dealing directly with HTML (or even knowing any), they also take away some of the flexibility and power that you can have by dealing with the HTML tags yourself. In a way, it's like the difference between programming in a low-level assembly language versus programming in Basic. Basic allows you to do some things much easier than an assembly language, but also cannot do as many things.

What Is the Future of HTML Tag Editing?

The HTML editors of the future will most likely be a hybrid of today's WYSIWYG and tag editors. On the one hand, as you will see in some of the examples that follow, more and more of the tag editors are implementing internal viewers that give you a WYSIWYG interface to your document. And, from the other end, WYSIWYG editors are becoming more and more capable with each new program, increasing their capabilities and the amount of sophisticated HTML programming you can do with them. At some point, these two paradigms of HTML programming will meet in the middle. Just as products like Visual Basic give you both ease-of-use and great capabilities, future generations of HTML editors will do the same.

Popular HTML Tag Editors

In the rest of this chapter, you take a brief look at three of the most popular HTML tag editors currently available. It would take a whole chapter—if not a whole book—to discuss each program completely. Here, you see some of the common features of the different programs, as well as some of the more advanced capabilities. Each of the programs discussed can be freely downloaded, either as the fully functional product for a limited evaluation period or as a less-functional freeware version (or both).

In the sections that follow, you should get an idea of the capabilities of the HotDog Web Editor, HoTMetaL, and HomeSite. Each section discusses downloading and installing the program, some of the basic features and configuration options, and some of the advanced features of the full versions of the software. Finally, a summary of some important information needed to obtain each program is given. After the discussions of all three HTML tag editors, a summary table will be given telling you where you can get the available versions of each editor and how much they cost.

HotDog Web Editor by Sausage Software

The HotDog Web Editor by Sausage Software has been one of the most popular HTML editors for quite some time. As each version of the program has been developed, it has increased its capabilities and provided more functions for easily incorporating some of the most sophisticated HTML elements.

Downloading and Installation

The HotDog Web Editor, available in a 16-bit version for Windows 3.1 and a 32-bit professional version for Windows 95, can be downloaded through the Sausage Software Web site at **http://www.sausage.com**. For the remainder of this section, HotDog Professional 3 is discussed.

HotDog is an application written in Visual Basic. Because of this, there are actually two sets of files that need to be installed. The first of these must be the support files necessary, which are the runtime libraries needed for Visual Basic applications. After those are installed, or if you already have them on your system, the program files themselves can be installed. In each case,

Part

VII

Ch

34

installation is very straightforward; each set of files comes in a self-installing executable archive. All you need to do is double-click each executable and follow the installation instructions.

One nice feature of HotDog you might discover when you install it is that the program detects whether or not you have Microsoft Internet Explorer installed in your system (see Figure 34.1). Because of the ActiveX technology used to create Internet Explorer, HotDog can use its capabilities within its previewer, increasing its bite.

▶ **See** "What ActiveX Controls Mean to You," for a discussion of Microsoft's ActiveX technology, **p. 496**

N O T E HotDog uses a dog theme through its operations. The previewer is called Rover, and the program unit that checks and verifies hypertext, multimedia, and other links is called the Link Sniffer. It also includes sound effects for many features and operations that are appropriate to this theme. While the sound effects are cute at first, you might find that they get on your nerves—or worse, slow down operation of the program. To turn them off, select the General tab of the Tools, Options menu and check the No Sound Effects box. ■

FIG. 34.1
HotDog can use Microsoft Internet Explorer to enhance its HTML document previewing capability.

HotDog User Interface

As shown in Figure 34.2, HotDog has a very involved user interface, and the different elements within it give you the ability to do many different things at the touch of a button. Each distinct area of the HotDog window, except for the document window where all the editing takes place, can be displayed or not, according to what you need to see. The different areas can also be resized to suit your needs.

Main Toolbar   The HotDog main toolbar includes five tabs for performing many different functions. The five tabs in the toolbar and their functions are as follows.

- **Elements:** In addition to the Windows standard buttons for creating, loading, and saving files, and cutting, copying, and pasting, this toolbar allows you to add many of the typical HTML tags, such as text formatting tags and headings, and perform other basic functions.

- **Insert:** The buttons in this toolbar allow you to insert some of the more sophisticated HTML elements, including tables, forms, inline images, and hypertext links. Two buttons on this toolbar also allow you to include embedded objects (a Netscape extension and ActiveX Controls).

FIG. 34.2

The HotDog window gives you ready access to all of its capabilities.

Link Sniffer

Floating toolbar

Document window

Document tab

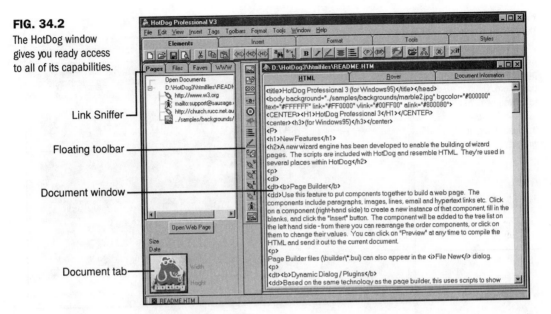

▶ **See** "Inserting Controls with the *OBJECT* Tag," for more information on using the <OBJECT> tag to include ActiveX Controls, **p. 505**

CAUTION

Be careful when using HotDog's capability to insert ActiveX objects. On my system, attempting to do this caused the program to abruptly exit. Be sure to save all of your files before trying it on your system.

■ **Format:** This toolbar gives you access to buttons for inserting many of HTML's formatting tags, as well as formatting various aspects of the HotDog display.

■ **Tools:** These buttons allow you to access HotDog's various configuration and customization menus. Configuring HotDog is discussed in the Configuration and Customization section, later in this chapter .

■ **Style:** The Style toolbar allows you to insert HotDog styles and predefined HTML style sheets.

Document Window The document window is the main window for HTML document creation and editing. It also has the following three tabs that display different information about the current file being edited:

■ **HTML:** This view of the document shows the actual HTML document itself, including all of the HTML tags.

■ **Rover:** This window shows the preview of the document as it actually would appear in a Web browser or other HTML-compatible viewer (see Figure 34.3).

FIG. 34.3

The <u>R</u>over tab in the document window allows you to get a preview of your HTML document. Options exist to let you see what it will look like in browsers that use different widths.

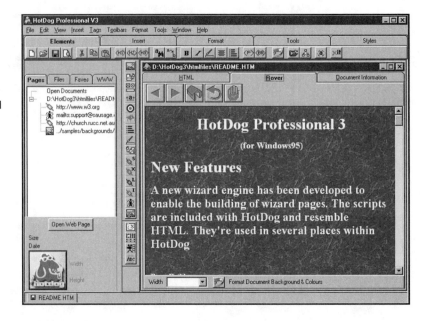

- **Document Information:** The document information window shows statistics about the current file being edited, including an estimate of how long it would take to download and view the complete document with different speed modems.

Link Sniffer   HotDog's Link Sniffer has the following four tabs that allow you to do many things:

- **Pages:** This tab shows the currently opened documents and gives a tree view of each of their hypertext links.

- **Files:** Viewing this tab shows you the files that you have locally. It can be configured to show HTML files, graphics, or all files.

- **Faves:** You can add items to this window for your favorite text, HTML tags, and hypertext links. Then you can add them to your HTML documents at the click of a mouse button.

- **WWW:** This tab uses HotDog's built-in FTP client to display a tree view of your HTML documents and other files on your Web server. Through this tab, you can access, edit, and save files on a remote site.

Floating Toolbars   In addition to the main toolbar, HotDog has a number of predefined toolbars that can be turned on or off. All of HotDog's functions can be accessed through buttons on one or more of these toolbars. These toolbars are also completely customizable.

These are called floating toolbars because they can be docked in different sections of the HotDog window. As shown in Figure 34.4, they can also be torn off and left in their own windows.

FIG. 34.4
HotDog's floating toolbars can be torn off the HotDog window and placed at any convenient location on your screen.

Document Tabs   The final element of the HotDog user interface is the row of document tabs along the bottom of the HotDog window. This gives you quick access to any of the currently open HTML documents that are being edited. Also, files that have been changed but not yet saved are indicated in the document bar by a small red x icon by the file name.

Basic HotDog Operations

Editing HTML documents with HotDog is very straightforward. For someone coming from using a simple text editor such as NotePad to HotDog, the transition can be made easily because you can decide for yourself how quickly to begin taking advantage of HotDog's features.

General HTML Formatting   For general formatting of HTML documents, HotDog offers many different options and methods for the insertion of HTML tags into the document. You may have an idea of what some of them might be from reading the information on the HotDog user interface in the preceding sections.

HTML tags can be inserted into documents with HotDog in a variety of ways. Toolbar buttons exist on either the main toolbar or one of the floating toolbars for any of the HTML tags that HotDog supports—its support includes all of the HTML 3.2 tags, as well as the Netscape and Microsoft extensions. Container tags, ones that use separate tags to open and close the region over which they operate (for example, <H1>...</H1> or <A HREF=*URL*>...</A>), can be entered along with their contents in one of two ways. If the tags are inserted first, the cursor is left between them and you can then type in the information that should be there. Or, if the container contents already exist in your file, you can highlight them and then select the HTML tag. HotDog inserts the opening and closing tags on each side of the selected region.

In addition to using the toolbar buttons, there are a number of other ways that you can enter HTML tags into your documents. HotDog's menus give you access to all of the HTML tags. Also, the Link Sniffer Faves tab and the pop-up menu that you get by right-clicking the mouse in the document window can each be configured to give you access to your most commonly used HTML tags.

Special HTML Format Options   In addition to the HTML tags that HotDog allows you to easily enter into your document, it has a number of special operations for entering some of the more involved and sophisticated HTML constructs. The different elements that can be entered in this way are as follows:

- ■ **Forms:** HotDog has a special window, shown in Figure 34.5, that allows you to easily place and format each of the different types of HTML forms elements.

Part
VII

Ch
34

FIG. 34.5

This window gives you an easy way to enter all of the necessary attributes for each HTML forms element, relieving you of needing to remember what information each element requires.

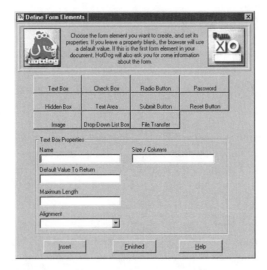

- **Lists:** HotDog's Create List Element window allows you to easily format and input the information to create an HTML numbered, unnumbered, or definition list.

- **Tables:** The Create Table window gives you an easy way to lay out and format an HTML table and to assign contents to each of the resulting cells.

The Create Table window is a great way to create a simple table. To create a more complex one, including mixed images and graphics or using row or column spanning, use this window to set up the table framework, then edit the HTML code to add the special effects.

- **Images:** HotDog's Insert Image and Image Properties windows allow you to include an inline image into your document, add alternate text, specify a hypertext link, and add other HTML graphics formatting options.

Configuration and Customizing

HotDog offers an overwhelming variety of ways you can configure and customize it so that it behaves exactly the way you want. Each of the different options can give you new ways to create your HTML documents and maximize your productivity.

Customized Toolbars   By selecting Tools, Customize Toolbars or pressing Ctrl+Alt+C, you can access HotDog's Customize Toolbar window (see Figure 34.6). From this window, you can create and delete toolbars and add and delete buttons from any defined toolbar. In addition to assigning any HotDog function to a button, you can also attach any HTML tag or even any of your own text. If you're using a special-purpose Web browser with some of its own tags, you could even define an entry for these completely new HTML tags!

FIG. 34.6

HotDog's Customize Toolbar window allows you to define toolbar buttons and complete a toolbar to suit your specific needs.

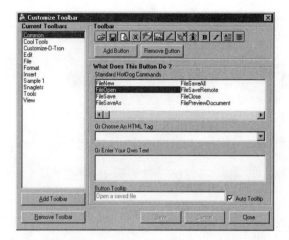

HotDog Environment Sound Effects   As mentioned earlier in this section, HotDog is enhanced by the use of environment sounds that are attached to different events that occur in HotDog (for example, opening or closing a file). Not only can you turn these sound effects on or off, you can also attach different sounds to the different events and even set HotDog up so that it only plays the sounds some of the time. The window through which you do this is accessed by selecting Tools, Mixing Desk.

Shortcut Keys   HotDog comes predefined with shortcut keys to perform different functions. Some of these are the standard Windows hotkeys—cut (Ctrl+X) and paste (Ctrl+V), for instance—and some are attached to different HotDog events. The Shortcut Key window, accessed by selecting Tools, Shortcut Keys, allows you to change any of these hotkeys, as well as create any new ones that you'd like. For those HotDog functions that have menu options, the menus are automatically updated to display the new shortcut key.

> **N O T E** In the document window, even if you assign new functions to some shortcut keys, the standard Windows function is still performed. For instance, Ctrl+X is always cut. ▪

Document Templates   Whenever a new document is created, HotDog gives you the option of using one of a series of predefined templates to create that document (see Figure 34.7). These formats use a series of windows to query you for standard information that goes in that template to create that kind of HTML document. In addition to the templates that HotDog gives you, you can also create templates from your own HTML files.

Part
VII

Ch
34

FIG. 34.7

The Document Template feature gives you a good way to make a quick start at creating HTML documents of a given sort.

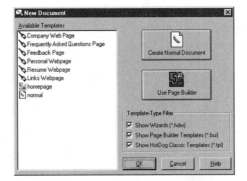

Advanced Features

In addition to the preceding features listed, HotDog has a number of advanced features that go beyond simple HTML support. The following sections cover some of these features.

Spell Checking   HotDog has a spell checker that understands HTML and all of the different HTML tags, and can be used to spell check the information in your HTML document files.

JavaScript Samples   HotDog includes a number of sample JavaScripts and allows you to include them in your HTML documents. These sample scripts can insert the current time of day into your document, create a splash screen that can be viewed while the rest of your document is downloaded, or create fade-in and fade-out background colors for your document.

Snaglets   Included with HotDog Professional 3 are what Sausage Software calls Snaglets. These are little applications that can be used to perform a given function. These four Snaglets can do the following things:

- **Client-Side Image Maps:** This Snaglet gives you a window in which you can use an image to define a client-side imagemap, and create the different areas that have hypertext links attached to them.

- **Frames:** The Frames Snaglet gives you an easy interface for defining a frameset and creating the frames that are displayed within it.

- **Animator:** The Animator Snaglet includes a Java class file that can be used to animate a set of images.

- **Text Effects:** This Snaglet uses another Java class file to attach one of a variety of special effects to a block of text within your HTML document.

HoTMetaL by SoftQuad

One of the first and most popular HTML tag editors is the HoTMetal editor by SoftQuad. The latest version of this program is available for the Windows 95/NT platforms, as well as the Macintosh and some UNIX platforms. Unlike the other tag editors discussed in this chapter, the commercial version of this program is not available for download or evaluation from the

SoftQuad Web site. It does provide a free version to get an idea of the capabilities of this program. In this section, you learn about the HoTMetaL Free Version and see the features of HoTMetaL Pro.

Downloading and Installation

HoTMetaL Free Version can be downloaded from the SoftQuad Web site located at **http://www.sq.com**. The program comes in a self-extracting archive file, and installation is straight-forward. Place the archive file in a temporary directory, execute it to decompress the archive files, and then execute the resulting Setup.exe file. From there, answer the installation questions to determine where the program is installed.

HoTMetaL User Interface

The HoTMetaL Free Version user interface is fairly uncomplicated. As shown in Figure 34.8, the screen is divided into three areas (other than the menu bar). These areas are the document window, toolbars, and information line.

FIG. 34.8
The HoTMetaL Free Version screen is divided into a number of areas to display your HTML document and information about it, and to provide the editing tools.

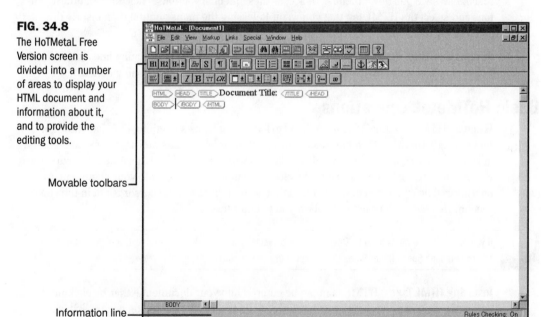

Movable toolbars

Information line

Part VII

Ch 34

Document Window The HoTMetaL document window is where your HTML document is displayed while you are editing it. As shown in Figure 34.8, rather than actually displaying the HTML tags used, HoTMetaL displays icons representing them.

Movable Toolbars HoTMetaL uses three toolbars, normally located at the top of the screen just below the menu bar, containing buttons for standard Windows 95 functions, common HTML elements, and other HTML elements. As shown in Figure 34.9, these toolbars can be torn off and displayed in windows of their own.

FIG. 34.9

HoTMetaL's toolbars can be moved around and placed anywhere on your screen that you want.

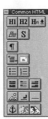

One button on the middle and five on the lower toolbar have small down-arrow icons. They are used to access menus giving options of certain types of HTML tags. These buttons are Macintosh-style pull-down menus. To access these menus, you must click and hold these buttons and select the HTML tag that you want. Releasing the mouse button then inserts the selected tag into your HTML document.

Information Line The last part of the HoTMetaL screen is the information line along its bottom. This bar reveals information about the current HTML document being edited.

Basic HoTMetaL Operations

When an HTML document is loaded into HoTMetaL, it looks something like that shown in Figure 34.10. HoTMetaL's menu selections and toolbar buttons, as well as the operation of the keyboard, are all context-sensitive, depending on where in the HTML document the cursor is. For instance, those functions that place <BODY> section HTML tags into your document are only accessible when the cursor is within that section. In fact, if the cursor is not in the <BODY> section, HoTMetaL does not even allow you to enter text.

 If you don't like the restrictions HoTMetaL places on where you can enter tags and text, you can disable this by selecting Special, Turn Rules Checking Off or pressing Ctrl+K.

Inserting HTML Tags HTML tags can be entered into your document either by clicking the appropriate toolbar button or by going through the Insert Element dialog box, which is accessed by selecting Markup, Insert Element or by pressing Ctrl+I. You can enter the contents of these tags by typing them in after the tags are inserted—the cursor is placed between the tags when they are inserted. You can also enter the contents first, highlight them, and then insert the tags which are placed around them.

HoTMetaL also automatically inserts certain tags. For instance, if you begin to type text when the cursor is in the <BODY> section of the document, paragraph container tags (<P>...</P>) are inserted around the text.

FIG. 34.10
HoTMetaL's HTML icons indicate the tags being used to format your Web pages and other HTML documents.

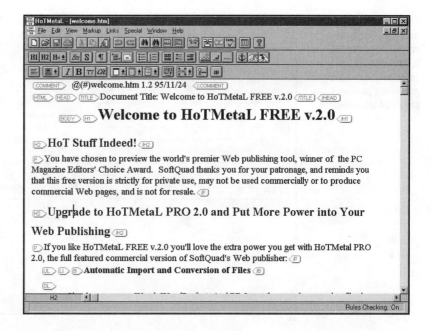

Editing HTML Tag Attributes After an HTML element is placed in your document, HoTMetaL gives you a quick way to edit all of its attributes. You do this by placing the cursor within the area to which the tag applies and selecting Markup, Edit SGML Attributes, or pressing F6. This brings up a dialog box similar to that shown in Figure 34.11, though customized for the appropriate HTML tag, of course. The one in Figure 34.11 shows the attributes of the <BODY> tag.

FIG. 34.11
HoTMetaL gives you an easy way to enter all of the different attributes for each HTML element that it supports.

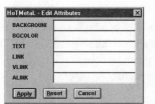

HoTMetal Table Support HoTMetaL Free Version's table support is relatively rudimentary, though it does ease the process of putting simple tables into your HTML documents. To put the framework of a simple HTML table into your document, select Markup, Insert Table, and you are queried for the number of rows and columns in your table. Then, as shown in Figure 34.12 for an eight-by-three table, HoTMetaL places a grid in your document, into each cell of which you can place the appropriate contents.

FIG. 34.12
HoTMetaL Free Version makes the process of table creation a bit easier by giving you a grid for the placing of individual table cells.

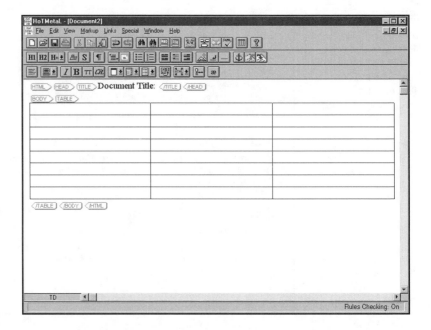

You can use HoTMetaL's capability to edit the attributes of HTML tags—either on the whole table or on the individual cells—using the Edit SGML Attributes dialog box discussed earlier. To edit the table attributes, place the cursor immediately after the opening table icon or immediately before the closing tag before calling up the dialog box. To edit the individual cells, first place the cursor in the appropriate cell.

Advanced Features

The HoTMetaL Free Version doesn't have a lot of advanced features beyond the ones mentioned here. It does have the capability to enforce adherence to the HTML 2 standard (also supporting some extensions). However, the latest commercial version of HoTMetaL, HoTMetaL Pro 3.0, adds many very powerful functions.

Rules Checking and Document Validation   As mentioned previously, HoTMetaL includes a rules-checking option. When this option is enabled, it enforces adherence to the HTML 2 standard when you are building your Web pages and HTML documents. This option is toggled with the Special, Turn Rules Checking On/Off menu option, or by pressing Ctrl+K.

HoTMetal PRO 3.0 Features   The commercial version of HoTMetaL, available for Windows 95 and NT, the Macintosh, and some UNIX platforms, has many sophisticated and advanced features for the creation of HTML documents. This product goes some of the way towards integrating the capabilities of an HTML tag editor with that of a WYSIWYG editor. Some of the advanced features of HoTMetaL PRO 3.0 are the following:

■ **WYSIWYG Display:** As you edit your document, HoTMetaL Pro 3.0 lets you see how it will look in a Web browser.

- **Drag-and-Drop Support:** Files, images, hypertext links, and text can be placed within HTML documents by dragging and dropping them directly into your document window.

- **Frames Support:** HoTMetaL Pro 3.0 lets you easily create HTML framesets visually and fill individual frames by dragging and dropping HTML documents into each frame.

- **Multimedia Support:** Includes support for audio, video, ActiveX Controls, ShockWave content, Java applets, and JavaScripts.

- **WYSIWYG Forms:** HTML forms can be laid out and created and, as you edit them, you can see exactly what they will look like.

- **Color Palettes:** HoTMetaL Pro 3.0 uses an RGB color wheel to allow you to select colors for fonts and backgrounds without worrying about hexadecimal color codes.

- **Built-In Graphics Editor:** The MetalWorks graphics editor is included with HoTMetaL Pro 2.0, allowing you to create imagemaps, transparent images, and buttons, and prepare your existing graphics for the Web.

- **Templates and Samples:** SoftQuad ships HoTMetaL Pro 3.0 with hundreds of HTML document templates and samples to make the creation of your own Web pages and HTML documents a snap.

HomeSite by Nick Bradbury

One of the newer HTML tag editors on the scene—but one that is quickly gaining a large following—is HomeSite, by Nick Bradbury. HomeSite is a pure tag editor that uses an internal browser and a quick interface to external browsers that makes it easy to create HTML documents. Numerous wizards and other advanced functions automate the creation of the latest and most sophisticated HTML elements.

Downloading and Installation

HomeSite 1.2 is a freeware program, and HomeSite 2.0 is the latest released shareware version of this program. (HomeSite 2.5 has been recently released in beta; some of its new features are discussed later in this chapter.) An evaluation copy of HomeSite 2.0, good for 50 executions, and all other versions of the program, can be downloaded from **http://www.dexnet.com/ homesite.html**.

HomeSite User Interface

When you start HomeSite and begin editing a file, you see a screen similar to that shown in Figure 34.13. The HomeSite screen is divided into a number of different areas, all of which provide a different capability to the user.

Part
VII

Ch
34

HTML Speedbar

FIG. 34.13

HomeSite's window is divided into many different areas, each providing a different function.

Document window

Document list

Rulers

Document tabs

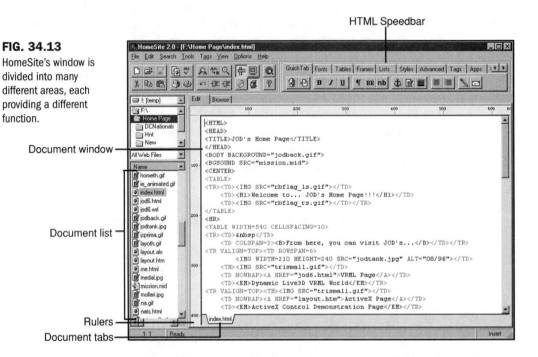

Main Toolbar   The HomeSite main toolbar gives you access to the standard cut/copy/paste and file create/open/save functions, as well as allows you to use some of HomeSite's other functions that can be used to format your document, to do a spelling check on it, and do various other things.

Document Window   The document window has two tabs: Edit and Browse. The edit window is where all of the editing of your HTML document is done. By clicking the Browse tab, you can see what your HTML document looks like, either in HomeSite's default internal browser or by setting HomeSite up to use Internet Explorer as its internal browser. (You'll learn how to do this later in this section.)

Document List   The document list, along the left side of the HomeSite window, can be configured to show all of the HTML documents, image files, both, or all of the files in the current directory. Any of the HTML documents can then be opened and edited in the document window of HomeSite by double-clicking them.

HTML Speedbar   The heart of HomeSite's HTML tag editing capabilities rests primarily in its HTML Speedbar. This is a tabbed toolbar with 10 predefined and 6 customizable tabs. Each of the predefined tabs has buttons for inserting a given category of HTML tags into your documents. The 10 predefined tabs (some of which are not displayed by default—see the HTML Speedbar section for details) are that follows:

- ■ **QuickTab:** This tab contains buttons for some of the most used HTML tags.
- ■ **Fonts:** The buttons available on this tab control the HTML text formatting tags.

- **Tables:** HTML tables can be inserted and edited through the button on this tab.
- **Frames:** The buttons on this tab can be used to set up an initial frameset and configure each of the frames within it.
- **Lists:** Using these buttons, HTML lists can be set up and list items can be defined.
- **Styles:** HTML style sheets can be created, edited, and included in your HTML document through the buttons on the Styles tab.
- **Advanced:** Including some advanced HTML elements—such as scripts, Java applets, and ActiveX Controls—can be done by using these buttons.
- **Tags:** This tab gives you access to a drop-down, scrollable list of all of the HTML tabs that HomeSite supports.
- **ASP:** The buttons in this tab are used to place server comments and commands into your documents.
- **CFML:** This tab gives you access to functions for interacting with the Cold Fusion product.

Document Tabs   The document tabs along the bottom of the document window tell you which HTML documents you have open. You can select the current document by clicking one of the tabs. If you have changed the file and haven't saved your changes, HomeSite indicates this by placing a red box next to the file name on the tab.

Rulers   The rulers can be placed in or removed from your document window by selecting the View, Rulers menu item. These rulers aren't terribly helpful in Edit mode, but they can be used with the internal browser to find out what your HTML document will look like when viewed with a Web browser or other HTML document viewer set at a given screen width.

Basic HomeSite Operations

If you'd like, you can create and edit HTML documents within the HomeSite document window by simply typing in all of your HTML tags by hand. In this case, you only know you are in an HTML tag editor by the fact that your HTML tags appear in different colors, depending on their type (and even that can be turned off).

But, of course, the real power of HomeSite comes in taking advantage of its many features for inserting HTML tags into your documents and setting the attributes of these tags. All HTML 3.2 tags, as well as all of the Microsoft and Netscape extensions, are understood by HomeSite and can be inserted. Also, HomeSite has some advanced features for inserting some of the more sophisticated HTML constructs.

General HTML Formatting   There are two ways to easily add HTML tags, and their contents, by using HomeSite. The first way is to click the button for that HTML tag, which places the opening and closing tags—or a single tag if it is not a container tag—into the document at the current cursor position and leaves the cursor between them, ready to input the contents. Or, you can enter and highlight the contents first, and then press the button.

Part

VII

Ch

34

For many of the HTML tags HomeSite supports, a variety of buttons can be selected to enter the elements in a few different ways. For instance, there are four ways to enter an HTML table by using the buttons in the Tables tab of the HTML Speedbar:

■ Call HomeSite's Table Wizard (described in the next section).

■ Add <TABLE> tags, or the tags for table rows, columns, or headers, by calling a dialog box in which the attributes are set and the contents are included and then are placed directly into the document.

■ Click buttons that simply add empty tags for the table, its rows, columns, or headers. Then, the contents of the tags and their attributes can be set by hand (or by right-clicking the cursor within the tag, which is described later in this section).

■ Use the Quick Table button to quickly enter the tags for an HTML table anywhere from 1×1 to 12×6 cells large.

In addition to the buttons that can be accessed through the HTML Speedbar, you can also add any HTML tag or any tag attribute by calling up the Tags window. This is done by pressing the Show Tag Selection button on the main toolbar, selecting View, Tag Selection, or pressing Ctrl+E. The Tags window has two tabs, one for tags and one for attributes, as shown in Figure 34.14. You can enter any of these into your document by double-clicking them.

FIG. 34.14

In addition to its many HTML tag buttons, HomeSite gives you access to all recognized HTML tags and attributes through the Tags window.

Special HTML Format Options   HomeSite also includes some special-purpose wizards and editors to make the addition of certain HTML constructs a lot easier. These include the following:

■ **List Editor:** Called up by selecting Tools, List Editor or pressing Shift+Ctrl+L, this editor allows you to easily add either an ordered or unordered list to your HTML document.

■ **Table Wizard:** The Table Wizard is called up by selecting Tools, Table Wizard or pressing Shift+Ctrl+T, and gives you an easy, step-by-step process to design and create HTML tables.

■ **Frame Wizard:** Called up by selecting Tools, Frame Wizard or pressing Shift+Ctrl+W, the Frame Wizard gives you an easy way to create an HTML document that uses frames. The syntax for using frames in HTML is fairly confusing if you haven't used them much, so the Frame Wizard's capability to completely specify a frameset and individual frame format, size, and contents, without needing to know any of the HTML syntax, is helpful (see Figure 34.15).

FIG. 34.15
The HomeSite Frame Wizard allows framesets and individual frames to be set up and filled very easily.

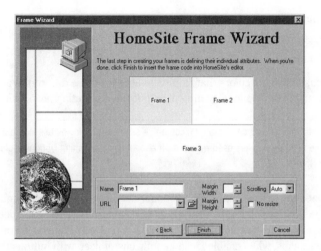

TROUBLESHOOTING

I've used the HomeSite Frame Wizard to create an HTML document using frames, but I don't see anything in the Browse window? HomeSite's internal browser is a great way to take a quick look at what your HTML documents will look like in a Web browser, but it does have limitations. One of these limitations is that it doesn't support frames. There are two ways to get around this. The first is, if you have Internet Explorer 3.01 or later installed in your system, you can configure HomeSite to use that as its internal browser (how to do this is explained in the Configuration and Customizing section immediately following). Then, any HTML tag that Internet Explorer understands will appear correctly. Otherwise, you can configure any other frames-capable Web browser as an external browser in HomeSite and use the Open in External Browser button on the main toolbar to view your document.

Configuration and Customizing

HomeSite is highly configurable, which allows you to maximize your productivity when editing HTML documents within it. You can create your own custom buttons and tags, and otherwise change the appearance of HomeSite to suit your needs.

Fonts and Colors HomeSite automatically color codes your HTML documents when they are loaded into the document window. The following types of tags and information can be set up to be given their own, unique colors:

- Images
- Anchors
- Tables
- Quotes

Part
VII

Ch
34

- Comments
- Scripts, objects, and styles
- All other tags and information

You can customize the colors that HomeSite uses for these different types of tags by selecting the Editor tag of the Options, Setting dialog box and selecting new colors.

 TIP If you find this color coding causes an unacceptable slowdown when you use HomeSite, you can decrease the number of colors used or turn it off altogether by selecting Options, Color Coding, Minimal or None.

HTML Speedbar   By selecting the Speedbar tab of the Options, Settings menu, you can see the 16 tabs, 15 of which can be enabled or removed from the HTML Speedbar. Included in this number are the Apps tab and five Custom tabs (nominally named Custom 1 through Custom 5). These six tabs, when enabled, can be fully customized with buttons that you create yourself.

The Apps tab allows you to create buttons that can be used to call any application on your system. For instance, you can set up buttons to call your favorite graphics editing program, the ActiveX Control Pad (if you want to easily add an ActiveX Control or script to your HTML document), or your FTP program to upload files to your Web server. By including the string %CURRENT% in the command line specified for the application, you can call it with the file name of the current document.

The Custom tabs allow you to add buttons to create custom tags or to enter custom text into your HTML documents. For instance, see Figure 34.16, which defines a button to put an <ADDRESS> block into the current HTML document. One of the predefined icons that can be used for the buttons is a little letter, appropriate because this includes an e-mail address (you can also specify a text label for the button). Though the dialog box asks for start and end tags, you don't actually have to add any HTML tags to the text used. After you create the button, when you click it, the material in the Start and End Tag areas are placed at the current cursor position of your document, and the cursor is left between them.

Internet Browser   HomeSite comes with an internal browser that you can use by selecting the Browse tab of the document window. The HomeSite browser is relatively capable, but is not capable of showing some of the more sophisticated HTML constructs, such as frames.

HomeSite can make use of the feature of Microsoft Internet Explorer (version 3.01 or higher) that allows it to be called by other applications. By selecting the Internal Browser tab of the Options, Settings menu, you can check the box to allow HomeSite to use Internet Explorer (if installed on your system) as its internal browser. Then, documents can be shown in all of their HTML glory, as in Figure 34.17 (which, though you obviously can't see it in this screenshot, also played the background MIDI file that is part of the document).

FIG. 34.16
HomeSite gives you five tabs for creating your own custom buttons, and one for setting up custom applications.

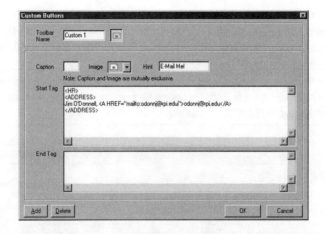

FIG. 34.17
By using Internet Explorer as its internal browser, HomeSite offers you a very good view of how your document will look.

Part
VII

Ch

34

Advanced Features

In addition to the many HTML editing features described in the preceding sections, HomeSite adds some other advanced features to make working with your HTML documents and document sets easier and more productive. Some of these advanced features are described in the following sections.

Projects and Extended Replace   HomeSite has a Projects capability, accessed by selecting File, Projects. This gives you the Projects window, shown in Figure 34.18. Through this window, you can create and delete projects, and add and delete files from these projects.

T I P   To add other file types to the list of those HomeSite recognizes as HTML documents, select the File tab of the Options, Settings menu and add the desired file type. That is how the ALX file type (used for HTML Layouts), shown in Figure 34.18, was added.

FIG. 34.18

HomeSite's Projects window allows you to create projects and assign multiple files to them.

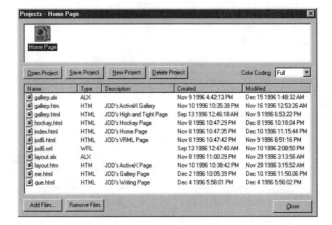

What does the project grouping allow you to do in HomeSite? A few different things. As shown in Figure 34.18, you can easily open all of the HTML files in a project by clicking the Open Project button in the Projects window. Another thing you can do with projects is accessed through the Extended Replace dialog box, by selecting Search, Extended Replace or by pressing Shift+Ctrl+R.

Extended Replace allows you to search and replace blocks of text in multiple HTML documents. You can elect to perform the search and replace in the current document, all open documents, all documents in a given directory, or all documents in a project. As shown in Figure 34.19, this is a good way to change information, such as your e-mail address, that exists in all of the documents in your Web site.

Spell Check   As you might expect in an HTML editor, HomeSite's spell checker, accessed by selecting Tools, Spell Check, pressing the Spell Check toolbar button, or pressing F7, understands HTML commands and is able to check the spelling of the content of your HTML document.

Web Document Publish   HomeSite has an easy interface to Microsoft's Web Publishing Wizard. If you have that product installed on your machine, you can click the Publish Current Document button on the main toolbar and use the wizard to upload your HTML and supporting files to your remote Web server.

FIG. 34.19

The Extended Replace dialog box allows you to search and replace blocks of text through multiple files, including all of those in a project.

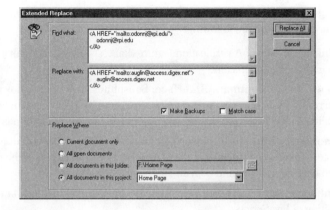

Right-Button Tag Editing One of the nicest capabilities of HomeSite is the context-sensitive pop-up menu it gives you when you right-click the mouse in the document window. As shown in Figure 34.20, the top entry in this menu depends on where your cursor rests within the HTML document. If you are within an HTML tag, the top menu entry gives you the option of editing that tag.

FIG. 34.20

Placing the cursor within any HTML tag and right-clicking the mouse brings up this pop-up menu.

When you select this menu item, or press F3 with the cursor within the HTML tag, you get a dialog box specific to the particular tag. This dialog box gives you the ability to set any and all of the recognized attributes for the tag (see Figure 34.21). In this way, you are relieved of the effort of memorizing what all of the attributes are for each tag, and can set the ones you need for the format you want.

Part

VII

Ch

34

FIG. 34.21

HomeSite's customized HTML tag dialog boxes allow you to set all of the attributes for any given tag.

Upcoming Improvements   In the near future, HomeSite will be upgraded to include numerous new features, including the following:

- **Link Verification:** A verification feature that tests your document's links and lets you change them dynamically.

- **New Custom Command Interface:** Substitutes custom drop-down menus for the current custom buttons to offer quick access to all of your custom tags, including the ability to insert the contents of a file whenever a given menu item is selected.

- **Improved Windows Explorer Interface:** New file management functions, allowing access to file and directory creation, deletion, and renaming on-the-fly, as well as drag-and-drop file moving and copying.

- **Enhanced JavaScript Support:** A new Script Wizard that facilitates the creation and editing of JavaScripts.

- **Improved Extended Replace:** The ability to search and replace text recursively through multiple subdirectories.

Program Information Summary

Table 34.1 summarizes the important information for the three HTML tag editors discussed—where on the Web to get them, what versions are available, and the price.

Table 34.1   Where to Find Popular HTML Tag Editors

	HotDog	HoTMetaL	HomeSite
URL	http://www.sausage.com	http://www.sq.com	http://www.dexnet.com/homesite.html
Versions	Professional 3 16-Bit v2	PRO 3.0 Free Version 2.0	Version 2.0 (2.5 now in beta) Version 1.2 (free)
Free Evaluation?	Yes, 30 Days	Yes, free version only	Yes, 50 uses
Price	$99.95 for either	$159 for PRO version	$39.95 for version 2.0+

Other HTML Editors

The HTML tag editors used as examples in this chapter are just the tip of the iceberg. There are many other freeware, shareware, and commercial products that can be used to create and edit HTML documents. If one of the programs described in this chapter doesn't suit your fancy, there are plenty of places you can look for alternatives.

ActiveX Control Pad

The ActiveX Control Pad is a rudimentary HTML tag editor available free from Microsoft. Its capabilities for editing HTML documents are not very advanced, but it was designed for other things. The ActiveX Control Pad allows you to very easily add and configure ActiveX Controls to your HTML documents, and gives you a WYSIWYG interface to these controls, including the HTML Layout Control. Additionally, it includes a Script Wizard, which gives you a point-and-click way to create sophisticated scripts by using either VBScript or JScript/JavaScript.

▶ **See** "Editing Scripts with the Control Pad's Script Wizard," to see how you can script your Web pages without learning a scripting language, **p. 521**

▶ **See** "Controlling Page Layout with the HTML Layout Control," to find out how to create precise layouts by using the HTML Layout Control, **p. 524**

Web Resources

There are plenty of places on the Web where you can find information about software meant to be used to create and edit HTML documents. Some of the best Web sites for information about HTML tag editors are the following:

- Windows95.com: **http://www.windows95.com**.
- ClNet's Shareware.Com: **http://www.shareware.com**.
- The Ultimate Collection of Winsock Software: **http://www.tucows.com**.
- ZD Net Software Library's Hot Files: **http://www.hotfiles.com**.

## CHAPTER 35

WYSIWYG HTML Editors

by Eric Ladd and Todd Stauffer

When you author an HTML document, all you're really doing is creating a plain text file. In the early days of HTML authoring, a simple text editor like vi (for UNIX) or Notepad (for Windows) was all document authors had to assist them. Later came add-on templates and libraries for existing word processing packages. These allowed users to stick with a familiar interface while giving them special functions to handle the more common authoring tasks. As the HTML standard grew to include more tags, dedicated tag editor programs emerged. These programs have interfaces that are similar to most word processing programs, but are loaded with special options to help set up not only the HTML tags, but the many attributes you can use with the tags to alter their effects. ■

Is "What You See Is What You Get" what you want?

WYSIWYG document editors enable those with little to no knowledge of HTML to do Internet publishing—but not everyone is happy about that.

Better than Gold!

Netscape's new Internet desktop suite, Netscape Communicator, includes a WYSIWYG HTML editor that expands on the capabilities of Netscape Navigator Gold.

An improved FrontPage

Microsoft has upgraded the FrontPage software suite to FrontPage 97—a change that brings many welcome additions to the FrontPage WYSIWYG editor.

Cranking pages through the Mill

Adobe, a prominent figure in Internet publishing, has recently released version 2.0 of its WYSIWYG editor called PageMill.

▶ **See** "What Is an HTML Tag Editor?" **p. 776**

The latest stage in this evolution is the "what-you-see-is-what-you-get" (WYSIWYG) HTML editor. This is something of a misnomer because with these programs you rarely see any HTML code. Rather, you compose the page as you would have it look on a browser screen and the program writes the corresponding HTML. This type of program promises to revolutionize Internet publishing because now all you need to know is how to format text and drag-and-drop objects on a page. The editor takes care of knowing the HTML.

This chapter takes an in-depth look at some of the features of the three most prominent WYSIWYG HTML editors available today. In this chapter, you will learn the basics of how to use the following:

■ Netscape Communicator

■ Microsoft FrontPage 97

■ Adobe PageMill

By considering your own authoring needs and the capabilities of each of these programs, you should be able to make a solid decision on which one to use in your publishing efforts.

A Word About WYSIWYG HTML Editors

For people who don't want to learn HTML or for those who abhor the thought of typing out all those tags longhand, WYSIWYG editors are a blessing. But there's another group that would have you believe that WYSIWYG editors are the scourge of the Internet publishing community. Members of this group are typically folks who have been doing HTML authoring for a (relatively) long time and who are accustomed to coding by hand in a simple text editor.

While lamenting the rapid, forward surge in technology is questionable, part of their argument is valid. WYSIWYG editors are tools that allow anyone, regardless of their HTML proficiency and their knowledge of what constitutes suitable content, to publish a document online. What this means is that you're much more likely to see documents that are poorly designed, that have lewd or self-indulgent content, or that generally have no business being on the Internet. WYSIWYG editors empower everyone to place information on the Internet, and it's important to realize that when everyone gets into the act, the information you see will be less homogeneous than what was there before.

In spite of this, WYSIWYG editors are here to stay, and you're very likely to find yourself using one. If you do, you should not treat it as an excuse to not learn HTML. Indeed, as you work with such an editor, you may find your knowledge of HTML helping you to better use the program. For example, you may look at a dialog box showing the properties of an image on your page and recognize how the controls in the dialog box relate to the different attributes of the <IMG> tag. Once you see the relationships between the program features and HTML, you'll become a smarter and faster user of WYSIWYG software.

Netscape Communicator

Netscape's latest entry in the feverish competition for your Internet desktop is Netscape Communicator—a suite of software that includes the following:

- Netscape Collabra—Collabra allows you to create and participate in online forums that are much like UseNet newsgroups.
- Netscape Composer—an extended version of Netscape Navigator Gold, Composer lets you author documents for a corporate intranet, the World Wide Web, and even for electronic mail.
- Netscape Conference—similar to Microsoft's NetMeeting, Conference supports real-time interaction between users through shared documents, a common whiteboard, and chat channels.
- Netscape Messenger—Messenger is Netscape's new e-mail client that is completely compatible with open standards while being tightly integrated with Composer, allowing you to create HTML-based e-mail.
- Netscape Navigator 4.0—Netscape's popular browser, updated with a highly customizable interface and even stronger support for Java, JavaScript, and embedded objects.

When you fire up Netscape Communicator, you'll see the screen shown in Figure 35.1. Note the floating toolbar you see in the figure. Using this toolbar, you can switch quickly from your browser to your inbox (Messenger), your discussion groups (Collabra), or your WYSIWYG editor (Composer). If you find that the toolbar is getting in your way, click the Netscape logo on the toolbar to minimize it. The minimized toolbar will still be available to you at the bottom of whatever Netscape window you have open.

 You can move the floating toolbar by clicking the ridged bottom-left corner of the toolbar and dragging it to where you want it to be. You can also right-click this corner to reveal a context-sensitive menu that lets you change the orientation (horizontal or vertical) of the toolbar and whether or not the toolbar is always in front of your Netscape window.

The balance of this section focuses on Netscape Composer—the WYSIWYG tool you can use to create and publish Internet documents.

Part
VII

Ch
35

Floating toolbar

FIG. 35.1

Netscape Communicator opens up the Navigator 4.0 browser by default.

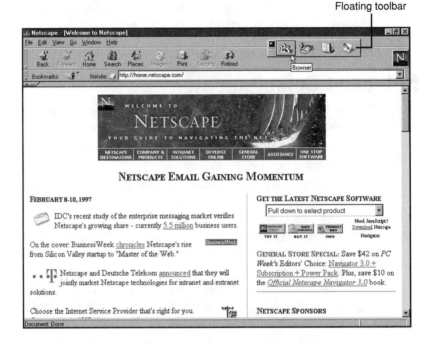

Getting Started

You have a number of different ways to get started with Netscape Composer. From the File menu, you can choose the New Page or Open Page options. Holding your mouse pointer over New Page reveals a drop-down list of three different ways to start a new document. These are:

- Start with a blank page (Blank).
- Create a new page from an existing template (From Template).
- Create a new page using a Page Wizard (From Wizard).

Selecting the blank page opens up the Composer window with nothing in it. Choosing the template option causes a second instance of the Navigator to start and open up a template's page on Netscape's Web site. If you opt for the Page Wizard, you also get sent to Netscape's site—this time to Netscape's online Page Wizard that walks you through the creation of a page.

N O T E   When you choose the Page Wizard, a second instance of Netscape Navigator does not launch like it does with the Templates option. ■

Also, under the File menu is the Open Page option. When you select this, you'll see the dialog box shown in Figure 35.2. Here you can enter the URL of an online document you want to edit or the directory path and file name of a local document. If you want to edit the document, and not just view it, be sure you've clicked the radio button next to the word Editor.

FIG. 35.2
You can open a remote or local document in either your Netscape browser or editor.

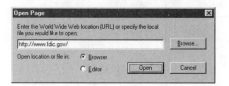

Another way you can start your editing session with Composer is to choose the Composer option from under the Window menu. When you do, you'll see the choices shown in Figure 35.3. These options essentially replicate the ones available to you under the File menu.

FIG. 35.3
Before the Composer window opens, the Create New Page dialog box prompts you for what kind of document you want to start with.

Your final option for getting started is to click the Web Page Composer button on the floating toolbar. This launches the Composer with a blank page, as shown in Figure 35.4.

Building Your Document

With the Composer open one way or another, you're ready to author your document. Composer supports you in this activity in a host of different ways. The next several sections show you how to take care of the following authoring tasks:

- Formatting text, both at the character and paragraph levels
- Placing graphics in your document
- Linking text and images to other documents
- Creating HTML tables
- Calling up a document's basic properties

Part
VII

Ch
35

FIG. 35.4

For a quick start with a blank page, just click the Composer button on the Netscape floating toolbar.

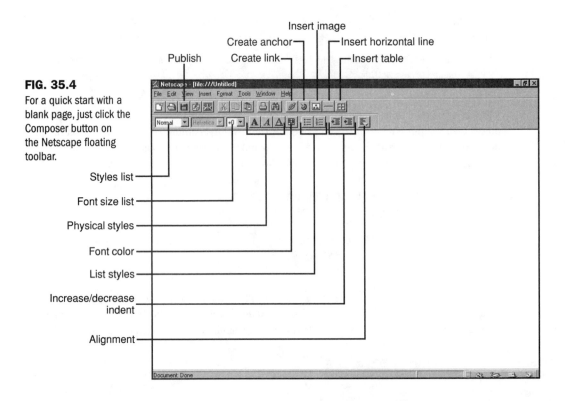

Publish

Create link

Create anchor

Insert image

Insert horizontal line

Insert table

Styles list

Font size list

Physical styles

Font color

List styles

Increase/decrease indent

Alignment

Formatting Text Placing and formatting text with Composer is as easy as it is with just about any word processor. To get some text in the Composer window, click your mouse pointer at the position you want the text to begin and type away. The words you see will be in the default type size, face, and color.

Modifying text you type in is just a matter of highlighting it (passing the cursor over the text while holding down the left mouse button) and applying the effect you want. You can apply text effects in many ways. Referring to Figure 35.4, you'll note the Composer Format toolbar. The first drop-down list on the toolbar contains the six heading levels, preformatted text, address, list item, and description text styles. The Normal+ style adds some extra line spacing to the Normal style, creating a little extra white space above and below the text.

Following the styles drop-down list is the font drop-down list, from which you can choose in which typeface the highlighted text should appear. The small drop-down list to the right of the font drop-down list is for changing the font size. Selecting positive values increases the size, while selecting negative values decreases it.

The next three buttons on the Format toolbar apply bold, italics, and underline styles, respectively, to highlighted text. The button immediately to the right of the underline style button lets you change the color of highlighted text from its default black. When you click this button, you get the Color dialog box, from which you can choose one of the available colors in the palette or define a custom color for your text.

Formatting at the paragraph level also happens from the Format toolbar. You can format a block of text as a bulleted or numbered list, increase or decrease indent levels, and set left, right, or center alignment with the rightmost buttons on the toolbar. All of these formatting options are available to you from the Format menu as well. In fact, if you choose Format, Paragraph, you'll get a few extra styles—Title and Block Quote—that aren't available anywhere on the toolbar.

Placing Graphics   Graphic elements help break up your page and prevent it from becoming an unattractive sea of text. Even a simple horizontal line can go a long way toward making a document more readable. To add a horizontal line, just place your cursor where you want the line to go and either click the Insert Horizontal Line button on Composer's upper toolbar (the Compose toolbar) or choose the Horizontal Line option from under the Insert menu.

By default, a horizontal line will reach all the way across the page, be two pixels high, and have a three-dimensional shading effect. You can change any of these attributes of the line by right-clicking your mouse pointer on the line and selecting the Horizontal Line properties option from the context-sensitive menu you see. In the resulting dialog box, you can adjust the line's height, width, and shading. Also, if you reduce the line's width, so that it no longer reaches all the way across the screen, you can change the alignment so that the line appears either flush left or flush right.

Graphics also include images, of course, and Composer makes it almost as easy to place an image as it is to place a horizontal line. By clicking the Insert Image button on the Compose toolbar or by choosing Insert, Image, you get the dialog box shown in Figure 35.5. Here you specify the location of the image, as well as a low resolution version of the image, a text alternative to the image, how the image should be aligned, how much space to leave around the image, whether or not the image should have a border and how big that border should be, and the height and width of the image. You can also choose to edit the image if you've set up a default image-editing program in the Composer preferences.

N O T E   If you choose to make the image float in the left or right margin with text wrapping around it, you'll have to view the page in the browser window, as Composer's display does not support this feature. █

N O T E   Including a text alternative for every image is an important service to users whose browsers don't support images or to those with images turned off. █

T I P   It's a good idea to click the Original Size button and check the box next to Lock width/height. This way the browser won't try to change the size of the image—something that browsers don't do very well. If you need an image to be bigger or smaller, your best bet is to make the change in an image editor.

FIG. 35.5

The Image Properties dialog box gives you very fine control over placement and appearance of images.

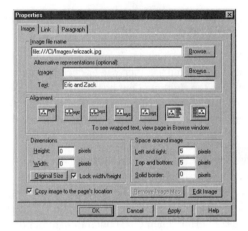

If you ever need to change the attributes of an image after you've placed it, just right-click the image and select the Image properties option from the pop-up menu you see. This will return you to the Properties dialog box you saw in Figure 35.5, where you can make the desired changes.

Setting Up Hyperlinks   Linked documents are a hallmark of the Web, and Netscape Composer makes it easy for you to set up links on both words (hypertext) and images (hypergraphics). If the text you want to convert to hypertext is already on the page, simply highlight it and click the Make Link button on the Compose toolbar or choose Insert, Link. What you'll see next is the dialog box shown in Figure 35.6. The text you highlighted is shown in the Link Source section of the box. All you need to do to complete the link is furnish the URL of the document you're linking to and any anchors you're targeting within that document.

N O T E   If you just click the Make Link button or choose Insert, Link without selecting any text, there will be an empty field in the dialog box where you can type in the link text. ■

Setting up a link on an image is just as simple. First, click the image to select it and then click the Make Link button or choose Insert, Link. This time you'll see the path to the image file in place of the text you're linking. Again, all you need to supply is the URL of the target document and any named anchors you might be using.

Set the border around a linked image to zero pixels if you don't want a colored border around a linked graphic.

Using Tables   It used to be that coding HTML tables was one of the most tedious jobs an author could encounter. But now with WYSIWYG tools, composing tables becomes an easy matter because you can do it right on-screen, and the editor writes out all of the tags for each cell and row. To insert a table with Netscape Composer, click the Insert Table button on the Compose toolbar or choose the Table option under the Insert menu. You'll then see the Table Properties dialog box shown in Figure 35.7. On the Table tab of this box, you can set up the basic configuration of the table—the number of rows and columns, how wide and tall it should be, whether or not it should have a caption, and how it is aligned on the page. Once you choose the parameters you want, clicking OK puts a skeleton of the table you designed on the page.

FIG. 35.6

The Link Properties dialog box shows the text or image that you're linking and the document you're linking to.

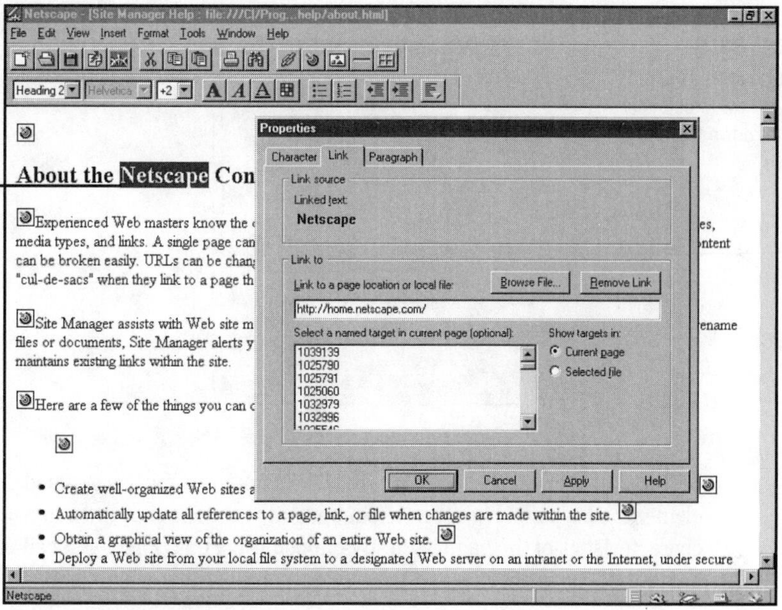

Highlighted text

FIG. 35.7

You begin an HTML table in Composer by specifying the global attributes of the table.

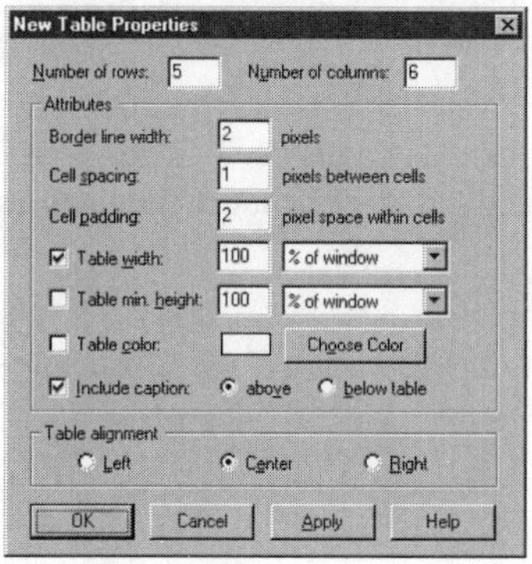

Once you have all of your data entered into the table, you can go to work on getting row and cell properties the way you want them. To change the attributes of a row, right-click anywhere in the row, choose the Table Properties option, and select the Row tab. From here you can set vertical and horizontal alignment and the background color of cells in the row. Similarly, you can right-click a cell, choose Table Properties, and select the Cell tab to change vertical and horizontal alignment, background color, text wrapping, use of the column heading style, spanning characteristics, and the height and width of the cell (see Figure 35.8).

FIG. 35.8
You have full control over how a table looks right down to the cell level.

Setting Page Properties   All of the discussion thus far has focused on setting up different elements on a page. However, it's important to realize that you can use Composer to set up characteristics of the page itself. By choosing Format, Page, you call up the dialog box you see in Figure 35.9. From here, you can select from the following tabs:

- General—This tab contains fields for specifying the document's title, author, description, keywords, and classification. The title information you supply is what appears between the <TITLE> and </TITLE> tags. The rest of the information is stored in <META> tags and can be used by Web robots to index your document.

- Appearance—Background colors and images and link colors are specified on this tab. You can configure your own color scheme or choose from several predefined color schemes.

- Advanced—If you need to set up your own <META> tags, or if you want to specify Netscape system variables (<META> tag with HTTP-EQUIV attribute), you can do so from this tab.

FIG. 35.9

Don't forget to title your document! It's an important service to readers and to programs trying to index your page.

Publishing Your Document

When you're satisfied with your document, and it's time to publish it, Composer can help you with that, too—even if you're publishing to a remote server!

N O T E Composer will prompt you to save your document before publishing it. This way, you can be assured that you're publishing your most recent changes. ■

Setting Publishing Options If you're going to be publishing a lot of documents to a remote machine, you should take a moment to set up Composer publishing preferences. To do this, choose Edit, Preferences, Editor Preferences to call up the dialog box you see in Figure 35.10. The tab you're interested in is the Publish tab.

FIG. 35.10

Composer supports remote publishing via FTP and can automatically change your pages to work on the remote machine.

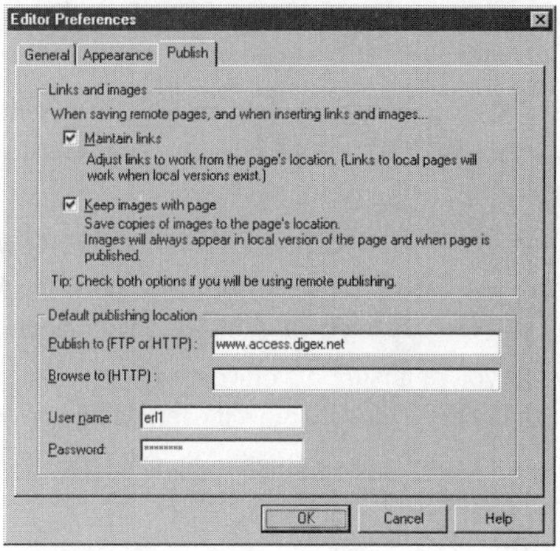

The tab is divided into two parts. The upper part deals with how links and images are treated during the transfer. Checking the Maintain links box tells Composer to change the HTML code as it publishes it so that the links you created will work on the remote machine. The Keep images with page option will send copies of all images on the page to the same directory that you save the page in. A good rule of thumb is to keep both of these checked. Otherwise, you may end up doing a lot of extra work yourself to make links work and to make images show up where they're supposed to be.

The lower half is where you set up your remote login session. Most users will choose the publish-by-FTP option, in which case you need to give the server name or IP address of the remote machine and your login ID and password on that machine.

Sending Your Document to a Remote Server To perform the actual transfer to the remote machine, click the Publish button on the Compose toolbar or choose File, Publish to reveal the Publish Files dialog box. You can choose to send just the file or the file together with other files in the same folder. You can also change the default publishing location if you happen to be publishing to a different machine than the one you set up in your editor preferences. Once you've decided what to publish and to where, click OK to initiate the transfer.

N O T E The preceding sections provide a very basic introduction to Composer. Indeed, we could probably write an entire book on Composer alone! If you want to learn more about Composer, you should visit Netscape's Web site, **http://home.netscape.com/**. In addition to reading the online documentation, you can download Composer from the site, install it on your machine, and experiment with it yourself—perhaps the best learning experience of all! ▪

Microsoft FrontPage 97

Microsoft has updated its Web development suite FrontPage to be compatible with the Office 97 suite and Windows 97. Together with Internet Explorer, FrontPage provides a total Web site creation solution that includes the following components:

- FrontPage Explorer—With the Explorer you can set up a structure for a site (called a Web in FrontPage vernacular) and use the Explorer's different views to get complete information about the site.
- FrontPage Editor—The Editor is the WYSIWYG part of FrontPage.
- Microsoft Image Composer—New to the FrontPage family, the Microsoft Image Composer is a utility you can use to do simple manipulations on graphics and images.
- TCP/IP Test Utility—If you're unsure of your network connection, the FrontPage TCP/IP test can run a quick check to let you know if everything is working correctly.
- FrontPage Web Server—FrontPage's CGI-compliant Web server lets you test your site locally before you make it live.

This section of the chapter will focus mainly on the FrontPage Explorer and Editor, since these are the components you'll use to set up sites and create documents. Other FrontPage components are considered briefly.

The FrontPage Explorer

When you start FrontPage Explorer, you will see the screen shown in Figure 35.11. The two major areas of the window provide two very different ways of looking at a Web. With no Web loaded, the Explorer window is largely empty, so your first step is to give yourself something to work with.

> **CAUTION**
>
> Before you start working on a Web, make sure you have a Web server program running. The Web Server that comes bundled with FrontPage is fine for this purpose.

FIG. 35.11

At startup, the FrontPage Explorer displays the Hyperlink View of a Web site.

Hyperlink view —

Folder view —

Links to images —

Repeated links —

Links within document —

Launch editor —

To do list —

Launch image composer —

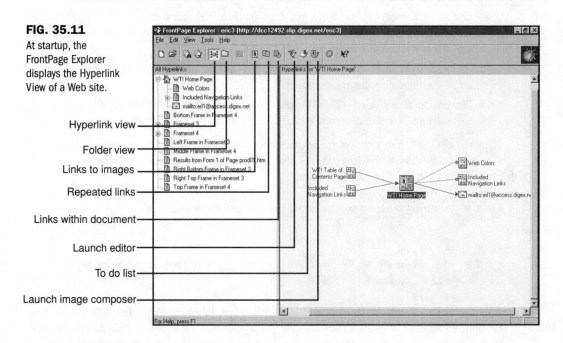

Creating a New Web To start a new Web, choose File, New, FrontPage Web or click the New FrontPage Web toolbar button. You will then see the New FrontPage Web dialog box, from which you can choose one of six Web templates or one of three Web wizards. These include:

- Normal Web—This simple Web is made up of only one page. You can make this page a home page and build the rest of the Web around it.

Part **VII**

Ch **35**

- Customer Support Web—If you're planning to provide customer support over the Internet, you may wish to investigate this Web, which is especially useful for companies supporting software products.

- Empty Web—Choose this option to start completely from scratch. An Empty Web is useful if you have a preexisting page done in the Editor or in another authoring program and want to incorporate it into a Web.

- Personal Web—The Personal Web is much like the average person's resume. It has information fields and hypertext links that you can customize or delete as you please.

- Project Web—Corporate intranet users can put project management online with the Project Web. The Web helps to track individual tasks and progress toward the goals of the project.

- Learning FrontPage—If you're just learning FrontPage, or if you want to make online support available to those who are, you can use the Learning FrontPage Web to help you attain your goal.

- Corporate Presence Wizard—By walking you through several dialog boxes, this Wizard collects information that is typically found on a corporate Web site and builds a Web with the responses you provide.

- Import Web Wizard—You can use this wizard to create a Web from existing documents on your computer or from a remote machine.

- Discussion Web Wizard—This Wizard also takes you through a series of dialog boxes that create a Web to support threaded discussions and a full-text search.

If you're creating a Web with a purpose that's consistent with one of the templates or Wizards, then you should choose the appropriate one. To begin with a blank page that you can place content on, select the Normal Web option.

N O T E The Normal Web template is the default choice when creating a new Web.

N O T E When you create a new Web, you'll be required to supply the network address of your server and a unique name for the Web.

One nice feature FrontPage has is the built-in To Do List. For more complicated Webs, like the Corporate Presence Web, the wizard will ask you if you want the To Do List displayed after the Web is created. If you choose Yes, you'll see the screen shown in Figure 35.12. The List tracks what pages need work, who had responsibility for them, and what level priority the work is.

TIP You're not limited to using the To Do List for Webs that you create using a FrontPage wizard. You can invoke the To Do List at any time by clicking the Show To Do List button on the Explorer toolbar. Once you call it up, you can add and update tasks on the List as needed.

FIG. 35.12

The FrontPage To Do List tracks unfinished tasks and who is responsible for completing them.

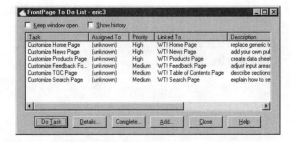

Viewing a Web   Once you have loaded a Web into the Explorer, you can look at it in one of two following ways:

- Hyperlink View—the Hyperlink View is the default Explorer view (refer to Figure 35.11). In this view, you'll see a hierarchical rendition of your Web site on the left-hand side of the window—much the same way as the left-hand side of the Windows Explorer shows you the hierarchical folder structure on your hard drive. If you click a plus sign (+), it expands the hierarchy found below the object with the plus sign. Clicking a minus sign (-) collapses an expanded hierarchy.

  On the right-hand side, you'll see a more graphic portrayal of your site—illustrating with arrows links to other pages within the site and off the site. You can click items whose icons have a plus (+) sign to expand the view further.

  The Hyperlink View makes it easy to see how your documents are linked together, and where you might be missing some critical links. Also, if you're looking for broken links pointed out by the Explorer link checker, this is the view you want to use.

  If you're using a "drill-down" kind of design for your site, the Hyperlink View gives you the best way to look at it. If you're looking for a certain page, you can follow the hierarchy right to it. The outline structure also makes it easy to see the most logical places to insert new pages.

- Folder View—You can switch to the Folder View by clicking the Folder View button on the Explorer toolbar or by selecting View, Folder View. This view more closely resembles the Windows Explorer, showing the folder hierarchy in the left-hand side of the window and document-specific information such as titles, file names and sizes, and last change dates on the right-hand side (see Figure 35.13).

  The Folder View can be handy in a number of situations. The last change date information can tell you how "fresh" information is on a page or whether a person responsible for an update has made the necessary changes. File size information is important for graphics and multimedia files and the Folder View can help you identify files that are too big to be part of your Web.

Part

VII

Ch

35

FIG. 35.13

The Summary View gives you all of the details on all of the component files in a Web site.

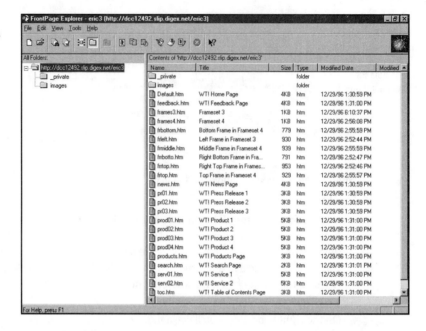

Link Tools   Visiting a Web site that has broken or outdated links can be one of a Web surfer's most frustrating experiences. It's frustrating for the site administrator, too. Keeping track of all links on a large site requires incredible attention to detail.

Keeping track of links to other sites is all but impossible without checking each link individually on a regular basis. Fortunately for both parties, the FrontPage Explorer comes with the following link utilities that help to alleviate these problems:

- Verify Hyperlinks—Choosing Tools, Verify Hyperlinks instructs the Explorer to perform a check on all of the links in your Web, including links to pages that are not on your Web. The Explorer reports its findings back to you in a window like the one you see in Figure 35.14. Links to pages within your site are shown with a red circle and the word "Broken" if they are broken, or are not shown at all if they are working. Links that couldn't be checked are shown with a yellow circle and a question mark in front of them. To verify these links, click the Verify button you see in the dialog box.

  You can verify each external link by selecting it in the window and clicking the Verify button. If an external link is verified, the Explorer places a green circle with the word "OK" in front of the link. If an external link is broken, it gets a red circle with the word "Broken."

- Recalculate Hyperlinks—The Recalculate Hyperlinks command (choose Tools, Recalculate Hyperlinks) updates the displays in each of the three views to reflect any changes made by you or other authors. It also regenerates all dependencies in the open Web. Dependencies are items that are read into a page, like the WebBots discussed later.

FIG. 35.14
You can generate a report on the integrity of all internal and external links by choosing Tools, Verify Hyperlinks.

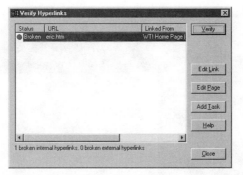

Other Useful Explorer Features   The FrontPage Explorer comes with some other handy features that can make your life as a Web site author much easier. These include the following:

- View Menu Options—The Hyperlinks to Images, Repeated Hyperlinks (multiple links to the same page), and Hyperlinks Inside Page (links from one point to another point on the same page) options under the View menu toggle the display of these types of links on and off. When these options are on, it modifies the three views to show the type of link selected. You can toggle these options from the Explorer toolbar as well.

- Proxy Server Setup—Security is a critical issue to most Webmasters. Consider the recent case of the Central Intelligence Agency Web site that was hacked and modified to contain very offensive content. Because of events like this, many Webmasters choose to set up a proxy server (or firewall) to act as an intermediary between their servers and the rest of the Internet. Choosing Tools, Options opens a dialog box with a Proxies tab where you can specify a proxy server for your Web server.

- Import/Export of Individual Documents—You can import an existing document into the Web you're working on by selecting File, Import. This is what you want to use if you start with an Empty Web and want to incorporate an existing page into it. Likewise, choosing File, Export, exports a selected document so that you can have a stand-alone version of it. Be careful when importing documents though, as some page-element properties may need to be manually edited for FrontPage to recognize them. This is particularly true for images.

With your Web created, it's time to put some content on its component pages. You do this by using the FrontPage Editor—a full-featured, WYSIWYG page composition program.

The FrontPage Editor

When you fire up the FrontPage Editor, you see a WYSIWYG environment in which you can create your Web documents—all without even typing an HTML tag (see Figure 35.15).

Part
VII

Ch
35

N O T E   Veteran HTML authors will be happy to learn that FrontPage 97 allows you to edit HTML code directly, rather than having to open the file in a separate text editor. ▪

FIG. 35.15
The FrontPage 97
Editor is where you
add content to the
documents you set
up in the Explorer.

Starting a New Document   When you select File, New to start a new document, you don't just get a blank screen to work in. Rather, you are given the option to activate one of the Editor's many templates and page creation wizards. Templates give you a structured document with several informational "holes" that you can fill in with appropriate text (see Figure 35.16). Page creation wizards collect information from you through a series of dialog boxes and then use the information you supply to author a page.

Figure 35.17 shows a dialog box from the Frames Wizard—a useful feature for developing framed pages without having to worry about all of those confusing <FRAMESET> tags. There are only a few standard framed layouts to choose from though, so you may not find your desired layout prepackaged in FrontPage. In this case, you'll have to set it up yourself by choosing the Make a custom grid option in the wizard's first dialog box.

The FrontPage Editor comes with three other wizards—Forms Page, Database Connector, and Personal Home Page. The Forms Wizard is quite handy and can spare you much of the drudgery of coding a form. Many common form fields come prepackaged and all you need to do is place them on your form. This isn't very helpful if the prepackaged form fields don't include the types of fields you need, but FrontPage also lets you build a customized form from the ground up. You can pass the form results to a CGI script or you can use the FrontPage Save Results bot to write the form data to a file. Results can be saved in HTML, plain text, or rich text formats.

FIG. 35.16

The Employment Opportunities template gives you a structure into which you can enter the job openings available at your company.

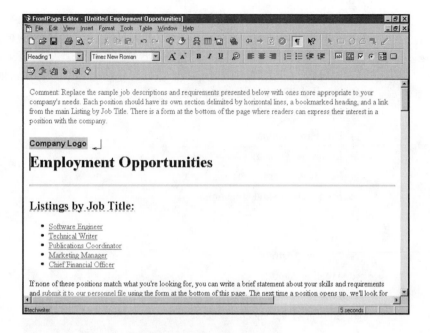

FIG. 35.17

Frames can be simple when you use the FrontPage Editor's Frames Wizard, as long as you're using one of the standard framed layouts.

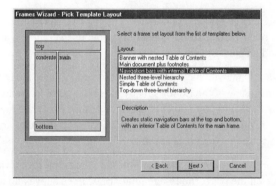

You can set up an interface to an Open Database Connectivity (ODBC) compliant database by using the Database Connector Wizard. Over a series of dialog boxes, you are prompted for the ODBC data source, the template file for the results, and what Structured Query Language (SQL) queries you want to make against the database.

The Personal Home Page Wizard walks you through a sequence of dialog boxes to gather information to create a personal Web page. The personal page FrontPage can generate for you is more like a resume than your average Web page, as it includes page elements like "Employee Information" and "Current Projects." If you want to author a more typical home page, you might want to skip FrontPage's Home Page Wizard.

In addition to the wizards, FrontPage can get you started with more than 20 standard page templates, including the following:

- Bibliography
- Database Results
- Employee Directory
- Feedback Form
- Frequently Asked Questions
- Glossary
- Guest Book
- Lecture Abstract
- Meeting Agenda
- Product Description
- Software Data Sheet
- What's New

Corporate site designers can make good use of a number of these templates. Specifically, press releases and press release directories, guest books, tables of contents, and What's New pages are frequently found on corporate sites.

The Editor Toolbars   Once you have a document started, or have loaded one in from an existing Web, you can make use of the Editor's many useful features to create or change the page. Figure 35.18 shows the Editor with all of its toolbars active. Many are just like the toolbar buttons you would see in other Microsoft Office applications. Others that are more specific to HTML authoring are labeled with callouts in the figure.

Of particular note are the Image toolbar, the Forms toolbar, and the Advanced toolbar. When you select an image on the page, the Image toolbar becomes active and allows you to trace hot regions for imagemaps, or to make a color in the image transparent. The Forms toolbar places form controls at the cursor's position on your page. Using buttons on the Advanced toolbar, you can place ActiveX controls, scripts, embedded objects, a Java applet, or an HTML tag not supported by one of the Editor's menus.

N O T E   You can toggle the display of any of the toolbars under the Editor View menu. ▪

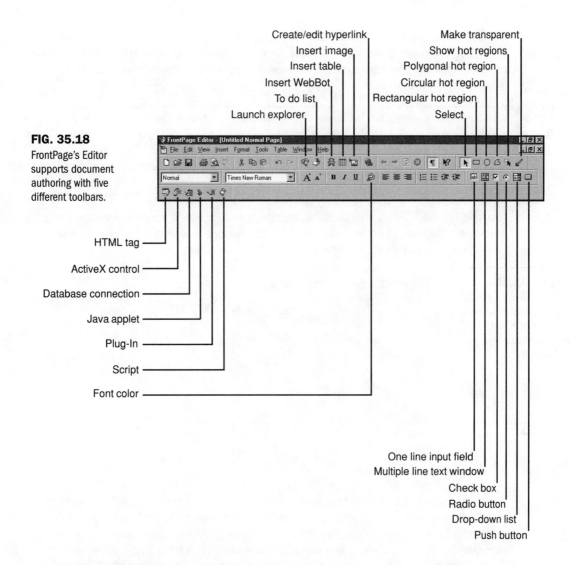

FIG. 35.18
FrontPage's Editor supports document authoring with five different toolbars.

Formatting Text   You can apply styles to text in a variety of ways. The physical styles (bold italics, underline) are available on the toolbar. All you need to do is highlight the text to format and click the appropriate button. The Style drop-down box works similarly and gives you access to a much greater range of styles, including heading and list styles.

To either side of the physical style toolbar buttons are the Increase/Decrease Text Size buttons and the Text Color button, which lets you paint highlighted text with a different color.

For several formatting options at once, select Format, Font and then select the Special Styles tab to reveal a dialog box in which you can click different styles to apply them to highlighted text.

Part
VII

Ch
35

When you want to insert vertical space between page elements and you use the Enter key to do it, it will be interpreted as a paragraph break (or tag) in your HTML code. If you just want a line break (or <BR> tag), you have to insert that manually by choosing Insert, Break and then selecting Normal Line Break.

T I P Some text elements are best handled outside of the Editor. If you have text elements that are common to each page, such as copyright information or a Webmaster e-mail address, you may want to consider copying and pasting these items into your pages, using a plain-text editor like Notepad. The FrontPage Editor can take a long time to load an entire page because it also loads images. A plain-text editor just loads the HTML code and is therefore much faster.

Inserting Images   To place an image on your page, choose Insert, Image to open the dialog box you see in Figure 35.19. In the box, you get the option to load the file from the current Web, a local drive, a remote machine, or from a clip art collection.

FIG. 35.19

You can place images from local or remote sources in your FrontPage Editor document.

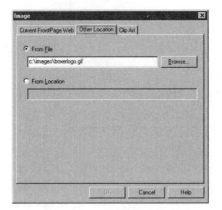

By default, the image is placed at the current cursor location and is left-justified with an ALIGN value of BOTTOM (text next to the image will line up with the bottom of the image). You can exercise greater control over the placement of the image in the image's Properties box. To reveal the image's properties, double-click the image or right-click the image and select the Properties option you see in the context-sensitive pop-up menu. The various tabs in the Image Properties dialog box, shown in Figure 35.20, allow you to specify image alignment, border size, horizontal and vertical spacing, low-resolution, and text alternatives for the image. If the image is hyperlinked, you can also specify what URL it is linked to. There's even a Video tab in case you're placing an AVI movie via the <IMG> tag.

If you need to edit an image that you've placed in a document, you can fire up Microsoft's Image Composer to make the changes. Image Composer is a full-featured graphics editor with support for scanning devices and special effects filters, as well as the more common graphic manipulations.

▶ **See** "Useful Graphics Tools," **p. 360**

FIG. 35.20
An Image Properties dialog box gives you finer control over image attributes.

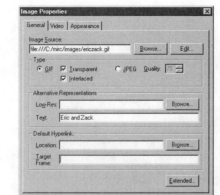

Setting Up Hyperlinks   To create hypertext, highlight the text to serve as the anchor and click the Create or Edit Hyperlink toolbar button. You'll then see a dialog box like the one in Figure 35.21. In the box, you can choose to link to a page that is currently open in the Editor, a page that is part of the Web that you're working on, any page on the World Wide Web, or a page that you ask the Editor to create for you.

FIG. 35.21
The Create Hyperlink dialog box lets you link to files on your site, files out on the Web, or files you have yet to create.

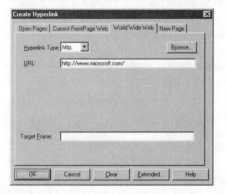

If you need to change the attributes of a link, you can right-click it and select the Hyperlink Properties option from the pop-up menu you see.

To color your links, right-click anywhere on the page and select the Page Properties option to reveal the dialog box you see in Figure 35.22. Options on the Background tab enable you to paint your visited, unvisited, and active links with whatever color you choose.

Part
VII

Ch
35

FIG. 35.22

Items in the Page
Properties dialog box
correspond to tags in
the document head
and attributes of the
<BODY> tag.

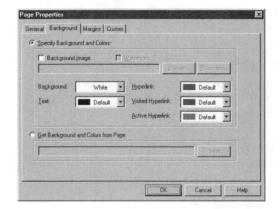

 T I P You can also set up titles, page margins, base URLs and targets, text color, and <META> tags from the
Page Properties dialog box.

Setting up a linked image is virtually the same as setting up linked text. Simply click the image
you wish to link and then click the Create or Edit Link button to open the dialog box you saw in
Figure 35.19. If you're setting up an imagemap, click the image once to select it and then use
the tools on the Image toolbar to set up the different hot regions. After you trace out a hot
region, the Editor will display the same dialog box you saw in Figure 35.19, so you can enter
the URL to associate with the hot region.

N O T E The FrontPage Editor uses client-side imagemaps. If you need to implement a server-side
imagemap, look at the HTML source code to get the hot-region coordinates, and then type
out your map file by hand. ■

Creating Tables To insert a table, choose Table, Insert Table or click the Insert Table toolbar
button. When you do, you'll see a dialog box like the one in Figure 35.23. After entering the
table size and border, alignment, padding, and spacing attributes, the Editor will place a blank
table in your document and you can fill in the cells with text, images, form fields, and even
other tables.

N O T E Most of the options under the Table menu are grayed out unless the cursor is in a table
cell. ■

You can delete the content of individual cells of a table by highlighting them and pressing
Delete, but it is more of a challenge to delete an entire table. Even if you remove all cell contents, FrontPage still leaves you with an empty table on-screen and all of the related table tags
in the HTML code. To remove the entire table, double-click your mouse just to the left of the

table to highlight the whole thing. Once highlighted, you can press Delete or Backspace to remove the entire table from both your screen and your HTML code.

FIG. 35.23

You set up a table in your document by filling out the Insert Table dialog box.

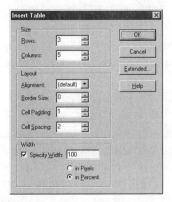

You can color the individual cells in your tables, thanks to HTML extensions now supported by Netscape and Microsoft browser products. To color a cell, right-click inside the cell and choose Cell Properties from the pop-up menu that appears. You can then choose your background color (or image) in the Custom Background section of the dialog box.

 TIP Coloring the individual cells can overstate the "block-like" nature of the cells. To reduce this effect, you may want to color your table cells with the same color you use to color your page background.

N O T E The way FrontPage displays a table is not exactly the same as the way Netscape Navigator or Microsoft Internet Explorer would do it. If you make a substantial change to a table, be sure to look at it in a browser to determine if you've achieved the desired effect. ■

Saving Your Document   To save your document for the first time, select File, Save As to open the dialog box shown in Figure 35.24. Notice that in this box you can save the document as a normal file or as a document template. Clicking OK will save the file to your current Web. If you want to save the page as a separate file, click the As File button and specify the name of the file to save the page to.

FIG. 35.24

When saving for the first time, you can make your document into a template for reuse at a later time.

Part

VII

Ch

35

Using WebBots

WebBots are preprogrammed dynamic objects that run when you save a file or when a user views your file online. The FrontPage Editor comes with several bots that you can build into your pages, including:

- Annotation—The Annotation bot places what is essentially a comment into your HTML code. Site visitors won't be able to see an annotation, but other people editing the annotated document will see it.

- Confirmation Field—To confirm the contents of a key form field, you can build a Confirmation Field bot into the confirmation page.

- HTML Markup—As more and more HTML extensions are introduced, you can use the HTML Markup bot to add nonstandard tags to your documents. FrontPage will not check this HTML for validity, so it's up to you to make sure the HTML code you insert uses proper syntax. The inserted HTML code will appear on the FrontPage Editor screen as a question mark in angle brackets (<?>) that is colored in yellow.

- Include—The Include bot reads in the contents of another file and displays them on the page. This is useful if you're including a standard element on every page, like a mailto link to your Webmaster or a navigation bar. By using the Include bot to place standard items on pages, you can keep these items in one file, and changes made to that file will be enough to make changes throughout your entire site.

- Scheduled Image—If you want an image to appear on a page, but only for a certain amount of time, you can use the Scheduled Image bot to do it. You tell the bot what image to use, when to start displaying it, when to stop displaying it, and what it should display outside of the scheduled period.

- Scheduled Include—The Scheduled Include bot works the same way as the Schedule Image bot, except it displays the contents of another file during the scheduled period.

- Search—The very useful Search bot gives you a simple way to set up full-text searching capabilities on your Web. The bot generates a query form and then does the search based on the user's input. FrontPage lets you specify the prompting text, the width of the input field, and the labels on the submit and reset buttons. You can also customize the search output with a given match's search score, file date, and file size.

- Substitution—A Substitution bot is replaced with the value of a page variable such as Author, ModifiedBy.

- Description, or Page-URL.

- Table of Contents—The Table of Contents bot prepares a table of contents for your site, starting from any page you choose. It will even recalculate the table when pages are edited, if you tell it to do so while setting it up.

- Timestamp—The Timestamp bot is particularly useful if you intend to note the time and date of the most recent changes to a page. The Timestamp bot gives you the choice between the date the page was last updated or the date that the page was last automatically updated.

Bots are unique in that their functionality is built right into FrontPage. This is very different from programming that supports similar functions, as these programs are typically written separate from the coding of the HTML. FrontPage integrates these two activities into one.

NOTE Much of the power of the FrontPage suite is derived from its set of standard bots. Additionally, you can write your own bots by using the FrontPage Software Developer's Kit. ■

Adobe PageMill

When you think of documents, it's logical to also think of the Adobe Corporation—the folks who brought us programs like PageMaker and the Internet document format PDF (Portable Document Format). It shouldn't surprise you then that Adobe has an entry in the WYSIWYG Web document editor field. Adobe PageMill is an easy-to-use document authoring tool with many neat features, including the ability to manipulate images without using a separate utility program.

The PageMill Window

With PageMill, you have a point-and-click, drag-and-drop, mousing-about interface to help you in your document authoring—much like you'd have with a word processor (see Figure 35.25).

FIG. 35.25
All HTML coding is accomplished through the PageMill interface elements.

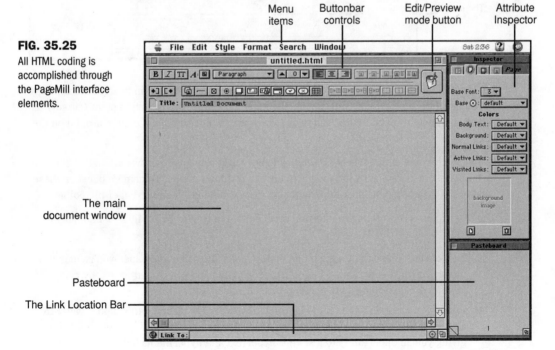

Menu items · Buttonbar controls · Edit/Preview mode button · Attribute Inspector

The main document window

Pasteboard

The Link Location Bar

Part
VII

Ch

35

The PageMill window is the heart of the program...it's where you'll type all your text (or paste it in from another program) and position your multimedia elements. The window is very drag-and-drop aware, so often you'll be able to simply drag text or graphics from their original program into the PageMill window. In certain cases, you can even drop the icon of a document or graphic file into the PageMill window, and the image or text will appear in the PageMill window (see Figure 35.26).

FIG. 35.26
Drag-and-drop is a big improvement over the raw HTML method of entering graphics.

Dropping the image places the picture

Dragging the image to PageMill

The image file's icon

For the most part, however, you'll use the PageMill document window in nearly the same way as you use a word processor. You can use the mouse to place your insertion point (cursor) on the page, highlight text for some action or to pick up graphics, and move them around on the page.

You may have noticed the PageMill window looks a little like a Web browser. That's been done on purpose. The document window is actually two windows in one. To change between these windows in PageMill, you click the Toggle Preview Mode button on the PageMill toolbar.

The two windows represent two different modes that really alter PageMill's functionality drastically:

- Edit mode—When the toggle mode button looks like a pen and paper, you're in edit mode. This is the mode that PageMill needs to be in so you can enter text by using the keyboard, make changes to text appearance, and add graphics.
- Preview mode—Now the toggle button looks like a 3-D globe. In this mode, PageMill acts more like a browser, allowing you to see how your pages will look on the Web while giving you an opportunity to test your hypertext and hypermedia links.

N O T E If you use the File, Open command in PageMill to open an existing HTML document,
PageMill starts out in Preview mode. Click the toggle mode button to edit the document.
New documents start in Edit mode. ▣

The PageMill Toolbar

The toolbar is where you'll find a lot of the common tools that you'll need to use in creating
your Web page. Not everything that's possible with HTML is available from the toolbar—many
commands are buried in the menus—but you'll find a lot of everyday stuff is right up front, just
like in your favorite word processing program (see Figure 35.27).

FIG. 35.27

The PageMill toolbar
can be used to
accomplish many
common Web authoring
tasks.

One important toolbar button deserves special mention. More than one PageMill-experienced
Web author has missed something fairly obvious at the bottom of the toolbar…the Title field.

Giving your Web documents a title is an important part of creating the page. Titles appear in
the bar at the top of a user's Web browser window. They are also used as entries in bookmark
lists and are scanned by robots that index your pages. Unfortunately, for some reason, a lot of
folks skip over it when creating pages in PageMill. Try to keep in mind the title textbox is
there. All you have to do to give your page a title is click in the textbox and type away.

The toolbar has one other special feature worth mentioning now. At the bottom-left corner of
the toolbars, right next to the title textbox, is the page icon. It doesn't look like much, but it's at
the heart of creating links in your PageMill documents.

In edit mode, move the mouse pointer up to the page icon, click it and drag (holding down the
mouse button). Notice the page icon comes along for the ride. What you're holding with the
mouse is a hyperlink to this particular document.

If you were working in another document, you'd be able to drag this page icon directly to the
other document, drop it in that document window, and create a link to this page. It's that
simple.

N O T E Actually, it's not quite that simple. There's one other factor—the page represented by the
page icon needs to be saved before the page icon is active. ▣

The Link Location Bar

Down at the bottom of the page is the heart of PageMill's hyperlink abilities…the link location
bar. It's here that you'll enter URLs for your hyperlinks.

Part
VII

Ch
35

N O T E You need to be in Edit Mode to place a hyperlink. ▦

The link location bar actually performs two different functions, depending on the current mode:

- Edit mode—In edit mode, you use the link location bar to enter URLs for hyperlinks. To create a link, you'll usually highlight text (or select an image) with the mouse, and then enter the URL for the link by typing it in the link location bar.

- Preview mode—In preview mode, the link location bar is primarily used to show you the URLs for the links on the page. Notice the link location bar changes to show you the associated URL when you move the mouse pointer over a hyperlink.

The Attribute Inspector

If you can't get something done with PageMill's toolbar, chances are that you'll find it in the Attribute Inspector. The Inspector is easily the most powerful element of the PageMill interface, allowing you to do everything from changing typefaces to adding background images to your Web pages to managing the HTML forms you create for user feedback (see Figure 35.28).

 T I P You can toggle the Attribute Inspector on and off by pressing command (Apple) + ; (semicolon) or by choosing the command Show Attribute Inspector or Hide Attribute Inspector in the Window menu.

FIG. 35.28

The Attribute Inspector uses different modes to change its options based on the type of element you need to alter—the Web page itself, text on the page, graphics, or form data.

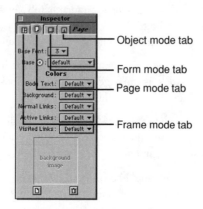

Object mode tab
Form mode tab
Page mode tab
Frame mode tab

The Attribute Inspector is a small floating window that's based on the idea that you'll use it in different modes depending on the elements you need to change. Those modes are:

- Page attributes—Clicking the Page mode button gives you a variety of options that relate to how the overall Web page will appear to viewers. Options include things like adding a background graphic to your page and changing the text color.

- Text attributes—Click the Text mode button and you are given the choice of changing highlighted text into nearly any conceivable HTML format.

■ Graphic/Form (Object) attributes—This mode button is only available if you've selected a graphic or form element (like a text box) in the document window. Then, pressing the button gives you options based on what you selected. For graphics, you'll get the opportunity to alter the height and width, enter ALT text, or add a border (see Figure 35.29). For form elements you can give the field a variable name, choose the size for the element, or enter other form-related attributes.

FIG. 35.29
Most HTML options for images are available right from the Attribute Inspector.

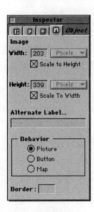

The Image Viewer

Adobe's experience with graphics comes shining through in the PageMill Image Viewer. From within your document you can view images, choose a transparent color in a GIF, and even create clickable imagemaps.

There's only one question: How do you find the Image Viewer? The answer is simple: If you've placed an image in the document window, make sure you're in Edit mode and then just double-click the image (see Figure 35.30).

 On a PC, you can use the File, Open command to open an image directly into the Image Viewer, without placing it in the document. On a Macintosh, File/Open is Command+O.

We could fill an entire chapter with information on how to use the Image Viewer, but space constraints compel us to just look quickly at an overview of the Image Viewer's capabilities:

■ Creating imagemaps—Imagemaps are graphics that are mapped with different "hot regions," which are mapped to different URLs. Click a certain part of a graphic, and you'll head off toward one Web page; click another and you'll load a multimedia file or a help page. This is the technology used on a lot of Web sites to create clickable interfaces.

■ Transparency—The Image Viewer has the ability (when dealing with GIF files) to turn a particular color of the image transparent (usually the background color). This gives the impression the graphic is sitting directly on the page—a popular effect on most Web documents.

Part
VII

Ch

35

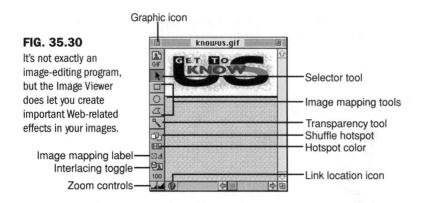

Graphic icon

FIG. 35.30

It's not exactly an image-editing program, but the Image Viewer does let you create important Web-related effects in your images.

Image mapping label
Interlacing toggle
Zoom controls

Selector tool
Image mapping tools
Transparency tool
Shuffle hotspot
Hotspot color
Link location icon

- Image linking—In contrast to imagemaps, it's also possible to make an entire image point at just one URL. The image becomes a hyperlinked "button" of sorts.

- Interlacing—The GIF file format is also capable of being saved in a special way, called "interlacing." This allows many Web browsers to gradually display the image as it is transferred across the Internet. An interlaced GIF appears to "fade" onto a page over the course of several passes.

Another of the Image Viewer's special features is the image icon located at the top left of the viewer window. It's another neat little tool that you can use for drag-and-drop to your HTML pages.

If you've loaded a graphic directly into the Image Viewer and you'd like to place that graphic on a Web page you're creating in PageMill, click the Arrow tool in the Image Viewer. Then, click and drag the image icon into the document window of the destination page. Drop the image on the page, and it should appear now as part of the new Web page.

The Pasteboard

One final key interface element is the Pasteboard, which you can access on a PC by choosing Window, Show Pasteboard; on a Macintosh, choose Command+/. Basically the Pasteboard works like the Clipboard in Windows or Mac—it's designed to aid in cut-and-paste. But, it's also something that the Clipboard never has been. It's easy to use with multiple images, clips of text, and HTML elements (see Figure 35.31).

FIG. 35.31

The Pasteboard gives you the freedom to keep common elements, graphics, or text clips handy for quick drag-and-drop operations.

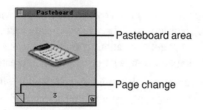

Pasteboard area

Page change

Aside from drag-and-drop support and the ability to store different types of elements on the same page, the Pasteboard also features five different pages for you to work with. Clicking the page controls at the bottom of the Pasteboard window lets you change pages.

TIP Get to know the Pasteboard. You'll be amazed by how quickly things go when you don't have to open a new image or retype text when you're authoring multiple Web pages.

You've probably gathered from the discussion of the PageMill interface that many common document authoring tasks—like formatting text or placing an image—are pretty easy with PageMill. And you would be correct! PageMill's word processor-like interface and drag-and-drop capabilities make authoring a snap. For this reason, you'll focus on the more advanced document components—tables, forms, and frames— for the rest of the chapter.

Creating Tables

Creating the initial table in PageMill is the easy part. First, place the insertion point (cursor) at the point in your document where you want the table to appear. Then, from PageMill's toolbar, click and hold the Insert Table icon. While you hold down the mouse button, drag down and to the right. You should see an expanding grid that appears to grow out of the Insert Table icon. When the table reaches the dimensions you desire, let go of the mouse button. PageMill will create the table and place it in your document window (see Figure 35.32).

FIG. 35.32
PageMill's Insert Table command makes it simple to create a table of nearly any size.

Insert table icon —

Grow the grid —

PageMill creates and places the table —

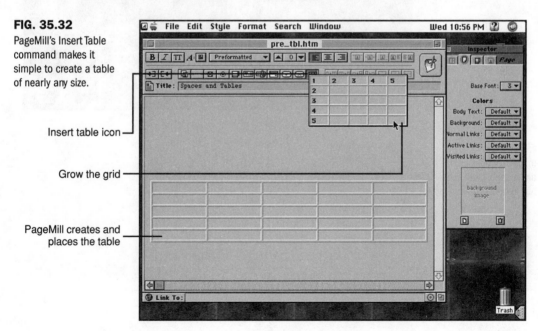

Once you have the table available to you in the document window, there are two things you should notice. First, clicking once on the border of the table selects it as an object and (assuming you have the Attribute Inspector visible) changes the Object tools to those that are relevant for a table.

Second, clicking the interior of a table makes the table active, which allows you to enter data and change the attributes of rows, columns, and individual cells. Once again you'll notice that the Attribute Inspector changes Object tools to reflect this (see Figures 35.33 and 35.34).

FIG. 35.33

The Inspector tools for table-as-object.

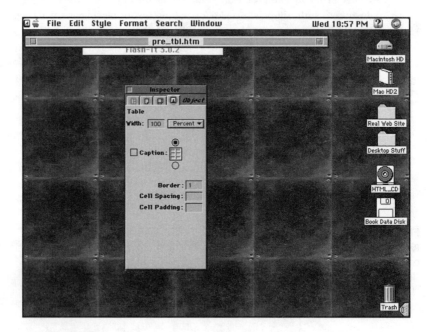

FIG. 35.34

Inspector tools for an active table (with cells highlighted).

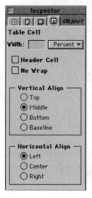

Filling in cells   If you've already made your table active, you probably noticed that one of the cells has a blinking cursor in it. Entering data for this cell is as easy as typing away. Anything alphanumeric is free game (that is, anything you enter on your keyboard should look fine in a cell), and you can even use text-emphasis commands to add some spice to your entries (see Figure 35.35).

 TIP   You can use the Tab key to move right one cell or Shift+Tab to move left one cell.

FIG. 35.35

Entering and emphasiz-
ing text in a table cell.

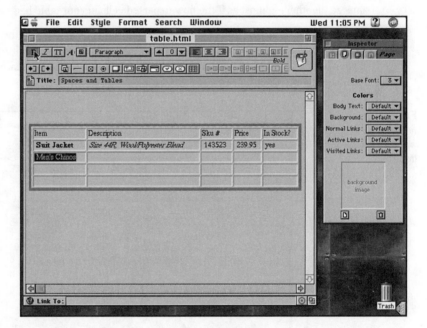

As you read in Chapter 9, "Creating Tables," a cell can be either a header cell or a data cell. To create a header cell, you begin by clicking the cell to select it. If you like, you can click in one cell, then drag to select a number of cells across a particular row or down a column. When you have the range selected for your header cells, use the Attribute Inspector to select the Make Header option.

Data that appears in these header cells will, by default, appear bold in your user's browser window (assuming the browser supports tables). Otherwise, the cell acts the same as any other data cell.

Adding (or Deleting) Rows and Columns   Adding rows and columns is easy enough to do in PageMill, provided you're already working in an active table. (And, even if you're not, activating the table is just a matter of double-clicking, as you've already seen.)

Start by selecting the column directly to the left of the area where you want the new column to appear. To do this, begin by clicking in the top cell of the column, and then drag the mouse pointer to the bottom cell. When you release the mouse button, you should see that the entire column has been highlighted. (With rows, highlight the row directly above the point at which you want to insert the new row.) Now, click the Insert Row/Column button. It's that simple!

Deleting columns and rows is rather a similar process, only this time you get to highlight the actual column or row in question. Drag to select the offending column or row, and then click the Delete Column/Row button once. It should disappear right away. The other columns or rows squeeze together—almost as if the now departed cells in your table had never even existed.

Adding a Table Caption You can give your table a title or footer with the table caption option. With the table selected as an object (but not active) use the Attributes Inspector to activate the Caption option by clicking its checkbox. When checked, a caption appears at the top of your table (see Figure 35.36).

FIG. 35.36

Adding a table caption with the Attributes Inspector.

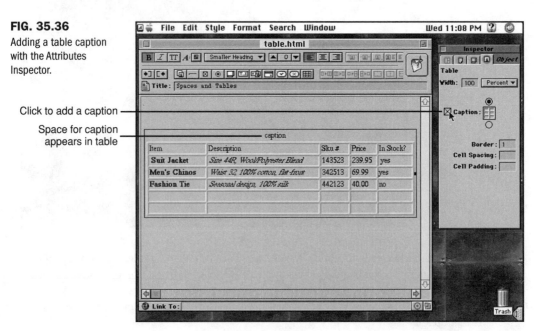

Click to add a caption

Space for caption appears in table

Next to the caption textbox you have two options: top or bottom. By default, your caption will appear at the top of the table. If you'd prefer to have it at the bottom, change that option by using the pull-down menu.

To edit the caption, make the table active by double-clicking it. Now you can place the cursor in the caption box (if it isn't already there) and type a new caption or title for your table. When you're done, use the standard movement keys to continue on to other cells within the table.

Changing Alignment Once you've got some data in your table, you may quickly decide that it needs to be formatted in some way that's different from the default way. When you first enter data, everything is aligned to the left of the cell, and in between the top and bottom borders. If you want to change this, all you've got to do is highlight and click.

To do the highlighting, click and hold the top-left corner of the cell's border and slowly drag the mouse pointer into the cell. When the entire cell highlights (and just that cell) you're ready to change alignment attributes (see Figure 35.37).

FIG. 35.37

Highlighting a single cell in your table.

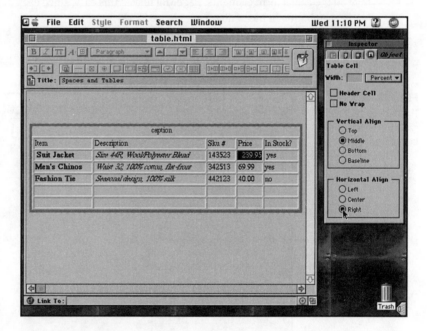

Next, look at the Attribute Inspector, where you'll see a number of cell parameters you can configure. Among these are alignment—both vertical and horizontal. Click the radio button next to the option you want to change, and then select the new alignment type you want to apply.

N O T E Aligning entire rows or columns of cells is similar to aligning individual cells, except that you have to highlight the entire row or column. ■

Another capability you have in PageMill is the option of adding space around your data, between your cells, or making the visible border larger or smaller. To use the cellpadding, cellspacing, and border features, you'll need to have selected the table as an object (it should be inactive). Then, move over to the Attribute Inspector and play around with the numbers. If you'd like a larger border, for instance, enter "5" instead of "1." You can create a borderless table (a table with no visible lines) by entering "0" for the border. Remember to hit Return or

Enter after changing one of these numbers. The results will appear immediately in the document window.

Creating Forms

PageMill also makes the composition of online forms much easier than coding them by hand. To get started, go into the Attribute Inspector and specify an ACTION URL and a METHOD for your form. Once you've got these basic form attributes in place, your next step is to concentrate on the actual form elements. PageMill makes this easy, since each of the major elements has its own button in the toolbar (see Figure 35.38).

FIG. 35.38
The PageMill toolbar gives you access to all the form elements.

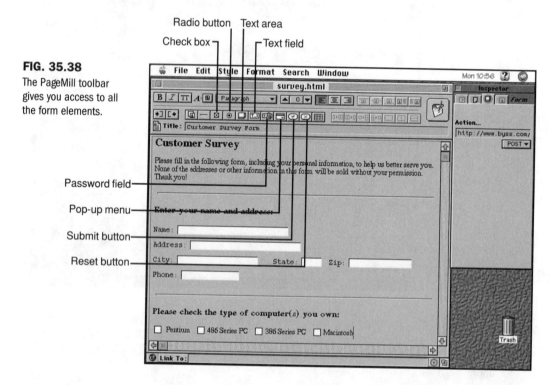

One of the more common uses for forms is to accept multiple lines of text from a user, perhaps for feedback, bug reports, or other uses. We'll look at how to place a text area in PageMill as a prototypical example of how to place a form element. Placing other form controls on a page is done almost the same way.

 TIP Don't forget that an important part of every form is the descriptive text you use to introduce each element.

To add a text area to your document, place the insertion point (cursor) at the point in the document where you'd like the text area to appear, and then click the Insert Text Area button in PageMill's toolbar (see Figure 35.39).

FIG. 35.39
Adding a text area to your document.

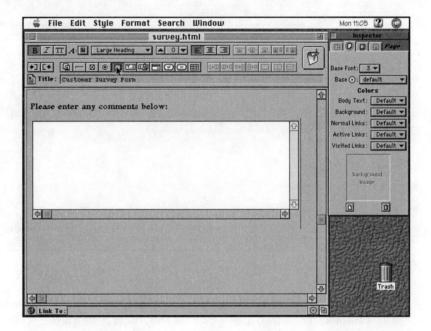

Now, you'll need to click once on the text area (to select it as an object) and head over to the Attribute Inspector.

The Inspector needs three things from you: a name for this form element, the number of rows you'd like displayed on the screen, and the number of columns you'd like displayed. The name can really be just about anything you want it to be—although it will eventually have to be a name recognized by the CGI script that deals with this information.

 TIP If someone else is creating your form's script, discuss the names of your form elements with them beforehand.

Notice that you can also use the mouse to set the rows and columns for your text area by clicking and dragging the drag boxes that surround the text area (see Figure 35.40).

FIG. 35.40

Putting your finishing touches on the text area.

Give the text area a name

Default text

Use grab boxes to resize

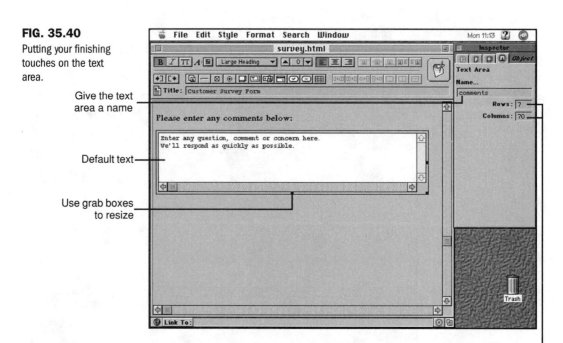

Choose dimensions

If you'd like to place default text in the text area (text your users will see before they enter something themselves) double-click the text area to make it active. A cursor should begin blinking inside the text box. Then just type away and your default text will appear.

As noted previously, placing other form elements follows a similar process. Just select where you want the form element to appear on the page, click the appropriate button on the toolbar to place the element, and then polish it off in the Attribute Inspector.

 T I P

Your knowledge of the different attributes of the form-related tags will be immensely helpful when working in the Attribute Inspector.

Creating Framed Documents

Perhaps the most daunting task for a document author is creating a framed document. It's easy to get lost in the mire of doing your framesets to set up the frames and then doing even more work to populate the frames with content. As with tables and forms, PageMill is a useful tool that can simplify the process for you.

Creating a framed document in PageMill is basically a three-step process. Specifically, you need to:

- ■ Decide how to organize your frameset.
- ■ Tweak the framed layout to meet any special requirements.
- ■ Place content in each frame and save the document.

Once you're comfortable with the content in Chapter 10, "Frames," you can move on to creating them in PageMill. The first thing you need to decide is how you want to organize the frameset interface. Then you need to use the Inspector to alter or fine-tune some of the frames-oriented options. Finally, you'll create the pages for each pane and save the whole mess.

Creating the Frameset   The way you create your frameset is somewhat dependent on what you want to do. For instance, if your sole reason for creating a frame document is to have a nonscrolling logo at the top of the page, you'll want two different frames in your document—two rows.

To do that, you hold down the Option key while pointing and clicking the top edge of the document window (see Figure 35.41). Hold down the mouse button and drag the mouse down into the document. Release the button and you've created a divider that splits the window into two frames.

FIG. 35.41
Hold down Option and drag the top of the document window down to create two rows of frames.

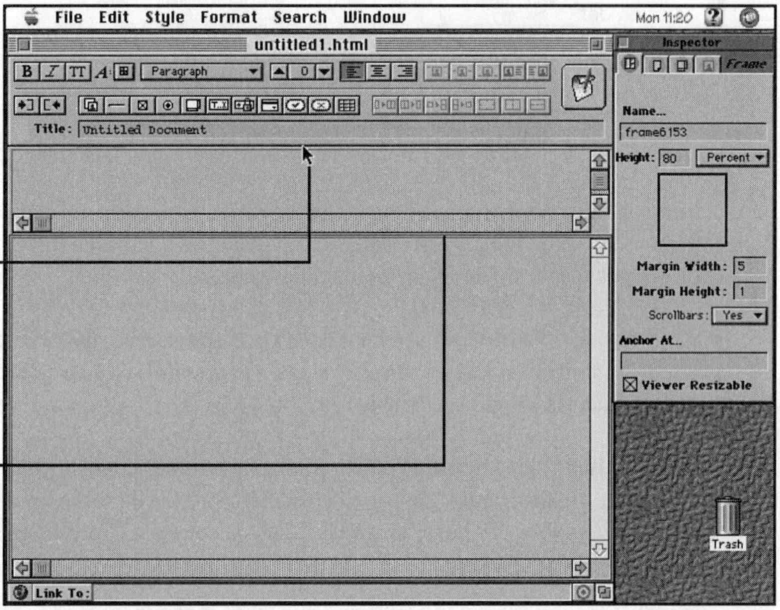

Click and drag here

Divider is created

You can also create your frames in columns—in fact, you can do both. Let's say that you not only want part of your frameset to include a nonscrolling logo, but you also want to add a list of hyperlinks to serve as a table of contents for your site. We'll do that by adding a column to the bottom row.

Below that first dividing line, click and drag the left border of the document window while holding down the Option key. You should be pulling a new divider across the screen to the right. The divider only appears in the second row (see Figure 35.42).

Part
VII

Ch
35

FIG. 35.42

Creating a column frame divider gives our example three different panes for loading Web documents.

Click and drag left border

Column frame divider is created

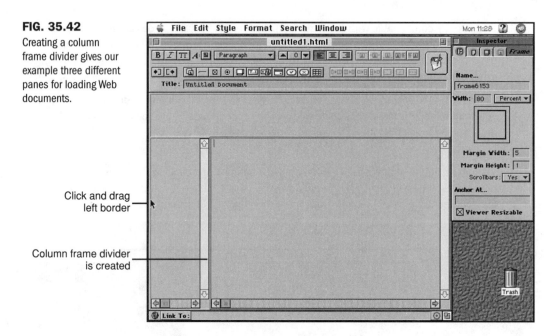

Now you have empty frames for each of the different documents you want to load. The top frame is for your logo page, the left column is for the table of contents, and the right column (the largest pane) will hold any of the other content.

N O T E If you need to delete one of the frames, just drag the frame divider back to its window border. Drop it on the border (or as close as possible) and PageMill will ask you if you're trying to remove the frame from the document. ▦

Frame Options and Attributes   With the empty frames created, you can move on to make adjustments to the frames' appearance and behavior. To do this, you turn your attention to the Attribute Inspector. It's here, as always, that you can tweak your frames and make your framed layout more to your liking.

In particular, you can set the following attributes in the Inspector:

■ Name   The Name attribute gives the selected frame a name. This is the internal name used by PageMill for targeting purposes. It isn't necessary for you to change the name, but it might be useful if you plan to edit any of the HTML by hand, since PageMill makes up really creative names like "Frame345298."

■ Width   In the Width field, you enter a number and the units to associate with the width of a frame. Generally, it's best to stick with percentages, but, if you really want things fixed on the screen, you can choose pixels.

- Scroll bars   You can also choose whether or not each of your frames will have scroll bars. The Auto setting is used when you want scroll bars if there's something to scroll, but you want them to disappear when everything fits in the frame.

- Viewer Resizable   Most frames-capable browsers permit users to resize a frame by dragging one of its borders to a new location. If you want to suppress this capability, turn off the Viewer Resizable option.

You're by no means obliged to any changes to the frameset parameters. If you're happy with them as you created them, then you can skip the Attribute Inspector and move right on to the next step—placing content in the frames.

Adding Content to Your Frames   With your empty frames all prepped and ready to go, it's time to put some content in them. So how do you get documents into their respective frames? There are two ways: just start typing in a frame to create the document, or use the File menu to load a document in the selected frame.

The first method is straightforward enough, so let's focus on the second. Select one of your frame areas, then choose the Insert Page option from PageMill's File menu. In the dialog box, find the document you want to load, and then click OK. Now that frame has a default document associated with it (see Figure 35.43).

> **CAUTION**
>
> You may be asked if you'd like to save "Frame345256" or something similar when you choose to load a new page in your frame. If you've done any work in that frame, you'll lose it if you don't save it at this point. If you haven't done anything in that frame, though, it's okay to go ahead and click Don't Save.

FIG. 35.43

After inserting an existing document in the frame, it becomes the default document associated with that part of the frameset document.

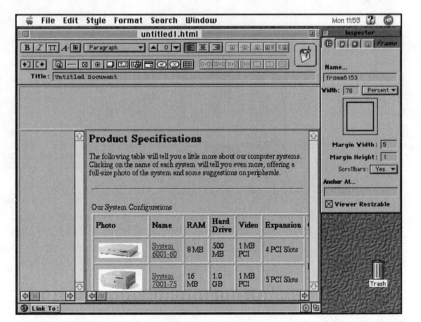

So what does it mean to be the default document associated with a frame? When the user loads the frameset into their browser, the default documents come along for the ride. They're the first documents that automatically appear in their frames when the frameset is loaded.

Creating Targets

The point of frames, though, is eventually to replace those default documents with new ones...at least in one of the panes of the frameset. To do that, we'll have to create links with targets.

In PageMill, that's pretty simple. You start by creating a link in any of the ways described earlier in the chapter. Then, highlight the link again (if it isn't already) and click and hold the mouse on the Target icon at the bottom of the document window. You can also click and hold the mouse button on the highlighted link (see Figure 35.44).

 T I P You can "triple-click" a hyperlink to quickly highlight all its text.

FIG. 35.44
Choosing a target for your hyperlink.

Choose the frame where you want the selected link to display

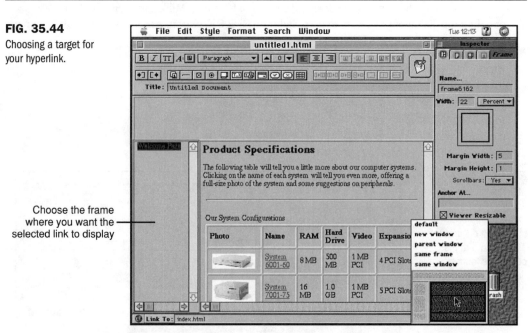

In the Target pop-up menu, select the text or part of the page that you want to appear as your link. Notice that the Target menu is actually a little representation of your page...you can simply highlight the frame you want to select as a target, and then release the mouse button. Now, when the user clicks that link, the resulting Web document will be loaded in the targeted frame.

So what are all those words doing? In a nutshell, here's what happens if you choose them instead of one of the frames:

- default   The target is whatever is the current default...usually the frame in which the link originates.

- new window   When this link is clicked, the resulting document is displayed in a new browser window created specifically for that purpose.

- parent frameset   The resulting document is displayed in the current frame, after any other frames on the current level are removed.

> **N O T E**   This one's a little confusing. Consider our three-paned scenario—two rows, and in the second row, two columns. A link that appears in one of the columns in that second row is targeted to the "parent frameset." When the user clicks that link, the two column frames disappear, and the new document is displayed in the "parent" of those column frames—the entire second row frame.

- same frame   Resulting document is displayed in the same frame as the hypertext link (and the document holding the hypertext link is unloaded).

- same window   Resulting document is displayed in the current browser window, after the frameset is unloaded. The new document will no longer be using a frames interface.

Saving All This Stuff

It's very important to remember to save everything when you're working in a frameset document. After all, even though you are working in one PageMill document window, you're actually editing two, three, or more documents at one time, and they all need to be saved.

> **CAUTION**
>
> Pay close attention when PageMill prompts you to save something—even in Preview mode. If you don't save the file that's in one of your frames, you'll have to re-create it from scratch.

Take a quick look at the File menu when you're working with frames. See anything different? You've suddenly got a bunch of options for saving your frames documents (see Figure 35.45).

What do all these different options do for you? Well, there are three to concentrate on...the rest are useful, too, but most of them are just "Save As..." options that let you rename the files in question. Here are the big ones:

- Save Frame   The currently selected frame (outlined in blue) will be saved by using its current file name. This is for default documents that you've edited on-screen.

■ Save Frameset   The frameset document—the container that describes where the frame dividers are supposed to be—is saved under the current file name. (If it's still "Untitled" you'll be given an opportunity to name it.)

■ Save All. This option saves the frameset and all the default documents currently being displayed in the different panes. Probably the safest choice.

FIG. 35.45

There's a ton of saving you have to do when you edit framed documents.

Save frame commands ——

Save frameset commands ——

Save it all ——

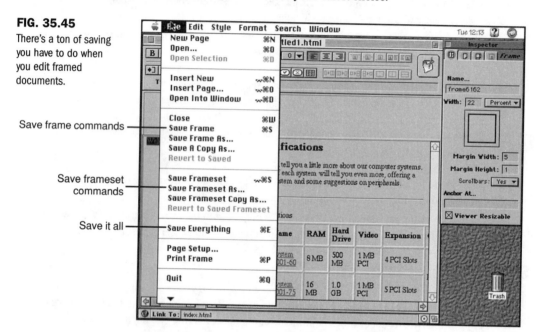

Examples

## CHAPTER 36

Accessing Databases

by Robert Niles

Almost every organization, no matter what size, uses a database for one reason or another. An untold amount of information is stored in a database, whether that information is about people (employment information, personal information, performance issues) or events that happened to make the news (bad weather, deaths, births, marriages, or social events). That information may be your company's inventory of products, how your company is doing in sales, or who your most prominent customers are. Whatever the case, individuals and organizations alike want, or need, to store information—most of which is kept in some sort of database.

Now comes the World Wide Web and, as you can tell, just about every company wants some sort of presence on it. You can easily see this by all the www-dot-*whatever*-dot-coms placed in just about every commercial on television!

If your organization, or the organization you are developing a Web presence for, has information in a database that it would like to provide on the World Wide Web, it can do so in one of two ways. The first way is to simply take a look at what information it has in its databases and place the relevant information in an HTML document. Using this method, if any of the information changes, it will not only have to edit the contents of the database, but it will have to edit the HTML document as well.

What databases are available

No matter what your budget is, there's a database for you—everything from something completely free to those super-powered databases that cost $5,000 or more.

What tools are available to help you

Various tools exist to help you build applications designed to retrieve, display, and manage data. You'll take a look at some of the most common database tools available, and what you need to make use of them.

Databases for those on a budget

If you are an entrepreneur or a smaller company, you'll see what you can do to make your services and products available by using databases. You'll cover databases that can be easily built using almost any platform.

SQL Databases

Almost every major organization uses SQL databases to store its information. You'll be introduced to methods of accessing SQL databases and how to use them in your Web applications.

The second way is to simply develop applications that query the database and generate a document, returning the latest information available. If information changes in the database, the Web documents automatically change to reflect those changes. ■

Available Databases

There are a multitude of databases available on the market today which can be used with your Web application to provide dynamic information to those visiting your site. What you end up using will depend mostly on what you are currently using, or what may fit into your organization's budget. This section lists some of the more common database solutions that are widely used on the Web.

Oracle

Oracle is the largest database developer in the world, providing databases for Windows NT and various UNIX flavors. Oracle has created its own set of tools (mainly PL/SQL, in conjunction with the Oracle Web Agent) which, coupled with the Oracle Webserver, allows you to create Web pages with little effort from information from the database. PL/SQL allows you to form stored procedures which help speed up the database query. The Oracle database engine is a good choice for large businesses that handle large amounts of information but, of course, you're going to pay for that. Today's price for Oracle 7 and the Oracle Webserver together is more than $5,000.

See **http://dozer.us.oracle.com/** for more information on Oracle and how you can use Oracle with the World Wide Web. Visit its Web page online!

Sybase

Sybase System 11 is an SQL database product that has many tools that can be used to produce dynamic Web pages from the information data in your database. A new product by Powersoft, the *NetImpact Studio* integrates with Sybase to provide a rich set of tools to help anyone create dynamic HTML documents. The NetImpact Studio consists of an HTML Browser/Editor accompanied by a Personal Web server. These allow you to create pages using a *WYSIWYG* or *"What You See Is What You Get"* interface. The Studio also comes with a Web database, support for JavaScript (which they see as the future of CGI scripting), and support for connecting to application servers.

NetImpact can be used in conjunction with *PowerBuilder*, an application that is used to create plug-ins and ActiveX components. It also can be used to complement *Optima++*, which is used to create plug-ins and will support the creation of Java applets.

Sybase can also be used with web.sql to create CGI and NSAPI (Netscape Server Application Programming Interface) applications that access the Sybase database server by using Perl.

Sybase is available for Windows NT, and UNIX.

For more information on Sybase, see its Web page at:

http://www.sybase.com

mSQL

mSQL is a middle-sized SQL database server for UNIX that is much more affordable than the commercial SQL servers available on the market. Written by David Hughes, it was created to allow users to experiment with SQL and SQL databases. Version 1.0.16 is free for non-commercial use (nonprofit, schools, and research organizations), but you will have to pay for individual and commercial use. The price is quite fair, at about $170. Version 2.0 has just been released with new tools and even more powerful queries.

For additional information on mSQL, along with documentation and a vast array of user-contributed software, see:

> **http://Hughes.com.au/**

Illustra

Illustra, owned by Informix, is the commercial version of Berkeley's Postgres. Available for both Windows NT and UNIX, Illustra uses an *ORDBMS*, or *Object-Relational Database Management System*. By using ORDBMS, queries are performed at very quick speeds. Illustra also uses DataBlade modules that help perform and speed up queries. The Web Datablade module version 2.2 allows the incorporation of your data on the Web with reduced effort. For more information, see:

> **http://www.informix.com/**

which contains detailed information on Illustra, along with additional information on how you can use Illustra with your Web-based applications.

Microsoft SQL

Available for Windows NT, Microsoft released its own SQL database server as a part of its BackOffice suite. Microsoft is trying heavily to compete with Oracle and Sybase. It has re-leased the server for about $1,000 (at the time of this writing) but you also must buy the SQL Server Internet Connector which costs about $3,000. These two products allow you to provide unlimited access to the server from the Web.

For additional information on Microsoft's SQL Server and how you can use Microsoft's SQL Server in conjunction with the World Wide Web, see:

> **http://www.microsoft.com/sql/**

Postgres95

Postgres95 is a SQL database server developed by the University of California at Berkeley for use on UNIX systems. Older versions of Postgres are also available but no longer supported. The site:

> **http://s2k-ftp.CS.Berkeley.EDU:8000/postgres/**

will provide additional information about Postgres95, along with the source code which is available for downloading.

Ingres

Ingres (Interactive Graphics Retrieval System) comes in both a commercial and public domain version. The University of California at Berkeley originally developed Ingres to work with graphics in a database environment, but Berkeley no longer supports the public domain version. You can still find it on the university's Web site.

Ingres uses the QUEL query language as well as SQL. *QUEL* is a superset of the original SQL language, making Ingres even more powerful. The public domain version is available for UNIX systems at:

ftp://s2k-ftp.cs.berkeley.edu/pub/ingres/

Computer Associates owns the commercial version of Ingres, called *OpenIngres*. This version is quite robust and capable of managing virtually any database application. The commercial version is available for UNIX, VMS, and Windows NT. For more information about the commercial version, visit the following site:

http://www.cai.com/products/ingr.htm

For more information about both the commercial and public domain versions of Ingres, visit the North American Ingres Users Association at the following site:

http://www.naiua.org/

FoxPro

Microsoft's Visual FoxPro has been a favorite for Web programmers, mostly because of its long-time standing in the database community, as well as its third-party support. FoxPro is an xBase database system that is widely used for smaller business and personal database applications. FoxPro is also available for most Windows platforms.

Visit the FoxPro home page on Microsoft's Web site for more information:

http://www.microsoft.com/catalog/products/visfoxp/

and visit Neil's FoxPro database page at:

http://adams.patriot.net/~johnson/neil/fox.html

Microsoft Access

Microsoft Access is a relational database management system that is part of the Microsoft Office suite. Microsoft Access can be used to create HTML documents based on the information stored in the Access database with the help of Microsoft's Internet Assistant. Microsoft's *Internet Assistant* is an add-on available free of charge for Access users. Microsoft Access can also support ActiveX controls which makes Access even more powerful when used with the Microsoft Internet Explorer.

A Job forum page was created to allow you to see how Access can be used in conjunction with the World Wide Web. For more information on Microsoft Access and the Job forum, see:

> **http://www.microsoft.com/Access/Internet/JobForum/**

If for some reason the database that your organization uses isn't listed here, don't fret. Most likely someone out there has created an interface in which you can use your database on the World Wide Web. The best way to find out is to perform a search using one of the many search engines available. For a starting point, take a look at:

> **http://www.yahoo.com/Computers_and_Internet/World_Wide_Web/**
> **Databases_and_Searching**

Side-by-Side Comparison

Choosing a database to suit your organization's needs is difficult, and should be carefully planned. It's quite difficult to tell you which database would best suit your needs without spending a bit of time with a company and seeing how that company operates. The best person to know which database is best for your organization is you. Even so, Table 36.1 might help you narrow your choices.

Table 36.1 A Comparison of Some of the Most Widely Used Databases on the Web

Database	Platforms	Suggested Use
Oracle	UNIX, NT	Large business
Sybase	UNIX, NT	Large business
mSQL	UNIX	Personal, small business
Illustra	UNIX, NT	Medium to large business
MS SQL	NT	Medium to large business
Postres95	UNIX	Personal, and small to medium business
Ingres	UNIX, NT	Small to large business
FoxPro	Windows, Macintosh	Small to medium business
MS Access	Windows	Personal, and small to medium business

Database Tools

Just as there are multiple databases available, there are also multiple methods of integrating your database with the World Wide Web. What tools you should use depends heavily on what platform your database resides on, your knowledge of programming, and your programming language skills. In this section, you'll take a look at a few of the most common tools that have been developed to make accessing databases easy for Web developers.

PHP/FI

PHP/FI was developed by Rasmus Lerdorf, who needed to create a script that enabled him to log visitors onto his page. The script replaced a few other smaller ones that were creating a load on Lerdorf's system. This script became *PHP*, which is an acronym for *Rasmus' Personal Home Page tools*. Lerdorf later wrote a script that enabled him to embed commands within an HTML document to access a SQL database. This script acted as a forms interpreter (hence the name *FI*), which made it easier to create forms using a database. These two scripts have since been combined into one complete package called PHP/FI.

PHP/FI grew into a small language that enables developers to add commands within their HTML pages instead of running multiple smaller scripts to do the same thing. PHP/FI is actually a CGI program written in C that can be compiled to work on any UNIX system. The embedded commands are parsed by the PHP/FI script, which then prints the results through another HTML document. Unlike using JavaScript to access a database, PHP/FI is browser-independent because the script is processed through the PHP/FI executable that is on the server.

PHP/FI can be used to integrate mSQL, along with Postgres95, to create dynamic HTML documents. It's fairly easy to use and quite versatile. You can visit

http://www.vex.net/php/

for more information on PHP/FI, along with examples of how PHP/FI can be used.

Cold Fusion

Allaire created *Cold Fusion* as a system that enables you to write scripts within HTML. Cold Fusion, a database interface, processes the scripts and then returns the information within the HTML written in the script. Although Cold Fusion currently costs $495, the product is definitely worth the price. Allaire wrote Cold Fusion to work with just about every Web server available for Windows NT and integrates with just about every SQL engine—including those database servers available on UNIX machines (if a 32-bit ODBC driver exists).

Cold Fusion works by processing a form, created by you, that sends a request to the Web server. The server starts Cold Fusion and sends the information to Cold Fusion which is used to call a template file. After reading the information the visitor entered, Cold Fusion processes that information according to the template's instructions. It then returns an automatically generated HTML document to the server and then returns the document to the visitor.

For more information on Cold Fusion, visit the Allaire Web site at

http://www.allaire.com/

W3-mSQL

W3-mSQL was created by David Hughes, the creator of mSQL, to simplify accessing an mSQL database from within your Web pages. W3-mSQL works as a CGI script your Web pages go through to be parsed. The script reads your HTML document, performs any queries required, and sends the result back out to the server and then on to the visitor to your site. W3-mSQL is much like PHP/FI but on a smaller scale. W3-mSQL makes it easy for you to create Web documents that contain information based on what is in your database.

A sample bookmarks script and database dump is included within the W3-mSQL archive.

For more information on W3-mSQL, see:

> **http://hughes.com.au/software/w3-msql.htm**

MsqlPerl

MsqlPerl is a Perl interface to the mSQL database server. Written by Andreas Koenig, it uses the mSQL API and allows you to create CGI scripts in Perl, complete with all the SQL commands available to mSQL.

You can download MsqlPerl at:

> **ftp://Bond.edu.au/pub/Minerva/msql/Contrib/**

MsqlJava

MsqlJava is an API which allows you to create applets that can access an mSQL database server. The package has been compiled with the Java Developer's Kit version 1.0 and tested using Netscape 3.0. Additional information on MsqlJava can be found on the following Web site. You can also download the latest version and view the online documentation, as well as see examples of MsqlJava in action.

> **http://mama.minmet.uq.oz.au/msqljava/**

Microsoft's dbWeb

Microsoft's *dbWeb* allows you to create Web pages on-the-fly with the use of an interactive Schema Wizard. The *Schema Wizard* is a GUI that specifies what is searched for within the database and which fields will appear within the Web page.

dbWeb allows you to publish information from a database in HTML format without having to know any HTML programming or making you learn how to use the ISAPI interface.

dbWeb can be used with the Microsoft Internet Information Server and supports the Oracle database server, the Microsoft SQL server, Access, Visual FoxPro, and any other databases which support the 32-bit ODBC driver.

For additional information on dbWeb, see:

> **http://www.microsoft.com/intdev/dbweb/dbweb.htm**

WDB

WDB is a suite of Perl scripts that help you create applications that allow you to integrate SQL databases with the World Wide Web. WDB provides support for Sybase, Informix, and mSQL databases, but has been used with other database products as well.

WDB uses what its author, Bo Frese Rasmussen, calls *form definition files* which describe how the information retrieved from the database should display to the visitor. WDL automatically creates forms on-the-fly that allow the visitor to query the database. This saves you a lot of the work preparing a script to query a database. The user submits the query and WDB, then performs a set of *conversions*, or links, so the visitor can perform additional queries by clicking one of the links.

Visit the WDB home page for further information at:

http://arch-http.hq.eso.org/wdb/html/wdb.html

Web/Genera

Web/Genera is a software toolset used to integrate Sybase databases with HTML documents. Web/Genera can be used to retrofit a Web front end to an existing Sybase database, or it can be used to create a new one. When using Web/Genera, you are required to write a schema for the Sybase database indicating what fields are to be displayed, what type of data they contain, what column they are stored in, and how you want the output of a query formatted. Next, Web/Genera processes the specifications, queries the database, and formats an HTML document. Web/Genera also supports form-based queries and whole-database formatting which turns into text and HTML.

The main component of Web/Genera is a program called *symfmt*, which extracts objects from Sybase databases based on your schema. Once the schema is written, compile the schema by using a program called *sch2sql*, which creates the SQL procedures that extract the objects from the database.

Once you have compiled the schema, you can retrieve information from the database using URLs. When you click a link, the object requested is dynamically loaded from the Sybase database, formatted as HTML, and then displayed to the visitor.

Web/Genera was written by Stanley Letovsky and others for UNIX.

This Web/Genera site contains additional information on Web/Genera. Along with downloading the latest version, this site talks about the history of Web/Genera and how it can be used today. You can find the Web site at:

http://gdbdoc.gdb.org/letovsky/genera/

MORE

MORE is an acronym for *Multimedia Oriented Repository Environment* and was developed by the Repository Based Software Engineering Program (RBSE). MORE is a set of application programs that operate in conjunction with a Web server to provide access to a relational (or Oracle) database. It was designed to allow a visitor access to the database using a set of CGI scripts written in C. It was also designed so that a consistent user interface can be used to work with a large number of servers, allowing a query to check information on multiple machines. This expands the query and gathers a large amount of information. Visit the MORE Web site for additional information on MORE and RBSE at:

> http://rbse.jsc.nasa.gov:81/DEMO/

DBI

DBI's founder, Tim Bunce, wanted to provide a consistent programming interface to a wide variety of databases using Perl. Since the beginning, others have joined in to help build DBI so that it can support a wide variety of databases through the use of a *Database Driver*, or *DBD*. The DBD is simply the driver that works as a translator between the database server and DBI. A programmer only has to deal with one specification, and the drivers handle the rest transparently.

So far, the following databases have database drivers. Most are still in testing phases, although they are stable enough to use for experimenting:

Oracle	mSQL	Fulcrum	C-ISAM
Ingres	Informix	DB2	Quickbase
Sybase	Empress	Interbase	

Visit the DBI Web page for the latest developments on DBI and various Database Drivers. Authors continue to develop this interface where DBDs are being built for additional databases. You can find this site at:

> http://www.hermetica.com/technologia/DBI/

DBGateway

DBGateway is a 32-bit Visual Basic WinCGI application that runs on a Windows NT machine as a service that provides World Wide Web access to Microsoft Access and FoxPro databases. It is being developed as part of the *Flexible Computer Integrated Manufacturing (FCIM) project*. DBGateway is a gateway between your CGI applications and the Database servers. Because your CGI scripts only "talk" with the Database Gateway, you only need to be concerned with programming for the gateway instead of each individual database server. This provides two advantages—programming a query is much easier because the gateway handles the communication with the database, and scripts can be easily ported to different database systems.

The gateway allows a visitor to your site to submit a form that is sent to the server. The server hands the request to the gateway which decodes the information and builds a query forming the result based on a template, or it can send the result of the query raw.

Visit **http://fcim1.csdc.com/** to view the DBGateway's user manual, view the online FAQ, and see how DBGateway has been used.

Databases for Everyone

As you have seen, there are many options available, both in which database you might want to consider and what tools are available. Even so, most of the options available are expensive or, for small businesses, some of the databases and tools discussed might not be practical.

For the smaller organization, you can still provide dynamic content using less expensive options. Two of these are *flat file* and *dbm databases* which cost no more than the convenience of having a machine which already provides Web services. Whether you have your own Web server or are hosting your pages on an ISP's Web server, flat file and dbm databases are an option to consider. If the databases are relatively small, no visitor to your site will be the wiser.

Flat File Databases

Other than being cheap, flat file databases are just about the easiest you can create. Other than the necessity to have a language with which to program, there is nothing else needed to create a small ASCII text database.

A flat file database consists mainly of lines of text where each line is its own entry. There is no special technique to index the database. Because of this, flat file databases usually are relatively small. The larger the database, the longer it takes to perform queries to the database.

A Simple Flat File Example   With any database, there are three important factors in designing Web-based database applications. First, you will need to be able to read from the database. Second, you will need to search the database. Last, if you want visitors to your site to order products, or even if you want to easily manage the information in your database, you will want to be able to write to the database.

With these factors in mind, you will want to design a simple phonebook database which allows you to write, read, and search a database for information. With the ability to perform these three functions, you can easily design your own database to suit your specific needs, or simply change these examples, customizing each one. With minor changes, these scripts can be used for inventory management, storing personnel information, or whatever suits your fancy.

Designing the HTML Pages   For your phonebook, the first thing that you need is an HTML page, which will allow someone to enter information into, or read from, the database. You must first decide what you want the visitor to enter.

In this example, the HTML document consists of three forms. The first form will allow the visitor to enter information into the phonebook database. The second form will allow the visitor to display the contents of the database, and the third form will allow the visitor to perform a keyword search on the database.

You can expand on this later, but right now you simply want the visitor to be able to enter a first name, last name, and telephone number, all of which will be stored in your flat file database.

The first form assigns the input from the visitor into three names: fname, lname, and phone. A hidden input type (see Listing 36.1), named act (for action), is created that tells your script which action it is expected to perform.

Listing 36.1 Pbook.html—HTML Code That Allow Visitors to Query a Phonebook Database

```
<HTML>
<HEAD><TITLE>Flat file Phonebook</TITLE></HEAD>
<BODY>
<H1>Your Flat file Phonebook</H1>
<HR>
<H2>Insert Information</H2>
<FORM ACTION="/cgi-bin/pbook.pl" METHOD="POST">
<PRE>
  First Name: <INPUT TYPE="text" NAME="fname">
   Last Name: <INPUT TYPE="text" NAME="lname">
Phone Number: <INPUT TYPE="text" NAME="phone">
</PRE>
<INPUT TYPE="hidden" NAME="act" VALUE="add">
<INPUT TYPE="submit" value="Add to Phonebook">
</FORM>
<HR><P>
<H2>Display Information</H2>
<FORM ACTION="/cgi-bin/pbook.bat" METHOD="POST">
<INPUT TYPE="hidden" NAME="act" VALUE="display">
Click on <INPUT TYPE="submit" value="Display">
to view all entries in the phonebook
</FORM>
<HR><P>
<H2>Search the Phonebook</H2>
<FORM ACTION="/cgi-bin/pbook.bat" METHOD="POST">
Enter a keyword to search for: <INPUT TYPE="text" NAME="keyword">
<INPUT TYPE="hidden" NAME="act" VALUE="search">
<INPUT TYPE="submit" VALUE="Start Search">
</FORM>
</BODY>
</HTML>
```

Writing to a Flat File Database   The first section of your script (see Listing 36.2) separates the information coming from the form that was filled out by the visitor. After that, the script checks to see if the action requested was to add information to the database. If so, the database file is opened and the information from the visitor is placed in the database file on a single line.

Listing 36.2 Pbook.pl—The Script Reads *STDIN* and Separates Its Contents

```perl
if ($ENV{'REQUEST_METHOD'} eq 'POST')
{
    read(STDIN, $buffer, $ENV{'CONTENT_LENGTH'});
    @pairs = split(/&/, $buffer);
    foreach $pair (@pairs)
    {
        ($name, $value) = split(/=/, $pair);
        $value =~ tr/+/ /;
        $value =~ s/%([a-fA-F0-9][a-fA-F0-9])/pack("C", hex($1))/eg;
        $contents{$name} = $value;

    }
}
print "Content-type: text/html\n\n";
$phonebook = "phonebk.txt";
if ($contents{'act'} eq "add") {
open(BOOK, ">>$phonebook") || do {&no_open;};
print BOOK "$contents{'fname'}:$contents{'lname'}:$contents{'phone'}\n";
close(BOOK);
print <<"HTML";
<HTML>
<HEAD><TITLE>Information added</TITLE></HEAD>
<BODY>
<H1>Information added</H1>
The information entered has been added to the phonebook.
<HR>
<CENTER>
<A HREF="/pbook.html">[Return to the Phonebook]</A>
</CENTER>
</BODY>
</HTML>
HTML
exit;
}
sub no_open {

print <<"HTML";
<HTML>
<HEAD><TITLE>Error!</TITLE></HEAD>
<BODY>
<H1> Error! Could not open the database!</H1>
<CENTER>
<A HREF="/pbook.htm">[Return to the Phonebook]</A>
</CENTER>
</BODY>
</HTML>
HTML

exit;
}
```

At this time, the information entered by the visitor has been placed in the database. If you were to take a look at the text file holding the information provided by the visitor, it would look something like:

```
John:Doe:555-5555
```

This format is called *colon-delimited*, meaning that each field is separated by using a colon. Any character can be used to delimit each field in a flat file database, and it is best to use a character that will not be present in a field. Using the colon, for example, would not be wise if you wanted to include an URL in the database. In that case, a comma might be more suitable.

Reading from a Flat File Database   If the visitor clicked Display, the information from the database is retrieved and simply appears to the visitor in a table. By using a table, the contents of the phonebook can easily be formatted into something that is easy to view.

As you can see in Listing 36.3, you check to see if the value of act is equal to `display`; if so, a page is created, and the contents of your database appear, where each line of information is broken into its respective parts. To accomplish this, use Perl's `split` function. The value of `$line` is split and assigned to the array `entry`. By splitting each line, you can control how you want the information to appear to the visitor (see Figure 36.1).

FIG. 36.1
By separating the contents of the database, you can control how the information is displayed.

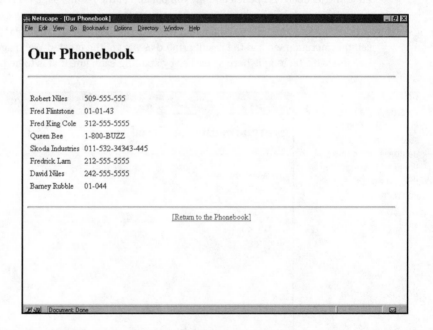

Listing 36.3   All Entries Are Displayed to the Visitor

```
if ($contents{'act'} eq "display") {

...
```

continues

Listing 36.3 Continued

```
open (BOOK, $phonebook) || do {&no_open;};
until (eof(BOOK))
{
  $line = <BOOK>;
  @entry = split(/:/, $line);
  print "<TR><TD>$entry[0] $entry[1]</TD><TD> $entry[2]</TD></TR>";
}

close(BOOK);
```

...

Once the information from the database is displayed, you finish the HTML document and exit the script.

Searching a Flat File Database Last, you will want to check to see if the visitor requested to perform a keyword search (see Listing 36.4). If so, you need to open the database and check each line against the keyword entered by the visitor.

First, the database is opened and the top portion of the results page is created. Next, you have a counter, which is initially set to zero (more on this in a moment). Now each line is read and checked against the value contained in the variable $contents{'keyword'}. If so, then the count is incremented and the result printed as part of the created Web page (see Figure 36.2). Use the same technique here as earlier by splitting each line that is to be printed into an array.

FIG. 36.2
By providing a method in which the visitor can search through a database, you remove the need to weed through excess information.

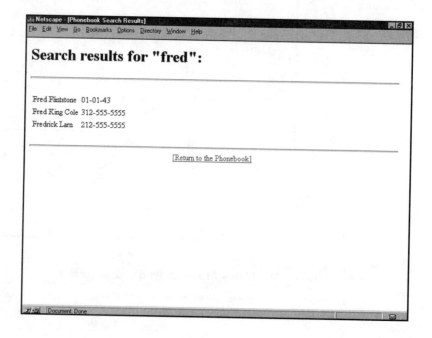

Netscape - [Phonebook Search Results]
File Edit View Go Bookmarks Options Directory Window Help

Search results for "fred":

Fred Flintstone 01-01-43
Fred King Cole 312-555-5555
Fredrick Lam 212-555-5555

[Return to the Phonebook]

Document: Done

Once you exit the loop, you check the count. If the count is equal to zero, then you know there were no entries in the database that matched the keyword search, and you inform the visitor that his or her search produced no results. Listing 36.4 will give you an idea of how this can be accomplished.

Listing 36.4   Each Line Is Checked and Only Matching Results Are Returned

```
if ($contents{'act'} eq "search") {

open (BOOK, "$phonebook") || do {&no_open;};

$count=0;

 until (eof (BOOK))
 {
   $line = <BOOK>;
   chop($line);
   if ($line =~ /$contents{'keyword'}/gi)
    {
     $count++;
     @entry = split(/:/, $line);
     print "<TR><TD>$entry[0] $entry[1]</TD><TD> $entry[2]</TD></TR>";
    }

 }

if ($count==0)
  {
   print "No Matches";
  }

close(BOOK);
```

Once the script has checked each line against the keyword, the database is closed, the script finishes the Web page, and the script is exited.

To see the script in its entirety, the script is available on the CD-ROM accompanying this book. A version for those using Perl on a Windows NT or Windows 95 platform is available as well.

dbm Databases

Most UNIX systems have some sort of dbm database—in fact, I have yet to find a system that runs without one. *dbm* is a set of library routines that manage data files consisting of key and value pairs. The dbm routines control how users enter and retrieve information from the database. Although not the most powerful mechanism for storing information, using dbm is a faster method of retrieving information than using a flat file. Because most UNIX sites use one of the dbm libraries, the tools you need to store your information to a dbm database are readily available.

There are almost as many flavors of dbm libraries as there are UNIX systems. Although most of these libraries are not compatible with each other, all basically work the same way. You'll first explore each of the dbm flavors to get a good understanding of their differences. Afterward, you'll again be shown how to create an address book script, which should give you a better idea of how dbm databases work.

The following list describes the most common dbm libraries available and explains some of the differences between each of the dbm libraries:

- dbm—The library routines for dbm are simple but can handle most jobs without a problem. The library contains the most functions allowing you to create databases, store, retrieve, and delete information, as well as a few functions that help you move around within the database. dbm stores the database in two files. The first has the extension .PAG and contains the bitmap. The second, which has the extension .DIR, contains the data.

- ndbm—Much like dbm with a few additional features, but this was written to provide better, and hence, faster storage and retrieval methods. Also, dbm can only have one database open while with ndbm, you can open many databases. Like dbm, ndbm stores its information in two files, using the extensions .PAG and .DIR.

- sdbm—If you have installed Perl, you will most likely have sdbm installed. sdbm comes with the Perl archive, which has been ported to many platforms. This means you will be able to use dbm databases as long as there is a version of Perl for your computer. sdbm was written to match the functions provided with ndbm, so portability of code shouldn't be a problem, either. For more information on sdbm and Perl, see the Perl language home page at:

  http://www.perl.com/perl/

- gdbm—The GNU version of the dbm family of database routines. This library does its own file locking to ensure that two or more users cannot write to the database simultaneously. gdbm has the same functions as ndbm, as well as the capability to reorganize the database and cache data. Also, the database has no size limit, depending only on your system's resources. gdbm databases create only one file, having the extension .DB.

- Berkeley Db 1.85—This expands on the original dbm routines significantly. As well as creating hashed tables, the library can also create databases based on a sorted, balanced binary tree (BTREE) and store information with a record line number (RECNO). The method you use depends completely on how you want to store and retrieve the information from a database. Berkeley's db creates only one file, which has no extension.

If for some reason you can't find a particular dbm database on your system, do a search on the Web for dbm databases. With the exception of dbm, the other dbm interfaces are freely available. Most likely you will find at least one of the dbm interfaces on your favorite FTP site.

dbm databases are relatively easy to use. Unfortunately, the use of dbm is poorly documented. Even so, you can find some additional information at:

http://www.polaris.net/docs/gdbm/

A dbm Example Now that the preceding section has briefly introduced the various dbm interfaces, this section will demonstrate how you can use them. As mentioned earlier, dbm databases can decrease the amount of time it takes to insert and retrieve information to and from a database. When your database starts growing, and using one of the larger database engines is still overkill (especially on your pocketbook), you might want to look into using dbm.

Inserting Information into a Dbm Database dbm databases have two fields: a key and the data (sometimes called the *value*). The *key* is simply a string that points to the data. The string within the key must be unique within a database. Note the following example:

Key	Data
Robert Niles	rniles@selah.net
Jason Lenny	jason@yakima.net
Ken Davis	kdavis@your.com
John Doe	jdoe@imtired.selah.net
Santa Claus	sclaus@north.pole.com
Bert	rniles@selah.net

The *data*, on the other hand, can contain any type of information. The data might contain an URL, an e-mail address, or even a binary file. Examine the following script, DBBOOKADD.PL, which adds information to a dbm database. This script is available on this book's companion CD-ROM.

The main components for using dbm are the Perl module, DB_FILE.PM, and the file control module, FCNTL.PM (see Listing 36.5). DB_FILE.PM acts as an interface to the dbm routines. The FCNTL.PM module provides you with functions which enable you to control access to the database so that two or more people cannot write to the database at the same time.

Listing 36.5 The Information from the Form Is Parsed in Order to Perform the Appropriate Function

```perl
#!/usr/bin/perl

use DB_File;
use Fcntl;

if ($ENV{'REQUEST_METHOD'} eq 'POST')
{
        read(STDIN, $buffer, $ENV{'CONTENT_LENGTH'});
        @pairs = split(/&/, $buffer);
        foreach $pair (@pairs)
        {
                ($name, $value) = split(/=/, $pair);
```

continues

Listing 36.5   Continued

```
                $value =~ tr/+/ /;
                $value =~ s/%([a-fA-F0-9][a-fA-F0-9])/pack("C",
                ➥hex($1))/eg;
                $form{$name} = $value;

        }
}
$file="addresses";
```

To connect to the database, you use the `tie()` function. The syntax for `tie()` is as follows:

`tie(%hashname, DB_File, filename, flags, mode)`

You can assign any `hashname`, although the name must start with the percent sign (%). Because you are using the DB_FILE.PM module, you must specify the file name. The `filename` identi-fies the file in which you are storing the data. You next specify the `flags`, which vary depend-ing on which dbm routines you are using. In this example, you use the flags that enable you to read from and write to files (`O_RDWR`) or, if the file doesn't exist, to create files (`O_CREAT`). The `mode` sets the database file's permissions. The mode `0660` specifies that the owner can read from and write to the database file, and that the group can only read from the file.

`$database=tie(%db, 'DB_File', $file, O_RDWR¦O_CREAT, 0660);`

This next very simple line is what magically adds the information to the database. You use the `hash` variable to enter the information into the database. The syntax for this line is as follows:

`$hashname{key}=value`

The following line places `$form{'name'}` into the database as the key, and assigns `$form{'email'}` to that key as its value:

`$db{$form{'name'}}=$form{'email'};`

Now you use the `untie()` function, which releases control of the database, and then `undef()`, which undefines the variable `$database`:

```
untie(%db);
undef($database);
```

Although a dbm database can contain only the key and a pair, you can trick the database into adding more fields. For example, if you want to include a telephone number, you have to add it to the value; by inserting some sort of separator, you can later identify the two separate entries. The following example uses the `join()` function, which joins separate strings together with a colon:

`$db{$form{'name'}}=join(":",$form{'email'},$form{'phone'});`

For example, if `$form{'email'}` contains the string jdoe@selah.net and `$form{'phone'}` contains the string 555-5555, the `join()` function produces the following string:

`jdoe@selah.net:555-5555`

Because e-mail addresses and telephone numbers do not include colons, the colon is probably the best choice for separating each entry. Of course, what you use to delimit each entry will depend on what kind of data you need to store.

What happens if a user tries to enter a name already stored in a key? As your script currently stands, it would simply continue on as if nothing happened. However, because each key must be unique, the script will not add the information to the database. To tell the visitor that the entry failed, you have to add a line that checks whether the name entered matches an existing key:

```
&error if $db{"$form{'name'}"};
```

Your error subroutine tells the visitor what happened and gives the visitor a chance to try again:

```
sub error {
print <<"HTML";
<HTML>
<HEAD><TITLE>Error!</TITLE></HEAD>
<BODY>
<H1>Error! -Name exists</H1>
I'm sorry, but the name you entered already exists.
➥If you wish to try again, click
<A HREF="/dbbook.html">here</A>.
</BODY>
</HTML>
HTML

exit;
}
```

Retrieving Information from a dbm Database   Now that you have entered information into the database, you want to enable your site's visitors to retrieve the information. Listing 36.6 starts this by accessing the database and generates the top portion of the Web page.

Listing 36.6   The Database Is Accessed, and the Top Portion of the Web Page Is Generated

```
#!/usr/bin/perl
# dbbook.pl
use DB_File;
use Fcntl;
print "Content-type: text/html\n\n";
$file="addresses";
$database=tie(%db, 'DB_File', $file, O_READ, 0660) || die "can't";
print <<"HTML";
<HTML>
<HEAD><TITLE>Simple dbm address book</TITLE></HEAD>
<BODY>
<CENTER>
<H1>A Simple Address Book</H1>
<TABLE BORDER=1>
HTML
```

Because you've entered the phone number and e-mail address into the value separated by a colon, you now must separate the phone number and e-mail address. The easiest way to do so is with the split() function. After you split this information, you pass the contents to the array @part:

```
while (($key,$value)= each(%db)) {
 @part = split(/:/,$value);
```

You can use an if statement to check whether the visitor entered an e-mail address. If the visitor did so, you print a link, using the HREF anchor. Otherwise, you simply print the key, then use the array to print the e-mail address and phone number:

```
if ($part[0]) {
   print "<TR><TD><A HREF=\"mailto:$part[0]\">$key</A></TD>";
   }
 else {
print "<TR><TD>$key</TD>";
   }

 print "<TD>$part[0]</TD><TD>$part[1]</TD></TR>\n";
}
```

Finally, you finish the Web page, closing the table, body, and HTML file. Last, you need to use untie() to release control of the database, undefine the $database variable, and exit the script.

```
print <<"HTML";
</TABLE>
<P>
<A HREF="/dbbook.html">[Add to address book]</A>
</BODY>
</HTML>
HTML
untie(%db);
undef($database);
exit;
```

Searching a dbm Database   You have learned how to enter information into the database and also how to retrieve information from the database. What would happen if the database starts to become extremely large? If you have 100 entries in the database, it could make for an extremely large Web page if you were to display everything within the database. Also, looking for a single name in the database could be a pain.

To solve this problem, you can enable the visitor to search through the database (see Listing 36.7). For example, a visitor could enter the last name **Doe**, thus narrowing the number of names the visitor has to weed through.

Listing 36.7   Input from the User Is Parsed, and the Database Is Accessed

```
#!/usr/bin/perl
# dbbooksearch.pl

use DB_File;
use Fcntl;
```

```
if ($ENV{'REQUEST_METHOD'} eq 'POST')
{
        read(STDIN, $buffer, $ENV{'CONTENT_LENGTH'});
        @pairs = split(/&/, $buffer);
        foreach $pair (@pairs)
        {
                ($name, $value) = split(/=/, $pair);
                $value =~ tr/+/ /;
                $value =~ s/%([a-fA-F0-9][a-fA-F0-9])/pack("C",
                ➥hex($1))/eg;
                $form{$name} = $value;

        }
}
print "Content-type: text/html\n\n";

$file="addresses";
$database=tie(%db, 'DB_File', $file, O_READ, 0660)
➥|¦ die "can't";
print <<"HTML";
<HTML>
<HEAD><TITLE>Simple dbm address book results</TITLE></HEAD>
<BODY>
<CENTER>
<H1>A Simple Address Book Results</H1>
<TABLE BORDER=1>
HTML
```

As each key/value pair loads from the database, each key is checked to see whether the key matches the string that the visitor entered:

```
while (($key,$value)= each(%db)) {
if ($key =~ /$form{'name'}/i) {
```

N O T E The /i switch, using Perl, allows for case-insensitive matching. Therefore, if the user enters *Bert*, *bErT*, or *bert*, the entry would match *Bert*, *bert*, *Robert*, or *Bertman*. ■

If you find a match, you print it:

```
@part = split(/:/,$value);
 if ($part[0]) {
   print "<TR><TD><A HREF=\"mailto:$part[0]\">$key</A></TD>";
   }
 else {
   print "<TR><TD>$key</TD>";
   }
 print "<TD>$part[0]</TD><TD>$part[1]</TD></TR>\n";
 }
}
```

Then you complete the Web document, untie the database, undefine the variable, and exit the script:

```
print <<"HTML";
</TABLE>
```

```
<P>
<A HREF="/dbbook.html">[Add to address book]</A>
</BODY>
</HTML>
HTML

untie(%db);
undef($database);

exit;
```

You could also search the value. Such a search gives you even more flexibility on what information is returned.

The script in its entirety is located on the CD-ROM that accompanies this book. As well, I have placed a version for Windows NT and Windows 95 (pbook.zip) which performs the same functions using the sdbm database that is distributed with Perl.

Using SQL Databases

Most SQL database servers consist of a set of programs that manage large amounts of data. These programs offer a rich set of query commands that help manage the power behind the SQL server. The programs also control the storage, retrieval, and organization of the information within the database. Thus, you can change, update, and remove the information within the database—after the support programs or scripts are in place.

A relational database doesn't link records together physically, like a dbm database does with the key and value pair. Instead, a *relational database* simply provides a field that can match information and returns the results as though the information were organized that way.

Relational databases store information in tables. A *table* is like a miniature database stored within a main database that groups the information together. For instance, you can have one database that contains one, two, or many tables.

Each table consists of columns and rows. The columns identify the data by name, as in the following example:

Name	Home Phone	E-Mail
Fred Barns	555-5555	**fbarns@somewhere.net**
Melissa Devons	555-5556	**missy@thisplace.com**
John Doe	555-5557	**jdoe@whatcha.want.com**

The name, phone number, and e-mail address are the columns, and each entry set is the *row*.

Although this book's purpose isn't to explain how relational databases work, you need a basic understanding of the concept. Suppose you stored the preceding information in a table called `personal`. You can join information from two or more tables within your query. Suppose that the following table is called `work`:

Name	Work Phone	Department
Fred Barns	555-5558	sysadmin
Melissa Devons	555-5559	programmer
John Doe	555-5560	janitor

Within your query, you can have something like the following:

```
select * from personal,work where personal.name=work.name
```

This query would print information about individuals from both tables. Keep in mind that this example is a very simple one. Queries from relational databases can get extremely complex. In fact, there are professionals whose sole job is to manage multiple databases with multiple tables, and ensure that when this information is queried from a database the results are intelligible.

SQL (Standard Query Language) is a query language that has become standardized. The simple language contains commands that query a database for information. SQL was written to be easily understandable, using simple English terms. If you were to read a query, the syntax of the query would sound much the same as if you were explaining the query to another person. Examine the following:

```
select personal.name,personal.home_phone,personal.email,
➥work.work_phone, work.department from personal,work
➥where personal.name=work.name
```

Even the following example would work on most systems:

```
select * from personal,work where personal.name=work.name
```

where the asterisk is a wild card that matches everything.

To insert information into a database, you use a query as follows:

```
insert into table (name, home_phone, email) VALUES ('rniles',
➥'555-5555','rniles@selah.net')
```

Just by examining these queries, you can easily determine what they do.

Using Microsoft's Internet Database Connector

IIS enables people who want to provide information on the Web to integrate their existing applications as Web applications. The IIS works well with the BackOffice Suite, which is a rich set of tools for businesses. One of the items included within the BackOffice Suite is Microsoft's SQL Server.

The IIS uses the *Internet Database Connector (IDC)*, which communicates with the database Open Database Connectivity (ODBC) driver. The IDC is an Internet Server API (ISAPI) file (HTTPODBC.DLL) that reads a file. IDC files have the extension .IDC and contain commands that can be used with any database that has an ODBC driver.

The ODBC driver retrieves the information from the database and formats the output of the information by using an .HTX (HTX means HTML extension) file.

The .HTX file formats the information from the ODBC driver as an HTML page. That file then returns to the Web server, which sends the document to the client.

Suppose you want to create a form that takes an order from a visitor and then stores that order in the database for later retrieval. The form action would point to an .IDC file, such as that shown in Listing 36.8. Figure 36.3 shows the resulting form.

Listing 36.8 An Order Form Processed by the IDC

```
<FORM ACTION="/orders/order.idc" METHOD="POST">
Name: <INPUT TYPE="text" NAME="name"><BR>
Street: <INPUT TYPE="text" NAME="street"><BR>
City: <INPUT TYPE="text" NAME="city"><BR>
State: <INPUT TYPE="text" NAME="state">
Zip: <INPUT TYPE="text" NAME="zip" SIZE=10><P>
Select which items you would like to order:<BR>
<INPUT TYPE="checkbox" NAME="ram" VALUE="ram"> 8MB RAM<BR>
<INPUT TYPE="checkbox" NAME="hd" VALUE="hd"> 1.2GB HD<BR>
<INPUT TYPE="checkbox" NAME="modem" VALUE="modem"> 28.8 Modem<P>
<INPUT TYPE="submit" VALUE="Place Order">
```

FIG. 36.3

Using a form, you can send information to Microsoft's SQL Server using an .IDC file.

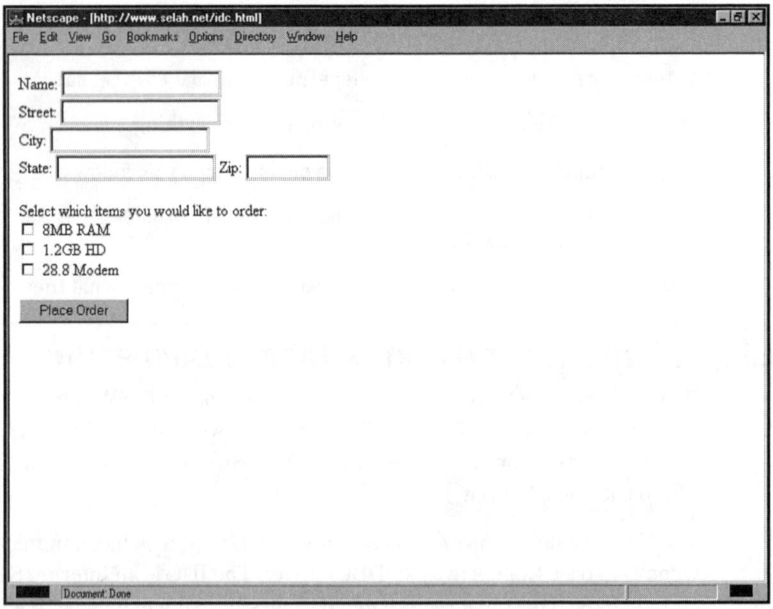

When the user clicks the Place Order button, the information entered in the form is sent to the server, which then opens the ORDER.IDC file.

ORDER.IDC contains commands that specify the database, the .HTX template, and the SQL query. Here's the ORDER.IDC file for the preceding example:

```
Datasource: Orders
Template: orderthx.htx
SQLStatement:
+INSERT name,street,city,state,zip,ram,hd,modem
+INTO orderinfo VALUES ('%name%', '%street%', '%city%', '%state%',
➥+'%zip%', '%ram%', '%hd%', '%modem%');
```

IDC's Required Directives

The .IDC file contains three directives that the IDC requires. The `Datasource` directive specifies the database to which to connect. The `Template` directive specifies which .HTX file to use to create the HTML page that returns to the server and ultimately goes to the client. The `SQLStatement` directive contains the query that inserts information into the database or retrieves information from the database.

Additional IDC Directives

Along with the `Datasource`, `Template`, and `SQLStatement` directives, additional directives are available. These directives are not required, but add a bit of flexibility when dealing with HTTPODBC.DLL. The rest of this section examines each of these directives and explains how you can use them.

The *DefaultParameters* Directive   You can use the `DefaultParameters` directive to specify the default parameters to use if the visitor doesn't fill out the form completely. For example, you can set the following default in case a visitor fails to enter a name:

```
DefaultParameters: name=%John Doe%
```

You can specify more than one parameter, but you must separate each with a comma.

The *RequiredParameters* Directive   The `RequiredParameters` directive enables you to specify which items the visitor must fill. If you want to ensure that the visitor enters a name and address, for example, you specify the following:

```
RequiredParameters: name, street, city, state, zip
```

The *MaxFieldSize* Directive   With the `MaxFieldSize` directive, you can specify a record's maximum length. If you don't specify the `MaxFieldSize`, the default value is 8,192 bytes.

The *MaxRecords* Directive   You can use the `MaxRecords` directive to set the maximum amount of records that a query returns. If you don't set the `MaxRecords` directive, the IDC allows the return of all records that match the query. This default setting isn't a problem with smaller databases, but can be with larger ones. Set this directive to a reasonable number of records, based on the kind of information that you are retrieving.

The *Expires* Directive   If you don't set the Expires directive, the database is accessed each time for information. If you do set this directive, the query returns to the user from a cache instead of accessing the database again. This can help reduce the system's load and return information to the visitor more quickly. By using the Expires directive, you specify the amount of seconds before the cache is refreshed.

The *Username* Directive   If you're not using the SQL Server's integrated security, you can specify a user name for accessing the SQL Server.

The *Password* Directive   You use the Password directive only if a password is required. When specifying the Password directive, you must enter a user name.

The *BeginDetail* and *EndDetail* Tags

Now all you need to do is create an .HTX file that creates the HTML document that you return to the visitor. As with the .IDC file, the .HTX file uses special commands or tags that help format the HTML document.

If a visitor to your site wants to query the database, the <%begindetail%> and <%enddetail%> tags store the returned information. For example, suppose that a visitor perusing your company product catalog enters a query to search for modems and that your database includes a field called modem. You can format the .HTX file to report each instance that matches the field:

```
<table>
<%begindetail%>
<tr><td><%modem%><td><%price%></td></tr>
<%enddetail%>
</table>
```

This code opens the <TABLE> tag. For each instance of a match, the file creates a row with the modem (which could simply be a name) and the price. The <%enddetail%> tag specifies the end of a section. You then use the <\TABLE> tag to close the table. If no records are found, this section is skipped.

The *CurrentRecord* Directive

The CurrentRecord directive counts the number of times that records are processed. You can use this directive to check whether the query generated any results and then inform the visitor of any results.

Soon you'll see how to use the CurrentRecord directive, but first examine other tags that enable you to check information and return results based on conditions.

Conditional Operators

Within the .HTX file, you can use the following simple conditional operators: <%if%>, <%else%>, and <%endif%>. By using these operator tags, you can check whether certain conditions are met. For example, you can check whether any records were returned, and if not, you can inform the visitor:

```
<table>
<%begindetail%>
<tr><td><%modem%><td><%price%></td></tr>
<%enddetail%>
</table>
<%if CurrentRecord EQ 0 %>
I'm sorry, but there isn't anything in the database
➥that matches your query.
<center>
<a href="products.html">[Product Database]</a>
</center>
```

The `<%if%>` tag uses four conditional words you can use to check information.

`EQ` checks whether a value is equal to the test, as in the following example:

```
<%if modem EQ "US Robotics" %>
US Robotics 28.8
<%endif%>
```

`GT` enables you to check whether one value is greater than another, as in the following example:

```
<%if price GT 500 %>
```

`LT` checks whether a value is less than another value, as in the following example:

```
<%elseif price LT 10 %>
<%endif%>
```

`CONTAINS` enables you to check whether a value is anywhere within another value, as in the following example:

```
<%if modem CONTAINS "Robotics" %>
US Robotics
<%endif%>
```

The *MaxRecords* Variable

The `MaxRecords` variable contains the value of the `MaxRecords` directive that the IDC file specifies, as in the following example:

```
<%if CurrentRecord EQ MaxRecords %>
Results have been abridged
<%endif%>
```

Fields

After a visitor enters fields within an HTML form, you can pass them directly to the .HTX file by adding the *idc.* prefix. For example, if you want to return information to the visitor who entered it, you could use the following code line:

```
Hello %idc.namd%. How is the weather in %idc.city%,
➥%idc.state%?<BR>
```

HTTP Variables

You can also use HTTP variables within .HTX files. To do so, you enclose the variable within the <% %> delimiters, as in the following example:

```
You are using <%HTTP_USER_AGENT%>
```

To continue with the order-entry example, you simply thank the visitor for entering the order and let the visitor know that you have processed it. Listing 36.9 gives you an example of how this is done.

Listing 36.9   A Simple Page Generated with an HTX File

```
<HTML>
<HEAD><TITLE>Thank you!</TITLE></HEAD>
<BODY>
<H1> Thank you for your order!</H1>
Thank you, %idc.name%. The following items will be added to your bill:
<UL>
<%if% idc.ram EQ "">
<%else%>
<LI> 8MB of RAM
<%endif%>
<%if% idc.hd EQ "">
<%else%>
<LI> 1.2GB Hard Drive
<%endif%>
<%if% idc.modem EQ "">
<%else%>
<LI> 28.8 Modem
<%endif%>
</UL>
These items will be sent to:
<%name%><BR>
<%street%><BR>
<%city%>, <%state%> <%zip%><P>
Again, thank you for your order, please visit us again soon!<BR>
<HR>
<P>
<A HREF="http://www.selah.net">[Return to main page]</A>
</BODY>
</HTML>
```

The .HTX file produces a page similar to that shown in Figure 36.4.

Again, you have only touched on the subject of using IDC and HTX files with Microsoft's IIS, but this should give you an idea of where you can go from here. One final note though: With the advent of FrontPage for Office 97, Microsoft has made using IDC and HTX files even easier through the use of its Database Wizard. I suggest taking a look at Que's *Special Edition Using FrontPage 97* for more information on how you can use FrontPage to access a database using the IDC.

FIG. 36.4
By using the .HTX file, you can embed a database's information into the final HTML document.

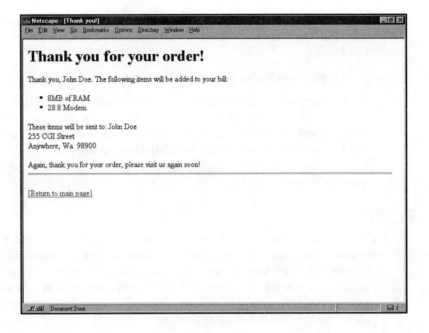

Using Oracle

Oracle, the industry's database heavyweight, provides a collection of tools that allow an administrator to easily tie the Web with an Oracle database. *Easy* might be a relative term here, because all the lingo that Oracle provides makes you feel like you're back in school learning your native language for the first time. Even so, once the generic terms provided by Oracle are understood, connecting to a database through the Web and displaying the results of a query to those visiting your site should seem like a breeze.

Web Listener

Oracle uses what is called a *Web Listener*. Simply put, a Web Listener is a Web server that recognizes various methods in which Web Listener may be accessed. Much like how normal Web servers operate, to find out whether a request will be a request for an HTML document or a CGI script, Oracle's Web Listener detects this and various other methods in which it might be used to access the database, or process a request.

For example, if Web Listener detects the string *owa*, and is properly placed with the HTTP request, then the Web server knows that it's supposed to activate the *Oracle Web Agent* (often referred to as OWA—more on this in a moment), and process the request using information stored in the *Database Connection Descriptor (DCD)*. The DCD tells the Web Agent both the database access privileges the PL/SQL agent has when executing a request, and the schema used for accessing the database.

As stated, the terminology can be a bit confusing. In order to clear things up a bit, take a look at the following URL. The URL can be broken down into three parts which are important to Web Listener.

http://www.foobar.com/owa-bin/owa/sample_empinfo

The first section, **http://www.foobar.com/owa-bin** defines the path to the Oracle Web Agent. The portion **owa** tells Web Listener that the Oracle Web Agent will be used. And **sample_empinfo** contains information on connecting to the database using PL/SQL. This URL can even be used within an HTML form, for example:

```
<FORM ACTION="http://www.foobar.com/owa-bin/owa/sample_empinfo"
➥METHOD="POST">
```

PL/SQL

The language for connecting to an Oracle database is PL/SQL. *PL/SQL* is a programming language that contains a superset of the structured query language (SQL) and is used to access the Oracle database. Where SQL is a language to simply query a database, PL/SQL allows you to create functions; use flow control and loops; assign variables, constants, datatypes, and various other statements that help you program applications that submit data to a database; and allows you to format the output of a query.

Another feature of PL/SQL is that you are allowed to store compiled PL/SQL code directly in the database. By doing so, you can call programs you created directly from the database which can be shared by other individuals (at the same time even!), removing the need for having multiple applications that do the same thing.

Unfortunately, PL/SQL is not an industry standard. Currently (and I'm not aware of any changes to this), PL/SQL can only be used with Oracle. This creates a problem with portability of code where you might want to have one interface that can be used to access various databases.

If you have installed the PL/SQL Web Toolkit with Oracle, you can use PL/SQL to format the output of queries into HTML format. The toolkit provides a full range of commands which will be converted to HTML tags that will include information from a query. For example, if you had an employee database which contained the name, ID number of an individual, a phone number, and the e-mail address of each of these employees, the following DCD would provide an HTML document like that in Figure 36.5.

The following PL/SQL query provides the visitor with this information:

```
Create or replace procedure emplist is
employees boolean;

begin
employees := htp.tablePrint('emp', 'BORDER=1');
end;
```

FIG. 36.5

Using Oracle's Web Toolkit enables the administrator to create HTML documents based on information in an Oracle database.

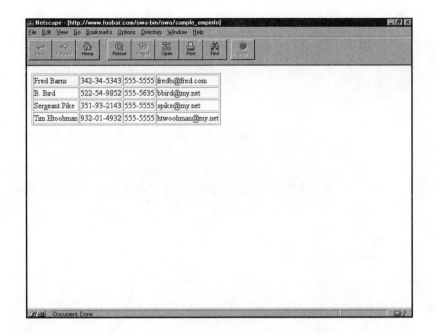

Fred Barns	342-34-5343	555-5555	fredb@fred.com
B. Bird	522-54-9852	555-5635	bbird@my.net
Sergeant Pike	351-93-2143	555-5555	spike@my.net
Tim Htoohman	932-01-4932	555-5555	htwoohman@my.net

Additional Information

Delving into Oracle's Web tools too deeply would require a book on its own. PL/SQL alone would require its own book, so unfortunately we can't go too deeply into every aspect of what Oracle can do. The information here should whet your appetite though, and if you have more questions about Oracle, I suggest you visit the following Web sites. Together with the information contained herein, you should be able to decide if Oracle is the best solution for you.

Thomas Dunbar has taken the time to provide information on how PL/SQL works with the World Wide Web. This page contains a couple of examples which should give you a better understanding of how PL/SQL and Oracle works. You can visit his page at:

http://gserver.grads.vt.edu/

For more information on PL/SQL itself, see:

http://www.inf.bme.hu/~gaszi/plsql/plsql_manual.html

## CHAPTER 37

Creating a Web Site for Business

by Mark R. Brown

Whether you are part of a Mom and Pop mail-order business, a Fortune 500 corporation, or something in between, the odds are good that you're considering putting your company on the World Wide Web. After all, everybody else is doing it, and if you don't get on the Web right away, you stand a good chance of being left behind. Right?

Not really. In truth, not every company needs to be on the Web. And many others who already have Web sites haven't really defined why they're there, or what benefits they expect to derive from their Web presence. There are even a few companies who have put up trial Web sites only to take them back down again once they realized how much they were costing in time, money, and other resources. In short, they just didn't think it through.

The World Wide Web is actually just one more tool in the vast arsenal available to business. And like TV advertising, self-published newsletters, mainframe computers, corporate jets, and other business tools, whether or not you need to make use of the Web depends on what kind of business you are in, and what you can reasonably expect a Web presence to do for you. ■

Define your goal
You should have a clear goal in mind before you set up a business site.

Design your Web site before beginning work
Once you have a goal firmly established, design follows logically.

Collect feedback from your customers
Most business sites are concerned not only with communicating to their viewers, but also with receiving feedback from them.

Build a Web site for your nonprofit organization
Nonprofit organizations can follow almost the same design steps as for-profit institutions in creating Web sites, as the goals are usually similar.

Why Be on the Web?

If you're in business, there's probably at least one good reason to put your company on the World Wide Web. The key to doing so successfully is to find out what that reason is *first*, before you go online with your Web site.

It's important to ask yourself this question: What do you want to accomplish with your Web presence?

There are four main reasons for putting your company on the Web:

- To sell a product or service
- To build name recognition
- To provide customer support
- To encourage investment in your company

You can do all of these things at once, but it's best to create clearly delineated areas on your site for each purpose. Then your client can jump to each area from a main "table of contents" type page.

Look at some real-world sites that attempt to accomplish each of these goals.

N O T E   If you have the budget, consider hiring a Web design firm to help you design your Web site, just as you would when launching an ad campaign. There are, after all, millions of potential customers out there on the Web. Grabbing their attention would certainly be worth the investment.

However, if you do hire a design firm, make sure you find one with both Web and PR savvy. The Web is a whole different ball game than any other medium, and Web design companies have sprung up like weeds. Many startups have technical online expertise, but lack solid PR and advertising skills. Older firms may have the PR and advertising experience, but may be struggling with the technical problems associated with putting Web sites online successfully.

You might want to check out some Web sites of companies that are about your size and already on the Web (those that are not your competitors). Most Web pages designed by professional designers have a tag line somewhere that indicates who did the page design work. Clicking their link will take you right to the responsible party. ■

Direct Sales

If you have a service or product line that you can sell directly to consumers, the World Wide Web can be just as effective as classified advertising, telemarketing, or mail order catalogs. Maybe even more so if your product or service is high-tech in nature.

N O T E   Keep in mind when designing your site that the customers you draw from the Web are not likely to have the same demographics as your normal customer mix. They are much more likely to be upscale, young, and technically oriented, though this may change to some degree as the Web matures. ■

With a Web site, you can put your catalog online, making it available 24 hours a day, 7 days a week. With a secure online form for taking credit card numbers and orders, you can effectively set up a full-time order desk without having to hire full-time order takers. But even if you opt to use your site in combination with a more traditional toll-free telephone number, or even with "snail mail" orders to your business address, putting your company on the Web is like opening an office that never closes its doors.

Figure 37.1 shows a typical catalog-oriented Web site whose main purpose is generating direct online sales.

FIG. 37.1
This Web-based catalog helps Software Select sell CD-ROMs.

Name Brand Recognition

Many large companies have developed Web sites for one reason and one reason only: building name brand recognition and loyalty. For Coca-Cola, Maytag, Chrysler, and other Fortune 500 corporations, a small increase in market share can mean a big increase in profits.

Since the Web draws in so many upscale consumers, it only makes sense for big companies to expend some time, money, and effort to create an impressive image on the Web. In fact, it is almost a requirement that such companies have huge Web sites. The public expects it of them.

Fortune 500 companies can't settle for simple sites—they build big, fancy, "fun" sites full of corporate image-builders. Oscar Mayer's site includes a multimedia history of wieners. Coca-Cola's includes seasonal promotions. Disney's has interactive online games. All have fully funded, well-staffed departments whose only job is to make sure their sites present as impressive a public image as their corporate offices, store displays, and TV commercials.

Figure 37.2 shows Hershey's home page on the Web. Its purpose is clearly to build name brand recognition and loyalty.

FIG. 37.2

Hershey's site includes an online cookbook, an interactive company history, and other brand-name reinforcement elements.

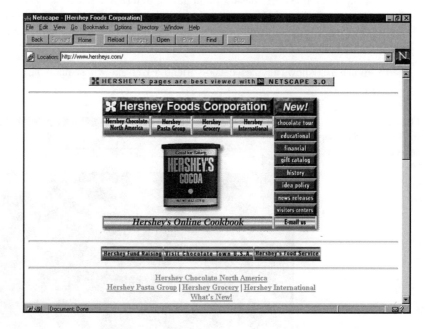

Customer Support

If your company spends a great deal of effort and time on customer support, odds are that you can cut those costs by a substantial margin by moving your first line of support onto the Web.

A Web site can provide 24-hour customer service at a fraction of the cost of keeping a full-time customer support staff on the payroll. Experience has proven that the majority of customer service problems can be solved by consulting a short list of "frequently asked questions" (or FAQs). The perfect place to post your company's FAQs is on the Web. If someone has a product question at 2 A.M., they can look it up on the Web. They're happy because they get an immediate solution to their problem. You're happy because you don't have to pay someone to man a telephone help desk at 2 A.M.!

Of course, the concept of customer support extends well beyond just a simple posting of FAQs. You can include forms your customers can fill out and send via e-mail to request product literature or custom fixes to more complex problems. You can even include product manuals online. These provide good reference material for customers who may have lost their manuals, or who may have outdated manuals. Online product manuals can serve as solid sales tools, providing extra information for potential customers who like to make purchasing decisions based on detailed information.

Online catalogs can also be considered a form of customer support for the same reason.

If your company provides a service instead of a product, your Web site can provide your customers and potential customers with the details of your services that might otherwise tie up a salesperson for hours. You can update that information with a few keystrokes.

Kelly Services is one service company that uses its Web site primarily for customer service (see Figure 37.3). As one of the major employment services in the country, it has two types of customers: the individuals it places, and the companies which it places with them. The Kelly Services site is chock full of information for both, from how to create a résumé, to a directory of services Kelly can provide for employers.

FIG. 37.3

Kelly Services provides customer service for prospective employers and prospective employees on its Web site.

Promoting Investment

A real phenomenon of the '90s is the incredible number of initial public stock offerings (or IPOs) being promulgated by high-tech companies. Each year sees hundreds or even thousands of new stock offerings. Even though there seems to be more investment money available all the time, competition among all these companies for investors is high.

That's why almost every IPO is preceded by the launch of a Web site promoting the company involved. Though such sites may also pursue the purposes already stated for business sites—sales, support, and recognition—they most often focus on simply supplying potential investors with information that will influence them to invest in the company.

Most such sites include profiles of the corporate officers, overviews of the company's products or services, and other promotional materials. Though companies are severely limited in what they can claim or communicate when an IPO is in the works, you'll find just about everything this side of the legal limits on the sites of companies taking the IPO plunge.

Figure 37.4 shows a fairly typical page of information from a company making an IPO. On this page, the company talks about the investment it has made in research and the products it has in the pipeline.

FIG. 37.4

Armed with information on this site, a potential investor can hopefully make a more informed decision about whether or not to invest in this company.

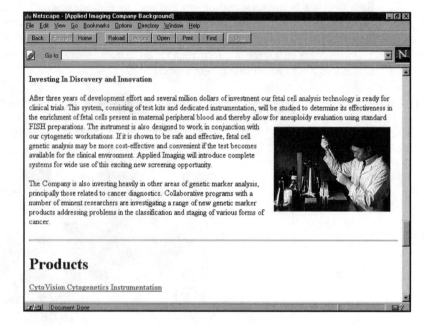

NOTE   No matter what kind of company you are putting on the Web, the following are a few sure-fire items that always draw attention.

● Provide News of cutting-edge research your company is conducting. Make sure you emphasize the *latest* developments and keep it up to date.

● Announcements of interesting new products are always hot ticket items on the Web. Mark new features with graphical "NEW!" icons.

● Remember that your audience on the Web is insatiably curious about nearly everything. If your company makes wieners, a "Multimedia History of Wieners" is guaranteed to make your site a hit.

● If you have imprinted items, sell them on the Web. Even if you're a local brew pub in Maine, you'll be astounded at how many beer aficionados in Oregon will order your "Lobster Brew" sweatshirts.

● Provide links to related sites—even your competitors! Nothing sells a Web site like a well-organized set of relevant links. It's the surest way to get someone to bookmark your site, and once you're bookmarked, you have your customer hooked for life. (Always make sure you have something new and fascinating on your link page to grab their attention and keep them around when they use that bookmark in the future.)

As always, make sure that everything you put on the Web brings you closer to your goals for being there. ■

More Examples Online

Need a few more examples? You'd expect the premier magazine of the advertising industry to host a good Web site, and *Advertising Age* does at **http://www.adage.com** (see Figure 37.5). It's flashy, fun, entertaining, and informative, and it never loses sight of why it's on the Web. You should check it out, not only because it's a good example, but because it also reviews *other* corporate Web sites.

FIG. 37.5
The *Advertising Age* Web site provides reviews of corporate Web sites.

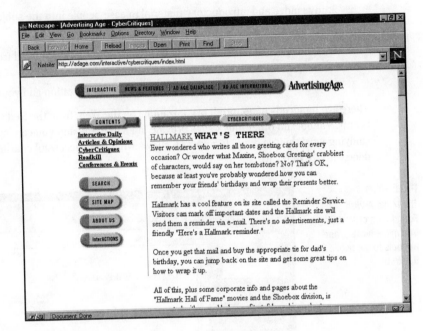

Nonprofit Organizations

Much of what's been said about corporate Web sites also applies to nonprofit organizations. But for organizations, the Web offers one additional advantage—it's the most effective and least expensive means ever invented for getting your message to the people.

Whether your organization wants to clean up the environment or clean up Washington; whether you want to raise the whole world's awareness of hungry children or just round up a few hundred kindred spirits who might want to join the Emily Dickinson Appreciation Society, you'll find plenty of sympathetic listeners on the Web.

Of course, an organization's site should usually be more serious (unless your topic is decidedly nonserious, of course) than a commercial site. It should certainly be heavier on information. It might help to think of your site as more of a resource than a selling tool. However, don't lose sight of your goal: to gain support. Depending on your organization, the support you desire might be cash contributions, volunteers, or even just letters to Congress, but the means to any of those ends is usually the same. You need to inform, educate, and evangelize the public about your cause.

The following are some items you'll definitely want to have on the Web site for your nonprofit organization:

■ Information about your organization: its history, membership, growth, awards, and so on.

■ Information about your cause: statistics, reports, digitized images, historical data, and news items.

■ Study guides and introductory material to ease people into the subject matter.

■ Links to related sites.

■ Testimonials from those whom your organization has helped and from celebrities who support your cause.

■ Information about how to join or support your organization and your cause.

There are hundreds of nonprofit organizations on the Web, from the Red Cross to the Boy Scouts. Yahoo! and other index sites provide links to them, and you can learn a great deal by studying what they've done. Figure 37.6 shows what one successful charitable organization has done with its Web site.

FIG. 37.6

The Make-A-Wish Foundation of America informs, educates, and appeals to the public on the Web.

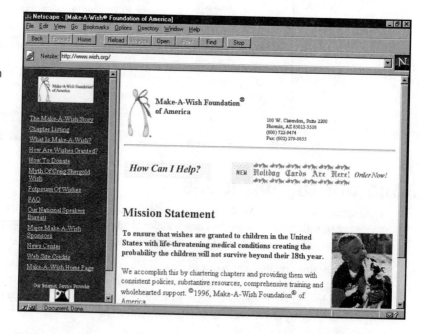

Creating a Business Site

Now it's time to take the plunge and design an actual Web site for a fictional business. First, create a company called "Honest Joe's Used Cars." Assume that Joe has hired you to put his company on the Web.

Focusing the Pitch

"You're putting a used car lot on the Web? Har, Har, Har!" was the reaction of Joe's main competitor when he found out that Joe was going to put his business on the Web. Since then, Joe has had the last laugh—all the way to the bank.

You see, even though Joe knows that it's called the "World Wide" Web, he also knows two other things: (1) Being on the Web is almost free, and (2) the "world" includes Milwaukee, where he sells cars. In fact, a lot of high-tech companies are located in the Milwaukee area. He's already sold cars to hundreds of their employees. Thousands upon thousands of Web-browsing potential car-buying customers reside in the Milwaukee area. Joe knows that lots of them are techie-types who might not be comfortable shopping for a car on a used car lot; but they love shopping for one on the Web.

Joe says he wants to communicate four major things on his site:

1. He offers easy credit terms.
2. He has a wide selection of cars, from sporty models for young, single programmers to family vans for middle-management types.
3. His cars are good, quality-checked vehicles.
4. His stock turns over constantly and, therefore, viewers should check back often for new listings.

Joe knows that the convenience of car shopping on the Web will draw in customers and that the immediacy of seeing new listings daily will keep them coming back until they buy from him.

Joe's site is typical in that it doesn't fit strictly into one of the business categories defined earlier. There's certainly an element of "building brand loyalty," since he wants the people who visit his site to come to his car lot when they're ready to buy. There's also an element of "direct sales," since he lists his products online. But he can hardly sell them directly over the Web—his customers still have to come to him. There's even an element of customer service, since he's helping his potential customers make informed buying decisions. About the only thing missing is "encouraging investment." Joe is the sole proprietor, and he intends to stay that way.

Organizing the Site

The first thing you need to do is review the information Joe wants to present and look over the resources he has available. You'll use that information to create a "flow chart" of how the site is to be organized.

Joe wants to put a few "hot" listings up front, right on his home page, along with a flashy, easy-to-use, clickable imagemap to send his customers off to information pages about credit, quality, and so on. He also wants to put his salesmen online, as well as a tie-in to his company "mascot," the "Happy Red Car." After a bit of discussion with Joe, you come up with the flow chart shown in Figure 37.7.

FIG. 37.7
This chart shows the navigational flow of information on the Web site for Joe's Used Cars.

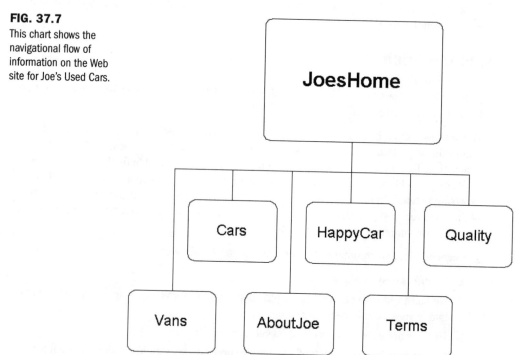

This site is pretty simple, with a home page that calls six documents. There are no fancy inter-connections, and no tree structure to worry about. Links are uncomplicated and easy to follow.

Joe's Home Page

Listing 37.1 shows the HTML for the home page for Honest Joe's Used Cars.

Listing 37.1 Home Page for Joe's Used Cars

```
<html>
<head>
</head>
<title>Honest Joe's Used Cars</title>
<!-- milwaukee wisconsin used cars pre-owned autos automobiles
bargains deals easy credit terms -->
<body>
<center>
<MAP NAME="joesmap">
```

```
<AREA SHAPE="RECT" COORDS="0,0,149,84" HREF="cars.htm">
<AREA SHAPE="RECT" COORDS="150,0,299,84" HREF="aboutjoe.htm">
<AREA SHAPE="RECT" COORDS="300,0,449,84" HREF="quality.htm">
<AREA SHAPE="RECT" COORDS="0,85,149,169" HREF="vans.htm">
<AREA SHAPE="RECT" COORDS="150,85,299,169" HREF="happycar.htm">
<AREA SHAPE="RECT" COORDS="300,85,449,169" HREF="terms.htm">
</MAP>
<IMG SRC="joesmap.gif" USEMAP="#joesmap">
<br>
<a href="quality.htm">[ Quality ]</a>
<a href="aboutjoe.htm">[ Honest Joe's Used Cars ]</a>
<a href="vans.htm">[ Family Vans ]</a>
<br>
<a href="cars.htm">[ Sporty Sedans ]</a>
<a href="happycar.htm">[ Home of the Happy Red Car! ]</a>
<a href="terms.htm">[ Easy Credit Terms! ]</a>
<hr>
<h3>Honest Joe's Used Cars · 2300 Lakeside Ave. ·
<a href="http://www.milwaukee.net/">Milwaukee, Wisconsin</a> ·
333-555-1111</h3>
<hr>
</center>
Over 100 <img src="new.gif" alt="NEW"> models this week!<br>
<img src="bulletbl.gif" alt="*"><a href="cars.htm#92Cutlass">
1992 Olds Cutlass</a><img src="hot.gif" alt="HOT!">
<b>*executive car*</b><br>
<img src="bulletbl.gif" alt="*"><a href="vans.htm#95Caravan">
1995 Dodge Caravan</a> <b>*loaded*</b><br>
<img src="bulletbl.gif" alt="*"><a href="cars.htm#94Cavalier">
1994 Chevy Cavalier</a> <b>*low mileage*</b><br>
<img src="bulletbl.gif" alt="*"><a href="cars.htm#96Taurus">
1996 Ford Taurus</a><img src="hand.gif" alt="<-">
<b>*the boss's wife's car!*</b><br>
<img src="bulletbl.gif" alt="*"><a href="cars.htm#77Dodge">
1977 Dodge Ramcharger</a> <b>*muscle car*</b><br>
<img src="bulletbl.gif" alt="*"><a href="cars.htm#73VW">
1973 VW Beetle</a> <b>*clean*</b><br>
<b>Click here for even more new <a href="cars.htm">
cars</a> and <a href="vans.htm">vans</a>!</b>
<p>
<center>
<hr>
<i>New cars and vans are arriving every day!<br>
<b>Bookmark</b> this page and come back often!</i><br>
<strong>Thanks for visiting Honest Joe's Used Cars.</strong>
</center>
<hr>
<strong>Page last updated January 1, 1997</strong>
<address>Email comments to: <a href="mailto:joe@joescars.com">
joe@joescars.com</a></address>
</body>
</html>
```

Figure 37.8 shows how Joe's home page looks in Netscape Navigator.

FIG. 37.8
Honest Joe's home page incorporates a client-side imagemap for easy navigation.

Take a look at the HTML for Joe's site step-by-step.

Up-Front Material

This page starts out simply, with the standard `<HTML>`, `<HEAD>`, and `<TITLE>` elements.

```
<html>
<head>
</head>
<title>Honest Joe's Used Cars</title>
```

However, the following line of HTML is intended not for human Web browsers, but for indexing "robots":

```
<!-- milwaukee wisconsin used cars pre-owned autos automobiles
bargains deals easy credit terms -->
```

Automatic indexing robot programs like Webcrawler will pick out all these terms and add them to their index lists. That way, if a user checks for any of these keywords in an index that has "crawled" his home page, he or she will find a link to Joe's site.

You didn't bother setting any fancy background images or colors in the `<BODY>` tag, nor did you set any text colors for this page. You want everyone to be able to see these pages, not just those with graphical browsers.

N O T E You need to make sure that the backgrounds of your GIF graphics are (including the
bullets) transparent so that whichever colors your viewers pick in their browsers will shine
right through. ■

The Navigational Imagemap

You use a client-side navigational imagemap to provide a big, colorful, graphic introduction
to Joe's home page, with an alternative text menu right below it for those who can't handle
imagemaps.

```
<MAP NAME="joesmap">
<AREA SHAPE="RECT" COORDS="0,0,149,84" HREF="cars.htm">
<AREA SHAPE="RECT" COORDS="150,0,299,84" HREF="aboutjoe.htm">
<AREA SHAPE="RECT" COORDS="300,0,449,84" HREF="quality.htm">
<AREA SHAPE="RECT" COORDS="0,85,149,169" HREF="vans.htm">
<AREA SHAPE="RECT" COORDS="150,85,299,169" HREF="happycar.htm">
<AREA SHAPE="RECT" COORDS="300,85,449,169" HREF="terms.htm">
</MAP>
<IMG SRC="joesmap.gif" USEMAP="#joesmap">
```

▶ **See** "Using Alternatives to Imagemaps," to learn how to avoid using an imagemap by slicing up
the image into rectangles, **p. 255**

This is the complete imagemap definition. Each individual area shape is a rectangle 150 pixels
wide by 85 pixels high, in a graphic imagemap 450 pixels wide by 170 pixels high.

The upper-left and lower-left areas link to separate HTML pages that list Joe's latest assort-
ments of cars and vans, respectively. The top-center area links to a page that tells all about
Joe's dealership, including Joe himself and his salespeople. The lower-center area of the
imagemap links to the story of the "Happy Red Car," the mascot of Joe's business. The
upper-right area links to a page extolling Joe's 12-point quality inspection program. Finally,
the lower-right area links to a page that details how to set up easy credit terms.

Each area is clearly defined by a unique graphic.

For those whose browsers don't support client-side imagemaps, you supply a text-only navigational "map" that repeats the functionality of the imagemap:

```
<br>
<a href="quality.htm">[ Quality ]</a>
<a href="aboutjoe.htm">[ Honest Joe's Used Cars ]</a>
<a href="vans.htm">[ Family Vans ]</a>
<br>
<a href="cars.htm">[ Sporty Sedans ]</a>
<a href="happycar.htm">[ Home of the Happy Red Car! ]</a>
<a href="terms.htm">[ Easy Credit Terms! ]</a>
<hr>
```

Part
VIII

Ch
37

Figure 37.9 shows how this text menu appears in Lynx, a UNIX-based, non-graphical Web browser.

FIG. 37.9

If you're concerned about letting everyone browse your site, you'll have to add elements like this text menu for those who use nongraphical browsers.

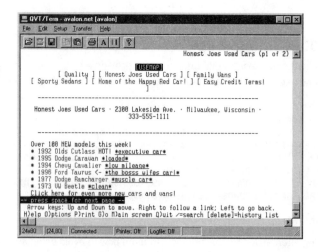

Establishing Site Identity

You follow the navigational tools with a tagline giving the address and phone number of Joe's car lot. Being civic-minded, he asks you to make the "Milwaukee, Wisconsin" part of his address a link to the local Chamber of Commerce promotional page for the city, as follows:

```
<hr>
<h3>Honest Joe's Used Cars · 2300 Lakeside Ave. · <a
href="http://www.milwaukee.net/">Milwaukee, Wisconsin</a> ·
333-555-1111</h3>
<hr>
</center>
```

After these lines, you're done with header stuff, so you add a horizontal rule to divide the rest of the page and turn off centering.

The Teasers

Now come the car listings. First, you tell people that over 100 new cars are available; then you list just six of them. Only the best "featured" cars are listed on Joe's home page, and you offer an irresistible blurb and hotlink to each. The link for each featured car is targeted to its listing on the appropriate page ("vans.htm" or "cars.htm"). These pages are updated weekly.

```
Over 100 <img src="new.gif" alt="NEW"> models this week!<br>
<img src="bulletbl.gif" alt="*"><a href="cars.htm#92Cutlass">
1992 Olds Cutlass</a><img src="hot.gif" alt="HOT!"> <b>*executive car*
</b><br>
<img src="bulletbl.gif" alt="*"><a href="vans.htm#95Caravan">
```

```
1995 Dodge Caravan</a> <b>*loaded*</b><br>
<img src="bulletbl.gif" alt="*"><a href="cars.htm#94Cavalier">
1994 Chevy Cavalier</a> <b>*low mileage*</b><br>
<img src="bulletbl.gif" alt="*"><a href="cars.htm#96Taurus">
1996 Ford Taurus</a><img src="hand.gif" alt="<-">
<b>*the boss's wife's car!*</b><br>
<img src="bulletbl.gif" alt="*"><a href="cars.htm#77Dodge">
1977 Dodge Ramcharger</a> <b>*muscle car*</b><br>
<img src="bulletbl.gif" alt="*"><a href="cars.htm#73VW">
1973 VW Beetle</a> <b>*clean*</b><br>
```

You could have used an HTML bulleted list for Joe's featured autos, but you wanted to use fancy graphic bullets instead.

Finally, you provide links that lead to two separate pages for all the rest—one for sedans and one for vans. These links are the same as those for the graphic sedan and van links in the imagemap at the top of the page:

```
<b>Click here for even more new <a href="cars.htm">cars</a> and <a
href="vans.htm">vans</a>!</b>
<p>
```

The Wrap Up

Finally, you finish with the electronic equivalent of a hearty handshake and an invitation to come back again:

```
<center>
<hr>
<i>New cars and vans are arriving every day!<br>
<b>Bookmark</b> this page and come back often!</i><br>
<strong>Thanks for visiting Honest Joe's Used Cars.</strong>
</center>
<hr>
<strong>Page last updated January 1, 1997</strong>
<address>Email comments to: <a href="mailto:joe@joescars.com">
joe@joescars.com</a></address>
</body>
</html>
```

More Work Ahead

This is all just for the home page. You still have a lot of work to do to create pages for credit, quality, and the other issues you want to address on this site. Joe is also going to have to hustle to keep his car and van lists up-to-date. But at least his home page looks good, and he's off to an excellent start.

Every business site is a unique challenge. Joe's concerns won't be your concerns. But if you set concrete goals and keep them firmly in mind when you're designing your Web site, you won't go far wrong.

Putting Existing Documents on the Web

So much for creating a business Web site from scratch. But, truth be told, almost any business setting up a Web site for the first time already has a great storehouse of "legacy documents"— brochures, sales literature, catalogs, etc.—available that can serve as the nucleus of that site. However, legacy documents present you with a different kind of problem: How do you get them from their original form onto your Web pages?

There are really four issues at work here, not one. Because the Web is a different medium than that for which your original information (brochures, videos, and so on) was prepared, you need to do some soul searching first to determine the following:

- What parts of those documents you should definitely put on the Web.
- What you should definitely omit.
- How it all should be reorganized to make use of hyperlinks.
- How to physically get the job done.

What to Include

Your brochures, newsletters, and videos are certain to be a rich source of material about your company or your organization. By carefully mining these resources, you can glean a great many text blurbs, graphics, and clips that will help you communicate your message on the Web.

Just make sure the information you keep is targeted and focused on helping you meet your defined goals. Focus, and don't yield to the temptation to include everything because it's so "good."

What to Omit

You should certainly throw away anything that is of use only to insiders. Remember that you are speaking to a worldwide audience, not preaching to the choir. Make especially certain you don't post anything of a private or proprietary nature.

Keep off your Web pages all irrelevant or off-topic information. Old annual reports, staff photos and biographies, and other irrelevant (boring) information should be disposed of, too.

How to Reorganize

Remember to think multimedia. Break text into short blocks and mix liberally with relevant graphics. Put the essentials up front, then provide hypertext links to the rest.

> **N O T E** Don't forget the "multi" in "multimedia"! Multimedia means more than just a few extra eye-catching graphic elements. It means video, audio, animation, and interactive applications, all integrated into a presentation that draws your viewers into your material. The more involved your audience gets with your Web pages, the better they will remember your message. ■

Build a good table of contents so that people will have no problem finding things on your site. Give them a clear, concise, topically oriented menu on your home page so navigation will be easy.

Where possible, organize data into tables, or present information as charts and graphs. Make it friendly.

The Mechanics

Part
VIII

Ch
37

If you have huge scanned-in graphics, redo them so they load in a reasonable amount of time. Remember the lowest common denominator. Scale them down in both size and number of colors so they will look good on a 640×480, 256-color screen.

If you have huge amounts of legacy text as word processor files, carve them down to a manageable size first, then feed them through a word processor-to-HTML converter.

Templates for Word Processors

If your legacy information is in word-processor file format, templates are probably available for converting them directly into HTML. These templates plug right into your existing word processor, effectively turning it into an HTML editing machine. In fact, Office 97 users can save their documents to HTML by choosing File, Save as HTML from the main menu.

As usual, Yahoo! has an index of such templates; it's at **http://www.yahoo.com/ Computers_and_Internet/Internet/World_Wide_Web/HTML_Converters/**. ●

## CHAPTER 38

Setting Up a Company Intranet

by Matthew Brown

By now, you've learned quite a lot about the Internet, HTML, CGI, and scripting languages. With all of that information embedded into your brain, you may be asking yourself, "How can there be anything more to learn?" In actuality, what you should be asking yourself is, "How can I tie all of this information together and use it for a business solution?"

Generally, when a software company begins the design process, it starts by looking at the needs of a very wide user base. While the software developers try to incorporate solutions for all users into their products, it's not possible for them to create an application that's perfect for everyone. In fact, that's quite an understatement. Many companies find themselves paying custom developers large amounts of money to customize off-the-shelf software to fit their needs. Believe it or not, by using HTML and Internet server tools, you can create a business solution so customizable that it can rival any proprietary solution on the software market today.

With the rise of the intranet, CIS departments are beginning to take charge of their network applications by developing solutions themselves. This results in two things— a decrease in operating expenses once the application is developed, and a solution that is scalable enough to

Leverage the power of an intranet

Developing an intranet is a cross-platform groupware solution.

Lower the cost of network collaboration

Develop your own solutions and save money.

Centralize all of your company's computer applications

Network users will find it easier to find information on an intranet.

Reduce training time through the use of an intranet

Your users will only have to learn one simple interface and become more productive.

Develop beyond the scope of the World Wide Web

Utilize high-speed LAN bandwidth to its maximum potential.

handle virtually any need that arises. In this chapter, it is the author's goal to give you enough information about using and developing an intranet that you are empowered with the ability to create Enterprise-sized applications on a shoestring-sized budget. ■

Defining the Intranet

An intranet, simply defined, is an internal network solution that utilizes the TCP/IP protocol and existing Internet technologies. These technologies range from Web servers to HTML and interactive scripting. The key idea to keep in mind is that anything that you've seen used on the Internet can be used on an internal level for customized solutions.

Uses of an Intranet

The most basic use of an intranet is file sharing. Everyone on your network needs access to shared files and resources. Making these files available, and easily accessible, can sometimes be a challenge. But through the use of proven Internet technologies, tasks such as file sharing are obtained easily. At its most basic level, the Internet itself is built on file sharing. Every time you click a hyperlink, the file that is anchored to the link is essentially shared and made available to your Web browser.

Maybe your files are already organized into specific directories that make searching for the right file a lot easier. Do those files happen to fall into the 8.3 file name category? If so, you'll find that by creating an intranet to organize and share files, you will have a much more user-friendly network that is accessible by everyone. That's really the purpose of an intranet—to share information that is accessible by anyone on your network and, at the same time, is easy to navigate. It's a lot easier to locate a file called "Company Fiscal Year: 1996" than "cofisyr96.doc." It also makes a lot more sense.

Most network users are not computer-savvy. They know just enough to get their work done. Sometimes the intricacies of a networked operation can actually slow down the end user by complicating situations because of too much technology. Deploying an intranet solution for your company will not only make network computing simpler, but it will also possibly increase work output through simplicity.

Getting Started

The base component of any good intranet is a robust, secure Web server. You can use virtually any type of computer hardware configuration available today. You have the option of paying for a Web server from a company such as Netscape Communications, Inc. (**www.netscape.com**) and O'Reilly (**www.ora.com**), or downloading free server software like the Internet Information Server by Microsoft (**www.microsoft.com**) and Apache for UNIX (**www.apache.org**). Intranets are essentially portable and can work within any Web server environment, unless you begin customizing your site with proprietary software extensions. Figure 38.1 illustrates one of many choices you have for Web serving software.

FIG. 38.1

Choosing the right Web server software for your LAN/WAN intranet can often be a confusing process.

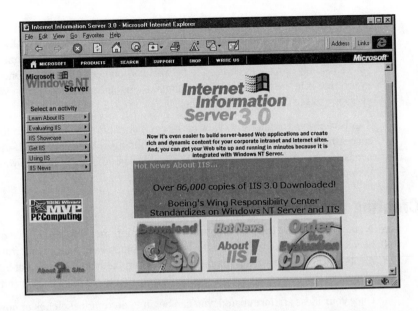

Once your Web server is in place, you will have to install the TCP/IP protocol and client software on each network node. Almost every operating system available today has TCP/IP built into the OS itself, though you may have to choose to install it as an option. Once TCP/IP is installed, you will need to give each workstation a unique IP address to identify itself within the network. You can manually add an IP address to each user's system, or configure your network to distribute IP addresses dynamically when a user logs on to the network or tries to access intranet services. Once the client workstation has been configured for TCP/IP, you will need to install a Web browser (and possibly other Internet software applcations) so that the company intranet can be reached.

N O T E It's a good idea to set up each user's default home page when you are installing the client software. As soon as the intranet goes live and your users try to access it, they will immediately be taken to your company home page as soon as they launch their browser. ▪

The next step is to give your Web server Ethernet connectivity. Play it safe and place your intranet server on a separate hub off of your router to ensure that it does not have Internet connectivity. Unless you have a specific goal in mind by connecting your intranet to the Internet, you will be introducing significant security risks into your LAN/WAN environment by doing so. The stories that you hear about hackers are true and you don't want to be their next victim. You will also need to make sure that your intranet server is physically located in a safe place. Make sure that the server is not publicly available where anyone can access it and view potentially sensitive files. For more information on Internet security, please refer to Chapter 33, "Security."

The last step to setting up a perfect intranet is moving your testbed Web site from a local development machine to the live server. Since the TCP/IP protocol is already in place, you have the option of moving files and directories through FTP if you're running an FTP server, or you can simply move files across the network as you normally would. Once you've verified that everything is in the right place, you can make a public announcement in your office inviting everyone to see the fruits of your labor.

This is really just a quick overview of the components that you will need to construct a successful intranet. Gathering the software, building a Web server, and setting up your client's needs are the basics of any intranet. The key to a good intranet boils down to the content that it provides.

Creating the Intranet Skeleton

A good way to start the planning process of your intranet is to make a list of your audience's needs. A great way to get ideas is to send out a memo requesting input from all of the departments that will be accessing the intranet. You'll probably find a wealth of information in the responses that you receive, which will only help you to develop a better intranet from the onset.

Once your ideas are formulated, you can begin to do rough sketches of how you want the information presented and organized. Charting tools such as Visio (**www.visio.com**) can help you in the development process. By mapping out your content, you will have an instant visual reference as to how your site will function and flow, as well as how all of the presented documents will be hyperlinked together. When your virtual "skeleton" is complete, you will instantly be able to tell how balanced your intranet is, and which department to go to for additional content if necessary. Figure 38.2 shows an example "skeleton" site built in Microsoft's Front Page.

FIG. 38.2
Creating a skeleton mock-up will assist you in the overall planning of your Web site.

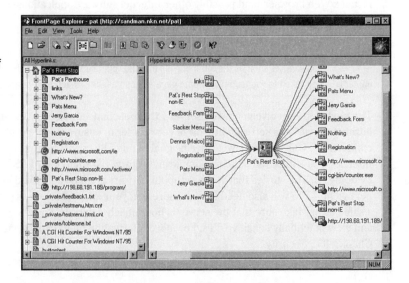

After you have balanced your Web site content, the next phase of development is the storyboard stage. Using a pen and paper, create a rough mock-up of the key components of your Web site. Outlining any framed content and drawing squares to represent where your graphics will lie truly helps in the design process to get a feel for how your Web site looks before any actual HTML coding occurs. Make special notes on the pages that require scripting languages and form components. This can help you in the HTML coding process immensely by providing a visual reference for creating the advanced pages. It is also helpful to mount your mock-up onto a larger "canvas." If you can organize your rough pages into a linked format, you will find that your HTML coding will flow better when your hands reach for the keyboard.

After the initial storyboarding is done, begin the actual HTML coding process by creating dummy pages for all of the major link-points in your site. This allows you to add text first, create links, and know that they will work. Remember that the key to an intranet is to provide information as opposed to creating an entertainment piece. It is often helpful to add the majority of the text for your intranet first. You can always build graphics around text after the initial site is given structure. For example, you can create an ordered list using the <OL><LI></OL> tags as a placeholder for an imagemap. The content will be in place first, allowing the graphics and other components to be added later in the development cycle. This process is illustrated in Figure 38.3.

FIG. 38.3

Adding text-based links to your Web site before you insert graphics is a great way to test the functionality of your intranet.

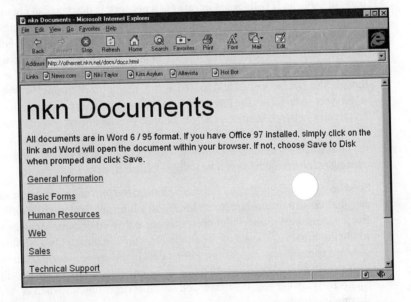

Once the majority of the text is in place, begin the process of adding complexity, or enhancements, to your Web site, such as graphics, scripts, and forms. One of the nice things about creating content for an intranet is that you don't have to worry about bandwidth restrictions like you do on the Internet. When developing for the World Wide Web, you would never think of using an imagemap that is 200K in size. On an intranet, however, files this size (and greater) can move across the network at very high speeds and can be displayed within the client browser immediately as a Web page opens. It's best to check with your System Administrator to get an idea of the internal bandwidth usage of your company and what limits you should place on your file sizes. Scripts and other interactive components of the intranet must be tested, debugged, and tested again. Make absolutely sure that your hyperlinks, forms, and scripts function as intended, without any problems. You'll be thankful that you went through so much agonizing testing before deployment, and so will the rest of the company.

Sharing Information

If you've worked in any networked environment, you know that file sharing is the most basic need of users. The accounting department needs to share files with financial officers, while Human Resources has to share files with their entire workforce base to get information to them quickly. Step back and take a look at how your office environment uses file sharing to enhance its productivity. You'll find that it's the most widely used network resource in almost every company. With this in mind, create your intranet with information sharing in mind.

Not every file on your intranet has to be put into a Web page format. One of the greatest advantages of using an HTML-based intranet in a network is that you can create hyperlinks to any file type. When a Web browser encounters a file type that it cannot display or does not know what to do with, the users will be prompted with a dialog box asking them what to do with the file. The users then have the opportunity to open the file with an external program or save it to their hard drive. Most applications used in a typical office environment are not intranet-friendly, though files can be opened and moved across the network through a Web interface. This is where you begin to see the low price point advantage of using an intranet instead of traditional proprietary network solutions such as Lotus Notes and Microsoft Exchange. You are the one in charge of creating the solution to your network problems as they arise, and you are not at the mercy of often limiting groupware solutions. Figure 38.4 shows one of many ways that existing software solutions can be utilized in an intranet.

Sometimes, proprietary solutions can be integrated into an intranet. For example, if your company has chosen to standardize on Microsoft's Internet Explorer and Office 97 products, any Excel spreadsheet, PowerPoint presentation, and Word document can be displayed seamlessly within the browser. This takes file sharing through an intranet to a whole new level. Many software companies are spending a great deal of money on Internet/intranet integration with their existing line of products. In time, all major computer applications will have this type of connectivity, giving you, the developer, limitless opportunities when creating a solution for sharing information.

FIG. 38.4
Microsft Word can be accessed from within Internet Explorer for document editing and browsing.

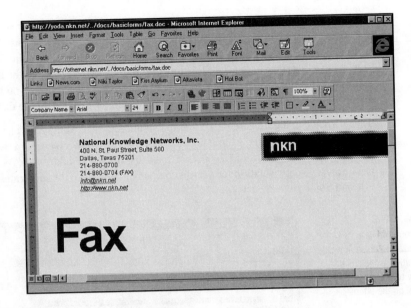

Addressing Security Concerns

One of the first questions that you will be asked once word gets around that you're developing an intranet is, "How do we keep the bad guys out?" Your initial response should be that you will not connect the intranet server to the Internet at all. This is by far the safest solution to keeping potential security problems away. There are special situations that will arise, however, that will make it impossible for you not to connect the intranet server to the Internet.

Suppose that you have an outside sales force that needs information to sensitive internal documents. Normally, either hard copies of the documents would have to be mailed to them or they would have to do without until they were able to get back to the office. With today's technology available, however, it is not realistic to hold information back from remote employees just because they cannot access your intranet. Thankfully, there are a few solutions that you can incorporate to protect your internal network, while providing intranet material to the outside workforce that needs it.

Incorporating a Firewall into Your LAN

A hardware-based firewall solution is by far the safest way to protect your internal network if it is connected to the Internet. The firewall is placed between your internal router and the router that connects you to the Internet. The firewall contains a list of IP addresses that are allowed to reach the Internet from your internal network, as well as a list of IP addresses that can reach your internal network via the Internet. This is a great solution for telecommuters and salespeople who need access to intranet information.

In order for this to work correctly, you will have to make sure that your remote workforce has a static IP address on the machine that they're accessing the Internet from. It has to be static so that the System Administrator doesn't have to update the database in the firewall every time an employee needs remote access. Most Internet service providers have the ability to provide static IP addresses, especially if you can show a real need for it. Once you have the IP address, simply notify the System Administrator and have him or her update the database.

The downside to a hardware-based firewall solution is cost. Many firewalls can cost tens of thousands of dollars. The leading firewall, Cisco's PIX (**www.cisco.com/warp/public/751/pix/index.html**), starts at $15,000, and that's just for 256 IP addresses. As you can see, this can be a very costly solution for a large company. Figure 38.5 demonstrates Cisco's PIX Firewall home page.

FIG. 38.5

Incorporating a hardware-based firewall solution is the safest way to protect your LAN on the Internet.

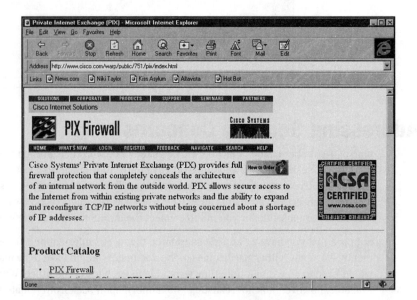

Implementing Security Through a Proxy Server

Most companies will not want to spend the money that it takes for hardware-based security, but they will still desire the functionality. You'll be happy to know that there is a solution. Implementing a proxy server will not only tighten the reigns on IP security, but it will also provide a money-saving way of reducing the Internet bandwidth used within a networked environment.

A proxy server holds a database that contains all of the IP addresses allowed to access your network, much like a firewall. The difference is that instead of adding a dedicated firewall system, you can set up a typical PC running proxy server software to do roughly the same function. Though the proxy server software may cost a few thousand dollars and you will have to dedicate a PC to running it, it is still a much cheaper alternative to an expensive firewall. Microsoft and Netscape both offer proxy servers that can be downloaded and evaluated for free from their Web sites. Microsoft claims that its proxy server is 99 percent secure. That's an interesting estimate if you step back and really look at it. That essentially means that 1 out of every 100 expert hackers would be able to break through the security and get into your network. While the proxy server is priced as a great alternative to a firewall, the threat of security violations is still in place. Microsoft's Proxy Server, shown in Figure 38.6, is one of many software-based security solutions available today.

FIG. 38.6
Implementing a proxy server is a low-cost alternative to a firewall.

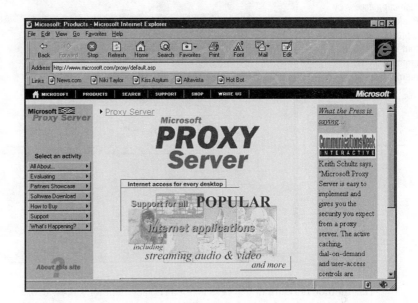

It was previously mentioned that a proxy server can reduce bandwidth usage, which results in an overall savings of money and resources. The computer that the proxy server resides on can cache Web sites as they are requested from the network. When a client requests a Web page that has been cached, the proxy server looks to the Web site to see if it has been accessed by this network before. If it has, the proxy server will check the file information on the Web site against what it has cached. If nothing has changed, the proxy server sends the cached copy of the Web site to the user instead of downloading redundant content. This is especially useful when your network users often access the same Web site multiple times a day.

Restricting Access on Your Web Server

There are essentially two ways to restrict access to users on the Web server itself. You can usually control which IP addresses are allowed to access the server, and you can control which users can see specific files or directories.

Restricting Network Access   Most commercial Web servers allow you to control who accesses the intranet site, generally through IP addresses. To restrict a user, simply enter their IP address into the correct area of the Web server. They will immediately be restricted from using the intranet Web server. Some server products, such as IIS by Microsoft, allow you to restrict access to every process that runs on the intranet server. This can come in very handy when you want to restrict FTP, Web, and mail access globally, as you only have to enter the restrictions once. Using IP-level access security, as shown in Figure 38.7, is an easy way to restrict access on an individual basis.

FIG. 38.7

Restricting access by IP address is a safe way to prevent known users from entering your intranet from the Internet.

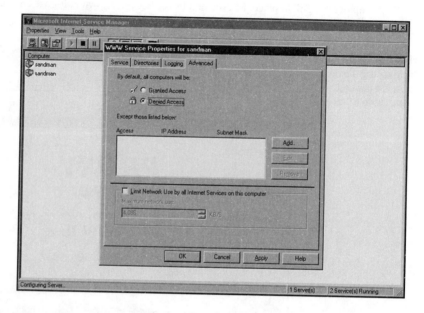

This method of restricting access is not a replacement for a firewall or a proxy server. This is very low-level security, though you may find that it works perfectly for your company. If a network user wants access bad enough, he can simply move to another workstation and try to access resources that way.

Restricting File and Directory Access   Many times, you will want to restrict specific files and directories from some users, while making them available to others. This is especially useful in situations where top executives or the accounting department need access to sensitive financial files, while the data-entry pool does not. In this case, you would use the built-in security found in most modern operating systems, like UNIX and Windows NT, to restrict resources by user groups. Figure 38.8 illustrates how you can restrict files by user groups in Windows NT.

If your files are organized into directories by department, you can easily restrict some departments from accessing another's files. This would be done on a global directory level. If network users need access to a few files within a department, but not all, then it is best to restrict individual files from being accessed by these groups. For more information about restricting user groups from accessing files and directories, consult your operating system documentation.

FIG. 38.8
Restricting access on
a file and directory
basis allows you to
close off certain areas
of your intranet to
unauthorized users.

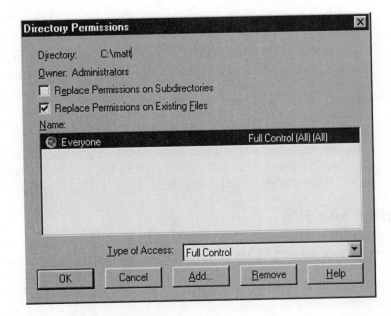

Part
VIII

Ch
38

Targeting Your Audience

To create a successful intranet, it is imperative that you are addressing the needs and user levels of your audience. As a co-worker once put it—you have to make it a no-brainer. Remember that the average intranet user knows very little about computers; generally just enough to complete his or her work. It's very important to concentrate on organizing your intranet in such a way that it will make sense to someone who has never seen an intranet, or network, before.

One way to do this is to get input from a variety of network users while the intranet is in development. Ask some of your co-workers to visit your mock intranet and send you their feedback. Remember, you're just developing the intranet, other people have to use it. Many developers make the mistake of making their site much too complicated. Reduce your intranet to its simplest level by finding out exactly what your users need, and leave it at that.

Creating Functional Content

Creating multiple ways of finding information is a great way to help your users. Use a mixture of graphical links and text-based links so that your users always have a way to get to the information without having to guess how. An example of this would be a mixed network of users who are heavy Windows clients and those who use DOS almost exclusively. The Windows users are more apt to look for a graphical path to information, whereas DOS-based users tend to follow text-based links. It's what they've learned and what they know.

Concentrate on making your intranet as "natural" as possible. Instead of concentrating on complex navigation solutions, create an interface that resembles something that a user is familiar with, such as a table of contents in a reference book. Everyone knows how to look up information that is well-organized in a reference book. All of the information is arranged in a document hierarchy that begins with a topic and delves down into information until it cannot be broken down any further. Your intranet site should follow these guidelines, while still providing a nice interface for the user. It is a good idea to create a table of contents for your entire Web site to provide ease of use and to help users quickly find the information that they're looking for so that they can get back to their work.

Indexing Your Site

Have you ever been to a Web site that you knew contained information that you were looking for, but you just couldn't find it? Wasn't it frustrating that you couldn't just type a term or phrase into a form field and search for the information that you needed? Your intranet users will experience the same frustrations that you did if you choose not to implement a search engine on your site.

There are many search engines available today on the Internet, both commercial and free, that you can download and incorporate into your Web site. One example of a search engine that's easy to put into place, as well as inexpensive, is Excite for Web Servers (**www.excite.com**). This is a scaled-down version of the Web search engine that millions of Web surfers utilize every day. The Excite search engine is available for the Windows NT and Sun Solaris platforms, and best of all—it's free. Figure 38.9 shows the Excite search engine page, where you can test the functionality and download a version that's right for your machine.

FIG. 38.9
Implementing a search engine makes it easier for your users to locate exactly what they're looking for.

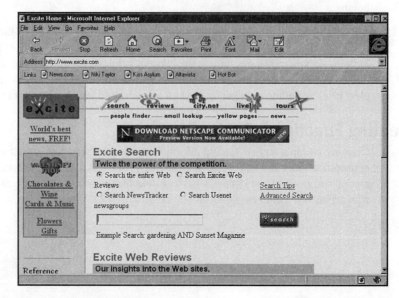

Once a search engine is installed on your intranet server, the program will scan your Web content directories and create a massive index file of the words in your documents. These words are held in a database that is cross-referenced with the corresponding document and its location. Once the index file is created, you will need to incorporate the index form field into your Web pages. Generally, the commands to do this are included with the search engine documentation, allowing you to cut and paste the HTML code into your documents.

> **N O T E** It's a good idea to put a link to your search page on every one of your intranet Web pages. This may seem a little redundant, but remember who your target audience is and the purpose of the site. Your users will love it that they have the ability to search the site for what they're looking for whenever they want to. ▇

A great aspect of the search engine is the fact that your users don't have to know any special techniques to find what they are looking for. They simply type the keyword or phrase into the text box, click the Submit button, and click one of the returned links. This can really save you some headaches by relieving you of the users who ask, "Now where was that again?" That's not to say that search engines on a local intranet can't be powerful. In fact, the truth is quite the opposite. Once your users learn how to use the search engine through trial and error, they will be able to locate exactly the content that they're looking for, no matter how closely related it is to another document.

Part
VIII

Ch
38

Getting Users Connected

You have the ability to create a wonderful intranet for your company, but how do you get your users to use it? The answer is to brainwash them. No, not really. A good place to start is to announce the intranet at a company meeting and briefly describe what its purpose is and how to use it. If your company is too large for a global meeting, consider going to each department to introduce the concept of the intranet and to explain the benefits of using it over traditional network resources. You might be surprised to find out that your users welcome the idea of the intranet upon learning how it will ease their network navigation.

When addressing the new user base of intranet users, remember exactly who your target audience is. You will be dealing with users who span a wide range of computer knowledge. The ideas that seem simple to you may seem extremely complex to them.

Training Your Users

There's no escaping the fact that you will have to train some of your users extensively in how to use your intranet effectively. For most of your network users, the intranet (and Internet for that matter) is a new technology that can quickly overwhelm them. Begin by sitting down with the users and explaining the concept of hyperlinks. After they've learned how to navigate between pages, you can follow up by explaining how a framed page operates and how to search for information by using the search engine. Put a special focus on the users' department and how to access all of the resources found within it. After they have their bearings, introduce the other departments and answer any questions that they ask.

If your users are also gaining Internet connectivity, you can gently introduce them to the broader scope of things. After showing them the search engine on your site, show them a search engine on the global Internet. Explain how hyperlinks on the Internet work just as they do on the intranet, simply on a much bigger scope.

Make sure that your users know where to go when they encounter a problem with their connection and the intranet itself. They don't really need to know the complexities of the Web browser. That's your job. You can also add a support page to your intranet where users can list any problems, comments, or complaints.

Group Participation

Most of your new intranet users will love your new work of art as long as you do a good job. In fact, many users might want to participate in the development of the intranet, especially when it relates to their own department. This really is a pretty good idea as it can relieve you of the burden of consistently updating the entire site.

A great way to encourage participation in the growth process of the intranet is to create a set of templates for each department so that the information they submit has a similar look and feel to the rest of the existing content. Most of your users will need some kind of a visual HTML editor like FrontPage to create their own content, although some adventurous ones will take on the task of learning HTML. Once the users are empowered with HTML templates, let them go to work, but have them submit the pages to you for approval before they go live. Figure 38.10 shows Microsoft's FrontPage in action, one of many visual HTML editors available today.

FIG. 38.10

FrontPage makes a great HTML editor for newbie Web developers.

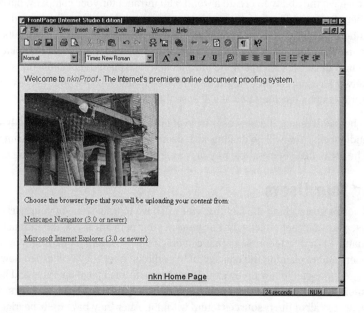

Encourage your users to come up with new ideas related to making your intranet more usable and provide more information. Since these users are essentially the ones for whom the intranet was designed, allow them to come up with their own solutions. With a little guidance and a good amount of patience, you might find that your intranet changes into something greater than you initially planned for.

Advanced Intranet Uses

Your intranet site doesn't have to solely revolve around Web pages. Remember that an intranet uses Internet technologies in an internal environment. That's *all* Internet technologies. Though Web pages are a great place to start your intranet, don't limit it to just Web-based content. E-mail is a great way to improve communications at the workplace. True collaboration through whiteboarding is a great way for two people at opposite ends of the office to work on the same file together. You can also host virtual discussions through NNTP technology. The following three sections will briefly explain how to expand your intranet by incorporating other forms of Internet content.

Hosting Discussion Groups

All Internet Service Providers offer access to what is known as UseNet newsgroups. These newsgroups are public discussion forums where Internet users can read messages about like topics and post replies or new messages. This is a commonly used way to get technical support via the Internet. If you have a question about how a piece of software operates, you can locate the relevant group, post your question, and check back at a later time to see if there are any responses. While the responses are not immediate, posts are generally made available for weeks after they've been posted. You can use this to your advantage by searching through older posts to find information closely related to what you're looking for.

The same technology used on the Internet for these discussion groups can be incorporated into your intranet environment. You will have to run what is known as an NNTP server on your intranet server and create the groups that you want to open to your users. This also involves loading an additional piece of client software on each user's machine so that they can read and respond to posts. You may want to moderate some of these groups to prevent users from posting off-topic. Moderating discussion groups involves reading every post, but ensures that only relevant information goes into a group. Be warned, however, that if a group receives 100 messages a day, and you're the moderator, you could spend all day simply reading and approving posts. Figure 38.11 illustrates the act of using a newsreader to host discussion groups.

There are quite a few freeware NNTP clients available on the Internet. Microsoft's Internet News and Forte's Free Agent are two clients widely used to read newsgroups. They are both extremely easy to use and configure.

Using custom newsgroups to host in-house discussions is a great way to provide technical support, gather input on a specific idea, or to simply give users an area to voice their opinions. Since newsgroup posts are generally very small, you can keep articles for quite a while, which will make a great reference site in the future for anything that is discussed.

FIG. 38.11

Enabling group discussions via NNTP is a unique way of adding discussion groups to your intranet.

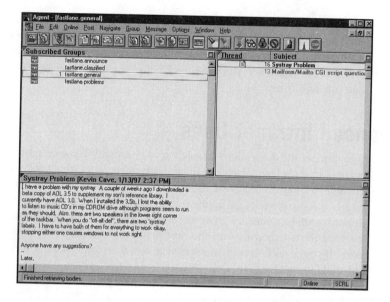

Using E-Mail to Communicate

Most people take e-mail for granted in an intranet setting. E-mail within an intranet is just as important as Web-based content. Allowing people to respond to each other's ideas quickly and privately is a great way to open up communication lines even more within the workplace. The most significant advantage to using e-mail is the reduction in paper use. No more interoffice memos, less traditional mail use, and more communication. E-mail is still the most widely used Internet application, and probably the most widely used intranet application. Microsoft Outlook, as shown in Figure 38.12, is a great tool for seamlessly incorporating e-mail into your intranet.

Mail servers are traditionally commercial applications that require more processing power than a Web server, depending on the number of users and volume of traffic. You may or may not be able to host a mail server on your intranet server. There are numerous e-mail client applications available on the Internet for free. Two widely used e-mail programs are Microsoft's Internet Mail and Eudora Lite (**www.eudora.com**). Both are equally functional and have many configurable options such as custom folders for mail and advanced mailing list capabilities.

Whenever a user encounters a Web page with an e-mail address on it, he or she can click the e-mail link and a new mail message will appear. The user types in a subject line and then the body of the message. Once the message is complete, the user sends the mail to the server and it is then routed to the addressee. A great way to encourage electronic mail use in the office is to create a Web page that lists company employees in alphabetical order, with their e-mail address listed next to their name. If one user needs to send another e-mail, he or she simply clicks the link and begins the message.

FIG. 38.12
Adding e-mail communication to your intranet can cut down on paper usage and encourage more inter-office communication.

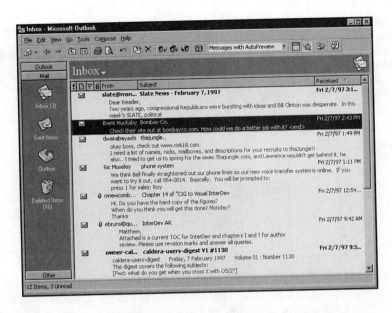

E-mail is quite simply the easiest Internet/intranet technology to learn because it closely resembles our own traditional mail system.

Collaboration with Whiteboarding

Whiteboarding is a way of allowing two users to see and use the same Windows application through the use of an external TCP/IP program.

Two products that are very competitive in this category of Internet tools are Microsoft's NetMeeting and the Intel Proshare (**www.intel.com**). NetMeeting is a stand-alone software-based application that is freely downloadable from the Internet. It features not only white-boarding, but also voice communications and text-based communications (like IRC) in one integrated package. NetMeeting allows multiple users to view and work on a file simultaneously, though it is limited in the application that you have to work with. The whiteboarding interface looks much like Windows Paint that comes bundled with Windows 95. You have general tool and color palettes that allow you to draw, type, and sketch in multiple shapes and colors. This can be very helpful when you need to collaborate visually with another employee on the other side of the building when you don't have time to walk over there. Microsoft's NetMeeting software, as shown in Figure 38.13, is an easy way to incorporate whiteboarding applications into your intranet.

FIG. 38.13

Products like Microsoft's NetMeeting allow you to collaborate over information online with another user.

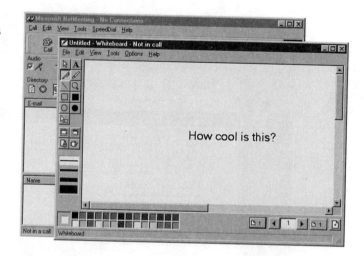

Intel's Pro Share product is similar to Microsoft's, yet vastly different in the way that it works. Pro Share is a hardware- and software-based product that requires that you install two expansion cards into your computer for it to work—the ethernet card and the video capture card. Video capture card? That's right, the Pro Share unit supports simultaneous whiteboarding, application sharing, and videoconferencing. The Pro Share unit costs about $1,000 and can be a pricey alternative to the free NetMeeting product when looking for a whiteboarding solution.

As the Internet continues to grow and mature, you will begin to see more advanced forms of whiteboarding applications that can help you to share information and collaborate on projects over your intranet. ●

## CHAPTER 39

Creating a Personal Web Site

by Mark R. Brown

When the chapters in this book were being assigned to individual authors, I hoarded this one for myself. The plumber's sink is always the one that leaks, they say, and the same thing holds true when you write books about the Web—for months my personal Web site has been a shining example of how *not* to do a Web site. I just haven't had the time to update it. I've been too busy writing.

But now all that is going to change—I've cleverly arranged to get paid for redoing my personal Web site by writing this chapter. And as I go through the steps of redesigning and planning my site, gathering together all the artwork and text files, and actually writing the HTML code for my new site, you can come along and hopefully get some good ideas for creating your own personal Web site.

This chapter will focus on using basic and intermediate HTML to create a useful, entertaining, and well-organized Web site. We won't get into CGI scripting, Java applets, or other advanced topics. The intention here is to learn to use a couple of basic "hand tools" to create a functional, fun, personal Web site. In fact, the only tools we'll use for creating this site are two excellent shareware programs: the HTML tag editor HTML Writer and the graphics editing program Paint Shop Pro.

Create a great site with simple HTML

You can create a perfectly awesome Web site by using only basic HTML commands.

Keep your site organized and each page simple

Organization and focus are much more important than anything else when designing a Web site or any HTML document.

Make sure that your personal Web site is solid

Though a personal Web site can and should be fun, it must also be bug free, or it won't present a good experience for your audience.

Planning and designing any HTML document involves the same up-front steps, no matter what the content or complexity. While documents that include Java and other advanced features are harder to build, the goal is the same—to create informative documents that are compelling, useful, and easy to use. This chapter will get you grounded in the basics so that you can move on to creating your own killer, high-tech HTML documents, with all the bells and whistles. ■

Getting Started

My Web site is a mess (see Figure 39.1). My links are outdated, my graphics are all jammed onto one page, and the bibliography I'd carefully assembled was lost in a server crash months ago. Since I earn my living telling other people how to create good Web sites, the situation is especially embarrassing. It's well past time to redo my personal site, and make it the showplace it ought to be!

▶ For some basic pointers on how to approach creating HTML documents, I suggest you first read Chapter 2, "HTML Page Design and Implementation," on **p. 19**

FIG. 39.1

Though enhanced by a photo of a strikingly good-looking man, my Web site is long over-due for a complete refurbishing. I even admit it on my home page!

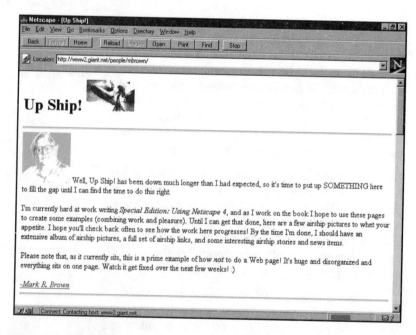

In fact, there's enough wrong with my Web site that I think it's best to just start over. So we'll begin at the beginning.

Choosing a Focused Topic

Surprisingly enough, the first step in setting up a personal Web site is often the most difficult—choosing a topic for each page.

Notice first of all that I said *a* topic, not a *bunch* of topics. The World Wide Web is a unique medium in that just about anyone can put up a site and sit back and see who visits. The problem is, that's just what happens. Most Web sites—especially personal Web sites—aren't very well thought out. Many people put up a site that includes everything they're interested in: their family, hobbies, line of work, and so on. Let's face it, the odds are against you that anybody surfing into your site will be interested in all the things that interest you.

The first thing you need to do is pick a topic. If you really, really want to cover more than one topic, set up two separate Web pages, or even more. Nobody's stopping you. You can even create a tasteful "Table of Contents" page that directs people to your various topics if you really want to. But keep things carefully separated, or you'll lose your audience by making a bad first impression.

And, let's face it, on the Web all you have is a first impression. With hundreds of thousands— soon, millions—of sites on the Web, nobody's going to stick around your site long if you don't grab them quickly. They'll surf off to a more appealing site.

Once you have your topic, it's important to narrow it down even more. If your interest is rock and roll, it might be best to concentrate on a single group. There are literally thousands of generic rock and roll sites out there, and you've got to attract a more elite clientele if you're going to make a name for yourself. If the group you choose to focus on is the Beatles, you'll have to create an extremely good site. If it's the Shirelles, you may stand a chance of becoming a Web legend—at least among Shirelles fans.

For me, my passion is airships, which means I've already got a nicely focused topic. It's not as generic as "airplanes" or even "fighter planes." In fact, when I first set up my site two years ago, an eternity in Web years, it was the first site on the Web devoted to the topic. Now a search of Yahoo! (see Figure 39.2) shows a short list of sites with similar topics, but I'm convinced I can still compete.

Part **VIII**

Ch **39**

N O T E If you're creating a personal Web site for personal gratification or artistic outline more than as a resource for other users, you don't need to worry as much about keeping your pages focused. Just have fun and experiment to your heart's content. ■

Selecting Content

After selecting a focused topic, the next step is to choose the types of content you'll provide on your site.

Depending on your subject matter, you may want to include video clips, audio files, graphics, lists of hyperlinks, text files, or database information.

It's best to go with what you have access to that is unique. If the same material has already appeared on other sites, there's no reason to include it on yours. With the hyperlinked nature of the Web, if someone has something online that you'd like to refer to, all you have to do is add a link to it. Why reinvent the wheel?

FIG. 39.2

When choosing a topic for your Web site, check out Web indexes like Yahoo! (**http://www. yahoo.com**) to see who your competition is, and find out what they've already done.

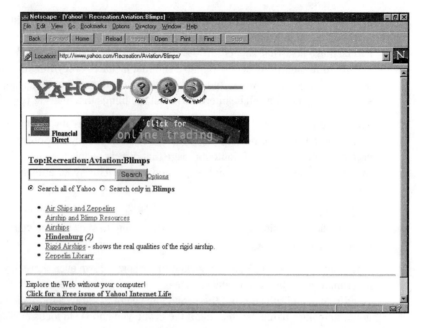

In the case of my airship site, I've got an extensive library of airship photos I've scanned in, digitized from videos, or downloaded from public domain sources, so I definitely want to include a library of airship images. I've also archived some interesting text articles over the years, so I'll include them. And I have collected a much more extensive list of airship-related links than Yahoo!, so I'll put those online, too.

> **N O T E**   All of the material I'll be putting online is in the public domain. If I'm not sure of the copyright status of an item, it won't go online. Though there's a lot of "borrowing" on the Web, there's no need to violate copyright laws when you're putting up your Web site. Make sure you have permission from the copyright holder if you plan to use any copyrighted material on your Web site. ▄

Later on, I want to add a bibliography of airship-related books, so I'll make sure there's a place for that on my site, too.

Organizing the Site

Form follows function. Now that I know what I'm going to put online, it's time to organize it. I have four categories of information I'm planning to use:

- Photos
- Links
- Text
- Bibliography

I think having a home page with a link to a directory page for each category would work fine. I'd like to keep a navigational directory handy for those who are roaming around my site, so I think I'll use frames in my design. I'd also like a title graphic so people remember where they are on the Web.

If I were designing a more complex site, I'd sit down and map out the organization of my site. But since this is a fairly simple site, with only four information "areas," I don't think that's really necessary.

Creating the Bones

Before I can hang any flesh on my skeleton design, I have to create the bones that make up that skeleton. That means getting out an HTML editor and starting to create the code for my home page.

I'm most familiar with HTML Writer, so let's boot that up and get started. Figure 39.3 shows the HTML code that creates my basic home page.

FIG. 39.3
HTML Writer displays the basic HTML code that will serve as the framework for my new Web site.

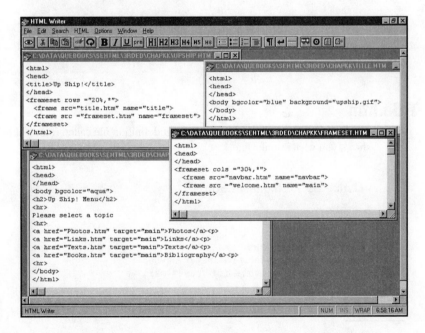

There are four main HTML files that define my site, two that create the framesets to create the screen layout, and two that contain the content for the title and navigation bar frames. Here's the HTML file for the outermost frameset:

```
<html>
<head>
<title>Up Ship!</title>
</head>
```

```
<frameset rows ="20%,*">
  <frame src="title.htm" name="title">
  <frame src ="frameset.htm" name="frameset">
</frameset>
</html>
```

UpShip.htm

This file sets the title of my site as "Up Ship!" which is the command that was shouted to the ground crew to launch an airship. This has been the title of my site for over two years, and I see no reason to change it now.

The FRAMESET definition in UpShip.htm produces two frames arranged as two rows. The top frame holds the file title.htm, which will contain just the GIF graphic titlebar of my site (see Listing 39.1).

Listing 39.1 title.htm

```
<html>
<head>
</head>
<body bgcolor="blue" background="upship.gif">
</body>
</html>
```

Title.htm

The bottom frame calls a second frameset definition file called frameset.htm. Listing 39.2 shows you what it looks like.

Listing 39.2 frameset.htm

```
<html>
<head>
</head>
<frameset cols ="30%,*">
  <frame src="navbar.htm" name="navbar">
  <frame src ="welcome.htm" name="main">
</frameset>
</html>
```

Frameset.htm

This file creates a frameset which breaks the bottom frame into two frames that form two columns. The end result of the FRAMESET tags in both files is that we have a single frame running across the entire top of the screen, which will hold title graphics, and two frames in the bottom portion of the screen, one for the navigation bar and one for the main content frame.

The navigation bar frame is defined in the file navbar.htm (see Listing 39.3).

Listing 39.3   navbar.htm

```html
<html>
<head>
</head>
<body bgcolor="aqua">
<h2>Up Ship! Menu</h2>
<hr>
Please select a topic
<hr>
<a href="Photos.htm" target="main">Photos</a><p>
<a href="Links.htm" target="main">Links</a><p>
<a href="Texts.htm" target="main">Texts</a><p>
<a href="Books.htm" target="main">Bibliography</a><p>
<hr>
</body>
</html>
```

Navbar.htm

This file contains a heading that identifies the menu and a list of targeted hyperlinks that can change the content in the main frame. For the time being, I've created a batch of dummy files like the following one so that when we test the page we won't get a bunch of errors telling us that files can't be found. We'll fill in content later, but here's what each looks like so far:

```html
<html>
<head>
</head>
<body>
Photos
</body>
</html>
```

Part
VIII

Ch

39

Photos.htm

One exception is the file welcome.htm, which is just my current home page, stuck in for the time being as filler.

Figure 39.4 shows what all this preliminary code nets us when displayed in Netscape Navigator.

Making Adjustments

Well, it's a start. The blue background in the title frame looks like a mistake, and I forgot to create the title graphic upship.gif. I don't think I really want it as a background graphic, either, since it will tile differently at different browser window sizes. I just didn't think that one through. We'll make it an inline image instead. And, of course, we've got to create it in the first place. That means firing up Paint Shop Pro.

Paint Shop Pro (at version 4.0 as this is written) is one of the best all-around image manipulation tools around. The fact that it is shareware doesn't hurt anything, either. I'm going to use it to turn a couple of airship images I have into a title graphic (see Figure 39.5).

FIG. 39.4

My first pass at a new home page. Now, we start tweaking!

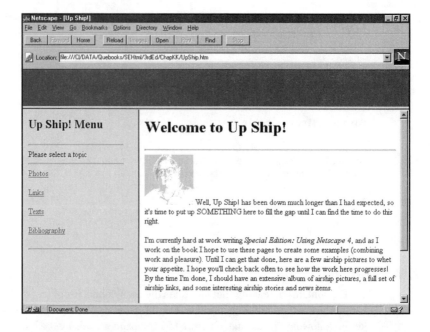

FIG. 39.5

Paint Shop Pro at work resizing images and combining them into a new work of art.

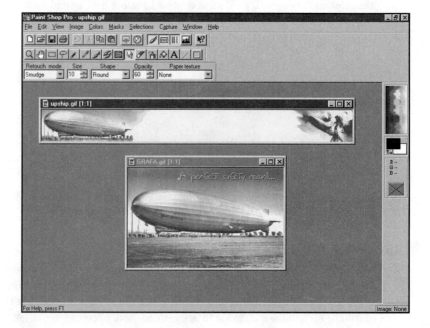

I've decided to take one image of the Graf Zeppelin and one of the Hindenburg in flames and combine them, adding some text at the same time. I can accomplish all of this in Paint Shop

Pro, right down to "smearing" the images to give the graphic some continuity. Saving it as a GIF file called UpShip.gif gives us the image we need to complete the Up Ship! home page.

A look at the navigation bar shows that I forgot to include a link to the Welcome page. Even though it comes up by default when a visitor enters the Up Ship! site, I've given them no way to go back to that page if they want to. So I'll add a link for "Welcome" to the "navbar.htm" file. The text lines on the navigation bar seem too far apart, as well, so I think I'll change the <P> tags into <BR> tags. That'll push the lines closer together. I'm still not sure about the "aqua" background color for the navbar, either, but I'm pretty sure I want it a different color than the other frames, so I'll let that be for now.

Figure 39.6 shows Up Ship! after these changes.

I think I can live with the look and feel of this set of frames for the time being. Now it's time to start to work on content.

FIG. 39.6

After a few relatively minor changes, my home page is starting to look like I intended.

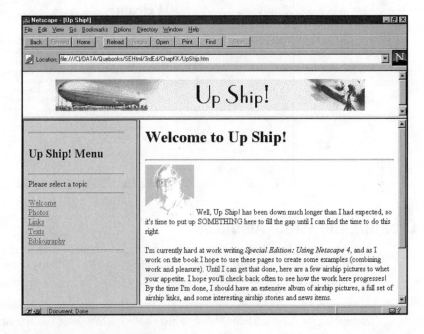

Bringing Together the Content

"Begin at the beginning," said Humpty Dumpty to Alice, "and go on until you reach the end." That's pretty good advice for content creation, too, which means I should probably work on the Welcome page first.

I really like that picture of the handsome guy, and the <H1> level heading that says "Welcome to Up Ship!" is okay, though it looks a bit redundant to have two huge "Up Ship!" signs so close together. I think I'll change that to just "Welcome." And, of course, it's time to update the text. No need for apologies, now that the site is being updated! And I think I'll move that e-mail address over to the navbar, where it will be available all the time. This means a subtle change to navbar.htm as well as rewriting the text in welcome.htm.

I also happened to notice that ugly scrollbar in the title frame, so I went into the upship.htm file and set SCROLLING="NO" for the FRAME definition for that frame.

Figure 39.7 shows what the Welcome screen looks like after making these changes.

FIG. 39.7

With a friendly new welcome screen and a few other minor changes, Up Ship! is starting to look ship-shape!

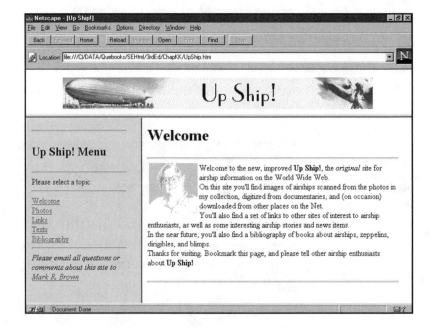

Creating the Photo Album

Now comes the toughest part of the site: creating an album of airship photos. I've got a *lot* of digitized airship photos. For the time being, I'm going to pick 10 to put online then I'll add to the collection as time permits.

My graphics are already the right size, but I need to create a set of thumbnails to use as a graphic menu. After all, I don't want to just shove kilobyte after kilobyte of photos down my viewers' throats! I want to let them choose which ones they want to see. So it's time to fire up Paint Shop Pro again. This time, I'll use the Resize command on the Image menu to create the thumbnails I need (see Figure 39.8).

The thumbnails I created are all a uniform 60 pixels in height, and use only 16 shades of gray. They should load very fast and make a good looking page.

Speaking of which, it's time to create one.

After much thought, it seems to make sense to divide the main frame into two frames for displaying images. I'll create a frame on the right to hold the thumbnails, and will keep enough of the main frame intact to display individual images. By grouping the thumbnails with their captions to create a scrolling list, I should be able to create a compact, easy-to-use, and interesting-looking display.

It's time to load up HTML Writer and go to work on creating the frameset and two frames that will make up the image viewer.

FIG. 39.8
Creating thumbnails is an essential part of building an online image album, and Paint Shop Pro does the job extremely well.

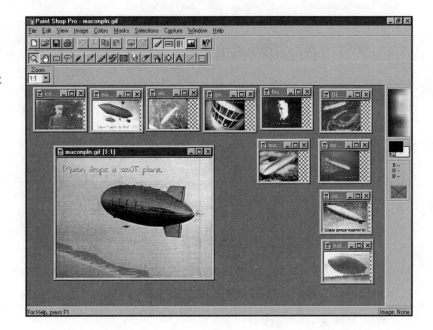

Part
VIII

Ch
39

Photos.htm

Photos.htm, shown in Listing 39.4, creates the two frames I need. The first frame will initially contain a beginning image called image.gif. (I've chosen to have this image unavailable from the scrolling menu—it's a photo of the burning Hindenburg, and I'd like it to be a sort of unselectable memorial.)

Listing 39.4   photos.htm

```
<html>
<head>
</head>
<frameset cols="3*,*">
  <frame src="image.gif" name="image" scrolling="no">
  <frame src="thumbs.htm">
</frameset>
</html>
```

The second frame calls the file thumbs.htm, described in the next section.

Thumbs.htm

Listing 39.5, thumbs.htm, creates the scrolling image menu. Each link combines the thumbnail image of a larger graphic with a targeted link that loads the full-size version into the named frame "image."

Listing 39.5   thumbs.htm

```
<html>
<head>
</head>
<body>
<hr>
<h2>Airship Image Directory</h2>
<hr>
<a href="Pic01.gif" target="image"><img src="Thumb01.gif"></a><br>
Santos-Dumont over Paris?<br>
<hr>
<a href="Pic02.gif" target="image"><img src="Thumb02.gif"></a><br>
Count Ferdinand von Zeppelin<br>
<hr>
<a href="Pic03.gif" target="image"><img src="Thumb03.gif"></a><br>
Airship photographed from biplane<br>
<hr>
<a href="Pic04.gif" target="image"><img src="Thumb04.gif"></a><br>
Hugo Eckener<br>
<hr>
<a href="Pic05.gif" target="image"><img src="Thumb05.gif"></a><br>
Nobile's airship Italia<br>
<hr>
<a href="Pic06.gif" target="image"><img src="Thumb06.gif"></a><br>
Zeppelin travel poster<br>
<hr>
<a href="Pic07.gif" target="image"><img src="Thumb07.gif"></a><br>
Hindenburg over the Olympics<br>
<hr>
<a href="Pic08.gif" target="image"><img src="Thumb08.gif"></a><br>
Hindenburg over New York City<br>
<hr>
<a href="Pic09.gif" target="image"><img src="Thumb09.gif"></a><br>
Graf Zeppelin's gondola<br>
<hr>
<a href="Pic10.gif" target="image"><img src="Thumb10.gif"></a><br>
U.S. Navy airship Macon<br>
<hr>
</body>
</html>
```

That's all we need, besides the individual GIF image files themselves. Figure 39.9 shows the result.

FIG. 39.9

Our image menu splits the main window into two frames, one for a scrolling thumbnail menu and one to display the full-size image.

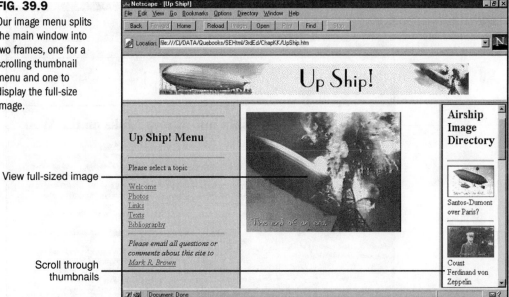

View full-sized image ——

Scroll through thumbnails ——

You know, it looks like there's enough room under those images to add a nice scrolling text file someday. We'll have to add another frame, but that should be no problem. The problem is finding time to write the text files to associate with each image. We'll leave that for future expansion.

N O T E You may have noticed that I'm giving little thought to anybody who uses a nongraphical browser, or those who are still operating at 640x480, rather than 800x600 resolution. Because this site is image-intensive, and because so many people are operating at the higher resolution these days, and because this is just a fun site anyway, I've decided it probably doesn't make any difference.

But, if I were concerned about folks with nongraphical browsers, I'd provide text alternatives for each image. At the very least, consider adding a disclaimer to your Web site stating that it's graphically intensive.

If you think otherwise, e-mail me from the link on my Web site, and let me know your opinion. ▪

Some Useful Links

What would the Web be without links? Over time, I've compiled a list of good airship links, and my next step is to add at least part of that list of links to my site. For this, all I need is my trusty HTML editor.

I've always been of the opinion that links without comments are somewhat less than useful, so I'll add a bit of personal commentary to my links. Figure 39.10 shows what I ended up with.

Part
VIII

Ch
39

FIG. 39.10

I chose to put my links into a bulleted list, with some commentary.

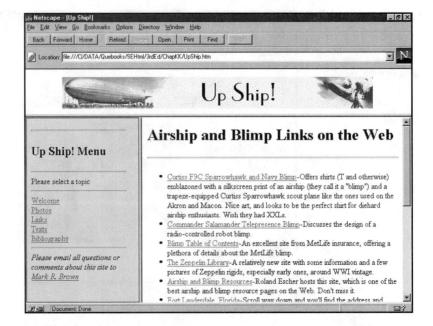

Listing 39.6 shows the HTML that created my list:

Listing 39.6   List of Links

```
<html>
<head>
</head>
<body>
<h1>Airship and Blimp Links on the Web</h1>
<hr>
<ul>
<li><A HREF="http://www.white-hawk.com/image-pages/rw-2.html"
target="_top">Curtiss F9C Sparrowhawk and Navy Blimp
</A>-Offers shirts (T and otherwise) emblazoned with
a silkscreen print of an airship (they call...
</ul>
<h3>Return soon! More links to come!</h3>
</body>
</html>
```

Links.htm

The entire page consists of nothing but an unordered (bulleted) list of links. Each link uses the TARGET="_top" attribute to wipe the screen clean and fill it with whatever is at the linked site. Otherwise, the linked site would just appear in the main frame, and that can get mighty crowded mighty fast. The page concludes with an admonition to return soon, because I've got a lot more airship links bookmarked that I'd like to add later.

Adding Some Articles

Now it's time to add some of the text articles I've got waiting on my hard drive. This should be easy—in fact, text loads so quickly that I think I'll just shove it into the main frame all in one file, with a "table of contents" of internal links at the head end. After a bit of manipulation and formatting in HTML Writer, the end result is shown in Figure 39.11.

FIG. 39.11

Though just a loose amalgam of more-or-less random articles, there's enough interesting information in this text file to hold an airship fan hostage for more than a few minutes.

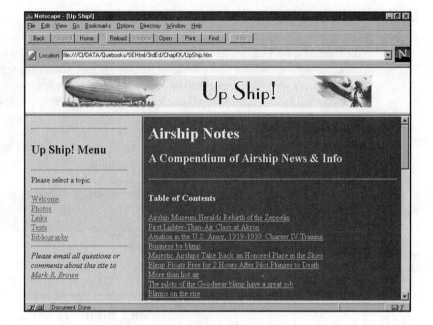

Here's a short sample of the HTML that creates this content:

```
<html>
<head>
</head>
<body bgcolor="blue" text="white" link="yellow" vlink="aqua">
<h1>Airship Notes</h1>
<h2>A Compendium of Airship News & Info</h2>
<hr>
<h3>Table of Contents</h3>
<a href="#museum">Airship Museum Heralds Rebirth of the
Zeppelin</a><br>
...
<a name="museum"><h3>Airship Museum Heralds Rebirth of the
Zeppelin</H3></a>
<hr>
Germany at last has a museum honoring the Zeppelin,
one of the defining images of the 1920s and 30s, and a
glimpse of a new airship that aims to...
```

Part **VIII**

Ch **39**

Texts.htm

The "Table of Contents" section of Texts.htm consists of a set of anchor tag links that HREF to the headings of each article, which are themselves named using the <A> tag NAME attribute. It's all pretty straightforward. Each article has its own name; each link in the Table of Contents links to that name.

Under Construction

It's inevitable that every Web site have an "Under Construction" icon somewhere. Mine comes in the Bibliography. I had a killer bibliography of airship books that I lost in a server crash. What about my backup, you say? I *thought* I had one. But I couldn't find it anywhere, so maybe I was hallucinating. It took me several days of research to put together the first time, so I hope my viewers will forgive me if I put off re-creating it until another time. But I've been told it was my most useful resource, so I'll definitely add it to my site as soon as I can. In the meantime, I'll create an apologetic "books.htm" file that tells the whole sad story of why there isn't currently a bibliography on Up Ship! and add an "Under Construction" icon to the Bibliography header. Figure 39.12 shows the state of my site after this addition.

FIG. 39.12

Though I hated to do it, I just didn't have time to create the bibliography I want to add to my site. I hope I can soon.

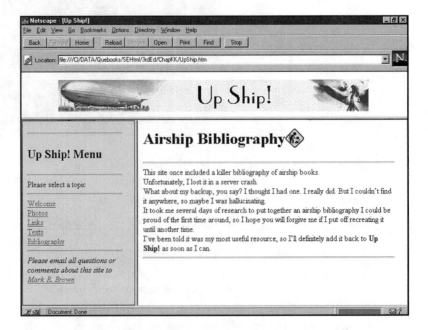

> **N O T E** Under construction icons can be annoying. Use them sparingly and only when they truly indicate a Web page that is coming soon. Consider just not putting a Web page online until it's available, unless you want people to know that it'll be available soon. ▪

Putting It on the Web

Now that I'm relatively happy with my new site, it's time to put it all online. Like most people putting up a personal Web site, I rely on my local ISP (Internet Service Provider) to host my site for me. My $19.95 flat access fee includes a UNIX account with 10M for my pages, so I've got plenty of room.

I use FTP to transfer my files to my ISP, so it's time to fire up my FTP program of choice, WS_FTP32 (see Figure 39.13). A few quick clicks and my site is updated. Finally!

FIG. 39.13
With a program like WS_FTP32, uploading your files to your ISP only takes a couple of minutes.

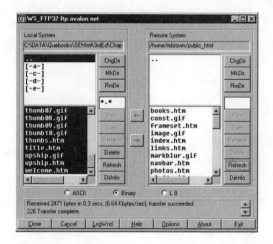

Your Personal Web Site

Well, that's about it for my personal Web site. But what about yours? While you're certainly welcome to borrow anything you want from my site, I'll reiterate: Form follows function.

Your site is bound to be different than mine, or anybody else's, because the information you want to present on your site is unique.

Strive to give your Web site its own personality, its own flavor, its own look and feel. And, I'll see you on the Web! ●

## CHAPTER 40

Interactive Site

by Jerry Honeycutt

Time changes all things. Web pages were once pretty dull. They contained a bunch of text and a few graphics. Over time, HTML provided Web developers the ability to include multimedia on the Web page: movies and sounds. Over the last year, though, HTML has made a huge leap. Now, you can use objects (ActiveX, plug-ins, and Java, for example), scripting, style-sheets, layers, and more to create great-looking HTML documents.

Thus, the dull, static HTML document isn't as acceptable to users as it used to be. They've seen the good life and they won't go back. That is, their expectations are higher than they used to be. Users know what an interactive HTML document looks like and they're starting to expect it.

That's where this chapter comes in. It contains numerous examples that you can add directly to your Web site to make it more interactive. For example, this chapter contains code you can add to an HTML document that will save the contents of a form and then prefill the form with the saved information the next time the user visits the site. ■

Gather feedback using an advanced user interface

This chapter shows you how to create a form that gathers feedback from the user. It has a few twists, however, that you can use in other forms.

Add extra value to your Web site

These value-added forms and controls won't bring more people to your Web site, but they'll help those people who do visit get more out of it.

Use advanced navigation on your Web pages

Image maps and links aren't the only way to move around a Web site. You can use drop-down lists and remote controls, too.

Bring people together through chat

If your Web site is frequented by people with a similar interest, they'll benefit from chat capabilities on your site.

Allow folks to search your site

If your site is very large, you must provide some way for people to search its contents. This chapter points you in the right direction.

Creating a Feedback Form

Whether you run a commercial site or a personal home page, you might want to gather feedback from the folks who visit your site. You might want to know if your graphics are too large, for example, or if your visitors found your site interesting enough to come back for another visit. Gathering this type of feedback helps you continuously improve your Web site.

The example shown in Listing 40.1 is an HTML document that contains a form for doing just that. It provides space for the user to type her mail address and comments, a drop-down list to choose the search tool the user used to find your site, and a few option buttons the user can use to tell you how she feels about your site. Figure 40.1 shows you what this document looks like in Navigator.

Listing 40.1   Feedback Form Example

```
<HTML>
<HEAD>
<TITLE>Feedback Form Example</TITLE>

</HEAD>
<BODY>

<FORM NAME=FEEDBACK METHOD=POST ACTION="mailto:jerry@honeycutt.com">
  <TABLE CELLPADDING=10>
   <TR>
      <TD VALIGN=TOP>
         <B>Please provide your e-mail address:</B><BR>
         <INPUT NAME=FEEDBACK_MAIL TYPE=TEXT SIZE=40>
      </TD>
      <TD VALIGN=TOP>
        <B>How did you find our site:</B><BR>
        <SELECT NAME=FEEDBACK_HOW SIZE=1>
           <OPTION VALUE=1>AltaVista
           <OPTION VALUE=2>Excite
           <OPTION VALUE=3>Lycos
           <OPTION VALUE=4>Yahoo!
           <OPTION VALUE=5>WebCrawler
           <OPTION VALUE=6>Friend
           <OPTION VALUE=7>Other Link
        </SELECT>
      </TD>
    <TR>
      <TD VALIGN=TOP ROWSPAN=2>
         <B>Tell us what you think about our Web site:</B><BR>
         <TEXTAREA NAME=FEEDBACK_MEMO COLS=45 ROWS=8>
         </TEXTAREA>
      </TD>
      <TD VALIGN=TOP>
         <B>How did we rate?</B><BR>
         <TABLE BORDER=1>
           <TR ALIGN=CENTER>
             <TH></TH><TH>Yes</TH><TH>No</TH>
```

```
          </TR>
          <TR ALIGN=CENTER>
            <TD ALIGN=LEFT>
              Did this site load fast enough?
            </TD>
            <TD>
              <INPUT NAME=FEEDBACK_SPEED TYPE=RADIO>
            </TD>
            <TD>
              <INPUT NAME=FEEDBACK_SPEED TYPE=RADIO>
            </TD>
          </TR>
          <TR ALIGN=CENTER>
            <TD ALIGN=LEFT>
              Did you find the graphics interesting?
            </TD>
            <TD>
              <INPUT NAME=FEEDBACK_GRAPHIC TYPE=RADIO>
            </TD>
            <TD>
              <INPUT NAME=FEEDBACK_GRAPHIC TYPE=RADIO>
            </TD>
          </TR>
          <TR ALIGN=CENTER>
            <TD ALIGN=LEFT>
                Was the content suitable?
            </TD>
            <TD>
              <INPUT NAME=FEEDBACK_CONTENT TYPE=RADIO>
            </TD>
            <TD>
              <INPUT NAME=FEEDBACK_CONTENT TYPE=RADIO>
            </TD>
          </TR>
        </TABLE>
      </TD>
    </TR>
    <TR ALIGN=RIGHT>
      <TD>
        <TABLE>
          <TD>
            <INPUT NAME=FEEDBACK_RESET TYPE=RESET VALUE=Clear>
            <INPUT NAME=FEEDBACK_SUBMIT TYPE=SUBMIT VALUE=Submit>
          </TD>
        </TABLE>
      </TD>
    </TR>
  </TABLE>
</FORM>

</BODY>
</HTML>
```

Part

VIII

Ch

40

FIG. 40.1
Placing each field's
prompt above the field
prevents you from
having to reformat the
form if the length of
the prompt changes
radically.

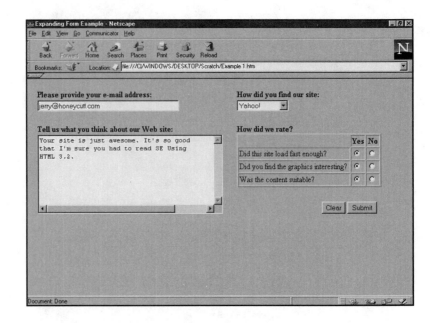

N O T E   Listing 40.1 uses the POST method with a `mailto` action. This example uses the `mailto`
             action to keep things simple. When you implement this document on your site, however,
you'll want to post the form to a CGI script that possibly stores the form in a database, against which
you can run queries. Also note that Internet Explorer doesn't support the `mailto` action. ■

Listing 40.1 is nothing more than a basic form that uses tables to keep the form's layout tidy.
The sections that follow show you how to do a bit more with this HTML document, however,
such as adding advanced options to the form that the user only sees when she clicks More and
validating the user's input with scripts.

▶ **See** "Combining Forms with Tables" to learn more about formatting a form using tables, **p. 229**

Auto-Expanding the Form with Layers

There are two types of users in this world: basic and advanced. With forms, you'll find many
cases in which a basic user needs to fill in only a few of the simpler fields, while the advanced
user needs to fill in all of the fields, including the more advanced fields.

What to do? You can display all of the form's fields at one time and let the basic user ignore the
advanced fields or you can hide the advanced fields and let the advanced user get to them by
clicking a special button. The latter is the approach that Windows 95 and Windows NT 4.0 take
in many cases. Have you ever seen a dialog box in Windows with a button labeled Advanced or
More? When the user clicks one of these buttons, the dialog box unfolds to show more fields.

With Netscape Navigator 4.0, hiding a portion of a form until a user clicks a button is easy. You use a combination of layers and scripts. Listings 40.2 and 40.3 are examples of such. Listing 40.2 shows the HTML you add to the previous example (Listing 40.1) to create the layer. It contains two additional fields formatted inside of a table. Add the HTML in Listing 40.2 to the code in Listing 40.1, just before the closing </FORM> tag.

Listing 40.2   The Hidden Layer within the Form

```
<!-- This layer contains the hidden part of the form that the user sees when they
     click on More>>. The event-handler at the top of this file shows the layer. -->

<LAYER NAME=MORE VISIBILITY=HIDE>
    <TABLE CELLPADDING=10>
      <TR>
        <TD>
          <B>Type the URL of your home page:</B><BR>
          <INPUT NAME=FEEDBACK_URL TYPE=TEXT SIZE=60>
        </TD>
        <TD>
          <B>Type your phone number:</B><BR>
          <INPUT NAME=FEEDBACK_PHONE TYPE=TEXT SIZE=32>
        </TD>
      </TR>
    </TABLE>
</LAYER>
```

▶ **See** "Creating a Basic Layer" for more information about basic layers in Navigator 4.0, **p. 260**

Part
VIII

Ch
40

Now that you have the layer, you need to be able to toggle its visibility property. You'll do that with a button. Add the following button to the form in Listing 40.1 (see Figure 40.2). Initially, this button contains the text More>>, which indicates to the user that if she clicks it, she'll see more fields. The button's OnClick event is associated with the OpenMore() function, which you'll create next.

```
<INPUT NAME=FEEDBACK_MORE TYPE=BUTTON VALUE="More>>" OnClick="OpenMore()">
```

Listing 40.3 shows you the scripts, which contain the OpenMore() function, necessary to show and hide the layer. It contains a global variable called blnMoreIsUp that describes the current state of the layer: false means that the layer isn't showing and true means that the layer is showing. The function OpenMore() toggles the state of blnMoreIsUp and sets the visibility property of the layer accordingly. Last, it changes the text value of the button you added to reflect the state of the layer: More>> if the layer is hidden and Less<< if the layer is showing.

FIG. 40.2

"Advanced" is another common word used on buttons like these.

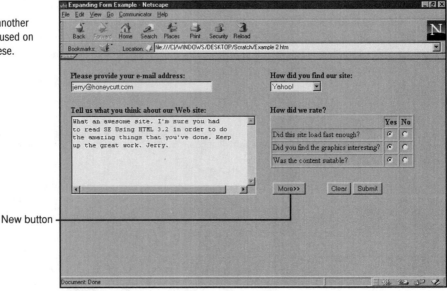

New button ───

Listing 40.3 Script to Toggle the Layer's State

```
<SCRIPT LANGUAGE=JAVASCRIPT>

blnMoreIsUp = false;

// Display the hidden form if it's not already displayed. Otherwise, hide it.
// Also, change the text in the button to reflect the current state of the
    ➡hidden form.

function OpenMore()
{
  blnMoreIsUp = !blnMoreIsUp;
  document.layers.MORE.visibility = blnMoreIsUp ? "INHERIT" : "HIDE";
  document.FEEDBACK.FEEDBACK_MORE.value = blnMoreIsUp ? "Less<<" : "More>>"
}
</SCRIPT>
```

Figure 40.3 shows you what the form looks like when the layer is showing. Note that the button now says Less<< and the fields contained in the layer appear at the bottom of the form.

N O T E In this case, the layer appears inline because you didn't specify a coordinate in the <LAYER> tag using the TOP and LEFT attributes. Had you specified these attributes, the browser would draw the Web page as though the layer didn't exist and then overlap the layer with the page—not exactly what you had in mind. ■

FIG. 40.3

If the user clicks Less to hide the advanced fields, the browser still keeps any data that the user typed in these fields.

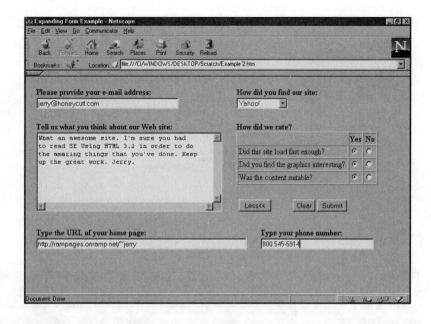

▶ **See** "Positioning a Layer" to learn the difference between displaying a layer inline or overlapping a layer, **p. 261**

Layers are a Netscape Navigator 4.0 feature. What about Internet Explorer users? Fortunately, Internet Explorer ignores the <LAYER> tag and displays anything contained within it (this is standard behavior for a browser). Thus, the user still sees the advanced fields as shown in Figure 40.4, but they can't hide them.

Part
VIII

Ch
40

Validating User Input with Scripts

Who says you can't control what the user types in an HTML form? You can. You can do it on the server using a script, but this unnecessarily wastes Internet bandwidth because you can easily validate a form on the user's client using a script. Listing 40.4 shows you how to validate the form from Listing 40.1 using JavaScript, but you can just as easily do it with VBScript, too.

Listing 40.4   Functions to Validate the Script

```
// Validate the contents of the form.

function IsValid()
{
  blnValid = true;

  with( document.FEEDBACK )
  {
    if( FEEDBACK_MAIL.value == "" )
    {
```

continues

Listing 40.4   Continued

```
      window.alert( "You must provide a mail address" );
      blnValid = false;
   }

   if( !(FEEDBACK_SPEED[0].checked || FEEDBACK_SPEED[1].checked) ||
       !(FEEDBACK_CONTENT[0].checked || FEEDBACK_CONTENT[1].checked) ||
       !(FEEDBACK_GRAPHIC[0].checked || FEEDBACK_GRAPHIC[1].checked))
   {
      window.alert( "Please select Yes or No for each rating" );
      blnValid = false;
   }
  }
  return blnValid;
}

</SCRIPT>
```

FIG. 40.4

If an Internet Explorer user clicks `More`, a JavaScript error will report that `layers` is undefined because IE doesn't support this object.

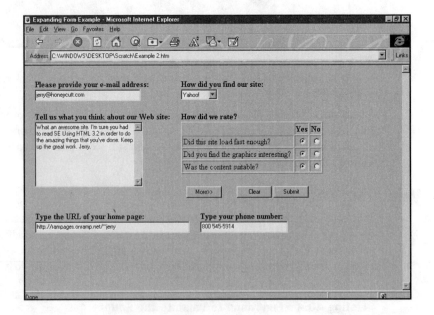

Add the script shown in Listing 40.4 to the top of the HTML document you created from Listings 40.1, 40.2, and 40.3. It contains a single function, called `IsValid()`, that checks that the user has typed a mail address and checked off the option buttons. If any of these fields are missing, `IsValid()` displays an error message (see Figure 40.5) to the user and returns `false`. If all these fields are okay, the function returns `true`.

FIG. 40.5
You could also ask the users to confirm that they intended to keep those fields blank by using the `window.confirm` method and allow them to continue if they did.

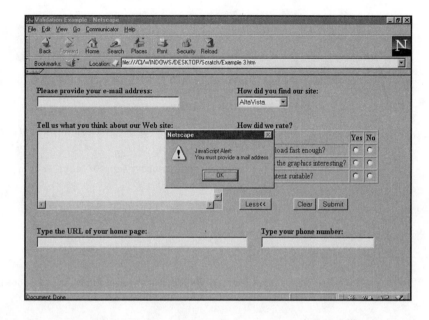

You have to associate `IsValid()` with the form's `OnSubmit` event, too. Replace the `<FORM>` tag in Listing 40.1 with the following `<FORM>` tag. The only difference is that the following `<FORM>` tag associates `OnSubmit` with `return IsValid()`, which is the syntax required for use with the `OnSubmit` event. If `IsValid()` returns `true`, the browser submits the form to the server; otherwise, the browser does nothing.

```
<FORM NAME=FEEDBACK METHOD=POST ACTION="mailto:jerry@honeycutt.com"
➥OnSubmit="return IsValid()">
```

Part
VIII

Ch
40

Saving the Form's Contents with Cookies

Most applications you run on your desktop remember your last settings and recall those settings each time you open the appropriate dialog box. Unfortunately, HTML forms don't follow this behavior. Some browsers will remember your settings during the current session; however, when you close and reopen the browser those settings are lost.

You can emulate this behavior using cookies. You use cookies to save information on the user's computer that you can recall and use during a later session (this causes some users great consternation). The browser's built-in objects don't provide all of the functions you need to use cookies, though. You need to define functions to save and parse cookies. The script shown in Listing 40.5 contains all the functions you need in order to use cookies in your own HTML documents.

Listing 40.5 Using Cookies to Save a Form's State

```
<SCRIPT LANGUAGE=JAVASCRIPT>
// Extract the value from the cookie at the given offset.
```

continues

Listing 40.5 Continued

```
function GetValue( Offset )
{
  var End = document.cookie.indexOf (";", Offset);
  if( End == -1 )
    End = document.cookie.length;

  // Return the portion of the cookie beginning with the offset
  // and ending with the ";".

  return unescape( document.cookie.substring( Offset, End) );
}

// Return the value of a cookie by name.

function GetCookie( Name )
{
  var Len = Name.length;

  // Look at each substring that's the same length as the cookie name
  // for a match. If found, look up the value and return it.

  var i = 0;
  while( i < document.cookie.length )
  {
    var j = i + Len + 1;
    if( document.cookie.substring( i, j) == (Name + "=") )
      return GetValue( j );
    i = document.cookie.indexOf( " ", i ) + 1;
    if( i == 0 )
      break;
  }
  return null;
}

// Create or change a cookie given its name and value. The name and value
// are required, but the expiration date isn't. Note that if you don't specify
// an expiration date, the cookie only exists for the current session.

function SetCookie( Name, Value, Expire )
{
  document.cookie = Name + "=" + escape( Value ) + ";expires=" + Expire;
}

// Write all the cookies for the FEEDBACK form.

function WriteCookies()
{
  var Expire = "Friday,25-Feb-2000 12:00:00 GMT";

  with( document.FEEDBACK )
  {
    SetCookie( "Mail", FEEDBACK_MAIL.value, Expire );
    SetCookie( "How", FEEDBACK_HOW.selectedIndex, Expire );
```

```
      SetCookie( "Memo", FEEDBACK_MEMO.value, Expire );
      SetCookie( "Speed", FEEDBACK_SPEED[0].checked ? "1" : "0", Expire );
      SetCookie( "Content", FEEDBACK_CONTENT[0].checked ? "1" : "0", Expire );
      SetCookie( "Graphic", FEEDBACK_GRAPHIC[0].checked ? "1" : "0", Expire );
   }
}

// Load the form with the values in the cookie.

function GetCookies()
{
  with( document.FEEDBACK )
  {
    FEEDBACK_MAIL.value = GetCookie( "Mail" );
    FEEDBACK_HOW.selectedIndex = GetCookie( "How" );
    FEEDBACK_MEMO.value = GetCookie( "Memo" );
    FEEDBACK_SPEED[0].checked = (GetCookie( "Speed" ) == "1");
    FEEDBACK_SPEED[1].checked = (GetCookie( "Speed" ) == "0");
    FEEDBACK_CONTENT[0].checked = (GetCookie( "Content" ) == "1");
    FEEDBACK_CONTENT[1].checked = (GetCookie( "Content" ) == "0");
    FEEDBACK_GRAPHIC[0].checked = (GetCookie( "Graphic" ) == "1");
    FEEDBACK_GRAPHIC[1].checked = (GetCookie( "Graphic" ) == "0");
  }
}
</SCRIPT>
```

SetCookie(*Name*, *Value*, *Expire*)

SetCookie() saves a value to the document's cookie by the given *Name* with the value contained in *Value*. It sets the expiration date to the date contained in *Expire*. If you don't provide an expiration date, the value lasts as long as the current session. Note that the date must be formatted like the following:

```
Day,DD-MMM-YYYY HH:MM:SS GMT
```

GetCookie(*Name*)

GetCookie() looks for a value called *Name* and returns its value. It looks at each value in the document's cookie until it finds the right one. Then, it uses GetValue() to parse out the value.

GetValue(*Offset*)

GetValue() returns the portion of the cookie beginning at the given *Offset* and ending with the first semicolon it encounters. This is the value.

The remaining two functions in this script, WriteCookies() and GetCookies(), are specified to the form in Listing 40.1. WriteCookies() writes a value to the cookie for each field in the form. GetCookies() reads all of the values from the document's cookie and sets each field in the form appropriately.

You're now armed with the functions to save the form's values to the document's cookie. Now you need to hook them up. The perfect place to save the values to the cookie is in the form's validation function: `IsValid()`. Add the following two lines of HTML to the end of this function (just before the last `return` statement); then, when the user submits a valid form, the validation function will save the form's values to the cookie.

```
if( blnValid )
    WriteCookies();
```

How about prefilling the form with the values in the cookie? That's easy. Change the `<BODY>` tag so that it looks like the following line. This associates the window's `OnLoad` event with the `GetCookies()` function, which prefills the form with the values in the cookie each time the user loads the HTML document containing the form.

```
<BODY OnLoad="GetCookies()">
```

 TIP Visit Netscape's site to see a complete cookie specification: **http://home.netscape.com/newsref/ std/cookie_spec.html**.

Dressing Up and Adding Value to Your Site

The examples in this section are easy to implement; yet, the people that visit your site will appreciate them. You can provide a Yahoo! search form right there on your home page, for example, or provide links that display news related to your Web site.

The last example in this section describes Microsoft Agent. You can use this ActiveX control to help along those users who aren't comfortable with computers or the Internet.

Add a Yahoo! Search Form

You've used Yahoo! before. Who hasn't? Did you know that you can add a form to your Web site that makes it possible for folks visiting your site to do a Yahoo! search, without actually visiting Yahoo!? Listing 40.6 shows the HTML for this form, which is contained within a frame as shown in Figure 40.6. The `<FORM>` tag uses the `TARGET` attribute to display the search results in the frame called `MAIN`. The `ACTION` attribute points to Yahoo!'s search engine.

Listing 40.6   Yahoo! Search Form

```
<HTML>
<FORM TARGET=MAIN METHOD="GET" ACTION="http://search.yahoo.com/bin/search">
  <IMG SRC="http://www.yahoo.com/images/recip/1yahoo.gif" WIDTH=104 HEIGHT=21
  ➥ALIGN=TOP ALT="[ Yahoo! ]" >
  <INPUT TYPE=TEXT NAME=p SIZE=18>
  <INPUT TYPE=SUBMIT NAME=name>
  <FONT SIZE=1>
  <A HREF="http://www.yahoo.com/search.html">Options</A>
</FORM>
</HTML>
```

FIG. 40.6

Options opens
Yahoo!'s advanced
search form.

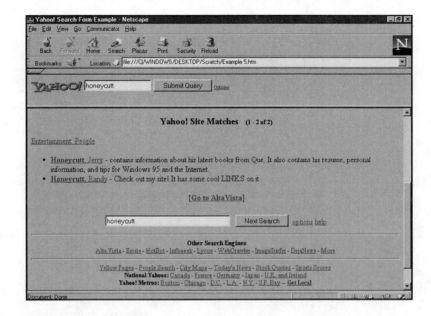

Add a Yahoo! News Page

You can also use Yahoo! to search the current news headlines for specific keywords. Your
visitors will get real value from the form shown in Listing 40.7 to your HTML document.
They can use it to search Yahoo!'s news for keywords that they choose, or they can click
one of the links on the right side of the form (see Figure 40.7) to submit a predefined search
for a topic.

Like the example in Listing 40.6, this example uses frames. Listing 40.7 shows the top frame,
called NEWS. The bottom frame is nothing more than an empty HTML document, called MAIN.
When the user submits a search or clicks one of the predefined topics, the browser loads the
search results in the bottom frame as shown in Figure 40.7.

Part

VIII

Ch

40

Listing 40.7   Form for Yahoo! News

```
<HTML>
  <FORM NAME=NEWS TARGET=MAIN METHOD=GET ACTION="http://search.main.yahoo.com/
➥search/news">
    <TABLE>
      <TR>
        <TD>
          <IMG SRC="http://www.yahoo.com/images/yahootogo/buttons/
          ➥yahoo_news.gif" WIDTH=175 HEIGHT=23 ALIGN=BOTTOM alt="[ Yahoo! News
          ➥Search]">
        </TD>
        <TD ROWSPAN=3>
          <UL>
            <LI><A TARGET=MAIN HREF="http://search.main.yahoo.com/search/
            ➥news?p=Microsoft+Internet">Microsoft and the Internet<A>
```

continues

Listing 40.7 Continued

```
            <LI><A TARGET=MAIN HREF="http://search.main.yahoo.com/search/
            ➥news?p=Netscape+Internet">Netscape and the Internet</A>
            <LI><A TARGET=MAIN HREF="http://search.main.yahoo.com/search/
            ➥news?p=Book+Internet">Books about the Internet</A>
            <LI><A TARGET=MAIN HREF="http://search.main.yahoo.com/search/
            ➥news?p=IPO+Internet">Internet Related IPOS</A>
            <LI><A TARGET=MAIN HREF="http://search.main.yahoo.com/search/
            ➥news?p=Windows+95">Windows 95</A>
            <LI><A TARGET=MAIN HREF="http://search.main.yahoo.com/search/
            ➥news?p=Windows+NT+4.0">Windows NT 4.0</A>
            <LI><A TARGET=MAIN HREF="http://search.main.yahoo.com/search/
            ➥news?p=QUE+Publishing">QUE Publishing</A>
          </UL>
        </TD>
      </TR>
      <TR>
        <TD>
          <B>Search news for these keywords:<B><BR>
          <INPUT NAME=p TYPE=TEXT SIZE=32>
        </TD>
      </TR>
      <TR>
        <TD ALIGN=RIGHT>
          <INPUT TYPE=SUBMIT VALUE="Get News">
        </TD>
      </TR>
    </TABLE>
  </FORM>
</HTML>
```

FIG. 40.7

You can prefill the input field to suggest keywords to the user.

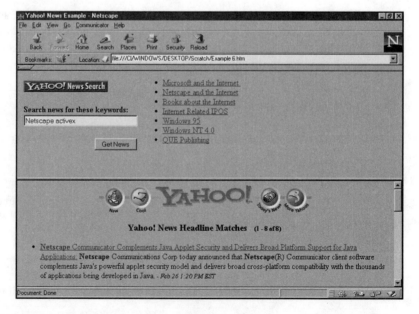

Provide Guidance by Using the Microsoft Agent

Microsoft Agent is a whopper of an ActiveX control (see Figure 40.8). It's a 4M download, but once the user has it on her machine, she'll be thrilled with it. You use the Microsoft Agent to guide the user around your Web site. You can suggest an action to the user, for example, or give the user a brief tour of the page after it loads. It doesn't just display a bunch of help text, either; it actually speaks the words (the user must have a sound card and speakers).

You do all this in event handlers. For example, if you want to give the user a tour when she loads your Web page, you program the Agent in the window's OnLoad event. If you want the Agent to tell the user that she didn't provide the correct input in a form, you program the Agent in that form's OnSubmit event.

FIG. 40.8

Microsoft Agent speaks the words you see in the balloon. Its mouth even moves in sync.

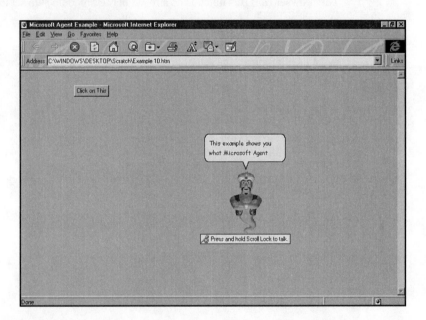

Part

VIII

Ch

40

Take a look at Listing 40.8. The <OBJECT> tag inserts the Agent into the HTML document. You don't have to specify any properties for the control, because you'll be controlling it with scripts. It contains three functions:

Load()

Load() is the event handler for the window's OnLoad event. It gives the user a guided tour. It introduces the user to the Microsoft Agent. It uses the methods shown in Table 40.1 to program the Agent. This event handler also sets a time out that calls MoreHelp() after 30 seconds elapse.

Table 40.1   Agent Methods Used in Listing 40.8

Method	Description
MoveTo	Moves the agent to the given screen coordinates
Speak	Specifies the text for the Agent to say
Play	Plays the previously defined text

MoreHelp()

MoreHelp() causes the Agent to suggest to the users that they click the button. The browser calls this function as a result of the timeout value set in Load().

Button_Click()

Button_Click() is the event handler for the button. When the user clicks the button, the event handler moves the Agent to a random location on the screen and programs it to say one of three phrases randomly.

Listing 40.8   Microsoft Agent Example

```
<HTML>
<HEAD>
<TITLE>Microsoft Agent Example</TITLE>
</HEAD>
<BODY OnLoad="Load()">

<OBJECT CLASSID="clsid:855B244C-FC5B-11CF-91FE-00C04FD701A5" ID=Agent>
</OBJECT>

<SCRIPT LANGUAGE=JAVASCRIPT>

function Load()
{
  // Enable the agent.

  Agent.Commands.Caption = "Microsoft Agent Example";
  Agent.Commands.Enabled = true;
  Agent.Active = true;

  Agent.MoveTo( 400, 300 );
  Agent.Speak( "Howdy, from Texas." );
  Agent.Play( "RestPose" );
  Agent.Speak( "This example shows you what Microsoft Agent is all about." );
  Agent.Play( "Explain" );
  Agent.Speak( "I boogie around the page and react to the things that you do." );
  Agent.Play( "RestPose" );
  Agent.Speak( "Click on the button to see for yourself." );
  Agent.Play( "Explain" );
```

```
    // Set a timer to give the users a bit of extra help if they don't click on
    ➡the button

    window.setTimeout( "MoreHelp()", 30000, "JAVASCRIPT" );
}

function MoreHelp()
{
  Agent.Speak( "Please, click on the button to see more of this example.¦Move
  ➡your mouse pointer to the button and click." );
  Agent.Play( "Explain" );
}

function Button_Click()
{
  // If this agent isn't active, make it so.
  if( !Agent.Active )
    Agent.Active = true;

  // Move the agent to a random spot (kinda cute) and say one
  // of a handful of random phrases.

  Agent.MoveTo( Math.random() * 800, Math.random() * 600, true );
  Agent.Speak( "Cool!" );
  Agent.Play( "RestPose" );
  Agent.Speak( "You clicked on the button!¦You did good!¦Click on the button
  ➡again." );
  Agent.Play( "Explain");
}

</SCRIPT>

<INPUT TYPE=BUTTON VALUE="Click on This" OnClick="Button_Click()">
</BODY>
</HTML>
```

▶ **See** "Connecting Controls to Scripts" to learn more about controlling an ActiveX control with a
script, **p. 511**

Providing Advanced Navigation

You use two basic concepts to provide navigation on your Web site: links and imagemaps.
The user clicks a link or anywhere within an imagemap, and the browser loads the URL
associated with that link or that area of the imagemap. Getting bored with these yet?

There are other ways to help the user navigate around your Web site, other than links and
imagemaps. For example, you can make navigation easy on the user and advance her to the
next page automatically. You can also let the user pick a page from a drop-down list and then
display that page in the browser window. The sections that follow contain examples of these
and more.

Part

VIII

Ch

40

Advancing the Page Automatically

Have you sat in on a presentation recently? It takes an hour to listen to the speaker barely spit out the words as she reads each slide; one by one. You might as well sit there and look at each page for fifteen seconds, automatically advancing to the next.

You can create a similar slide show using HTML documents. You use the window object's setTimeout method to specify a time and function. After the given amount of time passes, the browser calls the given function. You code this function so that it opens the next HTML document in the sequence. The example in Listing 40.9 does just that. The inline script at the top of the document sets a time out that calls Advance() after five seconds (5,000 milliseconds) pass. Advance() sets the top window object's location property to the URL of the next HTML document in the sequence.

Listing 40.9 Automatic Advance Example

```
<HTML>
<HEAD>
<TITLE>Automatic Advance Example</TITLE>

<SCRIPT LANGUAGE=JAVASCRIPT>
window.setTimeout( "Advance()", 5000, "JAVASCRIPT" );

function Advance()
{
   top.location="Example 7b.htm";
}
</SCRIPT>

</HEAD>
<BODY>
Your browser will open the next Web page in 5 seconds.
</BODY>
</HTML>
```

Using Forms and Scripts for Navigation

If you've been to Microsoft's site recently, you've seen forms used for navigation. Here's how it works: You select an item from the drop-down list and click a button. The browser opens the URL associated with that list item.

Take a look at Listing 40.10. It shows the HTML for a frame called NAVIGATE that contains a form with a single drop-down list (see Figure 40.9). It loads HTML documents in a frame called MAIN. The function OpenURL() is associated with the <SELECT> tag's OnChange event. When the user selects an item from the form's list, OpenURL() sets top.MAIN.location (our target frame is named MAIN) to the associated URL.

Listing 40.10 Form and Script for Navigation

```
<HTML>

<SCRIPT LANGUAGE=JAVASCRIPT>

function OpenURL( Index )
{
  if( Index == 0 ) top.location = "http://rampages.onramp.net/~jerry";
  if( Index == 1 ) top.location = "http://www.microsoft.com";
  if( Index == 2 ) top.location = "http://www.mcp.com";
  if( Index == 3 ) top.location = "http://www.netscape.com";
}

</SCRIPT>

<FORM NAME=NAVIGATE>
  <SELECT NAME=LIST SIZE=1 OnChange="OpenURL(
document.NAVIGATE.LIST.selectedIndex )">
  <OPTION NAME=JERRY>Jerry's Homepage
  <OPTION NAME=MS>Microsoft
  <OPTION NAME=QUE>Macmillan Publishing
  <OPTION NAME=NETSCAPE>Netscape
  </SELECT>
</FORM>
</HTML>
```

FIG. 40.9

You can get real fancy and store the URLs in an array, which you can index using the `selectedIndex` property.

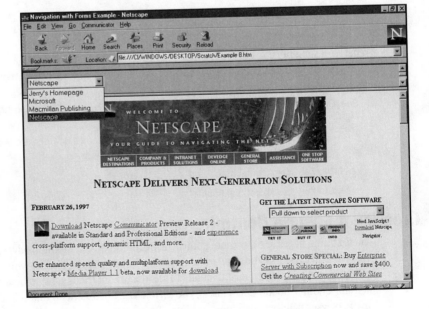

Part

VIII

Ch

40

Using Forms and CGI for Navigation

If you're more comfortable with CGI than with JavaScript or VBScript, you can do the same thing with a CGI script. Listing 40.11 shows the HTML to use a CGI script called `dispatch.cgi`. The form posts the current value from the `<SELECT>` tag to the CGI script, which opens that URL.

Listing 40.11   HTML Form for Use with CGI Dispatch Script

```
<HTML>
<HEAD>
<TITLE>CGI Dispatch Page</TITLE>
</HEAD>
<BODY>

<!-- Get your own dispatching CGI script at http://www.ahg.com/ftp/load.zip -->

<FORM METHOD=POST ACTION="cgi-bin/dispatch.cgi">
  <SELECT NAME=GO>
    <OPTION VALUE="http://www.microsoft.com">Microsoft
    <OPTION VALUE="http://www.netscape.com">Netscape
    <OPTION VALUE="http://rampages.onramp.net/~jerry">Jerry's Home Page
  </SELECT>
  <INPUT TYPE=SUBMIT VALUE="Go">
</FORM>

</BODY>
</HTML>
```

What's missing here is the CGI script. Your ISP might already provide a script you can use. Alternatively, you can get a free CGI script that loads an URL at **http://www.worldwidemart. com/scripts**.

▶ **See** Chapter 25, "All About CGI Scripts," to learn how to write your own CGI scripts.

N O T E   You'll find many sources for free CGI scripts on the Internet. However, two of my favorite sources are at the following URLs:

> **http://ahg.com/listcgi.htm**
>
> **http://www.selah.net/cgi.html** ▪

Creating a Remote Control

The first time users see a remote control, they mutter "wow" to themselves. Really. It's impressive. Wouldn't you like those users to say "wow" while they're visiting your site? A remote control is really nothing more than an HTML document that's built to be a small control document for another document. That is, you format the document so that it'll display in a very small browser window. Also, the contents of a remote control should be special. The remote control should contain resources that help the user get around your Web site easier—a search form, for example, or links to topic areas within your site.

Listing 40.12 shows the HTML for the remote control shown in Figure 40.10. It uses a table to neatly format the links and the form. Each link's TARGET attribute points to the window called MAIN (the inline script in Listing 40.13 sets the main browser window's name to MAIN). You've seen the Yahoo! search form before (refer to Listing 40.6).

Listing 40.12   The Remote Control

```
<HTML>
<HEAD>
<TITLE>Jerry's Remote Control</TITLE>
</HEAD>
<BODY>

<TABLE BORDER=0>
  <TR VALIGN=TOP>
    <TD>
      <B>Microsoft:</B>
    </TD>
    <TD>
      <A TARGET=MAIN HREF="http://www.microsoft.com/workshop/author/newhtml/
      ➥htmlref.htm">HTML Reference</A> -
      <A TARGET=MAIN HREF="http://www.microsoft.com/ie/default.asp">Internet
      ➥Explorer Home Page</A> -
      <A TARGET=MAIN HREF="http://www.microsoft.com/kb/">Knowledge Base</A>
    </TD>
  </TR>
  <TR VALIGN=TOP>
    <TD>
      <B>Netscape:</B>
    </TD>
    <TD>
      <A TARGET=MAIN
      HREF="http://home.netscape.com/comprod/products/communicator/
      ➥index.html">Communicator Home Page</A>
      <A TARGET=MAIN HREF="http://developer.netscape.com/index.html">Devedge
      ➥Online</A>
      <A TARGET=MAIN HREF="http://home.netscape.com/eng/mozilla/Gold/handbook/
      ➥javascript/index.html">JavaScript Authoring Guide</A>
    </TD>
  </TR>
  <TR>
    <TD COLSPAN=2>
      <HR>
      <FORM TARGET=MAIN METHOD="GET" ACTION="http://search.yahoo.com/bin/
      ➥search">
        <IMG SRC="http://www.yahoo.com/images/recip/1yahoo.gif" WIDTH=104
        ➥HEIGHT=21 ALIGN=TOP ALT="[ Yahoo! ]" >
        <INPUT TYPE=TEXT NAME=p SIZE=18>
        <INPUT TYPE=SUBMIT NAME=name>
        <FONT SIZE=1>
        <A TARGET=MAIN HREF="http://www.yahoo.com/search.html">Options</A>
      </FORM>
    </TD>
  </TR>
```

continues

Listing 40.12   Continued

```
</TABLE>
</BODY>
</HTML>
```

FIG. 40.10

Get fancy. Use an imagemap to make the remote control look like a TV's remote control.

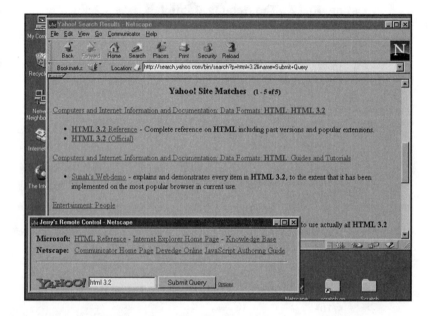

Save Listing 40.12 in an HTML file called `Example 9a.htm`. Then, you can open that remote control using the HTML document shown in Listing 40.13. It contains a button that has a function called `OpenRemote()` associated with its `OnClick` event. The `OpenRemote()` function uses the window's `Open` method to open the remote control in a new browser window called `MyRemote`. The width is 550 pixels, the height is 125 pixels, and the user can't resize it.

The script saves the new window object in `RC` for future use. For example, you can open a new HTML document in the remote control's window using the following line of HTML:

```
RC.location = "NewRemote.htm"
```

Listing 40.13   HTML Document that Opens the Remote Control

```
<HTML>
<HEAD>
<TITLE>Remote Control Example</TITLE>
</HEAD>
<BODY>

<SCRIPT LANGUAGE=JAVASCRIPT>
```

```
window.name = "MAIN"; // Give the current window a name that the remote can use.

var RC = null;
function OpenRemote()
{
  RC = window.open( "Example 9a.htm", "MyRemote",
"WIDTH=550,HEIGHT=125,RESIZABLE=0" );
}
</SCRIPT>

<FORM>
  <INPUT TYPE=BUTTON Value="Remote Control" OnClick="OpenRemote()">
</FORM>

</BODY>
</HTML>
```

▶ **See** "Understanding the Scripting Object Model" to learn more about using the browser's object model, **p. 548**

 T I P Put your favorite links, search tools, etc., on a remote control and save it to your disk. Add a link to the remote control to your bookmark file or favorites folder. Then you can get quick access to your favorite resources using your own personal remote control.

Searching Your Site

The most basic thing you can do to make your site interactive is to add searching capabilities. If your site only contains ten or so pages, it's probably not worth the effort. If your site contains dozens or hundreds of pages, however, you can make finding information on your site much easier with searching.

Part
VIII

Ch
40

You can use many different methods to provide search capabilities on your site. You can use a simple CGI script that does a search. You can use Windows NT Server's built-in Index Server or Netscape's Catalog Server to do a search. You can also use FrontPage's search WebBot (on a FrontPage-enabled Web server) to do a search.

CGI Scripts

Using a CGI script to do a search isn't the most efficient method you can choose. Each time that a user searches your site, the script scans all of the files in the Web and reports each file in which it finds a hit. This can get terribly expensive if you have a lot of visitors.

If you run a small site, however, with few visitors, using a CGI script is the most cost-effective method. You can get a free CGI search script at **http://worldwidemart.com/scripts/search.shtml**. Download and install this script on your Web server per the instructions in the enclosed file. Then add the HTML document shown in Listing 40.14 to your site. You must change the form's ACTION attribute to point to the location of the script on your server.

Listing 40.14   HTML Form for CGI Search Script

```
<HTML>
<HEAD>
<TITLE>Search Example</TITLE>
</HEAD>
<BODY>

<!-- Get the search CGI script for free at http://worldwidemart.com/scripts/
➥search.shtml -->

<FORM METHOD=POST ACTION="http://worldwidemart.com/scripts/cgi-bin/demos/
➥search.cgi">
  <TABLE BORDER=0>
    <TR>
      <TD COLSPAN=3>
        <B>Search for:</B><BR>
        <INPUT TYPE=TEXT NAME=terms size=80>
      </TD>
    </TR>
    <TR>
      <TD>
        <B>Boolean:</B><BR>
        <SELECT NAME=boolean>
          <OPTION>AND
          <OPTION>OR
        </SELECT>
      </TD>
      <TD>
        <B>Case:</B><BR>
        <SELECT NAME=case>
          <OPTION>Insensitive
          <OPTION>Sensitive>
        </SELECT>
      </TD>
      <TD VALIGN=BOTTOM>
        <INPUT TYPE=SUBMIT VALUE="Search">
      </TD>
  </TABLE>
</FORM>
</BODY>
</HTML>
```

Figure 40.11 shows the search form (refer to Listing 40.14). Figure 40.12 shows the search results.

FIG. 40.11
Consider placing this
search form on the
remote control that you
created earlier in this
chapter.

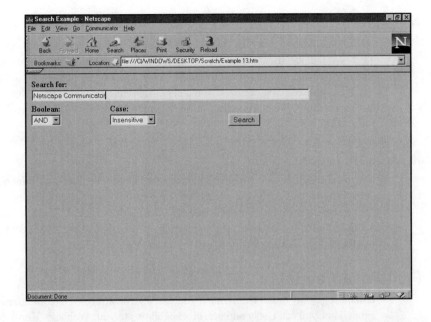

FIG. 40.12
If you don't like the
way the search results
appear, you can change
them in any way you
like because you have
the source code for the
script.

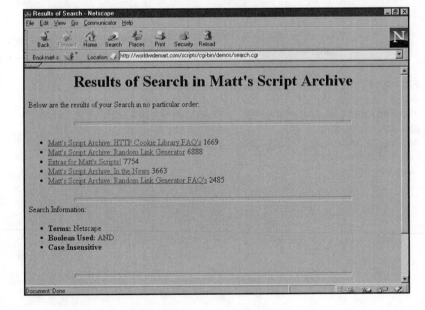

Part

VIII

Ch

40

Netscape

Netscape Catalog Server isn't cheap, costing about $1,000, but it's easy on your Web server. That is, it indexes the information on your server (not just HTML documents, either) and stores the results in a database. When the user does a search, she's actually searching the database, not scanning the disk. You can get more information about Netscape's Catalog Server at **http://home.netscape.com/comprod/server_central/product/catalog/ index.html**.

Microsoft Index Server

Microsoft Index Server is free and works with Windows NT 4.0 and Internet Information Server to index all of the documents on the server. When a user submits a search request with a search form, Index Server searches the index for matching documents and opens the result in the Web browser. You can get more information about Index Server at **http://www. microsoft.com/ntserver/info/indexserver.htm**.

FrontPage WebBots

It doesn't get any easier than this. If you use Microsoft FrontPage and the FrontPage Server extensions, you can easily add search capabilities to your Web site. Here's how:

1. Choose Insert, WebBot Component from FrontPage's main menu.

2. Choose Search from the list and click OK. You'll see the dialog box shown in Figure 40.13.

FIG. 40.13
You can change virtually every detail of the generated search form, including the submit buttons label, the text field's size, and so on.

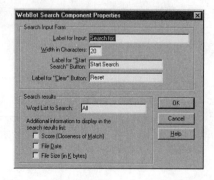

3. Complete the WebBot Search Component Properties dialog box and click OK.

After you've inserted the Search WebBot, FrontPage will create a Web page that looks similar to the one shown in Figure 40.14.

FIG. 40.14

After FrontPage generates the search form, you can add graphics, help text, and other embellishments.

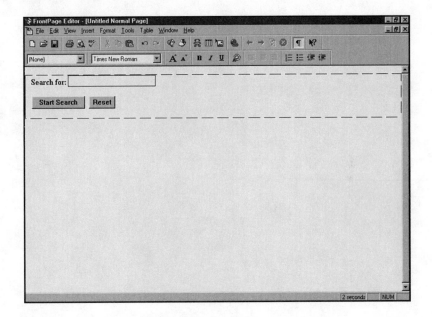

N O T E Check out Que's *Special Edition Using Microsoft FrontPage 97* to learn more about using FrontPage on your Web site. ▧

▶ **See** "Microsoft FrontPage 97" for an overview of Microsoft FrontPage, **p. 812**

Part

VIII

Ch

40

Appendixes

Looking Ahead to HTML 4.0

by Eric Ladd

Now that you've presumably mastered all that this book has to offer, you may be wondering, "What's next for HTML?" Part of the answer lies in what you have already read, since some of the HTML covered in this book is not yet "standard" HTML. The browser-specific HTML you learned in Chapter 15, "Netscape/Microsoft Extensions," or the concepts given in Chapter 16, "Dynamic HTML," are good examples of tags that are supported by some browsers, but are not yet adopted into HTML officially. And companies competing for your Internet desktop will very likely continue to implement special HTML instructions that only work with their browsers in an effort to woo you to their products. But, always keep in mind that these instructions aren't true HTML until they are adopted by the guardian of the language—the World Wide Web Consortium (W3C).

The W3C is made up of members from industry and academe who want to ensure that the Web evolves in a way that serves the electronic publishing needs of its users. This is a tall order when you consider that Internet standards are open standards. *Any* member of the Internet community can toss out an idea for the rest of the community to respond to. We've already seen the free-for-all between Microsoft and Netscape each trying to outdo the other in terms of browser capability. With so many opportunities for input and with corporations spawning new browser-specific HTML tags, the integrity of Web publishing becomes threatened. The members of the W3C recognized the need for a standard implementation of HTML so that document authors don't start writing to one browser or another. Stated another way, any document marked up with standard HTML should look largely the same on any browser that supports the standard. ■

Where HTML Is and How It Got There

The prevailing HTML specification—HTML 3.2—became the official recommendation of the W3C in early 1997. This means there is a consensus among consortium members that the specification is appropriate for implementation across the Web.

Getting to the recommendation stage was a fairly long haul, though. The HTML 3.2 draft specification was released in May 1996, after much speculation about a specification called HTML 3.0. HTML 3.0 was to include the tags from the HTML 2.0 standard *plus* many of the browser-specific tags that had been introduced, *plus* tags and entities for marking up documents with mathematical symbols and equations. The W3C found it unwieldy to develop a proper specification for so many markup instructions and instead released HTML 3.2—a subset of HTML 3.0 instructions that had become relatively stable in their implementation.

After several months of review, the HTML 3.2 specification became a proposed recommendation in September 1996 and finally an official recommendation in January 1997.

This book provides thorough coverage of the tags included in the HTML 3.2 standard. It also goes beyond the standard and discusses many browser-specific HTML instructions, plus some other markup that has been implemented in most popular browsers. When the next release of the HTML standard (HTML 4.0, code named *Cougar*) comes out, you should expect it to include the tags put forward in the HTML 3.2 specification, plus a good portion of the nonstandard instructions covered in this book. The next section takes a peek at a number of the enhancements you can expect to see.

Where HTML Is Going

In its HTML Activity Statement (**http://www.w3.org/pub/WWW/MarkUp/Activity/**), the W3C points to several different features it hopes to make part of the next HTML standard. These include:

- ■ **Client-side scripting**   When the W3C published the HTML 3.2 spec, it reserved the `<SCRIPT>` tag for use in future standards to support client-side scripting. As you saw in this book, both Netscape Navigator and Microsoft Internet Explorer support this tag for embedding client-side scripts in the `<HEAD>` section of an HTML document. You can expect the basic `<SCRIPT>` tag to work much the same way once it's included in the standard.

  Some possible new twists on scripting may be drawn from ways to implement style sheets. Specifically, the W3C mentions that they are looking into linking scripts from a separate file and embedding script code right in an HTML tag (much like Microsoft's dynamic HTML).

■ **Frames**   Frames are so commonplace on the Web that it might surprise you to learn that they are *not* standard HTML. Many of the hurdles surrounding the implementation of frames have been cleared through Netscape's and Microsoft's implementation in their browsers, so the W3C will most likely merge and polish these approaches to produce the standard.

One issue related to frames is layouts for different types of media. For example, an author may want a document to look one way on-screen and have a completely different layout when it is printed or displayed on a Braille terminal. The W3C is looking into the issue of changeable layouts, possibly implemented by means of style sheets.

■ **Support for Mathematical Content**   Mathematicians, scientists, and engineers everywhere will be thankful when a standard set of mathematical tags and entities becomes available. Currently, some authors go so far as to read each mathematical character (Greek letters, operator symbols, and so on) as a *separate image*. This creates alignment nightmares on a grand scale!

Once implemented, HTML math will very likely be much like mathematical document composition with programs like TeX or LaTeX, with tags to handle special operators and constructs and entities to handle special characters. The initial implementation of math-related HTML will probably require the use of a plug-in as well.

■ **Improved Form Functionality**   With so many Web applications making queries against back-end databases, the need to overhaul the way HTML forms work became clear fairly quickly. Look for the new-and-improved form tags to support nesting of forms, grouping of related fields, and a new way to enter records into and query a database.

■ **Typed Links and Document Meta-Information**   The <LINK> and <META> tags in the document <HEAD> are useful, but very often forgotten. The W3C is looking into "typed" links—that is, links with a specific meaning within the context of the document. For example, one type of link may point to standard navigational options (like a button bar at the bottom of a page) or a standard document component (like a table of contents).

■ **Embedded Objects**   There are many types of objects you can embed into a document (such as images, programs, and multimedia presentations) and equally many ways to implement the embedding through browser-specific HTML extensions (such as the <IMG>, <FIG>, <APPLET>, and <EMBED> tags). The W3C hopes to standardize the approach to embedding any object in a document with a smaller set of tags.

All of these features are put forward with the W3C's goal of producing a markup language that is easy to use, robust in its ability to present information, and platform-independent. With cooperation from the industry members of the Consortium (particularly those noted for introducing all sorts of browser-specific HTML) and a little patience, this is a very achievable goal. And, the attainment of this goal means a less chaotic electronic publishing environment for both authors and users alike.

N O T E   To keep up to date on the status of the evolving HTML standard, bookmark and frequently visit **http://www.w3.org/pub/WWW/MarkUp/**. ■

Creating Content for WebTV

by Jerry Honeycutt

WebTV opens up the Internet to millions of people who otherwise wouldn't have access to it. In fact, you don't even have to own a computer to access the Internet. You connect a WebTV Internet Terminal (see Figure B.1), which currently costs about $300, to your television and phone line; that's all. You get access to the World Wide Web and e-mail.

Developing content for WebTV users is a bit different than for Internet Explorer or Netscape users. Most importantly, WebTV doesn't support the full gamut of HTML 3.2 tags. There are more subtle differences, too. The user doesn't have as much screen real estate, for example. The user doesn't have the benefit of a screaming Pentium processor backed up with lots of memory and disk space, either.

If you want to target WebTV users with your Web site, you need to understand a few things before sitting down and writing your HTML. You need to understand WebTV's philosophy regarding content so that you can provide a somewhat consistent experience to the user. You also need to understand the limitations of WebTV with regard to the HTML tags and related technology that it supports. Last, you need to understand and use WebTV's style guide so that your Web pages look as good as possible on the WebTV Internet Terminal. ■

Understand the philosophy behind WebTV content

Creating content for WebTV is different than creating content for traditional browsers. This appendix shows you the differences.

Understand WebTV's limitations

WebTV doesn't support all HTML tags. As well, it has several other limitations that you need to know about.

Use the WebTV style guide to build pages

WebTV publishes a style guide that'll help you build great pages for WebTV Internet Terminal users.

FIG. B.1

You can hook a WebTV Internet Terminal to your television and get on the Net.

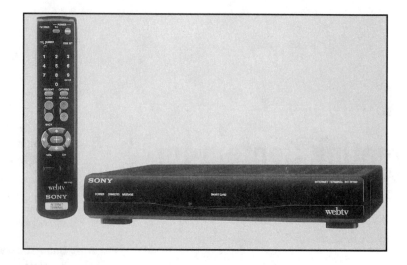

Reviewing WebTV's Content Philosophy

If you're developing a Web site for WebTV users, you're not doing business as usual. Just like a movie such as *Tin Cup* is specially formatted to fit the TV screen, you have to format your Web pages to fit the TV screen. That is, you have to make special provisions for WebTV users that you don't make for Internet Explorer or Netscape users.

WebTV's overriding philosophy is that you're creating a television-like experience. You're dealing with folks who are used to getting information in bite-sized chunks. The information they receive contains enough appealing action and sound to keep them interested. TV viewers tune out or change channels as soon as they get a little bit bored with, overwhelmed with, or confused about what they're watching.

With that in mind, here are some points that'll help you create that television-like experience, and keep your WebTV users tuned into your Web site:

- **Display small chunks of information on each page.** TV viewers are used to taking in a small bit of information from the TV screen. Keep it simple, and keep it small so that you don't overwhelm the user.

- **Build slim Web pages that load fast.** WebTV is a bit more sluggish than traditional browsers, so you need to build your Web pages so that they load as fast as possible. The WebTV users will have as much patience with a slow Web page as they'll have with Mr. Rogers when they're in the mood for a good action flick.

- **Use sound and videos.** Sound and videos help you better create a television-like experience. Most TV viewers skip right over dull television programs, and they'll skip right over your Web page if they don't have a compelling reason to view it. Keep in mind the next bullet point, however, as you create your images for WebTV users.

■ **Use low-bandwidth sound and video technology.** Even though you're creating a television-like experience, you need to use technology that downloads fast. Stick with MID files instead of WAV files, for example. Use images with lower color depth. You can also use animated GIFs instead of AVI files to create simple animations.

> **TIP** WebTV Internet Terminals can display Web pages designed for other browsers, but not very well.

Working Within WebTV's Limitations

Creating Web pages for the TV screen requires you to work within some limitations. In order to build an appliance that'll display Web pages on the TV screen, WebTV designers made a few changes to the technology you know and love. For example:

■ **The screen size is different than you're used to.** It's 560 by 420 pixels. You can only use 544 by 378 for your Web pages, though, as the rest of the screen is used for margins and a status bar.

■ **The user can scroll a Web page vertically, but she can't scroll a Web page horizontally.** Thus, you must make sure that your Web page fits entirely within the width of the screen (544 pixels).

■ **Many WebTV users will not have a keyboard.** They'll only have the WebTV remote control with which to navigate your Web site. Thus, you should limit the amount of actual input required at your Web site.

> **TIP** Future versions of WebTV might increase the size of the screen as new television standards are introduced.

Given these limitations, WebTV doesn't support all of the HTML tags available, and it also introduces many new tags that you'll have to use to create effective Web pages for the TV screen. You learn more about these in the following sections.

Unsupported HTML Tags and Attributes

WebTV supports most of the popular tags from HTML 2.0 and 3.2. It also supports some of the popular extensions introduced by Internet Explorer 3.0 and Netscape Navigator 3.0. You'll find many tags that WebTV doesn't support, however, including tags from HTML 2.0, HTML 3.2, and browser-specific extensions.

Table B.1 shows you the HTML tags that WebTV doesn't support. The table has two columns. The first column shows you each unsupported or partially supported tag. The second column indicates the unsupported attributes for that tag or it indicates that the tag isn't supported at all. If you see one or more attributes in the second column, that means that WebTV doesn't support those attributes. If you see "Unsupported" in the next column, that means that WebTV doesn't support that tag at all.

Table B.1   HTML Tags Not Supported by WebTV

Tag	Attribute
A	REL, REV, TITLE, URN
APPLET	Unsupported
BLINK	Unsupported
BODY	ALINK
EMBED	Unsupported
FONT	FACE
FORM	ENCTYPE
FRAME	Unsupported
FRAMESET	Unsupported
IMG	ALT, DYNSRC, LOOP
ISINDEX	PROMPT
LI	VALUE
META	NAME
NEXTID	Unsupported
OL	COMPACT
PARAM	Unsupported
PLAINTEXT	Unsupported
PRE	WIDTH
SCRIPT	Unsupported
STYLE	Unsupported
TABLE	HEIGHT
TD	NOWRAP
TEXTAREA	WRAP
UL	COMPACT
WBR	Unsupported

N O T E   You can check the user agent header to determine if the client is WebTV. Doing so allows you to provide different content for WebTV users than for Internet Explorer and Netscape users. Check to see if user agent field contains "WebTV" anywhere within it. If so, the client is WebTV. ■

WebTV HTML Extensions

Remember that you're creating Web pages for a low-resolution TV screen. Regular HTML 3.2 doesn't look as good on the TV screen as it does on a computer screen. Thus, the designers of WebTV introduced several HTML extensions that help you create content that does look good on the TV screen. The sections that follow provide you an overview of these extensions. For comprehensive information, see WebTV's Web site.

<A> WebTV adds two new attributes to the <A> tag: NOCOLOR and SELECTED. Use the NOCOLOR attribute to specify that WebTV should not display the link using color. Use the SELECTED attribute to indicate that WebTV should initially select that link (highlight it when the Web page first loads).

<AUDIOSCOPE> <AUDIOSCOPE> is a WebTV specify tag. It displays a graphical representation of stereo sound. That is, it displays the amplitude of a sound over time, graphically. Here are its attributes:

ALIGN=*Value*	The alignment with the previous text. You can set this attribute to one of these values: TOP, MIDDLE, BOTTOM, LEFT, RIGHT, TEXTTOP, ABSMIDDLE, BASELINE, ABSBOTTOM.
BORDER=*pixels*	Draws a border around the audioscope. You set this attribute to the width of the border in pixels. The default is 1.
GAIN=*value*	A multiplier to use with the audioscope. The default value is 1.
HEIGHT=*value*	The height of the audioscope in pixels. This reserves space for it on the screen as the WebTV loads the Web page. The default height is 80 pixels.
LEFTCOLOR=*color*	The color used for the left-channel of the stereo sound. You can use a named color or a color value like #FF0000.
LEFTOFFSET=*value*	The offset for the left-channel of the stereo sound. This determines how high (positive value) or low (negative value), in pixels, the left-channel is displayed above the center line. The default value is two pixels.
MAXLEVEL=*value*	Specifies whether or not the audioscope will clip the sound. The default value is false.
RIGHTCOLOR=*color*	The color used for the right-channel of the stereo sound. You can use a named color or a color value like #FF0000.
RIGHTOFFSET=*value*	The offset for the right-channel of the stereo sound. This determines how high (positive value) or low (negative value), in pixels, the right-channel is displayed above the center line. The default value is -two pixels.
WIDTH=*value*	The width of the audioscope in pixels. This reserves space for it on the screen as the WebTV loads the Web page. The default height is 100 pixels.

Part

IX

App

B

<BLACKFACE>   <BLACKFACE> is a WebTV container tag that renders the enclosed text in a double-weight, boldface font. Here's how to use it:

```
<BLACKFACE>This text is in blackface</BLACKFACE>
```

<BODY>   WebTV introduces several attribute extensions to the <BODY> tag:

CREDITS=url	The URL of a Web page that contains credit information (corporation information, personal background, and so on) for the Web site. The users will see this Web page when they click the Credits button in the Info Panel.
FONTSIZE=value	The size of the font to use on the Web page: SMALL, MEDIUM, or LARGE. This attribute overrides the user's setup.
HSPACE=value	The horizontal margin you'd like to use around the entire body of the Web page. The default value is eight pixels. WebTV recommends that you don't change this value.
INSTRUCTIONS	The URL of a Web page that contains usage information for the Web site. The users will see this Web page when they click the Instructions button in the Info Panel.
LOGO=url	The URL of an image to use as an icon in the list of favorites and the Send Panel. The image size should be 70 by 52 pixels.
NOHTILEBG	Prevents the background image from tiling horizontally.
NOVTILEBG	Prevents the background image from tiling vertically.
VSPACE=value	The vertical margin you'd like to use around the entire body of the Web page. The default value is six pixels. WebTV recommends that you don't change this value.
XSPEED=value	The speed at which the background image should scroll horizontally while the actual content of the Web page does not scroll. The default value is 0 (no scrolling).
YSPEED=value	The speed at which the background image should scroll vertically while the actual content of the Web page does not scroll. The default value is 0 (no scrolling).

<BQ>   WebTV introduces the <BQ> tag, which is an alias for the <BLOCKQUOTE> tag. Incidentally, WebTV also supports the <BLOCKQUOTE> tag.

<FONT>   WebTV adds two new attributes to the <FONT> tag: EFFECT and TRANSPARENCY:

EFFECT=value	Indicates any special effect to use with the font: RELIEF, EMBOSS, or SHADOW.
TRANSPARENCY=value	Indicates the percentage by which the background should show through the foreground text: 0 (none) to 100 (fully).

<HR> WebTV adds a new attribute to the <HR> tag called INVERTBORDER. The presence of this attribute indicates that WebTV will draw the rule with a raised border.

<IMG> WebTV adds a few new attributes to the <IMG> tag, mostly to support WebTV animations:

ANI=*url*	The URL of an animation sequence.
ANIMATEONSELECT	Indicates that WebTV will play an animation only when the user selects the image.
ANISTARTX=*value*	The starting location of the animation relative to the Web page or the containing table.
ANISTARTY=*value*	The starting location of the animation relative to the Web page or the containing table.
LOOP	Indicates that the animation should play over and over again, indefinitely.
RELOAD=n	Specifies how frequently the image should be reloaded.
SELECTED=*x,y*	The coordinate within an imagemap that should be selected when the user first loads the Web page.
TRANSPARENCY	The percentage by which the background should show through the foreground text: 0 (none) to 100 (fully).

T I P Add the SRC attribute to your WebTV <IMG> tags so that nonWebTV browsers can load the image.

<INPUT> WebTV introduces a handful of new attributes to the <INPUT> tag:

ACTION=*url*	Specifies the URL to which WebTV will submit the element when the user selects the control. This attribute overrides the action associated with the form.
NOARGS	Prevents arguments from being submitted to the server when using ACTION.
NOHIGHLIGHT	Prevents the element from being highlighted when the user selects it.
SUBMITFORM	Indicates that the contents of the entire form should be submitted along with the contents of the control if the contents of the element are submitted and you're using the ACTION attribute. If you don't use SUBMITFORM, only the contents of the control are submitted.
WIDTH=*value*	Specifies the width of the element in pixels.

<LIMITTEXT> <LIMITTEXT> is a WebTV extension that limits the width of text in an area. It has these attributes:

SIZE=*value*	The maximum number of characters to display on a line.

VALUE=*value*	The text string to which the limit is applied.
WIDTH=*pixels*	The maximum number of pixels to display on the text line.

<MARQUEE>   WebTV extends the Internet Explorer <MARQUEE> tag by adding the TRANSPARENCY attribute. TRANSPARENCY contains the percentage by which the background should show through the foreground text: 0 (none) to 100 (fully).

<NOSMARTQUOTES>   <NOSMARTQUOTES> is a WebTV extension. It's a container tag that specifies the enclosed text should not use smart quotes.

<SELECT>   WebTV adds several new attributes to the <SELECT> tag:

AUTOACTIVATE	Causes the list to automatically drop down when the user selects it, instead of having to press the Go button of the WebTV remote control.
BGCOLOR=*color*	The background color for the list. It can be a color value or a named color.
EXCLUSIVE	Specifies the list should not contain duplicate values.
SELCOLOR=*color*	The color for any selection in the list. It can be a color value or a named color.
SHOWEMPTY	Specifies that WebTV will display empty lists with the empty string.
TEXT=*color*	The color for text in the list. It can be a color value or a named color.
USESTYLE	Specifies that WebTV will display the list by using the current style for the page.

<SHADOW>   <SHADOW> is a new container tag that causes the enclosed text to be displayed with a shadow.

<SIDEBAR>   WebTV doesn't support frames. It does let you set up an area on the left side of the Web page, however, that doesn't scroll. You use the <SIDEBAR> tag to do this. It's a container tag. Any HTML tags enclosed between <SIDEBAR> and </SIDEBAR> are displayed on the left side of the Web page. This area doesn't scroll, either. <SIDEBAR> supports the following attributes:

ALIGN=*value*	Sets the alignment for the sidebar: LEFT, CENTER, or RIGHT.
WIDTH=*value*	The width of the sidebar in pixels.

<TABLE>   WebTV adds several new attributes to the <TABLE> tag:

CELLBORDER=*pixels*	The width of the cell border in pixels.
HREF=*url*	Causes the entire table to become an anchor. When the user clicks the table, WebTV opens the Web page indicated by HREF.

ID=*value*	The name for the table.
NAME=*value*	Same as the ID attribute.
TRANSPARENCY	The percentage by which the background should show through the foreground text: 0 (none) to 100 (fully).

<TEXTAREA> WebTV introduces a handful of new attributes to the <TEXTAREA> tag:

ALLCAPS	Specifies that the text entry should be displayed in all capitals.
AUTOACTIVATE	Specifies that the text area should be activated when the Web page first loads.
AUTOCAPS	Specifies that all text entry should use initial capitals (title case).
BGCOLOR=*color*	The background color for the text area. It can be a color value or named color.
CURSOR=*COLOR*	The color of the cursor while in the text area. It can be a color value or named color.
GROWABLE	Specifies that the text area can expand vertically as the user types text.
NOHARDBREAKS	Specifies the user can't enter hard breaks in the text area.
NOSOFTBREAKS	Specifies that WebTV won't enter soft breaks in the text area when submitting the text to the server.
NUMBERS	Specifies that the 1 should be selected when the user pops up the on-screen keyword.
SHOWKEYBOARD	Specifies that WebTV should automatically pop up the on-screen keyword.
USESTYLE	Specifies that WebTV will display the list by using the current style for the page.

<TD> & <TH> WebTV extends the <TD> with the following new attributes:

ABSHEIGHT=*value*	The absolute height, in pixels, of the table cell.
ABSWIDTH=*value*	The absolute width, in pixels, of the table cell.
MAXLINES=*value*	The maximum number of text lines to display in the table cell.
TRANSPARENCY	The percentage by which the background should show through the foreground text: 0 (none) to 100 (fully).

<TR> WebTV extends the <TR> with the TRANSPARENCY attribute. Set this attribute to the percentage by which the background should show through the foreground text: 0 (none) to 100 (fully).

Part

IX

App

B

Understanding WebTV's Style Guide

WebTV provides a comprehensive style guide, in both HTML and PDF format, at its Web site (**http://www.webtv.net**). At this site, you'll also find a complete listing of all the HTML tags and extensions that WebTV supports. The style guide helps you create content that looks great on the WebTV Internet Terminal. As a side note, many of the suggestions in WebTV's style guide will also help you create Web pages that look great in traditional browsers.

Here's an overview of WebTV's style guide recommendations (see WebTV's Web site for its complete style guide):

- **Display the most important information first.** TV viewers are not used to scrolling when they watch their favorite TV programs. If users have to scroll to see the most important information on your Web page, they might miss it.

- **Design your pages so they fit on a single screen.** For the same reason as the previous item, create pages that display on a single screen. You can organize your Web site so the user can navigate from page to page; but each page contains a single screenful of information.

- **Create a single focal point on each page.** Most TV programs direct the user's eyes to a single focal point on the screen. It can be an action or an object. Direct the user's eyes by providing a single focal point on your Web page, too.

- **Use <NOBR> to prevent line breaks.** If you use <BR> to break lines in your Web page, the page might look strange in WebTV. <NOBR> causes WebTV to ignore the <BR> tag.

- **Use form elements sparingly.** TV viewers aren't accustomed to forms and many don't have keywords. Design forms with pop-up menus, radio buttons, and check boxes whenever possible. As well, place the submit button in the lower-right corner of the Web page.

- **Avoid bright white and bright red backgrounds.** Bright white and bright red backgrounds don't display well in WebTV because these colors often create distortion on a TV. Consider using 90 percent white or 90 percent red, instead.

- **Don't use small fonts.** TV sets can't display fine details as well as a computer monitor. Thus, small fonts are hard for WebTV users to read.

- **Don't use images with fine detail.** For the same reasons as the previous item, avoid images with fine detail as the detail will be hard for a WebTV user to see.

- **Keep titles short.** WebTV truncates titles that don't fit in the status bar, so keep it short.

- **Use images with size hints.** Use the <IMG> tag's HEIGHT and WIDTH attributes to specify the size of the image so that the user will see the text of the Web page faster.

- **Use REL=NEXT to preload Web pages.** If you add REL=NEXT in a link by using the <LINK> tag, WebTV will preload the Web page pointed to by the link. Thus, the users will see the Web page much faster when they click the link.

What's on the CD?

The CD-ROM included with this book is packed full of valuable programs and utilities. This appendix gives you a brief overview of the contents of the CD. For a more detailed look at any of these parts, load the CD-ROM and browse the contents by using your favorite Web browser. ■

Web Browsers

We have included Microsoft's latest browser, Internet Explorer, on the CD along with:

Internet Explorer 3.0 (Internet Mail, Internet News, Active Movie, Net Meeting, HTML Layout Control)

SlipKnot

HTML Editors and Utilities

Save yourself the trouble of creating HTML pages with Notepad by choosing among the following HTML editors and special-purpose utilities:

BBEdit Lite

HotDog Pro

HomeSite

WebMedia Publisher Pro

HTML Grinder

HTML Notepad

Microsoft Internet Assistants

Webber

Color Manipulation Device

EasyHelp/Web

Map This!

WebForms

Webmania

Web Plug-Ins

Plug-ins are great. You've seen them described in some detail in Chapter 18, "Browser Plug-Ins," and you've seen what they can do. But finding and downloading these can be a hassle and is definitely time-consuming. We have provided over 80 plug-ins covering the following topics:

Audio

Graphics

Miscellaneous

Productivity

Remote Access

Video

VRML

Web Servers

The CD contains software necessary to build and maintain a regular Web site or an Intranet.

Apache

Internet Information Server

NCSA HTTPd

WebQuest

Java

Here you find the following Java tools that help you create animated applets and design scrolling marquees.

Clikette

Egor Animator

Ewgie

Flash

Hot_Java Browser

Swami

Web Utilities, Helper Applications, and Other Useful Utilities

Here you will find mailing-list engines, the popular Excite search engine, Web stats, security programs, and compression utilities.

ARJ

Stuffit

UUCode

WinCode

WinZip

COPS

CRACK

SATAN

Tiger

xinetd

HyperMail

LISTSERV

LSMTP

MailServ

Mthon Arc

Excite

Swish

WWWWAIS

GetStats

Cool Edit

Midigate

Mod4Win

AWave

GoldWave

Macromedia Director 6.0 Demo Software

ACDSee

GraphX

SnapCap

PaintShopPro

VuePrint

WebImage

WinECJ

WinJPEG

Perl

VB5 Control Creation Edition

Free HTML Versions of Popular Que Books

The CD-ROM contains the entire text of popular best-selling books from Que in HTML format. The chapters and sections are all hyperlinked and an HTML index is included for each book to make using them even easy.

The free books included are:

Special Edition Using Java, Second Edition

Special Edition Using CGI

Special Edition Using VBScript

Special Edition Using ActiveX

Part
IX

App
C

Index

X-Y-Z

Check out Que® Books
on the World Wide Web
http://www.quecorp.com

As the biggest software release in computer history, Windows 95 continues to redefine the computer industry. Click here for the latest info on our Windows 95 books

Make computing quick and easy with these products designed exclusively for new and casual users

Examine the latest releases in word processing, spreadsheets, operating systems, and suites

The Internet, The World Wide Web, CompuServe®, America Online®, Prodigy® —it's a world of ever-changing information. Don't get left behind!

Find out about new additions to our site, new bestsellers and hot topics

In-depth information on high-end topics: find the best reference books for databases, programming, networking, and client/server technologies

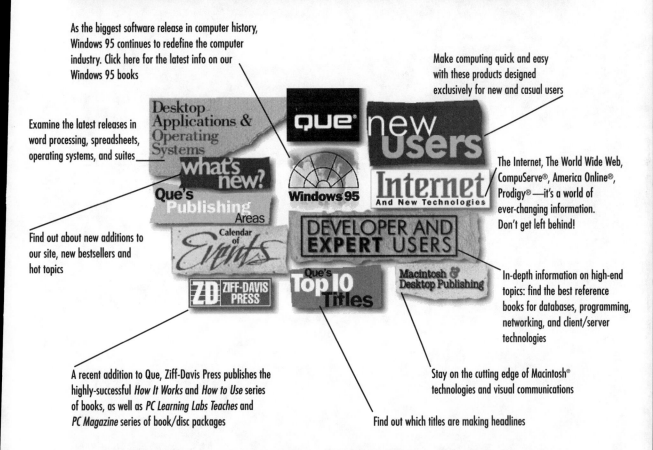

A recent addition to Que, Ziff-Davis Press publishes the highly-successful *How It Works* and *How to Use* series of books, as well as *PC Learning Labs Teaches* and *PC Magazine* series of book/disc packages

Stay on the cutting edge of Macintosh® technologies and visual communications

Find out which titles are making headlines

With 6 separate publishing groups, Que develops products for many specific market segments and areas of computer technology. Explore our Web Site and you'll find information on best-selling titles, newly published titles, upcoming products, authors, and much more.

- Stay informed on the latest industry trends and products available
- Visit our online bookstore for the latest information and editions
- Download software from Que's library of the best shareware and freeware

Complete and Return this Card for a *FREE* Computer Book Catalog

Thank you for purchasing this book! You have purchased a superior computer book written expressly for your needs. To continue to provide the kind of up-to-date, pertinent coverage you've come to expect from us, we need to hear from you. Please take a minute to complete and return this self-addressed, postage-paid form. In return, we'll send you a free catalog of all our computer books on topics ranging from word processing to programming and the internet.

r. ☐   Mrs. ☐   Ms. ☐   Dr. ☐

Name (first) ☐☐☐☐☐☐☐☐☐☐☐☐☐   (M.I.) ☐   (last) ☐☐☐☐☐☐☐☐☐☐☐☐☐☐☐☐☐☐

Address ☐☐☐☐☐☐☐☐☐☐☐☐☐☐☐☐☐☐☐☐☐☐☐☐☐☐☐☐☐☐☐☐☐

City ☐☐☐☐☐☐☐☐☐☐☐☐☐   State ☐☐   Zip ☐☐☐☐☐☐☐☐☐

Phone ☐☐☐ ☐☐☐ ☐☐☐☐   Fax ☐☐☐ ☐☐☐ ☐☐☐☐

Company Name ☐☐☐☐☐☐☐☐☐☐☐☐☐☐☐☐☐☐☐☐☐☐☐☐☐☐☐☐☐☐

E-mail address ☐☐☐☐☐☐☐☐☐☐☐☐☐☐☐☐☐☐☐☐☐☐☐☐☐☐☐☐☐☐

1. Please check at least (3) influencing factors for purchasing this book.

Front or back cover information on book .... ☐
Special approach to the content .... ☐
Completeness of content .... ☐
Author's reputation .... ☐
Publisher's reputation .... ☐
Book cover design or layout .... ☐
Index or table of contents of book .... ☐
Price of book .... ☐
Special effects, graphics, illustrations .... ☐
Other (Please specify): _____ ☐

2. How did you first learn about this book?

Saw in Macmillan Computer Publishing catalog .... ☐
Recommended by store personnel .... ☐
Saw the book on bookshelf at store .... ☐
Recommended by a friend .... ☐
Received advertisement in the mail .... ☐
Saw an advertisement in: _____ ☐
Read book review in: _____ ☐
Other (Please specify): _____ ☐

3. How many computer books have you purchased in the last six months?

This book only .... ☐   3 to 5 books .... ☐
2 books .... ☐   More than 5 .... ☐

4. Where did you purchase this book?

Bookstore .... ☐
Computer Store .... ☐
Consumer Electronics Store .... ☐
Department Store .... ☐
Office Club .... ☐
Warehouse Club .... ☐
Mail Order .... ☐
Direct from Publisher .... ☐
Internet site .... ☐
Other (Please specify): _____ ☐

5. How long have you been using a computer?

☐ Less than 6 months   ☐ 6 months to a year
☐ 1 to 3 years   ☐ More than 3 years

6. What is your level of experience with personal computers and with the subject of this book?

	With PCs	With subject of book
New	☐	☐
Casual	☐	☐
Accomplished	☐	☐
Expert	☐	☐

Source Code ISBN: 0-7897-0000-0

7. Which of the following best describes your job title?

Administrative Assistant .... ☐
Coordinator .... ☐
Manager/Supervisor .... ☐
Director .... ☐
Vice President .... ☐
President/CEO/COO .... ☐
Lawyer/Doctor/Medical Professional ..... ☐
Teacher/Educator/Trainer .... ☐
Engineer/Technician .... ☐
Consultant .... ☐
Not employed/Student/Retired .... ☐
Other (Please specify): _____ ☐

8. Which of the following best describes the area of the company your job title falls under?

Accounting .... ☐
Engineering .... ☐
Manufacturing .... ☐
Operations .... ☐
Marketing .... ☐
Sales .... ☐
Other (Please specify): _____ ☐

9. What is your age?

Under 20 ....
21-29 ....
30-39 ....
40-49 ....
50-59 ....
60-over ....

10. Are you:

Male ....
Female ....

11. Which computer publications do you read regularly? (Please list)

_____
_____
_____
_____
_____
_____
_____
_____
_____
_____

Comments: _____
_____
_____

Fold here and scotch-tape to mail

INDIANAPOLIS IN 46290-9042
201 W 103RD ST
MACMILLAN PUBLISHING USA
MACMILLAN COMPUTER PUBLISHING
ATTN MARKETING

POSTAGE WILL BE PAID BY THE ADDRESSEE

FIRST-CLASS MAIL PERMIT NO. 9918 INDIANAPOLIS IN

BUSINESS REPLY MAIL

NO POSTAGE
NECESSARY
IF MAILED
IN THE
UNITED STATES

Instant Web Site!

100 Mb for $19.95!
For more details on this great offer, visit our Web site at www.win.net/que97.html. Special offer available only on the enclosed CD-ROM – run the file D:\WINNET\SETUP.EXE to get started.

Tired of searching for a dependable and affordable home for your World Wide Web site? Look no further. This QUE® Books Special Offer gives you an incredible 100 Mb World Wide Web site on WinNET's professional Web Hosting System for only $19.95 a month — save $10 per month!

There are no setup fees and no hidden charges. You'll be able to make changes to your site within minutes of opening your account using the software on the enclosed CD-ROM. This is a totally risk-free offer and your satisfaction is guaranteed.*

HERE'S WHAT YOU'LL GET FOR ONLY $19.95 PER MONTH:

- *100 Megabyte Web Site (includes an FTP site)*
- *100 Megabytes of transfers*
- *UUCP E-mail System Account*
- *POP3 E-mail Account*
- *Unlimited FTP transfers to and from site*
- *Web site development accomplished through any Internet connection*
- *Access to the Public cgi-bin which includes*
  - *Form E-mailer Program*
  - *Image Map Program*
  - *Page Counter Program*
- *4 hours of toll-free 800 modem; 9 cents per minute thereafter; or*
- *20 hours of local access, $1 per hour thereafter*

Win NET™
COMMUNICATIONS, INC.

http://www.win.net
info@win.net
330F Distillery Commons
Louisville, Kentucky 40206
(800) 589-5999

Satisfaction Guarantee: *If you are not completely satisfied with WinNET's Internet service for any reason you can cancel your account within the first 30 days and we will refund 100% of your money without exception.*

There's absolutely no risk and nothing to lose!

This special offer is valid until 1/1/99 and is subject to change without notice. WinNET is a trademark of WinNET Communications Inc. QUE is a registered trademark of Macmillan.

NETCOM Interactive
Website Hosting Services

http://www.netcomi.com
1.888.638.2664 (toll free)

■ Complete Access

NETCOM owns and operates one of the largest and most robust
networks in the industry today. The international network of SMDS,
ATM, T3 and T1 highspeed lines connect hundreds of thousands
of worldwide businesses and individuals to the Internet with reliable
service and readily available access.

■ Complete Support

At NETCOM, we can assist you with designing inter-marketing
strategies. We specialize in setting up complete websites that include
domain registration and routing, configuration of your server
(or virtual server), CGI scripting, image mapping, interactive forms,
databases, secure transactions and usage statistics. We support the
emerging technologies for your business to utilize.

■ Complete Control

The exclusive NETCOM Business Center is a full service, on-line
support center, open 24 hours every day. Our clients have a number
of hosting options to select features such as: e-mail boxes, daily site
back-up, CGI and FTP access, security keys, traffic logs, stats, disk
space and monthly transfer rates. We allow you to customize your site
so you have complete control.

Visit our website or give us a call @ 1.888.638.2664
Mention this reference code QNI00297 and receive a 20% discount.

NETCOM Interactive
1607 LBJ Freeway
Dallas, TX 75234
972.481.5700

NETCOM

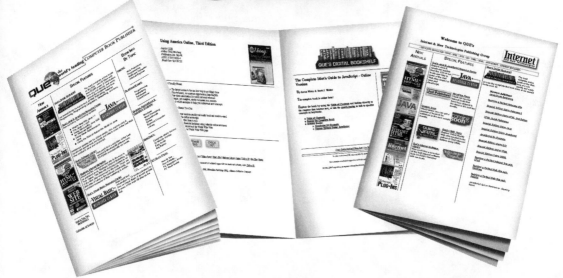

Never underestimate the power of a little chat.

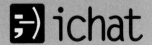

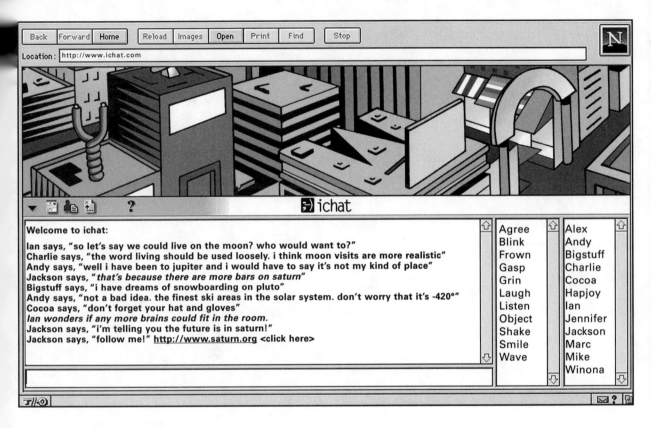

Great things happen when great minds get together. Add chat to your Web site and great things will happen there too.

Introducing *ichat* ROOMS. The first server to integrate both HTML and chat together.

When users visit a ROOMS-enabled site, an *ichat* frame opens in the lower portion of the browser to display a real-time, ongoing chat session among site visitors. Users enter the conversation and communicate with each other simply by typing.

More traffic. By adding two-way communications, *ichat* transforms a web site from a static medium into a dynamic, interactive community. Continuing access to this community will provide users with a powerful reason to return to your site and to stay longer once there.

See for yourself the power of a little chat.
**Visit our demonstration area at
http://www.ichat.com**
Or contact us at (512) 425-2200
or sales@ichat.com. For a little chat.

Download your *ichat* plug-in and come chat with us at http://www.ichat.com

Before using any of the software on this disc, you need to install the software you plan to use. See Appendix C, "What's on the CD?" for directions. If you have problems with this CD, please contact Macmillan Technical Support at (317) 581-3833. We can be reached by e-mail at **support@mcp.com** or by CompuServe at **GO QUEBOOKS**.

Read this Before Opening Software

By opening this package, you are agreeing to be bound by the following:

This software is copyrighted and all rights are reserved by the publisher and its licensers. You are licensed to use this software on a single computer. You may copy the software for backup or archival purposes only. Making copies of the software for any other purpose is a violation of United States copyright laws. THIS SOFTWARE IS SOLD AS IS, WITHOUT WARRANTY OF ANY KIND, EITHER EXPRESSED OR IMPLIED, INCLUDING BUT NOT LIMITED TO THE IMPLIED WARRANTIES OF MERCHANTABILITY AND FITNESS FOR A PARTICULAR PURPOSE. Neither the publisher nor its dealers and distributors nor its licensers assume any liability for any alleged or actual damages arising from the use of this software. (Some states do not allow exclusion of implied warranties, so the exclusion may not apply to you.)

The entire contents of this disc and the compilation of the software are copyrighted and protected by United States copyright laws. The individual programs on the disc are copyrighted by the authors or owners of each program. Each program has its own use permissions and limitations. To use each program, you must follow the individual requirements and restrictions detailed for each. Do not use a program if you do not agree to follow its licensing agreement.